Hidden Treasure of the Profound Path

A Word-by-Word Commentary on the Kalachakra Preliminary Practices

༄༅། །ཟབ་ལམ་སྔོན་འགྲོའི་ཚིག་འགྲེལ་སྔོན་མེད་རབ་གསལ་སྣང་བ།

by Shar Khentrul Jamphel Lodrö

ཤར་མཁན་སྤྲུལ་རིན་པོ་ཆེ་འཇམ་དཔལ་བློ་གྲོས

TIBETAN BUDDHIST RIMÉ INSTITUTE

Belgrave, Australia

ISBN: 978-0-9946106-9-0 (paperback)

ISBN: 978-0-9946107-0-6 (e-book)

Published by:

THE TIBETAN BUDDHIST RIMÉ INSTITUTE

This work was produced by the Tibetan Buddhist Rimé Institute, a not-for-profit organisation run entirely by volunteers. This organisation is devoted to propagating a non-sectarian view of all the world's spiritual traditions and teaching Buddhism in a way that is completely authentic, yet also practical and accessible to Western culture. It is especially dedicated to propagating the Jonang tradition, a rare jewel from remote Tibet which holds the precious Kalachakra teachings.

For more information on scheduled activities or available materials, or if you wish to make a donation to support our work, please contact:

Tibetan Buddhist Rimé Institute Inc.
1584 Burwood Highway
Belgrave VIC 3160
AUSTRALIA

www.rimebuddhism.com
temple@rimebuddhism.com

Contents

ཕྱི་དབྱིངས་འཁོར་འདས་དྭངས་མའི་གྲོང་ཁྱེར་བྱེ་བ་དགུ་བཅུའི་ཕོ་བྲང་ལ། །
ནང་དབྱིངས་དྲུག་བརྒྱ་སོ་དྲུག་ལྷ་ཡི་དཀྱིལ་འཁོར་སྟོང་གཟུགས་ལོངས་སྐུའི་ཞིང་། །
གཞི་དབྱིངས་རྣམ་པ་ཀུན་ལྡན་ཆ་མེད་འཁོར་འདས་ཀུན་ཁྱབ་ཆོས་སྐུའི་དབྱིངས། །
མངོན་བྱེད་ཟབ་ལམ་ཉག་གཅིག་རྡོ་རྗེའི་རྣལ་འབྱོར་དང་བས་ཕྱག་གིས་མཆོད། །

ཟབ་དོན་ཤེས་པ་མིན་ཡང་འདུན་པ་ཡིས། །
ཟབ་མོའི་དོན་ལ་འཇུག་པའི་རིམ་པ་ཙམ། །
གོ་སླ་ཤེས་ཐབས་ཚིག་གིས་འབྲི་སྟོན་གྱིས། །
བྲིས་པའི་ངལ་བ་བརྟེན་ལ་ཉོངས་པ་ཅི། །

ཕྱི་རིག་དུས་ཀྱི་འཁོར་ལོ་འཛམ་གླིང་བྱེ་བ་ཕྲག་བརྒྱའི་ཞིང་། །
ནང་རིག་དུས་ཀྱི་འཁོར་ལོ་རྡོ་རྗེའི་རྩ་རླུང་ཐིག་ལེའི་ཁམས། །
གཞན་རིག་དུས་ཀྱི་འཁོར་ལོ་ཐུགས་གསུང་སྐུ་ཡི་དཀྱིལ་འཁོར་གསུམ། །
དབྱེར་མེད་བར་དུ་རྟོགས་ལྡན་དམ་པའི་ཆོས་ལ་སྤྱོད་ནུས་ཤོག །

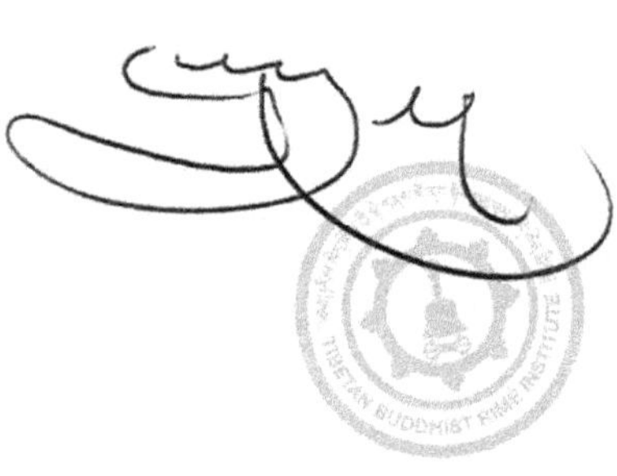

Homage

To the Outer Realm, the 96 million cities of Shambhala that are
the essence of samsara and nirvana;
To the Inner Realm, the sambhogakaya abode of the
Empty-form Mandala of six hundred and thirty-six deities;
To Basic Space, the indivisible Dharmakaya Realm possessing all
aspects and pervading all of samsara and nirvana;
With faith in the Vajra Yogas, the unique and profound path that
manifests realisations, I pay homage.

While not one who knows the deepest of meanings,
What fault is there in the aspiration to make effort to write down
Words of method and wisdom, making it easy to understand
The mere stages of entering into that profound meaning.

Outer Awareness of Kalachakra,
the billion-fold worlds of this universe;
Inner Awareness of Kalachakra,
the vajra realm of channels, winds and essences;
Enlightened Awareness of Kalachakra,
the three mandalas of mind, speech and body;
Until they are inseparable, may we enjoy the Sacred Dharma
of the Golden Age.

— Shakyamuni Buddha —

The Supreme Teacher of the Kalachakra Tantra

Introduction

This text provides a commentary on Jetsun Taranatha's root text "*The Divine Ladder: Preliminary and Main Practices of the Profound Kalachakra Vajrayoga.*" Originally written in the 17th century, *The Divine Ladder* has been used for hundreds of years by countless Jonang practitioners in order to actualise their realisations of the Kalachakra Path. It is a concise practice manual that encapsulates all of the pith instructions of the tradition as practiced in both India and Tibet.

In this time of considerable conflict and strife, the practice of Kalachakra is said to be particularly effective. As these teachings arose from the spiritual realm of Shambhala, they are closely linked to the cultivation of peace and harmony. These teachings are exceedingly rare in this world and therefore it is very difficult to encounter them, let alone in a language that you can understand. While many people have taken Kalachakra empowerments from great masters such as His Holiness the Dalai Lama, materials for how to practice have been very limited. For these reasons, I hope that you can appreciate both the rarity and preciousness of this text.

The title of the practice manual is "The Divine Ladder". It is called this because it presents the profound path to Kalachakra enlightenment in a gradual, step-by-step manner. It includes all of the preliminary practices leading to the Kalachakra completion stage practices, known as the *Six Vajra Yogas*. With these extraordinary methods, it is possible to attain complete enlightenment within a single human lifetime.

The instructions for these practices were originally taught by the Buddha to the Dharma Kings of Shambhala where they were preserved until eventually being introduced into India around the tenth century and soon afterwards into Tibet. While the Six Vajra Yogas are the main practice of the Kalachakra Path, to be qualified to engage in these practices, one must first complete the *Preliminary Practices* (ngöndro).

The purpose of the Kalachakra Path is to discover the enlightened truth of your reality, also known as Buddha-nature. This nature is currently hidden from your experience like a treasure buried deep underground or a jewel wrapped in many layers of garbage. The path is designed to facilitate the gradual process of removing obscurations from the mind that prevent you from experiencing that pristine nature.

Right now, our minds are filled with all sorts of concepts and dualistic notions that distort our perceptions and limit our capacity. Everything we experience is seen through the lens of afflicted states of mind such as pride, aggression and ignorance. Through a Buddhist path like Kalachakra and with the help of an authentic spiritual guide, we are able to train ourselves to gradually release these fixations. Initially this means establishing an ethical foundation for life by developing inner qualities such as discipline, kindness and wisdom. As we become familiar with these qualities, the veils of obscurations start to dissolve, allowing us to catch glimpses of our fundamental nature. The more we practice, the thinner the obscurations become and the more expansive our experience of Buddha-nature can be. What begins as a mere drop, eventually becomes a vast ocean. When all of the obscurations have been removed, you will have attained enlightenment.

AN OVERVIEW OF THIS BOOK

The Divine Ladder is split into four main parts. The first three parts cover the preliminary practices which are performed before engaging in the main practice of the Vajra Yogas. The last part provides supplementary practices that are used to strengthen your connection with the blessings of the two main lineage masters of the Jonang Tradition.

Part One: The Outer Preliminaries and Lineage Invocation

This begins with the Outer Preliminaries which focus on what are known as the *Four Convictions of Renunciation*. These four contemplations inspire us to practice Dharma with a strong resolve and deep sense of urgency. We then make supplications to the realised masters of the *Vajra Yoga Lineage* in order to draw inspiration from the unbroken transmission of the Kalachakra teachings.

Part Two: The Inner Preliminaries

Before engaging in the practice of Buddhist Tantra, it is vital to establish the necessary qualities that will support the more advanced techniques. These practices form a common foundation for all systems of Highest Yoga Tantra such as Kalachakra. In Tibet, practitioners traditionally perform these practices intensively over a given period of time in order to accumulate familiarity with them. They include:

1. *Taking Refuge and Making Prostrations* to ensure we are on the right path and relying on valid sources of protection.
2. *Cultivating Bodhicitta* to establish a firm motivation to achieve enlightenment for the benefit of all sentient beings.
3. *Vajrasattva Purification* to clear away negative propensities from our minds.
4. *Offering Mandalas* to accumulate vast stores of merit that will be needed to achieve realisations.
5. *Practicing Guru Yoga* to unify our minds with the enlightened qualities of the Buddha.

Without developing a strong familiarity with these five practices we will not have the necessary conditions for authentically engaging in Buddhist Tantra.

Part Three: The Unique Kalachakra Preliminaries and Main Practice

Once the common preliminaries have been completed, we are then ready to engage in the uncommon preliminaries which are specific to the

Kalachakra system of practice. These begin with the generation stage practice of *Innate Kalachakra*, where you visualise yourself in the enlightened form of Kalachakra, becoming familiar with your own enlightened qualities. Through this practice of deity yoga, we learn to identify more with our own pure nature rather than with the distorted reality that is created by our afflicted states of mind. When we have familiarised ourselves with this pure perception, we can then enter into the profound practices of the Kalachakra completion stage. These practices provide very skilful means to achieve a direct experience of one's enlightened nature and to completely eradicate all forms of obscuration.

Part Four: Two Additional Guru Yogas

The final section of the book is dedicated to two alternative practices of Guru Yoga that are used to strengthen one's connection with the Jonang masters *Kunkhyen Dolpopa* and *Jetsun Taranatha*. More than any other masters, these two enlightened beings are the heart of the Jonang Tradition and the source of unbelievable blessings.

In this book I will be focusing on providing a concise summary of the essential points with a brief discussion of topics that I believe will be beneficial for Western practitioners. The root text is presented in inset italics and is followed by a brief commentary. The full text is also included as an appendix at the end of this book. If you would like to study a more comprehensive presentation of these practices, I would recommend you read my book *Unveiling Your Sacred Truth through the Kalachakra Path*, a three volume set that provides detailed information regarding the Buddhist philosophy that informs all of these practices.

* * *

While reading this text, you should try to avoid the three defects of the pot. Firstly, you should avoid being like an overturned pot—close minded so the teachings do not penetrate. Secondly, avoid being like a pot with holes in the bottom—retaining little of what you read. And finally, avoid being like a pot filled with poison—contaminated with bias and assumptions that distort your understanding of the material.

Instead, try to apply the three wisdoms. Develop the wisdom of studying by going over the material again and again. Develop the wisdom of contemplation by reflecting on the meaning of words from many angles, and develop the wisdom of meditation by grounding your understanding in the experience of actually engaging in the practice of the root text. In this way, by studying, contemplating and meditating with a pure intention, I sincerely hope that you will gradually come to discover your own sacred truth of enlightenment.

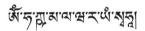

ཨོཾ་ཏ་ཀྲཱ་མ་ལ་ཤྭ་ར་ཡེ་སྭཱཧཱ།

PART ONE

The Outer Preliminaries And Lineage Invocation

— *The Wheel of Life* —
A Traditional Depiction of Cyclic Existence

CHAPTER ONE

The Four Convictions of Renunciation

The Kalachakra Path to enlightenment begins with the deep contemplation of four topics known as the *Four Convictions of Renunciation* or the *Four Thoughts which Turn the Mind towards Dharma*. First we reflect on the opportunity offered by a precious human life to engage in spiritual practice. Second, we reflect on the impermanence of all things, especially the certainty that we will die and the uncertainty of the moment of death. Third, we reflect upon the fundamental nature of dissatisfaction of this and future lives, causing us to turn away from everything that leads to suffering (including what we call ordinary happiness). Finally, we contemplate the Buddha's teachings on karma, which show how we are directly responsible for everything good or bad that happens to us in this or future lives, thereby opening the door to the possibility of following a path to liberation.

While all of these topics are covered in considerable detail in Book One of *Unveiling Your Sacred Truth*, the aim here is to encapsulate their meaning in a single verse:

> *O Think! During countless aeons, for this one time I have attained this precious human birth, which is so very hard to achieve and so easy to lose. The time of death is uncertain and the conditions leading to death are beyond my comprehension; this cherished body can die even today! So I shall abandon all worldly concerns that keep me chained to samsara, including all non-virtues and heavy heinous crimes. Instead I shall use the little time I have left wisely and practise Dharma with urgency, reflecting on the benefits of liberation.*

According to the Buddha's teachings, we are all involved in a constant cycle of suffering and uncertainty that spans across the process of birth, ageing, death and rebirth. Contrary to our limited belief that we are in control, each moment of our experience is dominated by our karmic propensities, including our emotional states and their objects. We therefore dwell in a state of anguish and uncertainty, never knowing what will happen next, bound by feelings of hope, fear and other emotions that take control of us. Even a delicious ice-cream has the potential for causing dissatisfaction when it becomes messy or leaves a nasty stain on our clothes; it can also become a source of aversion or make us sick when eaten in excess. This is what is understood as the fundamental suffering or unsatisfactory nature of life, which leads to a process called cyclic existence—or "samsara" in Sanskrit. This process condemns us to experience pain and suffering over and over again, and is likened to the movement of the wheel of a water mill or a fly trapped in a closed jar.

There is no beginning to this cycle of samsara and it only ends when we eliminate our ignorance of the true nature of reality. This ignorance refers to the fact that we hold onto a distorted idea of ourselves as being both "real" and "in-control", when in fact the nature of reality is impermanent and there is no truly existing "person" that controls everything. Once we let go of this idea of a solid self, there is no longer any firm ground for our emotions and karma to keep influencing us without choice, from moment to moment or lifetime to lifetime. Breaking free from this cycle is what we mean by the word "liberation".

As a human being, we have the most amazing capacity to understand the nature of our suffering. Based on this recognition, a precious human birth gives us the opportunity to practise Dharma purely and subsequently gain freedom. So long as we possess the unique set of eight freedoms and ten advantages, we will have the ability to follow the Buddha's path. This includes certain external conditions, such as being born in a place where the Buddha's teachings are accessible, and internal conditions which are mainly to do with having a conducive frame of mind.

These conditions, however, are very hard to achieve as they depend upon a great deal of merit accumulated over many lifetimes from actions such as maintaining a pure ethical discipline. To illustrate the rarity of this human birth, the Buddha told the story of the blind turtle who lives on the bottom of the ocean, rising up to the surface only once every hundred years. He said that the chance of a human birth is rarer than that of the turtle emerging at the exact moment for his head to poke through a wooden ring that is knocked about by the waves. To achieve all of the freedoms and advantages is even rarer than this.

Now that we have actually achieved this precious human rebirth, it is crucial to use it not only wisely, but urgently, as it is extremely easy to lose. It is so rare in fact, that this may well be our only opportunity to attain liberation. The amount of time we have left in this life to utilise in practising Dharma is extremely unpredictable as the time of death is uncertain and the conditions leading to death are beyond our comprehension. Even activities of daily life such as going to work, gardening or shopping are all potential causes of death. It rarely occurs to people to consider whether the next day or death will come first. Therefore, we must abandon all worldly concerns which are the source of suffering and keep us chained to samsara. There are *Eight Worldly Dharmas* which we normally seek to acquire or try to avoid: (1) gain and (2) loss; (3) pleasure and (4) pain; (5) attention and (6) being ignored; and (7) praise and (8) criticism. Instead of being led astray by these mundane concerns, we should use our time wisely and make Dharma our most important priority.

Generally speaking, there are *Ten Non-Virtuous Actions* you should strive to avoid. Three are of the body: (1) killing; (2) taking that which has not been freely given; and (3) sexual misconduct. Four are of the speech: (4) deceiving others through lying or misleading words; (5) divisive speech that destroys the harmony between others; (6) harsh speech that needlessly says things that are unpleasant to others; and (7) meaningless speech that is without purpose and wastes time. Finally, there are three of the mind: (8) covetousness that lusts after the belongings of others; (9) malice that wishes for others to experience suffering; and (10) holding wrong views that mistake the actual nature of things, such as supposing the existence of something that doesn't exist, denying the existence of something that does exist, and so forth. Each of these actions involves harming others with your body or speech, or generating the minds that will lead you to engage in such actions. Therefore the essence of this conduct is to abide in non-violence.

There are also a number of different sets of negative actions that create particularly heavy karmic consequences and thus should be abandoned completely. The first set are known as the *Eight Mistaken Behaviours*: (1) interrupting feast offerings of the faithful, thus hindering their accumulation of virtue; (2) disturbing the virtuous intentions of others, thus harming their mind; (3) Lacking faith in virtue and deprecating it; (4) aspiring to non-virtue and rejoicing in it; (5) abandoning the samaya-bond with the guru; (6) discouraging the wish of Dharma friends to withdraw from samsara; (7) transgressing samaya bonds of the yidam deity; and (8) leaving mandala practice and retreat. The essence of this set is to not abandon the supports for achieving enlightenment.

The second set is known as the *Four Heavy Actions*. These are: (1) swearing to act inhumanely; (2) allowing the shravaka discipline to degenerate and breaking the root pratimoksha vows; (3) allowing the bodhisattva discipline to degenerate and breaking the root bodhisattva vows; and (4) allowing the tantric samaya to degenerate and breaking the root tantric vows. Essentially, this is saying to uphold the ethical discipline of the Three Vows.

Another version of these four focuses on the way in which you engage with very important karmic situations. They include: (1) improperly taking the heavy practices of ordination; (2) improperly developing the heavy thoughts of the scholars; (3) improperly consuming the heavy food of the faithful, and (4) improperly using the heavy wealth of tantric practitioners. Each of these actions is heavy in the sense that actions done in relation to them will have a strong impact on your mind. It is very important to be careful in these four situations to avoid generating heavy negative karma.

And finally we have the *Five Heinous Crimes* of: (1) killing one's father; (2) killing one's mother; (3) killing an arhat; (4) causing a Tathagata to bleed due to having a harmful intention; and (5) causing a schism in the Sangha. These actions result in such powerful negative karma that they will dominate your mind at the time of death, generating extreme pain and torment in your next rebirth. Therefore, they should be abandoned at all costs.

Instead of engaging in these causes for suffering we should strive to practice virtuous actions such as protecting life, being generous, speaking truthfully and gently and also cultivating virtuous mental qualities such as compassion, humility and a wise view of reality. This has nothing to do with feeling guilty or being rigid in how we act, but rather with gaining confidence in which actions are beneficial to ourselves and others. With time and experience, our trust in this natural law of karma will grow.

If we die tomorrow without developing our spiritual qualities, we will definitely continue without freedom in this endless cycle of birth, ageing, sickness and death. In the little time we have left, having reflected deeply on the benefits of liberation, we must practise the Dharma with urgency, perseverance and great discipline so as to reach the ultimate freedom of enlightenment.

What is most important with these four contemplations is that we become genuinely disillusioned or weary with samsara, realising the futile aspects of this life and aspiring to "emerge" out of this pattern with a strong determination. Fortunately, even though you see all the pain and torment, you also see a way to get out, and so you develop a great sense of hope that liberation is possible and a wish to convey this hope to others.

These four thoughts also remind us that of all the things we could do with our life, practising the Dharma in an authentic and sincere way is really the most important and beneficial activity. While it may at times feel like we are swimming against the current by doing something that others can find strange or useless, we can have confidence in the profound purpose behind our actions.

EXHALING THE FOUL AIR

Having contemplated the Four Convictions, we can now prepare ourselves for the next practice with this simple breathing exercise:

> *Begin by closing the left nostril using the Pacifying Mudra and exhale three times through the right nostril, then change to the other nostril. Finish by exhaling three times through both nostrils. Visualise all afflictions and negativity leaving your body in the form of black smoke.*

This technique is called exhaling the foul air. It involves visualising all your impurities in the form of black smoke being forcefully blown out through your nostrils so that you can begin your practice with a clear mind.

This helps to remove counterproductive currents of energy which are associated with the breath and carry imprints of afflictive minds like attachment, aversion and ignorance. A simple version of this practice is to take three deep breaths, each time inhaling to the pit of the stomach and holding it for a while, then forcefully exhaling through both nostrils while visualising all impure energies such as lust and hatred leaving your mind and body.

A more elaborate version involves three rounds of three exhalations making nine exhalations in total:

1. First, fold the middle, ring finger and thumb of the left hand towards the palm. This will leave only the little finger and index finger of the hand pointing outward, which is known as the "pacify-

ing mudra". In a smooth, flowing and elegant motion, bring the left index finger up toward the left nostril. Inhale deeply but quietly through the mouth. Close the left nostril with the left index finger and release the air in three long exhalations, out through the right nostril.

2. Return the left hand to a natural position in the lap while bringing the right index finger upward in the same elegant motion. After inhaling, depress the right nostril, and exhale through the left nostril in the same manner as before.

3. Finally, return both hands to a natural position in the lap, inhale deeply through both nostrils, and then exhale through both nostrils in three long exhalations.

— Kunpang Thukje Tsondru —
Great Kalachakra Master who founded the Jonang Mountain Retreat

CHAPTER TWO

Brief Invocation of the Jonang Lineage Masters

Having recited and reflected upon the *Four Convictions of Renunciation*, you then invoke eight important lamas who were responsible for founding or establishing the great monastic institutions of the Jonang Tradition. A lineage refers to the teachings that have been transmitted in an unbroken line from the Buddha up to the present day. Such a lineage is authentic if it is based on real experience or realisation of the truth of those teachings. This experiential knowledge is handed down from teacher to student over many generations, along with the transmission of authentic commentaries or scriptures based on the words of the Buddha.

Without a firm commitment to an authentic lineage, we cannot realise the final aim of full and complete enlightenment. However, by following the teachings which have been handed down through such a lineage, it is possible to gradually progress along the path and eventually achieve the final goal of Buddhahood.

In science we are familiar with the value placed on knowledge produced through preceding research into a given field. Without that body of knowledge, it is very difficult to achieve any new discoveries. Likewise, a spiritual lineage represents the continuity of discoveries made by great spiritual practitioners which we can use to replicate their experience.

The lineage of the Kalachakra teachings began when Suchandra, the King of Shambhala, requested the teachings from Buddha Shakyamuni. Suchandra and his successors preserved this lineage in Shambhala for many hundreds of years, before eventually transmitting it to India in the tenth century. A few centuries later, the teachings spread to Tibet where they were primarily upheld by the dedicated practitioners of the Jonang Tradition. Within this tradition, the two most prominent figures were the Omniscient Dolpopa Sherab Gyaltsen and the Exalted Lord Taranatha. Both of these unparalleled masters attained great spiritual realisations, composed many influential texts and were responsible for establishing the extraordinary study and practice curriculum that is used in Jonang monasteries to this day.

INVOCATION OF THE JONANG MASTERS

To invoke a lineage means to make a connection with the spiritual influence of the great masters of the past, as well as to the omniscient Buddha, who is the ultimate source of that lineage. These masters devoted their lives to achieving enlightenment and to preserving the precious Kalachakra teachings. Therefore, by bringing them to mind we form a bond with their timeless aspirations. If we do this with a pure enough intention, it is then possible to actually feel the presence of these masters and receive their guidance.

Ultimately, however, we are not invoking anything outside of ourselves, for these masters are nothing more than a magical display of our own enlightened nature and therefore by remembering what these great beings achieved, we remember our own potential to manifest those very same qualities.

Some practitioners do not recite this brief invocation, as many of the eight lamas mentioned here are also included in the long lineage prayer, which follows, so if time is limited you may choose to go straight to the long lineage invocation.

The Root Lama

Glorious and precious root lama, having taken your seat upon the lotus of devotion at the crown of my head, bless me with your great compassion, take care of me with your great kindness, and grant me the siddhis of your body, speech and mind!

First you invoke your glorious and precious root lama, "Palden Lama" in Tibetan. *Palden* means "one who possesses glory or richness". *Lama* is a Tibetan word equivalent to guru in Sanskrit, which literally means "heavy" or full of good qualities. In Tibetan *la* means "above" and *ma* means "one who possesses". When combined we have the word *lama*, meaning "one who is above". Although lama is singular here, in Tibetan there is actually no distinction between singular and plural. Therefore our root lama does not necessarily refer to only one teacher— you could in fact have one, three or even more root teachers, as well as many other branch teachers who occupy various levels of importance in your spiritual journey.

That being said, after careful examination you may find a single teacher who is kindest to you personally or whose wisdom you find the most penetrating. If this is the case, you should regard them as your root lama and show them honour and respect at every opportunity, since this is the most important relationship you will ever have.

Visualising the lama taking a seat upon the lotus of devotion at the crown of your head symbolises the importance of the lama and the need to follow their instructions if you wish to further your spiritual development. In Asian and particularly Tibetan culture, placing oneself below another is a sign of great respect; for this reason the lama is visualised above one's crown. This is also the reason why it is customary for lamas to sit in an elevated position when giving teachings, reminding students to show great respect for both the teacher and the precious Dharma that he or she imparts.

If you aspire to be a tantric practitioner, as you fall asleep you should visualise the lama at your heart-centre, seated in the centre of a lotus flower, then as you awaken, imagine that he rises upwards through your central channel to take his place at the crown of your head throughout the day. In this way you can develop a strong connection with his presence, and through this you gain confidence in your own Buddha-nature, which the lama represents.

Praying to the lama to bless us with his great compassion and kindness is a way to remind ourselves that the lama represents the Buddha. In some forms of Buddhism the lama is regarded as a coach or a spiritual friend travelling along the same path, while in Vajrayana Buddhism he is considered to be the embodiment of all enlightened beings. It is said that if we view him as a human being we will receive the blessings of a human being, whereas if we see him as a Buddha, we will receive the blessings of a Buddha. Receiving blessings means our own good qualities increase as a result of our faith and devotion—this comes from inside of us and not from some external source.

The honour and devotion we have towards the lama is not based on a blind or theistic faith but rather a clear and confident faith. This means we have carefully analysed, tested and gained confidence in the Buddha's teachings, and have also gained confidence in the lama's good qualities, especially his kindness and his wish to show us the path to enlightenment. Although the kindness and compassion displayed by lamas may not be quite like the kindness shown by a mother to her child, it will definitely lead to the greatest possible benefit for the student. For this reason, we can view their body, speech and mind as sacred.

The *siddhis* bestowed by the lama are spiritual accomplishments or powers we develop through spiritual practice, whether they be "ordinary" or "supreme". Ordinary siddhis include supernatural abilities such as clairvoyance, while supreme siddhis refer to the qualities of enlightened realisation.

The text continues with prayers to eight key lamas of the Jonang Tradition. We should note that it is Tibetan custom for lamas to have many different names, and that some of these lamas are given different titles later on in the practice.

Kunkyen Dolpopa Sherab Gyaltsen

I pray to you Dolpopa. You are the omniscient Lord of Dharma, who perfectly understands the three turnings of the wheel of Dharma and the four classes of tantra. Please show the unmistaken path to all beings!

Dolpopa Sherab Gyaltsen is a central figure in the Jonang Tradition. He was known as *omniscient* because he was such an outstanding scholar and highly realised meditation master. His main accomplishment was to establish the unified system of Jonang practice that brought together the sutra lineage of Zhentong Madhyamaka with the tantric lineage of the Kalachakra Tantra. Born in 1292, in a remote region of western Tibet,

Dolpopa's birth had been prophesied by many sutras and tantras such as the *Great Drum Sutra*. He is commonly believed to have been an emanation of the Bodhisattva Avalokiteshvara as well as the Shambhalan King Pundarika.

Initially trained in Sakya Monastery as a very pure monk with perfect moral conduct, Dolpopa often travelled to many of the surrounding monasteries to receive teachings and to meditate. When he was thirty, he journeyed to the Jomonang Valley to visit the *Jonang Mountain Retreat.* He was so amazed by the realisations of the Jonang practitioners that he chose to give up his prestigious position as abbot of Sakya and moved to Jomonang to become a meditator.

Dolpopa would spend much of his life in retreat, eventually attaining realisations of the first four Vajra Yogas and complete mastery of the first three. It was at this time the Zhentong View manifested clearly in his mind, revealing to him the definitive meaning of the Buddha's final teachings on Buddha-nature and showing him how all the teachings could be understood without conflict. This philosophy, which relied heavily on the *Five Great Treatises of Maitreya*, would become the cornerstone of the Jonang curriculum and provide a crucial method for connecting the theory and practice of both sutra and tantra. It was due to Dolpopa's brilliant writings that the Zhentong View grew in prominence and was accepted by most to be the pinnacle of philosophical thought.

As the fourth abbot of Jonang Monastery, Dolpopa travelled throughout the region of Ü-Tsang, giving teachings, composing texts and debating with all the prominent scholars of his time. During the construction of the Great Stupa of Jonang, Dolpopa finished work on his excellent text known as *The Mountain Doctrine*. Within an ocean of scriptural quotations, Dolpopa systematically overcame all objections that had been raised by his contemporaries and demonstrated the profound truth behind the Zhentong philosophy. It is said, that during this time, there was no one in the province of Ü-Tsang who did not count Dolpopa as one of their most revered teachers.

In his later years, Dolpopa gave up the responsibilities of abbot and dedicated himself to meditation and teaching. Subsequently, his realisations became even more profound and subtle. As a result, he displayed many extraordinary capacities such as no longer needing to eat or drink. When he did take food however, it seemed as if there was no limit to the amount he could eat, and yet, no matter how much he ate, there was never any waste, as it was all consumed by the blazing of his inner fire.

In 1361, soon after Dolpopa had returned from a long journey to Lhasa, he passed into parinirvana amidst countless auspicious signs. While his physical body has long since dissolved, his spiritual presence continues until this day. For this reason we pray that he will continue to show the unmistaken path to all beings.

Kazhipa Rinchen Pal

I pray to you Kazhipa. Embodiment of all the Buddhas' activities, you make the precious jewel of the Dharma shine like the sun by displaying the four sublime powers.

Kazhipa Rinchenpal (Ratnashri in Sanskrit), was born into a royal family in the Gyalrong region of eastern Tibet. Before his birth it was prophesied that he would clarify the meaning of numerous secret tantras and would liberate many sentient beings. After developing a strong foundation in the Dharma, he travelled to Ü-Tsang where he studied under many of the direct heart-disciples of Dolpopa, such as Choklé Namgyal and Nyabön Kunga. Receiving the complete teachings of the omniscient Jonangpa, he become a highly realised holder of the lineage. When he returned home he founded the famed *Chojé Monastery* in Dzamthang, followed by many branch monasteries in the neighbouring regions.

According to the fundamental teachings of Buddhism, the Buddha was an Indian prince who renounced the conventional world and subsequently achieved enlightenment. However from the viewpoint of Mahayana Buddhism, the Buddha was already enlightened and his life was merely a display or an example of how to follow the path he taught. Similarly, all the great teachers of this world can be perceived as already being enlightened, appearing in human form out of their great compassion, to lead others along this path. For example, we can view someone like the Dalai Lama as an enlightened being, taking birth in our realm to demonstrate a life of tolerance and compassion as a leader and a pure "simple monk". It is from this perspective that we speak of masters like Khazipa being the *embodiment of all the Buddhas' activities.*

The *Four Sublime Powers*, also known as the four Buddha-activities, describe different ways that Buddhas can bring benefit to beings within varying situations. They include: (1) pacifying or creating peace; (2) expanding or enriching possibilities; (3) controlling situations or circumstances; and (4) subduing or destroying negativity with wrathful compassion.

Tséchu Rinchen Drakpa

I pray to you Rinchen Drakpa. You are adorned by Dharma teachings and profound realisations and your activities are vast and incomparable; whoever sees or hears you will surely be liberated!

Rinchen Drakpa (Ratnakirti in Skt.) was born in 1462 and was the closest disciple of the Gyalwa Chöje Khazhipa Rinchen Pal. It was Ratnakirti who was responsible for founding the second major monastic institution in the Dzamthang region—*Tséchu Monastery.* He was a skilled scholar, composing many texts on the Kalachakra practice and various other topics, and was therefore "*adorned by Dharma teachings*". Under the skilful guidance of both Khazipa and Rinchen Drakpa, the Jonang Tradition flourished in the eastern regions of Tibet.

The statement "*whoever sees or hears you will surely be liberated!*" refers to the karmic connection created by meeting a great being who vows to lead whoever he encounters to enlightenment. The seed planted by this connection is sure to mature and eventually ripen into supremely beneficial fruit.

Chojé Gyalwa Sangyé

I pray to you Gyalwa Sangye. Ordained in the Dharma, your devotion towards your masters is supreme and your actions are a glorious display of purity, discipline, wisdom and compassion.

Chöje Gyalwa Sangyé was the first reincarnation of Ratnashri, the founder of Chöje Monastery. Born as Rinchen Sangpo in the Zhakshöd region of Gyalrong, he is perhaps most well known for training hundreds of scholar-practitioners and sending them out into neighbouring regions to teach the Dharma. It is said that Gyalwa Sangyé and his students successfully established more than one hundred and eight branch monasteries. He displayed many enlightened qualities such as incredible renunciation, purity of his monastic vows, strict discipline to avoid even the slightest transgression, unwavering concentration and unmatched wisdom. He was thus a shining example for all who knew him.

Jetsun Taranatha

> *I pray at your feet Kunga Nyingpo. You are the source of all that is good, the embodiment of all Buddhas and the sole refuge for all beings, a protector from samsara and nirvana.*

Kunga Nyingpo, also known as Jetsun Taranatha or Drolway Gonpo, was one of the most important Jonang lineage masters. He lived from 1575 until 1635 and was believed to be the reincarnation of the great Rimé Master, Jonang Kunga Drolchok. Studying intensively at Chölang Jangster Monastery, he quickly covered the five main subjects of the Buddhist scriptures as well as the tantras, and thereby received transmission for all lineages of Vajrayana Buddhism.

One of Taranatha's most renowned accomplishments was the composition of a Dharma history of India, based on recollections from one of his previous lives as the Indian Mahasiddha Drupchen Nakpopa. To this day, this Dharma history is still considered authoritative and is widely used by many scholars. Taranatha also established the great Jonang monastery of *Takten Damchö Ling* where he composed roughly forty volumes of texts on a wide variety of subjects. In particular, texts like *The Essence of Other Emptiness* were influential in clearing away confusion regarding the Zhentong View and reviving Dolpopa's original philosophy. He benefited beings in countless ways and was hailed as a great ornament of the Buddha's definitive teachings and the source of all that is good.

As we have seen, from the perspective of Vajrayana, all great beings are manifestations of the Buddhas who are one in their wisdom nature. We can therefore say that Taranatha embodies all of the Buddhas and is the sole refuge of all beings. He protects them from the suffering and pain of samsara, as well as the temptation to seek nirvana, a limited version of enlightenment where one's mind-stream is "cut off" from the vaster goal of liberating all beings.

Chalongwa Ngawang Trinlé

I pray to you Chalongwa, Wish-fulfilling tree of the Dharma. Your speech blossoms like flowers and new followers delight in your teachings like bees to pollen.

Chalongwa Ngawang Trinlé was born in 1657 and studied for much of his early years in the Chalong Monastery of Tsang. He later become a very close disciple of Khidrup Lodrö Namgyal, who was responsible for founding *Tsangwa Monastery*, the third great monastic institution to be built in Dzamthang. Following in his teacher's footsteps, Ngawang Trinlé travelled to the east where he spent considerable time guiding a vast number of students and establishing Tsangwa as a major centre for the study and practice of the Jonang Dharma. He was recognised for his great wisdom and exceptional abilities and was eagerly invited to visit many regions by kings and leaders.

A wish-fulfilling tree is one that bears fruit according to one's wishes, needs or desires. In the same way, a great teacher can present the Dharma to perfectly meet the needs and aspirations of their audience. Similarly, Chalongwa's speech is likened to blossoming flowers which bloom when conditions are right, and his teachings are compared to pollen that resembles a sweet elixir, attracting new followers.

Ngawang Tenzin Namgyal

I pray to you Gawi Chöpel. Your mastery of speech is limitless and your appearance is perfect. You are the source of all supreme qualities as your moral conduct is sublime and your knowledge is unsurpassed like a great treasure.

Gawi Chöpel, also known as Ngawang Tenzin Namgyal, was born in 1691 and was the first Kalachakra Vajra Master to reside at Tsangwa Monastery. Recognised as the first reincarnation of Tsangwa's founder, Lodrö Namgyal, Gawi Chöpel received the complete teachings of the Jonang from his master Ngawang Trinlé. When he was only ten years old, he entered into retreat and achieved many realisations. For much of his adult life, Tenzin Namgyal dedicated himself to continuous practice of the Six Vajra Yogas in remote locations such as the Amitabha Cave, where Padmasambhava had meditated.

Gawi Chöpel was renowned for overcoming obstacles with magical powers in order to establish the Jonang system of teaching and practice. Guided by direct contact with deities and his supreme skill in meditation, he had great impact on his surrounding environment and his teachings benefited many. He was also known for his sublime moral conduct and his unsurpassed knowledge. In 1738, following his own prediction, he passed away after spending the entire day giving advice and prophecies to his students.

This is another verse that uses Vajrayana language, regarding Gawi Chöpel as a Buddha-emanation with perfect appearance, speech and other supreme qualities. Generally we describe Buddhas in terms of five types of characteristics—of body, speech, mind, qualities and activities. We can then speak of great lamas as being speech emanations, mind emanations and so forth.

Kunzang Trinlé Namgyal

I pray to you Trinlé Namgyal. Your wisdom shines like Manjushri, embodying the wisdom of countless Buddhas. You are a treasure of compassion, the power of all the enlightened ones.

Kunzang Trinlé Namgyal was born in the Gyalrong region of eastern Tibet and was the second reincarnation of the famed Lodrö Namgyal of Tsangwa Monastery. He trained diligently in the Dharma from a very young age, forming spiritual relationships with many great masters and receiving countless empowerments and instructions. He attained extraordinary realisations and was especially known for his wisdom, which was said to equal that of countless Buddhas, particularly the bodhisattva Manjushri. He was therefore highly sought after as a Dharma teacher and attracted many students.

Manjushri is a high-level bodhisattva who embodies the wisdom of all the Buddhas. Other bodhisattvas embody different qualities, such as Avalokiteshvara (Chenrezig in Tibetan) who embodies the compassion of the all the Buddhas and Vajrapani, who embodies their power. Therefore, in this verse, Trinlé Namgyal is being honoured as one who displays the enlightened qualities of wisdom, compassion and power.

All Dharma Teachers

I now pray to all of my precious teachers who have bestowed upon me transmissions, empowerments and teachings; whoever even remembers you will be released from suffering, and whoever has devotion will surely reach enlightenment.

This final verse refers to all of the precious Dharma teachers you have encountered throughout your life, whether they have given you transmissions, empowerments, personal instructions or other forms of authentic teaching. It does not matter if the Dharma you received was a small morsel or great volumes of precious teachings. Thinking of your teachers should provide a refuge from suffering and bring you peace of mind, so long as you have developed confidence in their teachings. If you have devotion and are motivated to practise diligently, there is no doubt you will eventually reach enlightenment as a result of this sacred connection

WRITER'S HOMAGE

> *OM GURU BUDDHA BODHISATTVA BHAYANA NAMO NAMAH*
> *I pay homage to the lama who generously bestows the wish-fulfilling jewel of Dharma for all beings.*

This is a writer's homage and is not normally included as part of the practice. The lama or guru is whoever leads you on the path to Buddhahood by generously bestowing the wish-fulfilling jewel of Dharma, and is therefore the source of all good qualities. It is common for writers to offer homage to holy beings in order to clear obstacles to their work.

— The Jonang-Shambhala Tradition —
Masters of the Six Vajra Yogas of the Kalachakra Completion Stage

CHAPTER THREE

Full Invocation of the Vajra Yoga Lineage

This next prayer is specifically designed to help you cultivate a strong connection with the lineage lamas of the profound Kalachakra Path of the Six Vajra Yogas. As I mentioned earlier, these teachings were first transmitted by Buddha Shakyamuni to the Dharma King Suchandra of Shambhala. Suchandra took those teachings back to Shambhala where they were preserved for around seventeen hundred years. The teachings were then transmitted to the Mahasiddha Manjuvajra who became known as the Great Kalachakrapada. The teachings flourished in India for a time and were eventually transmitted to Tibet through more than seventeen different lineages.

One particularly complete lineage of pith instructions was transmitted through the great pandita Somanatha to the Tibetan translator Dro Sherab Drak. This tradition became known as the Dro tradition and was subsequently propagated through a series of extraordinary yogis who all achieved the highest of realisations. After more than eight generations had passed, the great scholar-practitioner Kunpang Thukje Tsondru combined all seventeen lineages into a single unified stream. In this process, Thukje Tsondru founded the Jonang Mountain Retreat in the incredibly blessed valley of Jomonang.

Many great masters flocked to Jonang to meditate on their profound system of the Six Vajra Yogas. Greatest of all was the Omniscient Dharma King Dolpopa Sherab Gyaltsen, who unveiled the definitive meaning of the Zhentong View and established the unified system of study and practice that became the foundation of the Jonang Tradition. The Jonang Dharma continued to flourish in the provinces of Ü and Tsang well into the seventeenth century; however, due to political instability and sectarian clashes, many Jonang masters were forced to seek refuge in the far eastern regions of Amdo and Kham.

Since that time, the lineage has been preserved purely in an unbroken stream by the great Vajra Masters of the famed Dzamthang monasteries—Chöjé, Tséchu and Tsangwa. From these main centres, the lineage flowed into hundreds of branch monasteries, giving rise to different listings of lineage holders. One lineage of particular note passed through the prolific twenty-first century scholar-practitioner Ngawang Lodrö Drakpa and then to his students, Yonten Zangpo and Kunga Sherab Saljé.

The lineage that is presented in this book was passed through the accomplished yogi Ngawang Chözin Gyatso, extending to my own precious teacher Kybajé Lama Lobsang Trinlé. It is the lineage currently held in Tashi Chöthang Monastery, a branch of the larger Dzamthang Tsangwa Monastery. Due to the efforts of modern Jonang masters in India, Australia and the United States, the teachings of these lineages are now starting to be transmitted outside of Tibet.

INVOCATION OF THE VAJRA YOGA LINEAGE

The invocation of the lineage masters begins with a visualisation which at first may seem quite elaborate, but as you build a familiarity with the different elements over time, it will become easier. To this end you should visualise the entire assembly of lineage masters beginning with the Primordial Buddha, Vajradhara, Kalachakra and Buddha Shakyamuni. Once you have established the visualisation you can then request their blessings.

Visualisation

In the space immediately in front of you, in the centre of a five-coloured display of rainbow light and on top of a five-layered seat made from a lotus, and moon, sun, Rahu and Kalagni discs, visualise your root lama in the form of blue Vajradhara seated upon a throne.

Your root lama appears as Vajradhara, his body is blue in colour, with one face and two arms, holding a vajra and bell crossed at the level of his heart. He is seated with his legs in the full lotus posture, dressed in silk garments, adorned by precious ornaments such as a crown, earrings, necklaces, armlets, bracelets and anklets and possessing all the marks and signs of a Buddha.

He is surrounded by all the lineage masters of the Six Vajra Yogas, including the immaculate Primordial Buddha, the enjoyment body Kalachakra, the emanation body Shakyamuni, the thirty-five Dharma Kings of Shambhala and all the Indian and Tibetan lineage masters. Their bodies appear radiant, splendid and pleasing.

Each component of this visualisation has profound significance. For example, the four seats of moon, sun, rahu and kalagni each represent the four drops of the waking state, dream state, deep-sleep state and primordial wisdom state respectively. Guru Vajradhara, who is the tantric embodiment of enlightenment, sits majestically upon a lion throne and is inseparable from the nature of your own root lama. Although it may seem contrived, this visualisation is not something make-believe or the creation of some new phenomenon; rather it is a profoundly skilful means to develop "pure perception" of the enlightened reality which is beyond all ordinary dualistic notions and distinctions.

Each attribute of Vajradhara's body also has profound meaning. The crossed five-pronged vajra and bell represent the union of indestructible wisdom and compassion, and the marks and ornaments symbolise other aspects of enlightened reality, such as the purified five aggregates and eight consciousnesses. Although it is good to visualise the form of Vajradhara to counteract our ordinary perception, some people may derive more benefit from visualising the lama in their ordinary human form.

Traditionally one would take a few minutes to establish this visualisation before reciting the prayers, and it is best if you can visualise all the lineage masters gathered together, with their bodies appearing radiant, splendid and pleasing. Too much focus on the details however can become an obstacle. What is most important is to occupy your mind with a strong feeling of connection with the lineage, thinking that all of these holy beings are actually present. As you recite the prayer, you can bring to mind each lineage master individually as well as any details of their stories that you can remember. Practising in this way creates a link between you and the precious lineage. It is this connection which will bring you closer to the sacred reality of your own Buddha-nature.

Prayers to the Root and Lineage Lamas

I pay homage and pray to my root lama.
I pray to the root and lineage lamas.
I pray to the wish-fulfilling lineage.

Paying homage and praying to the root and lineage lamas is a way of showing our deepest honour and respect, reminding ourselves how precious this spiritual relationship is. The Tibetan word for root lama is "*tsawi lama*", and this refers to the Dharma teacher or teachers you have the most gratitude towards—those who have personally shown you the path to liberation. Of all the teachers you have encountered, your root lama is whoever you regard as the most important, whoever you have received the greatest number of teachings from, or whoever has benefited you the most in an enlightened way. This can be one or more lamas as there is no limitation on the number.

The other lineage masters may not have taught you directly, yet they are an integral part of the transmission lineage. Without this lineage of transmission, enlightenment cannot be attained, and therefore the lineage is like a wish-fulfilling gem, granting any wish a person desires. Even if you haven't met them, you should feel deep humility and gratitude towards these masters, in order to make a spiritual connection with this holy lineage.

Please bless me so the lineage transmission will enter within me.
May all these blessings enter my heart!
Please bless me so the darkness in my heart be cleared away!

As explained previously, you receive blessings when your own good qualities increase, or when you become closer to the reality of your Buddha-nature. The transmission lineage is like a staircase that helps you uncover this nature, leading to deep transformation as the blessings enter your heart. This is much more than temporarily "feeling good." Through this practice you can clear away the darkness of ignorance and other defilements that prevent you from experiencing the jewel of your own Buddha-nature.

I pray to the lama.
I pray to the lord of Dharma.
May all the spiritual fathers and their heart-sons bless me!

The lama is someone "above oneself" who is superior in spiritual qualities and therefore worthy of praise and homage. *Lord of Dharma* means they are like a king of spirituality. *Heart-sons* refer to those in the lineage who are close disciples of great lamas, who are their own spiritual fathers. They are like a prince who will ascend to their master's throne to continue their work. For example, Dolpopa had fourteen heart-sons who were each responsible for propagating the Jonang Dharma after Dolpopa passed into parinirvana. These included Chokgyalwa Choklé Namgyal, Tsungmed Nyabön Kunga and so forth.

Prayers to the Ground, Path and Result

I pray to the Tathagatagarbha, the essence of the primordial ground.
I pray to the profound Kalachakra vajra path.
I pray to the unveiled dharmakaya body of the reality of enlightenment, the result of the exhaustion of samsara.

The *Tathagatagarbha* refers to the fully awakened enlightened mind of Buddhahood, whose essence resides in all beings as the primordial ground of enlightenment, yet is currently obscured by temporary defilements. Buddha Maitreya likens this primordial ground to a treasure underground, honey amidst bees, grain in its husk or a precious image under a layer of clay. The *profound Kalachakra vajra path* refers to the teachings and practices you must follow to awaken this true nature according to the Kalachakra Tantra. This includes all of the preliminary practices described in the Divine Ladder as well as the main practice of the Six Vajra Yogas.

The *unveiled dharmakaya body of the reality of enlightenment* is the final result of following the path, at which point all afflictions are completely purified and realisation of Buddhahood is attained. Although the ground and the result are inseparable, on a relative level we need to practice the path in order to unwrap the many layers of defilements which prevent us from seeing this truth.

The dharmakaya is one of three bodies or dimensions of enlightenment (*kaya* in Sanskrit). It refers to the permanent, unchanging, empty aspect of the enlightened mind. This is the dimension of reality that is experienced by a Buddha. The other dimensions are the sambhogakaya enjoyment body and nirmanakaya emanation body, both of which represent the dimensions of reality that are experienced by sentient beings.

Prayers to the Four Bodies of the Buddha

Primordial Buddha

Guru Vajradahra

Shri Kalachakra

Buddha Shakyamuni

I pray to the sublime primordial Buddha.
I pray to the dharmakaya body of the reality of enlightenment Vajradhara.

Primordial Buddha and Vajradhara are different names used to describe the dharmakaya body of the reality of enlightenment. Each of these names points to a different aspect of this sacred truth, which is completely beyond any attempt to conceptualise. This is similar to the many names you use to describe the different roles you play in different circumstances—for example as a doctor, a husband or a first-born child.

Primordial Buddha means beginningless, timeless and never stained by the relative truth or the afflictions of samsara, just as space pervades all other elements, yet is not in the slightest way affected by them. This is known as the Svabhavikakaya or nature body. It is the aspect of how reality actually is.

Vajradhara is similar to the primordial Buddha, but the emphasis is placed on the wisdom that knows reality as it is. This is known as the jñana-dharmakaya or wisdom-truth body. In this way, even though the Primordial Buddha and Vajradhara are inseparable, they each help to highlight the subtle characteristics of the definitive meaning.

I pray to the sambhogakaya enjoyment body Kalachakra.

In the root text "longku" means sambhogakaya, which is the subtlest and purest display of the dharmakaya, also known as the enjoyment body. As sentient beings engage in spiritual practice, they slowly peel away the many layers of obscurations, purifying their minds and allowing them to experience increasingly more subtle levels of reality. The sambhogakaya represents the most subtle and purest level of dualistic experience, perceived only by highly realised bodhisattvas on the tenth level of spiritual development.

The Tibetan word for Kalachakra is "Dukyi Korlo", which is literally translated as "Wheel of Time". Here the notion of *time* refers to change or transformation, while *wheel* refers to the idea of an endless cycle or process. On a gross level, *Wheel of Time* indicates the infinite patterns of transformation that we all perceive; at a more subtle level, these two concepts point to the conventional nature of phenomena as being a union of great compassion and emptiness; then at the most subtle level, they refer to the ultimate nature of reality which is a union of immutable bliss and empty-form. The important thing to remember here is that Kalachakra is a term that refers to the totality of all experience and therefore can be understood in different ways depending on the subtlety of your perspective.

At Amaravati in Southern India, when the Buddha first taught the Kalachakra Tantra to an audience that included a vast array of both humans and non-humans, he manifested in the sambhogakaya form of the Kalachakra deity, along with a mandala of 636 deities. The main recipient of these teachings was King Suchandra, the great Dharma King who transmitted these teachings to the divine realm of Shambhala. Through the power of these teachings the Kings of Shambhala were able to develop a system of practice that effectively united people from a range of religious backgrounds, bringing peace and harmony to their kingdom.

Only beings with extremely high spiritual attainment, such as King Suchandra, could perceive and experience the enlightened form of Kalachakra directly, therefore saying that Buddha Shakyamuni appeared in the sambhogakaya form of Kalachakra to teach the Kalachakra Tantra, signifies that these teachings were communicated on an extremely subtle level of experience.

I pray to the nirmanakaya emanation body, Buddha Shakyamuni.

Put simply, the nirmanakaya emanation body is the being we commonly refer to as Prince Siddhartha, who demonstrated to ordinary human beings how they could become completely awakened Buddhas. He is often referred to as Buddha Shakyamuni, where *Buddha* means "awakened one" and *Shakya* refers to the name of his clan. On a deeper level, the nirmanakaya emanation body is how the sambhogakaya appears to ordinary beings; first appearing in human form and then displaying a life with birth, ageing and death.

In this way, nirmanakayas provide the bridge between the enlightened mind of the Buddha and the infinite sentient beings who are suffering in cyclic existence. Since the nirmanakayas appear in accordance with the karmic propensities of sentient beings, there is no limit to the shapes they can adopt. No matter what form a nirmanakaya manifests as, they are always perfectly suited to communicate the dharma to the sentient beings that encounter them.

Prayers to the Lineage Masters of Shambhala

I pray to the thirty-five Dharma Kings of Shambhala.

Shambhala is a term used to refer to the manifestation of peace and harmony in the experience of sentient beings. On an ultimate level, it is indivisible from the primordial ground of our own Buddha-nature. Conventionally, it is experienced in a wide variety of ways. When we refer to the Dharma Kings of Shambhala, we are referring to a specific manifestation of Shambhala known as the *Sublime Realm of Shambhala*.

This form of Shambhala is a pure realm of experience that has been generated from the enlightened aspirations of tenth level bodhisattvas, in combination with the karmic connections they have fostered with the sentient beings of this planet. It is a unique realm of opportunity which provides the humans of this world with all the necessary conditions to progress rapidly along the path to achieving enlightenment. While it can

— The Thirty-Five Dharma Kings of Shambhala —
Seven Dharma Kings, Twenty-Five Kalki Kings and Three Kings of the Golden Age

be considered a human realm, it is more subtle than this realm and therefore can only be experienced by the minds of beings with a corresponding level of subtlety.

It was from this subtle level of experience that the Bodhisattva King Suchandra emanated when he requested the Kalachakra from Buddha Shakyamuni in the Great Dhanyakataka Stupa of Amaravati in the south of India. At that time the Buddha, as Kalachakra, prophesied that there would be thirty-five Dharma Kings to uphold these teachings until the time of the next Golden Age. These kings are broken into three groups: the Seven Dharma Kings, the Twenty-Five Kalki Kings and the Three Kings of the Golden-Age.

The *Seven Dharma Kings* were the first seven generations of kings who were responsible for establishing the practice of Kalachakra in the land of Shambhala. Through their shining example they demonstrated the profound capacity we all have and inspired the citizens of Shambhala to transcend their limitations. These seven included: (1) Suchandra, (2) Sureshvara, (3) Taji, (4) Somadatta, (5) Sureshvara, (6) Vishvamurti, and (7) Sureshana.

The *Twenty-Five Kalki Kings* began when the great Dharma King Manjushri Yashas successfully united the people of Shambhala under a common recognition of their ultimate nature. By condensing the teachings of the Kalachakra Tantra, he made them available to a much broader audience, and in so doing showed them how to cut through their bias and unveil their sacred truth. Since the reign of Yashas, the Kings of Shambhala have been known as *Kalki*, meaning "unifier of castes". At this time we are currently living during the reign of the 20th Kalki, Aniruddha. The full list of Kalki Kings are: (1) Manjushri Yashas, (2) Pundarika, (3) Bhadra, (4) Vijaya, (5) Sumitra, (6) Raktapani, (7) Vishnugupta, (8) Arkakirti, (9) Subhadra, (10) Samudravijaya, (11) Aja, (12) Surya, (13) Vishvarupa, (14) Shashiprabha, (15) Ananta, (16) Mahipala, (17) Shripala, (18) Harivikrama, (19) Mahabala, (20) Aniruddha, (21) Narasimha, (22) Maheshvara, (23) Anantavijaya, (24) Yashas and (25) Raudra Chakri.

During the reign of the last Kalki King, it is prophesied that the world will reach a tipping point in the balance between ignorance and wisdom. Afflicted ways of thinking will dominate the world, resulting in unprecedented violence and degeneration, and yet at the same time, the minds of the people will have ripened, making it possible for the 25th Kalki, Raudra Chakri to emerge from Shambhala to re-invigorate the Dharma, ushering in an age of unparalleled peace and harmony. The three Kings who are prophesied to rule during this time are known as the *Three Kings of the Golden-Age*: (1) Brahma, (2) Sureshvara and (3) Kashyapa.

Prayers to the Lineage Masters of India

Dushapa Chenpo

Dushapa Nyipa

Gyaltse Nalendrapa

Panchen Dawa Gonpo

I pray to the Drupchen Dushapa Chenpo.

Drupchen Dushapa Chenpo, also known as Kalachakrapada the Elder, was the first holder of the complete Kalachakra lineage in this human realm. Born as Manjuvajra, the son of a Brahmin yogi, he grew up studying at the famed universities of Odantapuri and Nalanda in the northeast of India. Having attained considerable expertise in each of the five sciences, he received a vision of Manjushri telling him to travel north in search of Shambhala. Manjuvajra journeyed deep into the mountains where he met an emanation of the 11th Kalki King, Aja. The emanation bestowed on Manjuvajra all the empowerments and pith instructions, allowing him to achieve exceptional levels of realisation. After practicing for six months, he was able to travel to Shambhala where he received a treasure trove of teachings directly from the Kalki himself.

After memorising all of the precious teachings, Manjuvajra returned home and began to share the teachings with all who requested them. Through the guidance of his unrivalled realisation, the practice of the Six Vajra Yogas flourished in India. Dushapa Chenpo eventually mastered all six yogas, achieving complete enlightenment by actualising the state of rainbow body. *Drupchen* is the Tibetan word for "Mahasiddha", meaning someone with a high level of spiritual attainment, while *chenpo* is Tibetan for "great".

I pray to the Drupchen Dushapa Nyipa.

Manjuvajra's main disciple was a lay person, born of royal caste, known as Shri Badra. Due to his extraordinary attainments, he also became known as Kalachakrapada the Younger or Drupchen Dushapa Nyipa in Tibetan (*Nyipa* meaning "second"). In his spiritual practice, Shri Badra experienced many enlightened deities and realms and was recognised by all to have attained the twelfth stage of the Bodhisattva levels. While he had many students, twelve achieved rainbow body under his guidance. It was in fact Shri Badra who first worked with Tibetan translators to introduce the Kalachakra Tantra into Tibet.

I pray to Gyaltse Nalendrapa.

The practice of Kalachakra increased significantly under the guidance of Shri Badra's heart-disciple, the great Nalanda abbot Bodhibhadra, known in Tibet as Gyaltse Nalendrapa. In a famous story, Bodhibhadra posted a sign on the doorway to Nalanda University that effectively stated that if you did not understand Kalachakra, you did not understand the Buddha's ultimate intent. In response to this bold challenge, 500 scholars debated with Nalendrapa and were each defeated. This event firmly established the Kalachakra teachings in India, making it one of the most widespread systems of practice.

I pray to Panchen Dawa Gonpo.

From the great seat of Nalanda, the Kalachakra teachings were spread into the western land of Kashmir by the great pandita Somanatha (Dawa Gonpo in Tibetan). Originally of Islamic descent, Somanatha had become a brilliant scholar at a very young age. Travelling to Nalanda, he studied under some of the greatest masters of his time, in particular, Kalachakrapada the Younger and Nalendrapa. Through his practice of the Six Vajra Yogas, Somanatha achieved many remarkable powers such as gaining full control over his subtle winds. Recognising the karmic connection between Tibet and Shambhala, he travelled to Tibet on three occasions, giving general teachings on the *Perfection of Wisdom Sutras* and the *Five Collections of Arya Asanga*. To three very special students he transmitted the profound pith instructions of the Kalachakra completion stage practices.

Prayers to the Vajra Yoga Lineage of the Dro Tradition

Droton Lotsawa

Lama Lhaje Gompa

Lama Droton Namseg

I pray to the great translator Droton Lotsawa.

Born in western Tibet, Dro Lotsawa Sherab Drakpa had many great Indian teachers, however he regarded Somanatha as his main guru. Together the two translated Kalki Pundarika's commentary on the Abridged Kalachakra Tantra known as the *Stainless Light*. By making both the written and oral instructions available to Tibetan practitioners in their native tongue, he made an incredible contribution to the Kalachakra teachings in Tibet. For this reason he became known as a great translator. For much of the later part of his life, Dro Lotsawa spent his time close to Somanatha until the time of his death.

I pray to Lama Lhaje Gompa.

Lama Lhaje Gompa, also known as Konchok Sum, was born in the western Tibetan region of Penyul. Originally a highly accomplished tantric practitioner in the Nyingma Tradition, he was known for his capacity to pacify demons and practitioners of black magic. While Dro Lotsawa focused on translation, Lhaje Gompa focused on practising the teachings he had received from Somanatha and therefore dedicated all his time to meditation. As a result, he attracted many students who wished to receive from him the precious instructions for the Six Vajra Yogas.

I pray to Lama Droton Namseg.

Lhaje Gompa's main disciple was Lama Droton Namla Tsek who was a tantric lay practitioner wearing white robes. While he received the Kalachakra transmission from Lama Lhaje Gompa, he also studied extensively with Somanatha who taught him Asanga's *Five Collections* and Nagarjuna's *Six Madhyamika Treatises.* Although his heart practice was the Kalachakra Tantra. It was said that he had a direct connection with numerous yidam deities, and that enlightened dakinis would assist him whenever he needed their help. As fame of his scholarship and realisations began to spread, Droton Namseg became a much sought after teacher. Of the three Tibetan disciples of Somanatha, he was mostly the one responsible for propagating the Kalachakra teachings of the Dro Tradition. However, due to his enormous respect and veneration for the Vajra Yogas, he followed his teacher's example and kept the pith instructions as a whispered lineage passed only from master to heart-disciple.

Lama Drupchen Yumo | *Seachok Dharmeshvara* | *Khipa Namkha Öser* | *Machig Tulku Jobum*

I pray to the Lama Drupchen Yumo.

Lama Drupchen Yumo Mikyo Dorjé was born in a region of Tibet near the Himalayas. When he was very young, he was ordained as a monk and grew up to become highly regarded for his pure monastic discipline. As a young man he studied all of the sutras and then eventually the tantras. Making a brief connection with Somanatha, Yumowa went on to receive the complete Kalachakra transmission from Lama Droton Namseg. On the basis of these teachings, he accomplished remarkable powers such as the ability to manifest in different forms, as well as developing great knowledge of the Kalachakra Tantra. Yumo is perhaps most well known for being one of the first Tibetans to write about Buddha-nature in accordance with the teachings of Kalachakra, based on his own experience. These writings can be seen as a precursor to Dolpopa's writings on the *Zhentong View.*

I pray to Seachok Dharmeshvara.

Seachok Dharmeshvara was Drupchen Yumo's son. An exceptional scholar, by the age of sixteen he wrote a commentary on the Kalachakra Empowerments known as the *Wang Dorten* (*Sekkodesa* in Sanskrit). When he was twenty it is said he could comprehend everything his father knew. Many people believed he was an emanation of Manjushri as he mastered every detail of both the sutras and tantras, allowing him to defeat many renowned scholars with his sharp logic. Dharmeshvara received teachings from many lamas, but was particularly drawn to the *Guhyasamaja* and

Kalachakra Tantras. Following in his father's footsteps, he choose to pass the Vajra Yoga lineage on to his three children. In Tibetan *seachok* literally means "supreme son".

I pray to Khipa Namkha Öser.

Khipa Namkha Öser was born in Kangsar and was Seachok Dharmeshvara's eldest son. A tantric yogi and scholar, he focused primarily on Asanga's Five Collections as well as the Guhyasamaja and Kalachakra Tantras. It was said he had a direct connection to the female deities Vajravarahi and Sarasvati. The word *khipa* means "extraordinary scholar".

I pray to Machig Tulku Jobum.

Machig Tulku Jobum was Dharmeshvara's daughter, and was also considered the reincarnation of King Indrabhuti's sister. After memorising the great commentary of the Kalachakra Tantra word for word, she received the pith instructions from her father and attained the ten auspicious signs in a single day. In a further seven days of intensive practice, she mastered her inner winds, directing them into the central channel and so became a great yogini—a highly realised female practitioner.

Lama Drubtop Sechen

Chöje Jamyang Sarma

Kunkyen Chöku Öser

I pray to Lama Drubtop Sechen.

Lama Drubtop Sechen was born with a speech and hearing impairment, and no-one believed his life would amount to anything. However, after receiving the instructions for the Six Vajra Yogas from his sister Machig Tulku Jobum and practising under the guidance of his brother Namkha Öser, he swiftly attained realisations. This included the ability to recall his previous lives and to gain knowledge of his future. Later in his life he became known as Semochen when he established the monastery of Tsang Orlang Semoché.

I pray to the Chöje Jamyang Sarma.

Chöje Jamyang Sarma was born into a Nyingma family, but after his ordination he studied in many different monasteries. After contracting leprosy, he undertook an extensive Vajrapani retreat to overcome his illness. During this retreat he saw a vision of Manjushri who told him to seek instruction from Lama Drubtop Sechen. As he travelled to meet Semochen, he was required to overcome many demons and obstructive forces, but upon receiving empowerment, he was able to perceive his lama in the form of Kalachakra. From that moment on he practised the Six Vajra Yogas, attaining even greater realisations. Jamyang Sarma was responsible for founding many hermitages where yogis dedicated their lives to the practice of Kalachakra. *Chöje* literally means "Dharma lord" or "sovereign of the Dharma".

I pray to Kunkyen Chöku Öser.

Kunkyen Chöku Öser was the son of Serdingpa Zhonnu Ö. At his birth it was predicted that he would have the ability to dwell in the dharmakaya state and was therefore given the name *Chöku Öser* meaning "radiant dharmakaya". A great scholar of the sutras and tantras, he later developed incredible realisations after receiving the Kalachakra empowerment and instructions from Jamyang Sarma. It was said that he could directly perceive the wrathful form of Kalachakra, and on one occasion he was seen circumambulating a stupa while simultaneously meditating in a sealed room. *Kunkyen* literally means "omniscient", or "knowing everything".

Prayers to the Lineage Masters of Jonang Monastery

Kunpang Thukje Tsondru

Jangsem Gyalwa Yeshe

Khetsun Yonten Gyatso

I pray to Kunpang Thukje Tsondru.

Kunpang Thukje Tsundru was born in 1243 and is considered an emanation of a Kalki King of Shambhala. After receiving ordination he studied extensively in the monasteries of Sakya and Ngor, where he received the transmission of the Kalachakra in accordance with the Ra Tradition. He was later invited to become the abbot of Chöje Jamyang Sarma's monastery Kyangdur where he received the experiential transmission of the Kalachakra Dro lineage from Kunkyen Chöku Öser. Entering into retreat, Kunpangje quickly achieved many realisations on the basis of the Six Vajra Yogas. Still not satisfied he travelled the land, collecting the transmissions of all seventeen lineages of pith instructions for the Six Vajra Yogas, then at the request of the local goddess Nagmen Gyalmo, along with the communities of Chi, Drak and Nak, Kunpangje settled into the Jomonang valley where he established the Jonang Mountain Hermitage. It was here that Thukje Tsondru recorded all the pith instructions he had received, becoming the first Tibetan to preserve the Six Vajra Yogas in writing. As a result, countless students flocked to Jonang to study with this great master. Soon the name of the Gyalwa Jonangpa became synonymous with the study and practice of Kalachakra. The word *kunpang* is a title, which means "complete renunciation of all worldly concerns".

I pray to Jangsem Gyalwa Yeshe.

Jangsem Gyalwa Yeshe was ordained and practised Dharma for many years within the Karma Kagyu order. When he failed to achieve any realisations, the Karmapa Karma Pakshi informed him that he was missing the necessary karmic connections. He advised Gyalwa Yeshe to travel to Jonang Monastery to study under the great Thukje Tsondru. When he heard the name of Kunpangje, he was filled with great faith and devotion. Once he had received all of the Kalachakra empowerments and instructions, Gyalwa Yeshe quickly progressed in his practice of the Six Vajra Yogas. Eventually his realisations equalled that of his teacher, and he began to spread the Dharma widely. He was appointed abbot of Dechen Monastery and later became the head of Jonang Monastery. *Jangsem Gyalwa* means "Great Bodhisattva".

I pray to Khetsun Yonten Gyatso.

Khetsun Yonten Gyatso was born into a family who followed the Nyingma tradition and studied under many tantric masters from a variety of monasteries. After receiving the Kalachakra instructions from Thukje Tsundru, he completed all the night yoga practices over the course of twenty-one days. While practising the day yogas, his body levitated an arrow's length above the ground and for seven days he was able to move unimpeded through the mountains and valleys around Jonang. He also developed exceptional clairvoyant powers and supreme knowledge of all the Buddha's teachings and his body reportedly emitted a beautiful fragrance as a result of his excellent moral conduct. Yonten Gyatso was a close Dharma friend of Gyalwa Yeshe and later became his successor, assuming the Dharma throne as abbot of Jonang Monastery. In Tibetan, *khetsun* means "scholar with excellent moral conduct".

Kunkyen Dolpopa

Chogyal Choklé Namgyal

Tsungmed Nyabon Kunga

I pray to Kunkyen Dolpopa, emanation of the Buddhas of the three times.

Kunkyen Dolpopa was considered an emanation of the Buddhas of the three times as his realisation and mastery of the Buddha's teachings was so profound, and because everyone in the provinces of Ü and Tsang regarded him as their master. After gaining supreme realisation in retreat on the Kalachakra Vajra Yogas, he developed the incomparable Zhentong View and became the fourth abbot of Jonang Monastery. There he developed a unified system of Buddhist study and practice which combined the study of the Zhentong View with retreat practice focusing on the Six Vajra Yogas. This system has been maintained as the most precious jewel of the Jonang Tradition up to the present day.

I pray to the Chogyal Choklé Namgyal.

Choklé Namgyal was born to the King of Ngari Yatse, and received many high teachings from his father and uncle while still considerably young. As a child he studied at a variety of different monasteries and amazed everyone by giving large public teachings. As he was always victorious in debate, he was given the title *Chogyalwa*, meaning "The Invincible One". Choklé Namgyal received the Kalachakra empowerments and instructions from Dolpopa and became one of his closest students, perfectly memorising all the great texts. Eventually he became the fifth abbot of Jonang monastery, presiding over the community first for six years and later for another fifteen. During this time he became teacher to many great masters, such as the founder of the Geluk Tradition, Je Tsongkhapa, who received many Kalachakra teachings from him. In Tibetan *chogyal* means "Dharma King", while *choklé* means "victorious in all directions".

I pray to Tsungmed Nyabon Kunga.

Tsungmed Nyabon Kunga showed great intelligence from a very young age. After he was recognised by Khetsun Yonten Gyatso to be the reincarnation of the great Vajra Yoga master Jamsar Sherab, he excelled in all of his studies. His monastic education suffered a setback when he became extremely sick in his early twenties. He was miraculously cured, however, when Dolpopa Sherab Gyaltsen visited his monastery and spat on him. Eventually Dolpopa would become his main teacher, although he also received extensive teachings and guidance from Choklé Namgyal. Nyabon Kunga wrote prolifically, with many of his writings still treasured today. Many realised practitioners from other traditions were the recipients of his teachings, including Sakya Rendawa and Lama Tsongkhapa. Later in his life he founded the Jonang Monastery of Tsechen. The word *tsungmed* literally means "incomparable".

Drupchen Kunga Lodrö

Jamyang Konchog Zangpo

Drenchog Namkha Tsenchan

Panchen Namkha Palzang

I pray to Drupchen Kunga Lodrö.

Drupchen Kunga Lodrö was born into the royal family of Sharkha and was believed to be the reincarnation of Butön Rinchen Drup. He primarily studied the Buddha's teachings, especially the Kalachakra Tantra, under Nyabon Kunga, while also receiving teachings from many other masters. Having completely renounced attachment to worldly possessions and status, he took ordination, eventually becoming Nyabon's successor as abbot of Tsechen Monastery. After unsuccessfully attempting to broker peace between two warring clans, he became even more disillusioned with cyclic existence and went into retreat for close to fifty years. During this time he attained mastery not only of the Six Vajra Yogas, but of all the tantric systems of practice. As a great rimé master, he became the teacher to an ocean of students from all of the major traditions.

I pray to Jamyang Konchog Zangpo.

Jamyang Konchog Zangpo was born in Drakmar and was thought to be the reincarnation of the great Sakyapa Drakpa Gyaltsen. He trained at Zangden Monastery as well as many other monasteries from a variety of traditions, particularly the Sakya. After becoming a great scholar, he received the Kalachakra transmission from Kunga Lodrö and this became his heart practice. He went on to receive the esoteric transmissions from all of the major traditions and quickly achieved realisations. During his life he held the monastic seat in many monasteries, including Jonang, Tsechen, Samding and the non-sectarian monastery of Pelkhor Dechen. In this way he became an important lineage holder not only for the Jonang, but also the Sakya and Shangpa Kagyu.

I pray to Drenchog Namkha Tsenchan.

Namkha Chökyong was the heart-disciple of Jamyang Konchok and studied in various monasteries throughout central Tibet. As a result of the guidance he received from his teachers, he quickly mastered the Zhentong view and practice of the Six Vajra Yogas. He achieved great realisation through the practice of Kalachakra and eventually became the abbot of Tsechen Monastery. Later he would assume the vajra throne of Jonang Monastery itself where he was responsible for constructing a gold-plated roof for the great stupa of Dolpopa. The word *drenchog* literally means "supreme rescuer".

I pray to the Panchen Namkha Palzang.

The great Panchen Namkha Palzang was originally from the Sakya tradition. He became an expert in the Kalachakra Tantra after receiving empowerments and instructions from Namkha Chökyong. He attained great realisation by practising the Six Vajra Yogas and went on to found a monastery called Drepung (not to be confused with the monastic university in Lhasa), as well as becoming the ninth abbot of Jonang Monastery. For more than eighteen years, he also held the monastic seat of Namgyal Draksang in Jang, where he became the teacher to many prominent figures in western Tibet. The word *panchen* literally means "great pandita" or "great scholar".

Lochen Ratnabhadra

Palden Kunga Drolchok

Kenchen Lungrig Gyatso

I pray to Lochen Ratnabhadra.

The great adept Rinchen Zangpo, more commonly known as Lochen Ratnabhadra, was an accomplished practitioner of the Nyingma tantras. Training at several major monasteries, he became a respected scholar and also achieved great realisation after receiving the Kalachakra teachings from Namkha Palzang. It was said he had a direct connection to the wrathful deity Mahakala and was able to pacify many demons. Later in his life, Ratnabhadra established several monasteries and retreat centres, composed an important commentary on the Six Vajra Yogas and restored the monastery of the great Shangpa master Tangtong Gyalpo. The word *lochen* means "great translator".

I pray to Palden Kunga Drolchok.

Kunga Drolchok was born in Ngari Gongtung and lived from 1507 to 1566. He mastered many advanced teachings at an early age and studied with many great scholars in central Tibet. With a close connection to the enlightened dakini Niguma, he received the transmission of the *Six Dharmas of Niguma* directly from her. He also mastered the Kalachakra teachings and practice that he received from Rinchen Zangpo, and attained extraordinary realisation with a great many visions of enlightened beings. Over the course of his life he collected a vast array of teachings and practices, becoming an important lineage master of many traditions. While holding the monastic seat of Jonang Monastery for approximately twenty years, he compiled all of the teachings he had received into a single book known commonly as *"Drolchok's Quintessential Instructions"*. Subsequently, Kunga Drolchok was recognised throughout the land as a great rimé master. Near the end of his life he went on to found Cholung Jangtse Monastery. The word palden means "glorious".

I pray to Kenchen Lungrig Gyatso.

Kenchen Lungrig Gyatso trained primarily in Serdokchen, the monastery of the famed Zhentong master Shakya Chokden. During this time he became a realised practitioner of Vajrayogini whom he met during a dream. Later, when he met Kunga Drolchok, he received the complete empowerments, transmissions and pith instructions for the Kalachakra Six Vajra Yogas. When he put these teachings into practice, he attained remarkable realisations and powers; for instance, he could read Sanskrit instinctively without ever having studied the languages of India. He also received many visions of Indian mahasiddhas who bestowed on him pure transmissions of the teachings. Lungrig Gyatso became so respected that even the ninth Karmapa Wangchuk Dorjé and the Sakya Trizin would refer to him as the "Treasury of Dharma." The word *kenchen* means "great khenpo", someone who is an accomplished scholar or monastic leader.

Prayers to the Lineage Masters of Takten Damchö Ling

Kyabdak Drolway Gonpo

Ngonjang Rinchen Gyatso

Khidrup Lodrö Namgyal

Drupchen Ngawang Trinlé

I pray to Kyabdak Drolway Gonpo.

Kyabdak Drolway Gonpo, more commonly known as Jetsun Taranatha or Kunga Nyingpo, lived from 1575 to 1635, and is considered one of the most important Jonang lineage masters, second only to Kunkyen Dolpopa. Recognised by Lungrig Gyatso as the reincarnation of Kunga Drolchok, Taranatha received the complete transmission of the teachings and practices collected by his predecessor. After founding the monastic university of Takten Damchö Ling, Taranatha went on to author more than forty volumes of texts, creating an ocean of dharma that detailed every aspect of esoteric wisdom and practice. He was also instrumental in reviving the original view of Dolpopa's Zhentong philosophy which he felt had degenerated due to a lack of clarity on a number of key points. While he held the seat of Jonang Monastery for many years, he was known to wander the lands going from monastery to monastery, gathering teachings, debating with scholars and practicing in retreat. As a result he became a truly non-sectarian master who brought inspiration and blessings to all who met him. The word *kyabdak* means "all-pervasive rescuer of beings".

I pray to Ngonjang Rinchen Gyatso.

Ngonjang Rinchen Gyatso was born in the Tsang region and was ordained by Taranatha. He progressed swiftly in the Kalachakra practice and as a sign of his attainment, was suddenly able to absorb large volumes of knowledge instantly. Becoming abbot of Takten Damchö Ling, he taught extensively and guided retreat practice at the monastery for around fifteen years. In the later period of his life, as increasing restrictions were being placed on Jonang practitioners, Rinchen Gyatso chose to step down from his position and to go into retreat at Sangak Riwo Dechen. While there he continued to guide a steady stream of dedicated practitioners who wished only to practice the precious Dharma. The word *ngonjang* means "accomplished due to training in previous lives".

I pray to Khidrup Lodrö Namgyal.

Khidrup Lödro Namgyal lived between 1618 and 1683. He was recognised as a reincarnation of Dolpopa's mother and became a student of Taranatha when he was sixteen years old. He received full ordination from Rinchen Gyatso following many years of Dharma practice, and after receiving empowerments, was often guided by visions of White Tara. On one occasion it was said he impressed the great fifth Dalai Lama after discussing with him his realisation of the Zhentong view. Later in his life, Lödro Namgyal was invited to teach the Kalachakra Tantra at the inauguration of the new Dzamthang Tsangwa Monastery. The word *khidrup* literally means "scholar-yogi", someone who is very learned and also realised.

I pray to Drupchen Ngawang Trinlé.

Drupchen Ngawang Trinlé lived between 1657 and 1713 and had been prophesied to have great impact on the spread of the authentic Dharma by Dolpopa. At sixteen years of age he became the regent of Lödro Namgyal and practised the Six Vajra Yogas under his guidance. He spent six years in retreat in the cave of Amitabha, and afterwards travelled and taught widely, During this time he became the director of many monasteries, guiding Kalachakra retreat practice and composing many texts, such as the recitation of the seven Kalachakra preliminaries. He was also the recipient of teachings from lamas of all the different traditions and became widely known as a great Rimé master. The later portion of his life was spent at Dzamthang Tsangwa where he had been invited to teach. He ordained a very large monastic community and was responsible for founding many new monasteries and retreat centres in the Ngawa and Gyalrong regions. As he travelled through Mongolia on his way back to Central Tibet, he established several monasteries at the request of the emperor.

Prayers to the Vajra Masters of Dzamthang Tsangwa

Ngawang Tenzin Namgyal

Ngawang Khetsun Dargyé

Kunzang Trinlé Namgyal

Nuden Lhundrub Gyatso

I pray to Ngawang Tenzin Namgyal.

Ngawang Tenzin Namgyal, also known as Gawi Chöpel, was born in 1690. He was recognised as the first reincarnation of the famed Lodrö Namgyal. When he was only ten years old he received many teachings from Chalongwa Ngawang Trinlé, including the pith instructions of the Six Vajra Yogas. At sixteen he was ordained and he continued to dedicate himself to practice, achieving many extraordinary realisations. At the request of the Chöje Gyalwa Lhundrup, Tenzin Namgyal moved to Dzamthang Tsangwa Monastery where he began to teach the Six Vajra Yogas as their first resident Vajra Master. Under his guidance many students attained visions and other realisations. Like Dolpopa before him, he was highly influential in society, but unfortunately, in 1738, at the age of only forty-eight, he passed away, dissolving his mind into the dharmadhatu. The word *ngawang* means "great scholar endowed with powerful speech": it is an epithet relating the person to the wisdom of Manjushri.

I pray to Ngawang Khetsun Dargyé.

Ngawang Khetsun Dargyé was the second Kalachakra lineage holder at Tsangwa Monastery. He was renowned for his vast knowledge of Dharma and his display of perfect moral conduct, as well as his deep inner realisation. In particular, he had great insight into the practice of the Six Vajra Yogas and had several great disciples such as Kunga Chöpel and Chayur Chöjor.

I pray to Kunzang Trinlé Namgyal.

Kunzang Trinlé Namgyal was born in eastern Tibet and recognised as the second reincarnation of Tsangwa's founder Lodrö Namgyal. From an early age he made a connection with many holy beings, including his root lama, Ngawang Khetsun Dargyé. He received innumerable empowerments and instructions and attained remarkable realisation through diligent practice of the Six Vajra Yogas. Even the Karmapa, one of the highest lamas in all of Tibet, travelled a great distance from Ü-Tsang to visit and receive teachings from him. The word *kunzang* means "possessing all good qualities".

I pray to Nuden Lhundrub Gyatso.

Nuden Lhundrub Gyatso was the most influential disciple of Kunzang Trinlé Namgyal. He was highly accomplished in the practice of inner heat (tummo) and developed invincible wrathful tantric power, through which he could control all the local demons and deities. He was responsible for establishing Lower Tsangwa Monastery, performing many enlightened activities with the assistance of Jinpa Gyatso (the second reincarnation of Ngawang Trinlé). The word *nuden* literally means "possessing great energy and healing power".

Konchok Jigmé Namgyal

Ngawang Chöpel Gyatso.

Ngawang Chökyi Pakpa

Ngawang Chöjor Gyatso

I pray to Konchok Jigmé Namgyal.

Konchok Jigmé Namgyal was born in the Markok Valley and was believed to be the third reincarnation of Lodrö Namgyal. He made a connection with many masters and holy beings, especially Lhundrub Gyatso, who was also his brother from a previous life. As well as being a master of the Kalachakra teachings, he also received the teachings of the dakini Niguma and attained many exceptional qualities as a result of his flawless study and practice. The word konchok literally means "rare and sublime", while *jigmé* means "fearless".

I pray to Ngawang Chöpel Gyatso.

Ngawang Chöpel Gyatso, also known as the Tsangwa Gelong, was born in 1788 and trained at Dzamthang Tsangwa Monastery from the age of ten. He studied under many teachers and first received the transmission for the Six Vajra Yogas from Lama Ngawang Gyaltsen at the age of twenty-two. Attaining great realisation of the first two yogas during a three-year retreat, he later received the complete transmission from Jigmé Namgyal. He also received teachings such as Dzogchen and the Six Dharmas of Niguma from many other lamas, and became known for his extraordinary clairvoyant abilities. Later in his life, Chöpel Gyatso taught and travelled widely, becoming one of the main teachers of the great Rimé masters Jamgon Kongtrul and Patrul Rinpoche. He passed away in 1865 amidst a display of countless rainbows that appeared in the sky; a fitting testament to his great realisation. The word *chöpel* literally means "superior holder of Dharma".

I pray to Ngawang Chökyi Pakpa.

Ngawang Chökyi Pakpa was born in 1808 in the Zuka region and was ordained by Konchok Jigmé Namgyal when he was aged seven. He was especially proficient in the practice of the first two Vajra Yogas. While on retreat, he once experienced visions of the Kalki King Pundarika and Kunkyen Dolpopa, and also perceived visions of Shambhala and the pure-realm of Sukhavati. At twenty-five he studied over one hundred mandalas and memorised all their details, making him a much sought after master of rituals. Many of the detailed descriptions of mandalas used in Jonang rituals today can be attributed back to him. As Vajra Master of Dzamthang Tsangwa, Chökyi Pakpa was responsible for building a great prayer hall. He passed away in 1877 without any sign of sickness or pain, abiding for many days in the union of mother and son clear light.

I pray to Ngawang Chöjor Gyatso.

Ngawang Chöjor Gyatso was born in 1846 and received the Kalachakra teachings and empowerment from the Tsangwa Gelong, Chöpel Gyatso. On one occasion, when receiving this empowerment, he saw the lama as Kunkyen Dolpopa and experienced the non-dual Buddha-mind. He diligently practised the Six Vajra Yogas and attained many great realisations, including magical powers in his dreams and the continuous perception of his body in the state of clear-light. At the age of forty-five he became the Kalachakra Vajra Master at Tsangwa Monastery. He passed away in 1910.

Prayers to the Lineage Masters of Tashi Chöthang

Ngawang Chözin Gyatso

Ngawang Tenpa Rabgyé

Lama Lobsang Trinley

Khentrul Jamphal Lodrö

I pray to Ngawang Chözin Gyatso.

Ngawang Chözin Gyatso, also known as Washul Lhazö Lama, was considered to be an emanation of Akashagarbha, one of the eight great bodhisattvas. He studied at Dzamthang Tsangwa monastery, where he received all the instructions for the Six Vajra Yogas, principally from the Tsangwa Gelong. He composed many ritual practices and commentaries, and once revealed that millions of deities were emanating from his body. His realisations were so profound that he could perform miraculous feats such as walking through walls and travelling to pure-realms such as Shambhala to receive instructions. Many of the practices that were revealed to him in this way, are still used in Jonang monasteries to this day. Having spent time touring the land as a representative of Tsangwa Monastery, Chözin Gyatso went into retreat in the hermitage that would eventually become Tashi Chöthang Monastery. It was here that he taught many great masters such as Tenpa Rabgye and Bamda Gelek Gyatso. After his death, two complete sets of bones were found in his cremation stupa, indicating that he had attained the highest of realisations, the union of immutable bliss and empty-form.

I pray to Ngawang Tenpa Rabgyé.

Ngawang Tenpa Rabgyé was born in 1875. He received all the instructions for the Six Vajra Yogas from Ngawang Chözin Gyatso and experienced many signs indicating mastery of the practice. He also practised many other tantras and beheld innumerable visions of the different tantric deities. When he was twenty-five he studied and practised at Dzamthang Tsangwa Monastery. At fifty-six he became abbot of Chayul Monastery, and then later became abbot and Kalachakra master at Tashi Chöthang Monastery. Living a very humble life, he had no concern whatsoever for wealth or social standing. When he was seventy-six he passed away, remaining in the state of clear-light for six days.

I pray to the dispeller of darkness, the precious Lama Lobsang Trinley.

Lama Ngawang Lobsang Trinley was born in the Zuka valley of the Kham region in south-eastern Tibet in 1917. At the age of fourteen he studied at Chayul Monastery under Ngawang Tenpa Rabgyé. He focused intensively on Kalachakra practice and attained the ten signs of realisation within two weeks. In his thirties he contracted leprosy and consequently entered into solitary retreat for five years, practising Vajrapani. While in retreat, his sickness appeared in the form of thousands of worms flowing out of his body, dissolving and then transforming into tormas. He then spent the rest of his life treating and curing many people with leprosy and other ailments. He worked tirelessly to rebuild Mahayana and Vajrayana Buddhism in its pure form and re-establish Chöthang Monastery which had largely been destroyed due to fighting. Even though he appeared to be completely healthy, he passed away in 1999, fulfilling his own predictions. After thirteen days his body showed no sign of decay, and many miraculous appearances accompanied his death. He sent all his precious relics to the Potala Palace in Lhasa, keeping not even a single relic in his own monastery.

I pray to the Dharma warrior Khentrul Jamphal Lodrö.

Khentrul Jamphal Lodrö was born on 18th day of the second month in the year of the Water Rabbit. His family lived in a nomadic community in the Golok province of Eastern Tibet. He was recognised as a reincarnation of his mother's teacher Getse Khentrul, who in his previous life was the Kalachakra master Ngawang Chözin Gyatso. At the age of twelve he began his extensive Buddhist studies and practice under the guidance of Khenpo Sangten and several other lamas. Attending eleven monasteries in eastern Tibet he comprehensively studied the five traditions and undertook a three year

Kalachakra retreat at Chöthang Monastery under the guidance of his main master, Lama Lobsang Trinley. In 1997, Lobsang Trinlé awarded him the title of Khenpo, thereby authorising him to teach, and two years later he was chosen by the abbot of Dzamthang Tsangwa Monastery to teach there. Soon afterwards, he chose to abandon his prestigious position to spend time in solitary retreat, before undertaking a pilgrimage to India in 2000 to practice at many of the sacred Buddhist sites.

After several private audiences with His Holiness the Dalai Lama, in 2003 he came to Australia. His goal was to transmit the rare and precious Kalachakra teachings and establish the Jonang Tradition in the West. The title *khentrul* means both "Dharma scholar" or "abbot" and "recognised reincarnation". The name *Jamphal Lodrö* signifies the "gentle and glorious Manjushri", the bodhisattva of wisdom. During his time in the West, Khentrul Jamphal Lodrö has dedicated significant effort to learning the English language so as to effectively transmit the precious Dharma of the Jonang Tradition to his students.

Additional Supplications to the Lama

I pray to my primary root lama.
I pray to my glorious lama.
I pray to all the dharma lords.
May all the spiritual fathers and heart-sons bless me!

This verse encourages us to have an attitude of deep respect and honour for the lama and all the lineage masters, or dharma lords. This includes the spiritual fathers and their heart-sons, as the lineage has been transmitted from master to disciple from one generation to the next. Here *lama* refers not just to one "root" teacher, but to anyone from whom you have received empowerments or teachings.

Whoever honours and has life-long devotion to the precious lama
Constantly makes supplication and pays homage to the lama in this life.
May I be blessed with the primordial wisdom of the compassionate warrior.

The next verse is a reminder of the benefits of recollecting these lamas and cultivating devotion or gratitude toward them. Just remembering them evokes your own good qualities and therefore brings you peace. Meanwhile, having gratitude and life-long devotion to them will lead to even greater benefit. From an ordinary perspective, thankfulness and appreciation are causes for your own happiness. Such gratitude can also grow into extraordinary devotion and lead you to enlightenment, which is what we mean by primordial wisdom of the compassionate warrior.

In all my future lives may I never be separated from my glorious lama.
May I have great joy in my practice of the precious Dharma.
May I accomplish all enlightened paths and swiftly attain the state of Vajradhara!

When you pray to never be separated from your glorious lama, you are showing your teachers great honour and devotion. Also, if you have a strong connection or karmic link with your teachers and dharma friends, you are likely to meet them again lifetime after lifetime. If you are not separated from the Sangha (which includes all great Arya beings as well as any aspiring practitioner who follows the Buddha), you will never be separated from the precious Dharma and will have great joy practising it. You will then gradually accomplish all enlightened paths, traversing through the various levels of accomplishment, and finally attain the state of Vajradhara—complete enlightenment.

(Be resolute that the lamas of the holy lineage melt into light and bless your mind-stream.)

All of these preliminary practices have two stages—building a visualisation and connecting to the theme of the practice; and then dissolving what you constructed, recognising that it is all just a composition of your own mind. In this case, the lamas of the holy lineage, the focus of your visualisation, dissolve or melt into light and then bless your mind-stream, becoming inseparable from your own mind. During visualisation, you train your mind at the level of relative truth—the level of appearances. While dissolving your visualisation, you learn to recognise the empty nature of those appearances—the ultimate truth.

PART TWO

The Inner Preliminaries

— The Jonang Refuge Field —
Assembly of all the Sublime Objects of Refuge

CHAPTER FOUR

Refuge and Prostrations

Refuge is the first of the five inner preliminary practices. After contemplating the four convictions of renunciation, you are left with a sense of dread at the prospect of remaining in samsara for even one more second longer than necessary, but this fear is accompanied by the great hope that liberation is indeed possible if you place your trust and faith in the Three Jewels. This specifically means having faith in the *Buddha* as your guide, the *Dharma* as the teachings he gave and the *Sangha* as your spiritual companions. Without taking refuge it is not possible to follow the Buddha's path to enlightenment. For this reason, refuge is considered the foundation of all Buddhist paths.

Taking refuge means creating a spiritual link between you and all the great holy beings who embody the qualities of Buddhahood and committing yourself to following the teachings they have transmitted through an authentic lineage. We can think of the Buddha as a doctor, the Dharma as the medicine he prescribes for you and the Sangha as the nurses who help care for you while you are sick. This Sangha includes both the highly realised Arya Sangha (those who have seen the truth of emptiness and are on their way to achieving enlightenment), as well as those ordinary beings who act as your spiritual friends along the journey. While the Sangha provide conducive conditions for growth, in the end it is up to you alone to take the medicine and actually practice the instructions provided by the Dharma.

In general we can speak of two types of refuge: provisional refuge and definitive refuge. On the provisional level, you make prayers and prostrations to the Three Jewels with strong faith and with the motivation to liberate all beings. Here faith means having total trust and confidence in the teachings, which is the basis for allowing the blessings of the refuge to enter within you. With regards to motivation, the best motivation for taking refuge is to liberate all sentient beings from cyclic existence. On the definitive level, you are taking refuge in your own Buddha-nature and its potential to manifest as the three Buddha-kayas. In this way we use the provisional refuge as a mirror to reflect the definitive refuge.

The practice which follows is broken into three parts: establishing the refuge visualisation, reciting the refuge prayers while making prostrations and then finally dissolving the refuge field.

REFUGE VISUALISATION

As with anything new, the details of this refuge visualisation may seem daunting at first. However, you should know that there are many levels of meaning embedded in each detail, making it important to keep all its characteristics intact. Through hard work and a great deal of practice, you will definitely be able to unlock these deeper layers of profound spiritual significance. You should aim to develop a visualisation which is vibrant, clear and alive, while also rooted in an understanding of its non-dual nature. If you have difficulty with the visual component, don't worry. Simply focus your attention on the feeling that all of these objects of refuge are actually manifesting in the space before you, and have a sense of their presence. In the end, what is most important is to develop your awareness of what these objects mean in relation to your practice.

> *To take refuge, which is the foundation of all Dharma practice, first go to an isolated or quiet location and place the mind in its natural state, relaxed and focused. Visualise the space in front of you as a pure or enlightened realm, vast and expansive.*

The first step is to try and dissolve all ordinary appearances and consider your surroundings to be a pure or enlightened realm, vast and expansive.

This pure realm is free from all ordinary fixed concepts such as big and small, or things being limited to only one aspect. This is achieved by placing the mind in its natural state: relaxed and yet focused. You can create this feeling of openness by focusing on the space around you, or resting your mind at your heart-centre at the end of each out-breath.

In the centre of this realm is a great palace made of various precious substances and adorned with stunning jewels and ornaments. In the centre of the palace is an enormous wish-fulfilling tree with its vast draping branches and beautiful leaves, flowers and fruit radiating throughout the palace. At the top of this tree is a magnificent throne supported by lions. Upon this throne is a multi-coloured lotus with sun, moon, rahu and kalagni discs.

The precious substances and ornaments which adorn the great palace symbolise the perfection and purity of the surroundings. The wish-fulfilling tree represents a firmly rooted foundation and the oneness of all enlightened beings, with the branches, leaves and flowers characterising the many different aspects being displayed, to fulfil the wishes of all beings. The lion throne is a symbol of majesty and power while the lotus represents purity, and the sun and moon discs symbolise wisdom and compassion.

Root Lama

Lineage Lamas

One's root lama is seated upon the throne in the form of blue Vajradhara; he holds a vajra and bell crossed at the level of his heart. Primordial Buddha sits at the root lama's crown.

Vajradhara is the tantric form of enlightenment, as previously described in the lineage master invocation. He represents the enlightened mind of your root lama and is given this central position as he is your direct link to achieving enlightenment.

Yidam Deities

Nirmanakaya Buddhas

Surrounding your vajra master, in the branches of the tree are all the lineage lamas, the thirty-five Dharma Kings of Shambhala and the Yidam deities of Highest Yoga Tantra, such as Kalachakra. Surrounding them are the Yidam deities of the four classes of tantras.

In the earlier prayers we focused specifically on the lineage lamas. We now also include yidam deities which are tantric Buddha-forms, mostly wrathful in appearance, who help you accomplish tantric realisation. Each yidam represents a different collection of enlightened qualities that you can use to focus your mind and activate your hidden potential.

Buddha Shakyamuni sits below the Yidam deities.

The Buddhas are those fully enlightened beings who are all-knowing and omnipresent. They appear according to the merit of beings in the three times—the past, present and future—and the ten directions—the four cardinal directions, the four intermediate directions, as well as up and down. This includes the current Buddha Shakyamuni as well as all previous and future Buddhas such as Dipankara and Maitreya.

Arya Bodhisattvas

Shravaka and Pratyeka Arhats

To his right side, upon the branches of the tree, is the Mahayana Arya Sangha of Eight Bodhisattvas including Maitreya, Manjushri and Avalokiteshvara.

The Arya Sangha of bodhisattvas are those on the path to buddhahood who have directly realised the profound view of emptiness, such as the bodhisattva of compassion Avalokiteshvara and the bodhisattva of wisdom Manjushri. The sole intention of these sublime beings is to lead everyone to Buddhahood. For this reason you can regard them as your personal guides and protectors.

To his left side is the Hinayana Arya Sangha of shravakas and pratyekas, such as Shariputra.

We also take refuge in the Arya Sangha of Shravakas and Pratekyas. *Shravakas*, also known as hearers, hear the Buddha's teachings and attain the state of Arhat or individual liberation, following the path that is practised today in the Theravada tradition. *Pratyekas*, also called solitary realisers, find their own liberation through analysing the truth of dependent origination without relying directly on the teachings of a Buddha.

Wisdom Dakinis

Wrathful Dharma Protectors

At the base of this tree is an ocean of dakinis and Dharma protectors endowed with the divine eye, who guard the precious teachings. They abide in a manner protecting you.

Dakinis, known as *khandro* in Tibetan, literally means "sky walkers". They are divine feminine forms with the ability to assist genuine practitioners. They embody a type of spiritual energy which safeguards your spiritual progress and overcomes inner obstacles to your practice. Dharma protectors are wrathful forms that shield you from external obstacles and harmful forces; they embody a type of spiritual energy which prevents negativity from coming in, like an iron fence around you. The dakinis and dharma protectors surround you like an ocean, ensuring that you always receive spiritual protection.

Behind the branches, the holy Dharma appears as precious golden texts.

Finally, the Dharma jewel is represented by precious golden-coloured texts, which you can imagine are resonating with the beautiful sound of the Dharma, especially the definitive teachings on Buddha-nature and the glorious Kalachakra Tantra.

Be resolute that everything you visualise actually is like this. At the same time, be resolute that you take refuge on behalf of all sentient beings, with great longing and devotion towards the lama, the Three Jewels and the ocean of spiritual protection.

Even if you cannot recall all the details, you should be resolute that everything you visualise is actually like this and is not just an exercise in make believe. As someone who has entered the Mahayana path, you are not taking refuge alone but together with all beings who are intimately connected with you, as they have been your mothers, partners, friends and relatives over countless previous lifetimes. You can therefore visualise your father on your right side, your mother on your left side, your adversaries in front of you (giving them a position of honour as they have helped you develop patience), and hidden harmful forces at your rear. Extending this visualisation to every conceivable being in samsara, you lead them all to take refuge together in the Three Jewels. The ocean of spiritual protection refers to the entire refuge assembly—the root lama, lineage lamas, yidams, dakinis, dharma protectors and the Arya Sangha.

While you develop your visualisation, you must be sure to remember that the lamas, yidams, buddhas and so forth are not something external like some sort of god; rather each is a reflection of an important aspect of your own Buddha-nature, appearing in different forms to guide you while still being one in their wisdom nature.

Then pray with strong compassion and resolute intention to liberate all beings, passionately wishing that they find protection from the sufferings of samsara.

In accordance with the Mahayana path, you are taking refuge not only because you are seeking freedom from samsara, but because you wish that all beings find protection from samsaric suffering. As you perform the refuge practice you can therefore pray passionately with strong compassion and resolute intention: "How wonderful if they could all be free. May they be free. I will help them find freedom. I pray to the Three Jewels that they find freedom!"

RECITING REFUGE PRAYERS WHILE MAKING PROSTRATIONS

(While holding this visualisation as best you can, recite the long refuge prayer once and then repeat the short refuge prayer three or more times while making full prostrations. Full prostrations are only required while Refuge is your main practice.)

Once you have established the visualisation, you should recite the long refuge prayer once while holding this in your mind, and then repeat the short refuge prayer at least three times while making full prostrations. As you perform these prostrations, you should fill your mind with extraordinary thoughts, remembering all the amazing qualities of these precious Three Jewels.

Long Refuge Prayer

For the sake of all mother-like beings as limitless as space, from now until I reach the essence of enlightenment I take refuge in the noble root and lineage lords of Dharma, the glorious pure lamas, who embody the body, speech, mind, qualities and actions of the Buddhas of the three times and the ten directions, and are the source of the 84,000 Dharmas and kings of the noble Arya Sangha.

There is not a single being in samsara that has not been our mother since beginningless time, and as our mothers, they have loved us with every possible kindness, tenderness, care and affection. Just as space is limitless, so too is the number of kind mother-like beings, who can be found everywhere, just like space. It is for their sake that you take refuge until you reach enlightenment.

In this practice we consider the lama, our human teacher who is our direct connection to enlightenment, to be the perfect object of refuge since he embodies the qualities and actions of all the Buddhas and is the vessel through which we hear the Dharma. He is therefore the link to the 84,000 Dharmas that the Buddha taught as a remedy for 84,000 mental afflictions which emerge from the three root delusions—attachment, aversion and ignorance. The lama is also king of the Noble Arya Sangha, since he is our link to countless high-level beings who have the power to protect and guide us.

Short Refuge Prayer

I take refuge in the Dharma lords, the glorious lamas.
I take refuge in the enlightened mandala of yidams.
I take refuge in the bhagavans, the perfect Buddhas.
I take refuge in the immaculate holy Dharma.
I take refuge in the noble Arya Sangha.
I take refuge in the dakinis and all-seeing Dharma protectors.

(To be recited three times or more if you are focusing on Refuge practice.)

We recite each line over and over again for the length of a single prostration. For example, while repeating "I take refuge in the dharma lords, the glorious lama", you complete one full prostration. Likewise while reciting "I take refuge in the yidams…", you make another full prostration. Continue in this way while reciting the remaining lines.

Whilst you are completing your prostrations, you can think of the suffering of all mother-like beings and aspire to work tirelessly for their benefit. A total of six prostrations should be completed for each verse. That being said, it is the feeling and not the precise number of prostrations that is most important.

In the Jonang tradition, sessions of the refuge practice last up to two hours, and the prayer and prostrations are usually done together for a total of 100,000 times. This practice affirms our surrender and commitment to the Three Jewels and is also an effective way to destroy our pride.

Dissolution of the Refuge Field

After a session is completed, the following verse is recited three times:

> *I pay homage and take refuge in the lama and the precious Three Jewels. Please bless my mind-stream!*

With this verse you are making a transition to the final part of the practice, as you ask the lama and the precious Three Jewels to bless your mind-stream and therefore fill you with all of their good qualities. These qualities will continue to grow in the mind-stream until you reach enlightenment. Unlike the five sense consciousnesses, this mental consciousness can be developed in limitless ways, and is what makes enlightenment possible.

When refuge is your main practice, the final step is to dissolve the field of refuge, visualising all of the objects melting into light and dissolving into your mind-stream and into the minds of all other sentient beings as well. This is the ultimate practice of refuge, through which you learn to recognise that there is no longer any independent "you" and "them".

This process is usually carried out in four steps: (1) First the root and lineage lamas bless you with dazzling rays of light. Then you receive blessings from the yidams, followed by the Buddhas, dharma texts, Sangha, dakinis and dharma protectors. (2) Light then radiates from the entire field of refuge to purify the defilements of all beings, and radiates outwards to the Buddha-realms as they all become Buddhas. (3) The dakinis and dharma protectors then dissolve into the sangha, who then dissolve into the dharma texts. These texts then dissolve into the Buddhas, the Buddhas dissolve into the yidams, the yidams dissolve into the lineage masters and finally these lineage masters dissolve into the root lama Vajradhara. The vast palace and wish-fulfilling tree also dissolve into Vajradhara. (4) Finally Vajradhara comes to the crown of your head dissolving through your crown chakra and comes to rest at your heart chakra.

The idea is simply to watch what is happening and try to recognise how all of these objects are, in fact, inseparable from your own mind. This process is likened to water being poured into water, although initially it may feel much more solid than this. After practising this for some time, the solidity of the visualisation breaks down, and eventually it can feel like breaking a vase and watching the space inside the vase come together with the space outside.

If refuge is not your main practice, continue to hold the Refuge visualisation while you go on to the next preliminary practice, dissolving the field at the end of the Bodhicitta practice.

Dedication

> *Through the power of this virtue, May I complete the accumulation of merit and wisdom and so attain the two kayas of enlightenment for the sake of all beings.*

As with any Mahayana practice, you finish by dedicating the virtue or merit you have accumulated so that all beings may attain enlightenment. Merit is the positive energy created by doing this practice or performing any virtuous deeds with a good motivation. Wisdom, on the other hand, is to realise that the ultimate nature of all relative phenomena is empty of true existence, and this is achieved through deep contemplation and meditation practice. Wisdom and merit are the causes for attaining the two kayas of enlightenment—the dharmakaya, which is the primordial wisdom that sees the true nature of all phenomena, and the rupakaya, which is the compassionate display of enlightened form, manifesting for the benefit of all beings. The rupakaya includes both the sambhogakaya and nirmanakaya aspects of the Buddha.

If you fail to dedicate the merit of your practice, this is like leaving money on a window-sill where it can easily be stolen or blown away by the wind. Dedicating the merit towards enlightenment, however, is like investing this money in a bank. It will never be destroyed and will continue to grow until you reach enlightenment.

— Avalokiteshvara, Manjushri and Vajrapani —
The Three Great Bodhisattvas of Compassion, Wisdom and Power

CHAPTER FIVE

Generating the Mind of Enlightenment

Bodhicitta is the extraordinary altruistic intention to attain enlightenment for the sake of all beings. It is this attitude which is the essence of the Mahayana path. The seed of bodhicitta is great compassion, which is first established through deeply contemplating the nature of your relationship with sentient beings and cultivating the bond you feel towards them. This process leads to a form of bodhicitta known as *Aspirational Bodhicitta.* When this aspiration is strengthened, the mind will naturally give rise to the wish to act for their benefit. This proactive form of bodhicitta is known as *Engaged Bodhicitta.* It is this powerful motivation which then provides the basis for you to achieve your highest spiritual aims.

To generate the aspirational form of bodhicitta, you must first understand how all beings are just like you in wanting to be happy and wishing to avoid suffering. This fundamental equality forms the basis upon which we are able to develop unconditional love and compassion towards all sentient beings, regardless of their race, colour or creed. It embraces not only humans but also the vast range of animals and other non-human forms of life.

Furthermore, since beginningless time we have been taking rebirth in samsara, and each time we have been supported and nurtured by sentient beings who have been our mothers, our lovers, our friends and our families. So while we may not recognise them in this life, we can be sure that we have received immeasurable kindness from them and that we share a most intimate bond. By recognising this connection, and by developing a deep sense of gratitude for their kindness, it is only natural that you will develop the wish to repay them in whatever way you can.

When you look at the state of your dear kind mother sentient beings, you will see they are trapped in a perpetual cycle of endless suffering. It is as though they are trapped in a bad dream with no knowledge of the possibility of waking up. By reflecting carefully on this predicament, you will realise that the only way to really help them is to show them how to overcome their delusions and to practice a path that will lead them to long-lasting happiness. When you take this task on as your own personal responsibility, you will have developed the altruistic intention of bodhicitta—the wish to achieve the omniscient mind of enlightenment so you can best help your dear mothers in every possible circumstance, guiding them step-by-step until they too achieve the ultimate peace. By developing this far-reaching intention, you are doing much more than simply healing a temporary pain, you are providing beings with a genuine method to achieve permanent freedom from suffering.

Both Aspirational Bodhicitta and Engaged Bodhicitta are considered provisional in nature. They are temporary measures that provide you with the fuel you need to achieve your aim. Ultimately however, enlightenment is achieved through attaining a direct realisation of the nature of reality. This is known as the *Ultimate Bodhicitta*. It is like a fence that surrounds and safeguards your compassion. When you realise that although you aim to lead countless sentient beings to enlightenment, there were never any truly existent beings to begin with, then your compassion is free to manifest in a spontaneous and unbiased way. Your mind is able to rest in the definitive meaning, and from that perspective, engage in actions that are free from the concepts of a person who performs the action, the action that is being performed and the object that is the focus of the action. Each of these is recognised to be a manifestation of the mind, and since the concepts of success and failure are also in the mind, there is never any possibility of getting worn out or immobilised by views which are too goal-oriented or moralistic. It is this incredibly flexible outlook that allows you to become a fearless and compassionate warrior, known as a *Bodhisattva*.

Once your attitude begins to transform through the strength of your Bodhicitta, your practice will naturally shift to greater and greater engagement with the sentient beings in your life. This means taking advantage of the many opportunities that arise to offer your time and resources to benefitting others. This may come in the form of volunteering in your local community, or working on a day-to-day basis to bring more love and compassion to your relationships. In this context, you engage in the training of a bodhisattva, specifically focusing on what are known as the *Six Perfections*—generosity, ethical discipline, patience, diligence, meditative concentration and wisdom.

As we engage in increasingly more meaningful activities, we begin to broaden our awareness of the different ways in which people suffer. We begin to see that obvious sufferings—like the suffering of cancer, the sufferings related to living with a disability or the sufferings of approaching death—are simply one level of suffering. When we look more closely, we can see that there is also a more subtle form of suffering that is experienced, even by those we would normally label as well-off and successful, such as the sufferings of fear, anxiety and stress. The challenge for our training is to look deeply into the nature of the experiences of sentient beings and to develop a profound compassion for each of them. This compassion will drive your practice and inspire you into action.

For the preliminary practice of Bodhicitta, you recite and contemplate the meaning of various prayers which are designed to help you generate the aspiration to achieve enlightenment. In this practice, we ask the Three Jewels to bear witness as we develop a firm conviction to act for the benefit of sentient beings. To really give strength to these meditations, it is ideal if you can supplement your recitation with a great deal of study and reflection into topics like Bodhicitta, the Bodhisattva Vows and the Six Perfections. This material will provide you with a clear context for your practice and offer you many different angles to consider. If you are genuinely committed to this process, you will want to spend at least a few months of intensive practice on these contemplations or as long as it takes in order to become familiar with the essential points.

Remember that this particular practice is not about repeating prayers thousands of times. You don't accumulate them like you would prostrations or mantra. It is more about putting in the time to truly integrate this attitude into your behaviour. That being said, there are three parts connected to this preliminary: generating aspirational bodhicitta, strengthening your aspiration with the four immeasurables and renewing your vow to engage in the training of a Bodhisattva.

GENERATING ASPIRATIONAL BODHICITTA

You begin by first establishing your visualisation of the Refuge Field as a support for your Bodhicitta practice. Usually practitioners recite the refuge prayers before this practice, so the visualisation should be fresh in your mind. If not, then simply spend some time re-establishing the details of the visualisation. In this practice it is very important to have a clear sense of being surrounded by limitless sentient beings. It is, after all, their suffering which is the primary support for developing the quality of compassion. Once you have brought the visualisation to mind and have taken refuge at least three times, continue by reciting this prayer:

For the liberation of all beings, I will reach the state of complete Buddhahood;
I shall therefore meditate on the profound vajrayoga path.

(To be repeated three or more times.)

In this prayer you are giving rise to the aspiration to reach the state of complete Buddhahood so that you can benefit all sentient beings in the greatest and most expansive way possible. This first line highlights the two key components of the motivation: purpose and method. The purpose is to bring benefit to sentient beings, based on an overwhelming feeling of connection with others and the strong desire to free them from all forms of suffering. The method is what you need to do in order to fulfil your purpose. Since only the omniscient mind of a Buddha is completely free from all limitations, only a Buddha can truly bring benefit to all sentient beings without exception. By attaining the two kayas of Buddhahood, you achieve not only the ultimate benefit for yourself, but also the ultimate benefit for others.

The flavour of this wish is captured beautifully in Shantideva's *Guide to the Bodhisattva's Way of Life:*

May I be a guard for those without one,
A guide for all who journey on the road,
May I become a boat, a raft or bridge,
For all who wish to cross the water.

May I be an isle for those desiring landfall,
And a lamp for those who wish for light,
May I be a bed for those who need to rest,
And a servant for all who live in need.

May I become a wishing jewel, a magic vase,
A powerful mantra and a medicine of wonder.
May I be a tree of miracles granting every wish,
And a cow of plenty sustaining all the world.

Like the earth and other great elements,
And like space itself, may I remain forever,
To support the lives of boundless beings,
By providing all that they might need.

Just so, in all the realms of beings,
As far as space itself pervades,
May I be a source of all that life requires,
Until beings pass beyond samsara's pain.

In order to actualise the state of Buddhahood as quickly as possible, powerful methods are needed to cut through delusions and purify your mind of all karmic conditioning. For this reason we make the aspiration to meditate on the profound Vajra Yoga Path of the Kalachakra Completion Stage. This is the supreme method used in the Jonang Tradition to develop a profound level of concentration and insight into the nature of reality. With the pure motivation of Bodhicitta, a great deal of hard work and unwavering dedication, it is definitely possible to achieve enlightenment within a single lifetime.

As you recite this prayer, take your time to reflect on what these words mean to you. Consider why it is so important for you to help sentient beings. What will it take for you to fulfil their desires? What are the benefits of achieving Buddhahood? What are the benefits of practicing the Kalachakra Path? If you can sincerely answer these questions, then this aspiration will take on a profound meaning and will provide you with a solid foundation for your continued spiritual development.

CULTIVATING THE FOUR IMMEASURABLES

In the beginning of this practice, our aspiration to achieve enlightenment is quite weak. It is like a single seed we have just buried in the ground. If we ever hope to experience the fruit of that seed, we need to nurture our aspiration so it can empower us to engage in virtuous actions. This ripening process is achieved through what are known as the *Four Immeasurables*—love, compassion, joy and equanimity. We cultivate these qualities by reciting these four basic aspirations, where each line coincides with each of the Four Immeasurables respectively:

> *May all beings have happiness and the causes of happiness.*
> *May all beings be free from suffering and the causes of suffering.*
> *May all beings never be separated from the sublime happiness that is free from suffering.*
> *May all beings abide in the great equanimity free from attachment and aversion.*

In the beginning, our bodhicitta is quite limited due to our bias towards some sentient beings. As we cultivate these four qualities we break down the barriers of our bias, allowing us to embrace more and more beings into our aspiration. When that bias is completely removed, these qualities are free to become "*immeasurable*"—immeasurable in that our motivation is directed towards limitless sentient beings; immeasurable in that we are willing to dedicate countless future lives to achieving our goal, and finally, immeasurable in that the result of achieving Buddhahood is endowed with an infinite array of enlightened qualities.

It can be helpful when meditating on the four immeasurables to start by first reflecting on the nature of your relationships with sentient beings. In particular, try to establish a connection by considering the ways in which you are all equal. Also consider the incredible kindness that sentient beings have shown you in this life and by inference, in beginningless past lives. Try to cultivate a sense of affectionate love that sees sentient beings as your dear ones, like your mother or other close family members. The stronger your affection for sentient beings, the stronger your desire will be to see them free from suffering.

From this foundation, you can begin to recite the prayer of the Four Immeasurables. For each line, try to cultivate a progressively stronger intention. Begin by becoming accustomed to the possibility that sentient beings could actually experience your aspiration. For example, you can replace the word "May" with "How wonderful it would be if..." to create the verse, "How wonderful it would be if all sentient beings could have happiness and the causes of happiness!"

Having established the possibility, you can repeat the line again, but with a strong yearning for the aspiration to actually happen. So for the first immeasurable of love, you would recite "May all sentient beings have happiness and the causes of happiness!" The key here is to truly believe that this outcome is something worthwhile and desirable.

Then recite the line again, only this time recognise that sentient beings have been suffering in samsara since beginningless time and unless someone makes the effort, this aspiration will not be realised. Therefore, develop a sense of responsibility to take action. For example, you can think, "May I be the cause for all sentient beings to have happiness and the causes of happiness!" When this aspiration genuinely arises in your mind, then you will have generated the altruistic intention that marks the transition from Aspirational Bodhicitta to Engaging Bodhicitta.

Finally, we must recognise that to be successful in our aspiration, we will need considerable help. For this reason, recall your objects of refuge and from the bottom of your heart, pray to them to give you the strength and determination you require. If you can integrate these four aspects into each of the Four Immeasurables, gradually your conviction and confidence will increase.

To cultivate the Four Immeasurables, you can either use the four line version of the prayer in the Divine Ladder, or you could use the following expanded version:

How wonderful it would be if all sentient beings
had happiness and the causes of happiness!
May they have happiness and its causes!
I myself will be the cause for them to have these!
Please, Guru-Buddha, grant me your blessings so that
I may be able to do this.

How wonderful it would be if all sentient beings
were free from suffering and its causes!
May they be free from suffering and its causes!
I myself will free them from suffering and its causes!
Please, Guru-Buddha, grant me your blessings so that
I may be able to do this.

How wonderful it would be if all sentient beings were never separated
from the happiness of higher rebirth and liberation!
May they never be separated from the happiness of higher rebirth
and liberation!
I myself will be the cause for them to never be separated from these!
Please, Guru-Buddha, grant me your blessings so that
I may be able to do this.

How wonderful it would be if all sentient beings
were to abide in equanimity, free of hatred and attachment!
May they abide in equanimity!
I myself will be the cause for them to abide in equanimity!
Please, Guru-Buddha, grant me your blessings so that
I may be able to do this.

TAKING THE BODHISATTVA VOW

At the end of the session, if you have previously received the bodhisattva vow from an authentic teacher, it is now a good time to renew that vow. With the Refuge Field fresh in your mind, crouching on one knee with palms pressed together, recite the following two verses from the *Bodhisattva's Way of Life:*

Just as the sugatas of former ages
Aroused bodhicitta and then, in stages,
Trained themselves in skilful practice
On the genuine path of the bodhisattvas,

Like them, I take this sacred vow
To arouse bodhicitta here and now,
And train myself for others' good,
Gradually, as a bodhisattva should.

(Repeat these verses three times, and then develop the certainty that you have generated the Bodhisattva Vow.)

While this section is not traditionally part of the Divine Ladder, I have inserted it here because I believe it is important to renew your vows on a daily basis. This helps to keep your vows pure and to strengthen your commitment to practicing the Six Perfections. If you have not received these vows, you can skip this section completely.

CONCLUSION

To conclude your session, you should now dissolve the Refuge Field as described in the previous chapter on the Refuge practice. First the Dakinis and Dharmapalas dissolve into the Arya Sangha; the Sangha then dissolves into the Dharma; the Dharma dissolves into the Buddhas; and the Buddhas dissolve into the Yidams and Gurus respectively. Finally the Gurus and the entire visualisation dissolves into Vajradhara who comes to your crown and dissolves into you. Rest for a while in this state and then finish by dedicating any merit you have accumulated to the enlightenment of all sentient beings.

CHAPTER SIX

Vajrasattva Purification

Vajrasattva practice allows you to uncover the reality of your Buddha-nature, which is currently hidden as a result of defilements created by attachment, aggression and delusion. Our current situation is like a dirty piece of glass. This practice provides you with a powerful method to wash away the dirt while being confident that underneath there is crystal clear glass which is completely pure and unstained. Through the practice of Vajrasattva, this confidence will steadily grow as you come closer and closer to discovering the innate purity of your most profound nature.

What is it we need to purify? Currently we are dominated by our negative emotions and are controlled by the karmic conditioning we have developed over countless lifetimes. Most people rarely consider the role negative karma plays in their unfortunate experiences or the obstacles they encounter. As the influence of our karma is hidden from our ordinary awareness, we don't usually recognise that what we consider to be the causes of our happiness or suffering are only temporary conditions—they are not the root.

Furthermore, within our present mind-stream we carry specific karmic propensities which block us from developing a good understanding of the Dharma or engaging effectively in certain practices. This is especially true of profound practices such as the Six Vajra Yogas. According to Vajrayana Buddhism, all these negative propensities are held energetically in the form of "knots" in the channels of your subtle body. Since the mind is closely linked with the movement of energy, until these knots are cleared you will be unable to achieve higher realisations. For this reason we use the unique visualisation practice of Vajrasattva to "wash away" all of this negative energy and heal the subtle body, making it suitable for practice.

By purifying these karmic propensities you prevent their ripening in the future, ensuring your effectiveness in progressing along the spiritual path. Purification is achieved through the use of four components known as the *Four Powers*:

1. **Power of Reliance:** In order to transcend our own limitations, it is important to rely on objects which are actually capable of providing us with refuge from our suffering. In general the main object of our refuge is the Three Jewels—Buddha, Dharma and Sangha. For this practice, however, we specifically rely on the healing power and purity of our own Buddha-nature, manifesting in the form of a radiant white deity known as Vajrasattva. The name "Vajrasattva" literally means "enlightened warrior" or "the embodiment of the indestructible energy of enlightenment."

   In this practice we gradually build our visualisation of Vajrasattva by reciting many details. The essential point to remember is to feel the presence of Vajrasattva in the space above you. You can strengthen your personal connection with Vajrasattva by recognising that his nature is inseparable from the nature of your lama and therefore inseparable from your own nature. It is your connection to this nature that will purify your mind and guide you to enlightenment. If your reliance upon Vajrasattva is strong and stable, you can be sure that the subsequent purification will be equally as powerful.

2. **Power of Regret:** With Vajrasattva as your witness, the next step is to genuinely acknowledge your negative propensities without concealing anything. You completely abandon all sense of pride and expose your mistakes in the presence of Buddha Vajrasattva. You recognise that due to greed, hatred or carelessness, you have behaved unwisely and the propensities created by those actions will definitely lead to suffering in the future. You can think of these negative actions as a lethal poison you have just swallowed. In this way you develop the strong desire to rid yourself of the poison and to completely purify yourself of all negativity.

   For western cultures, we must be careful to distinguish between sincere regret and feelings of guilt or self-criticism. Purification is about remembering that our underlying nature is pure and free from defilements. It is full of enlightened qualities such as unconditional love and compassion and it is this nature we need to focus on.

3. **Power of the Remedy:** With strong regret in our mind, we then need to engage in a virtuous action that will help us create a positive counterforce to the propensities we are trying to purify. In this practice, the "remedy" is to recite the Vajrasattva mantra while visualising your body being cleansed by a radiant white nectar which washes away all impurities. Both of these techniques are skilful means to help you remember the purity of your nature.

   While this special practice is a particularly powerful method of purification, there are many others you can also do. For instance, you could strive to perform good deeds, be kind and compassionate to others, make amends to those you have harmed, cultivate patience in the face of adversity or ask for forgiveness when appropriate. No matter what method you choose as your remedy, be sure to dedicate the merits towards purifying your mind.

4. **Power of Restraint:** To conclude the process of purification, you need to establish a strong resolve to refrain from doing these negative actions again. If you have clearly identified the mistaken behaviour or broken vow, you should try to generate the determination to never repeat that action again in the future, even at the cost of your life. Developing this form of strong restraint is what gives power to your purification, making it possible to clear away lifetimes of negative karma.

   Practically speaking however, if you do not feel capable of abandoning a specific behaviour completely, you can start by strengthening your resolve to abstain from the action for a specific period of time. For instance, you could think, "For the next week, I will not do this or that." The main point is to develop a strong aspiration to refrain from negative conduct, then over time that resolve will eventually become powerful enough to abandon the non-virtue completely.

To help us generate these four powers, the following practice has been specifically designed to ensure that your purification is both strong and effective. You can recite it as a stand alone practice or as part of your daily recitation of the Divine Ladder.

A SHORT VAJRASATTVA PRACTICE WITH COMMENTARY

Prior to starting this practice, you should take refuge in the Three Jewels and generate Bodhicitta, as described previously. With this as your foundation you can then begin the actual practice.

Visualisation

We begin by first establishing the visualisation in our mind. Before generating a visualisation, you should dissolve any ordinary appearances by reciting the following mantra:

OM SVABHAVA SHUDDHA SARVA DHARMA SVABHAVA SHUDDHO HAM
All phenomena including oneself enter the natural state of emptiness.

The purpose of this mantra is to purify all appearances into the pure natural state of emptiness, the ultimate truth, which is empty of all deceptive phenomena. You should visualise your body and all appearances as an empty reflection, like the reflection of the moon on a lake.

From the natural state of emptiness, above my crown, the syllable PAM (པཾ) appears which transforms into an eight-petalled white lotus flower. The syllable AH (ཨཱཿ) appears on top of the lotus flower and transforms into a full moon disc. On top of the moon disc appears the syllable HUNG (ཧཱུྃ) which transforms into a white five-pronged vajra with a HUNG (ཧཱུྃ) syllable at its hub.

Slowly the natural state of emptiness becomes alive like a reflection in a mirror, and from this appears the syllable PAM, transforming into a white lotus flower which symbolises the innate non-attachment of Buddha-nature. The syllable AH represents the speech of all the Buddhas while the full moon disc is a symbol of compassion. The syllable HUNG represents the mind of all the Buddhas and the vajra represents their indestructible, unyielding spiritual power and wisdom. Vajras are usually made from metal and have five prongs at each end, representing the five Buddha-families or five wisdoms of a Buddha.

To unveil the dharmakaya or natural Buddha within us, we need to accumulate merit and purify all defilements on a relative level. The lotus, vajra and the seed syllables thus represent the generation of merit and the process of purification during the different stages of existence—birth, natural life, death, bardo and rebirth.

This HUNG (ཧཱུྃ) radiates luminous light to all universes and makes limitless offerings to all Arya beings. The light then radiates to all beings and purifies their negativities and obscurations. It then returns and dissolves into the syllable HUNG (ཧཱུྃ) and the white five-pronged vajra then completely melts into light.

The HUNG syllable is the essence of the mind of all the Buddhas. When you radiate light making offerings to all Arya beings, you are invoking the blessings of all the Buddhas. Visualising the light of these blessings dissolving back into you is a tantric way to strengthen the power of the practice. You then purify the negativities and obscurations of all beings with this same light, which is a unique method to accumulate merit. Activities such as making limitless offerings to enlightened beings and purifying the negativities and obscurations of sentient beings are the basis for attaining the rupakaya form bodies of a Buddha. Without engaging in these kinds of actions we will never achieve enough merit to attain complete enlightenment.

The light transforms instantly into Vajrasattva, with a white body, one face and two arms, holding a vajra in his right hand and a bell in his left. He embraces his consort Vajratopa in Yab-yum.

The forms of Vajrasattva and Vajratopa are aspects of the rupakaya enlightenment in this practice, representing all the merit you need to accumulate so that you can spontaneously benefit others.

Vajrasattva has a radiant white body which is youthful, translucent, perfectly proportioned and attractive—these features symbolise the purification of all negativities and obscurations. In Vajrayana practice,

— Vajrasattva Yab-Yum —
The purity of Buddha-nature symbolised by the union of method and wisdom

attributes like the vajra and bell are specific supports that connect you with the qualities of enlightenment. These connections are formed on the basis of the principles of interdependence.

The vajra embodies the quality of being indestructible, just like a diamond, and represents the Buddha's mind. The bell, bearing the image of a Buddha's face and the inscription of a mantra, represents the enlightened body and speech. The vajra is also the symbol of spontaneous great bliss and masculine spiritual qualities such as compassion. The bell also represents empty-form and feminine spiritual qualities, such as wisdom.

Although the practice still works if you visualise Vajrasattva as a solitary figure, it is more effective to visualise Vajrasattva together with his consort Vajratopa in enlightened embrace. This is known as Vajrasattva Yab-yum, and signifies the union of masculine and feminine qualities in the ultimate nature of reality.

> *Vajratopa is white in colour, holding a curved knife in her right hand and a skull cup in her left. They are both adorned with bone and jewelled ornaments and sit respectively with legs crossed in the vajra and lotus postures.*

The curved knife signifies method, or the ability to cut through the dualistic mind, while the skull cup represents wisdom, or the "consumption" of impure dualistic thought. Both Vajrasattva and Vajratopa are adorned with five silk garments and eight jewelled ornaments.

The *five silken garments* include: (1) a patterned blue silk scarf, (2) five coloured crown pendants, (3) a white silk upper-garment, (4) a lower skirt-like garment, and (5) long sleeves. These garments symbolise the five wisdoms.

The *eight jewelled ornaments* include: (1) a crown, (2) earrings, (3-5) short, middle and long necklaces, (6) shoulder ornaments, (7) bracelets and (8) anklets. These signify the eight pure consciousnesses.

The crossing of their legs in the vajra and lotus postures symbolises the indivisibility of samsara and nirvana.

At the Yab-yum's forehead the syllable OM (ཨོཾ) appears; at the throat, AH (ཨཱཿ); at the heart, HUNG (ཧཱུྃ); and at the navel, HO (ཧོཿ).

From the HUNG (ཧཱུྃ) at the Yab-yum's heart, light radiates outward to the ten directions and the purification power of all the Buddhas and bodhisattvas radiates back in the form of white nectar.

The OM, AH and HUNG syllables at the forehead, throat and heart represent the indestructible body, speech and mind of Vajrasattva, while HO at the navel signifies indestructible primordial wisdom. The light radiating to all the Buddhas and bodhisattvas collects their blessings and empowers the heart of Vajrasattva with the purification power of all the Buddhas (which Vajrasattva represents). This takes the form of luminous, translucent, brilliantly white nectar.

DZA (ཛཿ) HUNG (ཧཱུྃ) VAM (བྃ) HO (ཧོཿ)
The nectar now becomes inseparable from Vajrasattva Yab-yum.

With DZA, the nectar is drawn above the crown of Vajrasattva, with HUNG it dissolves into Vajrasattva, and with VAM it permeates all of Vajrasattva Yab-yum. Finally, as HO is recited the nectar becomes completely inseparable from Vajrasattva Yab-yum. With the completion of this visualisation, you have now generated the *Power of Reliance.*

Making Requests for Purification

Vajrasattva Yab-yum, please purify and cleanse all negativities, obscurations and transgressions accumulated by myself and all beings since beginningless time.

With Vajrasattva Yab-yum as your witness, you should now generate the Power of Remorse. In this verse you are calling on Vajrasattva Yab-yum to help you purify and cleanse all your negativities, obscurations and transgressions. You first recall all of the negative actions, habits and unwholesome energies of your body, speech and mind, then after recognising that these actions were harmful to yourself and others, make a heart-felt request to Vajrasattva, asking for help to purify them from your mindstream.

The Actual Purification

Having made your request, imagine the body of Vajrasattva and consort completely overflowing with nectar emerging from every pore of their body, especially at the point of union. The nectar then cascades downwards like a waterfall or a gentle shower of rain. Imagine the nectar washing over your body and entering through your crown. As it works its way down your body, envisage that all sicknesses, negative energies and afflicted minds are cleansed away and pushed out through the lower openings of your body, taking on the form of thick black liquid made of blood and pus. This liquid dissolves into the earth below you.

If you can, it is good to also imagine the field of Vajrasattva's purifying nectar extending outward to all sentient beings, purifying them in the same way. Hold this visualisation in your mind as you recite the long Vajrasattva mantra:

> ***OM SHRI VAJRA HERUKA SAMAYA MANUPALAYA | VAJRA HERUKA TENOPA | TISHTHA DRIDHO ME BHAVA | SUTOKAYO ME BHAVA | ANURAKTO ME BHAVA | SUPOKAYO ME BHAVA | SARVA SIDDHI MAME PRAYATSA | SARVA KARMA SU TSA ME | TSITAM SHREYANG KURU HUNG | HA HA HA HA HO | BHAGAVAN VAJRA HERUKA MAME MUNTSA | HERUKA BHAVA MAHA SAMAYA SATTVA AH HUM PHET***

You should recite this mantra as many times as you can depending on the time available. The meaning of this mantra is as follows:

Sanskrit	Meaning
OM	Homage!
SHRI VAJRA HERUKA	According to glorious wrathful Vajrasattva's sacred pledge
MANUPALAYA VAJRA HERUKA TENOPA	O Vajrasattva, protect the Samaya
TISHTHA DRIDHO ME BHAVA	Remain firm in me
SUTOKAYO ME BHAVA	Grant me complete happiness
ANURAKTO ME BHAVA	Be loving towards me
SUPOKAYO ME BHAVA	Grow within me (increasing my virtue)
SARVA SIDDHI MAME PRAYATSA	Bless me with all the siddhis
SARVA KARMA SU TSA ME	Show me all the karmas
TSITTAM SHREYANG KURU	Make my mind good, virtuous and auspicious
HUNG	Vajrasattva's essence (or seed syllable)
HA HA HA HA	The four immeasurables, four empowerments, four joys and four kayas
HO	Exclamation of joy
BHAGAVAN	O blessed one, embodiment of all the Buddhas
VAJRA HERUKA MA ME MUNTSA	Never abandon me
HERUKA BHAVA	Show me the vajra nature of the five wisdoms
MAHA SAMAYA SATTVA	O great wisdom being
AH HUNG PHET	Make me one with you!

The mantra connects you to the divine healing power of Vajrasattva and makes the cleansing process more effective than the visualisation alone, provided you invoke all of the four powers and you have good single-pointed concentration.

While this is the essential practice, there are also many other options for what to make the centre of your attention while reciting mantra. For example, you can choose to focus on the meaning of the mantra, on your feeling of regret and resolve, on the form of Vajrasattva Yab-yum or on the flow of nectar through your subtle body.

If you are overwhelmed by all these details, the most important thing is to recall the four powers and simply try to feel Vajrasattva's presence. If time is limited it is also possible to use a shorter version of the mantra:

OM VAJRASATTVA HUNG

While this short mantra is useful for quickly purifying negative actions, if you are focusing on this Vajrasattva practice as part of the Kalachakra Preliminaries, you should dedicate formal sessions to accumulating the long mantra. The goal is to accumulate at least 100,000 mantras, which usually takes about three months when the practice is done intensively. Alternatively, you can simply continue to practice for as long as it takes to experience the signs of purification.

Confessing All Wrongdoings

When you have completed your session, you can finish by generating the *Power of Restraint.* This is achieved by reciting verses of confession as follows:

Great protector, due to ignorance and confusion I have broken my samaya and let them decline. Compassionate Lama Vajrasattva Yab-yum, please purify my negativities and protect me. In you I take refuge, supreme Vajra holder, treasure of compassion and rescuer of all beings.

In this verse, you are confessing all the occasions where you have broken your commitments or let them decline due to ignorance and confusion, whether you were aware of it or not. This mainly refers to any vows or sacred commitments (samaya) that you have received from a Vajra Master. They include things like always cultivating respect and devotion for your teachers and maintaining pure perception of your experiences.

While this verse is specifically relevant for tantric practitioners, it really applies to whatever level of ethical discipline you are currently trying to develop, such as the Bodhisattva Vows or the precepts of Personal Liberation.

In the first part of the verse you are invoking the power of regret, thinking intensely of all the negativity you have accumulated. In the second part you are re-invoking the power of reliance by praying to compassionate Lama Vajrasattva and taking refuge in him. At the same time you are applying the power of remedy, as by reciting this prayer you are creating a positive energy that will counteract the negativity of your previous actions.

> *I confess and repent all transgressions of my body, speech and mind, including all breaches of my root and branch vows. Please purify and cleanse all stains, negativities, obscurations and transgressions amassed throughout beginningless cyclic existence.*

This is similar to the previous verse, only here you specifically recollect all your transgressions of body, speech and mind, as well as all breaches of root and branch vows. In the Kalachakra Tantra there are fourteen root vows and eight branch vows. To be qualified to keep tantric vows, however, you must also keep bodhisattva vows to the best of your ability, which include eighteen root vows and forty-six branch vows.

Finally you exhort Vajrasattva once again to purify and cleanse all the stains, negativities, obscurations and transgressions amassed throughout beginningless cyclic existence. We have developed many strong habits over countless lifetimes, and we are relying on Vajrasattva to help peel back all these layers of habitual patterns—to purify all our negative emotions, negative deeds and tendencies to break promises, as well as intellectual obscurations which prevent us from seeing the ultimate truth. At this point you should invoke the power of restraint by generating a strong resolve to never again be taken over by these negative habits and to refrain from committing negative deeds even if your life is at stake.

Dissolution of the Visualisation

> *As if the moon were melting into me, Vajrasattva Yab-yum looks down at me with a smile and begins to melt with joy, dissolving through the crown of my head. The body, speech and mind of Vajrasattva Yab-yum becomes inseparable from my own body, speech and mind.*

Having completed the relative level of the practice of purification, Vajrasattva then looks down at you with a smile, as if to say "well done". He then dissolves into you, becoming inseparable from your own body, speech and mind, as you realise that on the ultimate level Vajrasattva is none other than your own Buddha-nature. You thus recognise that your mind has always been pure.

When you focus on accumulating the Vajrasattva mantra, it is good to practice dissolving and then re-building the visualisation at regular intervals, for example at the end of each mala. This reminds you of the empty nature of the visualisation and prevents you from being fixated on appearances, as you observe the inseparability of you and Vajrasattva again and again.

Dedication of virtue

Complete your session with the following verse of dedication:

> *Through this virtue may I quickly reach the enlightened state of Vajrasattva Yab-yum and lead all beings without exception to this ground of purity. Through this virtue may all beings complete the accumulation of merit and primordial wisdom and so attain the two kayas of enlightenment.*

This dedication is similar to the prayer you recite at the end of the previous practices. This time, however, the emphasis is on the purity aspect of enlightenment. For this reason you aspire to reach the enlightened state of Vajrasattva and lead all beings to this state as well. Once they attain enlightenment they will have attained the two Buddha-kayas: the dharmakaya body of the reality of enlightenment and the rupakaya form bodies. These bodies are the result of accumulating wisdom and merit respectively.

CHAPTER SEVEN

Mandala Offering

The purpose of the practice of offering mandalas is to accumulate merit by making the most expansive and vast offerings possible with the best possible motivation. We direct these offerings toward the best possible recipients—the sublime Three Jewels. This combination of action, motivation and support make Mandala Offerings an extraordinarily effective method for accumulating vast quantities of merit in a relatively short period of time.

Merit is the positive energy that is generated when engaging in virtuous actions. This positive energy habituates your mind to virtue and therefore provides the basis for happiness to arise in the future. For instance, if you become habituated to generosity, you will create the causes to experience great wealth in the future; if you are habituated to patience, you will take on a beautiful appearance; and if you habituate yourself to strive for the achievement of enlightenment, then the result will be to experience all of the necessary conditions and opportunities to help you progress along the spiritual path. Merit is therefore a crucial component in helping you cultivate the virtuous qualities needed. In particular, it increases your ability to understand the Dharma correctly, helps you develop enthusiasm for your practice and gives you the strength to overcome all obstacles along the way.

The word "mandala" is a Sanskrit term referring to a symbolic representation of the universe. Unlike maps which focus mostly on spatial relationships, mandalas represent the full breadth of our mental experience.

This much broader scope allows them to capture the many dimensions of our experience in a visual way. While mandalas are commonly seen as two-dimensional paintings, this is not the only form they can take. A mandala can be constructed out of coloured sand or can be built in three dimensions. The type of mandala used in this practice is known as a "Mandala Offering" in that it is specifically designed to facilitate the offering process. Such a mandala is built by arranging various piles of offering substances (such as jewels, stones or grains) into layers stacked one on top of the other. Each layer consists of a ring which acts as a container for the offerings. Once a layer is filled, another ring is laid down and again filled with offerings. Finally, a wish-fulfilling jewel is placed on the summit of the piles.

Traditional Mandala Offering

The most basic form of mandala offering can be made by using the hands to create the mandala "mudra", which is simply a symbolic gesture.

The various substances offered in the mandala represent all the precious things that can be experienced in this world. As infinite sources of joy and happiness they are worthy offerings for the enlightened ones and include everything you could possibly imagine, whether physical or mental. For example you could offer fields of beautiful flowers as well as the positive karmic propensities you and others have generated in your minds, for these too are the basis for joy and happiness.

These substances are offered to the Refuge Field which includes all of the supports for achieving enlightenment: the lamas, buddhas, bodhisattvas and so forth. We make offerings to them, not because they need the offerings, but because they represent the enlightened qualities we aspire to achieve. By showing reverence to them and by offering everything we experience, we make a powerful karmic connection to them which functions as a basis for their qualities to arise in us.

The last step of a mandala offering is to recall why you are making the offering. We are not trying to accumulate merit for our own gain. We wish to accumulate merit so we can achieve enlightenment and bring benefit to all sentient beings. In other words, we are making the offering with the motivation of bodhicitta. Because there are limitless sentient beings, any offering made on their behalf will generate limitless merit. This is what makes the offering so expansive and so effective.

THE MANDALA OFFERING PRACTICE WITH COMMENTARY

We will now describe the mandala offering practice in accordance with the Jonang Tradition. As with any Mahayana Buddhist practice, you should first take refuge and then generate the aspiration to achieve enlightenment for the benefit of all beings.

Visualisation

> *In the space immediately in front of you, visualise your root lama in the form of blue Vajradhara. He is surrounded by the Three Jewels, yidam deities and dakinis. They appear unfabricated and magnificent.*

The first step is to establish the Refuge Field visualisation as described previously in the practice of taking refuge. Spend some time to rest the mind in an expansive and open state, and then allow the details of the visualisation to emerge from this space. Remember, the essential point is to feel the presence of the various objects of refuge. It is that feeling which allows us to connect with the enlightened qualities they represent.

Invoking the Field of Merit

> *You are the jewel-like lama, the one whose kindness leads to the dawning of great bliss in a single instant. I bow at your lotus feet, Lama Vajradhara.*

Having developed our visualisation, we then recite a number of verses that are designed to generate devotion towards the field of merit, which will be the recipient of your offerings. This field is embodied by the jewel-like lama who is our human link to enlightenment and the simultaneous representation of the Three Jewels. We especially remember the incredible kindness our lama shows us by teaching and guiding us along our spiritual journey. Due to our lack of merit the Buddhas are unable to guide us directly, and instead guide us through the form of the lama. It is for this reason that the lama is considered kinder than all of the Buddhas. By thinking of the lama in this way, they can lead us to incredible spiritual realisations such as experiencing in a single instant the awareness of great bliss, which transcends the ordinary conceptual mind. Although we speak of a singular lama, we should always remember that they represents all of our teachers, both male and female. He is a single embodiment of all those who have benefited you on your journey to enlightenment.

Bowing to the lama's lotus feet is a poetic way of saying that every part of the lama's body possesses great beauty, while also referring to the lotus flower upon which the lama traditionally sits in visualisations. Within Buddhist cultures, it is generally seen as a great honour to touch the lowest point of the lama's body (the feet) with the highest point of your own body (the head). In this verse we refer to the lama as Vajradhara because his enlightened body is indestructible, representing the dharmakaya body of the reality of enlightenment.

> *I pay homage to the lama for whom my gratitude is beyond compare. The light of your enlightened truth dispels my darkness. You are the faultless wisdom eye, the sun-like lama of great immutable bliss.*

According to Vajrayana Buddhism, your spiritual progress depends on your ability to show gratitude and appreciation for your lama and the light of his "enlightened truth", which is the truth you discover by practising the Dharma he teaches. The "faultless wisdom eye" refers to the lama's ability to see and point out our hidden weaknesses, while "sun-like" means the lama is like a source of radiant light; enabling us to see all that is around us.

> *You are our mother and father. You are the master of all beings, a true and noble friend. You are the great protector who acts for the benefit of all sentient beings. You are the great rescuer who steals away negative obscurations. You are the one who abides in excellence. You are the sole abode of all supreme qualities, completely free from all faults. You are the protector of the lowly, the supreme conqueror of self-cherishing and suffering; the source of all wealth, the wish-fulfilling jewel, the supreme victorious Dharma Lord; in you I take refuge.*

The Dharma teacher is like a parent in a spiritual sense—like a "mother", he provides you with love and spiritual nourishment; and like a "father", he guides and protects you on your spiritual journey. He is the "master of all beings" as he does not discriminate regarding who he will guide to enlightenment and accepts all beings regardless of caste, race or social standing. As a "noble friend" he shares the precious Dharma with you and provides unconditional love and support, caring for you until you reach enlightenment. Furthermore, he protects you from the sufferings of samsara and rescues you by showing how to achieve enlightened qualities.

In addition, the Dharma teacher "steals away negative obscurations" by teaching you how to overcome all negative qualities, and it is only by following his teachings that you can attain the "supreme qualities" of Buddhahood. As a manifestation of the Buddhas in human form, the lama is also the "great protector" who acts for the benefit of all sentient beings and is the supreme conqueror of self-cherishing and suffering, having achieved enlightenment for the sake of all beings. Finally, he is described as a "wish-fulfilling jewel" as he is able to manifest limitless enlightened qualities for the benefit of his followers.

In you I take refuge, immaculate and holy root lama; supreme, victorious Dharma Lord, embodiment of the Buddhas of the three times.

If you like, you can recite this verse alone instead of the previous verses, recalling that taking refuge in the Three Jewels is the foundation of all Dharma practice. Here, taking refuge in the lama is equal to taking refuge in the Three Jewels, as the lama is considered the embodiment of the Buddhas of the three times—past, present and future. All past Buddhas achieved enlightenment through reliance on their Dharma teachers, all present Buddhas manifest in the form of Dharma teachers and all future Buddhas are trained by Dharma teachers. This is why the lama, who teaches you the precious Dharma, is seen as holy and immaculate.

Medium-length Mandala Offering

OM VAJRA BHUMI AH HUNG.
The foundation is the pure, mighty golden earth.

Here we begin the medium-length mandala offering practice unique to the Jonang Tradition. This involves placing nine heaps of rice or jewels on a plate, which represents the universe being offered to the field of refuge. This is much briefer than the traditional long mandala offering which involves thirty-seven offering objects.

With the mantra "*OM VAJRA BHUMI AH HUNG*" you begin to assemble the mandala by creating a foundation, the pure, mighty golden earth, on which you can build a physical and mental picture of the universe. A circular plate is used to represent this foundation. You should rub its surface clockwise with your wrist a few times before proceeding with the offering.

OM means "perfect" or "with excellence", and is used at the beginning of any activity to help guide us to perfection. *VAJRA* means "indestructible." *BHUMI* means "earth, ground or basis." *AH* means "fundamental origin" or "emptiness". *HUNG* means "essential" or "fullness." Taken together, this mantra leads us to excellence and glory in any activity and assists us in reaching enlightenment.

The model for the universe we are using here is a little different from the conventional scientific model. According to the Kalachakra Tantra, the universe was formed as the four great elements united according to the collective karma of beings. From within space, the black wind element was first to arise, followed by the red fire element, the white water element and finally, the yellow earth element. Each of these elements is represented by concentric discs with a decreasing diameter, stacked one atop another. The circular plate symbolises this foundation of elements.

OM VAJRA REKHE AH HUNG.
The universe is encircled by a great iron fence of mountains and in the centre is Mount Meru, the king of mountains.

With this mantra you visualise the great Mount Meru appearing upon the centre of the yellow earth disc, encircled by a great iron fence of mountains or perimeter ridge which represents the outer boundary of the universe or world system. Mount Meru is circular in shape and at its peak are five summits. These features each represent different aspects of our universe which are experienced by different sentient beings, for instance, the base of Mount Meru represents the gross realms of experience of sentient beings, while the levels rising upward represent increasingly more subtle realms of experience.

As you build this visualisation in your mind, you should take the largest ring from your mandala set and place it on top of the circular plate. Taking a handful of offerings (for instance rice, stones or jewels), place a single heap in the centre of the plate to symbolise Mount Meru.

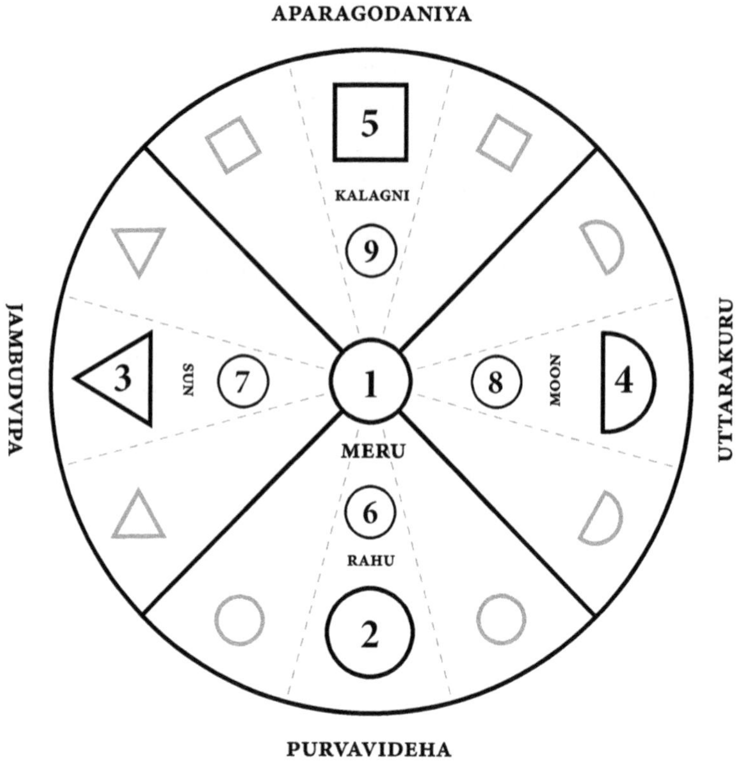

The Nine-Heap Mandala Offering according to Kalachakra Cosmology

To the east is Purvavideha, to the south is Jambudvipa,
to the north is Uttarakuru and to the west is Aparagodaniya.

These are the four continents surrounding Mount Meru. To the east is Purvavideha (meaning "great physical prosperity"), with three islands in the shape of circles. To the south is Jambudvipa ("a place of the sound Dzam"—likened to the sound of tree leaves falling into the sea) with three triangular shaped islands. This is where our realm of experience is said to be located. To the north is Uttarakuru (meaning "hidden news and bad sound"), with three semi-circular islands. Finally, to the west is

Aparagodaniya (meaning "great material prosperity"), with three square islands. It is important to understand that these "continents" and "islands" are not a representation of physical geographic land masses. They instead represent different realms of experience that exist at different levels of subtlety. The world as we know it, as described by modern science, is simply one description of one island within the continent of Jambudvipa. When we realise that our universe is only one small part of a much larger multi-dimensional universe, we begin to see how expansive Buddhist cosmology actually can be.

As you continue adding details to your visualisations, you should place four heaps of offerings into the four directions, following the order they are mentioned in the text. When working with mandalas as offerings, the eastern direction is considered to be on the edge of the plate that is closest to you. So here we place one pile in the East; then one in the South (on the left side of the plate); one in the North (on the right side of the plate) and finally one in the West (on the far side of the plate).

Rahu, Sun, Moon and Kalagni, and in the middle the total wondrous possessions of humans and gods, complete and lacking nothing.

The focus now shifts to all of the celestial bodies which make up our universe as we know it. In the cosmology described by the Kalachakra Tantra, this includes the sun, moon and two "planets" known as Rahu and Kalagni. The movement of these four bodies plays a critical role in the cycles of time that we experience as sentient beings. Due to their influence on our minds, they all have profound spiritual and astrological significance. The planet Rahu (represented by a black disc) refers to the appearance of a lunar eclipse and is associated with the northern node of the moon. The planet Kalagni (represented by a yellow disc) refers to the appearance of a solar eclipse and is associated with the southern node of the moon. Add four heaps of offerings to represent each of the four planets.

While it is good to know the traditional cosmology and visualise the universe in this way, you should also be creative with this practice and bring to mind everything that is pleasing in the world of humans and gods, including lakes, forests, mountains, palaces, jewels and works of art. You could also offer Asia, Europe, Africa, South and North America, national parks, waterfalls, money, flying carpets, mobile phones, banks and even objects of your mind such as virtuous qualities and spiritual attainments. With each object of offering you can think of, add a pile of offerings to the mandala until the first ring is completely full. Remember that anything you perceive as being beautiful or valuable is a worthy object to be offered. Don't think that you can only offer things you physically own. All of your experiences belong to you and therefore these are what you are offering, not the objects themselves.

All this wealth I offer with great devotion to my immaculate root and lineage lamas, And to the mandala of yidams, Buddhas, bodhisattvas, pratyekas, shravakas, dakinis and all-seeing Dharma protectors.

Next place your second largest ring on top of the first, and while mentally generating different objects of offerings, place more heaps of offerings into the mandala. Note how the movement of the rice is similar to the arising and dissolution of thoughts in rapid succession. Imagine that with each heap you are offering more and more of your experiences. Continue in this way until the second ring is completely filled.

Then put the third ring on top of the second, imagining that with each pile of offerings you offer the subtlest level of your experience. This includes all of the virtuous karmic propensities you have accrued since beginningless time and all of the virtuous qualities you have developed. Offer the very best parts of who you are as a person.

When the last ring is completely filled, place the wish-fulfilling jewel on top to represent your achievement of full and complete enlightenment. Think of the limitless benefit you will bring to sentient beings in the future and offer this virtue as part of the mandala. After the mandala set is completely filled, you should raise it as a gesture of offering all its wealth with great devotion to the field of refuge, the immaculate root and lineage lamas and so forth.

> *Out of compassion accept this mandala for the sake of all beings, and having accepted this offering, please bless me!*

Having made this offering, you then ask the field of refuge to accept this mandala. As the Buddhas' compassion is limitless, their blessings will naturally arise in us when the offering is made. Our offering of the universe should also include the merit accumulated by all sentient beings and all enlightened beings. Offering in this way increases the merit of all beings so that they may reach enlightenment, and therefore the offering is made for the sake of all beings.

> *Recollecting the virtue of body, speech and mind gathered by myself and all beings during the three times, together with the collection of excellent Samantabhadra offerings in this precious mandala, both real and visualised, I offer this all to my lama and the Three Jewels. Please accept this with your compassion and bless me!*

The collection of virtue of the three times refers to merit that has been accumulated with body, speech and mind since beginningless time, as well as the merit generated now and in the future until we reach buddhahood. As in the previous verse, you are asking the field of refuge, which is embodied by the lama and the Three Jewels, to accept your offering and bless your mind-stream, thus strengthening your spiritual practice.

This is the final verse of the medium-length mandala offering. If you wish, you can repeat these verses again and again, counting these as accumulations. However, when focusing on accumulations it is more common to use the brief nine-pile offering as explained below.

Brief Mandala Offering

> *The ground is anointed with perfume and strewn with flowers. Its centre is adorned with Mount Meru, surrounded by the four continents, the Sun and the Moon. This I offer as a buddha-field for all beings to enjoy.*

This short version of the mandala offering is generally used for accumulations, although it is good if you can recite the medium-length version beforehand. You only need the base of a mandala set or a plate for the nine piles of offerings.

First you should clean the offering plate with your wrist in a clockwise circular motion, and if you wish you can splash scented water on the plate before doing this. This symbolises the ground being purified or anointed with perfume and strewn with flowers. Then you place one heap of rice in the centre, symbolising Mount Meru, followed by one heap in the front, one to the left, one to the right and one behind. These last four piles represent the four quarters of the universe or four continents. You then end with four more piles—one between the front and centre piles, one between the left and centre piles, one between the right and centre piles, and one between the pile behind and the centre pile. These represent the planets of rahu, sun, moon, and kalagni respectively.

The visualisation is similar to that described in the previous practice. In particular, the base of the offering mandala is made of golden material and anointed with perfume, representing the vast array of natural perfumes, plants and flowers of this earth. You then visualise all sorts of pleasing things such as jewels, crystals, flowers, herbs and grains, as well as the sun, moon, rivers, lakes, minerals, creatures of all shapes and sizes and other objects of natural beauty. Finally, you visualise this entire offering transforming into a Buddha-field, a pure land inhabited by enlightened beings with magnificent trees, palaces and special beings as in the refuge practice. This Buddha-field has the power to benefit beings in limitless ways, and so you offer this for all beings to enjoy. To make an especially auspicious connection, you can bring to mind the features of the Sublime Realm of Shambhala, and imagine that all beings are fortunate enough to be born there.

> ***GURU IDAM RATNA MANDALA KAM NIRYA TAYAMI***
> *(Reciting this, offer the mandala.)*

After each recitation of the prayer you then recite this offering mantra and imagine that the visualised mandala dissolves into you. Rest for a moment in the awareness of the ultimate nature of the offerings you have made. Then quickly clean the offering plate and recite the prayer again as you place the nine heaps of rice on the plate for the next offering.

When accumulation of merit is the main focus of your practice, this process is repeated quite quickly. The shortest possible way is to simply repeat the mantra while you are creating and then dissolving the mandala. If you practice in this condensed manner, it is important that you are always aware of the meaning of the practice, so that it does not degenerate into empty ritual. You can also alternate this brief offering with a longer version, for example doing one medium-length offering after twenty-one shorter ones.

— Kyabje Lama Lobsang Trinlé —
Renowned Abbot of Tashi Chöthang Monastery and Kalachakra Vajra Master

CHAPTER EIGHT

Foundation Guru Yoga

The purpose of guru yoga, the fifth Kalachakra preliminary, is to unify your mind with the holy mind of your teacher. On a relative level you chant all kinds of prayers and supplications to open your mind and heart to the lama's blessings and generate great devotion. On an ultimate level you learn to recognise that the definitive lama is none other than your own wisdom mind. This means the lama is not only an important person in your life, but is your personal path to enlightenment. As we are unable to receive direct guidance from enlightened beings, we need to rely on a human form to link us to the enlightened wisdom of the Buddha. This outer teacher is the person you are asking to help you by dismantling your ego. This process of dissolution leads to the discovery of the inner teacher, your own enlightened wisdom. The practice of guru yoga is absolutely essential if you wish to follow the tantric path to enlightenment, as it is the lama's blessing that allows you to develop pure perception and open the door to all other tantric realisations.

If you have a sceptical mind, you might be very suspicious of the whole idea of guru devotion—it may seem like something fabricated, theistic or undemocratic. On a basic level, Buddhism is all about sound logic and practical methods that everyone can easily test. This is akin to a good manual for learning to drive a car. However, practices like guru devotion and guru yoga take you beyond this basic level of Buddhism—they are much more like the personal advice that you can receive from a driving instructor. This advice provides you with essential knowledge that has arisen from the experience of generations of lineage masters. It is this wisdom that we rely on in order to practise effectively.

When you recite the supplications of a guru yoga practice, you are not meant to simply have blind devotion—these verses are designed to help you to deeply penetrate your mind-stream and lead you to an understanding of truth beyond all words and concepts. You should remember that real devotion to the guru is not a theistic or dictatorial situation, but rather an honouring of the mutual agreement between you and your teacher to work towards enlightenment.

It is said that the blessings we receive from the lama correspond to our attitude toward him. For instance, we may see him as a very compassionate man, a noble Arhat or a fully enlightened Buddha. These attitudes would give rise to the blessings of a compassionate man, the blessings of an Arhat and the blessings of a Buddha respectively.

In the tantric path we work with developing the pure perception that sees our lama as inseparable from the Buddha. We start by focusing on the outer qualities of the Guru in order to inspire the mind, then focusing on the inner reality of the Guru as being inseparable from Buddha-nature. Finally, we recognise that our own Buddha-nature is inseparable from the guru's Buddha-nature and therefore there is no guru "out there" that is separate from us. In essence, this is the transformation that guru yoga facilitates. Right now we feel as though we are here, while Buddha-nature is somewhere else. Through working with the Guru, we create a bridge that connects us to our inner nature and helps us unlock its limitless capacity.

GURU YOGA PRACTICE WITH COMMENTARY

The following practice is the first of three guru yogas which are traditionally practiced in the Jonang Tradition. Each practice emphasises a slightly different connection to help strengthen your bond with the lineage masters. In this practice, Foundation Guru Yoga, the focus is on the root lama as being inseparable from Vajradhara. The other two (which are presented at the end of this book) are focused on the two most important lineage masters of the tradition: Kunkyen Dolpopa Sherab Gyaltsen and Jetsun Taranatha. All of the guru yogas use the same basic structure—establish the visualisation, make supplications to the lama (and other objects of refuge), receive the four empowerments and then merge your mind with the lama's wisdom mind.

Visualisation

Visualise yourself in a magnificent vast palace in the centre of a pure realm. Your vajra master appears in front of you, in the centre of the palace, as Lord Vajradhara. He is seated upon a lotus, with sun, moon, rahu and kalagni discs which rest upon a lion throne.

Your vajra master has a body blue in colour, with one face and two arms, holding a vajra and bell crossed at the level of his heart. His legs are in full lotus posture. Adorned with silken garments and jewelled ornaments, with marks and signs complete, his body is radiant and luminous. He smiles down upon you, pleased with you.

Lord Vajradhara is surrounded by the deities of the four classes of Tantra, all lineage lamas and the entire assembly of yidam deities, buddhas, bodhisattvas, shravakas, pratyekas, dakinis and Dharma protectors. Be confident that all of them are actually present.

The guru yoga practice begins by invoking your lama, the vajra master, in the divine form of Lord Vajradhara, who is the embodiment of all the lineage masters, Buddhas, bodhisattvas and so forth. As in the refuge practice, you consider that all appearances dissolve into emptiness, from which a pure realm with a magnificent vast palace emerges, like the reflection of the full moon in a lake. The lama then appears in the space in front of you as the primordial Buddha Vajradhara upon the lion throne, lotus, sun, moon, rahu and kalagni discs, and gazes affectionately at you, signifying your close personal connection with him. The details of the

Guru Vajradhara

assembly's make-up and the significance of each type of enlightened being are described in the refuge section. Unlike the assembly in the refuge visualisation, in this practice the field of enlightened beings is gathered like a crowd surrounding your root lama.

Your visualisation should be clear, vivid and vibrant, yet appearing like a reflection, as none of the visualised objects have a truly existing external nature. If they are familiar to you, it might also help to recall some of the stories of the great lineage masters to bring this to life. As with any visualisation practice, you should try to visualise the objects as best you can.

However, the details are not as important as the feeling of the practice or the meaning behind it.

> *Having visualised the field of assembly, make great offerings, both actual and visualised. As you begin to practice you should have confident faith that you possess Buddha-nature and that it can be uncovered through sincere unwavering devotion to your immaculate root lama.*

Having visualised the field of merit, you then imagine making great offerings to Lama Vajradhara and his enlightened companions. You can also make actual offerings to the lama, for example, by placing precious objects in front of a shrine. On a more practical level, you can pledge to offer the lama your time, services, financial assistance or other kinds of help according to your capacity.

As you begin the practice you should have sincere unwavering devotion, which is total trust in the truth of the path you are following, being convinced that you possess Buddha-nature which can definitely be uncovered. Faith is essentially trust in the process of cause and effect. Just as you have the confidence to bake a cake if all the right ingredients are present, so too you can be confident in the enlightened path when certain conditions are present. These conditions include renunciation, compassion, devotion and above all, knowing that you possess Buddha-nature.

Prayers to the Lineage Masters

> *Kind and precious root lama, everything good and virtuous in samsara and nirvana has arisen from your enlightened power. My protector, a wish-fulfilling source, I pray to you from the depths of my heart.*

According to Vajrayana Buddhism, your kind and precious root lama, whose nature is inseparable from all the Buddhas, is the source of everything conceivable that is virtuous, good and beneficial. Although he is equal to the great Buddhas in his wisdom, his kindness surpasses that of the Buddhas as he is appearing to you right now. He is the one who is actually manifesting in your life. Remembering his great kindness, including all circumstances when his teachings helped you and all the small acts of kindness and compassion you can recall, you should pray to him from the depths of your heart. In doing so you are actually invoking the wisdom aspect of your own mind.

I pray to the all-pervasive truth body of great bliss,
The primordial Buddha Vajradhara who abides in Akanishta.
I pray to Kalachakra the enjoyment body.
I pray to Buddha Shakyamuni, the emanation body,
the highest of the Shakyas.
I pray to my lama who embodies the four buddha-kayas.

The lineage that the root lama embodies begins with the primordial Buddha Vajradhara, whose form represents the all-pervasive dharmakaya body of the reality of enlightenment which is changeless and beyond form. Akanishta literally means "the highest", and in this case it refers to the enlightened sphere of dharmakaya Buddha, the realm of Vajradhara. Kalachakra represents the sambhogakaya enjoyment body of enlightenment, while Buddha Shakyamuni represents the emanation body, which together is the compassionate display of enlightened energy for the sake of others. We pray to the lama who embodies the four Buddha-kayas, which include the above three kayas as well as the svabhavikakaya, which is the union of these three.

I pray to the Dharma Kings, translators and panditas:
The thirty-five Shambhala Kings, emanations of the victorious ones,
The two Kalachakrapada, the Older and Younger, and the two unsurpassed scholars, Nalendrapa and Somonatha.

This verse connects us to some of the most important masters in the Jonang-Shambhala lineage. The Dharma Kings, translators and panditas include: the Thirty-Five Dharma Kings who were responsible for preserving the teachings of Kalachakra in Shambhala; the two Kalachakrapada, who brought the Kalachakra teachings into the human world; and the two great scholars of Nalanda who widely propagated the Kalachakra teachings, Nalendrapa and Somanatha.

I pray to the three lamas who attained supreme siddhis:
Protector of all beings Konchoksung,
Great and accomplished meditator Droton Namseg,
Great Mahasiddha Drupchen Yumo Chöki Rachen, great trumpeter of the Dharma.

We now begin invoking the lineage lamas in sets of three, in rough chronological order, while we recollect their unique qualities. Supreme siddhis refers to extraordinary spiritual attainment. Konchoksung, also known as Lama Lhaje Gompa, was a great nagpa (tantric lay practitioner) who spread the Kalachakra teachings widely. Droton Namseg, also a nagpa, is said to have developed a direct connection with many enlightened deities through exceptional meditation practice. Drupchen Yumo Chöki Rachen was a fully ordained monk famous for his extraordinary spiritual powers, who was widely recognised as a great mahasiddha.

I pray to the three wondrous sources of refuge:
Nirmanakaya Seachok Dharmeshvara the greatest son,
Flawless Dharma scholar Khipa Namkha Oser,
Master of magical powers and clairvoyance, Semochen.

Seachok Dharmeshvara was hailed as an emanation of Manjushri and was the son of Drupchen Yumo. Khipa Namkha Öser was an extraordinary, flawless scholar and great tantric yogi who was a master of Asanga's works as well as the Kalachakra Tantra. Semochen achieved swift realisation after practicing the Six Vajra Yogas, and thus gained clairvoyance and other supernatural abilities.

I pray to the three supreme rescuers:
Dispeller of darkness Jamsar Sherab,
All-knowing Kunkhyen Chöku Öser,
The one who perfected immutable bliss, Kunpang Thukje Tsondru.

Jamsar Sherab (also known as Chöje Jamyang Sarma) was a highly realised master who was healed from leprosy after engaging in extensive retreat practice. Chöku Öser was a great scholar of the sutras and tantras, hailed as omniscient or all-knowing, and was also a highly accomplished yogi. Kunpang Thukje Tsondru was regarded as an emanation of one of the Shambhala Kalki Kings, having unified all of the Kalachakra lineages in Tibet and perfected immutable bliss through the practice of the Six Vajra Yogas.

I pray to the three incomparable lamas:
Conqueror of great wisdom Jangsem Gyalwa Yeshe,
Ocean of great qualities Khetsun Zangpo,
Omniscient Buddha of the three times Dolpopa.

Despite limited success with Dharma practice early in his life, Jangsem Gyalwa Yeshe attained incomparable realisation and great wisdom after practising the Six Vajra Yogas under Thukje Tsondru's guidance. Khetsun Zangpo (also known as Khetsun Yonten Gyatso) was known for many great qualities such as impeccable moral conduct, as well as his extraordinarily swift realisation of the vajrayoga practices. The great Jonang luminary Dolpopa, who unified the Kalachakra Tantric Lineage with the Zhentong Sutra Lineage, was considered the emanation of the Buddha of the three times as his realisation and mastery of the Buddha's teachings was so profound as both a scholar and a saint.

I pray to the three roots of living Dharma:
All-triumphant Choklé Namgyal,
Universal source of joy Nyabonpa,
Treasury of knowledge and compassion, Kunga Lodrö.

Choklé Namgyal was known as the "invincible one" as he was able to memorise all the great texts and was undefeatable in debate, being all-triumphant. Nyabonpa (also known as Tsungmed Nyabon Kunga) was a prolific writer and highly respected Dharma teacher, whose teachings were a universal source of joy. Kunga Lodrö studied extensively early in his life, his mind becoming a treasury of knowledge, yet later on he became a wandering yogi, moved by supreme renunciation and compassion.

I pray to the three wondrous lamas:
Embodiment of the Three Jewels Trinlé Zangpo,
Protector of the definitive all-expansive Dharma Nyeton Damcho,
Great master of sutra and tantra Namkha Palzangpo.

Trinley Zangpo (also known as Jamyang Konchog Zangpo) trained in a variety of monasteries from all traditions, thus embodying all the teachings of the Three Jewels. Nyeton Damcho (also known as Drenchog Namkha Tsenchan) attained great realisation through the practice of the Six Vajra Yogas, and as abbot of two great monasteries was a protector of the definitive all-expansive Dharma. Namkha Palzangpo (also known as Panchen Namkha Palzang) initially trained in the Sakya tradition and became an eminent scholar of sutra and tantra, especially of the glorious Kalachakra Tantra.

I pray to the three who accomplished unsurpassable benefit for others:
Great translator Ratnabhadra,
Source of joy for all beings Lama Kunga Drolchok,
Witness of the true unborn meaning Lungrig Gyatso.

It was said that Ratnabhadra brought great benefit to others with his ability to pacify demons through his connection with the wrathful deity Mahakala, while also establishing several monasteries. Lama Kunga Drolchok was a great Rimé master who had a close connection with the Dakini Niguma and brought great joy to all beings through his Dharma work. Lungrig Gyatso attained extraordinary realisation through the practice of the Six Vajra Yogas, including complete control of the dream state, and was therefore a witness of the true, unborn meaning of the ultimate truth.

I pray to the three with unequalled kindness:
Great liberator Drolway Gonpo,
Treasure of ocean-like qualities Kunga Rinchen,
Embodiment of all holy beings Khidrup Namgyal.

Drolway Gonpo (also known as Taranatha or Kunga Nyingpo), was a great liberator of beings as he taught Dharma widely, was a prolific writer and revitalised the Jonang Tradition. Kunga Rinchen (also known as Ngonjang Rinchen Gyatso) was a great scholar and teacher known for his ability to absorb large volumes of knowledge, and for other ocean-like qualities due to his accomplishments during previous lives. Khidrup Lodrö Namgyal was said to be a reincarnation of Dolpopa's mother, and is considered the embodiment of all holy beings as he achieved great spiritual abilities with miraculous signs appearing whenever he performed certain rituals.

I pray to the three holders of the treasury of holy teachings:
Master of speech Thugye Trinlé,
Victorious one Tenzin Chogyur,
Ornament of Dharma practice Ngawang Chöjor.

Ngawang Thugye Trinlé (also known as Chalongwa), was born in Chosang in the year of the wooden horse and had many spiritual powers from an early age, such as pacifying demons. He took instruction from many Lamas including the Panchen Lama Lobsang Chogyen, especially receiving the Kalachakra six yogas from Chöjé Kunsang Wangpo. He had many followers from Golok to the Zuka Ta Tse. Tenzin Chogyur (also known as Ngawang Tenzin Namgyal), achieved many great realisations through practice of the Six Vajra Yogas and was thus victorious in his Dharma practice. Ngawang Chöjor (also known as Ngawang Khetsun Dargye) was considered an ornament of dharma practice due to his great realisations, which included magical powers in his dreams and the continuous perception of his body in the state of clear-light.

I pray to the three lamas who effortlessly accomplish holy activities:
Ornament of perfect conduct Trinlé Namgyal,
Great treasure and siddha of Dharma Chökyi Peljor,
Holder of perfect pith instructions Gyalwe Tsenchang.

Trinlé Namgyal received instructions from a variety of masters and attained profound realisation through the practice of the Six Vajra Yogas, and was thus revered as one possessing many good qualities, including perfect conduct. Chokyi Peljor received the Kalachakra six yogas from his master, Khetsun Dargye. He quickly attained the signs of true realization of the Kalachakra completion stage and became an authentic lineage holder. He was known as Shayul Chögor and was clairvoyant, reading others' minds. Gyalwe Tsenchang (also known as Nuden Lhundrup Gyatso) was born in Zuka Yakdo. He was recognized as the reincarnation of Tsangwa Ngawang Trinlé. He became a resident of Yakdo Palace and was widely known as a spiritual master held in high regard in many places. He was recognized as a great spiritual leader by the monarch Ahkyong, who was his patron.

I pray to the three lamas who liberate beings by sound and sight:
Quintessence of the Three Jewels Jigme Namgyal,
Embodiment of all saviours Chöpel Gyatso,
One who attained the body of union of enlightenment Chözin Gyatso.

Jigme Namgyal, believed to be the third reincarnation of Khidrup Lodrö Namgyal, attained many extraordinary qualities as a result of flawless study and practice. Chöpel Gyatso became known for his extraordinary clairvoyant abilities. At the time of his death, many rainbows appeared as testament to his great realisation. Chözin Gyatso was considered the emanation of Akashagarbha. His realisations were so profound that he could perform miraculous feats such as walking through walls and travelling to pure realms such as Shambhala, where he received instructions which he brought back to Tibet.

I pray to the three ornaments of the sacred Dharma:
Expounder of the golden Dharma Tenpa Rabgye,
Incomparable wisdom in holy activities Lobsang Trinlé,
Flourishing in the continent with the wisdom of Manjushri,
Jamphel Lodrö.

Tenpa Rabgye received all the instructions for the Six Vajra Yogas from Ngawang Chözin and experienced many signs indicating mastery of the practice. He lived a very humble life and passed away at the age of seventy-six, remaining in a state of clear light for six days. Lobsang Trinlé also focused intensively on the Kalachakra practice. After contracting leprosy in his thirties and entering into a solitary retreat to practice Vajrapani for five years, he dedicated the remainder of his life to treating and curing people with leprosy and other illnesses. He also worked tirelessly to rebuild Mahayana and Vajrayana Buddhism in its pure form. Jamphel Lodro was recognised as the reincarnation of Getse Khentrul, who in his previous life was the Kalachakra master, Chözin Gyatso. He studied the five Tibetan Buddhist traditions through attending eleven monasteries in Tibet. After a pilgrimage to India to practice at the major sacred Buddhist sites, he travelled to Australia with a dedicated commitment to teach and translate the Dharma into the English language.

Seven-Limb Practice & Supplication

I prostrate with body, speech and mind to you, ultimate, unfailing, and eternal refuge.
I offer limitless clouds of offerings, both real and mentally generated.

This verse is the beginning of what is known as a seven-limb practice. In the Tibetan Buddhist tradition this collection of prayers for seven practices is commonly recited as a preliminary to many practices, as it offers a condensed version of many instructions which are essential to the accumulation of merit and wisdom.

The first branch is similar to the refuge practice, in which you prostrate with body, speech and mind as a way of *paying homage* and expressing respect to the ultimate, unfailing and eternal refuge of the lama and the Three Jewels, who have the power to liberate you and all beings from samsara. This acts as an antidote to our pride. The second branch of the prayer involves *offering* limitless clouds of offerings, both real and mentally generated, as a way to accumulate merit. While reciting these prayers you should visualise the field of refuge as described earlier, with you and all sentient beings offering prostrations and other precious objects as in the mandala offering practice. This serves as an antidote to our stinginess or lack of generosity.

I confess all my negativities and transgressions amassed
since beginningless time.
I rejoice in all virtue within samsara and nirvana.
I pray that you turn the wheel of Dharma unceasingly.

The third branch of the seven-limb practice involves *confessing* all our negativities and transgressions, with the lama and Three Jewels as our witness. As in the Vajrasattva practice, all four powers should be present. With the lama and Three Jewels as your support, you should cultivate genuine regret for all the negativity you have accumulated through your body, speech and mind, as if you have just swallowed poison, and resolve not to repeat this in the future. As an antidote you can visualise rays of light emanating from the Three Jewels and washing away all your negativity, which gathers together in the form of a black pile on the tip of your tongue.

After this practice of confession is the fourth branch. Here you *rejoice* in all virtue within samsara and nirvana, which includes all the merit accumulated by yourself and others, both ordinary sentient beings and enlightened beings. This enables you to accumulate great waves of merit and acts as an antidote to jealousy.

Encompassing the fifth branch, you next pray that the lama and the Three Jewels *turn the wheel of Dharma* unceasingly, as without someone to teach us Dharma there would be no way to achieve liberation from samsara and we would be like a blind person left alone in the middle of a desert. After attaining enlightenment the Buddha initially decided not to teach, but changed his mind when the gods Brahma and Indra made offerings and requested him to turn the wheel of Dharma. In the same way we should request that all those who hold the Buddha's teachings continue to teach in this world as an antidote to our delusion.

I implore you to remain with us without passing into parinirvana.
May all virtue be dedicated so that myself and all others swiftly attain supreme enlightenment!

Having prayed for the lama and the Three Jewels to turn the wheel of Dharma, in this sixth branch we pray that they *continue to remain* with us in samsara forever, without passing into parinirvana; the state beyond all suffering which the Buddha entered when he passed away. Although in reality Buddha is beyond birth and death, our ability to perceive him depends on our merit, so by making this request we are praying that we will have the merit to keep on receiving his teachings.

The seventh and final branch of this practice is *dedication*, through which we offer all virtue so that myself and all others swiftly attain supreme enlightenment. As with previous dedication practices, you should not only offer your own virtue, but all merit accumulated by yourself and others throughout the past, present and future. This vast intention will no doubt lead to a vast result.

I pray to my precious glorious lama, lord of Dharma and embodiment of all the Buddhas.
I pray to my precious glorious lama, lord of Dharma possessing the four Buddha-kayas.

This verse reminds us again how in Vajrayana practice the lama is the most important object of refuge, as he is the embodiment of all the Buddhas, or our living link with the universal energy of enlightenment. By learning to see the lama as an enlightened being possessing the four Buddha-kayas, we have a path by which to discover the inner four kayas of our enlightened nature.

I pray to my precious glorious lama, lord of Dharma,
my unequalled ultimate refuge.
I pray to my precious glorious lama, lord of Dharma,
my unequalled ultimate rescuer.

The lama is your unequalled ultimate refuge and unequalled ultimate rescuer as he embodies the ultimate refuge of the Three Jewels, who offer us an unmistaken and unequalled path by which we can be rescued from the suffering of samsara and attain perfect enlightenment.

I pray to my precious glorious lama, lord of Dharma,
who teaches the supreme path to liberation.
I pray to my precious glorious lama, lord of Dharma,
the source of all sublime attainments.
I pray to my precious glorious lama, lord of Dharma,
who clears away the darkness of ignorance.

In this verse we are acknowledging our tremendous gratitude toward the lama, reminding ourselves that he teaches the supreme path to liberation, that he displays to us all sublime attainments as our personal connection to the Buddhas, and that he clears away the darkness of ignorance which prevents us from becoming enlightened.

Please bestow empowerment upon me!
Please bless me with the power to engage in the practice with complete dedication!

We are now supplicating the lama to bestow empowerment upon us, which is a formal ritual to connect us to his enlightened wisdom (as described in the section which follows). In Mahayana Buddhism, the empty nature of mind is presented through philosophical and contemplative analysis, so the mind first understands emptiness and then discovers it. Through empowerment (*abhisheka* in Sanskrit), not only the mind but also the body and speech are introduced as a manifestation of our Buddha-nature, as if to say "you have this!" We are not receiving something external, but rather we are activating a recognition of something within ourselves.

We also pray to the lama to empower us so we can engage in Dharma practice with complete dedication. This request is a powerful way to create conditions which are conducive to authentic Dharma practice.

May all obstacles be cleared away so I may dedicate my life to the practice!
May I experience the essence of the practice!

Obstacles to spiritual practice include external obstacles such as financial problems or adversaries acting against us, and internal obstacles such as thoughts of miserliness or lust, which steal our minds away from Dharma practice. We also pray to experience the essence of the practice, which means attaining true realisation rather than just intellectual understanding.

May my practice reach the ultimate perfection!
May I naturally emanate love, compassion and Bodhicitta!

To ensure our Dharma practice is successful we need dedication or devotion to the Dharma, good focus or single-pointed concentration. We also need the ability to cultivate love, compassion and bodhicitta, which should become such a part of us, that we naturally emanate these qualities.

May I unite perfect concentration and insight!
May I attain true experience and supreme realisation of the Dharma!

We can experience the reality of our Buddha-nature and completely eradicate our mental defilements if we are able to unite perfect concentration and insight. We therefore pray that we will attain shamatha, the state of perfect single-pointed concentration by which the mind can be powerfully focused like a spotlight upon any object we choose, and that this will lead to vipashyana, the state of clear insight into the true nature of reality.

May I perfect the practice of the profound vajrayoga path!
May I be empowered with the siddhis of the great seal in this single lifetime.

Finally, we pray to the lama that we may be able to practise and accomplish the profound path of vajrayoga, which is the extraordinary tantric method of the Jonang Kalachakra Tradition known as the Six Vajra Yogas.

Receiving the Four Empowerments

Through the four empowerments, we are introduced to the holy body, speech, mind and primordial wisdom of the lama, which are in fact a manifestation of our own Buddha-nature. The "body, speech and mind" we are being introduced to have many different levels of meaning, but in a simple way we are purifying the subtle body (made up of channels and chakras), the subtle speech (or inner wind), the subtle mind (or essences) and finally the residue of all three combined (known as the foundation consciousness). According to the Kalachakra system, the true four empowerments take place with a secret wisdom consort, therefore, the practice of receiving the empowerments here is meant as a symbolic representation of this more profound level.

From the syllable OM (ཨོཾ) at the forehead of my root lama, the great Vajradhara, white light streams forth and dissolves into my forehead chakra, purifying negativities and obscurations of the body. May I receive the vase empowerment and be blessed by the enlightened body!

With the first empowerment, known as the *vase empowerment*, white light radiates from the lama's forehead and dissolves into your forehead chakra, located at the mid-point between the eyes about a centimetre above the nasal bridge. This purifies obscurations of the body, related to negative actions such as stealing or inflicting physical harm on others, and dismantles the defilements of the channels and chakras. You are therefore blessed by the enlightened Body-Vajra, becoming a receptive vessel for visualisation practice and empowered with the propensities for attaining the nirmanakaya emanation bodies of a Buddha.

> *From the syllable AH (ཨཱཿ) at the lama's throat, red light streams forth and dissolves into my throat chakra, purifying negativities and obscurations of speech. May I receive the secret empowerment and be blessed by the enlightened speech!*

With the second empowerment, known as the *secret empowerment,* red light radiates from the lama's throat and dissolves into your throat chakra, located just above the Adam's apple. This purifies negativities and obscurations of speech related to negative actions such as speaking harshly or untruthfully. It also dismantles the defilements of the inner winds. You are therefore blessed by the enlightened Speech-Vajra, becoming a receptive vessel for mantra recitation practice and empowered with the propensities for attaining the sambhogakaya enjoyment bodies of a Buddha.

> *From the syllable HUNG (ཧཱུྃ) at the lama's heart, dark-blue light streams forth and dissolves into my heart chakra, purifying negativities and obscurations of mind. May I receive the wisdom empowerment and be blessed by the enlightened mind!*

With the third empowerment, known as the *wisdom empowerment,* dark-blue light radiates from the lama's heart and dissolves into your heart chakra, located at the centre of the chest. This purifies obscurations of the mind related to thoughts such as greed, hatred and fixed views, and dismantles the defilements of the subtle essences. You are therefore blessed by the enlightened Mind-Vajra, becoming a receptive vessel for practices such as tummo (involving the subtle winds and channels) and empowered with the propensities for attaining the dharmakaya wisdom truth body of the Buddha.

From the syllable HO (ཧོཿ) at the lama's navel, yellow light streams forth and dissolves into my navel chakra, purifying all propensities of conceptual thought and attachment. May I attain the sacred fourth empowerment; May I be imprinted with the four Buddha-kayas and blessed by the indestructible primordial wisdom!

With the fourth empowerment, known as the *word empowerment*, yellow light radiates from the lama's navel and dissolves into your navel chakra, which is actually located about four finger-widths below the navel. This purifies all propensities of conceptual thought and attachment, which refers to the cognitive obscurations and karmic imprints stored in the foundation consciousness, the "ground of all things." This dismantles the defilements which are left as a residue of the three poisons already mentioned. You are therefore blessed by the indestructible Primordial Wisdom-Vajra, becoming a receptive vessel for direct meditation on the ultimate truth and empowered with the propensities for attaining the svabhavikakaya, sublime nature body of the Buddha.

Merging the Mind with the Lama's Wisdom Mind

The lama melts into light and dissolves into me. My own mind becomes inseparable from the dharmakaya mind of the lama. May I remain effortlessly in this non-conceptual, uncontrived state.

As in the preceding practices, you end the guru yoga practice by dissolving the entire visualisation and observing and contemplating the inseparability of you and the lama. The lama therefore melts into light and dissolves into you. As this happens, your mind becomes inseparable from the dharmakaya mind of the lama. When you begin the practice there is still a separate notion of "you" and the lama, just as rice and wheat can still be separated, although they are mixed together. When you advance on this path, there is no notion at all of being separate and your mind becomes completely merged with the wisdom mind of the lama. Just like water poured into water, they become inseparable. Finally you come to realise that there was never any separation between your mind and the lama's mind which is none other than your own Buddha-nature. You are not only merging your mind with the lama's but the whole of your being, including body and speech, even though in reality there was nothing to merge, as they have never been separate.

After merging your mind with the lama's wisdom mind you should remain effortlessly in this non-conceptual and uncontrived state as best as you can. Let your mind merge with the mind of the lama for as long as you can sustain it. Once you lose this sense of oneness, you can recite prayers for a few minutes and then experience the lama dissolving into you once again, just watching without any preconceived ideas.

It may take a while to understand or get the hang of this practice, and we should not complain if nothing happens right away. To have success in this practice many conditions must be present on the part of the giver, the receiver and the connection. The lama has to be purely connected to an authentic lineage, we need to generate a great deal of merit while maintaining the right kind of devotion, and we need a good relationship or close karmic connection with the lama.

Dedication

May I become just like you, glorious root and lineage lamas.
May my followers, life-span, noble title and pure realm become just like yours!

We dedicate the virtue of this guru yoga practice by aspiring to emulate the glorious root and lineage lamas. It is our limited perception preventing us from seeing the truth that these lamas are in fact fully enlightened

Buddhas. We should therefore aspire to follow their example so we can uncover our own Buddha-nature.

In the second line, we are developing the aspiration to attain all the enlightened qualities of our lama. This includes an entourage of "followers" around us that we have the power to influence in an enlightened way in order to achieve our enlightened purpose. This is a result of our merit. "Life-span" refers to a long life so that we may benefit beings in the best possible way. "Noble title" refers to how we manifest for other's benefit, whether this be as a Kalki King of Shambhala, a simple monk or a wandering hermit. Finally, "pure realm" refers to the manifestation of the merit the lama has accumulated while on the path to Buddhahood, just as Buddha Amitabha dedicated oceans of merit so that beings may be reborn in his pure realm if they remember his name at the moment of their death.

Through the power of my prayers to you,
May all disease, poverty and conflict be pacified wherever we might be!
May the precious Dharma and everything auspicious increase throughout the universe!

With this verse we dedicate the virtue of the practice so that all disease, poverty and conflict are pacified throughout the world and that everything that is virtuous and auspicious, especially the precious Dharma, will increase throughout the universe and lead all beings to the ultimate happiness of enlightenment.

* * *

The *Unique Preliminaries* detailed in the following section are reserved for those who have taken the commitments of Highest-Yoga Tantra. If you have not yet received these empowerments, then you should stop your recitation here at the end of Guru Yoga. At a future time, when the conditions are present, you can then take the empowerments and engage in the practices without restrictions.

PART THREE

Unique Kalachakra Preliminaries and Main Practice

— Kalachakra Yab-Yum —
Innate Kalachakra deity in union with Vishvamata

CHAPTER NINE

Innate Kalachakra Practice

In the next practice we visualise ourselves in the enlightened form of the two-armed Kalachakra deity, known as Innate Kalachakra. This is the first of the two unique preliminaries for the Six Vajra Yogas according to the Jonang Tradition, and is also known as the generation stage in highest yoga-tantra. We should only engage in this practice if we have previously received a highest yoga-tantra empowerment, preferably in accordance with the Kalachakra Tradition. In the Jonang Tradition, we practice the generation stage as a preliminary to the completion stage practices of the Six Vajra Yogas. For these practices, receiving Kalachakra Empowerments is essential.

When you "generate yourself" as an enlightened deity, you are not generating a fabricated, make-believe reality, but instead, using an extraordinarily skilful method to bring you closer to the non-dual reality of enlightenment that is your most profound nature. With this method you learn to view the universe as pure and all beings in it as enlightened, even though they may appear to ordinary minds as having many defilements that have not yet been overcome. By seeing through conventional reality and embracing its ultimate nature, you are able to experience all levels of reality with a much clearer and more compassionate view.

Currently we are stuck in all sorts of dualistic notions, distinctions and negative emotions. Meditating upon yourself as a deity helps you dismantle this cocoon of delusion by introducing you to a pure Buddha-realm which is free from all dualistic limitations. It allows you to transform all impure experiences into pure perception until you realise that everything has been pure all along. Although this pure perception is not yet the actual experience of emptiness, you are coming closer to it and therefore it is used as a provisional stepping stone to reach a much deeper reality. Once you are thoroughly familiar with the pure nature of your experience, you will be qualified to practise the completion stage, where you meditate directly on the sublime emptiness.

While you are training to view yourself as the enlightened Kalachakra deity, you are transforming your world into the sacred Kalachakra mandala which represents the profound relationship between the Outer Kalachakra of the container universe, the Inner Kalachakra of the contained sentient beings, and the Alternative Kalachakra of their enlightened nature. By familiarising yourself with the following visualisation and mantra, especially during intensive retreat practice, you can gain conviction in this enlightened reality where all appearances become the enlightened deities of Kalachakra, all sounds become the enlightened speech of Kalachakra, and all thoughts arise and dissolve in the unborn realm of the enlightened mind of Kalachakra. Wherever you go, your entire experience becomes pervaded by the essence of Kalachakra.

A SHORT PRACTICE OF INNATE KALACHAKRA WITH COMMENTARY

As with any Mahayana practice, you should take refuge and cultivate the supreme intention of bodhicitta. You then begin the practice by first establishing the visualisation and then reciting the mantra. This visualisation practice should contain three key features: (1) presence, (2) clarity and (3) purity of perception. *Presence*, or divine pride, is to do with the strength of feeling or emotional connection you have with the visualisation. *Clarity* is the awareness of details, which is gradually imprinted in our minds through practice. They should be vibrant and translucent like a rainbow; not rigid and fixed. *Pure perception* is when you realise the true significance of the symbols that you visualise. If you are overwhelmed by all the details, remember that the feeling of presence and confidence is of greatest importance.

Visualisation

> ***OM SHUNYATA JNANA VAJRA SVABHAVA ATMAKO HAM***
> *OM, I consist of the nature of the awareness vajra of emptiness.*

Reciting this mantra, quickly visualise yourself and all phenomena dissolving into the natural state beyond concepts and remain in this state for a while. You should think with absolute confidence, "I am the primordial, natural state of reality; beyond subject and object." Try to dwell in this non-conceptual state as best you can.

> *Arising from emptiness, I instantly and spontaneously appear as Innate Kalachakra. I appear upon a cushioned floor formed by a lotus and moon, sun, Rahu and Kalagni* discs, which lies upon the summit of Mount Meru and the universe of four elements. My body is blue in colour, with one face, two arms and three eyes. I embrace the consort Vishvamata and hold a vajra and bell at my chest.*

From the empty state beyond concepts, you are infused with the intention of bodhicitta and instantly appear as Innate Kalachakra, known as "Dukor Langkye" in Tibetan. Within the enlightened mind of Innate Kalachakra appears a series of four concentric discs representing the universe of the four elements: (from the bottom) a vast wind mandala, a fire mandala, a water mandala and an earth mandala. In the centre of the earth mandala appears Mount Meru, on top of which appears a multicoloured lotus flower and then a white moon disc, red sun disc, black rahu disc and yellow kalagni disc. The moon disc symbolises bodhicitta, the sun disc symbolises the realisation of emptiness, the rahu disc immutable bliss and the kalagni disc empty-form.

Kalachakra stands majestically upon this seat. He is dark-blue in colour, symbolising the ultimate purity of the central channel, and has one face symbolising the one ultimate natural truth of all phenomena. His two arms symbolise the method and wisdom of the primordial state or the inseparability of immutable great bliss and empty-form. His three eyes symbolise direct perception of the past, present and future. He embraces the consort Vishvamata with hands stretched out, holding a vajra in the right hand and a bell in the left, symbolising the ultimate unity of method and wisdom, or the masculine and feminine aspects of enlightenment.

Kalachakra's neck has three colours—dark-blue in the middle, red on the right side and white on the left side—symbolising the elimination of three qualities known as the *Three Gunas:* (1) tamas, (2) rajas and (3) sattva. In Kalachakra these qualities represent the *Three Poisons*: (1) ignorance, (2) attachment and (3) aversion. These terms are familiar to the followers of the Hindu Samkhya system and were used specifically to help guide such practitioners onto a beneficial path.

> *My white left leg is drawn in and tramples the heart of the white creation god. My red right leg is extended and tramples the heart of the red desire god. My head is adorned with a topknot of plaited locks, a wish-fulfilling jewel and a crescent moon.*

Kalachakra has two legs and is standing on top of two samsaric gods linked to the Hindu tradition, symbolising freedom from both samsara and nirvana. The white left leg is slightly bent and crushes the chest of the god Ishvara, depicted as a wrathful, one-faced, three-eyed white god who wears a tiger skin and a snake ornament and is lying face up, after having fainted. This signifies the transformation of the left channel lalana and the elimination of the four afflictions (attachment, aversion, ignorance and pride). The red right leg is standing straight and crushing the chest of the red desire god Karmadeva, who has a peaceful face, two arms and wears jewelled ornaments, again lying face up after having fainted. This signifies the transformation of the right channel rasana and the elimination of the four maras (the aggregates, affliction, death and pleasurable objects).

Kalachakra's head is adorned with a top-knot of thick hair plaited into locks which hang loosely down his back, and on top of this is a precious wish-fulfilling jewel draped in silk and flowing downward. In front of the top knot is a multi-coloured crossed vajra, symbolising the *four sublime powers of a Buddha*: (1) pacifying, (2) increasing, (3) controlling and (4) wrathfully subduing. Above the double vajra is a crescent moon symbolising immutable bliss.

> *I am wearing vajra ornaments and a lower garment of tiger skin. My fingers are of five different colours and the three joints of each finger are also of different colours. Vajrasattva is seated upon the crown of my head, and I stand in the centre of a burning ring of flames of five different colours. My facial expression shows a mixture of wrath and passion.*

Kalachakra is adorned with numerous vajra ornaments made of indestructible diamonds such as earrings, necklaces, armlets, belt, anklets and malas. He is draped in a silk scarf, symbolising the indestructible immutable bliss of the enlightened mind, and is wearing a lower garment of tiger skin symbolising the elimination of pride and arrogance.

The five digits of the left and right hand are of five different colours: (1) the thumb is yellow, (2) the index finger is white, (3) the middle finger is red, (4) the ring finger is dark-blue and (5) the little finger is green. These symbolise the purification of the *five elements* of the left channel lalana, which results in the attainment of the *five wisdoms*: (1) the all-encompassing wisdom, (2) mirror-like wisdom, (3) wisdom of equanimity, (4) wisdom of discrimination and the (5) all-accomplishing wisdom. On the inside of each hand, the three joints of each finger are of three different colours: (1) the joint closest to the tip of the finger is white, (2) the middle joint is red and (3) at the base (nearest the palm) is dark-blue. These colours symbolise the purification of the right channel rasana and the attainment of the indestructible vajra (1) body, (2) speech and (3) mind. The crown is adorned with a blue-coloured Vajrasattva, symbolising that Kalachakra primarily belongs to the Vajrasattva Buddha-family.

Luminous rays of five different coloured lights radiate outwards by the span of a body, then become a ring of intense flames, with both the lights and flames continuing outwards still further. His face has an appearance of both wrath and power, with a frightening pair of upper and lower fangs, and the three eyes bulging and slightly bloodshot. His expression shows a mixture of uncompromising wrathful intensity and passionate love or divine sexual bliss. This signifies indestructible compassion and immutable bliss.

I am embraced by Vishvamata who has a body yellow in colour, with one face, two arms and three eyes. She holds a curved knife in her right hand and a skull cup in her left. With her right leg drawn in and her left leg extended, we are standing together in union. She is naked and adorned with the five bone ornaments. Half of her hair is tied in a topknot and the rest is falling loose.

Kalachakra is embracing the consort Vishvamata, and they are inseparably in union (known as Kalachakra Yab-yum). Vishamata's aspect has a golden yellow body, with one face, two arms and three eyes, and she is holding a curve-bladed skinning knife in her right hand which is embracing Kalachakra. She holds a skull cup in her left hand, offering divine nectar to Kalachakra. She stands together with Kalachakra in divine sexual union, her right leg bent and her left leg extended. She is naked and adorned with a golden wheel on her crown and five bone ornaments: (1) bone earrings, (2) armlets, bracelets, (3) anklets, (4) belt and (5) necklaces. Half of her hair is tied in a top-knot at her crown and half is flowing down her back, symbolising how all phenomena ultimately have a nature of empty-form.

At the forehead of my Yab-yum appears the syllable OM (ཨོཾ); at the throat, AH (ཨཱཿ); at the heart, HUNG (ཧཱུྃ); at the navel, HO (ཧོཿ); at the secret place, SVA (སྭཱ); and on the crown, HA (ཧཱ).

At Kalachakra Yab-yum's forehead is (1) a white-coloured OM, representing the pure nature of the water element and Amitabha, the vajra body of all the Buddhas. (2) At their throat is a red AH syllable representing the pure nature of the fire element and Ratnasambhava, the vajra speech of all the Buddhas. (3) At their heart is a dark-blue HUNG syllable representing the pure nature of the air element and Amoghasiddhi, the vajra mind of all the Buddhas. (4) At their navel is a yellow HO, representing the pure nature of the earth element and Vairochana, the indestructible vajra wisdom of all the Buddhas. (5) At their secret place is a blue SVA syllable, representing the pure nature of the primordial wisdom element and Vajrasattva, the ultimate purity of the Buddhas' primordial wisdom. (6) Finally, upon their crown is a green HA syllable representing the pure nature of the space element and Akshobya, the vajra activities of all the Buddhas.

The purpose of visualising the six syllables is not just to bless or transform these particular locations on your body, but to understand that Kalachakra and Vishvamata are the pure embodiment of the six realms of samsara and that this is no different from your own primordial nature.

Rays of light emanate outward from my heart transforming the entire universe into a Buddha-field, and all beings into innumerable deities of the Kalachakra mandala.

Next, rays of luminous light of six different colours emanate outwards from Kalachakra's heart and the six syllables, reaching out to the six realms of samsara. The Buddha-field of the Kalachakra Mandala pervades the entire universe of the six realms, and the light transforms all beings into innumerable deities of the Kalachakra mandala.

With confidence, remind yourself that you are Kalachakra and Vishvamata in union and make your visualisation clear, vibrant and translucent as rainbow light, unlike an ordinary picture or statue. Remain in this state of natural Kalachakra for as long as you wish.

Mantra Repetition & Dissolution

OM HA KSHA MA LA VA RA YANG (SVAHA)
(Recite the mantra for as long as you like)

Having stabilised the visualisation of Innate Kalachakra, you should then visualise the Kalachakra mantra symbol at your heart and recite the mantra. The best way to recite the mantra is to bring to mind an understanding of the many different levels of meaning of each syllable, while also holding a clear visualisation in your mind. It may be recited aloud or silently, though either way there must be a distinct sound for each syllable. The best method is to recite the mantra with a whisper, ensuring this is not too loud.

To visualise the mantra symbol (sometimes known as the Ten-Fold Powerful One), visualise a lotus at your heart with layered discs upon it—moon, sun, rahu and kalagni. On top of these discs appears the mantra symbol with interconnected coloured letters, as shown above. Depending on the practice you are doing, you can visualise the components with different colours. In the Jonang Tradition, for the Kalachakra Generation Stage we visualise the symbol as follows (from the top downwards): (1) there is a white HA; (2) a green KSHA; (3) a multi-coloured MA; (4) a yellow LA; (5) a white VA; (6) a red RA; (7) and a black YA; (8) at the top is a red crescent; (9) with a white drop on it; and a (10) dark-blue nadu (like a small flame) arising from the drop.

The mantra syllables have multiple levels of meaning, symbolising various aspects of the Outer, Inner and Alternative Kalachakra. In a general sense it signifies the entire Buddha-dharma, including the three vehicles and 84,000 teachings of the Buddha. It also represents the *six elements*, which make up all conventional phenomena and are the main objects of purification: (1) wind (YA), (2) fire (RA), (3) water (VA), (4) earth (LA), (5) consciousness (MA) and (6) space (HA). These elements are also associated with six aspects of the path to enlightenment and the six Buddha-families, the final result of enlightenment. In addition, the green KSHA represents the primordial mind element, the crescent moon represents the red essences and right channel, the drop represents the white essences and the left channel and the nadu represent the central channel.

The Ten-Fold Powerful One

Alternative Visualisations for Recitation

Jetsun Taranatha gives us the option to simply visualise the mantra as green in the centre of our heart if the specific details are too difficult, as green represents all the colours. Alternatively, you can continue practising one of the following visualisations. Among them, you can choose to focus on the visualisation you feel more connected to. While reciting the mantra, focus on the details of the visualisation and keep your mind resting in the state that it produces. Through the power of this practice, you can begin to experience all sounds as mantra, all appearances as deities and all thoughts as dharmakaya wisdom.

Mindfulness of the Kalachakra Mandala

From the Kalachakra mantra visualised at your heart, you radiate infinite beams of light to the Sambhogakaya Buddha-realms and invoke all of the 636 Kalachakra deities and any other Yidam deities of the four classes of tantra. Kalachakra Yab-yum absorbs all these deities so you become the embodiment of them all.

Mindfulness of the Root Guru

Visualising yourself as Kalachakra Yab-Yum and from the mantra at your heart, radiate light in all directions invoking your main spiritual guru. You receive the four empowerments from your guru who then dissolves into the blue Vajrasattva above your crown and you become inseparable.

Mindfulness of the Dharma Teachers

Visualising yourself as Kalachakra in union with Vishvamata, light radiates in every direction from the mantra at your heart, invoking all the Dharma teachers you have a connection with. They all dissolve into your main guru, the embodiment of all your spiritual teachers, who is inseparable from Vajrasattva on your crown.

Making Offerings to the Enlightened Beings

Visualise yourself as Kalachakra Yab-yum and radiate infinite rays of light to all the Buddha-realms from the Kalachakra mantra at your heart. The rays transform into countless offerings made externally, internally and secretly, satisfying and pleasing the pure minds of all the Buddhas. At the same time be certain that all beings accumulate oceans of merit. The rays of light then return carrying the blessings of the body, speech and mind of all the Buddhas in the form of images, mantras and symbols, which all dissolve into Kalachakra Yab-yum. You thereby receive the powers of the body, speech and mind of all the Buddhas.

Purification of All Impure Realms

Visualising yourself as Kalachakra Yab-yum, infinite rays of light now radiate from the mantra at your heart to all the impure universes. As the light touches each universe it instantly becomes a pure Buddha-realm filled with great palaces, and all beings instantly become Kalachakra deities. The rays of light return and dissolve into Kalachakra Yab-yum. This is known as purifying the impure universes and is equivalent to the Bodhisattva practice known as pure-land training, whereby all roots of virtue are transformed into means for establishing a Buddha-realm, where you will gain the state of enlightenment. For Mahayana sutra practitioners this practice is carried out over many aeons, yet a true Vajrayana practitioner could accomplish it in a very short time.

The Mantra Fire-Brand

The next two visualisations are commonly practised in all forms of Highest-Yoga Tantra. For the first of these, continue to visualise yourself as Kalachakra Yab-yum with the Kalachakra symbol at your heart, remembering that your true natural reality is empty of all deceptive phenomena. All samsaric and enlightened phenomena are a manifestation of Kalachakra Yab-yum. With great confidence see all the syllables of the Kalachakra mantra *OM HAKSHA MALA VARAYA* radiate forth in a stream from Kalachakra's mouth down to his heart, continuing down his body to his secret vajra jewel and streaming forth with a great sound of bliss into Vishvamata's secret lotus. The stream of syllables then moves upwards through her central channel, flowing out of her mouth and into Kalachakra's mouth before dissolving into the symbol at his heart. Each time a new mantra is formed it continues to flow in this manner.

The Reverse Mantra Fire-Brand

For the second, visualise yourself as Kalachakra Yab-yum with the Kalachakra mantra at your heart as before. Recall that your true natural reality is empty of all deceptive phenomena and that all samsaric and enlightened phenomena are a manifestation of Kalachakra Yab-yum. With great confidence, see all the syllables of the Kalachakra mantra, *OM HAKSHA MALA VARAYA*, radiate forth in a stream from Kalachakra's mouth into Vishvamata's mouth, continuing down her central channel through her secret lotus and streaming with a great sound of bliss into Kalachakra's secret vajra jewel. It then travels up through his central channel and dissolves into the Kalachakra symbol at his heart. Each time a new mantra is formed it continues to move as a circular stream in this manner.

The Recitation that is Like the Buzzing of Bees

Finally, there are two other forms of visualisation and mantra recitation which were practised by many great Indian and Tibetan masters. These are very powerful and are only performed by practitioners of Highest Yoga-tantra. They are also the most precious practices to prepare for the Kalachakra completion stage and the main recitation practice in Highest Yoga-tantra. This is because through them, one can gain the realisation of the inseparable union of great bliss and empty form.

For the first practice, continue to visualise yourself as Kalachakra Yab-yum with the mantra at your heart, and this time all the Buddhas and sentient beings in the ten directions instantly become Kalachakra. All recite the Kalachakra mantra *OM HAKSHA MALA VARAYA* so that all you can hear is the sound of mantra. Keep your mind focused on this state and recite the mantra single-pointedly: *OM HAKSHA MALA VARAYA*. One Indian master stated, "Your mantra recitations, practice and merit are multiplied by this visualisation and practice."

The Four Extraordinary Activities

The second practice is known as the four extraordinary activities, carried out for others by tantric practitioners. These activities include: pacifying, increasing, controlling and wrathfully subduing; each is identified with a specific colour as described below and can be practised individually or together.

Once again begin by visualising yourself as Kalachakra in union with Vishvamata with the Kalachakra symbol at your heart, and this time multitudes of deities appear amidst rays of light radiating outwards to the farthest reaches of space. These streams of light burst forth from the seed syllable: (1) white light emerges as white deities to pacify or dispel sickness, afflictions and obstacles; (2) yellow light emerges as yellow deities to increase longevity, merit, wealth and the good qualities of all beings; (3) red light emerges as red deities to bestow the ability to control and gain power, glory, great energy and influence for the benefit of all beings; and (4) finally, dark-blue light emerges as dark-blue deities to defeat the demons, maras and difficult obstacles which impede the capacity of sentient beings to achieve enlightenment.

The lights and deities return and dissolve back into you, eradicating your afflictions and obscurations to enlightenment. Your realisations are strengthened and you attain the ability to control your inner winds and chakras: all your ignorance and delusions are removed.

These two visualisations can be practised sequentially, with each part followed by recitation of the mantra, or as a whole with mantra recitation at the end.

Dissolution

The entire visualisation then melts into light and dissolves into me.

To conclude a practice session, dissolve all the visualisations you have created, including the environment and deities of the entire mandala into Kalachakra Yab-Yum, then Vishvamata dissolves into Kalachakra, and Kalachakra dissolves from the periphery to the centre, leaving the inner mantra symbol in the centre of his chest. Next the mantra symbol dissolves from the base upwards to the nadu. The nadu at the top of this symbol then gradually disappears into emptiness and you remain in this open state of awareness for as long as you can.

In this way the entire visualisation dissolves and merges with your being like water poured into water. Throughout this practice you should have a clear understanding that the embracing Kalachakra and Vishvamata are in fact you. As you dissolve the visualisation, you should simply rest in your awareness of this inseparability.

Dedication

By the power of this virtue, May I swiftly attain the state of Kalachakra, and lead all beings to Kalachakra enlightenment!

As with the preceding practices, you end by dedicating the merit so as to swiftly attain the state of Kalachakra through the practice of the Six Vajra Yogas. Your aim should be to lead all beings to the state of Kalachakra enlightenment, at which time the rupakaya form body of enlightenment will spontaneously bring benefit to countless sentient beings.

("The Divine Ladder —Preliminary and Main Practices of the Profound Kalachakra Vajrayoga", composed by Drolway Gonpo (Taranatha), describes how the great Jonangpa tantric lineage masters and their heart-sons practised, and includes the essence of all the pure lineage instructions.)

The author of this text is Taranatha, the great 17th century Jonang master who was both a brilliant scholar and highly realised practitioner. It gathers together the essential instructions which were passed on from one generation to the next, from the tantric lineage masters to their heart-disciples. The great practitioners of the past practiced in this way, and we should consider it a tremendous blessing to have the opportunity to follow in their footsteps. At this stage, the main text is complete.

CHAPTER TEN

Aspiration to Accomplish the Six Vajra Yogas

Through the generation stage practice of Innate Kalachakra, we strengthen our pure perception which allows us to use more of our experience as a basis for realising the ultimate nature of reality. On this foundation, we are now ready to enter into the main practice of the Kalachakra completion stage—the Six Vajra Yogas.

In order to practice these profound methods, it is first necessary to receive the *Four Higher Empowerments* from a qualified Kalachakra Vajra Master. You will also need to receive the unique pith instructions for the way to correctly practice these techniques. For this reason it is vital that you cultivate a spiritual relationship with an authentic teacher who holds the lineage of these instructions. Without them, there is no way to progress along this path.

ཨོྃ་ཨཱཿཧཱུྃ་ཧོཿཧྃ་ཀྵཿ

In accordance with the Jonang-Shambhala Tradition, the completion stage practices are ideally taught in an experiential fashion, with the student first receiving instructions and then engaging in the practice until the technique is mastered. As the student achieves the necessary level of realisation, the Vajra Master provides the next set of instructions. In this way the student progresses in a step-by-step fashion that ensures the desired outcomes are achieved.

While this is the most traditional method of practice, it has also become common to practice all six of the yogas intensively over the course of a three year retreat. Many Jonang practitioners will engage in this sort of retreat at an early age so they can establish the necessary connections with the Vajra Yoga Path. After developing familiarity with the practices, they will either immediately enter into long-term retreat or will continue to expand their understanding through study before entering into retreat at a later time.

Until such time as we are able to participate in such a retreat, we should focus our attention on developing the aspiration to practice the Six Vajra Yogas. The prayer that follows is designed to strengthen our connection to this path and to help us develop familiarity with the general structure of the practices.

THE UNCOMMON PRELIMINARY OF THE THREE ISOLATIONS

After receiving the completion stage empowerments, the first practice that is given is actually the last of the two uncommon preliminaries known as the *Three Isolations* (*Wen Sum* in Tibetan). This unique dark-room practice is specifically designed to establish the non-conceptual, single-pointed concentration that is necessary to authentically practice the Vajra Yogas. This advanced practice is not contained in the root text as it is traditionally transmitted directly from the Vajra Master to the student. I will now briefly describe the main elements of this practice to provide an indication of its structure and purpose.

The Three Isolations is essentially a very effective method for developing the mind of single-pointed concentration known as *shamatha*. What makes this practice so unique is that it combines a profound meditation similar to the traditions of *Mahamudra* or *Dzogchen*, with a powerful physical posture that works directly with the subtle energetic body of the practitioner. Together, these two aspects quickly isolate the meditator's body, speech and mind, making them pliable and conducive for advanced yogic practices. The results of this practice can be understood in the following way:

1. **Isolation of Body:** Through the use of an uncommon seven-point physical posture, the subtle energies that are distributed throughout the body are gradually gathered and begin to flow in the central channel. When this happens, the body becomes pliant and able to meditate for extended periods of time without fatigue. Because the physical body is no longer causing discomfort to the meditator, it then becomes possible to fully withdraw the mind into non-conceptual awareness.
2. **Isolation of Speech:** If we are caught up in or attached to ordinary speech, our inner wind will circulate through the left and right channels. This movement of energy brings with it the proliferation of conceptual thoughts which serve to mask our primordial nature. When we rest in silence, the circulation of energy slows down, causing the conceptual mind to become dormant and allowing the non-conceptual mind to manifest. As we become more familiar with this practice, the breath becomes extremely subtle and we are able to remain in silence for as long as we like, without experiencing boredom or other forms of hardship.
3. **Isolation of Mind:** As long as we are caught up in or attached to ordinary dualistic thoughts, it will be impossible to effectively manipulate the subtle winds. By resting in a mind that is free from all forms of grasping, we stop fuelling the unwanted proliferation of thoughts. This in turn allows our subtle winds to settle even further, until we can achieve a pristine mind that is blissful, non-conceptual and incredibly lucid.

Because these three components are so closely interconnected, by working with them all simultaneously, it is possible to achieve extraordinary levels of concentration in a relatively short period of time. When done correctly, it normally takes two months of intensive practice to achieve the desired realisations. That being said, this time-frame depends entirely on how well the practitioner prepares their mind with the previously discussed preliminary practices. If they cultivate the qualities of patience and determination, over time their mind will develop through the following four stages:

1. **Perceiving:** At this stage the mind has greater awareness yet it cannot remain in single-pointed focus for long.
2. **Habituation:** As thoughts arise they spontaneously vanish, enabling the mind to remain in single-pointed focus without effort.
3. **Stabilisation:** By continuing to practise, thoughts hardly arise at all and the mind no longer becomes disturbed or loses concentration. Occasionally thoughts will arise and then gently pass away.
4. **Perfect Stabilisation:** The mind becomes so skilled it can choose whether to rest in a stillness that is spontaneously single-pointed, or to focus without distraction on a topic of analysis.

THE MAIN PRACTICE OF THE SIX VAJRA YOGAS

By practising the Six Vajra Yogas, you develop the ability to see both yourself and your environment as non-dualistic empty-form. The initial dark-room practices focus on developing a familiarity with these empty-forms and then through special yogic techniques, you mix the perceptions of empty-form with awareness and the inner winds. When these three aspects are fully integrated, they provide the basis for those winds to enter into the central channel and dissolve the subtle essences located at different key points in the subtle body. These subtle essences subsequently give rise to increasingly more concentrated states of mind. The result of this practice is the ability to completely stop the flow of all inner winds and thereby dissolve the experience of a material body, until all that remains is the illusory rainbow body at the point of enlightenment.

There is no specific root text for the practice of the Six Vajra Yogas, as traditionally they were passed down orally from teacher to disciple. Due to the extremely advanced nature of this practice, it is necessary to strengthen your aspiration until such time as you are actually able to control your subtle energetic system, or your Vajra Master believes you are qualified to begin.

OM AH HUM HO HANG KYA

Through the power of Buddha-nature, may I cut the conceptual movement of my mind. May I experience the ten signs and clear-light mind, and attain the path of Withdrawal Yoga. I pray to my saviours, my kind lama and the heirs of the holy lineage. Bless me so that this is accomplished!

The six syllable mantra at the beginning of this verse symbolises both the six chakras and the six yogic practices. The power of Buddha-nature refers to the "Tathagatagarbha", the primordial ground or natural Buddha residing in the continuum of every being, through which all enlightened qualities are obtained.

The next three lines describe the first of the Six Vajra Yogas, known as *Withdrawal*. This includes a night-time practice, carried out in a dark room with eyes wide open, and a day-time practice which involves focusing one's vision on the clear blue sky. Through these practices the conceptual movement of your mind is cut, as the ten inner winds which circulate in the subtle body are absorbed into the central channel. The ten signs and clear-light mind are experienced, which then become stronger, clearer and more stable. Four of these signs are objects of the night-time practice while the remaining six are objects of the day-time practice. On the basis of these ten signs, an "inner world" that is quite independent of the outside world is developed. At this stage however, these signs are still perceived as being separate from the subjective awareness of the mind.

Finally, as this is an aspiration prayer, you pray to the kind lama and all the heirs of the holy lineage, since the practice can only be accomplished with a connection to the transmission lineage and devotion toward the lama.

Through the power of Buddha-nature, may my speech, inner wind and consciousness become unwavering. May my wisdom increase, along with the joy and bliss of analysis, and may I attain the path of Stabilisation Yoga. I pray to my saviours, my kind lama and the heirs of the holy lineage. Bless me so that this is accomplished!

This verse refers to the second of the Six Vajra Yogas, known as *Meditative Stabilisation*. Through this yoga, the perception of the empty-forms attained in the previous practice is unified indivisibly with the awareness of an inner perceiver, and therefore one's speech, inner wind and awareness become unwavering. While the first yoga allows one to perceive the empty-forms of the ten signs as the objects of the mind, the second yoga enables the practitioner to "mix" these signs with the mind and experience the joy and bliss of analysis (special insight). Prior to this stage, you practise with the eye sense consciousness and visual forms. Here, you practise with each of the sense consciousnesses and their objects individually—including sound, smell, taste and touch. At this stage, special conditions such as a dark room are not necessarily needed.

Through the power of Buddha-nature, may the ten winds of lalana and rasana enter avadhuti. May I experience the blazing fire of tummo and the melting and descent of the crown essence HANG (ཧཾ). May I thus attain the path of the Life-Force Yoga. I pray to my saviours, my kind lama and the heirs of the holy lineage. Bless me so that this is accomplished!

The third of the Six Vajra Yogas is known as harnessing the *Life-Force*. Previously the empty-forms were mixed with the perceiving awareness itself. These two are now combined with the inner winds so that there is no separation between the three entities. The ten winds of the left and right channels (lalana and rasana) are unified as they are drawn into the central channel (avadhuti), thereby causing the circulation of the inner winds in the left and right channels to cease. This is achieved by focusing on the navel centre, where the blazing fire of tummo (known as "inner heat") is experienced. As the energy in the central channel intensifies, the heat rises and melts the visualised syllable HANG at the crown of the head. As the energy begins to drip downwards, it generates an increasingly intense experience of bliss.

Through the power of Buddha-nature, may the white essence be retained and stabilised at my forehead. May I experience unchanging bliss as the essences melt, and attain the path of Retention Yoga. I pray to my saviours, my kind lama and the heirs of the holy lineage. Bless me so that this is accomplished!

This verse refers to the fourth yoga, known as *Retention*. During the previous stage the practitioner is able to retain the essential bodily fluids and thereby unify empty-forms, awareness and subtle winds. Through this yoga, these three elements are then integrated with the indestructible subtle fluid essences located in the six subtle chakra centres. Beginning with the white essences that are retained and stabilised at the forehead chakra, the practitioner learns to direct the essences down the central channel, moving from chakra to chakra. As one does this, aspects of great bliss are experienced. This bliss increases as the subtle essences continue to melt, giving rise to what are known as the sixteen aspects of joy.

Through the power of Buddha-nature, may all my chakras and channels be filled with the pure essence of great bliss. May I attain mastery of the three glorious consorts, and attain the path of Recollection Yoga. I pray to my saviours, my kind lama and the heirs of the holy lineage. Bless me so that this is accomplished!

The fifth of the Six Vajra Yogas is known as *Recollection*. At this stage the practitioner has gained complete control of the movement of the subtle essences which allows them to completely fill the six chakras with the pure essence of great bliss. In order to achieve the most powerful form of concentration, all of the gross and subtle essences must be gathered at the lower opening of the central channel. This is achieved by working with three types of consort: a physical consort, a visualised consort and great consort of empty-form. Through the first two, it becomes possible to manifest the third, which is the only consort capable of supporting the immutable bliss that abides without movement in the definitive meaning.

Through the power of Buddha-nature, may the six chakras of my subtle body be filled with the white essence of immutable great bliss. May I experience the unshakeable non-dualistic mind and attain the path of Absorption Yoga. I pray to my saviours, my kind lama and the heirs of the holy lineage. Bless me so that this is accomplished!

The final stage of the Six Vajra Yogas is *Meditative Absorption*. Having developed a stable absorption in the state of supreme immutable bliss, one progresses along the twelve bodhisattva stages of absorption. At the beginning of this process, the path of insight is achieved, during which time the unshakeable non-dualistic mind of sublime emptiness is experienced directly for the first time with perfect single-pointed concentration. At this point one attains an approximate Kalachakra form, similar to the actual form of the enlightened deity. By remaining in this state of absorption, each of the six chakras are filled from the bottom up with the white essence of immutable great bliss. As the process develops, one progresses along the path of habituation. In total, one experiences 21,600 moments of immutable great bliss, which purify 21,600 defilements, gradually dissolving the inner winds and exhausting the elements of the material body. When all afflictive and cognitive obscurations are thereby eliminated, buddhahood is achieved in the form of the co-emergent fully-actualised Kalachakra deity.

Through the power of Buddha-nature, may my body never be separated from the yogic postures, May my mind never be separated from the profound pith instructions of unmistaken Dharma, and may I accomplish the path of the Six Vajra Yogas. I pray to my saviours, my kind lama and the heirs of the holy lineage. Bless me so that this is accomplished!

This verse is a final aspiration prayer to accomplish the path of the Six Vajra Yogas. You pray that your body is never separated from the special yogic postures and your mind is never separated from the profound pith instructions given to you by your lama. In this context, pith instructions are the directions for the postures and profound yogic meditation techniques, transmitted orally by the lama rather than being written down.

Dedication

Through this virtue, may all beings abandon the meaningless concerns of samsara, may they meditate upon the supremely meaningful vajrayoga path and swiftly unveil the enlightenment of Kalachakra!

We end our Kalachakra practice with a dedication prayer, wishing that all beings abandon meaningless samsaric concerns and instead make the most of the precious opportunity they have to attain enlightenment. Specifically, you wish they become connected with the supremely meaningful vajrayoga path as presented here in this text, and have the ability to meditate upon the Six Vajra Yogas and so swiftly unveil the enlightenment of Kalachakra.

Through this virtue, may I swiftly attain the Six Vajra Yogas, and lead all beings without exception to the state of Kalachakra enlightenment!

This second part of the dedication emphasises your personal wish to attain the Six Vajra Yogas, not only for your own sake, but to lead all beings without exception to the state of Kalachakra enlightenment. This is also a reminder that the Six Vajra Yogas are a Mahayana practice, through which you take personal responsibility to lead all beings to enlightenment. This intention is what determines the result of your practice.

Through this virtue, may all beings complete the accumulation of merit and primordial wisdom, and so attain the two Buddha-kayas!

Finally, you dedicate the virtue so that all beings complete the accumulation of merit and primordial wisdom, which are the cause for attaining the dharmakaya body of the reality of enlightenment and the rupakaya form bodies of enlightenment. The form bodies are that which spontaneously manifest to accomplish the benefit for others, and in this case they emerge in the form of the Kalachakra deity.

PART FOUR

Two Additional Guru Yogas

— Kunkyen Dolpopa Sherab Gyaltsen —
The Dharma King of the Glorious Jonang Tradition

CHAPTER ELEVEN

Dolpopa Guru Yoga

Rain of Blessings for the Six Yogas of the Vajra Lineage

In the Jonang Tradition there are three separate guru yoga practices which are used within the context of a traditional three year retreat—the Foundation Guru Yoga (described earlier in this text), the Dolpopa Guru Yoga and the Taranatha Guru Yoga. These three practices offer a powerful method to connect us with the holy lineage as Dolpopa and Taranatha are considered to be the two most influential and extraordinary figures in the Jonang-Shambhala Tradition of Kalachakra.

During such a retreat, the guru yoga practice is undertaken for a maximum of three weeks. In the first week the Dolpopa Guru Yoga is recited, in the second week the Taranatha Guru Yoga is practiced, and in the third week, Foundation Guru Yoga. These profound practices are not just preliminaries. They also play a significant role in the practice of the Six Vajra Yogas. After completing the practice of guru yoga as a preliminary, it is customary to recite one guru yoga for each session, over the course of four sessions per day. First we recite the Dolpopa Guru Yoga, followed by the Taranatha Guru Yoga, and ending with the Foundation Guru Yoga. When we have completed all three, we begin the cycle again from the start.

THE DOLPOPA GURU YOGA PRACTICE WITH COMMENTARY

The Dolpopa Guru Yoga bears the title "Guru Yoga—Rain of Blessings for the Six Yogas of the Vajra Lineage." The practice can be considered a rain of blessings as the recitations and prayers are designed to take us beyond the ordinary mind by invoking the blessings of Dolpopa and the other lineage masters. This opens the door to tantric realisation by giving us the ability to authentically practice the Six Vajra Yogas as passed down through this lineage. The basic principles and structure of this practice are the same as in the Foundation Guru Yoga described earlier in this commentary.

Visualisation

Kunkyen Dolpopa appears in front of you in the form of blue Vajradhara surrounded by the entire field of merit. Looking in your direction, his gaze is filled with great love.

In this practice, we visualise the field of merit twice. First we establish it as a basis for taking refuge and generating bodhicitta, and then we generate it as the basis for our practice of guru yoga. Imagine the entire merit field instantly manifests in the space in front of you. Kunkyen Dolpopa is seated on a lion-throne at its centre, indivisible with Vajradhara. Once you have established the visualisation, continue by taking refuge:

NAMA SHRI KALACHAKRAYA

I go for refuge with vivid faith in the lama, yidam and the Three Jewels.
(Repeat the above line three times.)

"*Nama*" is an expression of homage and "*shri*" means glorious. "*Going for refuge with vivid faith*" means our mind is clear and filled with joy, gratitude and inspiration. This faith should also be eager and confident, with complete trust in the lama, yidam and Three Jewels.

May I generate immeasurable love, compassion, joy and equanimity
towards all beings!
May I diligently practise the profound path of guru yoga
for the sake of all beings!

You then arouse the altruistic aspiration of Bodhicitta by first cultivating the four immeasurables—love, compassion, joy and equanimity—and aspiring to attain complete enlightenment for their sake. You then strengthen your determination by generating the engaging form of Bodhicitta, praying that you will practise the profound path of guru yoga for the sake of all beings.

May all impure, temporary appearances dissolve into emptiness.

We dissolve the entire merit field back into emptiness as a way of reminding us of its true nature. Let all impure, temporary appearances melt back into the non-dual state, becoming like the reflection of the moon on a lake.

Seated on a throne on top of my crown, upon a five-layered seat of a lotus, moon disc and so forth, my root lama appears as the great Vajradhara. His body is blue in colour and has one face and two arms.

We now build the merit field again by visualising your root lama in the form of Vajradhara, with a blue body, one face and two arms. He abides above the crown of your head seated on a throne, which is supported by a five-layered seat consisting of a green lotus, white moon disc, red sun disc, black rahu disc and yellow kalagni disc. Each of these layers has spiritual significance—the lotus signifies purity, the moon disc symbolises the waking state, the sun disc symbolises the dream state, the rahu disc symbolises the deep sleep state and the kalagni disc symbolises the primordial wisdom state. Together they encompass the totality of our experience and the basis upon which we realise the ultimate nature of reality.

Although we are instructed to visualise Vajradhara, in this practice it is more common to visualise your root lama in the form of Dolpopa. You may however choose to visualise the form of Vajradhara while recollecting the qualities of the omniscient Dolpopa. As this practice was composed by Dolpopa, it makes no mention of using his form in the visualisation—this instruction was added later to honour Dolpopa's contribution to the lineage and connect with his spiritual presence.

> *He is seated in a full lotus posture. He is draped in elegant silk garments and his body is adorned with precious jewels and bone ornaments. He holds a vajra and bell crossed at his heart.*

More details are given here about the visualised form of Vajradhara, whose nature is inseparable from your root lama and Dolpopa. He is seated upon the throne in full lotus posture and he wears silk garments, jewels and bone ornaments, which all symbolise particular aspects of enlightened reality. The vajra and bell crossed at his heart symbolise the union of indestructible compassion and wisdom.

> *The four centres of his body are marked with four syllables, light rays emanate outwards from the syllable HUNG (ཧཱུྃ) at his heart, Invoking all the root and lineage lamas together with the entire field of refuge,*
>
> ***DZA (ཛཿ) HUNG (ཧཱུྃ) VAM (བཾ) HO (ཧོཿ)***
> *Becoming inseparable from them.*

At Dolpopa's forehead appears a syllable OM (ཨོཾ), at the throat AH (ཨཱཿ), at the heart HUNG (ཧཱུྃ) and at the navel HO (ཧོཿ). From the HUNG at the heart, light rays stream forth in all directions. When you say the syllable DZA, this light becomes empowered by all the root and lineage lamas. When the syllable HUNG is spoken, it gathers at the crown of Vajradhara. With VAM it dissolves into Vajradhara and with HO he becomes inseparable from their enlightened presence. Remind yourself that Vajradhara, Dolpopa and all of the lineage lamas, including your most precious root lama, are all of one inseparable nature.

Supplicating the Lama

Precious lama, I pay homage to your body, speech and mind. Your body is adorned with unchanging, perfect marks and signs. Your uninterrupted Brahma-like speech pervades the ten directions. You abide in the unmistaken mind of the great seal.

With this verse you begin the supplication prayers to the lama by praising the wonderful qualities of his body, speech and mind. The unchanging marks and signs of his body refer to the 32 major marks and 80 minor signs of a Buddha, while the uninterrupted Brahma-like speech refers to the pleasing, beautiful and melodious speech of the subtle form-realm gods. The unmistaken mind of the great seal refers to the unchanging quality of the enlightened mind, which is like the king's seal in that it cannot be altered. The great seal is also a reference to the ultimate Mahamudra—the direct realisation of the definitive meaning.

I prostrate to you who is the embodiment of the thirty-six Tathagatas, unveiled when the thirty-six aggregates are perfectly purified through the six vajra yogas such as withdrawal and so forth.

This verse is the beginning of a seven-branch offering practice in which we prostrate or pay homage to the lama as the embodiment of the thirty-six Tathagatas. In the Kalachakra Tantra there are six buddha families representing each of the *six aggregates*—(1) the form aggregate is Vairochana, (2) the perception aggregate is Amitabha, (3) the feeling aggregate is Ratnasambhava, (4) the compositional factors aggregate is Amoghasiddhi (5) the consciousness aggregate is Akshobhya and (6) the primordial wisdom aggregate is Vajrasattva.

The six bodhisattvas represent the *six sense powers*—(1) the ear sense faculty is Vajrapani, (2) the nose sense power is Khagarba, (3) the eye sense power is Kshitigarba, (4) the tongue sense power is Lokeshvara, (5) the body sense power is Sarvanivarana and (6) the mind sense power is Samantabhadra. When these bodhisattvas are combined with the buddhas, we arrive at a total of thirty-six combinations. For example in the case of Akshobhya, we have Vajrapani-Akshobhya, Khagarba-Akshobhya, Kshitigarba-Akshobhya, Lokeshvara-Akshobhya, Sarvanivarana-Akshobhya, Samantabadra-Akshobhya. These six represent the perfect purification of the consciousness aggregate through the six sense faculties, in accordance with the methods of meditation found in six vajra yogas. The other five buddha-families should be understood in the same way.

I offer with joy and pure intention an inconceivable ocean of Samantabhadra offerings, including all virtues of body, speech and mind gathered during the three times!

This refers to the second part of the seven-branch offering, during which you generate an inconceivable number of visualised offering objects to the lama and Three Jewels, with the pure intention of wishing to liberate all beings. This includes not only physical objects, but also virtues of body, speech and mind gathered during the past, present and future.

Samantabhadra refers to the primordial Buddha who abides in the limitless expanse of dharmakaya, and "Samantabhadra offerings" are a way to describe the limitless and pervasive nature of your offerings. In the Kalachakra tradition we can imagine twelve offering dakinis. From the heart of each goddess emerges twelve more offering goddesses. They continue to multiply in this way with each goddess emanating more goddesses until they become limitless in number.

I openly confess all my negativities amassed through
body, speech and mind, and pray that they be purified.
I rejoice in all virtue!
I wholeheartedly request that you turn the wheel of Dharma without ceasing!
I implore you to remain forever in samsara for the sake of all beings!

The seven-branch offering continues as you confess all negativities accumulated through harmful actions of body, speech and mind, praying for them to be purified, with the strong resolve to not repeat them in the future. We then multiply our merit through rejoicing in the virtues of ourselves and all sentient beings. Even though the lama's compassion is infinite, he will only teach if we sincerely request that he turns the wheel of Dharma. Although in reality the lama is beyond life and death, we nonetheless implore him to remain forever in samsara without passing into parinirvana for the sake of all beings.

I pray to my glorious lama. Your nature is inseparable from the four Buddha-kayas. You are the chief of all vajra holders, having completed the three accumulations and attained the twelve paths. Please bless me!

As the lama is the embodiment of all the Buddhas, his nature is inseparable from the *four Buddha-kayas*—(1) the svabhavikakaya nature body, (2) the dharmakaya wisdom-truth body, (3) the sambhogakaya enjoyment body and (4) the nirmanakaya emanation body. As he is the embodiment of all the masters who transmit the profound tantric teachings, he is the chief of all vajra holders. The *three accumulations* refer to (1) generosity, (2) great concentration and (3) wisdom, while the twelve paths refer to specific stages of attainment on the Kalachakra path, which correspond to the exhaustion of the material components of the body and their energies at the six chakra-centres.

I pray to my glorious lama. You have fully realised the five wisdoms and have completely transformed the eight objects of dualistic conception by abiding for a single moment in non-dual primordial awareness. Please bless me!

The five wisdoms of a Buddha are unveiled as the *five aggregates* are purified. They include: (1) the wisdom of all-encompassing space, (2) the mirror-like wisdom, (3) the wisdom of equanimity, (4) the wisdom of discrimination and (5) the all-accomplishing wisdom. The eight objects of dualistic conception are the objects of the eight forms of consciousness—(1) colours and shapes, (2) sounds, (3) smells, (4) tastes, (5) tactile sensations, (6) mental phenomena, (7) deluded conceptions and (8) the substrate (alaya). When purified they are experienced as the eight female bodhisattvas. All of this, however, is purified by mixing your awareness with the glorious lama who abides in non-dual primordial awareness.

> *I pray to my glorious lama. Your enlightened activity is one with the activity of all the lamas, liberating and maturing fortunate disciples through the twelve empowered attainments of the generation and completion stages. Please bless me!*

As the lama embodies all the masters, the lama's compassionate activity is one with the activity of all the lamas and leads to the liberation and spiritual maturation of all his fortunate disciples. The scope of this compassionate activity increases as one moves through the twelve empowered attainments of the generation and completion processes. These twelve attainments occur during the practice of the sixth vajra yoga known as Meditative Absorption, and correspond to the exhaustion of the material components of the body and their energies at the six chakra-centres. Empowerments from innumerable Buddhas are needed to accomplish each of these attainments.

> *I pray to the glorious lama. You are one with all the yidams, your aggregates are the six Buddha-families, your consciousnesses are the eight bodhisattvas, your arms, legs and so forth are the assembly of wrathful deities. Please bless me!*

In this verse we supplicate the lama as the embodiment of all the yidams; the peaceful and wrathful enlightened deities who are the source of all tantric attainments. The six Buddha-families (as mentioned previously) are the pure aspect of the six aggregates. The eight Bodhisattvas are the pure aspect of the eight sense powers, while the assembly of wrathful deities are the pure aspect of the *five action faculties*: (1) the mouth faculty, (2) the arm faculty, (3) the leg faculty, (4) the anus faculty, and (5) the supreme faculty.

I pray to the glorious lama. You are one with all the Buddhas, your nature is the magnificent body of truth; you have perfected the two accumulations and manifest countless emanations for the benefit of beings. Please bless me!

We now supplicate the lama as the embodiment of all the Buddhas. His nature is inseparable from the dharmakaya, the magnificent body of truth. Since he has perfected the two accumulations of wisdom and merit, he is able to manifest countless emanation bodies for the benefit of beings. Through accumulating wisdom and merit in this way he has unveiled the *two Buddha-kayas*—(1) the dharmakaya body of the reality of enlightenment and (2) the infinite rupakaya form bodies.

I pray to the glorious lama. You are one with all immaculate Dharmas, You manifest as the teachings and texts of ultimate meaning, You lead us to the inexpressible profound truth. Please bless me!

With this verse we consider the lama to be the embodiment of all immaculate dharmas, which include the 84,000 teachings of the Buddha which serve as a remedy for every conceivable mental affliction. This includes the teachings and texts of ultimate meaning, which refer to those teachings that are definitive in their interpretation, especially the teachings of the third turning which describe the inconceivable reality of Buddha-nature and form the basis of Dolpopa's undefeatable Zhentong View. Through the words and exposition of these teachings and texts, we are led to the direct experience of the inexpressible profound truth, just as a finger can point to the moon even though it is not the moon itself.

I pray to the glorious lama. You are one with all the great lords of the Arya Sangha who abide in the ten bodhisattva levels, having attained complete liberation and accomplishment; You are the immaculate virtuous friend, a refuge for all beings. Please bless me!

We now supplicate the lama as the embodiment of the great lords of the Arya Sangha, the immaculate virtuous friends who assist us on our spiritual path. These are noble beings who progress irreversibly towards Buddhahood through the power of their merit and wisdom and have entered the path of insight, where the true empty nature of reality is seen directly. This journey takes place in ten stages known as the ten bodhisattva levels, during which subtler and subtler obscurations are overcome and qualities such as generosity and patience are perfected. Complete liberation and accomplishment refers to the freedom from taking rebirth in samsara, which is achieved on the path of insight and the attainment of the bodhisattva view of emptiness.

> *I pray to the glorious lama. You are one with all the Dharma protectors who destroy all enemies and obstacles through the power of your non-dual compassion. Please bless me!*

Here we regard the lama as the embodiment of all the dharma protectors who destroy all enemies and obstacles. These are worldly or enlightened beings who take on a wrathful form. Their function is to protect the Buddha's teachings from becoming diluted or distorted and to help genuine practitioners overcome enemies as well as external and internal obstacles. External obstacles include poor health or other circumstances which prevent you from practicing, while distorted views or being pulled towards distracting activities are considered internal obstacles. Non-dual compassion refers to the kind of compassion that is simultaneously aware of the illusory nature of all phenomena and is therefore not bound by expectations or clinging.

> *I pray to the glorious lama. You are the origin of all siddhis, bestower of both supreme and common accomplishments, as you have mastered the actions of pacifying, expanding, controlling and subduing. Please bless me!*

Now we supplicate the lama as the origin of all siddhis, for it is through following his instructions that we are able to attain both supreme and common accomplishments. Common accomplishments refer to supernatural abilities such as clairvoyance and miraculous powers while supreme accomplishments are related to achieving enlightened qualities. The four sublime powers of a Buddha are: (1) pacifying, (2) expanding, (3) controlling and (4) subduing. They are the means by which a Buddha spontaneously engages in activities which bring limitless benefit to beings. As a Vajrayana practitioner you are training yourself to see that everything the lama does or says is an expression of these four powers, as you learn to perceive him as a living Buddha.

I pray to the glorious lama. You dispel all darkness as you clear away wrong views by composing, debating and explaining the sutras, tantras, treatises and pith instructions. Please bless me!

We now supplicate the lama in the aspect of a perfect Dharma teacher who dispels the darkness of ignorance and wrong views. He does so by composing texts, engaging in debate to defeat wrong views, explaining the words of the Buddha as presented in the sutras and tantras with reference to authentic treatises or commentaries, and finally by passing on pith instructions or heart advice, which are key oral instructions passed down through the lineage.

By drinking the nectar of his precious Dharma instruction on the profound meaning, from this day onwards may I follow the lama like a shadow. May my glorious lama bless me so that this is accomplished!

This verse is a statement of our resolute commitment to follow the lama's precious Dharma instructions, which lead to the profound truth of emptiness. As this Dharma is so precious, we also commit to making offerings and serving the lama, following him like a shadow. By strengthening our connection with the lama in this way, we can accumulate merit, putting us in a better position to understand the profound meaning of his teachings.

Without consideration for food, clothing and luxuries, having abandoned wrong and impure livelihoods, may I taste the nectar of Dharma with the tip of my tongue. May my glorious lama bless me so that this is accomplished!

We now commit to developing a genuine mind of renunciation by pledging to practise Dharma without consideration for food, clothing and luxuries. This pledge is supported by our abandonment of wrong and impure livelihoods, which includes any activity that involves harming life, cheating, stealing, lying or other forms of immoral conduct.

From this day onwards may I remain in an isolated place, meditating single-pointedly upon the profound meaning, so I may reach the great seal of liberation in this very lifetime. May my glorious lama bless me so that this is accomplished!

Having established the mind of renunciation, we now pledge to simplify our life and be content to dwell in an isolated place where conditions are conducive to developing good single-pointed concentration by meditating intensively upon the profound meaning of the Dharma. With this kind of dedication we can aim to reach the great seal of liberation, or the final result of Buddhahood, in a single lifetime.

May I see the four syllables at the chakras of the lama's body
as the four Buddha-kayas.
May I receive the four empowerments by focusing upon them.
May my glorious lama bless me so that this is accomplished!

This verse is an aspiration prayer to receive the four empowerments from the lama. These four empowerments are received when you focus on the four syllables located on the four main chakras of the lama's body—the forehead, throat, heart and navel. With each of these empowerments you are awakening the four Buddha-kayas within your own mind-stream—the nirmanakaya, sambhogakaya, dharmakaya and svabhavikakaya.

Receiving the Four Empowerments

> *From the OM (ཨོཾ) at my lama's forehead, a white OM (ཨོཾ) streams forth and dissolves into my own forehead chakra. Through this power may I receive the vase empowerment. May my glorious lama bless me so that this is accomplished!*

As in the Foundation Guru Yoga, we now receive the four empowerments. This begins with the vase empowerment, which takes place as the OM you visualise at the lama's forehead emanates dazzling white light and dissolves into your own forehead chakra.

> *Through this power may I purify the obscurations of the body and waking state, experience the four joys and unveil the vajra emanation body. May my glorious lama bless me so that this is accomplished!*

This vase empowerment purifies the obscurations of your body, which have accumulated through negative actions such as stealing and so forth, as well as the obscurations of the waking state, at which time the forehead chakra is most active. The four joys are experienced when the coarse bodily fluids are refined and become more and more subtle at each of the four main chakras. This process also destroys the negativity or obscurations which form "knots" around these chakras. In addition, this empowerment introduces you to the indestructible vajra emanation body, or the nirmanakaya aspect of your Buddha-nature.

> *From the AH (ཨཱཿ) at my lama's throat, a red AH (ཨཱཿ) streams forth and dissolves into my own throat chakra. Through this power may I receive the secret empowerment. May my glorious lama bless me so that this is accomplished!*

Next you receive the secret empowerment as dazzling red rays of light stream forth from the AH syllable at the lama's throat and dissolve into your own throat chakra.

Through this power may I purify the obscurations of speech and the dream state, experience the four excellent joys and unveil the enjoyment body of vajra speech. May my glorious lama bless me so that this is accomplished!

This empowerment purifies the obscurations of speech connected with lying, harsh words and so forth. It also purifies the obscurations of the dream state, which is associated with the throat chakra and determines our ability to engage in practices such as dream yoga. The four excellent joys are experienced as the subtle fluids or essences are refined further, and you are introduced to the enjoyment body of vajra speech, which is the sambhogakaya aspect of your Buddha-nature.

From the HUNG (ཧཱུྃ) at my lama's heart, a black HUNG (ཧཱུྃ) streams forth and dissolves into my own heart chakra. Through this power may I receive the primordial wisdom empowerment. May my glorious lama bless me so that this is accomplished!

Now you receive the primordial wisdom empowerment as dazzling black rays of light stream forth from the HUNG syllable at the lama's heart and dissolve into your own heart chakra.

Through this power may I purify the obscurations of mind and the deep sleep state, experience the four supreme joys and unveil the Dharmakaya body of vajra mind. May my glorious lama bless me so that this is accomplished!

This empowerment purifies the obscurations of mind connected with lust, wrong views and so forth and also purifies the obscurations of the deep sleep state, which is associated with the heart chakra. The four supreme joys are experienced as an even subtler refinement of the essences, which takes place at the four chakras. In this way you are introduced to the dharmakaya body of vajra mind, which is the unborn dharmakaya aspect of your Buddha-nature.

From the HO (ཧོཿ) at my lama's navel, a yellow HO (ཧོཿ) streams forth and dissolves into my own navel chakra. Through this power may I receive the sacred fourth empowerment. May my glorious lama bless me so that this is accomplished!

Finally you receive the sacred fourth empowerment as dazzling yellow rays of light stream forth from the HO syllable at the lama's navel and dissolve into your own navel chakra.

Through this power may I purify the propensities of attachment, experience the four innate joys and unveil the primordial vajra wisdom of blissful emptiness. May my glorious lama bless me so that this is accomplished!

This empowerment purifies the most subtle propensities of attachment which are stored in the foundation consciousness and underlie all the other negative tendencies of body, speech and mind. The four innate joys are experienced as the most subtle refinement of the essences, and you are introduced to the primordial vajra wisdom of blissful emptiness, which is the svabhavikakaya aspect of your Buddha-nature, representing the inseparability of all three kayas.

Dissolution

The lama at my crown melts into light and dissolves into me. He abides in the centre of an eight-petalled lotus at my heart. May my glorious lama bless me so that this is accomplished!

As in the Foundation Guru Yoga, you end the practice by dissolving the visualisation and recognising that the ultimate lama is none other than your own mind. To do this you watch the lama at your crown melt into light and travel down your central channel to the centre of an eight-petalled lotus at your heart. You should simply watch the inseparability of the lama and your own mind. Remain in this natural state for as long as you can. When the mind starts to stir again, you may continue to make prayers and supplications.

Dedication

> *Through this practice, may all beings purify all their stains and obstacles and swiftly reach the essence of the Tathagata.*

We conclude by dedicating the merit for the ultimate benefit of others. In this case we pray that all beings purify all their stains and obstacles which prevent them from recognising the reality of their Buddha-nature. We also pray that they swiftly reach the essence of the Tathagata, at which point the ground of our true being, the Tathagatagharba, is completely unveiled.

> *May I not give rise, even for an instant, to wrong views about the glorious Lama's liberating appearances. With a devotion that sees everything he does as excellent, may the blessings of the Lama enter my mind.*

In this aspiration, we pray to never lose sight of the fact that all the appearances we experience are merely expressions of the primordial awareness of the glorious Lama. It is through realising the nature of these appearances that we attain liberation. With this understanding, we strive to practice the pure perception that sees all the Lama's actions as opportunities to develop realisations.

> *In future lives may I never be separated from my glorious lama. May I never be separated from the joy of practicing the precious Dharma. May I accomplish all the enlightened bhumi levels and paths and quickly attain the state of Vajradhara.*

We complete the practice with the prayer to never be separated from the lama, both conventionally as our teacher and ultimately as our nature. We pray to never be separated from our practice of the precious Dharma so that we may continue on our journey towards enlightenment, traverse the ten bodhisattva bhumi levels that establish the five paths and ultimately attain the fully enlightened state of Vajradhara.

— Jetsun Taranatha Drolway Gonpo —
The Great Rimé Master who preserved the purity of the Jonang Tradition

CHAPTER TWELVE

Taranatha Guru Yoga

The Anchor for Collecting Siddhis

The Taranatha Guru Yoga is the third of the three guru yoga practices in the Jonang tradition, and is the briefest of the three practices. It is called "*The Anchor for Collecting Siddhis*" as it is a fundamental or root practice (an "anchor") for achieving spiritual realisation. The term "siddhis" refers to both ordinary spiritual attainments, such as clairvoyance or miraculous powers, as well as the supreme attainment of enlightenment. We can only uproot our mental afflictions with enlightened realisation, and this is why it is considered supreme.

As Taranatha was an extraordinary figure in the Jonang Kalachakra lineage, this guru yoga gives us the opportunity to connect with his spiritual presence and thereby make a link with all enlightened beings. In today's Jonang monasteries, this guru yoga is performed in the second week of an intensive three week guru yoga practice. We should always remember that guru yoga is a fundamental practice which allows us to develop our connection not only with the lineage, but most importantly with the very heart essence of tantric practice—our primordially present Buddha-nature. It is this realisation that will allow us to make our practice of the Six Vajra Yogas an effective cause for achieving enlightenment.

THE TARANATHA GURU YOGA PRACTICE WITH COMMENTARY

The basic principles and structure of this practice are the same as in the Foundation Guru Yoga details described earlier. What is most important to remember is that ultimately the lama is the wisdom aspect of your own mind, and the act of praying to and supplicating the external lama is actually a skilful method to help you see this inner wisdom.

Visualisation

I fervently pay homage to the glorious lama. All phenomena are only appearances within the mind. One's own mind is of an empty and clear nature, beyond words. Whatever various appearances are, they are never separable from the ever present moment to moment self-awareness.

This guru yoga begins by paying homage or prostrating to the glorious lama, who is the embodiment of all the Buddhas and your personal connection to enlightenment. We then describe the emptiness of relative truth, stating how all relative phenomena are only appearances within the mind. The ultimate truth of our Buddha-mind however, is not empty of itself but rather empty and clear. All that we perceive is therefore a display of the mind's projections and not the true nature of mind itself.

OM SHUNYATA JÑANA VAJRA SVABHAVA ATMAKHO HUNG

With this mantra all relative phenomena dissolve into the state of emptiness (*SHUNYATA*), appearing like the reflection of the moon on still water. Unlike the previous mantras, this mantra points to more than just emptiness, as it places greater emphasis on the "fullness" aspect—the reality of Buddha-nature as the ground of our being.

My mind in its natural state is the pure realm of Akanishta. In the centre of this pure realm is a radiant palace, and in it my glorious root lama is seated upon a lotus, sun disc and moon disc which rest upon a lion throne.

After resting the mind in its natural state for a while, you begin by visualising a radiant palace in the centre of Akanishta, the pure realm of the samboghakaya enjoyment body. The glorious root lama is seated in the centre of this palace upon a lion throne, lotus flower, sun disc and moon disc in the sky before you. This signifies majesty, purity, wisdom and compassion.

My glorious lama is radiant like a golden mountain reflecting a hundred-thousand rays of sunlight. He is pleased and smiles at me.

The lama is radiant in appearance and smiles at you, as if to say "well done". The form of the lama is not specified here so you can visualise him as Vajradhara, or alternatively in the form of Taranatha or even the physical form of your root lama. In any case, his nature is inseparable from the spiritual presence of Taranatha and the nature of your own root lama.

Above my lama the lineage masters miraculously appear, surrounded by herukas such as Vajravarahi and clouds of yidams.

The masters of the Jonang-Shambhala lineage appear above the lama while peaceful and wrathful yidam deities (also known as "herukas") surround the lama like a great cloud.

Buddhas and bodhisattvas from the ten directions appear in the space before me and glorious arhat emanations occupy the ground. They are surrounded by dakinis and all-seeing Dharma protectors with their retinues, poised to obey the lama's every instruction.

We are now building the assembly to include all the Buddhas and bodhisattvas from the ten directions (the four cardinal and four intermediate directions plus up and down). We also visualise arhat emanations, whom we consider as actual emanations of Buddhas and bodhisattvas. Surrounding these are dakinis and dharma protectors, whose function is to guard us against internal and external obstacles. They are poised to obey the lama's every instruction, as they are emanations of the lama with a particular role to perform.

The entire assembly is in vibrant motion like lightning and storm-clouds, filling all of space and the surrounding lands. All these beings have radiant bodies: to various sentient beings who need to be tamed, their appearances vary accordingly; They ceaselessly expound the Mahayana teachings and their minds abide in the clear-light of great bliss as they perform oceans of virtuous activities.

This verse describes the visualised assembly in general terms. Rather than being flat, solid or fixed, the assembly is radiant, in vibrant motion and incredibly vast, extending to the furthest reaches of space. While their minds abide in the clear-light of great bliss, which is beyond all dualistic notions, they ceaselessly expound the Mahayana teachings for the benefit of all beings and they effortlessly and spontaneously perform oceans of virtuous activities.

> *All of this is but a meaningful manifestation of the glorious lama, just as all appearances of samsara and nirvana are but a miraculous display of the lama's primordial wisdom.*

The entire visualisation you have been developing is in fact a manifestation of the glorious lama, since the lama is inseparable from your own Buddha-nature and embodies all the lineage masters, yidams, Buddhas, bodhisattvas, arhats, dakinis and dharma protectors. Of this vast and sublime assembly, we choose to focus on the lama since he is our personal link to enlightenment.

According to the highest view of Buddhism, all appearances of samsara and nirvana are a miraculous display of the lama's primordial wisdom, which is none other than our own Buddha-nature. On the ultimate level, for example, the five aggregates are the five male Buddhas and the five elements are their consorts, while the six sense powers are the six male bodhisattvas and the six objects represent their consorts.

Supplicating the Lama

> *I offer my body, my possessions, all the virtue of the three times and every conceivable object of offering from all the pure-lands of the ten directions.*

Having established the visualisation with the lama as your central object of refuge, you now fill your mind with every conceivable object of offering, including your body (which you cherish above all else), your possessions and all the virtuous deeds carried out by yourself and others during the past, present and future. In addition, you should also visualise the pure Buddha-realms of the ten directions and offer them up as well.

I offer everything my mind can conceive with pure aspiration: All beings of the six realms including adversaries, friends and relatives, extending to the farthest reaches of space, together with every pleasing object of offering in all of the three realms. Through the power of my visualisation and prayer, I manifest all of these countless, inconceivable and magnificent objects of offering.

The offering practice continues as you bring to mind and manifest countless, inconceivable and magnificent objects of offering, all with the pure aspiration of connecting to the Buddha's wisdom and benefiting others. Your offering includes all beings of the six realms—humans and animals, as well as unseen beings such as gods, demi-gods, hungry ghosts and hell beings. You should also include your loved ones, friends, relatives and adversaries. Normally in offering practices we only think of pleasing or likeable objects, yet in reality there is no distinction between pleasant and unpleasant as they are all merely a projection of the mind. We should therefore offer everything without bias or judgment, letting go of all our attachment and aversion.

All these offering treasures manifest from the primordial awareness of the Buddhas, bodhisattvas and dakinis who appear in the three times and ten directions. All these innumerable and inconceivable manifestations are none other than the glorious display of the lama's mind, inseparable from my own mind, the unborn display of dharmakaya.

This verse poses the question of where all of these offering objects come from. Ultimately they all manifest from the primordial awareness of the Buddhas and other objects of refuge, and in particular, they are none other than the glorious display of the lama's mind, which is inseparable from my own mind. Thus we begin by conceiving the vast display of offering objects as something outside of ourselves, and then recognise that it is all a reflection of our own Buddha-nature which is inseparable from the lama.

Precious lama, you embody all the Buddhas.
Precious lama, you embody all the Dharma.
Precious lama, you embody all the Sangha.

We now supplicate the lama as the embodiment of the *Outer Three Jewels*—(1) the Buddha, (2) Dharma and (3) Sangha. These are the external manifestations which act as the primary support for our spiritual practice. Each of them is embodied within the physical form of the lama.

> *Supreme Dharma King, you embody all the lamas. You embody all the yidams while all the dakinis and Dharma protectors manifest as your retinues. I pray to you Vajradhara, please bless me and all those who have faith in you!*

We now pray to the lama as the embodiment of the *Inner Three Jewels*—(1) Lama, (2) Yidam and (3) Dakinis. We pray to the lama as the supreme Dharma King, embodying all the lamas who hold the holy lineage and teach the precious Dharma. This same lama embodies the enlightened yidam deities who are the root of spiritual attainments, the dakinis who are the root of enlightened activity and an inner source of protection, as well as the dharma protectors who protect against all obstacles to spiritual progress. We say they manifest as (the lama's) retinues as they are inseparable from the enlightened nature of the lama. On a relative level they are sent forth to accomplish the lama's instructions like the messenger of a king. Finally we pray to the lama as Vajradhara, who is the essential nature of the enlightened guru and the source of all blessings.

> *Glorious lama, you are Vajradhara in the pure realm of the enjoyment body. You are the wrathful Heruka when subduing all evils. You are Shakyamuni to beings with pure renunciation. You are the great sage to the ascetics.*

Just as a crystal can reflect many different colours, the compassion of the glorious lama is reflected in countless forms depending on the merit, capacities and personalities of different beings. For those with pure perception, he appears as Vajradhara in the pure realm of the enjoyment body. For unruly or unwholesome beings who need to be tamed, he appears as the wrathful Heruka, an enlightened expression of wrathful compassion who is able to subdue all evils. For those with pure renunciation, such as the great arhats of the Buddha's time, he appears in the human form of Buddha Shakyamuni, and for those who live as ascetics he appears as a great sage who points out the true middle way.

To those who follow the path of the three vehicles, you manifest as the Bodhisattva, the Pratyeka and the great Shravaka. You also appear in the form of Brahma, Vishnu, Lord Shiva and all other sages and saints.

The Buddha described three types of paths to suit different types of spiritual aspirants, which are referred to as the *three vehicles*—(1) the Bodhisattva vehicle, (2) the Pratyeka vehicle and (3) the Shravaka vehicle. The Bodhisattva vehicle is a journey over a vast number of lifetimes that carries the aspiration to fulfil the vow of becoming an omniscient Buddha so that we can spontaneously and effortlessly help beings to be free from suffering and attain enlightenment themselves. The Pratyeka or "solitary realiser" vehicle is a path to developing deep wisdom through one's own analysis, without the need for external teachers and resulting in a more limited form of enlightenment. The Shravaka or "hearer" vehicle involves hearing and following the Buddha's foundational teachings and achieving individual liberation from samsara. For aspirants on each of these paths, the lama manifests as an appropriate spiritual mentor, whether this be a Bodhisattva, Pratyeka or great Shravaka.

The final line of this verse is testament to the depth of Taranatha's wisdom and his perfect non-sectarian outlook. Not only does the lama manifest as Buddhist teachers or mentors, but also as teachers, sages and saints from other traditions such as Brahma, Vishnu and Lord Shiva of the Hindu tradition. This also includes great sages such as Jesus Christ or the prophet Mohammed. As beings have a countless variety of personalities and learning styles, it makes sense that the Buddhas would teach a variety of religious systems in order to lead them all closer to the truth.

Sometimes you appear in the position of a king, at other times you appear as a yogi or ascetic. To others you appear as a pure monk with simple robes. I pray to you, performer of great, vast deeds according to the needs of each being. Just as the thoughts and aspirations of all beings are inconceivable, so too is the vastness and depth of your teachings.

In this verse we continue to supplicate the lama as the supreme embodiment of everything which is beneficial in the world. He appears in the position of a king who is keen on worldly affairs, in order to bring peace, justice and spiritual values to a great number of people. He also appears as a yogi or ascetic to demonstrate the path of renunciation and discipline to spiritual aspirants, and as a pure monk with simple robes to demonstrate perfect moral conduct and the benefits of a simple life focused on the benefit of others. We therefore pray to the lama who performs great, vast deeds according to the needs of each being. In the same way that the thoughts and aspirations of all beings are inconceivable, so too are the lama's methods of teaching the Dharma.

Just as rainbows and clouds appear in the sky, arising, abiding and then vanishing back into the sky, you are the dharmakaya body of the reality of enlightenment free from all extremes, performing great deeds spontaneously and without effort. Even though you act in a way that meets the needs of all beings, you abide in a state of clear, self-aware and non-dual expanse of dharmadatu.

These two verses offer a poetic description of the lama's spontaneous and effortless compassion, which takes the form of great deeds performed in a way that meet the needs of all beings. These spontaneous activities are likened to rainbows and clouds. They arise and vanish spontaneously into the vast expanse of the sky, depending on numerous causes and conditions, such as the presence of moisture, the angle of the sunlight and so forth. In the same way, the lama's great deeds emerge from the vast expanse of the dharmakaya truth body—the state of clear, self-aware and non-dual expanse of the basic space of reality (dharmadhatu)— depending on causes and conditions such as the merit and aspirations of different beings.

You are beyond birth and death, coming and going, near and far. I pray to you, pristine body of the reality of enlightenment. I pay homage from the depths of my heart with unceasing devotion!

The pristine dharmakaya body of the reality of enlightenment of the lama is completely beyond all concepts such as birth and death, coming and going, near and far. The unceasing devotion that we arouse towards the lama from the depths of our heart is none other than devotion and confidence in the reality of our own Buddha-nature. Praying to the lama is therefore a very skilful method to bring us closer to this sacred truth.

> *I take refuge in you, embodiment of all sources of refuge. I offer countless virtuous objects while being aware of their empty nature. I confess and purify all my negativities even though their nature is empty from the beginning.*

With this verse we begin a seven-branch prayer. First we pay homage to the lama who is the embodiment of all sources of refuge. We then offer countless virtuous objects and confess and purify all our negativities. It carries a deeper meaning however, as we are called to be aware of the empty nature of the offering objects and that ultimately there is nothing to confess as our nature is primordially pure. These incredibly profound statements help us view the practice in the light of their definitive meaning as they remind us of the illusory nature of all phenomena.

> *I rejoice in the virtue of all beings in samsara and nirvana.*
> *May the empty sound of your teachings never cease.*

The seven-branch prayer continues as we rejoice in the virtue of all beings and request that the lama never ceases to teach the precious Dharma. From the perspective of ultimate truth however, even the lama's words are none other than empty sound, a luminosity of the unborn dharmakaya perceived in the form of sound.

> *The dharmakaya body of the reality of enlightenment is beyond birth and death. May you ceaselessly turn the wheel of precious Dharma.*
> *May you remain forever for the sake of all beings.*

With this verse we request the lama to ceaselessly turn the wheel of precious Dharma according to the needs of sentient beings, and that he remain forever for the sake of all beings without abandoning samsara.

I dedicate all my virtue so my mind may become inseparable from yours, O holy lama. May all beings attain supreme enlightenment!

The seven-branch prayer ends here as we dedicate all our virtue so that our mind may become inseparable from the mind of the holy lama, meaning that we will discover the sacred reality of our own Buddha-nature by recognising the ultimate nature of the lama. We also dedicate this practice with the aspiration of a bodhisattva, wishing with great compassion that all beings be free from suffering and attain supreme enlightenment.

Glorious Drolway Gonpo, rescuer of all beings, please bless me with your body, speech and mind. Bestow upon me the four empowerments at this very instant!

We now supplicate glorious Drolway Gonpo, better known as Taranatha, who is the rescuer of all beings from the uncontrollable suffering of samsaric existence. We implore him to bless us with his body, speech and mind and bestow the four empowerments upon us. As the verse mentions Taranatha, the author of this guru yoga practice, it must have been added by someone else after Taranatha's time.

Receiving the Four Empowerments

May my body transform into innate bliss.
May my speech transform with the power of mantra.
May my heart transform into clear-light wisdom!
Perfect lama, I pray to you to bless me at this very instant.

When we receive the first three of the four empowerments our body transforms into the vajra body of innate bliss, our speech transforms into the vajra speech which possesses the power of mantra, and our heart transforms into the vajra mind which is inseparable from the clear-light wisdom of our Buddha-nature. This verse also implies a deeper level of meaning which accords with the pith instructions of tantra, especially the reference to the power of mantra.

Rays of light stream forth from the lama's forehead, throat, heart, and navel and then dissolve into my own four chakras, bestowing upon me the four empowerments of body, speech, mind and primordial vajra wisdom!

As you recite this verse you begin to receive the four empowerments. Brilliant rays of white light stream forth from the lama's forehead, while dazzling rays of red, black and yellow light stream forth from the three other centres—the throat, heart and navel centres respectively. These rays of light dissolve into your own four chakras as you receive the empowerments of body, speech, mind and primordial vajra wisdom. With each of these four empowerments, particular defilements are purified and particular spiritual powers are attained. You can refer to previous sections for more details.

May I receive the vase empowerment.
May I receive the secret empowerment.
May I receive the union of great bliss and wisdom empowerment.
May I receive the sacred fourth empowerment of the great seal beyond conception!

With this verse you actually receive the four empowerments—the vase, secret, wisdom and sacred fourth empowerment. Each of these points to a particular aspect of your Buddha-nature, as if to say "You have that!" The third empowerment here is literally translated as the "empowerment of the union of great bliss and primordial wisdom". The fourth empowerment is described as the great seal beyond conception as it points directly to the ultimate reality of your Buddha-nature, which is completely beyond all dualistic notions that give rise to conceptual thought.

Dissolution

Great Dharma King, I rely on no-one else but you. You are my only true refuge. Just like water poured into water, May I dissolve into inseparable union with you!

For one last time we are proclaiming our complete trust in the lama who we regard as a great Dharma King and our only true object of refuge or our only worthy rescuer from the pain of samsara. The lama then dissolves into light, becoming inseparably merged with your mind-stream, just like water poured into water. With more experience however, this dissolving process may become more like a vase shattering as the empty space inside the vase merges with the space around it. By repeating this exercise again and again and simply watching the mind of the lama and your own mind come together like this, you can develop great confidence in the reality of your Buddha-nature, which has been with you all along.

May the lama melt into the essence of nectar and fill my four chakras, bestowing empowerment upon me.

As the lama melts into light and dissolves into you, visualise his essence in the form of blissful, radiant white nectar filling your forehead, throat, heart and navel chakras, thus purifying all the defilements and unwholesome energies stored around these chakras. Incredible joy is experienced as these energy-centres are activated, and you are empowered once again with the blessings of the lama's body, speech, mind and primordial wisdom.

Meditate on the natural lama, the great dharmakaya body of the reality of enlightenment inseparable from one's own mind, and remain in this natural state beyond all concepts.

Once again you should meditate on the inseparability of the great truth body of the lama and your own mind. We call this the natural lama, the natural enlightened state beyond all dualistic notions, which can only be realised when our faith and devotion take us beyond the ordinary dualistic mind.

Dedications

In all my future lives may I be born into an excellent family, with a clear mind, lack of pride, great compassion and faith in the Lama. May I abide in my commitments to the Glorious Lama.

We complete this practice with verses of dedication. In this prayer, we aspire to be born with all the necessary conditions to progress along the spiritual path as fast as possible. In particular, we pray to be able to practice the most profound and skilful means of devotion to a glorious lama, which accumulates oceans of merit and wisdom.

May I not give rise, even for an instant, to wrong views about the glorious Lama's liberating appearances. With a devotion that sees everything he does as excellent, may the blessings of the Lama enter my mind.

With this next prayer, we are praying to be free from all obstacles to our spiritual practice. In particular we aspire to be free from the ordinary view which focuses on faults of the lama, and prevents us from achieving realisations. We instead pray to develop the pure perception that recognises the underlying purity of all of his actions, and functions as a foundation for profound insight.

In future lives may I never be separated from my glorious lama. May I never be separated from the joy of practicing the precious Dharma. May I accomplish all the enlightened bhumi levels and paths and quickly attain the state of Vajradhara.

Again, we end the practice by recognising that the lama is the basis upon which all obscurations are removed and all qualities are developed. For this reason we pray to never be separated from him, nor from his precious teachings which lead to the ultimate joy—full and complete enlightenment.

This is the perfect Guru Yoga enabling you to reach Buddhahood in one lifetime. Have no doubt. Composed by Jetsun Taranatha, aged 29

This practice was composed by the great Jonang scholar and siddha Jetsun Taranatha in the early 17th century. His concluding statement reminds us that this guru yoga practice is supremely profound, rare and precious as it forges a connection to the holy lineage of the Six Vajra Yogas. This is such an effective and powerful practice that can enable you to attain the omniscient state of Buddhahood in a single lifetime, emulating many great practitioners of the past. This should be a tremendous source of confidence, and you should therefore have no doubt about this practice.

Conclusion

Here it is said that the Kalachakra is the King of Tantra. It is renowned by both the wise and foolish in the Land of Snow Mountains due to the kindness of the excellent protectors of Tibet, who have bestowed the Great Empowerments of Kalachakra again and again.

And yet, where are the mature disciples with power and faith, who continually engage in genuine practice? It is important to now consider how in the Land of Snows, even this much good karma has become almost non-existent.

Due to the condition of being mixed up in the distractions of various things, my armour of perseverance has been stolen by laziness. Even though, this analysis and understanding is not an unsurpassed explanation, you can be certain that it will guide you on the excellent path.

Because of that, born from my virtuous intention, I offer this medicine of happiness and wellbeing to those new to the path.May the truth of dependent-arising give rise to great power and may the dakinis and dharma protectors help us at all times.

From now on, through the path of the profound definitive meaning, the six yogas which cease the movement of the winds in the subtle channels, and the great bliss of the union with the Great Consort of Empty-Form, may we experience the ecstasy of the sixteen joys.

Even if other sentient beings and myself are unable to reveal the essence of the secret and profound Dharma, in the future, may we be able to enjoy the definitive and secret Dharma of the Golden Age under the guidance of the mandala of the Fierce Kalki.

OM AH HUM HO

— *The Sublime Realm of Shambhala* —

Guardians of the Kalachakra Teachings

I prostrate and go for refuge to all those who are praiseworthy such as the Kalki Dharma Kings, the assembly of wisdom deities and their 96 royal emanations, dwelling within the superior lineage of the Sublime Tantrayana Realm of Shambhala—surrounded by a garland of snow mountains, like an eight-petalled lotus, the principal city of Kalapa, sits atop Mount Kailasha as a divine manifestation; around it are pleasure groves, lakes of white lotus flowers; in the centre of a sandalwood forest lies the enlightened mandala; in the outer petals, residing separately are nine-hundred and sixty million cities and so forth.

By the power of the sublime virtue created through this effort, when our bodies of this life are cast aside, may we be born into the retinue of the glorious Kalki Kings of Shambhala and accomplish the teachings of Kalachakra.

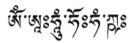

ཨོཾ་ཨཱཿཧཱུྃ་ཧོཿཧཾ་ཀྵཿ

Appendices

APPENDIX ONE

The Divine Ladder: Preliminary and Main Practices of the Profound Kalachakra Vajrayoga

༄༅། །དུས་འཁོར་འཇུག་རིམ་ཟབ་ལམ་རྡོ་རྗེའི་རྣལ་འབྱོར། །

by Jetsun Taranatha

PART ONE: OUTER PRELIMINARIES AND LINEAGE INVOCATION

I. Four Convictions of Renunciation

O Think! During countless aeons, for this one time I have attained this precious human birth, which is so very hard to achieve and so easy to lose. The time of death is uncertain and the conditions leading to death are beyond my comprehension, this cherished body can die even today! And so I shall abandon all worldly concerns that keep me chained to samsara, including all non-virtues and heavy heinous crimes. Instead I shall use the little time I have left wisely and practise Dharma with urgency, reflecting on the benefits of liberation.

(Begin by closing the left nostril using the Pacifying Mudra and exhale three times through the right nostril, then change to the other nostril. Finish by exhaling three times through both nostrils. Visualise all afflictions and negativity leaving your body in the form of black smoke.)

II. Brief Invocation of the Jonang Tradition of Kalachakra

(i) Visualisation

Visualise your root lama, seated upon a lotus flower at your heart centre, rising up through your central channel to the crown of your head. The lama appears luminous.

(ii) Invocation

Glorious and precious root lama, having taken your seat upon the lotus of devotion at the crown of my head, bless me with your great compassion, take care of me with your great kindness, and grant me the siddhis of your body, speech and mind!

I pray to you Dolpopa. You are the omniscient Lord of Dharma, who perfectly understands the three turnings of the wheel of Dharma and the four classes of tantra. Please show the unmistaken path to all beings!

I pray to you Kazhipa. Embodiment of all the Buddhas' activities, you make the precious jewel of the Dharma shine like the sun by displaying the four sublime powers.

I pray to you Rinchen Drakpa. You are adorned by Dharma teachings and profound realisations and your activities are vast and incomparable, whoever sees or hears you will surely be liberated!

I pray to you Gyalwa Sangye. Ordained in the Dharma, Your devotion towards your masters is supreme and your actions are a glorious display of purity, discipline, wisdom and compassion.

I pray at your feet Kunga Nyingpo. You are the source of all that is good, the embodiment of all Buddhas and the sole refuge for all beings, a protector from samsara and nirvana.

I pray to you Chalongwa. Wish-fulfilling tree of the Dharma. Your speech blossoms like flowers and new followers delight in your teachings like bees to pollen.

I pray to you Gawi Chöpel. Your mastery of speech is limitless and your appearance is perfect. You are the source of all supreme qualities as your moral conduct is sublime and your knowledge is unsurpassed like a great treasure.

I pray to you Trinley Namgyal. Your wisdom shines like Manjushri, embodying the wisdom of countless Buddhas. You are a treasure of compassion, the power of all the enlightened ones.

I now pray to all of my precious teachers who have bestowed upon me transmissions, empowerments and teachings, whoever even remembers you will be released from suffering, and whoever has devotion will surely reach enlightenment.

(Visualise your root lama melting into light and blessing your mindstream.)

(iii) Writer's Homage

OM GURU BUDDHA BODHISATTVA BHAYANA NAMO NAMAH
I pay homage to the lama who generously bestows the wish-fulfilling jewel of Dharma for all beings.

(This section is not usually recited.)

III. Full Invocation of the Jonang-Shambhala Lineage

(i) Visualisation

In the space immediately in front of you, in the centre of a five-coloured display of rainbow light and on top of a five-layered seat made from a lotus and moon, sun, Rahu and Kalagni discs, visualise your root lama in the form of blue Vajradhara seated upon a throne.

Your root lama appears as Vajradhara, his body is blue in colour, with one face and two arms, holding a vajra and bell crossed at the level of his heart. He is seated with his legs in the full lotus posture, dressed in silk garments, adorned by precious ornaments such as a crown, earrings, necklaces, armlets, bracelets and anklets, and possessing all the marks and signs of a Buddha.

He is surrounded by all the lineage masters of the Six Vajra Yogas, including the immaculate Primordial Buddha, the enjoyment body Kalachakra, the emanation body Shakyamuni, the thirty-five Dharma Kings of Shambhala, and all the Indian and Tibetan lineage masters. Their bodies appear radiant, splendid and pleasing.

(ii) Invocation

I pay homage and pray to my root lama. I pray to the root and lineage lamas.
I pray to the wish-fulfilling lineage.

Please bless me so the lineage transmission will enter within me.
May all these blessings enter my heart!
Please bless me so the darkness in my heart be cleared away!

I pray to the lama.
I pray to the lord of Dharma.
May all the spiritual fathers and their heart-sons bless me!

I pray to the Tathagatagarbha, the essence of the primordial ground.
I pray to the profound Kalachakra vajra path.
I pray to the unveiled dharmakaya body of the reality of enlightenment, the result of the exhaustion of samsara.

I pray to the sublime primordial Buddha.
I pray to the dharmakaya body of the reality of enlightenment Vajradhara.
I pray to the sambhogakaya enjoyment body Kalachakra.
I pray to the nirmanakaya emanation body, Buddha Shakyamuni.
I pray to the thirty-five Dharma Kings of Shambhala.

I pray to the Drupchen Dushapa Chenpo.
I pray to the Drupchen Dushapa Nyipa.
I pray to Gyaltse Nalendrapa.
I pray to Panchen Dawa Gonpo.

I pray to the great translator Droton Lotsawa.
I pray to Lama Lhaje Gompa.
I pray to Lama Droton Namseg.

I pray to the Lama Drupchen Yumo.
I pray to Seachok Dharmeshvara.
I pray to Khipa Namkha Öser.
I pray to Machig Tulku Jobum.

I pray to Lama Drubtop Sechen.
I pray to the Chöje Jamyang Sarma.
I pray to Kunkyen Chöku Öser.

I pray to Kunpang Thukje Tsondru.
I pray to Jangsem Gyalwa Yeshe.
I pray to Khetsun Yonten Gyatso.

I pray to Kunkyen Dolpopa, emanation of the Buddhas of the three times.
I pray to the Chogyal Choklé Namgyal.
I pray to Tsungmed Nyabon Kunga.

I pray to Drupchen Kunga Lodrö.
I pray to Jamyang Konchog Zangpo.
I pray to Drenchog Namkha Tsenchan.
I pray to the Panchen Namkha Palzang.

I pray to Lochen Ratnabhadra.
I pray to Palden Kunga Drolchok.
I pray to Kenchen Lungrig Gyatso.

I pray to Kyabdak Drolway Gonpo.
I pray to Ngonjang Rinchen Gyatso.
I pray to Khidrup Lodrö Namgyal.
I pray to Drupchen Ngawang Trinlé.

I pray to Ngawang Tenzin Namgyal.
I pray to Ngawang Khetsun Dargyé.
I pray to Kunzang Trinlé Namgyal.
I pray to Nuden Lhundrub Gyatso.

I pray to Konchog Jigmé Namgyal.
I pray to Ngawang Chöpel Gyatso.
I pray to Ngawang Chökyi Pakpa.
I pray to Ngawang Chöjor Gyatso.

I pray to Ngawang Chözin Gyatso.
I pray to Ngawang Tenpa Rabgyé.
I pray to the dispeller of darkness, the precious Lama Lobsang Trinley.
I pray to the Dharma warrior Khentrul Jamphal Lodrö.

I pray to my primary root lama.
I pray to my glorious lama.
I pray to all the Dharma lords.

May all the spiritual fathers and their heart-sons bless me!
Whoever honours and has life-long devotion to the precious lama,
Constantly makes supplication and pays homage to the lama in this life.
May I be blessed with the primordial wisdom of the compassionate warrior.

In all my future lives may I never be separated from my glorious lama.
May I have great joy in my practice of the precious Dharma.
May I accomplish all enlightened paths and swiftly attain the state of Vajradhara!

(Be resolute that the lamas of the holy lineage melt into light and bless your mindstream.)

PART TWO: INNER PRELIMINARIES

I. Refuge & Prostrations

(i) Visualisation

To take refuge, which is the foundation of all Dharma practice, first go to an isolated or quiet location and place the mind in its natural state, relaxed and focused. Visualise the space in front of you as a pure or enlightened realm, vast and expansive. In the centre of this realm is a great palace made of various precious substances and adorned with stunning jewels and ornaments. In the centre of the palace is an enormous wish-fulfilling tree with its vast draping branches and beautiful leaves, flowers and fruit radiating throughout the palace. At the top of this tree is a magnificent throne supported by lions. Upon this throne is a multi-coloured lotus, with sun, moon, rahu and kalagni discs. One's root lama is seated upon the throne in the form of blue Vajradhara; he holds a vajra and bell crossed at the level of his heart. Primordial Buddha sits at the root lama's crown.

Surrounding your vajra master, in the branches of the tree, are all the lineage lamas, the thirty-five Dharma Kings of Shambhala and the Yidam deities of Highest Yoga Tantra, such as Kalachakra. Surrounding them are the Yidam deities of the four classes of tantras. Buddha Shakyamuni sits below the Yidam deities. To his right side, upon the branches of the tree, is the Mahayana Arya Sangha of Eight Bodhisattvas, including Maitreya, Manjushri and Avalokiteshvara. To his left side is the Hinayana Arya Sangha of shravakas and pratyekas, such as Shariputra. At the base of this tree is an ocean of dakinis and Dharma protectors endowed with the divine eye, who guard the precious teachings. They abide in a manner protecting you. Behind the branches, the holy Dharma appears as precious golden texts.

Be resolute that everything you visualise actually is like this. At the same time, be resolute that you take refuge on behalf of all sentient beings, with great longing and devotion towards the lama, the Three Jewels and the ocean of spiritual protection. Then pray with strong compassion and resolute intention to liberate all beings, passionately wishing that they find protection from the sufferings of samsara.

(While holding this visualisation as best you can, recite the long refuge prayer once and then repeat the short refuge prayer three or more times while making full prostrations. Full prostrations are only required while Refuge is your main practice.)

(ii) Long Refuge Prayer

For the sake of all mother-like beings as limitless as space, from now until I reach the essence of enlightenment I take refuge in the noble root and lineage lords of Dharma, the glorious pure lamas, who embody the body, speech, mind, qualities and actions of the Buddhas of the three times and the ten directions, and are the source of the 84,000 Dharmas and kings of the noble Arya Sangha.

(iii) Short Refuge Prayer

I take refuge in the Dharma lords, the glorious lamas.
I take refuge in the enlightened mandala of yidams.
I take refuge in the bhagavans, the perfect Buddhas.
I take refuge in the immaculate holy Dharma.
I take refuge in the noble Arya Sangha.
I take refuge in the dakinis and all-seeing Dharma protectors.

(To be recited three times or more if you are focusing on Refuge practice.)

I pay homage and take refuge in the lama and the precious Three Jewels.
Please bless my mind-stream! (3x)

(When Refuge is your main practice, once recitation and prostrations are complete, visualise the objects of Refuge melting into light and dissolving

into your mindstream like water being poured into water. Be resolute that you become inseparable from the Refuge field. If Refuge practice is not your primary practice, continue to hold the Refuge visualisation as you move on.)

(iv) Dedication

Through the power of this virtue, May I complete the accumulation of merit and wisdom and so attain the two kayas of enlightenment for the sake of all beings.

II. Generating the Mind of Enlightenment

(i) Visualisation

While visualising the Refuge field in front of you, generate great Bodhicitta from your heart to liberate all sentient beings on behalf of the Refuge field.

(ii) Aspiring Bodhicitta

For the liberation of all beings, I will reach the state of complete Buddhahood; I shall therefore meditate on the profound vajrayoga path.

(To be repeated three or more times.)

(iii) Engaging Bodhicitta

Having generated the mind of enlightenment, now expand it to include all beings without exception.

May all beings have happiness and the causes of happiness.
May all beings be free from suffering and the causes of suffering.
May all beings never be separated from the sublime happiness
that is free from suffering.
May all beings abide in the great equanimity
free from attachment and aversion.

(This prayer is repeated one or three times, or more if you are focusing on Bodhicitta practice.)

(iv) Taking the Bodhisattva Vows

If you would like to renew your Bodhisattva pledges, recite the following verse from Shantideva's "Bodhisattva's Way of Life":

Just as the sugatas of former ages,
Aroused bodhicitta and then, in stages,
Trained themselves in skilful practice,
On the genuine path of the bodhisattvas,

Like them, I take this sacred vow:
To arouse bodhicitta here and now,
And train myself for others' good,
Gradually, as a bodhisattva should.

(Repeat this verse three times, and then develop the certainty that you have generated the Bodhisattva Vow.)

(v) Dedication

Dissolve the Refuge field while meditating upon the profound meaning of the Bodhicitta verses. At the end of the session dedicate the virtue of your practice using whatever dedication prayer you choose.

III. Vajrasattva Purification

(i) Visualisation

First recite:

OM SVABHAVA SHUDDHA SARVA DHARMA SVABHAVA SHUDDHO HAM
All phenomena including oneself enter the natural state of emptiness.

From the natural state of emptiness, above my crown, the syllable PAM (པཾ) appears which transforms into an eight-petalled white lotus flower.

The syllable AH (ཨཿ) appears on top of the lotus flower and transforms into a full moon disc. On top of the moon disc appears the syllable HUNG (ཧཱུྃ) that transforms into a white five-pronged vajra with a HUNG (ཧཱུྃ) syllable at its hub.

This HUNG (ཧཱུྃ) radiates luminous light to all universes and makes limitless offerings to all Arya beings. The light then radiates to all beings and purifies their negativities and obscurations. It then returns and dissolves into the syllable HUNG (ཧཱུྃ) and the white five-pronged vajra then completely melts into light.

The light transforms instantly into Vajrasattva, with a white body, one face and two arms, holding a vajra in his right hand and a bell in his left. He embraces his consort Vajratopa in Yab-yum.

Vajratopa is white in colour, holding a curved knife in her right hand and a skull cup in her left. They are both adorned with bone and jewel ornaments and sit respectively with legs crossed in the vajra and lotus postures.

At the Yab-yum's forehead the syllable OM (ཨོཾ) appears; at the throat, AH (ཨཿ); at the heart, HUNG (ཧཱུྃ); and at the navel, HO (ཧོཿ). From the HUNG (ཧཱུྃ) at the Yab-yum's heart, light radiates outward to the ten directions and the purification power of all the Buddhas and bodhisattvas radiates back in the form of white nectar.

DZA (ཛཿ) HUNG (ཧཱུྃ) VAM (བཾ) HO (ཧོཿ)
The nectar now becomes inseparable from Vajrasattva Yab-yum.

(ii) Request for Purification

Vajrasattva Yab-yum, please purify and cleanse all negativities, obscurations and transgressions accumulated by myself and all beings since beginningless time.

(iii) The Actual Purification

Visualise blissful nectar flowing from the union of Vajrasattva Yab-yum into the crown of your head, pushing sickness and defilements out of your body and into the ground below. As the nectar clears away all negativities, bring to mind the four powers and recite the following mantra:

OM SHRI VAJRA HERUKA SAMAYA MANUPALAYA | VAJRA HERUKA TENOPA | TISHTHA DRIDHO ME BHAVA | SUTO-KAYO ME BHAVA | ANURAKTO ME BHAVA | SUPOKAYO ME BHAVA | SARVA SIDDHI MAME PRAYATSA | SARVA KARMA SU TSA ME | TSITAM SHREYANG KURU HUNG | HA HA HA HA HO | BHAGAVAN VAJRA HERUKA MAME MUNTSA | HERUKA BHAVA MAHA SAMAYA SATTVA AH HUM PHET

(This mantra is recited one, three, seven or twenty-one times, or as much as you can if you are focusing on this practice. Conclude with the prayer that follows.)

Great protector, due to ignorance and confusion I have broken my samaya and let them decline. Compassionate Lama Vajrasattva Yab-yum, please purify my negativities and protect me. In you I take refuge, supreme Vajra holder, treasure of compassion and rescuer of all beings.

I confess and repent all transgressions of my body, speech and mind, including all breaches of my root and branch vows. Please purify and cleanse all stains, negativities, obscurations, and transgressions amassed throughout beginningless cyclic existence.

As if the moon were melting into me, Vajrasattva Yab-yum looks down at me with a smile and begins to melt with joy, dissolving through the crown of my head. The body, speech and mind of Vajrasattva Yab-yum becomes inseparable from my own body, speech and mind.

(iv) Dedication

Through this virtue may I quickly reach the enlightened state of Vajrasattva Yab-yum and lead all beings without exception to this ground of purity. Through this virtue may all beings complete the accumulation of merit and primordial wisdom and so attain the two kayas of enlightenment.

IV. Mandala Offering

(i) Visualisation

In the space immediately in front of you, visualise your root lama in the form of blue Vajradhara. He is surrounded by the Three Jewels, yidam deities and dakinis. They appear unfabricated and magnificent.

(ii) Invoking the Field of Merit

You are the jewel-like lama, the one whose kindness leads to the dawning of great bliss in a single instant. I bow at your lotus feet, Lama Vajradhara.

I pay homage to the lama for whom my gratitude is beyond compare. The light of your enlightened truth dispels my darkness. You are the faultless wisdom eye, the sun-like lama of great immutable bliss.

You are our mother and father. You are the master of all beings, a true and noble friend. You are the great protector who acts for the benefit of all sentient beings. You are the great rescuer who steals away negative obscurations. You are the one who abides in excellence, you are the sole abode of all supreme qualities, completely free from all faults. You are the protector of the lowly, the supreme conqueror of self-cherishing and suffering; The source of all wealth, the wish-fulfilling jewel, the supreme victorious Dharma Lord; in you I take refuge.

In you I take refuge, immaculate and holy root lama, supreme victorious Dharma Lord. Embodiment of the Buddhas of the three times.

(This verse is a shortened version of the previous three verses and may be used on its own.)

(iii) Medium-length Mandala Offering

OM VAJRA BHUMI AH HUNG.
The foundation is the pure mighty golden earth.

OM VAJRA REKHE AH HUNG.
The universe is encircled by a great iron fence of mountains and in the centre is Mount Meru, the king of mountains.

To the east is Purvavideha, to the south is Jambudvipa, to the north is Uttarakuru and to the west is Aparagodaniya. Rahu, Sun, Moon, Kalagni, and in the middle the total wondrous possessions of humans and gods, complete and lacking nothing.

All this wealth I offer with great devotion to my immaculate root and lineage lamas, And to the mandala of yidams, Buddhas, bodhisattvas, pratyekas, shravakas, dakinis and all-seeing Dharma protectors. Out of compassion accept this mandala for the sake of all beings and having accepted this offering, please bless me!

Recollecting the virtue of body, speech and mind gathered by myself and all beings during the three times, together with the collection of excellent Samantabhadra offerings in this precious mandala; both real and visualised, I offer this all to my lama and the Three Jewels. Please accept this with your compassion and bless me!

(iv) Brief Mandala Offering

This is an alternative briefer form of the mandala offering, which can be used for accumulations.

The ground is anointed with perfume and strewn with flowers. Its centre is adorned with Mount Meru, surrounded by the four continents, the Sun and the Moon. This I offer as a buddha-field for all beings to enjoy.

GURU IDAM RATNA MANDALA KAM NIRYA TAYAMI

(Reciting this, offer the mandala.)

At the completion of a Mandala session, visualise the Mandala and Refuge field dissolving into light and pouring into your mindstream.

V. Foundation Guru Yoga

(i) Visualisation

Visualise yourself in a magnificent vast palace in the centre of a pure realm. Your vajra master appears in front of you, in the centre of the palace, as Lord Vajradhara. He is seated upon a lotus, with sun, moon, rahu and kalagni discs* which rest upon a lion throne.

Your vajra master has a body blue in colour, with one face and two arms, holding a vajra and bell crossed at the level of his heart. His legs are in full lotus posture. Adorned with silk garments and jewel ornaments, with marks and signs complete, his body is radiant and luminous. He smiles down upon you, pleased with you.

Lord Vajradhara is surrounded by the deities of the four classes of Tantra, all lineage lamas and the entire assembly of yidam deities, buddhas, bodhisattvas, shravakas, pratyekas, dakinis and Dharma protectors. Be confident that all of them are actually present.

Having visualised the field of assembly, make great offerings, both actual and visualised. As you begin to practice you should have confident faith that you possess Buddha-nature and that it can be uncovered through sincere unwavering devotion to your immaculate root lama.

*(*Although rahu and kalagni discs do not appear in the original text, they have been added here for the sake of consistency and to reflect traditional pith instruction.)*

(ii) Prayers to the Lineage Masters

Kind and precious root lama, everything good and virtuous in samsara and nirvana has arisen from your enlightened power. My protector, a wish-fulfilling source, I pray to you from the depths of my heart.

I pray to the all-pervasive truth body of great bliss, the primordial Buddha Vajradhara who abides in Akanishta.
I pray to Kalachakra the enjoyment body.
I pray to Buddha Shakyamuni the emanation body, the highest of the Shakyas.
I pray to my lama who embodies the four buddha-kayas.

I pray to the Dharma Kings, translators and panditas: The thirty-five Shambhala Kings, emanations of the victorious ones, The two Kalachakrapada, the Older and Younger, and the two unsurpassed scholars, Nalendrapa and Somonatha.

I pray to the three lamas who attained supreme siddhis: Protector of all beings Konchoksung, Great and accomplished meditator Droton Namseg, Great Mahasiddha Drupchen Yumo Chöki Rachen, great trumpeter of the Dharma.

I pray to the three wondrous sources of refuge: Nirmanakaya Seachok Dharmeshvara the greatest son, Flawless Dharma scholar Khipa Namkha Oser, Master of magical powers and clairvoyance, Semochen.

I pray to the three supreme rescuers: Dispeller of darkness Jamsar Sherab, All-knowing Kunkhyen Chöku Öser, The one who perfected immutable bliss, Kunpang Thukje Tsundu.

I pray to the three incomparable lamas: Conqueror of great wisdom Jangsem Gyalwa Yeshe, Ocean of great qualities Khetsun Zangpo, Omniscient Buddha of the three times Dolpopa.

I pray to the three roots of living Dharma: All-triumphant Choklé Namgyal, Universal source of joy Nyabonpa, Treasury of knowledge and compassion, Kunga Lodrö.

I pray to the three wondrous lamas: Embodiment of the Three Jewels Trinlé Zangpo, Protector of the definitive all-expansive Dharma Nyeton Damcho, Great master of sutra and tantra Namkha Palzangpo.

I pray to the three who accomplished unsurpassable benefit for others: Great translator Ratnabhadra, Source of joy for all beings Lama Kunga Drolchok, Witness of the true unborn meaning Lungrig Gyatso.

I pray to the three with unequalled kindness: Great liberator Drolway Gonpo, Treasure of ocean-like qualities Kunga Rinchen, Embodiment of all holy beings Khidrup Namgyal.

I pray to the three holders of the treasury of holy teachings: Master of speech Thugye Trinlé, Victorious one Tenzin Chogyur, Ornament of Dharma practice Ngawang Chöjor.

I pray to the three lamas who effortlessly accomplish holy activities: Ornament of perfect conduct Trinlé Namgyal, Great treasure and siddha of Dharma Chökyi Peljor, Holder of perfect pith instructions Gyalwe Tsenchang.

I pray to the three lamas who liberate beings by sound and sight: Quintessence of the Three Jewels Jigme Namgyal, Embodiment of all saviours Chöpel Gyatso, One who attained the body of union of enlightenment Chözin Gyatso.

I pray to the three ornaments of the sacred Dharma: Expounder of the golden Dharma Tenpa Rabgye, Incomparable wisdom in holy activities Lobsang Trinlé, Flourishing in the continent with the wisdom of Manjushri, Jamphel Lodrö.

(iii) Seven-limb Prayer & Supplication

I prostrate with body, speech and mind to you, ultimate, unfailing, and eternal refuge. I offer limitless clouds of offerings, both real and mentally generated. I confess all my negativities and transgressions amassed since beginningless time. I rejoice in all virtue within samsara and nirvana. I pray that you turn the wheel of Dharma unceasingly. I implore you to remain with us without passing into parinirvana. May all virtue be dedicated so that myself and all others swiftly attain supreme enlightenment!

This seven-branch prayer was composed by Vakindadharma.

I pray to my precious glorious lama, lord of Dharma
and embodiment of all the Buddhas.
I pray to my precious glorious lama, lord of Dharma
possessing the four Buddha-kayas.
I pray to my precious glorious lama, lord of Dharma,
my unequalled ultimate refuge.
I pray to my precious glorious lama, lord of Dharma,
my unequalled ultimate rescuer.
I pray to my precious glorious lama, lord of Dharma,
who teaches the supreme path to liberation.
I pray to my precious glorious lama, lord of Dharma,
the source of all sublime attainments.
I pray to my precious glorious lama, lord of Dharma,
who clears away the darkness of ignorance.

Please bestow empowerment upon me!
Please bless me with the power to engage in the practice with complete dedication!

May all obstacles be cleared away so I may dedicate my life to the practice!
May I experience the essence of the practice!
May my practice reach the ultimate perfection!
May I naturally emanate love, compassion and Bodhicitta!
May I unite perfect concentration and insight!
May I attain true experience and supreme realisation of the Dharma!
May I perfect the practice of the profound vajrayoga path!
May I be empowered with the siddhis of the great seal in this single lifetime.

(iv) Receiving the Four Empowerments

From the syllable OM (ཨོཾ) at the forehead of my root lama, the great Vajradhara, white light streams forth and dissolves into my forehead chakra, purifying negativities and obscurations of the body. May I receive the vase empowerment and be blessed by the enlightened body!

From the syllable AH (ཨཱཿ) at the lama's throat, red light streams forth and dissolves into my throat chakra, purifying negativities and obscurations of speech. May I receive the secret empowerment and be blessed by the enlightened speech!

From the syllable HUNG (ཧཱུྃ) at the lama's heart, dark-blue light streams forth and dissolves into my heart chakra, purifying negativities and obscurations of mind. May I receive the wisdom empowerment and be blessed by the enlightened mind!

From the syllable HO (ཧོཿ) at the lama's navel, yellow light streams forth and dissolves into my navel chakra, purifying all propensities of conceptual thought and attachment. May I attain the sacred fourth empowerment; May I be imprinted with the four Buddha-kayas and blessed by the indestructible primordial wisdom!

Dissolve the entire visualisation as you recite the following verse:

The lama melts into light and dissolves into me. My own mind becomes inseparable with the dharmakaya mind of the lama. May I remain effortlessly in this non-conceptual, uncontrived state.

(Try to remain in this state beyond all ordinary concepts for as long as you can.)

(v) Dedication

May I become just like you, glorious root and lineage lamas.
May my followers, life-span, noble title and pure realm become just like yours!

Through the power of my prayers to you, may all disease, poverty and conflict be pacified wherever we might be!
May the precious Dharma and everything auspicious increase throughout the universe!

PART THREE: UNIQUE KALACHAKRA PRELIMINARIES AND MAIN PRACTICE

I. Innate Kalachakra Practice

(i) Visualisation

Having first established the mind of Refuge and Bodhicitta earlier in your practice, recite:

OM SHUNYATA JNANA VAJRA SVABHAVA ATMAKO HAM
OM, I consist of the nature of the awareness vajra of emptiness.

Arising from emptiness, I instantly and spontaneously appear as Innate Kalachakra. I appear upon a cushioned floor formed by a lotus and moon, sun, Rahu and Kalagni* discs, which lies upon the summit of Mount Meru and the universe of four elements. My body is blue in colour, with one face, two arms and three eyes. I embrace the consort Vishvamata and I hold a vajra and bell at my chest.

* *Although Kalagni does not appear in the original text, it has been included here for the sake of consistency and there is no clear explanation or reason why it should not be part of the visualization.*

My white left leg is drawn in and tramples the heart of the white creation god. My red right leg is extended and tramples the heart of the red desire god. My head is adorned with a topknot of plaited locks, a wish-fulfilling jewel and a crescent moon.

I am wearing vajra ornaments and a lower garment of tiger skin. My fingers are of five different colours and the three joints of each finger are also of different colours. Vajrasattva is seated upon the crown of my head, and I stand in the centre of a burning ring of flames of five different colours. My facial expression shows a mixture of wrath and passion.

I am embraced by Vishvamata who has a body yellow in colour, with one face, two arms and three eyes. She holds a curved knife in her right hand and a skull cup in her left. With her right leg drawn in and her left leg extended, we are standing together in union. She is naked and adorned with the five bone ornaments. Half of her hair is tied in a topknot and the rest is falling loose.

At the forehead of my Yab-yum appears the syllable OM (ཨོཾ); at the throat, AH (ཨཱཿ); at the heart, HUNG (ཧཱུྃ); at the navel, HO (ཧོཿ); at the secret place, SVA (སྭ); and on the crown, HA (ཧཱ).

Rays of light emanate outward from my heart transforming the entire universe into a Buddha-field, and all beings into innumerable deities of the Kalachakra mandala.

(You can keep the mind focused single-pointedly upon this visualisation for as long as you wish.)

(ii) Mantra Repetition and Dissolution

Having stabilised the visualisation of Innate Kalachakra, visualise the Kalachakra mantra symbol at your heart upon a lotus, moon disc, sun disc, Rahu disc and Kalagni disc. Then recite the mantra while visualising the mantra symbol.

The mantra is visualised as OM (ཨོཾ), then there is a blue HA (ཧ), a green KSHA (ཀྵ), a multi-coloured MA (མ), a yellow LA (ལ), a white VA (ཝ), a red RA (ར), and a black YA (ཡ). At the top is a white crescent moon with a red sun on it and a dark purple nadu (like a small flame) arising from the sun.

OM HA KSHA MA LA VA RA YANG (SVAHA)
(Recite the mantra for as long as you like.)

The entire visualisation then melts into light and dissolves into me.

(iii) Dedication

By the power of this virtue, May I swiftly attain the state of Kalachakra, and lead all beings to Kalachakra enlightenment!

"The Divine Ladder —Preliminary and Main Practices of the Profound Kalachakra Vajrayoga", composed by Drolway Gonpo (Taranatha), describes how the great Jonangpa tantric lineage masters and their heart-sons practised, and includes the essence of all the pure lineage instructions.

II. Aspiration to Accomplish the Six Vajra Yogas

OM AH HUM HO HANG KYA

Through the power of Buddha-nature, may I cut the conceptual movement of my mind. May I experience the ten signs and clear-light mind, and attain the path of Withdrawal Yoga. I pray to my saviours, my kind lama and the heirs of the holy lineage. Bless me so that this is accomplished!

Through the power of Buddha-nature, may my speech, inner wind and consciousness become unwavering. May my wisdom increase, along with the joy and bliss of analysis, and may I attain the path of Stabilisation Yoga. I pray to my saviours, my kind lama and the heirs of the holy lineage. Bless me so that this is accomplished!

Through the power of Buddha-nature, may the ten winds of lalana and rasana enter avadhuti. May I experience the blazing fire of tummo and the melting and descent of the crown essence HANG (ཧཱཾ). May I thus attain the path of the Life-Force Yoga. I pray to my saviours, my kind lama and the heirs of the holy lineage. Bless me so that this is accomplished!

Through the power of Buddha-nature, may the white essence be retained and stabilised at my forehead. May I experience unchanging bliss as the essences melt, and attain the path of Retention Yoga. I pray to my saviours, my kind lama and the heirs of the holy lineage. Bless me so that this is accomplished!

Through the power of Buddha-nature, may all my chakras and channels be filled with the pure essence of great bliss. May I attain mastery of the three glorious consorts, and attain the path of Recollection Yoga. I pray to my saviours, my kind lama and the heirs of the holy lineage. Bless me so that this is accomplished!

Through the power of Buddha-nature, may the six chakras of my subtle body be filled with the white essence of immutable great bliss. May I experience the unshakeable non-dualistic mind and attain the path of Absorption Yoga. I pray to my saviours, my kind lama and the heirs of the holy lineage. Bless me so that this is accomplished!

Through the power of Buddha-nature, may my body never be separated from the yogic postures, may my mind never be separated from the profound pith instructions of unmistaken Dharma, and may I accomplish the path of the Six Vajra Yogas. I pray to my saviours, my kind lama and the heirs of the holy lineage. Bless me so that this is accomplished!

III. Dedication

Through this virtue, may all beings abandon the meaningless concerns of samsara, may they meditate upon the supremely meaningful vajrayoga path and swiftly unveil the enlightenment of Kalachakra!

Through this virtue, may I swiftly attain the Six Vajra Yogas, and lead all beings without exception to the state of Kalachakra enlightenment!

Through this virtue, may all beings complete the accumulation of merit and primordial wisdom, and so attain the two Buddha-kayas!

PART FOUR: TWO ADDITIONAL GURU YOGAS

I. Dolpopa Guru Yoga: Rain of Blessings for the Six Yogas of the Vajra Lineage

(i) Visualisation

Kunkyen Dolpopa appears in front of you in the form of blue Vajradhara surrounded by the entire field of merit. Looking in your direction, his gaze is filled with great love.

NAMA SHRI KALACHAKRAYA
I go for refuge with vivid faith in the lama, yidam and the Three Jewels.
(Repeat the above line three times.)

May I generate immeasurable love, compassion, joy and equanimity towards all beings!
May I diligently practise the profound path of guru yoga
for the sake of all beings!
May all impure, temporary appearances dissolve into emptiness.

Seated on a throne on top of my crown, upon a five-layered seat of a lotus, moon disc and so forth, my root lama appears as the great Vajradhara. His body is blue in colour and has one face and two arms.

He is seated in a full lotus posture. He is draped in elegant silk garments and his body is adorned with precious jewels and bone ornaments. He holds a vajra and bell crossed at his heart.

The four centres of his body are marked with four syllables, light rays emanate outwards from the syllable HUNG (ཧཱུྃ) at his heart, invoking all the root and lineage lamas together with the entire field of refuge,

DZA (ཛཿ) HUNG (ཧཱུྃ) VAM (བྃ) HO (ཧོཿ)
Becoming inseparable from them.

(ii) Supplicating the Lama

Precious lama, I pay homage to your body, speech and mind. Your body is adorned with unchanging, perfect marks and signs. Your uninterrupted Brahma-like speech pervades the ten directions. You abide in the unmistaken mind of the great seal.

I prostrate to you who is the embodiment of the thirty-six Tathagatas, unveiled when the thirty-six aggregates are perfectly purified through the six vajra yogas such as withdrawal and so forth.

I offer with joy and pure intention an inconceivable ocean of Samantabhadra offerings, including all virtues of body, speech and mind gathered during the three times!

I openly confess all my negativities amassed through body, speech and mind, and pray that they be purified. I rejoice in all virtue! I wholeheartedly request that you turn the wheel of Dharma without ceasing! I implore you to remain forever in samsara for the sake of all beings!

I pray to my glorious lama. Your nature is inseparable from the four Buddha-kayas. You are the chief of all vajra holders, having completed the three accumulations and attained the twelve paths. Please bless me!

I pray to my glorious lama. You have fully realised the five wisdoms, and have completely transformed the eight objects of dualistic conception By abiding for a single moment in non-dual primordial awareness. Please bless me!

I pray to my glorious lama. Your enlightened activity is one with the activity of all the lamas, liberating and maturing fortunate disciples through the twelve empowered attainments of the generation and completion stages. Please bless me!

I pray to the glorious lama. You are one with all the yidams, your aggregates are the six Buddha-families, your consciousnesses are the eight bodhisattvas, your arms, legs and so forth are the assembly of wrathful deities. Please bless me!

I pray to the glorious lama. You are one with all the Buddhas, your nature is the magnificent body of truth, you have perfected the two accumulations and manifest countless emanations for the benefit of beings. Please bless me!

I pray to the glorious lama. You are one with all immaculate Dharmas, You manifest as the teachings and texts of ultimate meaning, You lead us to the inexpressible profound truth. Please bless me!

I pray to the glorious lama. You are one with all the great lords of the Arya Sangha who abide in the ten bodhisattva levels, having attained complete liberation and accomplishment; You are the immaculate virtuous friend, a refuge for all beings. Please bless me!

I pray to the glorious lama. You are one with all the Dharma protectors who destroy all enemies and obstacles through the power of your non-dual compassion. Please bless me!

I pray to the glorious lama. You are the origin of all siddhis, bestower of both supreme and common accomplishments, as you have mastered the actions of pacifying, expanding, controlling and subduing. Please bless me!

I pray to the glorious lama. You dispel all darkness as you clear away wrong views by composing, debating and explaining the sutras, tantras, treatises and pith instructions. Please bless me!

By drinking the nectar of his precious Dharma instruction on the profound meaning, from this day onwards may I follow the lama like a shadow. May my glorious lama bless me so that this is accomplished!

Without consideration for food, clothing and luxuries, having abandoned wrong and impure livelihoods, may I taste the nectar of Dharma with the tip of my tongue. May my glorious lama bless me so that this is accomplished!

From this day onwards may I remain in an isolated place, meditating single-pointedly upon the profound meaning, so I may reach the great seal of liberation in this very lifetime. May my glorious lama bless me so that this is accomplished!

May I see the four syllables at the chakras of the lama's body
as the four Buddha-kayas.
May I receive the four empowerments by focusing upon them.
May my glorious lama bless me so that this is accomplished!

(iii) Receiving the Four Empowerments

From the OM (ཨོཾ) at my lama's forehead, a white OM (ཨོཾ) streams forth and dissolves into my own forehead chakra. Through this power may I receive the vase empowerment. May my glorious lama bless me so that this is accomplished!

Through this power may I purify the obscurations of the body and waking state, experience the four joys and unveil the vajra emanation body. May my glorious lama bless me so that this is accomplished!

From the AH (ཨཱཿ) at my lama's throat, a red AH (ཨཱཿ) streams forth and dissolves into my own throat chakra. Through this power may I receive the secret empowerment. May my glorious lama bless me so that this is accomplished!

Through this power may I purify the obscurations of speech and the dream state, experience the four excellent joys and unveil the enjoyment body of vajra speech. May my glorious lama bless me so that this is accomplished!

From the HUNG (ཧཱུྃ) at my lama's heart, a black HUNG (ཧཱུྃ) streams forth and dissolves into my own heart chakra. Through this power may I receive the primordial wisdom empowerment. May my glorious lama bless me so that this is accomplished!

Through this power may I purify the obscurations of mind and the deep sleep state, experience the four supreme joys and unveil the Dharmakaya body of vajra mind. May my glorious lama bless me so that this is accomplished!

From the HO (ཧོཿ) at my lama's navel, a yellow HO (ཧོཿ) streams forth and dissolves into my own navel chakra. Through this power may I receive the sacred fourth empowerment. May my glorious lama bless me so that this is accomplished!

Through this power may I purify the propensities of attachment, experience the four innate joys and unveil the primordial vajra wisdom of blissful emptiness. May my glorious lama bless me so that this is accomplished!

The lama at my crown melts into light and dissolves into me. He abides in the centre of an eight-petalled lotus at my heart. May my glorious lama bless me so that this is accomplished!

(Meditate on the natural state of the inseparability of your own mind and that of your lama, the great dharmakaya truth body, and remain in the non-conceptual state of dharmadhatu for as long as you can.)

(iv) Dedication

Through this practice, may all beings purify all their stains and obstacles and swiftly reach the essence of the Tathagata.

May I not give rise, even for an instant, to wrong views about the glorious Lama's liberating appearances. With a devotion that sees everything he does as excellent, may the blessings of the Lama enter my mind.

In future lives may I never be separated from my glorious lama.
May I never be separated from the joy of practicing the precious Dharma.
May I accomplish all the enlightened bhumi levels and paths and quickly attain the state of Vajradhara.

"Guru Yoga—Rain of Blessings for the Six Yogas of the Vajra Lineage" was composed by the Dharma Lord Kunkyen Dolpopa Sherab Gyaltsen. May it lead to virtue and auspiciousness!

II. Taranatha Guru Yoga: The Anchor for Collecting Siddhis

(i) Visualisation

Jetsun Taranatha appears in front of you in the form of blue Vajradhara surrounded by the entire field of merit. Looking in your direction, his gaze is filled with great love.

OM SVASTI. The Anchor for Collecting Siddhis guru yoga.

I fervently pay homage to the glorious lama. All phenomena are only appearances within the mind. One's own mind is of an empty and clear nature, beyond words. Whatever various appearances are, they are never separable from the ever present moment to moment self-awareness.

My mind in its natural state is the pure realm of Akanishta. In the centre of this pure realm is a radiant palace, and in it my glorious root lama is seated upon a lotus, sun disc and moon disc which rest upon a lion throne.

(For the sake of consistency, rahu and kalagni discs can also be visualised here.)

My glorious lama is radiant like a golden mountain reflecting a hundred-thousand rays of sunlight. He is pleased and smiles at me.

Above my lama the lineage masters miraculously appear, surrounded by herukas such as Vajravarahi and clouds of yidams. Buddhas and bodhisattvas from the ten directions appear in the space before me and glorious arhat emanations occupy the ground. They are surrounded by dakinis and all-seeing Dharma protectors with their retinues, poised to obey the lama's every instruction.

The entire assembly is in vibrant motion like lightning and storm-clouds, filling all of space and the surrounding lands. All these beings have radiant bodies; to various sentient beings who need to be tamed, their appearances vary accordingly; they ceaselessly expound the Mahayana teachings and their minds abide in the clear-light of great bliss as they perform oceans of virtuous activities.

All of this is but a meaningful manifestation of the glorious lama, just as all appearances of samsara and nirvana are but a miraculous display of the lama's primordial wisdom.

(ii) Supplicating the Lama

I offer my body, my possessions, all the virtue of the three times and every conceivable object of offering from all the pure-lands of the ten directions. I offer everything my mind can conceive with pure aspiration: All beings of the six realms including adversaries, friends and relatives, extending to the farthest reaches of space, together with every pleasing object of offering in all of the three realms. Through the power of my visualisation and prayer, I manifest all of these countless, inconceivable and magnificent objects of offering.

All these offering treasures manifest from the primordial awareness of the Buddhas, bodhisattvas and dakinis who appear in the three times and ten directions. All these innumerable and inconceivable manifestations are none other than the glorious display of the lama's mind, inseparable from my own mind, the unborn display of dharmakaya.

Precious lama, you embody all the Buddhas.
Precious lama, you embody all the Dharma.
Precious lama, you embody all the Sangha.

Supreme Dharma King, you embody all the lamas.
You embody all the yidams while all the dakinis and Dharma protectors manifest as your retinues. I pray to you Vajradhara, Please bless me and all those who have faith in you!

Glorious lama, you are Vajradhara in the pure realm of the enjoyment body. You are the wrathful Heruka when subduing all evils. You are Shakyamuni to beings with pure renunciation. You are the great sage to the ascetics.

To those who follow the path of the three vehicles, you manifest as the Bodhisattva, the Pratyeka and the great Shravaka. You also appear in the form of Brahma, Vishnu, Lord Shiva and all other sages and saints.

Sometimes you appear in the position of a king, at other times you appear as a yogi or ascetic. To others you appear as a pure monk with simple robes. I pray to you, performer of great, vast deeds according to the needs of each being. Just as the thoughts and aspirations of all beings are inconceivable, so too is the vastness and depth of your teachings.

Just as rainbows and clouds appear in the sky, arising, abiding and then vanishing back into the sky. You are the dharmakaya body of the reality of enlightenment free from all extremes, performing great deeds spontaneously and without effort. Even though you act in a way that meets the needs of all beings, you abide in a state of clear, self-aware, and non-dual expanse of dharmadhatu.

You are beyond birth and death, coming and going, near and far. I pray to you, pristine body of the reality of enlightenment. I pay homage from the depths of my heart with unceasing devotion!

I take refuge in you, embodiment of all sources of refuge.
I offer countless virtuous objects while being aware of their empty nature.
I confess and purify all my negativities even though their nature is empty from the beginning.
I rejoice in the virtue of all beings in samsara and nirvana.
May the empty sound of your teachings never cease.
The dharmakaya body of the reality of enlightenment is beyond birth and death, may you ceaselessly turn the wheel of precious Dharma.
May you remain forever for the sake of all beings.
I dedicate all my virtue so my mind may become inseparable from yours, O holy lama. May all beings attain supreme enlightenment!

Glorious Drolway Gonpo, rescuer of all beings, please bless me with your body, speech and mind. Bestow upon me the four empowerments at this very instant!

(iii) Receiving the Four Empowerments

May my body transform into innate bliss.
May my speech transform with the power of mantra.
May my heart transform into clear-light wisdom!
Perfect lama, I pray to you to bless me at this very instant.

Rays of light stream forth from the lama's forehead, throat, heart, and navel, and then dissolve into my own four chakras. Bestowing upon me the four empowerments of body, speech, mind and primordial vajra wisdom!

May I receive the vase empowerment.
May I receive the secret empowerment.
May I receive the union of great bliss and wisdom empowerment.
May I receive the sacred fourth empowerment of the great seal beyond conception!

Great Dharma King, I rely on no-one else but you.
You are my only true refuge.
Just like water poured into water,
May I dissolve into inseparable union with you!

May the lama melt into the essence of nectar and fill my four chakras, bestowing empowerment upon me.

(Meditate on the natural lama, the great dharmakaya body of the reality of enlightenment inseparable from one's own mind, and remain in this natural state beyond all concepts.)

(iv) Dedication

In all my future lives may I be born into an excellent family,
With a clear mind, lack of of pride, great compassion and faith in the Lama.
May I abide in my commitments to the Glorious Lama.

May I not give rise, even for an instant,
To wrong views about the glorious Lama's liberating appearances.
With a devotion that sees everything he does as excellent,
May the blessings of the Lama enter my mind.

In future lives may I never be separated from my glorious lama.
May I never be separated from the joy of practicing the precious Dharma.
May I accomplish all the enlightened bhumi levels and paths and quickly attain the state of Vajradhara.

This is the perfect Guru Yoga enabling you to reach Buddhahood in one lifetime. Have no doubt. Composed by Jetsun Taranatha, aged 29

APPENDIX TWO

Tibetan Text

༄༅། །ཟབ་ལམ་སྒྲོན་འགྲོའི་ཚིག་འགྲེལ་

སྒྲོན་མེད་རབ་གསལ་སྣང་བ།

ཤར་མཁན་སྤྲུལ་འཇམ་དཔལ་བློ་གྲོས་ཀྱིས།

ཛོ་ནང་སྟོང་གཟུགས་བདེ་ཆེན་སྙིང་གིས་པར་དུ་བསྐྲུན།

དཀར་ཆག

འདི་ཉིད་འབྲི་བའི་དགོས་དོན།

ཚིག་འགྲེལ་དཔེ་དེབ་འདི་འབྲི་དགོས་དོན་ནི། བོད་བརྒྱུད་ནང་བསྟན་གྱི་དགོན་སྡེ་ཁག་ཏུ་གཏོགས་པའི་གྲྭ་བཙུན་མང་པོའི་ཐོས་བསམ་སྒོམ་པའི་ཉམས་ལེན་ལ་གྲུབ་འབྲས་དམན་པ་ནི། གྲྭ་བཙུན་སྒེར་སོ་སོའི་བློ་རིག་རབ་འབྲིང་ཐ་གསུམ་ལ་ལོས་ཤིང་འཚམ་པའི་སྣ་མང་གི་སློབ་གསོའི་ལམ་རིམ་མེད་པ། དབང་པོ་ཡང་རབ་ཅན་དང་། བློ་རིག་རྩེ་ཕྱུད་ཅན། ཡང་ན་འབད་བརྩོན་ཡང་རབ་ཅན་རྣམས་ལ་གྲུབ་འབྲས་གང་ལ་གང་འཚམ་ཡོད་ཀྱང་། དབང་པོ་འབྲིང་མན་ཆད་ལ་གྲུབ་འབྲས་ཏ་ཅང་ཆུང་། ཡང་དགོས་སུ་དབང་པོ་རྟུལ་ཞན་ཅན། ཡང་ན་བློ་རིག་རྣོ་ཡང་། ཆོས་གཞུང་ལ་བློ་མི་རྐྱེན་པ་རྣམས་ལ་ཡང་དཀའ་ངལ་ཆེན་པོ་ཞིག་འཕྲད་ཀྱིན་ཡོད།

དཔལ་ལྡན་རྒྱལ་བ་རྫོང་ནང་བའི་ཆོས་བརྒྱུད་འདི་ནི་ལོ་ངོ་བརྒྱ་ཕྲག་མང་པོའི་བར་དུ་གཙོ་བོ་སྒྲུབ་པའི་ཕྱོགས་ལ་ནན་ཏན་ཅན་ཡིན། སྒྲུབ་ཕྱོགས་ནས་ཉམས་ལེན་ལ་འབད་བརྩོན་ཆེན་པོ་གནང་དུས་སུ། བཤད་ཕྱོགས་ནས་ཚིག་དོན་ཞིབ་ཕྲ་ཀུན་ལ་གོ་བ་མ་ལོན་པའི་དཀའ་ངལ་འབྱུང་སྲིད་ཅིང་འབྱུང་ངེས་པ་ཞིག་ཀྱང་རེད།

ལྷག་པར་དུ་ཟབ་ལམ་རྡོ་རྗེ་རྣལ་འབྱོར་དུ་གྲགས་པའི་དུས་འཁོར་རྫོགས་རིམ་སྦྱོར་དྲུག་གི་ཉམས་ལེན་འདི་ནི་འཛམ་གླིང་ལ་མེད་པའི་ཁྱད་ནོར་གྱི་ཟབ་ཆོས་ཞིག་ཡིན། ཆོས་འདི་ཉམས་སུ་ལེན་པ་ལ་སྔོན་འགྲོ་ངག་འདོན་འདི་ཉིད་ཉམས་ལེན་གྱི་གནད་སྙིང་དུ་གྱུར་ཡོད་པ། འདིའི་ཕྱོགས་སུ་སྤྱིར་འགྲེལ་བ་དང་ལྷན་ཐབས་སོགས་ཡོད་ཀྱང་། འདི་ལ་དབུ་ནས་མཇུག་གི་བར་དུ་ཚིག་དོན་རེ་རེ་བཞིན་འགྲེལ་ཡོད་པའི་ཚིག་འགྲེལ་ཞིག་ད་བར་དུ་མེད། ལྷག་པར་དུ་ཐ་ན་བརྒྱུད་པའི་བླ་མ་རེ་རེ་བཞིན་གྱི་རྣམ་ཐར་མཛད་བསྡུས་དང་བཅས་པ་མཐར་ཆགས་སུ་བཀོད་ཡོད་པ་ཞིག་ད་སྟོན་ཡོད་སྐྱོང་མེད་པས། བདག་བློ་ཟབ་དོན་ལ་ནང་བྱན་ཆུབ་པ་ཞིག་མིན་ཡང་། ལྷག་བསམ་རྣམ་དག་གིས་འདི་ཉིད་འབྲི་བའི་ངལ་བ་དང་དུ་བླངས་པས། རང་དང་སྐལ་མཉམ་མང་དག་ལ་ཕན་ངེས་ཡིན་པ་ནི་ཐེ་ཚོམ་མི་དགོས་པས། ཚིག་གི་ཕྲེང་ཕྱོག་རེ་རེ་བཞིན་འགྲེལ་ནས་དོན་གནད་ཁག་གཅིག་དང་

བཅས་ཀུན་གྱི་ཉམས་ལེན་ལ་གྲུབ་འབྲས་འབྱུང་ཆེད་དུ་བྲིས་པའོ།།

མཐའ་དོན་རེ་སྐུལ་ཞུ་རྒྱུ་ནི། རྒྱལ་བ་ཇོ་ནང་བའི་བསྟན་པའི་ལྷག་ཞབས་སུ་སྐྱེས་པ་ཞིག་ཡིན་ཕྱིན། ཟབ་ལམ་རྡོ་རྗེ་རྣལ་འབྱོར་འདི་ཉིད་ཉམས་ལེན་གྱི་གཙོ་གནད་དུ་མི་འཛིན་པར་བྱུང་རྒྱལ་རྟོགས་པའི་རྗེས་འབྲང་གི་རིགས་ནི། རྩ་བ་བོར་ཏེ་ཡལ་ག་ར་འཐམ་པའི་དཔེ་དང་། འཛམ་གླིང་སྤྱིའི་ཁྱད་ནོར་དང་། ལྷག་པར་དུ་རང་རེ་ཁ་བ་གངས་ཅན་པའི་གཅེས་ནོར་ལ་བདག་སྐྱོང་མི་བྱེད་པར་གང་སྐྱིགས་སུ་དོར་བ་ལས་མ་འདས་པས། འདི་ཉིད་ཉམས་ལེན་གྱི་གཙོ་གནད་དུ་འཛིན་དགོས་པ་ནི་རྩོད་བྲལ་རེད། དེའི་ཕྱིར། རང་ཅག་ཀུན་མཁྱེན་དོལ་པོ་བ་རྟོན་པ་བཞི་ལྡན་གྱི་རྗེས་འཇུག་ཡིན་པས། རྟོན་བཞི་གོ་ལོག་ཏུ་མི་འཛིན་པར། ཕྲན་གང་ཟག་ཕལ་བ་ཞིག་གིས་བྲིས་པ་རྒྱུ་མཚན་དུ་བྱས་ནས་སྣང་ཆུང་དུ་མི་འདོར་བར། ཆོས་འདི་ཟབ་ལམ་དང་འབྲེལ་བའི་དགོས་མཁོར་གཞིགས་ཏེ། ཟབ་མོའི་ཉམས་ལེན་གནད་དུ་བཟུང་ཞིང་འདི་ནས་གོམ་པ་དང་པོ་སྤོ། དཔལ་ལྡན་རྒྱལ་བ་ཇོ་ནང་བའི་བསྟན་པ་ལ་ཞབས་འདེགས་དང་། མ་འོངས་པར་རང་ཉིད་ཤམྦྷ་ལའི་རྫོགས་ལྡན་གསར་བའི་ཟབ་ཆོས་ཀྱི་དཔལ་ཡོན་ལ་རོལ་ནུས་པ་ཞིག་ཅེས་ཀྱང་བྱ་འོས་སོ།།

ཡུལ་དམ་པ་ལ་མཆོད་པར་བརྗོད་པ།

ཕྱི་དབྱིངས་འཁོར་འདས་དྭངས་མའི་གྲོང་ཁྱེར་བྱེ་བ་དགུ་བཅུའི་ཤམྦྷ་ལ།།
ནང་དབྱིངས་དྲུག་བརྒྱ་སོ་དྲུག་ལྷ་ཡི་དཀྱིལ་འཁོར་སྟོང་གཟུགས་ལོངས་སྐུའི་ཞིང་།།
གཞི་དབྱིངས་རྣམ་པ་ཀུན་ལྡན་ཆ་མེད་འཁོར་འདས་ཀུན་ཁྱབ་ཆོས་སྐུའི་དབྱིངས།།
མཛོན་བྱེད་ཟབ་ལམ་ཉག་གཅིག་རྡོ་རྗེའི་རྣལ་འབྱོར་དང་བས་ཕྱག་གིས་མཆོད།།

ཟབ་དོན་ཤེས་པ་མིན་ཡང་འདུན་པ་ཡིས།།
ཟབ་མོའི་དོན་ལ་འཇུག་པའི་རིམ་པ་ཙམ།།
གོ་སླ་ཤེས་ཐབས་ཚིག་གིས་འབྲི་སྙོན་གྱིས།།
བྲིས་པའི་ངལ་བ་བརྟེན་ལ་ནོངས་པ་ཅི།།

ཕྱི་རིག་དུས་ཀྱི་འཁོར་ལོ་འཛམ་གླིང་བྱེ་བ་ཕྲག་བརྒྱའི་ཞིང་།།
ནང་རིག་དུས་ཀྱི་འཁོར་ལོ་རྡོ་རྗེའི་རྩ་རླུང་ཐིག་ལེའི་ཁམས།།
གཞན་རིག་དུས་ཀྱི་འཁོར་ལོ་ཐུགས་གསུང་སྐུ་ཡི་དཀྱིལ་འཁོར་གསུམ།།
དབྱེར་མེད་བར་དུ་རྫོགས་ལྡན་དམ་པའི་ཆོས་ལ་སྤྱོད་ནུས་ཤོག །

ཟབ་ལམ་རྡོ་རྗེའི་རྣལ་འབྱོར་མཚམས་སྦྱོར།

ཟབ་ལམ་རྡོ་རྗེ་རྣལ་འབྱོར་དུ་གྲགས་པ་དཔལ་དུས་ཀྱི་འཁོར་ལོའི་རྫོགས་རིམ་སྦྱོར་བ་ཡན་ལག་དྲུག་ཉམས་སུ་བླང་བ་ལ། དེང་གི་ཆར་དཔལ་དུས་ཀྱི་འཁོར་ལོའི་ཉམས་ལེན་ཆ་ཚང་ཞིང་བླ་མའི་མན་ངག་དང་དབང་ལུང་གི་བྱིན་རླབས་ཀྱི་རྒྱུད་མ་ཡལ་བར་ཡོད་པ། དཔལ་རྒྱལ་བ་ཇོ་ནང་བ་ལས་ལྷག་ཅིག་འཛམ་གླིང་ཡོངས་ན་མེད་པ་ཁ་ཚོན་བཅད་ནས་བཤད་ཐུབ་པས། དེའི་ལུགས་གཙོ་བོར་བྱས་པའི་ཐུན་མོང་གི་སྔོན་འགྲོ་ལྔ་དང་། རྫོགས་རིམ་སྦྱོར་བ་ཡན་ལག་དྲུག་གི་ཐུན་མོང་མ་ཡིན་པའི་སྔོན་འགྲོ་གཉིས་བཅས་སྔོན་འགྲོ་ཆོས་བདུན་དང་། དངོས་གཞི་སྦྱོར་བ་ཡན་ལག་དྲུག་མདོར་བསྡུས་སུ་བཀོད་ཅིང་། མཁས་བླུན་བར་མ་ཀུན་གྱིས་གོ་སླ་ཞིང་སྟབས་བདེ་བ་ཞིག་འབྲི་བའི་འདུན་པ་དང་དུ་ལེན་འདོད་བྱུང་།

ལྷག་པར་དུ་ཆོས་ལ་མོས་པ་ཙམ་ཡོད་ཀྱང་། དེར་གོ་བ་དང་རྒྱུས་མངའ་ཆུང་བའི་དབང་གིས་ཚིག་དོན་མི་གོ་མཁན་དག་ལ་ཆེད་དུ་དམིགས་ཏེ། བླ་རྒྱུད་ནས་བཟུང་ཚིག་དོན་གཉིས་ཀ་འབྲི་སྣོན་ནག་འགྲོས་སུ་བྲི་བར་བྱ་བ་ལ།

དེའང་ཐོག་མར་གསང་སྔགས་ཐུན་མོང་གི་སྐྱབས་འགྲོ་ལ་སོགས་པའི་སྔོན་དུ། སྔོན་འགྲོ་བློ་ལྡོག་རྣམ་བཞིར་གྲགས་པ། མཆོག་དམན་ཀུན་གྱིས་གོ་བདེ་ཞིང་། ཚེ་འདི་ཕྱི་ཀུན་ལ་ཕན་པའི་གནས་ལུགས།

ཀུན་ལ་མེད་དུ་མི་རུང་བ་དག་གིས་མདུན་དྲངས་ཏེ་བཤད་ན་འདི་ལྟར།

བློ་ལྡོག་རྣམ་བཞི་གནད་བསྡུས།

༄༅། །ཀྱེ་མ་སེམས་དང་གྲངས་མེད་བསྐལ་པ་རུ། །རྙེད་དཀའི་དལ་འབྱོར་ལན་གཅིག་ཐོབ་པ་འདི། །རབ་ཏུ་འཇིག་སླ་འཆི་རྐྱེན་བསམ་མི་ཁྱབ། །གཅེས་སྐྱོང་ལུས་འདི་དེ་རིང་ཉིན་འཆི་སྲིད། །མི་དགེ་ལོག་ལྟོ་མཚམས་མེད་སྡུག་བསྔལ་རྒྱུ། །འཁོར་བའི་བྱ་བ་ཐམས་ཅད་སྤངས་བྱས་ནས། །ཅུང་ཟད་ལོང་ཡོད་དུས་འདིར་ལུས་ངག་ཡིད། །ཐར་བའི་ཕན་ཡོན་བསམ་ནས་ཆོས་བསྒྲུབ་འཚལ། །

ཡིད་སྐྱོ་བའམ་ཧ་ལས་པའི་དོན། ཀྱེ་མ་ཞེས་པའི་ཚིག་གིས་མདུན་དྲངས་ཏེ། སེམས་དང་ཞེས་བསམ་བློ་རྣལ་མ་ཞིག་ཐོངས་དང་། དོན་གཏིང་ཟབ་ཅིག་གོ་ཞིང་རྟོགས་རྒྱུ་ཡོད། གྲངས་མེད་བསྐལ་པ་མང་པོ་རུ་ཤིན་ཏུ་རྙེད་པར་དཀའ་ལ། རྙེད་མ་མྱོང་བའི་ལུས་རྟེན་འདི་འདྲའི་མཆོག་ཅིག་སྟེ། དམ་པའི་ཆོས་སྒྲུབ་པའི་གོ་སྐབས་དང་ནུས་པ་ཆ་ཚང་ཡོད་པའི་ལུས་རྟེན་འདི་ལྟ་བུ་ཞིག་ནི་ཤིན་ཏུ་རྙེད་དཀའི་རང་བཞིན་ཏེ། སྐྱེ་བ་སྔོན་མ་དག་ཏུ་རྒྱུ་ཚུལ་ཁྲིམས་རྣམ་པར་དག་པ་བསྲུངས་པས་མ་གཏོགས། དལ་བ་བརྒྱད་དང་འབྱོར་བ་བཅུ་ཚང་བའི་མི་ལུས་ཚད་ལྡན་འདི་མི་རྙེད། གྲོགས་སྦྱིན་པ་སོགས་དགེ་བ་མང་པོས་གྲོགས་བྱས་མེད་ན་ལུས་རྟེན་འདི་འདྲ་བ་ཞིག་མི་ཐོབ། རྐྱེན་སྨོན་ལམ་དྲི་མ་མེད་པ་མང་པོས་མཚམས་སྦྱོར་མེད་ནའང་ལུས་རྟེན་ཁྱད་པར་ཅན་འདི་འདྲ་བ་ཞིག་མི་ཐོབ། འོན་ཀྱང་ད་ལྟ་རང་ལ་ཐོབ་ཡོད་པའི་དལ་འབྱོར་གྱི་མི་ལུས་ཚད་ལྡན་འདི་ནི་ཆེས་རྙེད་པར་དཀའ་བ་ཞིག་དང་། རྙེད་ན་དོན་ཆེ་བ། ད་ཐེངས་ལན་གཅིག་མ་གཏོགས་སྐྱེ་བ་གྲངས་མེད་དུང་ཕྱུར་མང་པོའི་བར་དུ་ཐོབ་མི་ཐུབ་པ་ཞིག་རེད། དེའི་ཕྱིར། འདི་འདྲའི་དལ་བའི་རྟེན་བཟང་ནི་ཤིན་ཏུ་རྙེད་དཀའ་བ་ཞིག་དང་། རྙེད་ཟིན་པའི་རྗེས་སུ་འདི་ཉིད་རྟག་པ་དང་བརྟན་པ། མི་འགྱུར་ཞིང་ཡིད་རྟོན་རུང་བ། གཏན་གནས་ཀྱི་ངོ་བོར་ཡོད་དམ་སྙམ་ན། དེ་ཡང་རྩ་བ་ནས་མེད་པ་འདི་ལྟར།

རབ་ཏུ་འཇིག་སླ་འཆི་རྐྱེན་བསམ་མི་ཁྱབ། །
གཅེས་སྐྱོང་ལུས་འདི་དེ་རིང་ཉིན་འཆི་སྲིད། །

ད་ལྟའི་ང་ཚོའི་ལུས་རྟེན་འདི་ནི་ཤིན་ཏུ་ཤོར་སླ་ཞིང་རབ་ཏུ་འཇིག་སླ་བ་ཡིན། རྒྱུ་མཚན་ནི། འཆི་རྐྱེན་བསམ་གྱིས་མི་ཁྱབ་པ་སྣེ་ཤིན་ཏུ་མང་བས་ཡིན། དཔེར་ན་དགྲ་དང་ནད། གདོན་དང་དུག མཚོན་དང་མྱོག ཡང་ན་ཐོག་དང་སེར་བ་ལ་སོགས་པའི་འཇིགས་པ། མ་ཟད་གཟའ་གདོང་ཐུག་ཏུ་གྲགས་པ་སྙིང་རྩ་འགག་ནས་གློ་བུར་དུ་འཆི་བ་སོགས། དཔེར་ན་ནད་ཙུང་ཟད་མེད་པའི་རྣམ་པར་ཡོད་པ་དང་། ནང་སྲུང་གི་འགན་ཁུར་ལྡན་པའི་དཔུལ་དང་སྨན་ཁབ་ཡོད་པ་ཆེས་མང་པོ་ཞིག་ཀྱང་གློ་བུར་དུ་འཆི་དགོས་པ་སོགས་གྲངས་ལས་འདས་པའོ།། གསོན་པའི་རྐྱེན་ནི་ཤིན་ཏུ་ཙུང་ལ། དེའང་གསོན་རྐྱེན་དུ་སྨན་པ་དག་ཀྱང་འཆི་རྐྱེན་དུ་འགྱུར་བ་ཧ་ཅང་མང་སྟེ་དཔེར་ན། ཟས་དུག་པ། སྨན་ལོག་པ། གྲོགས་ཀྱིས་བསླུས་ནས་ཤི་བ་སོགས་ཤིན་ཏུ་མང་བ་ནི་ཤེས་སླ་མོ་ཡིན། རྒྱུ་མཚན་དེ་དག་གིས། འཁོར་བ་མི་རྟག་པའི་རང་བཞིན་དུ་གྲུབ་པ་འདིར། གནས་སྐབས་ཙམ་གྱི་རིང་དལ་ཞིང་འབྱོར་བའི་ལུས་རྟེན་འདི་ཉིད་ཀྱང་། མི་བརྟན་ཅིང་མི་རྟག་པར་ཡིད་རྟོན་མི་རུང་བའི་ངོ་བོར་གནས་ཡོད་པ་ཤེས་དགོས། རང་གིས་ཤིན་ཏུ་གཅེས་པར་སྐྱོང་བའི་ལུས་རྟེན་འདི་ཉིད་ནི། དེ་རིང་ཙམ་དུ་ཡང་མི་འཆི་བའི་གདེང་ཚོད་ཙུང་ཟད་ཀྱང་མཆོག་དམན་སུ་ལའང་མེད་པས། ཉིན་དེ་རིང་ནས་འཆི་ཚོག་ཚོག་ཏུ་གནས་ཡོད་པ་ཞིག་རེད།

མི་དགེ་ལོག་ལྟ་མཚམས་མེད་སྡུག་བསྔལ་རྒྱུ།།
འཁོར་བའི་བྱ་བ་ཐམས་ཅད་སྤྱངས་བྱས་ནས།།

དེ་འདྲའི་དོན་ཆེ་ཞིང་སྟོར་ཉེན་ཆེ་བའི་ལུས་རྟེན་ཁྱད་འཕགས་འདི་ལ་སྙིང་པོ་ཇི་ལྟར་ལེན་དགོས་སྙམ་ན་འདི་ལྟར། ཆོས་ཀྱི་གནས་ལུགས་མཐར་ཐུག བདག་མེད་པའི་དོན་མི་ཤེས་པས་མ་རིག་པས་རྒྱུ་བྱས་ནས་ཉོན་མོངས་པ་མངོན་དུ་གྱུར་བའི་དབང་གིས་ལས་བསགས་ཏེ་འཁོར་བའི་ལུས་རྟེན་ཟག་བཅས་ཉེ་བར་ལེན་པའི་ཕུང་པོ་འདི་བྱུང་། ལྷག་པར་དུ་རྒྱུ་མི་དགེ་བའི་ལས་དག་ལ་ནི་འབྲས་བུ་སྡུག་བསྔལ་ཁོ་ན་ལས་མེད་པས་དུག་ལྟར་དུ་འཛེམས་དགོས་པར་བསྟན་པ་རེད། རང་ཅག་བདག་འཛིན་ལ་སྐྱེ་བ་ཐོག་མེད་ནས་གོམས་ཡོད་ཕྱིར། རང་གི་ལུས་པོ་འདིའང་བདག་མིན་བདག་ཏུ་བཟུང་སྟེ་ཡོད་པས་གཞན་དབང་དུ་གྱུར་ཡོད། གནས་སྐབས་སུ་རང་ཅག་གི་སེམས་འདི་ད་ལྟའི་ལུས་རྟེན་འདི་ལ་གནས་བཅས་ཡོད་པས་ལུས་འདི་ཚོར་བ་རྣོན་པོས་བཅིངས་ཡོད། རང་ཅག་གི་ལུས་རྟེན་ལ་གཅེས་འཛིན་དང་ཆགས་སྲེད་ཧ་ཅང་དམ་པོ་ཞིག་ཡོད། དེའི་དབང་གིས་ལུས་རྟེན་འདི་ལ་བརྟེན་ནས་ཆགས་སྡང་མང་པོ་གསོག་གིན་ཡོད། ཡིན་ཡང་རང་ཅག་གིས་གཅེས་པར་སྐྱོང་བཞིན་པའི་ལུས་རྟེན་འདི། ཉི་མ་དེ་རིང་ཙམ་ལའང་རང་ཉིད་དང་ཁ་མི་འབྲལ་བ་སུས་ཀྱང་འགན་ལེན་མི་ཐུབ་པར། དེ་རིང་ཉིད་ནས་འཆི་སྲིད་པ་ཡིན་ཕྱིར། རང་གི་ད་ལྟའི་ལུས་ངག་ཡིད་གསུམ་ལ་བརྟེན་ནས་སྙིང་པོ་ལེན་པའམ། དོན་སྙིང་ཆེན་པོ་ཞིག་ཨེ་ཆོད་ལྟ་དགོས་པ་ལས། འདི་ལ་གཅེས་འཛིན་དང་ཆགས་སྡང་བྱེད་པ་དོན་མེད་ཡིན་པ་ཤེས་པའི་ཐོག་ནས།

རང་གི་ལུས་འདི་ལ་གཅེས་འཛིན་ཆེ་དྲགས་པས་དམ་པའི་ཆོས་ལ་བསམ་སྒོམ་གཉིད་ཐབ་མི་བྱེད་པར་ཚོར་བ་བདེ་སྡུག་གི་རྗེས་སུ་འབྲངས་ནས་མི་ཚེ་འདའ་ན། མི་དགེ་བ་བཅུ་དང་། ལོག་པ་བརྒྱད། ལྷི་བ་བཞི། མཚམས་མེད་པ་ལྔ་སོགས་འཁོར་བ་སྡུག་བསྔལ་གྱི་རྒྱུ་འབའ་ཞིག་གིས་སྣེ་ཁྲིད་ནས་སྡུག་བསྔལ་མུ་མཐའ་མེད་པའི་རྒྱ་དུ་ཚུད་འགྲོ་བས། ད་ནས་བཟུང་སྙིང་པོ་མེད་པའི་འཁོར་བའི་བྱ་བ་དེ་དག་གཏན་དུ་སྤང་བར་བྱའོ་སྙམ་དུ་འདུན་པ་ཤུགས་ཆེན་བསྐྱེད་དགོས་པའོ།།

མི་དགེ་བ་བཅུ་ནི། ལུས་ཀྱི་སྒོ་ནས་གཞན་གྱི་སྲོག་གཅོད། གཞན་གྱི་རྒྱུ་ནོར་མ་བྱིན་པར་ལེན་པ། ལོག་གཡེམ་སྟེ་གཞན་ལ་གནོད་པ་དང་འབྲུག་རྐྱེན་སློང་བྱེད་ལ་སོགས་པའི་འཁྲིག་སྤྱོད། ངག་གི་སྒོ་ནས་རྫུན་གྱིས་བསླུ་ཁྲིད་བྱེད་པ། ཕྲ་མ་སྟེ་མིའི་མཛའ་བརྩེར་གཏོར་བཤིག་གཏོང་བྱེད་ཀྱི་ཚིག་བཤད་པ། ཚིག་རྩུབ་སྟེ་དོན་མེད་པར་གཞན་གྱི་ཡིད་དུ་མི་འོང་བའི་ཚིག་སྨྲ་བ། ངག་འཁྱལ་ཏེ་དོན་མེད་དུ་ལས་ཀ་དང་དུས་ཚོད་ཆུད་ཟོས་ཀྱི་གཏམ་བཤད་པ། ཡིད་ཀྱི་སྒོ་ནས་བརྣབ་སེམས་ཏེ་གཞན་གྱི་འབྱོར་ཕྱུག་སོགས་ལ་འདོད་རྔམ་དང་འཕྲན་སེམས། ཕྲག་དོག་སྐྱེ་བ། གཞན་སྡུག་བསྔལ་མྱོང་ན་འདོད་པའི་གནོད་སེམས་འཆང་བ། ལོག་ལྟ་སྟེ་གནས་ལུགས་མ་ཤེས་པའི་ལྟ་བ་ཕྱིན་ཅི་ལོག་པ། མེད་པ་ལ་ཡོད་པར་སྒྲོ་འདོགས་དང་། ཡོད་པ་ལ་མེད་པར་སྐུར་བ་འདེབས་པ་ལ་སོགས་པའི་ལྟ་བ་འཆང་བ། དཔེར་ན་ལས་རྒྱུ་འབྲས་མེད་པར་ལྟ་བ་ལྟ་བུའོ།།

ལོག་པ་བརྒྱད་ནི། རྒྱུ་འབྲས་ཁྱད་དུ་བསད་ནས་འཐབ་རྩོད་བྱེད་པ་དང་། སྲོག་གི་ལྷམ་པོར་ནོར་ཟ་བ་དང་། སློབ་མ་ལ་ཕྱིན་ཅི་ལོག་ཏུ་ལུང་བསྟན་པ་དང་། རི་བོའི་རྩེ་ནས་ཀུས་འདེབས་དང་། རྒྱ་མཚོའི་ནང་དུ་དུག་སྤྱོད་པ་དང་། ཆུ་བོ་ཆེན་པོ་གཡལ་བསྒྱུར་བ་དང་། རྩི་ཤིང་ནགས་ཚལ་མེས་བསྲེགས་པ་དང་། མ་ལ་མངལ་སྤྱོད་པ་དང་བརྒྱད་དོ།། ཡང་ན་དད་པ་ཅན་གྱི་ཚོགས་གཅིག་པ་སྟེ་དགེ་བ་ལ་བར་ཆད་བཟོ་བ། དགེ་བ་ཅན་གྱི་ཐུགས་དཀྲུག་པ་སྟེ་དགེ་སེམས་ཅན་གྱི་ཐུགས་ལ་གནོད་པ་བྱས་པ། དཀར་པོའི་ཆོས་ལ་མི་དད་ཅིང་སྨོད་པ། ནག་པོའི་ཆོས་ལ་འདུན་ཞིང་ཡི་རང་བ། བླ་མའི་དམ་ཚིག་སྤངས་པ། ཆོས་གྲོགས་ལ་གདུང་སེམས་བཅད་པ། ཡི་དམ་ལྷའི་དམ་ཚིག་དང་འགལ་བ། དཀྱིལ་འཁོར་གཉན་པོའི་སྒྲུབ་པ་དང་མཚམས་བཀྲོལ་བ་ལ་སོགས་པ་བཤད་སྲོལ་མང་དུ་ཡོད་དོ།།

གཞན་ཡང་ལྕི་བ་བཞི་སྟེ། མི་ཆོས་དང་འགལ་བའི་མནའ་ཟོས་པ། ཉན་ཐོས་ལ་འདུལ་ཁྲིམས་ཉམས་པ་སྟེ་སོ་ཐར་གྱི་རྩ་ལྟུང་བྱུང་བ། བྱང་སེམས་ལ་བསླབ་པ་ཉམས་པ་སྟེ་བྱང་སེམས་ཀྱི་རྩ་ལྟུང་བྱུང་བ། གསང་སྔགས་ལ་དམ་ཚིག་ཉམས་པ་སྟེ་གསང་བ་སྔགས་ཀྱི་རྩ་ལྟུང་སོགས་བྱུང་བ། ཡང་ན་བཙུན་པའི་ཕྲུག་ལྕི། མཁས་པའི་གོང་ལྕི། དད་པ་ཅན་གྱི་ཟས་ལྕི། སྔགས་པའི་ནོར་ལྕི་བ་ཡང་ཡོད།

མཚམས་མེད་པའི་ལས་ལྔ་ནི། ཕ་བསད་པ། མ་བསད་པ། དགྲ་བཅོམ་པ་བསད་པ། དེ་བཞིན་གཤེགས་པའི་སྐུ་ལ་ངན་སེམས་ཀྱི་ཁྲག་འབྱིན་པ། དགེ་འདུན་གྱི་དབྱེན་བྱས་པ་རྣམས་སོ།། འོ་ན་དེ་དག་དང་འགལ་བའི་ལས་གཅིག་ཀྱང་མི་བྱ་བ་གཞི་ལ་བཞག་ནས། དེ་ལས་གཞན་ཅི་ཞིག་དང་ཇི་ལྟར་བྱ་དགོས་སྙམ་ན།

ཆུང་ཟད་ལོང་ཡོད་དུས་འདིར་ལུས་ངག་ཡིད།།
ཐར་པའི་ཕན་ཡོན་བསམ་ནས་ཆོས་བསྒྲུབ་འཚལ།།

གོང་དུ་བཤད་པ་དག་རྒྱུ་མཚན་དུ་བཟུང་ན། ད་ལྟའི་དུས་ཚོད་འདི་ནི་ཙ་ཆེ་ཞིང་རིན་ཐང་བྲལ་བའི་གནས་སྐབས་སུ་ངོས་བཟུང་ནས། ཆུང་ཟད་དམ་པའི་ཆོས་ལ་བསམ་བློ་གཏོང་ལོང་ཙམ་ཡོད་པ་འདི་གོ་སྐབས་གལ་ཆེན་དུ་བརྩིས་ཏེ། དུས་འདིར་སྐེ་དུས་ད་ལྟ་ཉིད་ནས་རང་གི་ལུས་ངག་ཡིད་གསུམ་པོ། འཁོར་བ་སྡུག་བསྔལ་ལས་གཏན་དུ་ཐར་བའི་ཐར་བ་དམ་པ་ཞི་བའི་ཕན་པ་དང་ཡོན་ཏན་བསམ་གྱིས་མི་ཁྱབ་པ་ལ་བསམ་བློ་རྣལ་མ་ཞིག་བཏང་ནས། ཐར་བ་དམ་པ་དེ་ཉིད་ཐོབ་པའི་ཆེད་དུ། དམ་པའི་ཆོས་ཡང་དག་པ་ཞིག་བསྒྲུབ་པར་འཚལ་ལོ་སྙམ་པ་ལ་སོགས་པའི་འཁོར་བ་ལ་བློ་ལྡོག་བྱེད་རྣམ་བཞིའི་སྒོ་ནས་བློ་རྣལ་དུ་ཕབ་ནས། རིམ་པར་གསང་སྔགས་ཐུན་མོང་གི་སྔོན་འགྲོ་དག་ལ་དངོས་སུ་མ་འཇུག་པའི་སྔོན་དུ། ཐབ་ལམ་རྡོ་རྗེ་རྣལ་འབྱོར་གྱི་ལམ་གྱི་རིམ་པ་དག་རང་རྒྱུད་ལ་སྐྱེ་བའི་ཆེད་དུ། ཙ་བ་དང་བརྒྱུད་པའི་བླ་མ་དག་ལ་གདུང་ཤུགས་དྲག་པོས་གསོལ་བ་འདེབས་པའི་སྒོ་ནས་འཇུག་པ་ནི་དམ་པ་གོང་མ་དག་གི་ཐུག་སྲོལ་ཡིན།

དེ་ལྟར་བློ་ལྡོག་རྣམ་བཞིའི་དོན་རྣམས་ཤེས་པར་བྱས་ནས་མྱུར་དུ་རྒྱུད་ལ་སྐྱེས་རྗེས། ཐུན་མོང་གི་སྔོན་འགྲོ་ལྔ་དང་ཐུན་མིན་གྱི་སྔོན་འགྲོ་གཉིས་ལ་རིམ་བཞིན་ཞུགས་ཏེ། དངོས་གཞི་སྦྱོར་བ་ཡན་ལག་དྲུག་ལ་འཇུག་པ་ཡང་དག་འོང་ཕྱིར་དུ། དྲིན་ཅན་ཙ་རྒྱུད་ཀྱི་བླ་མ་ནས་བཟུང་ཤར་ཛམ་ཐང་ཆོས་ཀྱི་ས་བྲང་ནས་བརྒྱུད་པ་ཁག་གི་ཐུག་སྲོལ་ལྟར་དུ། ཐོག་མར་དམིགས་བཀར་གྱིས་བླ་མ་གལ་ཆེན་འགའ་ལ་རིམ་པ་བཞིན་གསོལ་བ་གདབ་པ་ལས། ཆེས་ཐོག་མར་རང་ཉིད་ཀྱི་ཐུན་མོང་མ་ཡིན་པའི་ཙ་བའི་བླ་མར་གསོལ་བ་གདབ་པ་ནི།

དམིགས་བཀར་བླ་བརྒྱུད་ཁག་ཅིག་གི་གསོལ་འདེབས།

དཔལ་ལྡན་རྩ་བའི་བླ་མ་རིན་པོ་ཆེ།།
བདག་སོགས་སྤྱི་བོར་པདྨའི་གདན་བཞུགས་ནས།།
བཀའ་དྲིན་ཆེན་པོའི་སྒོ་ནས་རྗེས་བཟུང་སྟེ།།
སྐུ་གསུང་ཐུགས་ཀྱི་དངོས་གྲུབ་བསྩལ་དུ་གསོལ།།

དཔལ་དང་འབྱོར་བ་ཐམས་ཅད་ཀྱི་མཆོག་ཏུ་གྱུར་པ་རྫོགས་པའི་སངས་རྒྱས་ཀྱི་གོ་འཕང་ལ་རེག་པའི་ཁྱད་ནོར། ལུང་དང་རྟོགས་པའི་བསྡུས་པ་དམ་པའི་ཆོས་ཀྱི་དཔལ་དང་ལྡན་པའི་བླ་མ་ནི། ཐུན་ལ་ཐར་པ་དམ་པའི་ལམ་སྟོན་མཁན་གྱི་དགེ་བའི་བཤེས་གཉེན་དག་གི་ཁྲིད་ནས། གསང་སྔགས་བླ་མེད་ཀྱི་གདམས་ངག་གནང་མཁན་ཉིད་སྟེ། རྩ་བའི་བླ་མ་ནི། བརྒྱུད་པའི་བླ་མ་ཐམས་ཅད་ཀྱི་རྩ་བ་དང་། ཐར་པ་དང་ཐམས་ཅད་མཁྱེན་པའི་མྱུར་ལམ་གྱི་སྒྲོག་རྩ་ལྟ་བུར་གྱུར་ཡོད་པས་རིན་པོ་ཆེ་ཡིད་བཞིན་གྱི་ནོར་བུ་ལས་ཀྱང་ལྷག་པ་ཁྱེད། ཐུན་གཉིད་པའི་རྣལ་འབྱོར་གྱི་སྐབས་སུ། སྙིང་པདྨ་འདབ་བརྒྱད་ཀྱི་ནང་དུ་གསལ་ཡོད་པའི་བླ་མ་དེ་ཉིད། རྩ་དབུ་མ་བརྒྱུད་དེ་ཡར་ཐེབས་ནས་བདག་སོགས་སེམས་ཅན་ཐམས་ཅད་ཀྱི་སྤྱི་གཙུག་ཁྲུ་གང་གི་ཡང་སྟེང་དུ། རང་ལ་ཐུགས་དགྱེས་པ་དང་བརྩེ་བ་ཟླ་མེད་དང་བཅས་བཞུགས་ནས། བཀའ་དྲིན་བསྐལ་བའི་བར་དུ་ཡང་གཞལ་མཐའ་བྲལ་བའི་མཁྱེན་པ་དང་བརྩེ་བ་ཆེན་པོའི་སྒོ་ནས་རང་ཅག་རྗེས་སུ་གཟུང་བ་པོ། སྐུ་དང་གསུང་དང་ཐུགས་ཀྱི་ཡོན་ཏན་བསམ་གྱིས་མི་ཁྱབ་པའི་བདག་ཉིད། ཁྱེད་ཀྱི་སྐུ་གསུང་ཐུགས་ཀྱི་དངོས་གྲུབ་ཕན་བདེ་བླ་ན་མེད་པ་དག་རང་ཅག་སེམས་ཅན་ཀུན་ལ་བསྩལ་དུ་གསོལ། ཞེས་གདུང་ཤུགས་དྲག་པོས་གསོལ་བ་བཏབ་པའོ།།

དེ་ནས་དཔལ་ལྡན་རྒྱལ་བ་རྗེ་ནང་བའི་དཔལ་དུས་ཀྱི་འཁོར་ལོའི་སྦྱོར་བ་ཡན་ལག་དྲུག་གི་བརྒྱུད་པའི་བླ་མ་རྣམས་ཀྱི་ཁྲིད་ནས་དམིགས་བསལ་འགའ་བཀར་ཏེ་གསོལ་བ་གདབ་པ་ལ།

དང་པོ་རྗེ་ནང་བསྟན་པའི་གསལ་བྱེད་ཀུན་མཁྱེན་དོལ་པོ་བ་ཤེས་རབ་རྒྱལ་མཚན་ལ་ཐོག་མར་གསོལ་བ་གདབ་པ་ནི།

ཆོས་འཁོར་གསུམ་གྱི་དགོངས་པ་ཇི་བཞིན་མཁྱེན།།
རྒྱུད་སྡེ་བཞི་ཡི་དེ་ཉིད་ཐུགས་སུ་ཆུད།།
འགྲོ་བ་ཀུན་ལ་མ་ནོར་ལམ་སྟོན་པ།།
ཀུན་མཁྱེན་ཆོས་ཀྱི་རྗེ་ལ་གསོལ་བ་འདེབས།།

དཔལ་རྒྱལ་བ་ཇོ་ནང་བའི་བསྟན་པ་འཛིན་པའི་ཡང་སྙིང་། གདན་རབས་བཞི་བ་པ། དཔལ་དུས་ཀྱི་འཁོར་ལོའི་བྱིན་རླབས་དོན་བརྒྱུད་བཅོ་ལྔ་བ། ཆོས་ཀྱི་རྒྱལ་པོ་ཆེན་པོ་ངེས་དོན་དབུ་མའི་ཤིང་རྟའི་སྲོལ་འབྱེད་པ་རིགས་ལྡན་སྤྲུལ་བའི་སྐུ་ཐམས་ཅད་མཁྱེན་པ་ཇོ་ནང་བ། དོན་གྱི་སྐད་དུ་མཚན་ནས་སྨོས་ན། མཚན་བརྗོད་པར་དཀའ་བ་དོལ་པོ་བ་ཤེས་རབ་རྒྱལ་མཚན་དཔལ་བཟང་པོ་གང་དེ་ཉིད། རང་ཅག་གི་བསོད་ནམས་ཀྱིས་བླ་མའི་སྐལ་བར་ཐོབ་པ་འདི་ནི་ཤིན་ཏུ་ཡ་མཚན་པའི་གནས་ལགས་ཏེ། དེ་ཡང་ཟ་བོ་ཆེའི་མདོ་སྡེ་སོགས་ལས་ལུང་བསྟན་པ་ནི། ལི་ཙ་བྱི་གཞོན་ནུ་འཛིག་རྟེན་ཐམས་ཅད་ཀྱིས་མཐོང་ན་དགའ་བ་ཞེས་བྱ་བ་མ་འོངས་པའི་དུས་ན་ཀ་ཡོ་རིའི་བརྒྱུད་དུ་ངའི་མིང་འཆང་བའི་དགེ་སློང་དུ་གྱུར་ཏེ། ཞེས་སོགས་གསལ་བར་གསུངས་པ་དང་། གཙུག་ཏོར་རྣམ་པར་རྒྱལ་མའི་རྒྱུད་ལས། བདེ་གཤེགས་མྱ་ངན་འདའ་འོག་ནས།།ལོ་ནི་སྟོང་ཕྲག་ཕྱེད་རིང་ཚེ།།གདོང་དམར་ཡུལ་དུ་ང་འདྲ་བའི།།བསྟན་པ་འཛིན་པའི་དགེ་སློང་ཞིག །ཆུ་བོ་ལྡོན་ཤིང་ཕྲེང་མཛེས་སུ།།ཀ་ཡོ་རི་ཡི་གྲོང་ཁྱེར་དུ།།ཡབ་ནི་ཡེ་ཤེས་དབང་ཕྱུག་ཆེ།།ཡུམ་ནི་ཚུལ་ཁྲིམས་རྒྱན་ཞེས་གྲགས།།སྲས་ནི་སངས་རྒྱས་མིང་ཅན་འབྱུང་།།ང་ཡི་བསྟན་པའི་རྒྱལ་མཚན་འཛུགས།།ཆོས་ཀྱི་དུང་འབུད་དར་ཐུར་འགྱུར།།ཞེས་སོགས་མདོ་རྒྱུད་དུ་མ་ནས་ཡང་ཡང་ལུང་བསྟན་པའི་ཀུན་མཁྱེན་ཇོ་ནང་བ་ཆེན་པོ་ཁམས་གསུམ་ཆོས་ཀྱི་རྒྱལ་པོ་ནི། ཡུལ་མངའ་རིས་དོལ་པོ་བར་ཚང་ཀ་ཡོ་རིའི་གྲོང་ཁྱེར་དུ་ཡབ་ཡེ་ཤེས་དབང་ཕྱུག་དང་ཡུམ་ལྷ་མོ་ཚུལ་ཁྲིམས་རྒྱན་གཉིས་ཀྱི་སྲས་སུ། ཕྱི་ལོ་ ༡༢༩༢ སྤུགས་སྙིང་མ་བའི་ཁྲིམ་རྒྱུད་དུ་སྐུ་འཁྲུངས། དེ་རྗེས་ས་སྐྱའི་ཆོས་ལ་གསན་བསམ་ཡང་དག་བྱས། མཐར་ཇོ་ནང་བའི་ལྷ་སྒོམ་སྦྱོད་གསུམ་གྱིས་བླ་ན་མེད་པའི་ཡིད་འཕྲོག་ནས་བསྟན་པ་དེ་ལ་ཞུགས། མཐར་བསྟན་པ་དེ་འཛིན་ཅིང་བསྟན་པ་དེ་ཉིད་ལ་འགྲན་གྱི་ཟླ་མེད་དུ་གྱུར་པའོ།། དམ་པ་ཁོང་ཉིད་དགུང་ལོ་བདུན་ཅུར་སོན་པ། ཕྱི་ལོ་ ༡༣༦༡ ལྕགས་མོ་གླང་གི་ལོའི་དགུན་ཟླ་ར་བའི་ཡར་ངོའི་ཚེས་དྲུག་གི་སྔོད་ཐུན་དང་པོའི་དུས་སུ་གཟུགས་སྐུ་ཆོས་དབྱིངས་སུ་བསྡུས་པར་མཛད་དོ།།

རྒྱལ་བ་རྫོགས་པའི་སངས་རྒྱས་བཅོམ་ལྡན་འདས་ཀྱིས། གདུལ་བྱ་སེམས་ཅན་རྣམས་ཀྱི་ཁམས་དབང་མོས་པ་དང་བསྟུན་ཏེ། ལེགས་པར་གསུངས་པའི་དམ་པའི་ཆོས་ཀྱི་འཁོར་ལོ་གསུམ་སྟེ། བཀའ་དང་པོ་བདེན་པ་བཞིའི་ཆོས་འཁོར། བཀའ་བར་བ་མཚན་ཉིད་མེད་པའི་ཆོས་འཁོར། བཀའ་ཐ་མ་ལེགས་པར

རྣམ་པར་ཕྱེ་བའི་ཆོས་འཁོར་ཏེ། དམ་པའི་ཆོས་ཀྱི་འཁོར་ལོ་རིམ་པ་གསུམ་གྱི་དགོངས་པ་མ་ནོར་ཞིང་མ་ཆད་པ་ཇི་བཞིན་ཐུགས་སུ་མཁྱེན་ཅིང་། རྒྱལ་བ་རྫོགས་པའི་སངས་རྒྱས་ཀྱིས་གདུལ་བྱ་ཐུན་མོང་མ་ཡིན་པ་ལ་གསུངས་པའི་གསང་བ་སྔགས་ཀྱི་བྱ་རྒྱུད། སྤྱོད་རྒྱུད། རྣལ་འབྱོར་རྒྱུད། རྣལ་འབྱོར་བླ་མེད་ཀྱི་རྒྱུད་དེ་རྒྱུད་སྡེ་བཞི་ཡི་དེ་ཉིད་དམ། དགོངས་དོན་མཐའ་དག་ཐུགས་སུ་ཇི་བཞིན་པ་ཆུད་ནས་ཉམས་ལེན་ཁྲིད་དུ་འཕགས་པའི་སྒོ་ནས། ཕྱོགས་དང་རིས་སུ་མ་ཆད་པའི་འགྲོ་བ་གདུལ་བྱའི་ཡུལ་དུ་གྱུར་ཚད་ལ་མ་ནོར་ཞིང་ཡང་དག་པའི་ལམ་སྟོན་པ་ལ། ཐབས་མཁས་ཤིང་ཐུགས་རྗེ་ཆེ་བའི་ཀུན་མཁྱེན་དོལ་པོ་བ་ཤེས་རབ་རྒྱལ་མཚན་ཞེས་རྫོགས་པའི་སངས་རྒྱས་ཀྱི་མཚན་གྱི་ཅོད་པན་འཆང་བ། དམ་པའི་ཆོས་ཀྱི་རྗེ་བོ་ཁོང་གི་གྲུབ་མཐའ་དེ་རྟོད་ཐྲལ་དུ་སོང་ནས་ཕྱོགས་བཞིའི་དགེ་བཤེས་དུ་མས་བསྐུལ་ནས་ངེས་དོན་རྒྱ་མཚོ་སོགས་གྲུབ་མཐའི་ཆོས་བཅུ་དྲུག བཀའ་བསྡུ་བཞི་བ། དུས་འཁོར་ས་བཅད་སོགས་དུས་འཁོར་ཆ་ལག་བཅོ་བརྒྱད། ཡུམ་གྱི་མཆན་བུ། གསོལ་འདེབས་ཉེར་ལྔ། ཐུགས་རྗེ་ཆེན་པོའི་ཆོས་སྐོར་ཉེར་གསུམ། བསྟོད་སྐོར་བཅུ་བཞི། སྐུ་འབུམ་ཆེན་པོའི་ཆོས་སྐོར་ལྔ། རྡོ་རྗེ་ཕྲེང་བ་དབང་སྐོར་གསུམ། སྤྲིངས་ཡིག་བརྒྱད། སྨོན་ལམ་གསུམ། བཀྲ་ཤིས་བཞི་སོགས་སྤྱི་ཀུན་ཏུ་གསུང་རབ་ཀྱི་ཡིག་ཆ་མང་པོ་མཛད་པས། ཐུབ་བསྟན་སྤྱི་དང་ངེས་དོན་དབུ་མ་ཆེན་མོ་མདོ་སྔགས་ཀྱི་གནས་ལུགས་མཐར་ཐུག་ཏུ་ལུང་རིགས་དྲི་མ་མེད་པས་གཏན་ལ་ཕབ་སྟེ། རྒྱུ་དང་འབྲས་བུའི་ཐེག་པའི་ཆོས་སྒོ་མཐའ་དག་གསལ་བར་བྱེད་པ་པོ། ཁྱེད་ལ་སྙིང་ཁོང་རུས་པའི་གཏིང་ནས་གསོལ་བ་འདེབས་ཞེས་གདུང་ཤུགས་དྲག་པོས་གསོལ་འདེབས་བྱས་པའོ།།

རྒྱལ་བ་ཀུན་གྱི་འཕྲིན་ལས་གཅིག་བསྡུས་པ།།
ཞི་རྒྱས་དབང་དྲག་ལས་ཀྱིས་མཐའ་འཁོབ་ཏུ།།
བསྟན་པ་རིན་ཆེན་ཉིན་མོར་བྱེད་པའི་དཔལ།།
དཀའ་བཞིའི་མཚན་ཅན་ཞབས་ལ་གསོལ་བ་འདེབས།།

ཤར་རྫམ་ཐང་གི་ཆོས་སྡེ་ཆེན་པོ་ཕྱག་འདེབས་གནང་མཁན། རིགས་ལྡན་གྱི་སྤྲུལ་བར་གྲགས་པ་དྲུང་དཀའ་བཞི་བ་རིན་ཆེན་དཔལ་གང་ཉིད་དེ། ཕྱི་ལོ་ ༡༣༥༠ ལོར་རྒྱལ་མོ་ཚ་བ་རོང་དུ་སྐུ་འཁྲུངས། འདས་དང་མ་འོངས་ད་ལྟ་དུས་གསུམ་གྱི་རྒྱལ་བ་རྫོགས་པའི་སངས་རྒྱས་ཀུན་གྱི་མཛད་པ་དང་འཕྲིན་ལས་ཕྱོགས་གཅིག་ཏུ་བསྡུས་པ་ལྟ་བུའི་མཛད་བཟང་དམ་པ་འཆང་བ། ནད་གདོན་ཉོན་མོངས་སོགས་ཞི་བའི་ཐུགས་རྗེ། དཔལ་དང་འབྱོར་བ་སོགས་རྒྱས་པའི་བསོད་ནམས། འདོད་དགུའི་ཡིད་འོང་དང་སྲིད་ཞིའི་ལེགས་ཚོགས་ཡོན་ཏན་དབང་དུ་བསྡུས་པའི་ནུས་པ། ཉོན་མོངས་བདུད་དང་མ་རུངས་པ་སོགས་འདུལ་

བའི་དུག་པོའི་མཐུ་རྩལ་སོགས་ལ་མངའ་བརྙེས་པ། མཐའ་འཁོབ་ཏེ་དམ་པའི་ཆོས་མ་དར་ཞིང་ཆོས་ཀྱིས་མ་ཐུལ་བའི་ཡུལ་ཁམས་རྡོ་འཛིར་སྒྲ་གསུམ་སོགས་སུ་རྒྱལ་བའི་བསྟན་པ་སྤྱི་དང་། ལྷག་པར་བྱང་ཤམྦྷ་ལའི་ཟབ་གསང་གི་ཆོས་མཆོག་རིན་ཆེན་ནོར་བུས་ཀྱང་མཚོན་དུ་མེད་པ་འདི་ཉིད། ཉིན་མོའི་སྣང་བ་ལྟར་གསལ་བར་བྱེད་པའི་དཔལ་མགོན་དམ་པ། དྭང་དཀའ་བཞི་བ་རིན་ཆེན་དཔལ་ཞེས་པའི་མཚན་གྱི་ཡོངས་པན་འཆང་བ་ཁྱེད་ཀྱི་ཞབས་ལ་སྙིང་གསུམ་གུས་པས་གསོལ་བ་འདེབས་སོ།།

ལུང་རྟོགས་ཡོན་ཏན་རིན་ཆེན་རྒྱན་གྱིས་སྤྲས།།
མཐོང་ཐོས་དྲན་རེག་ཐར་བའི་ལམ་ལ་བཀོད།།
ཟབ་བྱུང་རྣམ་དཀར་མཛད་པ་བསམ་མི་ཁྱབ།།
གྲགས་པའི་མཚན་ཅན་ཞབས་ལ་གསོལ་བ་འདེབས།།

དྭང་དཀའ་བཞི་བའི་བུ་ཆེན་ཆོས་བཅུ་རིན་ཆེན་གྲགས་པའམ་རཏྣ་ཀཱིརྟི་ནི། དར་སྐྱ་འཁྱོར་གོས་ཐང་དུ་དུས་རབས་བཅོ་ལྔ་བའི་ནང་དུ་སྐུ་འཁྲུངས། རྒྱལ་བ་རྫོགས་པའི་སངས་རྒྱས་ཀྱི་ལུང་སྡེ་སྣོད་གསུམ་དང་ལམ་བསླབ་པ་གསུམ་གྱི་ཉམས་ལེན་གྱི་རྟོགས་པའི་ཡོན་ཏན་རིན་ཐང་ཆེས་ཆེན་པོ་སྟེ་རིན་ཐང་གཞལ་མེད་ཀྱི་རིན་པོ་ཆེའི་རྒྱན་གྱིས་སྤྲས་པ། གང་ཟག་སུ་ཡིས་མཐོང་བ་དང་ཐོས་པ། དྲན་པ། ཐུག་འཕྲད་དེ་རེག་པ་ལ་སོགས་གང་རུང་ཅམ་གྱིས་ཀྱང་བག་ཆགས་བཟང་པོའི་ས་བོན་རྒྱུད་ལ་བཞག་ཅིང་། ཐར་བའི་ལམ་ལ་བཀོད་པའི་ཐུགས་རྗེ་ལྡན་པ། སྐུ་ཚེ་ཧྲིལ་པོར་དམ་པའི་ཆོས་ཀྱི་མཛད་པ་ཟབ་དུ་བྱུང་བའི་རྣམ་དཀར་གྱི་མཛད་པ་བསམ་གྱིས་མི་ཁྱབ་པ་སྟེ་བསམ་ཡུལ་ལས་འདས་པ་གནང་བ་པོ། རཏྣ་ཀཱིརྟིའམ་ཆོས་བཅུ་རིན་ཆེན་གྲགས་པའི་ཞབས་ཀྱི་པདྨོ་ལ་སྙིང་གསུམ་གུས་པ་ཆེན་པོས་གསོལ་བ་འདེབས་སོ།།

གང་གིས་བཤེས་གཉེན་དམ་པ་མང་དུ་བསྟེན།།
ཐུབ་པའི་བསྟན་ལ་རབ་བྱུང་ཚུལ་ཁྲིམས་གཙང་།།
ཤེས་རབ་དྲི་མེད་གཞན་དོན་ལེགས་བརྩོན་པ།།
རྒྱལ་བ་སེངྒེའི་ཞབས་ལ་གསོལ་བ་འདེབས།།

དྭང་རཏྣ་ཤྲཱིའི་དངོས་སློབ་ཆོས་རྗེ་རྒྱལ་བ་སེངྒེ་ནི། དགའ་ཤོད་དཔལ་མོ་འཛོམས་སུ་དུས་རབས་བཅོ་ལྔ་བའི་ནང་དུ་སྐུ་འཁྲུངས་འཚོ་གནས་གནང་སྟེ། ཕྱི་ལོ་ ༡༥༩༠ ལོར་གཟུགས་སྐུའི་བཀོད་པ་བསྡུས། གང་ཟག་ཁྱད་པར་བ་གང་ཞིག་གིས་ཐར་བ་དང་ཐམས་ཅད་མཁྱེན་པར་འདུན་པས། དམ་པའི་ཆོས་ཀྱི་དགེ་བའི་བཤེས་གཉེན་ཤིན་ཏུ་མང་པོའམ་མང་དུ་བསྟེན་ཅིང་། སྙིང་པོ་མེད་པའི་འཁོར་བའི་འཁྱོར་ཐུག་ལ་

ངེས་པར་འབྱུང་བས་དབང་གིས། ཉོན་མོངས་ཕྲ་རགས་ས་བོན་དང་བཅས་པ་བཅོམ་ཐུབ་པའི་ཐུབ་པ། རྫོགས་པའི་སངས་རྒྱས་ཀྱི་བསྟན་པ་དྲི་མ་མེད་པའི་ལམ་ལ་རབ་ཏུ་བྱུང་ཞིང་ཚངས་པར་སྤྱོད་པའི་ཚུལ་ཁྲིམས་མི་མཐུན་པའི་ཆ་ཤས་ཙམ་གྱིས་ཀྱང་མ་གོས་པར་གཙང་ཞིང་། ཕྲ་ཞིང་ཕྲ་བ་ནས་བསྲུངས་པ་དང་། ཚུལ་ཁྲིམས་རྣམ་པར་དག་པས་བསམ་གཏན་དང་ཤེས་རབ་གསལ་ཞིང་དྲི་མ་མེད་པ་དང་། གཞན་སེམས་ཅན་ཐམས་ཅད་ཀྱི་གནས་སྐབས་དང་མཐར་ཐུག་གི་ཕན་བདེའི་དོན་ལ་ལེགས་པར་ཏེ་ཡང་དག་པར་བརྩོན་པའི་བརྩོན་འགྲུས་དང་ལྡན་པ། དམ་པའི་ཆོས་ཀྱི་རྗེ་བོ་རྒྱལ་བ་སེ་ཏྲེ་ཞེས་གྲགས་པ་ཉིད་ཀྱི་ཞབས་ལ་སྒོ་གསུམ་གུས་པས་ཕྱག་འཚལ་ཞིང་གསོལ་བ་འདེབས་སོ།།

རབ་རྒྱས་ཕན་བདེ་འབྱུང་གནས་རིན་པོ་ཆེ།།
འགྲོ་བའི་སྐྱབས་གཅིག་སངས་རྒྱས་ཀུན་གྱི་དངོས།།
ཁྱབ་བདག་ངོ་བོ་རྗེ་བཙུན་སྲིད་ཞིའི་མགོན།།
ཀུན་དགའ་སྙིང་པོའི་ཞབས་ལ་གསོལ་བ་འདེབས།།

རྗེ་བཙུན་ཀུན་དགའ་སྙིང་པོ་སྟེ་ཡོངས་གྲགས་སུ་ཏཱ་ར་ནཱ་ཐ་ནི། དེ་ཡང་བོད་ཁམས་སྐྱོང་བའི་བརྟན་མ་བཅུ་གཉིས་ཀྱི་ནང་ནས་རྡོ་རྗེ་གཡུ་སྒྲོན་མའི་གནས་ཁ་རག་འབྲང་གི་ཕུ། སྔོན་རྭ་ལོ་ཙཱ་བ་ཆེན་པོའི་བརྒྱུད་པ་རིམ་པར་བྱོན་པའི་བསྟི་གནས། ད་ལྟ་ཆོས་འཁོར་སྡིངས་སུ་གྲགས་པ་རྭ་ཤར་ནུབ་གཉིས་ལས་ཤར་བ་ཀུན་དགའ་སེང་གེས་བཏབ་པའི་དགོན་གཞི་དེར། དེའི་གདུང་རྒྱུད་སྔགས་འཆང་ཚུལ་ཁྲིམས་རྒྱ་མཚོ་ལ་སྲས་བཞི་བྱུང་བའི་ཆེ་ཤོས་རྣམ་རྒྱལ་ཕུན་ཚོགས་དང་ཡུམ་རྡོ་རྗེ་བུ་དགའ་ལྷ་མོ་གཉིས་ཀྱི་སྲས་སུ་གཙང་དུ། ཕྱི་ལོ་ ༡༥༧༥ ལོར་སྐུ་འཁྲུངས་སོ།།དམ་པ་ཁོང་གིས་མདོ་སྔགས་རིགས་གནས་དང་བཅས་པ་ཡོངས་སུ་སྦྱངས་པ་མཐར་ཕྱིན་པ་བྱས་པས། འཕགས་བོད་མཁས་གྲུབ་ཀུན་གྱི་གཙུག་མཆོག་ཏུ་གྱུར། ད་དུང་དམ་པ་ཁོང་གི་གསུང་རྩོམ། རྗེ་བཙུན་རིན་པོ་ཆེའི་སྟོན་པའི་མཛད་བརྒྱ། རྒྱ་གར་ཆོས་འབྱུང་སོགས་པཎ་གྲུབ་མང་པོའི་རྣམ་ཐར་དང་། ཤེར་སྙིང་དང་བཟང་སྤྱོད་ཀྱི་འགྲེལ་བ་སོགས་མདོ་ཕྱོགས་སྤྱིའི་རྣམ་བཤད་དུ་མ་དང་། ཁྱད་པར་ཐེག་མཆོག་རྒྱས་པའི་དབུ་མ་སོགས་གཞན་སྟོང་དབུ་མ་ཆེན་པོའི་སྐོར་སོགས་ལྟ་གྲུབ་ཀྱི་སྐོར་དང་། དུས་འཁོར་བདེ་གསང་འཇིགས་གསུམ་སོགས་གསང་སྔགས་རྒྱུད་སྡེའི་ཆོ་ག་མང་པོ་དང་། དུས་འཁོར་བདེ་གསང་གི་བསྐྱེད་རྫོགས་ཀྱི་རྣམ་བཤད་སོགས་སྔགས་ཀྱི་གཞུང་འགྲེལ་མང་པོ་དང་། ཐ་ན་བསྟོད་ཚོགས་སྨོན་ལམ་སོགས་ཀྱིས་མཚོན་བསྡོམས་པོ་ཏེ་བཅུ་ཕྲག་བཞི་ལྷག་གི་གསུང་རབ་མཛད་པའི་སྒོ་ནས་མདོ་སྔགས་སྤྱི་དང་། ཁྱད་པར་ངེས་དོན་དབུ་མ་ཆེན་མོ་རྗེ་རྒྱལ་བ་གཉིས་པ་ཇོ་ནང་བའི་དགོངས་བཞེད་ལྟར་ལེགས་པར་གསལ་བར་བྱས་ཏེ་དར་རྒྱས་སུ་མཛད་དོ།།དགུང་

གྲངས་རེ་གཅིག་བཞེས་པ། ཕྱི་ལོ་ ༡༨༣༥ ཤིང་མོ་ཕག་ལོའི་ནག་པ་ཟླ་བའི་ཉེར་བརྒྱད་ལ་གཞན་དོན་དུ་དགོངས་ནས་སྣང་བའི་རྒྱལ་པོའི་ཞིང་དུ་གཤེགས།

དེ་འདྲའི་མཁྱེན་བརྩེ་ནུས་པའི་ཡོན་ཏན་རབ་ཏུ་རྒྱས་ཤིང་། གནས་སྐབས་དང་མཐར་ཐུག་གི་ཕན་པ་དང་བདེ་བའི་འབྱུང་གནས་དམ་པ་ཡིད་བཞིན་གྱི་ནོར་བུ་རིན་པོ་ཆེ་ལྟ་བུ། ཉེ་རིང་ཆགས་སྡང་བྲལ་བའི་འགྲོ་བ་མ་ལུས་པའི་སྐྱབས་དང་མགོན་གཅིག་པུ། རྫོགས་པའི་སངས་རྒྱས་ཀུན་གྱི་ཡོན་ཏན་དངོས་ལྟ་བུ་ཡིས་ཕྱུག་པ། དུས་གསུམ་རྒྱལ་བ་རྒྱ་མཚོ་འཁོར་འདས་མ་ལུས་ཀུན་ལ་ཁྱབ་པའི་བདག་པོ་དམ་པ། ཁྱབ་བདག་རྡོ་རྗེ་འཆང་ཆེན་པོའི་ངོ་བོ། ཆོས་ཀྱི་རྗེ་བོ་མི་དགེ་བའི་དྲི་མས་མ་གོས་པས་བཙུན་པ། སྲིད་པ་འཁོར་བ་ལས་ཞི་བསིལ་ཐར་པའི་ལམ་དུ་འཁྲིད་པའི་མགོན་སྐྱབས་དམ་པ། ཏཱ་ར་ནཱ་ཐ་སྟེ་མཚན་དངོས་སུ་ཀུན་དགའ་སྙིང་པོ་ཁྱེད་ཀྱི་ཞབས་སོར་ལ་བཏུད་དེ་གུས་པས་གསོལ་བ་སྙིང་ཐག་པ་ནས་འདེབས་སོ།།

ངག་གི་དབང་པོ་འདབ་བརྒྱ་ཁ་ཕྱེས་ནས།།
ཀུན་མཁྱེན་དོན་གཉེར་བློ་གསལ་བུང་བའི་ཚོགས།།
དགའ་སྟོན་འཕྲིན་ལས་སྦྲང་རྩིས་ཚིམ་མཛད་པ།།
འདོད་དགུའི་དཔག་བསམ་ཁྱེད་ལ་གསོལ་བ་འདེབས།།

ཆ་ལུང་བ་ངག་དབང་འཕྲིན་ལས་ནི། གཙང་བ་སྐུ་ཕྲེང་དང་པོ་མཁས་གྲུབ་བློ་གྲོས་རྣམ་རྒྱལ་གྱི་བླ་མ་དང་སྐུ་དབོན་གཉིས་ཀ་ཡིན། ཡུལ་ཆོས་བཟང་དུ། ཕྱི་ལོ་ ༡༨༥༢ ལ་སྐུ་འཁྲུངས། རྒྱལ་བ་རྫོགས་པའི་སངས་རྒྱས་ཀྱི་ཆོས་སྨྲ་བར་ངག་གི་སྒྲ་རྩལ་ལ་དབང་འབྱོར་བའི་དབང་པོའི་འདབ་བརྒྱ་མེ་ཏོག་ཁ་ཕྱེས་པ་ལྟ་བུའི་བློ་གྲོས་ཀྱི་ངག་སྒོ་ནས། ལམ་མཆོག་ཐར་པ་དང་ཀུན་མཁྱེན་རྒྱལ་བའི་གོ་འཕང་ལ་དོན་གཉེར་བཟོད་བརྩོན་ལྡན་པའི་བློ་གསལ་ཞིང་། འདོད་པ་ཆུང་བའི་ཐར་འདོད་པ་བུང་བའི་ཁྱུ་ཚོགས་ལྟ་བུ་ལ། ཐབས་མཁས་ཤིང་སྙིང་བརྩེ་བའི་སྒོ་ནས་ཟབ་རྒྱས་དམ་ཆོས་དགའ་སྟོན་གྱི་འཕྲིན་ལས་ཀྱི་སྦྲང་རྩིས་ཚིམ་པར་མཛད་པ་པོ། དགོས་འདོད་ཐམས་ཅད་ཡིད་ཀྱིས་སྨོན་པ་བཞིན་སྩོལ་བའི་འདོད་དགུ་འཛོམ་པའི་དཔག་བསམ་གྱི་ཤིང་ལྟ་བུ་ཁྱེད་ལ། གུས་པས་གསོལ་བ་འདེབས་ཞེས་པ་འདི་ནི་ཆ་ལུང་པ་འཕྲིན་ལས་རྣམ་རྒྱལ་མཆོག་ལ་ལག་ཟུང་སྙིང་གར་སྦྱར་ནས་གསོལ་བ་འདེབས་སོ།།

ངག་དབང་རྣམ་པར་རྒྱལ་བ་སྐུ་ཡི་མཆོག །
ཡོན་ཏན་འབྱུང་གནས་ཚུལ་ཁྲིམས་རྒྱ་མཚོ་ཆེ།།
མང་ཐོས་ནོར་བུའི་ཚོགས་ཀྱིས་ཡོངས་སུ་བརྒྱན།།
དགའ་བའི་ཆོས་འཕེལ་ཞབས་ལ་གསོལ་བ་འདེབས།།

གཙང་བ་མཁས་གྲུབ་བློ་གྲོས་རྣམ་རྒྱལ་གྱི་ཡང་སྲིད། གཙང་བ་སྐུ་ཕྲེང་གཉིས་པ་ངག་དབང་བསྟན་འཛིན་རྣམ་རྒྱལ་ནི། ཕྱི་ལོ་ ༡༨༥༡ ལ་ཡུལ་འཚོས་ཟ་བ་རྡུ་སྐུ་འཁྲུངས། རྒྱལ་བའི་གསུང་སློབ་བ་ལ་ངག་གི་དབང་འགྱུར་ཞིང་། ནད་སོགས་ཕྱི་ནང་གསང་བའི་མི་མཐུན་པའི་དགྲ་ལས་རྣམ་པར་རྒྱལ་བའི་སྐུ་ཡི་གཟི་བརྗིད་ནུས་པ་མཆོག་ཏུ་གྱུར་བ། ཐར་བ་དང་ཐམས་ཅད་མཁྱེན་པའི་ཡོན་ཏན་ཀུན་གྱི་འབྱུང་གནས་ལྷག་པ་ཚུལ་ཁྲིམས་ཀྱི་བསླབ་པ་རྒྱ་མཚོ་ལྟ་བུ་དང་ལྡན་པའི་ཆེ་བ་མཆོག་དང་ལྡན་པ། ལུང་སྟེ་སྟོད་དག་ལ་མང་དུ་ཐོས་པའི་རིན་ཆེན་ནོར་བུའི་ཚོགས་ཀྱིས་ཡོངས་སུ་སྟེ་ཡང་དག་པར་བརྒྱན་པ། ངག་དབང་བསྟན་འཛིན་རྣམ་རྒྱལ་དེ་མཚན་གཞན་དགའ་བའི་ཆོས་འཕེལ་ཞབས་ལ་གསོལ་བ་འདེབས།།

རབ་འབྱམས་རྒྱལ་བའི་མཁྱེན་བརྩེ་འཇམ་པའི་དབྱངས།།
མཐའ་ཡས་ཐུགས་རྗེའི་དབང་ཕྱུག་སྤྱན་རས་གཟིགས།།
ཐུབ་དབང་མཐུ་སྟོབས་གཅིག་བསྡུས་ཀུན་ཏུ་བཟང་།།
འཕྲིན་ལས་རྣམ་རྒྱལ་ཞབས་ལ་གསོལ་བ་འདེབས།།

གཙང་བ་སྐུ་ཕྲེང་གསུམ་པ་ཀུན་བཟང་འཕྲིན་ལས་རྣམ་རྒྱལ་ནི། ཕྱི་ལོ་ ༡༩༤༠ ལ་རྒྱལ་རོང་འབབ་གོ་རྡུ་སྐུ་འཁྲུངས། རབ་འབྱམས་རྒྱལ་བ་ཀུན་གྱི་མཁྱེན་པ་དང་བརྩེ་བའི་ཡོན་ཏན་གཅིག་ཏུ་བསྡུས་པ་རྗེ་བཙུན་འཇམ་པའི་དབྱངས་དང་། མཐའ་ཡས་པའི་ཐུགས་བརྩེ་བ་ཆེན་པོའི་ཐུགས་རྗེའི་གཞན་དབང་ཏུ་སོང་བའི་དཔལ་གྱིས་ཕྱུག་པ་འཕགས་མཆོག་སྤྱན་རས་གཟིགས་རྣམ་གཉིས་དང་། ཐུབ་པ་རྒྱལ་བའི་དབང་པོ་ཀུན་གྱི་ཚད་དང་མཐའ་ཡས་པའི་མཐུ་དང་སྟོབས་བསམ་གྱིས་མི་ཁྱབ་པ་ཐམས་ཅད་གཅིག་ཏུ་བསྡུས་པ། དུས་དང་རྣམ་པ་ཐམས་ཅད་དུ་རྒྱལ་སྲས་ཀུན་ཏུ་བཟང་པོ་དང་ཕྱག་ན་རྡོ་རྗེ་སོགས་རིགས་གསུམ་མགོན་པོས་བྱིན་གྱིས་བརླབས་པ། ཀུན་བཟང་འཕྲིན་ལས་རྣམ་རྒྱལ་ཞབས་ལ་གསོལ་བ་འདེབས།།

གང་ཞིག་དྲན་པས་སྡུག་བསྔལ་ཀུན་སེལ་ཞིང་།།
གུས་པས་བསྟེན་ན་བླ་མེད་མཆོག་སྩོལ་བ།།
དབང་རྒྱུད་མན་ངག་དོན་སྟོན་ལ་སོགས་པའི།།
རྩ་བའི་བླ་མ་རྣམས་ལ་གསོལ་བ་འདེབས།།

གོང་དུ་གསོལ་བ་གདབ་ཡུལ་གང་དང་སུ་ཞིག་ལ་དད་ཅིང་དྲན་པ་ཙམ་གྱིས་འཁོར་བའི་སྡུག་བསྔལ་ཀུན་སེལ་བའི་ནུས་པ་ལྡན་ཞིང་། དད་དམ་འགྱུར་མེད་དང་གུས་པ་ཆེན་པོས་བསྟེན་ན་འཇིག་རྟེན་གྱི་བླ་ན་མེད་པའི་དམ་པའི་ཆོས་མཆོག་ཉིད་ཐུན་ལ་སྩོལ་བར་མཛད་པ་པོ་ཁྱེད་ཀྱིས། རང་ཉིད་ལ་དབང་གི་རྒྱུད་

པ་གནང་བ་དང་མན་ངག་གིས་བསྐྱངས་པ། ཟབ་མོའི་དོན་སྟོན་པ་ལ་སོགས་བྱས་པའི་རྩ་བའི་བླ་མའམ་རང་ལ་དངོས་སུ་དམ་པའི་ཆོས་ཀྱི་འབྲེལ་བ་ཡོད་པ་རྣམས་ལ། རང་རྒྱུད་དུ་ཟབ་ལམ་གྱི་བྱིན་རླབས་སྒྱུར་དུ་འཇུག་པར་གསོལ་བ་འདེབས་སོ།། ཞེས་པའོ།།

ཞེས་སོགས་འདི་ཡན་གྱི་བླ་མ་དེ་དག་ལ་དམིགས་བསལ་གྱི་ཐུགས་སྨོན་འགའ་ཞིག་གིས་ཐུན་མོང་མ་ཡིན་པའི་ལུགས་སྲོལ་འགའ་ཞིག་གི་དབང་དུ་བྱས་པ་ཉིད་རྗོགས་སོ།། འདི་དག་མ་བསྒྲགས་པར་འོག་གི་བླ་མ་བརྒྱུད་པའི་རིམ་པ་ལ་ཐད་ཀར་ཞུགས་ཀྱང་གློག་མཁན་དང་ཉམས་སུ་ལེན་མཁན་དག་ལ་ཆད་ལྷག་མེད་ཀྱང་བླ་མ་གོང་མ་དག་གི་ཐུགས་སྨོན་དུ་བགྲིས་པ་ཤེས་པར་བྱའོ།།

དཔེ་སྦྱོར་དུག་གི་བླ་བརྒྱུད་དངོས་ལ་འཇུག་པར་བྱ་བ་ལ། རྩ་བརྒྱུད་ཀྱི་བླ་མ་དེ་དག་གི་གསོལ་འདེབས་དག་ནས་མ་བསྒྲག་སྔོན་དུ་རྩ་བརྒྱུད་ཀྱི་བླ་མ་དེ་དག་རང་ཉིད་ཀྱི་ཡིད་དྭངས་བསྒོམ་དགོས་པས། དེའི་རིམ་པ་དག་ནི་འདི་ལྟར།

སྦྱོར་དྲུག་བརྒྱུད་པའི་བླ་མ་ཡོངས་ཀྱི་རྣམ་ཐར།

ཨོཾ་གུ་རུ་བུདྡྷ་ཛྙོ་ཧྲི་ས་ཧཱ་ན་མོ་ན་མཿ

གང་ཞིག་ཕུན་ཚོགས་ཀུན་གྱི་གཞི།།བླ་མེད་གོ་འཕང་ཡིད་བཞིན་ནོར།།འགྲོ་བ་ཀུན་ལ་ཉེར་སྩོལ་བ།།བླ་མའི་ཞབས་ལ་གུས་པས་འདུད།།ཐོག་མར་སྦྱོར་དྲུག་བླ་མ་བརྒྱུད་པའི་གསོལ་འདེབས་བྱ་བའི་སྔོན་དུ་རང་གི་སེམས་ནང་དུ་སྦྱོར་དྲུག་གི་བླ་མ་བརྒྱུད་པ་རྣམས་ཅི་ནུས་ཀྱིས་གསལ་ཅི་ཐུབ་བལྟ། གལ་ཏེ་ཐུབ་མཁན་རབ་ཅིག་གི་དབང་དུ་བཏང་ན་འདི་ལྟར་དགོས། རང་གི་མདུན་གྱི་ནམ་མཁར་འཛའ་འོད་སྣ་ལྔ་འཁྲིགས་པའི་དབུས་སུ་སེང་ཁྲི་པད་ཟླ་ཉི་མ་སྒྲ་གཅན་དུས་མེའི་གདན་ལྔ་བརྩེགས་ཀྱི་སྟེང་དུ་ངོ་བོ་རྩ་བའི་བླ་མ། རྣམ་པ་རྒྱལ་བ་ཁྱབ་བདག་རྡོ་རྗེ་འཆང་སྐུ་མདོག་སྔོན་པོ་ཞལ་གཅིག་ཕྱག་གཉིས་རྡོ་རྗེ་དང་དྲིལ་བུ་ཐུགས་ཀར་བསྣོལ་ནས་འཛིན་པ། ཞབས་རྡོ་རྗེ་སྐྱིལ་ཀྲུང་གིས་བཞུགས་ཤིང་དར་དང་རིན་པོ་ཆེའི་རྒྱན་དྲུག་གིས་སྤྲས་པ། མཚན་དཔེ་ཡོངས་སུ་རྫོགས་པ། དེའི་མཐའ་སྐོར་དུ་དམ་པ་དང་པོའི་སངས་རྒྱས། ལོངས་སྐུ་དུས་ཀྱི་འཁོར་ལོ། སྤྲུལ་སྐུ་ཤཱཀྱ་ཐུབ་པ། ཆོས་རྒྱལ་རིགས་ལྡན་སོ་ལྔ་སོགས་སྦྱོར་དྲུག་བརྒྱུད་པའི་བླ་མ་རྣམས་ཀྱིས་བསྐོར་བ། ཐམས་ཅད་སྐུ་གཟི་བརྗིད་བཀྲག་མདངས་དང་ལྡན་པ། བདག་ལ་ཐུགས་དགྱེས་པའི་སྒོ་ནས་བཞུགས་པར་གསལ་བཏབ་ལ།

ཞེས་དེ་ལྟར་གསུངས་པ་ཇི་ལྟ་བ་བཞིན་དུ་དངོས་སུ་ཡིད་ངོར་བསྒོམ་ཐུབ་ན་རབ་ཡིན་ལ། དེ་མ་ཐུབ་ནའང་། ཚིག་གི་དོན་རྣམས་རྟོག་ངོར་མི་གོ་བ་ཅི་ཡང་མེད་པར་བྱས་ཏེ། རྩ་བརྒྱུད་ཀྱི་བླ་མ་དེ་དག་གོང་དུ་བཤད་པ་ནང་བཞིན་དུ་ཡོད་སྙམ་པ་དང་། དེ་དག་ལ་གདུང་ཤུགས་དྲག་པོའི་སྒོ་ནས་གསོལ་བ་གདབ་དགོས། དེ་ལྟར་བྱ་བ་ལ་སྔོན་དུ་དད་འདུན་དང་བ་ཆེན་པོའི་སྒོ་ནས་གསོལ་འདེབས་འདི་འདྲ་ཞིག་གིས་དབུ་བརྩན་པར་བྱ།

གསོལ་བ་འདེབས་སོ།།
དྲིན་ཅན་རྩ་བའི་བླ་མ་ལ་གསོལ་བ་འདེབས།།

ཞེས་ལྷ་དང་བླ་མ་ལ་མཁྱེན་བརྩེ་ཞུས་པ་བསམ་གྱིས་མི་ཁྱབ་པ་ཡོད་པར་ཡིད་ཆེས་དང་དད་པ་དག་སྣང་ཆེན་པོའི་སྒོ་ནས་ཞུ་བ་འདི་བྱེད་དོའམ་གསོལ་བ་འདེབས་སོ་ཞེས་པའི་དོན། འཁོར་བའི་འཇིགས་པ་ལས་སྐྱོབ་ཅིང་ཐར་བ་དམ་པའི་ལམ་སྟོན་མཁན་གྱི་དྲིན་ཅན་དང་། རང་ལ་ཡོད་ཚད་ཀྱི་གཙོ་བོའམ་ཡང་ན་ལེགས་ཚོགས་ཐམས་ཅད་ཀྱི་རྩ་བའི་འབྱུང་ཁུངས། འཇིག་རྟེན་ནས་བླ་ན་འཕགས་པས་བླ་མའམ་གོང་མ་ཉིད་ལ་ཞུ་བའམ་གསོལ་བ་འདི་འདེབས་སོ།།

རྩ་བ་བརྒྱུད་པའི་བླ་མ་ལ་གསོལ་བ་འདེབས།།

རང་ལ་ཐད་ཀར་དུ་ཟབ་ལམ་གདམས་ངག་གི་བཀའ་དྲིན་ཆེ་བའི་རྩ་བའི་བླ་མ་གང་ཉིད་ཀྱི་ཡོན་ཏན་ཐམས་ཅད་ཀྱི་འབྱུང་གནས་བརྒྱུད་པའི་བླ་མ་ཐམས་ཅད་ལ་གསོལ་བ་འདེབས་སོ། །

བརྒྱུད་པ་ཡིད་བཞིན་ནོར་བུ་ལ་གསོལ་བ་འདེབས།།

ལེགས་ཚོགས་ཀུན་གྱི་འབྱུང་ཁུངས། ཁྱད་པར་དུ་གསང་ཆེན་སྨྱུར་ལམ་རྡོ་རྗེའི་ལམ་གྱི་བརྒྱུད་པ་སྐྱེ་དམ་པའི་མན་ངག་དང་བྱིན་རླབས་ཀྱི་རྒྱུན། ཡིད་བཞིན་གྱི་ནོར་བུ་ལས་ཀྱང་ལྷག་པ་ཉིད་མཆིས་པའི་བརྒྱུད་ལྡན་བླ་མ་ཀུན་ལ་གསོལ་བ་འདེབས་སོ།།

བརྒྱུད་པའི་བྱིན་རླབས་འཇུག་པར་བྱིན་གྱིས་རློབས།།

སྐུ་བཞིའི་བདག་ཉིད་རྡོ་རྗེ་འཆང་ནས་བརྒྱུད་པ་བར་མ་ཆད་པའི་བྱིན་རླབས་ཐམས་ཅད་ཐུན་གྱི་སེམས་རྒྱུད་ལ་རས་ཡུག་ཚོན་གྱིས་ཁ་དོག་བསྒྱུར་བ་ཇི་བཞིན་དུ་འཇུག་པར་བྱིན་གྱིས་རློབས་ཤིག་ཅེས་པའོ།།

བྱིན་རླབས་སྙིང་ལ་འཇུག་པར་བྱིན་གྱིས་རློབས།།

དམ་ཚིག་ཉམས་པའི་གཡའ་ཡིས་ཡེ་ནས་མ་གོས་ཤིང་། བྱིན་རླབས་ཀྱི་དྲོད་མ་ཡལ་བའི་དམ་པ་གོང་མ་ཐམས་ཅད་ཐུན་གྱི་སྙིང་ཁོང་རུས་པའི་གཏིང་ལ་འཇུག་པར་གྱུར་ཏེ་བྱིན་གྱིས་རློབས་པ་དང་། རང་རྒྱུད་ཀྱི་ཉོན་མོངས་པ་དག་པར་གྱུར་ཅིག

སྙིང་གི་མུན་པ་སེལ་བར་བྱིན་གྱིས་རློབས།།

ཚེ་རབས་ཐོག་མེད་ནས་བསགས་ཤིང་གཏིང་ཟབ་པའི་སྙིང་ནང་གི་མ་རིག་ཉོན་ཤེས་ཀྱི་མུན་པ་མ་ལུས་པ་སངས་ཤིང་སེལ་བར་བྱིན་གྱིས་རློབས།

བླ་མ་ལ་གསོལ་བ་འདེབས།།

ཡོན་ཏན་རྒྱལ་བ་ཀུན་དང་མཉམ་ཡང་། བཀའ་དྲིན་རྒྱལ་བ་ལས་ཀྱང་ལྷག་པའི་བླ་མ་དམ་པའི་སྐུ་གསུང་ཐུགས་ལ་གདུང་ཤུགས་དྲག་པོས་གསོལ་བ་ཡང་ནས་ཡང་དུ་འདེབས་སོ།།

ཆོས་རྗེ་ལ་གསོལ་བ་འདེབས།།

ཐར་བ་དང་ཐམས་ཅད་མཁྱེན་པའི་ས་མཁན། དམ་པའི་ཆོས་ཀྱི་རྒྱལ་པོའམ། ཆོས་ཀྱི་རྗེ་བོ་གང་ཉིད་ལ་སྒོ་གསུམ་དད་གུས་ཆེན་པོས་གསོལ་བ་འདེབས་སོ།།

ཡབ་སྲས་ཆོས་བྱིན་གྱིས་རློབས།།

དེ་ལྟར་དད་པ་དང་དམ་ཚིག་གཙང་མས་གསོལ་བ་རྟེ་གཅིག་ཏུ་གདབ་ན་རིགས་ཀྱི་ཁྱབ་བདག་བླ་མ་དམ་པ་ཆོས་ཀྱི་རྗེ་བོ་སྟེ་ཡབ་ཆེན་དག་དང་། ཐུགས་ཀྱི་སྲས་མཆོག་ཐར་བའི་ལམ་སྟོན་པ་དག་གིས་ཐུན་ཐར་བ་དང་ཐམས་ཅད་མཁྱེན་པའི་ལམ་དུ་བདེ་བླག་ཏུ་འཇུག་ནུས་པར་བྱིན་གྱིས་རློབས་ཤིག

དེ་འདྲའི་གསོལ་འདེབས་དག་གིས་དབུ་བརྒྱན་པར་བྱས་ཏེ། ད་ནི་དངོས་སུ་ངེས་གསང་གི་ཟབ་ལམ་དམ་པའི་མན་ངག་འདི་ཉིད་གང་ནས་བརྒྱུད་པའི་བླ་མ་དག་ལ་རེ་རེ་བཞིན་རང་རྒྱུད་དུ་དེ་དག་གི་བྱིན་རླབས་དང་རྟོགས་པ་འཇུག་ཆེད་དུ་གསོལ་བ་འདི་ལྟར་འདེབས།

གཞི་བདེ་གཤེགས་སྙིང་པོ་ལ་གསོལ་བ་འདེབས།།

གང་ཟག་རང་གི་རྒྱུད་དུ་ཡེ་གདོད་མ་ཉིད་ནས་འགྱུར་བ་མེད་པའི་གཞི་རྒྱུད་དམ། རིགས་ཁམས་བདེ་བར་གཤེགས་པའི་སྙིང་པོ་སངས་རྒྱས་ཀྱི་སྐུ་གསུམ་རང་ཆས་སུ་ཡོད་པ་དེ་མངོན་དུ་འགྱུར་བར་སྒོ་གསུམ་གུས་པ་ཆེན་པོས་གསོལ་བ་འདེབས་སོ།།

ཟབ་ལམ་རྡོ་རྗེའི་རྣལ་འབྱོར་ལ་གསོལ་བ་འདེབས།།

དེ་ལྟ་བུའི་རིགས་ཁམས་དེ་མངོན་དུ་འགྱུར་བྱེད་བླ་ན་མེད་པ་ཟབ་ཅིང་མྱུར་བའི་ལམ་མཆོག མི་འཛིག་སྲ་ཞིང་བརྟན་པ་རྡོ་རྗེ་ལྟ་བུའི་རྣལ་འབྱོར་དེ་ལ་གུས་པས་གསོལ་བ་འདེབས་ཤིང་འཇུག་པར་བགྱིའོ།།

འབྲས་བུ་བྲལ་འབྲས་ཆོས་སྐུ་ལ་གསོལ་བ་འདེབས།།

གཞི་བདེ་གཤེགས་སྙིང་པོ་སངས་རྒྱས་རང་ཆས་སུ་ཡེ་གདོད་མ་ནས་ཡོད་པས། གསར་དུ་རྒྱུས་བསྐྱེད་དེ་སངས་རྒྱས་ཐོབ་མི་དགོས་པར་སྒྲིབ་གཉིས་དག་པའི་འབྲས་བུ་དམ་པ། བྲལ་འབྲས་སངས་རྒྱས་ཆོས་ཀྱི་སྐུ་དེ་ལ་གསོལ་བ་འདེབས་ན་མྱུར་དུ་མངོན་དུ་འགྱུར་བར་བྱིན་གྱིས་བརླབ་ཏུ་གསོལ།

དམ་པ་དང་པོའི་སངས་རྒྱས་ལ་གསོལ་བ་འདེབས།།

གོང་བཞིན་གདོད་ནས་བཞུགས་པའི་སངས་རྒྱས་ཡིན་པས་དམ་པ་དང་། ཡེ་ནས་རང་བཞིན་ལྷུན་གྲུབ་ཡིན་པའི་ཆ་ནས་དང་པོའི་སངས་རྒྱས་ཞེས་པའི་སྒྲས་བསྟན་པ་དེ་ལ་གསོལ་བ་འདེབས་སོ།།

ཆོས་སྐུ་རྡོ་རྗེ་འཆང་ཆེན་ལ་གསོལ་བ་འདེབས།།

རང་བཞིན་རྣམ་དག་གི་སངས་རྒྱས་ཆོས་ཀྱི་སྐུ་དེ་ལ་རྡོ་རྗེ་འཆང་ཆེན་ཞེས་པའི་ཚིག་གིས་བསྟན་པ་དེ་ལ་གཉིས་འཛིན་བྲལ་བའི་སྒོ་ནས་གསོལ་བ་འདེབས།

ལོངས་སྐུ་དུས་ཀྱི་འཁོར་ལོ་ལ་གསོལ་བ་འདེབས།།

ས་མཐོར་གཤེགས་པའི་འཕགས་མཆོག་ཁོ་ནའི་སྐལ་བཟང་གི་སྤྱོད་ཡུལ་ལོངས་སྐུ་ངེས་པ་ལྔ་ལྡན། རང་སྣང་རྣམ་པར་དག་པའི་དཔལ་དུས་ཀྱི་འཁོར་ལོ་ལ་རྣམ་རྟོག་གི་དྲི་མ་བྲལ་བའི་སྒོ་ནས་གསོལ་བ་འདེབས་སོ།།

སྤྲུལ་སྐུ་ཤཱཀྱ་ཐུབ་པ་ལ་གསོལ་བ་འདེབས།།

གདུལ་བྱ་ཐུན་མོང་གི་སེམས་ཅན་རྣམས་ཀྱི་ཁམས་དང་མོས་པ་བཞིན་དུ་བསམ་བཞིན་སྤྲུལ་པའི་སྐུར་བཞེངས་པའི་མཆོག་གི་སྤྲུལ་སྐུ། ཞིང་འདིའི་རྣམ་འདྲེན་བཞི་པ་ཤཱཀྱ་ཐུབ་པ་བརྩེ་ཆེན་ཐུགས་རྗེ་ཅན་ལ་སྒོ་གསུམ་གུས་པའི་སྒོ་ནས་གསོལ་བ་འདེབས།

ཆོས་རྒྱལ་སུམ་ཙུ་རྩ་ལྔ་ལ་གསོལ་བ་འདེབས།།

སྤྲུལ་པའི་ཞིང་མཆོག་ཤམ་བྷ་ལའི་རིགས་ལྡན་ལོངས་སྐུའི་ཟབ་ཆོས་དཔལ་དུས་ཀྱི་འཁོར་ལོའི་རྒྱུད་འཛིན་ཆེན་པོ། དཔལ་དུས་ཀྱི་འཁོར་ལོའི་ཟབ་གསང་གི་ཆོས་ཞུས་ནས་འཛིན་སྐྱོང་སྤེལ་བའི་བདག་པོ། ཆོས་རྒྱལ་ཟླ་བ་བཟང་པོ་དང་། ཁོང་ལས་གཞན་ཆོས་རྒྱལ་བདུན་ནི་རིམ་པ་བཞིན། ༡ རྒྱལ་པོ་ཟླ་བ། ༢ ལྷ་དབང་། ༣ གཟི་བརྗིད་ཅན། ༤ ཟླ་བའི་བྱིན། ༥ ལྷའི་དབང་ཕྱུག ༦ སྣ་ཚོགས་གཟུགས། ༧ ལྷའི་དབང་ལྡན་རྣམས་དང་།

རིགས་ལྡན་ཉེར་ལྔ་ནི། དང་པོ་པདྨ་ལའི་རིགས་ཐམས་ཅད་རྡོ་རྗེའི་རིགས་ཀྱི་ངོ་བོར་སྒྱུར་བ་པོའི་ཐོག་མ། ༡ རིགས་ལྡན་འཇམ་དཔལ་གྲགས་པ། ༢ པདྨ་དཀར་པོ། ༣ བཟང་པོ། ༤ རྣམ་རྒྱལ། ༥ བཤེས་གཉེན་བཟང་པོ། ༦ རིན་ཆེན་ཕྱུག ༧ ཁྱབ་འཇུག་སྟོབས་པ། ༨ ཉི་མ་གྲགས། ༩ ཤིན་ཏུ་བཟང་། ༡༠ རྒྱ་མཚོ་རྣམ་རྒྱལ། ༡༡ རྒྱལ་དཀའ། ༡༢ ཉི་མ། ༡༣ སྣ་ཚོགས་གཟུགས། ༡༤ ཟླ་བའི་འོད། ༡༥ མཐའ་ཡས། ༡༦ ས་སྐྱོང་། ༡༧ དཔལ་སྐྱོང་། ༡༨ སེངྒེ། ༡༩ རྣམ་པར་གནོན། ༢༠ སྟོབས་པོ་ཆེ། ༢༡ མ་འགགས་པ། ༢༢ མི་ཡི་སེངྒེ། ༢༣ དབང་ཕྱུག་ཆེན་པོ། ༢༤ མཐའ་ཡས་རྣམ་རྒྱལ། ༢༥ རིགས་ལྡན་དྲག་པོ་འཁོར་ལོ་ཅན་བར་ཉེར་ལྔ་དང་། དེའི་སྟེང་དུས་འཁོར་རྒྱུད་ཐོག་མར་ཞུ་བ་པོ། གོང་གི་ཆོས་རྒྱལ་ཟླ་བ་བཟང་པོ་དང་རིགས་ལྡན་ཉེར་ལྔ་བ་དྲག་པོ་འཁོར་ལོ་ཅན་གྱི་སྲས་ ༡ ཚངས་པ་དང་ ༢ ལྷ་དབང་གཉིས་བཅས་བསྡོམས་པའི་ཆོས་རྒྱལ་སུམ་ཅུ་རྩ་ལྔ་དང་། ཡང་ཁ་ཅིག་གིས་ཆོས་རྒྱལ་བདུན་དང་རིགས་ལྡན་ཉེར་ལྔ། སྲས་གསུམ་སྟེ་སྲས་ལྷ་དབང་དམ་ལྷ་དབང་རྒྱུད་ཀྱི་སྲས་ ༣ འོད་སྲུང་བགྲང་མཁན་ཡང་ཡོད། མདོར་ན་བྱང་པདྨ་ལའི་ཆོས་རྒྱལ་རིགས་ལྡན་ཀུན་ལ་ཐུན་མིན་དད་འདུན་དང་བ་ཆེན་པོས་ལུས་དད་པའི་ཕྱག་དང་། ངག་དད་པས་བསྟོད་དབྱངས། ཡིད་དད་པས་མོས་གུས་དང་ཁྲིད་ཤེས་ཀྱིས་གསོལ་བ་སྙིང་ནས་འདེབས་སོ།།

༡ གྲུབ་ཆེན་དུས་ཞབས་པ་ཆེན་པོ་ལ་གསོལ་བ་འདེབས།།

དུས་རབས་དགུ་བའི་ནང་དུ་རྒྱ་གར་ལྷོ་ཕྱོགས་ཨ་ཏ་ཞེས་པའི་ཡུལ་དུ་ཡབ་བྲམ་ཟེའུ་བདེ་བྱེད་གཤིན་རྗེ་གཤེད་ཀྱི་རྣལ་འབྱོར་བ་ཞིག་དང་། ཡུམ་པདྨ་ཅན་གཉིས་ཀྱི་སྲས་སུ་འཁྲུངས། མཚན་དུ་མཉྫུ་བཛྲ། བོད་སྐད་དུ་འཇམ་པའི་རྡོ་རྗེར་གྲགས་པ། མདོ་སྔགས་ཀུན་ལ་མཁས་ཤིང་། འཇམ་དཔལ་གྱི་ཞལ་གཟིགས་པ་ཞིག་ལ་ཡི་དམ་གྱིས་ལུང་བསྟན་ནས་བྱང་ཕྱོགས་སུ་གཤེགས་པས། ལམ་དུ་རིགས་ལྡན་གྱི་སྤྲུལ་པ་དང་མཇལ། དབང་བསྐུར་ཞིང་ཟབ་མོའི་རྣལ་འབྱོར་ཟླ་བ་དྲུག་ལ་བསྒོམས་པས་རྫུ་འཕྲུལ་ཐོབ་སྟེ་པདྨ་ལར་བྱོན། རིགས་ལྡན་དངོས་དང་མཇལ། དཔལ་དུས་ཀྱི་འཁོར་ལོའི་ཟབ་བཀའ་མང་དུ་གསན་ཅིང་ཉམས་སུ་བླངས་ལེན་མཛད། སེམས་འགྲེལ་སྐོར་གསུམ་སོགས་རྒྱུད་སྡེ་མང་པོ་གསན། དེ་དག་ལས་བཀའ་ཞིག་ཐུགས་ལ་བཟུང་། བཀའ་ཞིག་གླེགས་བམ་དུ་སྤྱན་དྲངས་ཏེ་འཕགས་ཡུལ་དུ་བྱོན། སྒོམ་པ་གཙོ་བོར་མཛད། གྲུབ་པ་ཐོབ་པས་མུ་སྟེགས་ཀྱི་དཔུང་ལྷ་སྟངས་ཀྱིས་གནོན་པ་སོགས་རྫུ་འཕྲུལ་མང་དུ་བསྟན། སྐལ་ལྡན་གྱི་སློབ་མ་རྣམས་ལ་གསང་བའི་སྒོ་ནས་རྒྱུད་སྨིན་པས་མྱུར་ལམ་བསྟུལ་ཏེ་མཐར་གཟུགས་སྐུ་འཇའ་ལུས་སུ་གཤེགས་པར་གྲགས་པ་ཁོང་གིས། འཛམ་གླིང་འདིའི་སྤྱོད་ཡུལ་དུ་མ་གྱུར་བའི་རྟོགས་ལྡན་པདྨ་ལའི་ཟབ་ཆོས། དུས་ཀྱི་འཁོར་ལོ་འཛམ་གླིང་འདིར་ནང་འདྲེན་གནང་མཁན་ཁོ་ནར་

གྱུར་པ་དེ་ཉིད། ཕྱིས་སུ་མཚན་གྲུབ་ཆེན་དུས་ཞབས་པ་ཆེན་མོ་སྟེ། གྲུབ་ཐོབ་ཆེན་པོ་དུས་འཁོར་ཞབས་པ་ཆེན་པོའི་ཞབས་ཀྱི་པདྨོ་དང་ཐུགས་ཀྱི་དབྱིངས་ཀློང་ལ་སྒོ་གསུམ་དང་བ་ཆེན་པོས་གསོལ་བ་འདེབས་སོ། །

༢ གྲུབ་ཆེན་དུས་ཞབས་པ་གཉིས་པ་ལ་གསོལ་བ་འདེབས།།

གྲུབ་ཆེན་དུས་ཞབས་ཆེན་པོ་མཱཧཱུ་བཛྲ། བོད་སྐད་དུ་འཛམ་པའི་རྡོ་རྗེར་གྲགས་པའི་ཟབ་མོ་སྔགས་བརྒྱུད་ཀྱི་ཐུགས་སྲས་མཆོག་གྱུར། དུས་ཞབས་ཆུང་བ་ཤཱི་ལ་བྷ་དྲ། ཙ་རོལ་སྨྲ་བ་ཟིལ་གྱིས་གནོན་པ་དང་། ཁོང་ནི་ཕྱི་ནང་ཡོངས་ཀྱི་གཞུང་ལུགས་ལ་མཁས་ཤིང་། མངོན་ཤེས་རྫུ་འཕྲུལ་ཐོགས་པ་མེད་པས་ཕྱུ་སྙེགས་པའི་ལྟ་བ་ཚར་བཅད་ཅིང་། ཁྱད་པར་དུ་དཔལ་དུས་ཀྱི་འཁོར་ལོའི་ཟབ་ཆོས་སྔན་ནས་སྔན་དུ་བརྒྱུད་པའི་སྐལ་བཟང་ཐོབ་པས། ལུགས་ཀྱི་ས་བཅུ་གཉིས་པ་ཐོབ་ཅིང་། དཔལ་དུས་ཀྱི་འཁོར་ལོའི་ཟབ་ཆོས་ཀྱི་ཡང་དག་པའི་བརྒྱུད་འཛིན་གཉིས་པ། དཔལ་ནཱ་རོ་བ་ལ་སོགས་པའི་སྐལ་བཟང་གི་སློབ་བརྒྱུད་མང་དུ་བྱུང་བ། གྲུབ་ཆེན་དུས་ཀྱི་འཁོར་ལོའི་སྐུ་ཞབས་པ་གཉིས་པར་གྲགས་ཤིང་། མཚན་གཞན་ཤཱི་ལ་བྷ་དྲ་ལ་སྒོ་གསུམ་གུས་པས་གསོལ་བ་འདེབས་སོ།།

༣ རྒྱལ་སྲས་ནཱ་ལེནྡྲ་པ་ལ་གསོལ་བ་འདེབས།།

གྲུབ་ཆེན་ཤཱི་ལ་བྷ་དྲའི་ཐུགས་སྲས་ནཱ་ལེནྡྲ་བྷ་དྲའམ་བོད་སྐད་དུ་བྱང་ཆུབ་བཟང་པོ། ཕྱི་ནང་གཉིས་ཀྱི་ཆོས་ལ་ཤིན་ཏུ་མཁས་ཤིང་། ནང་པའི་ཆོས་ཡོད་དོ་ཅོག་ལ་མཁས་པས་དཔལ་ནཱ་ལེནྡྲའི་གནས་གཞིའི་བདག་པོར་གྱུར། ལས་བཞི་གང་བསྒྲུབས་ཀྱང་རྣལ་འབྱོར་པོ་ནས་འགྲུབ་པར་ངེས་ཤིང་། ལྷག་པར་དུ་དཔལ་དུས་ཀྱི་འཁོར་ལོའི་ཟབ་ཆོས་ཐུགས་དམ་དུ་བཟུང་ཞིང་བརྒྱུད་འཛིན་མཆོག་ཏུ་གྱུར་པ་རྒྱལ་བ་རྫོགས་པའི་སངས་རྒྱས་ཀྱི་ཐུགས་སྲས་སུ་གྱུར་པ། མཚན་རྒྱལ་སྲས་ནཱ་ལེནྡྲ་པའམ་བོ་དྷི་བྷ་དྲ་ལ་དད་འདུན་གུས་པ་ཆེན་པོས་གསོལ་བ་འདེབས་སོ།།

༤ པཎ་ཆེན་ཟླ་བ་མགོན་པོ་ལ་གསོལ་བ་འདེབས།།

རྒྱ་གར་ཁ་ཆེའི་རིགས་སུ་སྐུ་འཁྲུངས་ཤིང་། ཕྱི་རོལ་བའི་གཞུང་ལུགས་མཐར་ཕྱིན་པ། མདོ་སྡེ་སྐྱང་འདས་ལས་ངེས་དོན་བསྟན་པའི་བརྒྱུད་འཛིན་ཡང་དག་ཏུ་ལུང་གིས་ཟིན་པ། མ་ཡུམ་ནང་བ་སངས་རྒྱས་པ་ལ་མོས་པ་ཆེ་བས་མ་ཡུམ་གྱིས་བསྐུལ་ཏེ་ནང་བའི་གཞུང་ལ་སྦྱངས་པས་མཐར་ཕྱིན་ནས་པཎྜི་ཏ་ཆེན་པོར་གྱུར། ལྷག་པར་དུ་དཔལ་དུས་ཀྱི་འཁོར་ལོའི་ཟབ་ཆོས་ཀྱིས་རིགས་སད་དེ་ཉམས་ལེན་མཐར་ཕྱིན། དབུགས་ཐེངས་རེ་ལ་ཤླཽ་ཀ་བཅུ་དྲུག་ཙམ་ཟིན་པའི་གཟུངས་ཐོབ་པ། དུས་འཁོར་སོགས་ལུགས་ཀྱི་ཟབ་

དོན་བསྒོམས་པས་སློག་འཛིན་གཉིས་ཀ་མཐར་ཕྱིན་པ། སྐུ་ལ་བཤང་གཅིའི་རྒྱུ་བ་ཆད། ཆོས་རྐུན་ལ་སྡིགས་མཛུབ་མཛད་པ་ཙམ་གྱི་བཏུལ་བ་སོགས་ནུས་མཐུ་ཆེ་བ། རྗེས་སུ་རིགས་ལྡན་གྱི་སྤྲུལ་བས་བོད་དུ་གདུལ་བྱ་ཡོད་པར་ལུང་བསྟན་པས་བོད་དུ་ལན་གསུམ་བྱོན། སྒྲོན་གསལ། རིགས་ཚོགས། འཕགས་པ་ཐོགས་མེད་ཀྱི་ས་སྡེ་སོགས་རྒྱ་ཆེར་གསུངས། ཁྱད་པར་དུ་དཔལ་དུས་ཀྱི་འཁོར་ལོའི་ཟབ་ཆོས་ཤིན་ཏུ་དར་བར་མཛད། ཟབ་གསང་རྫོགས་ལྡན་གྱི་ཆོས། དུས་ཀྱི་འཁོར་ལོའི་ཟླ་བ་གཞོན་ནུ་ཐོག་མར་བོད་གངས་རིའི་ལྗོངས་སུ་འདྲེན་པར་མཛད་པའི་མགོན་པོ་མཆོག་ལ་བཀའ་དྲིན་སྙིང་བཅངས་ཀྱིས་གདུང་ཤུགས་དྲག་པོས་གསོལ་བ་ལན་སྙིང་དུ་འདེབས་སོ།།

༥ སྒྲ་སྒྱུར་འབྲོ་སྟོན་ལོ་ཙཱ་ལ་གསོལ་བ་འདེབས།།

མཚན་དངོས་ནི། འབྲོ་ལོ་ཙཱ་བ་ཤེས་རབ་གྲགས་པ། དུས་རབས་བཅུ་གཅིག་པར་སྐུ་འཁྲུངས་ཤིང་། དཔལ་དང་འབྱོར་བའི་ལོངས་སྤྱོད་ཐམས་ཅད་དམ་ཆོས་ཟབ་མོའི་ཡོན་དུ་ཕུལ་ཞིང་། པཎ་ཆེན་ཟླ་མགོན་གྱི་མདུན་ནས་དཔལ་དུས་ཀྱི་འཁོར་ལོའི་ཟབ་ཆོས་ཡོངས་རྫོགས་གསན་ནས་བླ་མ་མཆོག་ཏུ་བཀུར། གངས་རིའི་ཁྲིད་དུ་སྤྱན་བརྒྱུད་དུས་ཀྱི་འཁོར་ལོའི་བཀའ་ཐོག་མར་བབས་ཤིང་། དཔལ་དུས་ཀྱི་འཁོར་ལོའི་རྫོགས་ལྡན་གྱི་ཟབ་ཆོས་སྐད་གཉིས་སྨྲ་བའི་སྒྲ་སྒྱུར་ཤིང་རྟ་ཆེན་མོ་འབྲོ་ལོ་ཙཱ་བ་ཤེས་རབ་གྲགས་པའམ། མཚན་གཞན་འབྲོ་སྟོན་ལོ་ཙཱ་བ་ཆེན་མོ་མཆོག་ལ་བཀའ་དྲིན་གཞལ་མཐའ་མེད་པའི་འདུ་ཤེས་དང་། མོས་གུས་དང་གདུང་ཤུགས་དྲག་པོས་གསོལ་བ་རབ་ཏུ་འདེབས།

༦ བླ་མ་ལྷ་རྗེ་སྒོམ་པ་ལ་གསོལ་བ་འདེབས།།

བོད་ནུབ་བརྒྱུད་འཕན་ཡུལ་དུ་སྐུ་འཁྲུངས། མཚན་ལ་བླ་མ་ལྷ་རྗེ་སྒོམ་པ་དཀོན་མཆོག་སྲུང་དུ་འབར་གྲགས། ཁོང་གིས་ལུས་ངག་ཡིད་གསུམ་ལོངས་སྤྱོད་དང་བཅས་པ་བླ་མ་ཁ་ཆེ་པཎ་ཆེན་ཟླ་བ་མགོན་པོ་ལ་ཕངས་མེད་དུ་ཕུལ་བས། ཟླ་བྲལ་གྱི་གཏོང་ཕོད་ལྡན། པཎ་ཆེན་ཟླ་མགོན་ལས་དབང་རྒྱུད་བཤད་མན་ངག་མཐའ་དག་ཐོབ། བླ་མའི་ཐུགས་ཟིན་ཏེ་གདམས་ངག་མ་ལུས་པ་གསན་ཅིང་། སྒྲུབ་པ་ཉམས་ལེན་བླ་ན་མེད་པ་བྱས་པའི་འབྲས་བུར། སྤུགས་ཀྱི་ཡི་དམ་ཡོངས་རྫོགས་ཀྱི་ཞལ་གཟིགས་པ་དང་ལུང་བསྟན་ཐོབ། དམ་པའི་ཆོས་སྒྲུབ་མཁན་རྣལ་མའི་མཆོག་ཏུ་གྱུར་པའི་བླ་མ་ལྷ་རྗེ་སྒོམ་པ་དེ་ཉིད་ལ་སྒོ་གསུམ་གུས་པ་ཆེན་པོས་གསོལ་བ་འདེབས་སོ།།

༧ བླ་མ་སྒྲོ་སྟོན་གནམ་བརྩེགས་ལ་གསོལ་བ་འདེབས།།

བླ་མ་སྒྲོ་སྟོན་གནམ་བརྩེགས་ནི། ཡུལ་འཕན་ཡུལ་སྟོར་བཟང་དུ་ཕ་མ་རིགས་བཟང་གི་སྲས་སུ་འཁྲུངས། འཁོར་བའི་ཆོས་ལ་ངེས་པར་འབྱུང་ཞིང་། དམ་པའི་ཆོས་ལ་དད་བརྩོན་དྲན་པ་བརྟན་པོས་དམ་པའི་བཤེས་གཉེན་མང་དུ་བསྟེན་ཅིང་གདམས་ངག་གིས་རྒྱུད་ཡོངས་སུ་གང་། ལྷག་པར་དུ་པཎ་ཆེན་བླ་མགོན་ནས་དབང་དང་རྒྱུད་བཤད་རྫོགས་པར་གསན། ཟབ་ཆོས་དུས་ཀྱི་འཁོར་ལོ་ལ་ཉམས་ལེན་རྒྱལ་མ་བྱས། ཁྱད་པར་དུ་བླ་མ་ལྷ་རྗེ་སྒོམ་པ་ཡུན་རིང་བསྟེན་ནས་གདམས་ངག་མང་དུ་ཐོབ། གསང་རྒྱ་དམ་པོས་ཉམས་ལེན་ཁོ་ན་གནང་ནས་སྐུ་ཚེ་ཉམས་ལེན་གྱིས་མཐར་ཕྱིན་ཀྱང་། ཟབ་གསང་དུས་ཀྱི་འཁོར་ལོའི་གདམས་པ་བླ་མ་གྲུབ་ཆེན་ཡུ་མོ་བ་མ་གཏོགས་སུ་ལའང་རྫོགས་པར་མ་གནང་། བླ་མ་སྒྲོ་སྟོན་ནས། མཚན་དངོས་འགྲོ་མགོན་ནམ་མཁའ་བརྩེགས་སུ་གྲགས་པ་དེ་ལ་ལུས་ངག་ཡིད་གསུམ་མི་ཕྱེད་པ་ཆེན་པོའི་སྒོ་ནས་གསོལ་བ་འདེབས་སོ།།

༡ བླ་མ་གྲུབ་ཆེན་ཡུ་མོ་ལ་གསོལ་བ་འདེབས།།

བླ་མ་གྲུབ་ཆེན་ཡུ་མོ་མི་བསྐྱོད་རྡོ་རྗེ་འམ། མཚན་གཞན་དད་པ་རྒྱལ་པོ་ནི། དུས་རབས་བཅུ་གཅིག་པའི་ནང་རབ་བྱུང་དང་པོའི་དུས་སུ། གངས་དཀར་ཏི་སེའི་ཤར་ཡབ་ཁྲིམ་པ་ཞེས་བྱ་དང་། ཡུམ་མཚན་ལྡན་མ་ཞིག་གི་སྲས་སུ་སྐུ་འཁྲུངས། ཁ་ཆེ་པཎ་ཆེན་ལས་ཆོས་འབྲེལ་ཙམ་ལས་མ་ཐོབ་ཀྱང་། བླ་མ་སྒྲོ་སྟོན་གནམ་བརྩེགས་མི་ལོ་ལྔའི་བར་དུ་བསྟེན་ནས་ཁོང་ལ་བཞུགས་པའི་དབང་རྒྱུད་མན་ངག་མཐའ་དག་ཐུགས་ཀྱི་བཅུད་དུ་འཁྱིལ། ཕྱིས་འུ་ཡུག་གི་རྒྱལ་གནས་སུ་བཞུགས། རྫུ་འཕྲུལ་མང་དུ་བསྟན་པ་ནི་ཡོངས་གྲགས་ཤིག་ཡིན། གཞན་སྟོང་དབུ་མའི་ལྟ་བ་དཔལ་དུས་ཀྱི་འཁོར་ལོ་དང་འབྲེལ་བའི་བསྟན་བཅོས་མང་དུ་མཛད། གསང་ཞིང་སྦས་པའི་ཟབ་ཆོས་སྣང་བརྒྱུད་ཀྱི་གདམས་པ་འདི་ཉིད་ཙུང་ཟད་ཀྱ་ཡངས་དང་ཁྱབ་བརྡལ་དུ་གནང་། དེའི་དབང་གིས་ལུགས་ཀྱི་གཞན་སྟོང་གྲུབ་མཐའི་སྲོལ་འབྱེད་དུའང་གྲགས། གངས་རིའི་ཁྲོད་ཀྱི་གྲུབ་པའི་ཁྱུ་མཆོག་ཆེན་མོ་བླ་མ་གྲུབ་ཆེན་ཡུ་མོ་བ་རུ་གྲགས་པའི་དཔལ་དུས་ཀྱི་འཁོར་ལོའི་རྣལ་འབྱོར་པ་ཆེན་མོ་ཁྱེད་ལ་སྒོ་གསུམ་གུས་པ་ཆེན་པོས་གསོལ་བ་འདེབས་སོ།།

༢ སྲས་མཆོག་དྷརྨེ་ཤྭ་ར་ལ་གསོལ་བ་འདེབས།།

གྲུབ་ཆེན་ཡུ་མོ་བ་དགུང་ལོ་ལྔ་བཅུ་ཙ་ལྔའི་སྐབས། ལས་སྨོན་བཟང་པོ་དང་འབྲེལ་བའི་སྐུ་སྲས་སུ་འཁྲུངས་པར་གྲགས་ཤིང་། མཚན་གཞན་སྲས་ཆོས་ཀྱི་དབང་ཕྱུག་ཅེས་བྱ། ཤེས་རབ་ཤིན་ཏུ་རྣོ་བས་ཡབ་གྲུབ་ཆེན་ལ་མངའ་བའི་གདམས་ངག་ཐམས་ཅད་དགུང་ལོ་ཉི་ཤུ་ཚུན་ལ་ཐུགས་སུ་ཆུད། དཔྱལ་ལོ་ཀུན་དགའ་རྡོ་རྗེ། བརྒྱ་གླིང་བ། ས་སྐྱ་པཎ་ཆེན་སོགས་ཀྱིས་རྩོད་ཀྱང་མ་ཐུབ། དུས་འཁོར་གསང་རྒྱ་དམ་

པོའི་སྒོ་ནས་སྒྲུབ་པ་ཉམས་ལེན་གནད་སྨིན་བྱས་པས་ཡབ་ཀྱི་ཐུགས་དམ་ཟིན་པ་བྱུང་། སྲས་ཀྱི་མཆོག་ཏུ་གྱུར་པ་དྷརྨེ་ཤྭ་ར་བ་ཆེན་མོ་ལ་སྒོ་གསུམ་གུས་པ་ཆེན་པོས་གསོལ་བ་འདེབས་སོ།།

༡༠ མཁས་པ་ནམ་མཁའ་འོད་ཟེར་ལ་གསོལ་བ་འདེབས།།

མཁས་པ་ནམ་མཁའ་འོད་ཟེར་མཆོག་ནི། སྲས་མཆོག་ཆོས་ཀྱི་འབྱུང་གནས་ཀྱི་ཐུགས་སྲས་མཆོག་དེ་ཡིན་ཞིང་། བུ་ཆེན་ནམ་མཁའ་འོད་ཟེར་ཞེས་མདོ་སྔགས་ལ་མཁས་ཤིང་གྲུབ་པའི་ཚད་དུ་བརྙེས་པ་ཞིག་བྱུང་། ཞེས་དམ་པ་གོང་མ་རྣམས་ཀྱིས་གསུངས་འདུག ཁོང་གི་གསུང་རྩོམ་ལ་འོད་ཟེར་ཐྲེང་བ་སོགས་བསྟན་བཅོས་ཀྱང་མང་དུ་བཞུགས། མདོ་སྔགས་ཀྱི་ཆོས་ལ་མཁས་པའི་ཁྱད་ཆོས་ལྡན་པའི་མཛད་རྗེས་མང་དུ་བཞག ལྷག་པར་དུ་བྱམས་ཆོས་སྡེ་ལྔ་ལ་ཤིན་ཏུ་མཁས་པ་ཡོངས་གྲགས་སོ།། མཁས་གྲུབ་གཉིས་ལྡན་གྱི་ཡང་སྲས་དམ་པ་གང་ལ་གསོལ་བ་སྙིང་ནས་འདེབས་སོ།།

༡༡ མ་ཅིག་སྤྲུལ་སྐུ་ཇོ་འབུམ་ལ་གསོལ་བ་འདེབས།

སྲས་མཆོག་དྷརྨེ་ཤྭ་རའམ་ཆོས་ཀྱི་དབང་ཕྱུག་ལ་སྲས་ལྕམ་སྲིང་གསུམ་ཡོད་པའི་ནང་གི་ཆེ་བ། ཨིནྡྲ་བོ་དྷིའི་ལྕམ་ལཀྵྨཱི་ཀ་རའི་སྤྲུལ་སྐུ་ཡིན་པར་གྲགས་པ། སྲས་མོ་ཇོ་འབུམ་ནི། གཟུགས་བྱད་ཤིན་ཏུ་མཛེས་མ་ཞིག་ཡིན་ཁར་གཞོན་དུས་སྤྱོད་པ་རྒོད་ཅིང་། ཡབ་གཤེགས་རྗེས་ཡུམ་ལ་དཀའ་ངལ་ཆེན་པོ་བྱུང་བས་མཐུ་ངན་སྔགས་བསླབས་པས་ཀུན་གྱིས་གླགས་མི་ཚུགས་ཤིང་བཀའ་གཉན་པར་གྱུར། ཉིན་ཞིག་འཇིག་རྟེན་ལ་སྙིང་པོ་མེད་པའི་རིགས་སད་དེ་ཆོས་རྣམ་དག་ལ་བརྩོན། དཔལ་དུས་ཀྱི་འཁོར་ལོ་ལ་ལས་སྐལ་བཟང་པོ་ཡོད་པས། སྒོམ་ཁང་དུ་ཞུགས་མ་ཐག་ལས་རླུང་དབུ་མར་རྒྱུ་འགོ་ཚུགས། རིམ་གྱིས་སྦྱོར་བ་ཡན་ལག་དྲུག་བསྒོམས་པས་ཞག་གཅིག་ལ་རྟགས་བཅུ་རྫོགས། དུས་འཁོར་རྒྱུད་འགྲེལ་ཡོངས་རྫོགས་ཐུགས་ལ་གསལ་བར་གྱུར། ཞག་བདུན་ལ་རླུང་དབུ་མར་ཐིམ། གྲུབ་ཐོབ་ཆེན་མོར་གྱུར་པས་དཔལ་དུས་ཀྱི་འཁོར་ལོའི་བསྟན་པའི་སྒོ་ནས་ཕན་བདེ་རྒྱ་ཆེན་བྱུང་། གྲུབ་པའི་དབང་ཕྱུག་མ་ཆེན་མོ་མ་ཅིག་སྤྲུལ་པའི་སྐུ་ཇོ་འབུམ་མམ། རྗེ་མོ་མཆོག་ལ་སྒོ་གསུམ་དང་མོས་གདུང་ཤུགས་དྲག་པོས་སྒོ་ནས་གསོལ་བ་འདེབས་སོ།།

༡༢ བླ་མ་གྲུབ་ཐོབ་སེ་ཆེན་ལ་གསོལ་བ་འདེབས།།

མ་ཅིག་ཇོ་འབུམ་དེ་ཉིད་ཀྱི་གཅུང་སེ་མོ་ཆེ་བའམ་ནམ་མཁའ་རྒྱལ་མཚན་ནི། སྦྱོར་བ་ཡན་ལག་དྲུག་བསྒོམས་པས་ཉམས་རྟོགས་དང་མཁྱེན་རབ་ནང་ནས་བརྡོལ། ནམ་མཁའ་འོད་ཟེར་ལས་རྒྱུད་འགྲེལ་

དང་། རྫོ་འབུམ་ལས་དབང་མདོར་བསྡུས་བཀའ་འགྲེལ་པདྨ་ཅན་གསན། གྲུབ་ཐོབ་རང་གི་སྐྱེ་བ་བཅུ་དྲུག་དྲན་པ་སོགས་གྲུབ་པའི་རྟགས་མཚན་མང་། ལུང་གིས་ཟིན་ཅིང་མ་འོངས་ལུང་བསྟན་ཡང་མང་། མཚན་སྙན་གྱི་གྲགས་པ་ཤིན་ཏུ་ཆེ་ཞིང་སྐུ་ཚེའི་སྨད་ལ་གཙང་རོ་ལུང་སེ་མོ་ཆེའི་དགོན་པ་བཏབ། ཕྱུ་ལུང་ཕུག་ཏུ་སྐུ་བསྟུང་བ་མེད་པར་འོད་གསལ་དང་སྒྱུ་གཤེགས། སྐུ་གདུང་ལ་རང་བྱོལ་ཁྱད་འཕགས་མང་དུ་བྱུང་བས་ཀུང་སེམས་ཅན་ཆེས་མང་པོར་ཕན་ཐོགས་རྒྱ་ཆེར་ཐོབ། སྒྲུབ་པ་ཟབ་མོའི་ཉམས་ལེན་གྱིས་སྐྱུ་ཚེ་འདས་ཤིང་། སྔོན་གནས་རྗེས་དྲན་གྱིས་རང་གཞན་གྲོལ་བའི་བརྒྱུད་པའི་གསང་ཆེན་བརྒྱུད་འཛིན་པ་ཆེན་པོ་མཆོག་ལ་སྙིང་ནས་དད་པས་གསོལ་བ་འདེབ་སོ།།

༡༣ ཆོས་རྗེ་འཇམ་དབྱངས་གསར་མ་ལ་གསོལ་བ་འདེབས།།

མཚན་གཞན་འཇམ་གསར་བ་ཤེས་རབ་འོད་ཟེར་དུ་ཡང་གྲགས། ཁོང་ནི་ཡུལ་ཉང་སྟོད་དུ་སྐུ་འཁྲུངས། ཡབ་ཀྱི་མཚན་ལ་སློབ་དཔོན་དཔལ་ཆེན་ཟེར། ལྷག་པའི་ལྷ་འཇམ་དཔལ་དབྱངས་ཀྱིས་ལུང་བསྟན་པ་ལྟར་སེ་མོ་ཆེ་བ་ལས་དུས་འཁོར་གྱི་དབང་གསན་བསྒོམས་པས་ཉམས་རྟོགས་མཐར་ཕྱིན། རྒྱང་འདུར་དུ་འཆད་ཉན་མཛད། བཤད་སྒྲུབ་སྤེལ་མའི་དང་ལ་བཞུགས། སྤྱིངས་ཡིག་བེཊཱུཪྻའི་ཕྲེང་བ་སོགས་མཛད། འདི་མན་ལ་དུས་འཁོར་ཝུང་ཟད་བཀའ་རྒྱ་ཡངས་སུ་བཏང་འདུག་པར་གྲགས་ཤིང་། དེ་ཡང་སྐྱེས་བུ་དམ་པ་འདིས་འགྲོ་བར་བྱམས་བརྩེ་དང་ཐུགས་བསྐྱེད་ཀྱི་བདག་རྐྱེན་ལས་བྱུང་བ་འདྲ། མཁས་གྲུབ་གཉིས་ལྡན་གྱི་ཆོས་རྗེ་དམ་པ་འཇམ་དབྱངས་གསར་མ་ལ་གསོལ་བ་འདེབས་པའོ།།

༼འགྲེལ་བ་འདིའི་ནང་དུ་འདི་མན་ཆད་ཀྱི་བླ་རྒྱུད་རྣམས་ཀྱི་མཇུག་ཏུ་གསོལ་བ་འདེབས་སོ་ཞེས་པའི་ཚིག་རྣམས་མ་བཞག་པར་རིགས་འགྲེས་བྱེད་དགོས་པ་ཤེས་པར་བྱའོ།། ༽

༡༤ ཀུན་མཁྱེན་ཆོས་སྐུ་འོད་ཟེར་ལ་གསོལ་བ་འདེབས།།

ཀུན་མཁྱེན་ཆོས་སྐུ་འོད་ཟེར་གྱིས་ཆོས་རྗེ་འཇམ་དབྱངས་གསར་མ་ལས། དུས་འཁོར་གྱི་དབང་རྒྱུད་མན་ངག་ཡོངས་སུ་རྫོགས་པར་གསན་པས་ཉམས་རྟོགས་བརྒྱ་འགྱུར་དུ་འཕེལ། དབང་གི་ཡེ་ཤེས་དབབ་པའི་སྐབས་སུ་རང་གི་བླ་མ་ཡི་དམ་ཁྲོ་བོ་རྡོ་རྗེ་ཤུགས་དངོས་སུ་གཟིགས། ཡེ་ཤེས་ཕེབས་པའང་ཉིན་ཞེད་ཙམ་ལ་མ་ཡལ། དུས་འདི་དག་ཏུ་གསང་བ་འདུས་པའི་རྒྱུད་ཡོངས་རྫོགས་རྒྱ་གར་གྱི་སྐད་དུ་སངས་ཀྱིས་བཏོན། མནལ་ཐམས་ཅད་འོད་གསལ་དུ་སོང་བའི་ངང་ནས་སྒོམ་བཟླས་སོགས་བྱས་ཤིང་སྐུའི་བཀོད་པ་ཡང་ཅིག་ཆར་མང་དུ་སྟོན་མཁན་ཞིག་ཡིན་པར་གྲགས།

༡༥ མཆུངས་མེད་ཀུན་སྤངས་ཆོས་རྗེ་ལ་གསོལ་བ་འདེབས།།

མཚན་བརྗོད་ལུགས་གཞན་ལ་ཀུན་སྤངས་པ་ཐུགས་རྗེ་བརྩོན་འགྲུས་སུ་གྲགས་པ་ཁོང་ནི། རིགས་ལྡན་གྱི་སྤྲུལ་བ་དངོས་ཡིན་པར་གྲགས་ཤིང་། མཁས་བཙུན་བཟང་པོའི་མཐར་ཐུག་པའི་རྟགས་མངོན་གྱུར་གྱི་གྲུབ་ཐོབ་ཆེན་མོ་ཞིག་ཡིན། མཚན་གྱི་རྣམ་གྲངས་ལ་ཞང་ཀུན་སྤངས་ཐུགས་རྗེ་བརྩོན་འགྲུས་ཞེས་དང་། མཚན་གཞན་ཀུན་སྤངས་ཆེན་པོ་ཀུན་ཏུ་བཟང་པོ་ཞེས་ཀྱང་བྱ། མདོག་གི་དང་བ་ཕྱུར་ཞེས་པའི་ས་ཆར། ཕྱི་ལོ་ ༡༢༤༣ ཆུ་ཡོས་ལོར་སྐུ་འཁྲུངས། ས་སྐྱ་དང་མདར་སོགས་དབུས་གཙང་གི་གྲྭ་ས་ཕལ་ཆེ་བར་ཐོས་བསམ་གནང་། མདོ་སྔགས་ཐམས་ཅད་ལ་མཁྱེན་པ་ཤིན་ཏུ་རྒྱས། ཆུ་མིག་པ་སེང་གེ་དཔལ་སོགས་མཁས་མཆོག་ཐམས་ཅད་ཞབས་ཀྱིས་མནན། ཀུན་མཁྱེན་ཆོས་སྐུ་བ་ལ་མངའ་བའི་གཞུང་གདམས་ངག་ཐམས་ཅད་གསན་ཅིང་། ཁོང་ལས་འབྲོ་ལུགས་ཀྱི་དབང་རྒྱུད་བཤད་དང་། སྦྱོར་དྲུག་ཉམས་ཁྲིད་དུ་མ་གསན་ནས་ཉམས་སུ་བླངས་པས་ཉམས་རྟོགས་ཀྱི་གློང་བརྡོལ། མི་མ་ཡིན་གྱི་ཇོ་མོ་ནགས་སྨན་རྒྱལ་མོ་དང་། ཕྱི་བྲག་ནགས་གསུམ་གྱི་དགེ་འདུན་དང་ཚོ་སྡེ་ཀུན་གྱིས་གདན་འདྲེན་བྱས་པ་བཞིན། དཔལ་ནགས་སྨན་རྒྱལ་མོའམ། ཇོ་མོ་ནང་དུ་ཆོས་སྡེ་ཆེན་པོར་གཏན་གྱི་གདན་ས་མཛད། ཁོང་ནི་སྦྱོར་བ་ཡན་ལག་དྲུག་པའི་གདམས་པ་མི་འདྲ་བ་བཅུ་བདུན་ཙམ་ལ་ཐོས་བསམ་མཐའ་རྒྱ་ཆོད་པ་གནང་ནས་ཉམས་མྱོང་གི་ཚད་དུ་ལོང་ཡོད་པ་ཞིག་གོ།

སྐབས་འདི་དག་ཏུ་ཁོང་ལ་དཔལ་དུས་ཀྱི་འཁོར་ལོས་ཞལ་གཟིགས་ལུང་བསྟན་མང་དུ་བྱུང་། རྣལ་འབྱོར་ཡན་ལག་དྲུག་གི་མན་ངག་སྐོར་བརྒྱད་དུ་ཡོད་པ་རྣམས་ཡི་གེར་འགོད་པར་མཛད། དེ་ནི་སྔགས་ཀྱི་གཞན་སྟོང་དབུ་མ་ཆེན་པོ་བདེ་སྟོང་ཟུང་འཇུག་གི་ངོ་བོར་མངོན་དུ་བྱ་བའི་ཐབས་མཆོག སྦྱོར་དྲུག་གི་ཁྲིད་ཡིག་བོད་དུ་བྱུང་བ་སྔ་ཤོས་ཡིན།

སྐུ་ཚེའི་སྨད་དུ་ཀུན་མཁྱེན་ཆེན་པོའི་སྒྲུབ་གནས་སྐྱིད་ཕུག་བདེ་ལྡན་དུ་གདན་ཕབ་སྐྱེ་དེས་དོན་སྒྲུབ་བརྒྱུད་ཀྱི་བསྟན་པའི་གདན་ས་བ་ལོ་ཉེར་གཅིག་ཙམ་མཛད། དཔལ་དུས་ཀྱི་འཁོར་ལོའི་རྫོགས་རིམ་སྦྱོར་བ་ཡན་ལག་དྲུག་གི་སྒོ་ནས་ཆོས་ཀྱི་འཁོར་ལོ་རྒྱ་ཆེར་བསྐོར་ཞིང་། སྐལ་ལྡན་སློབ་མ་སྟོང་ཕྲག་མང་པོ་རྣམ་ཀུན་མཆོག་ལྡན་གྱི་སྟོང་བ་ཆེན་པོ་དང་། མཆོག་མི་འགྱུར་བའི་བདེ་བ་ཆེན་པོ་ཟུང་འཇུག་གི་བདེ་དགའི་དཔལ་ལ་རོལ་བར་བྱས། གངས་ལྗོངས་བསྟན་པའི་ཡང་སྙིང་རྒྱ་ཆེར་སྤེལ་ཞིང་འཛམ་གླིང་ཕན་བདེའི་རྩ་བ་སྲ་བརྟན་དུ་བཞག་གོ།

དཔལ་རྒྱལ་བ་ཇོ་ནང་བ་ཞེས་པའི་མཚན་གྱི་སྙན་པ་གངས་རིའི་ལྗོངས་སུ་འདི་ནས་བྱུང་ཞིང་། དེ་ནས་

བཟུང་ཆོས་བརྒྱུད་འདི་ལ་དཔལ་ཇོ་ནང་བ་ཞེས་པའི་མཚན་ཆགས་དོན་ཡང་རྒྱུ་མཚན་དེ་དག་ཡིན། མགོན་པོ་མཆོག་དཀྱུང་གྲངས་དོན་གཅིག་བཞེས་པ། ཕྱི་ལོ་༡༣༡༣ ཆུ་མོ་གླང་གི་ལོ། དབྱིད་འབྲིང་པོའི་ཉེར་ལྔའི་ཐོ་རེངས་ལ་དགོངས་པ་སྟོང་གཟུགས་དགའ་ལྡན་བདེ་བར་གཤེགས་པའི་ངོ་བོར་ཐིམ།

༡༨ བྱང་སེམས་རྒྱལ་བ་ཡེ་ཤེས་ལ་གསོལ་བ་འདེབས།།

བྱང་སེམས་རྒྱལ་བ་ཡེ་ཤེས་ནི། ཕྱི་ལོ་ ༡༢༥༩ མེ་སྤྲུལ་ལོར་ཡུལ་མདོ་ཁམས་སུ་འཁྲུངས། ཆོས་རྗེ་ཀུན་སྤྱངས་ཆེན་པོ་དང་མཇལ་ནས་མི་ཕྱེད་པའི་དད་པ་ཐོབ། རྣལ་འབྱོར་ཡན་ལག་དྲུག་གསན་ནས་ཉམས་སུ་བླངས་པས་ཉམས་རྟོགས་མཐར་ཕྱིན། གཞུང་གདམས་ངག་ཐམས་ཅད་བུམ་པ་གང་བྱོའི་ཚུལ་དུ་གནང་ཞིང་ཐོབ། ཀུན་སྤྱངས་ཆེན་པོའི་བཀའ་གནང་བ་ལ་བརྟེན་ཇོ་ནང་གི་གདན་སར་ཕེབས། ཆོས་རྗེ་ཀུན་སྤྱངས་པའི་གདན་སར་ལོ་བརྒྱད་བཞུགས་རྗེས། མཁས་བཙུན་ཡོན་ཏན་རྒྱ་མཚོ་ལ་གདན་ས་གཏད་ནས་དཀྱུང་ལོ་རེ་བཞི་བ། ཕྱི་ལོ་ ༡༣༣༠ ལྕགས་ཕོ་སྤྲེལ་ལོའི་དབྱིད་འབྲིང་པོའི་ཚེའི་བཅུའི་ཉི་དྲོས་ལ་ཕྱུག་མོ་ཆོས་རྫོང་གི་རི་ཁྲོད་དུ་སྐུ་གཤེགས་སོ།།

༡༩ མཁས་བཙུན་ཡོན་ཏན་རྒྱ་མཚོ་ལ་གསོལ་བ་འདེབས།།

དེ་ནས་མཁས་བཙུན་ཡོན་ཏན་རྒྱ་མཚོ་ནི། བྱང་སེམས་ཆེན་པོ་རྒྱལ་བ་ཡེ་ཤེས་ཉིད་ཀྱི་མཆེད་གྲོགས་དང་སློབ་མ། རྒྱལ་ཚབ་གསུམ་པ་ཡིན། མདོག་གི་མཁར་སྟེང་ཞེས་པ་རུ། ཕུགས་སྟེང་མ་བའི་ཁྱིམ་རྒྱུད་ཅིག་ཏུ། ཕྱི་ལོ་ ༡༢༨༠ ལྕགས་སྤྲེལ་ལ་འཁྲུངས། གྲྭ་ས་མང་དུ་བསྟེན་པ་ལས་གཙོ་བོར་མདར་ཞེས་པ་རུ་སྦྱངས་པ་མཛད། གསང་ཕུགས་ཕྱོགས་ཀྱི་བླ་མ་མང་དུ་བསྟེན། མཐར་ཇོ་ནང་དུ་ཕེབས་ཏེ་ཀུན་སྤྱངས་ཆེན་པོ་ལ་ཟབ་ལམ་གྱི་ཁྲིད་གསན། མཚན་མོའི་རྣལ་འབྱོར་ཞག་ཉེར་གཅིག་ལ་རྟགས་བཅུ་རྫོགས་པར་མཐར་ཕྱིན། ཉིན་མོའི་རྣལ་འབྱོར་གྱི་སྐབས་འཕར་གཡོའི་ཉམས་ཆེར་བྱུང་སྟེ་མདའ་རྒྱང་ཙམ་དུ་འཕར་བའི་འཕར་གཡོའི་ཉམས་ཆེར་བྱུང་། མ་ཟད་ཇོ་ནང་གི་རི་གླུང་མེད་པར་ཐོགས་མེད་དུ་བྱོན་པའི་ཉམས་ཞག་བདུན་གྱི་བར་དུ་བྱུང་། ཉམས་དེ་ཉིད་སངས་ནས་ཆོས་རྣམས་མཉམ་ཉིད་ཆེན་པོ་གཅིག་གི་ངང་དུ་གྱུར། རྗེས་སུ་མངོན་མཁྱེན་ཐོགས་མེད་མངའ་བར་གྱུར། དམ་པའི་ཆོས་ལ་འདི་མ་གསན་དང་འདི་མི་མཁྱེན་པ་མེད་པ་ཙམ་ཡིན་པར་གྲགས། སྐུ་བཙུན་པ་རབ་ཀྱི་མཐར་ཐུག་པས་ཚུལ་ཁྲིམས་ཀྱི་དྲི་བསུང་རྒྱ་ཆེར་འཕྲོ་བ་ཞིག་ཏུ་གྲགས། དང་པོ་ཀུན་སྤྱངས་ཆོས་རྗེ་བླ་མ་བསྟེན་ཚུལ་རྒྱུད་ནས་བཤད་པ་ལྟར་བསྟེན། དེ་རྗེས་བྱང་སེམས་ཆེན་པོ་གདན་སར་ཕེབས་པ་ལའང་ཀུན་སྤྱངས་ཆེན་པོ་དང་ཁྱད་མེད་དུ་བསྟེན། བྱང་སེམས་ཆེན་པོ་སྐུ་འདས་རྗེས་ཁོང་ཇོ་ནང་གི་གདན་སར་ཕེབས། སྒྲུབ་བརྒྱུད་ཀྱི་བསྟན་པ་རྒྱ་

ཆེར་བསྐྱངས་ཏེ། ལོ་བདུན་ལྷག་ཙམ་ནས་ཀུན་མཁྱེན་ཆེན་པོ་དོལ་པོ་བ་ཤེས་རབ་རྒྱལ་མཚན་གདན་ས་འཛིན་པ་བོར་བསྐོས། དེ་རྗེས་ལོ་གཉིས་ཙམ་གྱི་རྗེས་དགུང་ལོ་རེ་བརྒྱད་པ། ཕྱི་ལོ་ ༡༣༢༧ མེ་མོ་ཡོས་ཀྱི་ལོར་སྟོན་ཟླ་འབྲིང་པོའི་ཚེས་ལྔ་ལ་དག་ཞིང་དུ་གཤེགས་སོ།།

༡༨ ཀུན་མཁྱེན་དུས་གསུམ་སངས་རྒྱས་ལ་གསོལ་བ་འདེབས།།

སྐྱེས་བུ་ཆེན་པོ་གང་གི་མཚན་གྱི་རྣམ་གྲངས་ནི། དོལ་པོ་བ་ཤེས་རབ་རྒྱལ་མཚན། ཆེ་བརྗོད་དུ་ཆོས་ཀྱི་རྒྱལ་པོ་ཆེན་པོ་ངེས་དོན་དབུ་མའི་ཤིང་རྟའི་སྲོལ་འབྱེད། རིགས་ལྡན་སྤྲུལ་པའི་སྐུ། ཀུན་མཁྱེན་ཆེན་པོ་ཇོ་ནང་བ་ཤེས་རབ་རྒྱལ་མཚན། གཞན་ཡང་ཀུན་མཁྱེན་དོལ་བུ་པ་ཤེས་རབ་རྒྱལ་མཚན་དཔལ་བཟང་པོ་སོགས་མཚན་གྱི་རྣམ་གྲངས་མང་། བདག་ཉིད་ཆེན་པོ་མཆོག་འདི་ནི་ཡུལ་མངའ་རིས་དོལ་པོ་བན་ཚང་ག་ཡོ་རིའི་གྲོང་ཁྱེར་དུ་ཡབ་ཡེ་ཤེས་དབང་ཕྱུག་དང་ཡུམ་ལྷ་མོ་ཚུལ་ཁྲིམས་རྒྱན་གཉིས་ཀྱི་སྲས་སུ། ཕྱི་ལོ་ ༡༢༩༢ ཆུ་ཕོ་འབྲུག་ལ་རྒྱལ་སྲས་དོན་གྲུབ་གཉིས་པ་ལྟ་བུའི་ཚེས་ངོ་མཚར་བའི་མཛད་ཚུལ་དང་བཅས་སྐུ་བལྟམས། ཡུལ་དུ་བླ་མ་སྐྱི་སྟེངས་པ་སོགས་བླ་མ་མང་རབ་བསྟེན། ཆོས་ཀྱང་སྙིང་མ་དང་དབུ་མ་རིགས་ཚོགས་སོགས་དང་། རིག་གནས་བཟོ་གནས་ཟླ་མོ་མང་པོ་ཆུང་ངུའི་དུས་ནས་ཚེགས་མེད་དུ་མཁྱེན། དགུང་ལོ་བཅུ་དྲུག་པ་ལ་སྐྱི་སྟོན་འཇམ་དབྱངས་གྲགས་པ་ཡ་རྩེར་ཕེབས་དུས་གློ་བོ་སྟོད་དུ་མཇལ། ཕྲེང་བ་སྐོར་གསུམ་སོགས་ཀྱི་ལག་ལེན་དང་ཆོས་མང་དུ་གསན། དགུང་ལོ་ཉེར་གཅིག་པ་ལ་གཅིག་བུར་བྲོས་ཏེ། བླ་མ་སྐྱི་སྟོན་པའི་དྲུང་དུ་ཕེབས་ནས་གཞུང་འགྲེལ་བ་དང་བཅས་པའི་ཚིག་དོན་མཐའ་དག་ཐུགས་སུ་ཆུད། སློབ་དཔོན་རིན་ཡེའི་དྲུང་དུ་རྗེ་འུའི་བཙུད་ལེན་སོགས་སྦྱོང་། བྱམས་ཆོས་དང་ཡུམ་རྒྱས་འབྲིང་བསྡུས་གསུམ་སོགས་ཞེར་ཕྱིན་གྱི་མདོ་རྣམས་སྐྱུར་བར་གསན་ཙམ་གྱིས་ཐམས་ཅད་ཐུགས་སུ་ཆུད། དབུས་གཙང་གི་སྟེ་མང་ཆེ་བར་གྲྭ་སྐོར་མཛད་པས་མཁྱེན་རབ་ཀྱི་རྟལ་དང་རིགས་པའི་རྣམ་འགྱུར་མཆོག་ཏུ་གྲགས། ཞེར་ཕྱིན་འབུམ་པ་སོགས་མདོ་སྡེ་དུ་མའི་ཚིག་མཐའ་དག་ཐུགས་ལ་བྱང་ཞིང་གཞུང་ཆེ་ཆུང་གང་ལ་ཡང་ཐོགས་པ་མེད་པར་མཁྱེན་པ་རྒྱས་པས། ཐམས་ཅད་ཀྱིས་ཀྱང་ཀུན་མཁྱེན་རང་དུ་འདུག་ཅེས་པས་ཀུན་མཁྱེན་གྱི་མཚན་དེ་དུས་ནས་ཀྱང་ཐོགས།

སྤྱིར་མདོ་སྔགས་ཀྱི་ཆོས་གསན་པའི་བླ་མ་སུམ་ཅུ་ལྷག་མངའ་བ་ལས་མཆོག་ཏུ་གྱུར་པ། སྐྱི་སྟོན་འཇམ་དབྱངས་ལ་མདོ་སྔགས་ཀྱི་གཞུང་ཆེ་ཆུང་དཔག་མེད་དང་། དབང་བསྐུར་རང་ཡང་ཟུར་བཀའ་བདུན་ཅུ་ཙམ་དང་། དུས་འཁོར་ཡང་བླ་མ་འདིའི་དྲུང་ནས་གསན་ཏེ་དབང་རྒྱུད་མན་ངག་ཐམས་ཅད་ལ་ཤིན་ཏུ་མཁས་པར་གྱུར། ཕྱི་ལོ་ ༡༣༢༢ ལ་ཇོ་ནང་དུ་ཕེབས་ཏེ། མཁས་བཙུན་ཆེན་པོ་ཡོན་ཏན་རྒྱ་མཚོ་ལས་

དབང་དང་གདམས་པ་མང་པོ་དང་། སྦྱོར་དྲུག་ལ་ཉམས་ཁྲིད་གསན། དམིགས་པ་ཞུ་སྐབས་མ་གཏོགས་སུ་དང་ཡང་མི་འཕྲད་པར་མཁའ་སྤྱོད་བདེ་ལྡན་དུ་བཞུགས་ཏེ་བསྒོམས། སོར་བསམ་གྱི་ཉམས་རྟོགས་མཐར་ཕྱིན་པས་བླ་མས་མགྱོགས་འཁྲིད་བྱ་གསུངས། མི་མཐུད་དུ་བསྒོམས་པས་སྲོག་རྩོལ་མཐར་ཕྱིན་པའི་རྟགས་རྒྱུད་ནས་བཤད་པ་བཞིན་མངའ། ཐོག་མར་ཇོ་མདའ་ནས་ཇོ་ནང་དུ་ཡར་ཐེབས་པས་ནམ་མཁའ་ལ་དུས་ཀྱི་འཁོར་ལོའི་དཀྱིལ་འཁོར་ཡོངས་རྫོགས་གཟིགས། དེ་ནས་བཟུང་ཡི་དམ་ཞལ་གཟིགས་པ་ནི་གྲངས་ལས་འདས། འཕགས་པ་སྤྱན་རས་གཟིགས་དང་མི་ལབ་པ་བཞིན་ཡོད་ལ། གུར་མགོན་དང་རྣམ་སྲས་བྲན་བཞིན་འཁོལ། ཕྱག་མཆོད་ཐུགས་དམ་མཛད་རེས་ཀྱིས། རིགས་གསུམ་མགོན་པོ་དང་། འཕགས་མ་སྒྲོལ་མ་དང་། སྨན་བླ། བྱམས་པ་རྣམས་རེ་མོས་ཀྱིས་འབྱོན། མཁའ་འགྲོ་རྒྱ་མཚོ། སྒྱུ་འཕྲུལ་དྲྭ་བ། སྡོམ་པ་ཆེ་ཆུང་། རྡོ་རྗེ་ཕག་མོ། རྡོ་རྗེ་དབྱིངས་ལ་སོགས་པའི་དཀྱིལ་འཁོར་གཟིགས་པ་ཡང་གྲངས་ལས་འདས།

བདེ་བ་ཅན་གྱི་སྨོན་ལམ་མཛད་ཚེ་བདེ་ཆེན་ཞིང་དངོས་སུ་གཟིགས་པ་དང་། གཟིམ་ཁང་བདེ་བ་ཅན་དུ་གུ་རུའི་ཚེས་བཅུའི་མཆོད་པ་མཛད་པའི་ཚེ། སློབ་དཔོན་པདྨ་མཁའ་འགྲོའི་ཚོགས་དང་བཅས་མངོན་སུམ་དུ་བྱོན་ནས་ཤིས་བརྗོད་མཛད་པ་དང་། མཆོད་རྟེན་བཞེངས་པའི་ལས་ལ་ཞུགས་ཚད་བདེ་བ་ཅན་དུ་འགྲོ་བའི་མཚན་མ་གཟིགས། དེ་ཡང་བླ་མའི་བཀའ་དྲིན་ཆེན་པོས་དགུང་ལོ་སོ་ལྔ་བ། ཕྱི་ལོ་ ༡༣༢༦ ལོར་ཇོ་ནང་གདན་ས་ཆེན་པོའི་གདན་ས་བ་མཛད་དགོས་པའི་བཀའ་ཕེབས། དེས་ཁོང་གི་སློབ་དཔོན་མཁས་བཙུན་ཆེན་པོ་ཤིན་ཏུ་དགྱེས་ནས་ལོ་གཉིས་མ་ཟིན་ཙམ་ལ་ཉིན་མཚན་མེད་པར་དབང་ལུང་ཁྲིད་བཤད་པ་སོགས་བླ་མ་ཉིད་ལ་མངའ་བའི་ཆོས་ཐམས་ཅད་བསྐྱལ། བཀའ་དང་བསྟན་བཅོས་འགྱུར་རོ་ཅོག་ལ་རྫོགས་པར་ནན་ཏན་དང་བཅས་པས་ཚར་གཅིག་གཟིགས། དེ་གའི་དོན་ཐམས་ཅད་མ་འདྲེས་པར་ཐུགས་སུ་ཆུད།

གཞན་སྟོང་གི་ལྟ་སྒོམ་ཁྱད་པར་ཅན་ནི། མཁའ་སྤྱོད་བདེ་ལྡན་དུ་བཞུགས་པའི་ཚེ་ཐུགས་ལ་འཁྲུངས་པ་ཡིན་ཀྱང་། ལོ་ཤས་ཤིག་ཏུ་གཞན་ལ་མ་གསུངས། དགེ་བའི་བཤེས་གཉེན་དམ་པ་བཅུ་ལྷག་ལ་སྙིང་པོ་མདོ་བཅུའི་བཤད་པ་རང་བཞེད་རྩལ་དུ་བཏོན་ཏེ་རྒྱས་པར་གསུངས། འདུས་པའི་སྐྱེ་མང་པོར་མདོ་སྔགས་ཟུང་འཇུག་མཆོག་གཞི་ལ་བཞག་པའི་དཔལ་དུས་ཀྱི་འཁོར་ལོའི་དབང་ལུང་མན་ངག་གི་བསྐྱེད་རྫོགས་རྒྱ་ཆེར་གསུངས་པས་རྟོགས་ལྡན་གྱི་སློབ་བུ་བསམ་གྱིས་མི་ཁྱབ་པ་ཆེས་མང་དུ་བྱུང་། གཞན་སྟོང་སྟོན་པའི་གསུང་རབ་ཐན་ཐུན་ཀྱང་མང་དུ་མཛད། ཁོང་གི་དཔེ་ཆ་རྣམས་དང་ཆོས་སྐད་ཕྱོགས་ཐམས་ཅད་དུ་ཁྱབ་པས་མཁས་པ་ཡལ་གྱི་གློར་མ་ཤོང་། དངོས་སུ་འབེལ་གཏམ་རྩོད་པར་ཞུས་པ་རྣམས

རྒྱ་མཚོ་ལ་ཁ་བ་བབས་པ་བཞིན་དུ་ལྷགས་གཅིག་ཀྱང་མ་ཚུགས། ཁོང་ལ་དངོས་སུ་མཇལ་བ་རྣམས་ཁོང་གི་གྲུབ་མཐའ་ལ་ངེས་ཤེས་དང་བླ་མ་ལ་དད་པ་ བླ་མེད་ཐོབ་པ་ཤ་སྟག་བྱུང་། རིང་ནས་ངག་ལན་དང་རྩོད་ཡིག་བསྐུར་བ་རྣམས་ལ་ལྟུགས་ལན་མཛད་པས་ངེས་པ་སྐྱེད། ཕྱིས་སུ་ཁོང་གི་གྲུབ་མཐའ་དེ་རྩོད་བྲལ་དུ་སོང་ནས། ཕྱོགས་བཞིའི་དགེ་བ་ཤེས་དུ་མས་བསྐུལ་བས་རི་ཆོས་ངེས་དོན་རྒྱ་མཚོ་སོགས་གྲུབ་མཐའི་ཆོས་བཅུ་དྲུག དུས་འཁོར་ས་བཅད་སོགས་དུས་འཁོར་ཆ་ལག་བཅོ་བརྒྱད། ཡུམ་གྱི་མཚན་བྱུ། གསོལ་འདེབས་ཉེར་ལྔ། ཐུགས་རྗེ་ཆེན་པོའི་ཆོས་སྐོར་ཉེར་གསུམ། བསྟོད་སྐོར་བཅུ་བཞི། སྐྱ་འབུམ་ཆེན་པོའི་ཆོས་སྐོར་ལྔ། རྡོ་རྗེ་ཕྲེང་བ་དབང་སྐོར་གསུམ། སྤྲིངས་ཡིག་བརྒྱད། སྨོན་ལམ་གསུམ། བཀྲ་ཤིས་བཞི་སོགས་སྤྱ་ཕྱི་ཀུན་ཏུ་གསུང་རབ་ཀྱི་ཡིག་ཆ་མང་པོ་མཛད་པས། ཐུབ་བསྟན་སྤྱི་དང་ངེས་དོན་དབུ་མ་ཆེན་མོ་མདོ་སྔགས་ཀྱི་གནས་ལུགས་མཐར་ཐུག་ཏུ་ལུང་རིགས་དྲི་མ་མེད་པས་གཏན་ལ་ཕབ་ཏེ་རྒྱུ་དང་འབྲས་བུའི་ཐེག་པའི་ཆོས་སྒོ་མཐའ་དག་གསལ་བར་བྱས། ཆོས་ཁྲིའི་ཁར་ཆོས་གསུངས་པ་དང་། བཟོ་བོ་རྣམས་ཀྱི་སར་བཀོད་པ་མཛད་པ་དང་། གཟིམ་ཚུང་དུ་ཐུགས་དམ་ལ་བཞུགས་པ་སོགས་སྐུ་ལུས་ཀྱི་བཀོད་པ་གསུམ་དུས་གཅིག་ཏུ་བྱུང་བ་ནི། མི་མང་པོར་མངོན་སུམ་དུ་གྱུར། སྐུའི་བཀོད་པ་བརྒྱད་དུས་གཅིག་ཏུ་བྱུང་བ་ཡང་འགའ་རེས་མཐོང་།

སྐུ་འབུམ་མཐོང་གྲོལ་ཆེན་མོ་མི་དང་མི་མ་ཡིན་གྱིས་བཞེངས་པའི་ཆ་རྐྱེན་འབུལ་ཞིང་ལས་ཀ་ལ་རེམ་པས། ངོ་མཚར་འཕྲུལ་གྱིས་ཕྱི་ནང་གི་བཀོད་པ་ཡོངས་རྫོགས་དཀའ་ངལ་མེད་པས་གྲུབ་ཅིང་། དགེ་མཚན་ལེགས་པའི་ལྟས་བཟང་དང་བཅས་པ་རབ་གནས་མཐའ་རྒྱས་དགའ་སྟོན་གྱི་ཞིང་དུ་བཞེངས་གྲུབ་གྱུར། དེ་ཡང་ཁོང་ཉིད་ཇོ་བོ་ཆེའི་མདོ་སྡེ་སོགས་ལས་ལུང་བསྟན་པ་ནི། ལི་ཙ་བྱི་གཞོན་ནུ་འཇིག་རྟེན་ཐམས་ཅད་ཀྱིས་མཐོང་ན་དགའ་བ་ཞེས་བྱ་བ་མ་འོངས་པའི་དུས་ན་ཀ་ཡོ་རིའི་བརྒྱུད་དུ་ངའི་མིང་འཆང་བའི་དགེ་སློང་དུ་གྱུར་ཏེ། ཞེས་སོགས་གསལ་བར་གསུངས་པ་དང་། གཙུག་ཏོར་རྣམ་པར་རྒྱལ་མའི་རྒྱུད་ལས། བདེ་གཤེགས་མྱ་ངན་འདའ་འོག་ནས།། ལོ་ནི་སྟོང་ཕྲག་ཕྱེད་རིང་ཚེ།། གདོང་དམར་ཡུལ་དུ་ང་འདྲ་བའི།། བསྟན་པ་འཛིན་པའི་དགེ་སློང་ཞིག ཀུ་བོ་ལྡོན་ཤིང་ཕྲེང་མཛེས་སུ།། ཀ་ཡོ་རི་ཡི་གྲོང་ཁྱེར་དུ།། ཡབ་ནི་ཡེ་ཤེས་དབང་ཕྱུག་ཆེ།། ཡུམ་ནི་ཚུལ་ཁྲིམས་རྒྱན་ཞེས་གྲགས།། སྲས་ནི་སངས་རྒྱས་མིང་ཅན་འབྱུང་།། ང་ཡི་བསྟན་པའི་རྒྱལ་མཚན་འཛུགས།། ཆོས་ཀྱི་དུང་འབུད་དར་ཕྱར་འགྱུར།། ཞེས་སོགས་མདོ་རྒྱུད་དུ་མ་ནས་ཀུན་མཁྱེན་ཇོ་ནང་བ་ཆེན་པོ་ཁམས་གསུམ་ཆོས་ཀྱི་རྒྱལ་པོ་ནི་ཡང་ཡང་ལུང་བསྟན་པ་ཞིག་གོ།

དགུང་ལོ་བདུན་ཅུར་སོན་པ། ཕྱི་ལོ་ ༡༣༨༡ ལྕགས་མོ་གླང་གི་ལོའི་དགུན་ཟླ་ར་བ་ཡར་ངོའི་ཚེས་དྲུག་གི་སྲོད་ཐུན་དང་པོའི་དུས་སུ་གཟུགས་སྐུ་ཆོས་དབྱིངས་སུ་བསྡུ་བར་མཛད་དོ།། དེའི་ཚེ་ས་གཡོ་བ་དང་

འཇའ་འོད་མེ་ཏོག་གི་ཆར་སོགས་ངོ་མཚར་བའི་ལྟས་དང་བཅས་ཞག་བདུན་རིང་ཐུགས་དམ་མ་གྲོལ། རྒྱུད་ནས་ཇི་ལྟར་གསུངས་པ་བཞིན་དུ། ཐུགས་དམ་མ་གྲོལ་བའི་བར་དུ་ཕྱག་ཞེས་པ་ནས་འཇད་ཞེས་པའི་བར་གྱི་གཙང་བོ་ཉིས་ལྷབ་གྱིས་བྲུག་པར་གྱུར། ཐུགས་དམ་གྲོལ་བའི་ཚེ་བྱང་སེམས་དབུ་གཙུག་ནས་ལྷུད་པའི་སྐབས་ཇོ་མདའ་ཞེས་པའི་ས་ཡི་གཙང་བོ་ཛ་ཡུན་ཙམ་ལ་གྱེན་དུ་ལོག་ནས་ཆད། གཙང་བོ་ཆད་ཤུལ་ནས་མི་འགའ་རེས་འགྲོ་འོང་བྱེད་ཐུབ་པ་བྱུང་བ་ལ་སོགས་ཆེས་ངོ་མཚར་བ་བྱུང་ངོ་།། དེ་ནས་སྤུར་སྦྱོང་མཛད་པའི་ཚེ་དུ་བ་ཐམས་ཅད་འཇའ་འོད་དུ་སོང་བ། འོད་གསལ་རྫམ་ལྟ་བུའི་ནམ་མཁར་ཁྱབ་ཅིང་བར་སྣང་ལ་རོལ་མོའི་སྒྲ་དང་དྲི་བཟང་སོགས་ངོ་མཚར་བའི་ལྟས་མང་བྱུང་། གདུང་རུས་ཀྱི་སྐལ་ཚོགས་དག་དུ་དུས་འཁོར་ཕྱག་མང་། དཔལ་བར་རྟ་མགྲིན་ཡང་གསང་། དབྱུང་གཡས་མི་གཡོ་བ། ལྷག་པར་སངས་རྒྱས་ཐོད་པ། ཕྱག་མཇུབ་སྤྱན་རས་གཟིགས་སོགས་ལྷ་སྐུ་འབུར་དོད་མང་བོ་དང་། སྟོང་ཆེན་ཡིག་ལྔ་སོགས་གསུང་རྟེན་མང་བོ། དུང་དཀར་གཡས་འཁྱིལ་སོགས་ཐུགས་རྟེན་མང་བོ་རིང་བསྲེལ་གྱི་ཚོགས་དང་བཅས་དཔག་ཏུ་མེད་པའི་ངོ་མཚར་བ་ཆེས་མང་བོས་འཛིགས་རྟེན་ལ་ངོ་མཚར་དང་བྱིན་རླབས་ཀྱིས་ཁེངས་པར་མཛད་པའོ།།

༡༨ ཆོས་རྒྱལ་ཕྱོགས་ལས་རྣམ་རྒྱལ་ལ་གསོལ་བ་འདེབས།།

ཀུན་མཁྱེན་ཆེན་པོའི་གདན་ས་འཛིན་པའི་མངའ་བདག བྱང་ཆུབ་སེམས་དཔའ་ས་སྙིང་གི་སྤྲུལ་བར་གྲགས་པ་ཕྱོགས་ལས་རྣམ་རྒྱལ་ནི། ཕྱི་ལོ་ ༡༣༠༨ མེ་བོ་རྟ་ཡི་ལོར་མངའ་རིས་ཡ་ཚེ་རྒྱལ་པོའི་བླ་མཆོད་ཅིག་གི་སྲས་སུ་འཁྲུངས། ཡབ་ཁུ་བོ་སོགས་ལས་ སྔགས་ཆོས་མང་བོ་དང་དབུ་མ་རྒྱ་འཇུག སྤྱོད་འཇུག་བཅས་མཁས་པར་སྦྱངས། དབུས་གཙང་དུ་ཕྱིན་ནས་ཕར་ཚད་དབུ་གསུམ་སྦྱངས་པས་གཞུང་ལུགས་ཐམས་ཅད་ལ་མཁྱེན་པ་རྒྱས། དགུང་ལོ་ཉེར་གཅིག་ལ་དབུས་གཙང་ཀུན་ཏུ་གྲྭ་སྐོར་མཛད། ཇོ་ནང་དུ་ཐེབས། ཆོས་རྗེ་ཀུན་མཁྱེན་ཆེན་པོས་སྐུ་འབུམ་མཐོང་གྲོལ་ཆེན་པོ་ལ་བསྐོར་བ་མཛད་བཞིན་པ་དང་མཇལ་ནས་བླ་བྲང་དུ་ཞག་བདུན་རིང་བཞུགས་ནས་འབེལ་གཏམ་མང་དུ་མཛད། དབུ་མ་གཞན་སྟོང་གི་གྲུབ་མཐའ། སངས་རྒྱས་ཐམས་ཅད་ཀྱི་དགོངས་པ། ཆོས་ཐམས་ཅད་ཀྱི་ཆོས་ཉིད་དུ་ངེས་པ་རྙེད། ཀུན་མཁྱེན་ཆེན་པོ་ལ་མི་ཕྱེད་པའི་དད་པ་འཁྲུངས། དེའི་སྐབས་ཆོས་འབྲེལ་ཅི་རིགས་གསན། རྗེས་སུ་སླར་ཡང་དུས་འཁོར་གྱི་རྒྱུད་སོགས་ཐུགས་ལ་བཟུང་ནས་ཇོ་ནང་དུ་ཐེབས་སྐབས། དུས་ཀྱི་འཁོར་ལོའི་དབང་ཞུས། ཟབ་ལམ་གྱི་ཁྲིད་བསྒྲུངས་པས་ཉམས་རྟོགས་ཕུན་སུམ་ཚོགས་པ་འཁྲུངས། རྒྱུད་འགྲེལ་སྦྱངས་པས་ཆེགས་མེད་མཁྱེན། བུ་སློན་ཐམས་ཅན་མཁྱེན་པའི་མདུན་དུ་ཕར་ཕྱིན་དང་མཚན་བརྗོད་གསན། རྗེ་བདག་ཉིད་ཆེན་པོ་ཅོང་ཁ་བས་དམ་པ་འདི་ལས་དཔལ་དུས་ཀྱི་འཁོར་ལོའི་ཆོས་

མང་དུ་གསན་པ་སོགས་བསམ་གྱིས་མི་ཁྱབ་ཅིང་ཁྱད་དུ་འཕགས་པའི་སྐྱེས་བུ་དམ་པ་ཞིག་གོ། རྒྱལ་བ་ཇོ་ནང་གི་གདན་ས་ལོ་དྲུག་ལ་འཛིན་སྐྱོང་མཛད། སྐུ་ཚེའི་སྨད་དུ་སླར་ཡང་ཇོ་ནང་གི་གདན་ས་འཛིན་པ་གནང་། དགུང་ལོ་གྱ་གཅིག་པ། ཕྱི་ལོ་ ༡༣༨༦ མེ་སྟག་ལོའི་ས་ཟླའི་བཅུ་གཅིག་གི་ཉི་ཤར་ལ་བདེ་བ་ཅན་དུ་ཐེབས་པར་གྲགས།

༢༠ མཆུངས་མེད་ཉ་དབོན་ཀུན་དགའ་ལ་གསོལ་བ་འདེབས།།

འཇམ་དཔལ་སྤྲུལ་བར་གྲགས་པ་མཆུངས་མེད་ཉ་དབོན་ཀུན་དགའ་དཔལ་ནི། ཕྱི་ལོ་ ༡༢༨༥ ཤིང་མོ་བྱའི་ལོའི་ཐ་སྐར་ཟླ་བའི་ཚེས་བརྒྱད་ལ་ཡུལ་ཉང་པོར་འཁྲུངས། ཁམས་པའི་དགེ་བཤེས་ཉ་དར་མ་རིན་ཆེན་གྱི་དབོན་པོ་ཡིན། ཆུང་དུའི་དུས་ནས་མཁྱེན་རབ་ཤིན་ཏུ་ཆེ། ཀུན་མཁྱེན་ཆེན་པོ་དང་ཡང་ཡང་མཇལ། ཕྱིས་མདོ་སྔགས་ཀྱི་གཞུང་ཐམས་ཅད་ལ་མཁྱེན་པ་རྒྱས་ཤིང་རིག་པའི་དབང་ཕྱུག་ཆེན་པོར་གྱུར། ཕྱོགས་ལས་རྣམ་རྒྱལ་ཡུན་རིང་བསྟེན། ཉམས་རྟོགས་ཀྱང་མཐར་ཕྱིན། དུས་འཁོར་སོགས་མདོ་སྔགས་ཀྱི་ཆོས་མང་པོ་མཁྱེན་པའི་མཁས་པ་ཆེན་པོར་གྱུར་ལ། ལྷག་པར་ཚད་མ་ཉ་ལ་ཁྲུངས་གཏུགས་ཟེར་བའི་ཚད་དུ་མཆིས། རྗེ་ཙོང་ཁ་བ་ཆེན་པོས་པར་ཕྱིན་གསན་པ་ལ་སོགས་པ་དམ་པའི་སྐྱེས་བུ་མང་པོའི་དགེ་བའི་བཤེས་སུ་གྱུར་བ་སོགས་འགྲན་བྲལ་གྱི་བདག་ཉིད་ཆེན་པོ་ཞིག་ཡིན། དགུང་ལོ་གོ་ལྔ་པ། ཕྱི་ལོ་ ༡༣༧༩ ས་ལུག་ལོའི་ཆུ་སྟོད་ཟླ་བའི་ཚེས་དྲུག་ལ་ངོ་མཚར་དུ་མའི་ལྟས་བཅས་སྐུ་ཞི་བའི་དབྱིངས་སུ་གཤེགས་སོ།།

༢༡ གྲུབ་ཆེན་ཀུན་དགའ་བློ་གྲོས་ལ་གསོལ་བ་འདེབས།།

ཆོས་རྗེ་ཉ་དབོན་པའི་ཐུགས་སྲས་གྲུབ་ཆེན་ཀུན་དགའ་བློ་གྲོས་ནི། རུས་ཤར་ཁ་བའི་རུས་རྒྱུད་དུ་སྐུ་འཁྲུངས། བླ་མ་དགེ་བའི་བཤེས་གཉེན་ཆེས་མང་པོ་ལས། ཕར་ཚད་མངོན་འདུལ་དབུ་མ་སོགས་མདོ་སྔགས་གཉིས་ལ་གསན་བསམ་རྒྱ་ཆེར་གནང་། ལྷག་པར་དུ་དཔལ་དུས་ཀྱི་འཁོར་ལོ་གཞིས་ཕྱིན་པ་ཆོས་རྗེ་ཉ་དབོན་པ་ལས་གསན། དམ་པ་འདི་ཉིད་རིགས་རུས་རྒྱལ་རིགས་སུ་འཁྲུངས་ཀྱང་། སྲིད་འཁོར་ལ་ཆགས་པ་བྲལ་བའི་སྒོ་ནས་བས་མཐའ་རྣམས་ཀྱི་འཚོ་བ་ལ་བརྟེན་ཏེ་སྒྲུབ་པ་ཁོ་ན་ལ་གཞོལ་བས་རྟོགས་པ་མཆོག་ལྡན་གྱིས་གྲུབ་བརྙེས་སུ་གྱུར། དཔལ་ལྡན་རྒྱལ་བ་ཇོ་ནང་བའི་ཆོས་བརྒྱུད་འཛིན་སྐྱེལ་ལ་བརྩོན་འགྲུས་དང་། དད་འདུན་ཆེན་པོ་ལྷོད་མ་སྐྱོང་བས་སྐུ་ཚེ་ཧྲིལ་པོར་རྣམ་དག་སྐྱོན་བྲལ་གྱིས་དུས་འདས་པའི་སྐྱེས་བུ་དམ་པ་ཞིག་ལགས་ཤིང་། བུ་སྟོན་རིན་ཆེན་གྲུབ་ཀྱི་སྐྱེས་སྤྲུལ་དུ་གྲགས་པ་ཞིག་ཀྱང་ཡིན་ནོ།།

༢༢ འཇམ་དབྱངས་དཀོན་མཆོག་བཟང་པོ་ལ་གསོལ་བ་འདེབས།།

འཇམ་དབྱངས་དཀོན་མཆོག་བཟང་པོ་ནི། འབྲུངས་ཡུལ་ལ་སྟོད་བྱུང་བའི་ཕྱོགས་ཡིན། རྒ་བའི་གྲྭ་ས་བཟང་ལྡན་ཡིན་ཡང་། ས་སྐྱ་སོགས་གྲྭ་ས་མང་ཆེ་བར་ཕྱིན། མཁན་འཇམ་དབྱངས་རིན་རྒྱལ་བ་ལས་ས་སྐྱའི་ཆོས་རྣམས་གསན། གྲུབ་ཆེན་ཀུན་དགའ་བློ་གྲོས་ལས་དུས་འཁོར་སོགས་ཟབ་དོན་མཐའ་དག་གསན་ཏེ་ཐུགས་སུ་ཆུད། སི་ཏུ་ཀུན་བཟང་རབ་བརྟན་འཕགས་ཀྱིས་བླ་མར་བཀུར། ཉང་སྟོད་ཀྱི་ཆོས་སྡེ་གསར་བའི་ཆོས་དཔོན་མཛད། ཇོ་ནང་བའི་གྲྭ་ཚང་གསར་དུ་བཙུགས། ཕྱིས་རྗེ་ཤར་ནུབ་ཞེས་པའི་གདན་ས་ཆེན་པོ་གཉིས་ཀྱིས་གུས་པས་བཏུད། ཆོས་སྡེ་དེ་དག་དང་ཇོ་ནང་གི་གདན་ས་འཛིན་པ་མཆོག་གི་མཛད་པ་བསྐྱངས། གྲུབ་པའི་རྟགས་མཚན་དུ་མཁས་གྲུབ་རྗེ་དཔོན་སློབ་ཀྱིས་བྱད་ཁ་བྱས་པར་བྱང་སེམས་དང་རྗེས་བཟླས་སྤེལ་བས་ཕྱིར་ལོག་ཏུ་སོང་། བླ་མ་ས་སྐྱ་པ་ཆེན་པོའི་ཡང་སྲིད་དུ་གྲགས་པ་ཞིག་ཡིན་སོད། གཙོ་བོ་རྒྱལ་བ་ཇོ་ནང་བའི་ལུགས་ཀྱི་དཔལ་དུས་ཀྱི་འཁོར་ལོའི་ཕུལ་བྱུང་བརྒྱུད་ལྡན་བླ་མ་ཞིག་ཏུ་གྱུར་པའོ།།

༢༣ འདྲེན་མཆོག་ནམ་མཁའི་མཚན་ཅན་ལ་གསོལ་བ་འདེབས།།

མཚན་གཞན་ནམ་མཁའ་ཆོས་སྐྱོང་དུ་གྲགས་པ་ནི། རྒ་བའི་གྲྭ་ས་གྲྭ་ཚང་ཆེན་མོ་ཡིན། ཀུན་མཁྱེན་བསོད་ཆེན་ལས་མཚན་ཉིད་ཀྱི་གཞུང་རྣམས་མཁས་པར་སྦྱངས། སླར་འཇམ་དབྱངས་དཀོན་བཟང་གི་ཆོས་གྲྭར་ཕྱིན། ཆོས་དང་གང་ཟག་ལ་དད་དེ་མཚན་ཉིད་ཀྱི་གཞུང་རྣམས་གསན་བསམ་མཛད། གཞན་སྟོང་ལ་ངེས་པ་གཏིང་ནས་ཆུགས། སྦྱོར་དྲུག་ཞུས་ཏེ་ཉམས་རྟོགས་ཤིན་ཏུ་བཟང་བའི་ཚད་དུ་ཕྱིན། དཔལ་དུས་ཀྱི་འཁོར་ལོའི་རྒྱུད་རྣམས་ལ་ཤིན་ཏུ་མཁས་པར་གྱུར། ངམ་རིང་སོགས་སུ་འཆད་ཉན་པ་འགའ་རེའི་སར་ཐེབས། རྗེ་ཤར་ནུབ་དང་ཁྱད་པར་སེང་གེ་རྗེ་བས་ཡོན་བདག་བྱས། རྗེ་ཆེན་དང་ཇོ་ནང་གི་གདན་ས་བ་ཡུན་རིང་མཛད་དེ་བཤད་སྒྲུབ་གཉིས་ཀས་བཟུང་། སྐུ་འབུམ་མཐོང་གྲོལ་ཆེན་མོའི་ཆོས་འཁོར་གསེར་ཟངས་ཀྱིས་གཡོགས་པ་ལ་སོགས་པ་མཛད་བཟང་གིས་སྐུ་ཚེ་འདས་ཤིང་ཉམས་དང་རྟོགས་པའི་གདེང་ཚད་བརྙེས་པ་ཞིག་གོ །

༢༤ པཎ་ཆེན་ནམ་མཁའ་དཔལ་བཟང་ལ་གསོལ་བ་འདེབས།།

ནམ་མཁའ་དཔལ་གྱི་བཟང་པོ་ནི། དང་པོར་རྒ་བའི་གྲུབ་མཐའ་ས་སྐྱ་བ་ཡིན། སོས་པ་རབ་འབྱམས་པ་ཐུགས་རྗེ་དཔལ་བཟང་གི་གྲྭ་སར་སློབ་གཉེར་མཛད། བརྒྱ་སྟེར་འཆད་ཉན་ཡང་ལོ་ཤས་ཆུགས་པ་བྱུང་།

ལྷུན་སྡིངས་སུ་བདག་ཉིད་ཆེན་པོའི་སློབ་མ་ཤཱངས་སྟོན་བྲོ་བ་ལས་དུས་འཁོར་བྱང་ལུགས་ཞུས་ཏེ། དེ་ལ་མཁས་པར་སྦྱངས། རྒྱལ་བ་ནམ་མཁའི་མཚན་ཅན་ལས་སྦྱོར་དྲུག་མན་ངག་ཇོ་ནང་བའི་ལུགས་འདི་ཞུས། ཆོས་འདི་ལ་སྔ་དུས་ཤིག་ནས་གསན་པས་ཉམས་རྟོགས་བཟང་པོ་འཁྲུངས་ཡོད་པ་ཞིག་གོ། གདན་ས་འབྲས་སྤུངས་དགོན་གཞི་བཏབ་ནས་ཀྱང་འགྲོ་དོན་བྱུང་བ་ལ་སོགས་པ་མཛད་འཕྲིན་ཆེས་བཟང་པོ་མཛད་དོ།།

༢༥ ལོ་ཆེན་རཏྣ་བྷ་དྲ་ལ་གསོལ་བ་འདེབས།།

ལོ་ཆེན་རཏྣ་བྷ་དྲ་ནི། འཁྲུངས་ཡུལ་འབྲོག་པའི་ས་ཁུལ་ཡིན་ཞིང་། གྲྭ་ས་བཞད་ཀྱི་གྲྭ་ཚང་ཆེན་མོ་ནས་ཡིན། ཨོ་རྒྱན་རྫོགས་པ་སོགས་བླ་མ་མང་པོ་བསྟེན། གསང་སྔགས་གསར་རྙིང་སོགས་ཀུན་ལ་མཁས། ཁྱད་པར་པཎ་ཆེན་ནམ་མཁའ་དཔལ་བཟང་ལས་དུས་འཁོར་གྱི་ཆོས་སྐོར་གསན་པས་ཉམས་རྟོགས་རྒྱས། སྤྱན་རས་གཟིགས་སོགས་ཡི་དམ་མང་པོའི་ཞལ་གཟིགས། མདོག་གི་སླན་སྡིངས་དང་། བཞད་རི་བོ་གྲུ་འཛིན་སོགས་དགོན་གནས་མང་དུ་བཏབ། ཐུགས་རྗེ་ཆེན་པོའི་དམར་ཁྲིད་དང་། སྦྱོར་དྲུག་གི་ཁྲིད་ཡིག་སོགས་ཀྱང་མཛད་དོ།།

༢༦ དཔལ་ལྡན་ཀུན་དགའ་གྲོལ་མཆོག་ལ་གསོལ་བ་འདེབས།།

རྗེ་ཀུན་དགའ་གྲོལ་མཆོག་ནི་མངའ་རིས་སྨད་ཀྱི་གློ་བོ་སྨན་ཐང་ཞེས་པར། གཉག་སྟོན་ཤཱཀྱ་སྲུ་ནེའི་རིགས་རྒྱུད་དུ་དགུང་ལོ་ང་བརྒྱད་བཞེས་པ་ཡབ་དཔོན་དྲུང་ཆེ་དབང་བཟང་པོ་དང་། ཡུམ་བཙུན་མོ་སྤྲ་ཕྲི་གཉིས་ལས་ཕྲི་མ་ལོ་ཉེར་གཉིས་བཞེས་པ་རྣམ་གཉིས་ཀྱི་སྲས་སུ་མེ་ཡོས་ལོར་འཁྲུངས། དགུང་ལོ་བདུན་པར་དྲུང་པ་ཆོས་རྗེ་ལས་ག་ཤེད་དམར་ལྷ་ལྷུའི་དབང་ཞུས། གསང་མཚན་ཞི་སྟོང་རྣམ་དག་རྡོ་རྗེ་གསོལ། དགུང་ལོ་བཅུ་བར་དྲུང་པ་ལས་དགེ་ཚུལ་གྱི་སྡོམ་པ་བཞེས། ཀུན་དགའ་གྲོལ་མཆོག་ཏུ་མཚན་གསོལ། ས་སྐྱའི་ཞེན་པ་བཞི་བྲལ་གསན་པས་ཉམས་རྟོགས་ཁྱད་པར་ཅན་འཁྲུངས། ཇོ་ནང་། ཤངས་པ། ས་སྐྱ་སོགས་བརྒྱུད་པ་ཀུན་ལ་ཐོས་བསམ་ཆེས་མང་བས་རྙིང་ཕྱོགས་ཀྱི་ཆོས་སྐོར་དང་བཅས་པའི་མཛོད་ཆེན་དུ་གྱུར། རྒྱལ་བ་དགེ་འདུན་རྒྱ་མཚོ་དང་ཡན་གཉིས་མཇལ་བའི་དང་པོའི་སྐབས། འབེལ་གཏམ་གནང་བས་ཡན་ཚུན་བར་དུ་ཐུགས་མཉེས་ཚད་མེད་བྱུང་། རྗེས་སུ་མཇལ་དུས་ཆོས་འབྲེལ་བཀའ་གདམས་ནོར་ཕྲེང་གི་རྒྱ་ལུང་ཞུས་པས་ཆོས་འབྲེལ་བྱུང་བ་སོགས་ཡན་ཚུན་ཆོས་འབྲེལ་ཅན་དུ་ཡང་གྱུར། ལོ་ཆེན་རིན་ཆེན་བཟང་པོ་ལ་ནམ་མཁའ་དཔལ་བཟང་ནས་བརྒྱུད་པའི་དུས་ཀྱི་འཁོར་ལོའི་ཆོས་སྐོར་ཡོངས་རྫོགས་གསན་ནས་ཉམས་བཞེས་མཛད། སྐབས་ཤིག་ལ་ཇོ་ནང་གི་གདན་ས་འཛིན་པར་མཛད། སྐུ་ཚེའི་སྨད་དུ་ཆོས་ལུང་བྱང་རྩེ་བཏབ་ནས་སྒྲུབ་སྡེ་གཙོ་བོར་མཛད།

བུ་སློབ་ཀྱི་གཙོ་བོ། རྗེ་རིང་ཀུན་དགའ་རྒྱལ་མཚན། ཆོས་སྐུ་ལྷ་དབང་གྲགས་པ། མཁས་དབང་བྱམས་པ་ལྷུན་གྲུབ། མཁན་ཆེན་ལུང་རིགས་རྒྱ་མཚོ། རྗེ་དྲུང་ཀུན་དགའ་དཔལ་བཟང་རྣམས་སོ།། དེ་ནས་ཐོན་གྱི་སྐྱེས་རབས་དང་རྗེས་ནས་ཡང་སྲིད་ངོས་འཛིན་སོགས་ཀྱི་ལུང་བསྟན་གསལ་བར་མཛད་དེ། བསྟན་འགྲོའི་དོན་རེ་ཞིག་རྫོགས་ཚུལ་གྱིས་དགུང་ལོ་དྲུག་ཅུ་མེ་སྟག་ལོའི་ཟླ་བ་དང་པོའི་ཚེས་བརྒྱད་ལ་གཟུགས་སྐུ་ཆོས་དབྱིངས་སུ་ཐིམ་པའོ།།

༢༧ མཁན་ཆེན་ལུང་རིགས་རྒྱ་མཚོ་ལ་གསོལ་བ་འདེབས།།

ལོ་ཙཱ་བ་ཆེན་པོ་རཏྣ་བྷ་དྲའི་དངོས་སློབ་མཁན་ཆེན་ལུང་རིགས་རྒྱ་མཚོར་གྲགས་པ་ནི། ཉང་སྟོད་དུ་སྐྱེ་བ་གཙང་ཁང་བའི་སྐུ་རུས་སུ་འཁྲུངས། གསེར་མདོག་ཅན་ཞེས་པ་རུ་མདོ་ཐུགས་ལ་གསན་སྦྱོང་རྒྱ་ཆེར་མཛད་པས་མཁས་པ་ཕུལ་དུ་བྱུང་བར་གྲགས། རྒྱལ་རྩེའི་མཁན་པོར་མངའ་གསོལ་མཛད། གཞན་སྟོང་ཁང་ཚོགས་པ་སོགས་ཀྱི་མཁན་པོར་ཡུན་རིང་པོར་བཞུགས། ཁྱད་པར་རྗེ་ཀུན་དགའ་གྲོལ་མཆོག་ཚུལ་བཞིན་དགེ་བའི་བཤེས་གཉེན་མཆོག་ཏུ་བསྐུར་ཏེ་དུས་འཁོར་གྱི་དབང་རྒྱུད་མན་ངག་མཐའ་དག་གསན་ནས་ཉམས་བཞེས་ཡང་དག་པ་གནང་། གདུལ་བྱ་ལའང་ཚུལ་བཞིན་དུ་སྤེལ་བའི་ཐུན་མོང་དང་ཐུན་མིན་གྱི་བརྒྱུད་འཛིན་པར་གྱུར། དགོངས་པ་ཆོས་དབྱིངས་སུ་མ་བསྡུས་པའི་ཐོན་ནས་མ་འོངས་ལུང་བསྟན་དང་། ཡང་སྲིད་ངོས་འཛིན་སོགས་ཀྱི་ཞལ་བཀོད་གསལ་རྒྱས་གནང་བ་སོགས་ངོ་མཚར་བའི་མཛད་རྗེས་ཡང་ཤིན་ཏུ་མང་། རྗེས་སུ་རྗེ་དམ་པའི་ཡང་སྤྲུལ་ཁྲི་འདོན་མཛད་པ་དང་བཀའ་ཆོས་ཐམས་ཅད་ཡུལ་བྱུང་དུ་འགྲུབ་པ་བྱུང་། དེ་ལྟར་དུ་ཐམས་ཅད་ལ་སྟ་གོན་དང་ལེགས་འགྲུབ། རང་དབང་དང་མངོན་ཤེས་ལ་སོགས་པ་ལྡན་པའི་སྒོ་ནས་རེ་ཞིག་གདུལ་བྱ་རྫོགས་ཏེ་གཟུགས་སྐུ་ཆོས་ཀྱི་དབྱིངས་སུ་བསྡུས་སོ།།

༢༨ ཁྱབ་བདག་སྒྲོལ་བའི་མགོན་པོ་ལ་གསོལ་བ་འདེབས།།

ཁྱབ་བདག་སྒྲོལ་བའི་མགོན་པོའམ་རྗེ་བཙུན་ཀུན་དགའ་སྙིང་པོ། ཡོངས་གྲགས་སུ་ཏཱ་ར་ནཱ་ཐ་ནི། བོད་ཁམས་སྐྱོང་བའི་བརྟན་མ་བཅུ་གཉིས་ཀྱི་ནང་ནས་རྡོ་རྗེ་གཡུ་སྒྲོན་མའི་གནས་ཁ་རག་འབྲང་གི་ཕྱུ། ཐོན་ར་ལོ་ཙཱ་བ་ཆེན་པོའི་བརྒྱུད་པ་རིམ་པར་བྱོན་པའི་བསྐྱེ་གནས། ད་ལྟ་ཆོས་འཁོར་སྒྲིངས་སུ་གྲགས་པ་རུ་ཤར་ནུབ་གཉིས་ལས་ཤར་བ་ཀུན་དགའ་སེ་ཐྨིས་བཏབ་པའི་དགོན་གཞི་དེར། དེའི་གདུང་རྒྱུད་ཐུགས་འཆང་ཚུལ་ཁྲིམས་རྒྱ་མཚོ་ལ་སྲས་བཞི་བྱུང་བའི་ཆེ་ཤོས་རྣམ་རྒྱལ་ཕུན་ཚོགས་དང་། ཡུམ་རྡོ་རྗེ་བུ་དགའ་ལྷ་མོ་གཉིས་ཀྱི་སྲས་སུ། སྤྱི་ལོ་ ༡༥༧༥ ཤིང་མོ་ཕག་ལོ་ཆུ་སྟོད་ཟླ་བའི་ཚེས་བརྒྱད་ལ་གྲོད་པུ་འཇའ་ཚོན་ཁ་དོག་ལྔ་ལྡན་གྱི་ནང་དུ་འཁྲུངས། ཁ་འབྱེད་མ་ཐག་ཁྱེའུ་སྐུ་ལ་ཤ་མཚན་ཁྲག་ཞགས་ཀྱི་ཐིག

ལེ་ཡི་ཁྲིའི་ཚངས་སྐུད་ཀྱི་རྣམ་པ་ཅན། ཕྱག་ཞབས་ལ་འཁོར་ལོ་དང་། སྐུ་ལ་ཀུར་ཀུམ་གྱི་དྲི་དང་ལྡན་པ་སྤྱན་གྱིས་ཕྱོགས་ཐམས་ཅད་ལ་གཟིགས་བཞིན་ཞལ་ནས་སུམ་ཛ་ནིའི་སྔགས་ལན་གསུམ་བརྗོད་པ་ཞིག་བལྟམས་སོ།། དེ་སྐབས་མེས་པོས་པདྨ་སྲི་གཅོད་རྡོ་རྗེ་ཞེས་པའི་མཚན་གསོལ། སྨྲ་ཤེས་ཙམ་ནས་ང་བླ་མ་ཀུན་དགའ་གྲོལ་མཆོག་ཡིན་ཞེས་ཡང་ཡང་གསུངས།

དེ་ནས་དགུང་ལོ་བརྒྱད་པར་དཔོན་སློབ་རྣམས་བགྲོས་ནས། དཔལ་སྟག་ལུང་བ་ཆེན་པོ་ཀུན་དགའ་རྒྱལ་མཚན་གདན་དྲངས་ནས་རབ་ཏུ་བྱུང་སྟེ། མཚན་ཀུན་དགའ་སྙིང་པོ་བཀྲ་ཤིས་རྒྱལ་མཚན་དུ་གསོལ་ཞིང་། དག་སྣང་དུ་སྤྲུལ་པའི་བཤེས་གཉེན་རྒྱ་གར་བ་ཛྙ་ལ་ནཱ་ཐས། ཏཱ་ར་ནཱ་ཐ་ཞེས་པའི་མིང་བསྩལ། མཁས་མཆོག་བྱམས་པ་ལྷུན་གྲུབ་བླ་མར་བསྟེན་ནས་མདོ་རྒྱུད་ལ་གསན་སྦྱོང་མཛད་དེ་མཁས་པའི་གནས་ཐོབ། འདུལ་འཛིན་ཀུན་དགའ་རྒྱལ་མཚན་གྱིས་མཁན་པོ་དང་། བྱམས་པ་ལྷུན་གྲུབ་ཀྱིས་སློབ་དཔོན་གནང་དེ་བསྙེན་པར་རྫོགས་ཏེ། ཕྱི་ལྟར་ཉན་ཐོས་ཀྱི་སྤྱོད་པ་དང་། ནང་ལྟར་རྒྱལ་སྲས་བྱང་སེམས། གསང་བ་ལྟར་ན་སྔགས་འཛིན་རྣལ་འབྱོར་བ་ཆེན་པོར་གྱུར། རྗེ་ནོར་རིང་བ་ལས་ལམ་འབྲས་དང་དབང་ལུང་གདམས་པ་མང་དུ་གསན། རྗེ་བྲག་སྟོད་པ་ཆོས་སྐུ་ལྷ་དབང་གྲགས་པའི་དྲུང་ནས་ཆོས་དྲུག་ཕྱག་ཆེན་རྣམས་ཀྱིས་གཙོས་མན་ངག་མང་པོ་གསན་པས་མངོན་པར་རྟོགས་པའི་ཀློང་རྡོལ། མཁན་ཆེན་ལུང་རིགས་རྒྱ་མཚོས་དུས་ཀྱི་འཁོར་ལོའི་དབང་དང་རྒྱུད་བཤད། མན་ངག་སྦྱོར་བ་ཡན་ལག་དྲུག་པའི་བྱིན་རླབས་དོན་བརྒྱུད་བཅས་བསྩལ་ཅིང་ཉམས་སུ་བླངས་པས་ཉམས་རྟོགས་མཐར་ཕྱིན། བུ་རྡོར་ལུགས་གཉིས་ལ་མཁས་ཤིང་བཅུ་གཉིས་ཀྱི་ཡེ་ཤེས་མཆོག་རིམ་གྱིས་བརྙེས་ཏེ་གྲུབ་པའི་དབང་ཕྱུག་ཏུ་གྱུར། རྗེ་དྲུང་ཀུན་དགའ་དཔལ་བཟང་གིས་དུས་འཁོར་དང་མགོན་བཀའ་རྣམས་གནང་། སློབ་དཔོན་ཆེན་པོའི་བཀའ་བགོད་ལ། གདན་ས་འཛིན་པར་ཇོ་ནང་དུ་ཐེབས་དགོས་གསུངས་པ་ལྟར་ཇོ་ནང་རི་ཁྲོད་དུ་གདན་ས་འཛིན་པར་ཐེབས། དགུང་ལོ་ཉེར་དགུའི་དབྱིད་དུས་ཤིག་ལ་ཇོ་ནང་དུ་ཐོ་རེངས་སྤྲིན་གསེབ་ནས་རྗེ་བཙུན་བྱམས་པ་བྱོན་ནས་རང་ལ་ཐིམ། ལྷ་ཀླུ་འདྲེ་སྲིན་མང་པོ་ལ་ཆོས་འཆད་བཞིན་པའི་ཉམས་བྱུང་། རྗེས་སུ་གཞན་སྟོང་དབུ་མའི་གྲུབ་མཐའ་ལ་ངེས་ཤེས་གཏིང་ནས་སྐྱེད། ཀུན་མཁྱེན་ཆེན་པོའི་ཞལ་གཟིགས་ཤིང་སྔ་ཕྱིའི་ལུང་བསྟན་མང་དུ་མཛད་པ་དང་། རྨི་ལམ་གྱི་ངང་ནས་ཤམྦྷ་ལར་ཡང་ཕྱིན་པས་ཡུལ་གྱི་བཀོད་པ་གསལ་བར་མཐོང་བ་དང་། པོ་བྲང་ཀ་ལཱ་པར་ཕྱིན་པས་ས་བཅུའི་བྱང་ཆུབ་སེམས་དཔའི་སྐུ་རིགས་ལྡན་དང་མཇལ་ནས་གསུང་གི་བདུད་རྩི་ཐོབ་པའི་དག་སྣང་བྱུང་། སྐྱིད་ཕུག་ཏུ་མཚམས་ལ་བཞུགས། ལོ་དུས་ལྟར་ཆགས་མེད་དུ་ཇོ་ནང་དུས་ཁྲིད་ཆེན་མོ་བཙུགས་པས་ཁྲིད་མ་ཐེབས་པ་གཅིག་ཀྱང་མེད། རྒྱ་གར་སློབ་དཔོན་སུ་ནི་ཤྲཱ་ཏ་ཤྲཱི་དང་། བུདྡྷ་བཛྲ་སོགས་ལས་ཟབ་བཀའ་མང་པོའི་གདམས་པ

ནོད་དེ་ཐུགས་བཅུད་རྒྱས། སླར་རྫོ་ནང་སྒྲུབ་མཆོད་ཀྱི་ཚེ་དུས་འཁོར་རྟུལ་ཚོན་བཞེངས་སྐབས། སྒྲུབ་སྡེ་གང་ཡོད་ཡོངས་སྒྲིལ་བདུན་བརྒྱ་ཙམ་ལ་དབང་བཅུ་གཅིག་རྫོགས་རིམ་བཞིན་རྫོ་ནང་གི་དུས་ཁྲིད་སྒྲར་ལས་ལྷུག་པ་མཛད་ཅིང་། འཁོར་ལོ་སྡོམ་པའི་གསང་གསུམ་གྱི་རོལ་བ་མཐུལ་བའི་ཉམས་བཟང་ཡང་བྱུང་། གཙང་བ་སྟེ་སྲིད་ཕྱུན་ཚོགས་རྣམ་རྒྱལ་གྱིས་ཆོས་གཞིས་དང་ལྷ་འབངས་སོགས་རྒྱ་ཆེར་ཕུལ་ཏེ། ངེས་དོན་གྱི་ཆོས་གཞི་དགོན་གནས་ཕུལ་བས། དགུང་ལོ་ཞེ་གཅིག་པ། ཕྱི་ལོ་ ༡༨༡༥ ཤིང་མོ་ཡོས་ཀྱི་ལོ། རྗེར་བླ་གསུམ་པའི་ཆོས་བརྒྱུད་ལ་ཐིག་བཏབ་ཏེ་དཔལ་རྟག་བརྟན་དམ་ཆོས་གླིང་ངེས་དོན་དགའ་བའི་ཚལ་གསར་བཞེངས་གནང་། བསམ་འགྲུབ་རྩེའི་རྒྱལ་བུའི་སྐུ་གེགས་བསལ། དགུང་གྲངས་ཉེར་དྲུག་སྐོར་ལ་ཧ་སྦྲེང་སོགས་ཀྱི་འདུས་ཚོགས་ལ་ཆོས་འབྲེལ་དང་། བྲག་སེང་གེའི་ཞོལ་དུ་རྫེ་ཅོང་ཁ་བའི་བཞུགས་ཁྲིའི་སྟེང་ནས་ལམ་རིམ་གསུངས། རྒྱ་དགེ་མེ་ཐུབ་མ་རྣམས་མཇལ་ཚེ་དགྲ་ནག་གི་རྒྱུད། སྐད་གཉིས་ཀྱིས་སྨྲ་བའི་སྤོབས་པ་ཆེ་ཞིང་ཤུགས་སྦྱར་བས། ཧ་སྦྲེང་བ་རྣམས་ངོ་མཚར་བས་བསྔགས་བརྗོད་ཀྱི་སྐད་པ་གང་སར་ཁྱབ་པས་བསྟན་འགྲོ་ལ་ཕན་པ་རྒྱ་ཆེར་བྱུང་ངོ་།།

འཕགས་བོད་གཉིས་ཀྱི་རྒྱུད་སྡེ་བཞིའི་དབང་ཁྲིད་མན་ངག་མ་ལུས་པ་གསན། རྒྱ་གར་གྲུབ་ཆེན་གུ་རུ་ལྷ་ཕྱོགས་པ་སངས་རྒྱས་སྦས་པའི་མགོན་པོ་ལས་གསང་སྔགས་རྒྱུད་སྡེའི་དབང་བསྐྱེད་རྫོགས་མཐའ་ཡས་པ་གསན་པ་སྟེ། བླ་མེད་སྔགས་ཀྱི་གཞུང་ལུགས་ལ་བོད་འདིར་སྔོན་མེད་ཀྱི་ལེགས་བཤད་གྲངས་སུ་བཏབ་པའང་ལྔ་བརྒྱ་ཙམ་བྱུང་བར་ཉིད་ཀྱིས་གསུངས་སོ།། དེ་སོགས་ཀྱིས་མཚོན་ཆེ་བའི་རྣམ་ཐར་མང་ལ། གཞན་ཡང་སྤྱ་ཕྱི་ཀུན་ཏུ་རྒྱ་གར་གྱི་རྣལ་འབྱོར་བ་འགའ་ལ་ཟབ་ཆོས་དང་ཕྱི་ནང་གི་རིག་གནས་སོགས་ཞུས་པས། དགོངས་དོན་ཀུན་མངོན་པར་བྱང་ཆུབ། དབོན་པོ་ལྷུན་གྲུབ་ཀྱིས་བསྐུལ་ནས་སྦྱོར་དྲུག་གི་ཁྲིད་ཡིག་མཐོང་བ་དོན་ལྡན་བརྩམས། རྒྱ་གར་ཆོས་འབྱུང་སོགས་དུས་འཁོར་བདེ་གསང་འདུས་གསུམ་སོགས་གསང་སྔགས་རྒྱུད་སྡེའི་ཚོ་ག་མང་པོ་དང་། དུས་འཁོར་བདེ་གསང་གི་བསྐྱེད་རྫོགས་ཀྱི་རྣམ་བཤད་སོགས་སྔགས་ཀྱི་གཞུང་འགྲེལ་མང་པོ་དང་། ཐ་ན་བསྟོད་ཚོགས་སྨོན་ལམ་སོགས་ཀྱིས་མཚོན་བསྡོམས་པོ་ཏི་བཅུ་ཕྲག་བཞི་ལྷག་གི་གསུང་རབ་མཛད། མདོ་སྔགས་སྤྱི་དང་ཁྱད་པར་ངེས་དོན་དབུ་མ་ཆེན་པོ་རྗེ་རྒྱལ་བ་གཉིས་པ་ཇོ་ནང་བའི་དགོངས་བཞེད་ལྟར་ལེགས་པར་གསལ་བར་བྱས་ཏེ་དར་རྒྱས་སུ་མཛད། མ་ཟད་བོད་གངས་ཅན་གྱི་རྒྱུད་སྡེ་ཀུན་ལ་སྨན་པའི་མཛད་རྗེས་མང་དུ་བཞག དགུང་གྲངས་རེ་གཅིག་བཞེས་པ། ཕྱི་ལོ་ ༡༨༣༥ ཤིང་མོ་ལུག་ལོའི་ནག་པ་ཟླ་བའི་ཉེར་བརྒྱད་ལ་གཞན་དོན་དུ་དགོངས་ནས་སྨན་པའི་རྒྱལ་པོའི་ཞིང་དུ་གཤེགས་པར་གྲགས།

༣༨ སྔོན་སྦྱངས་རིན་ཆེན་རྒྱ་མཚོ་ལ་གསོལ་བ་འདེབས།།

སྟོན་སྦྱངས་རིན་ཆེན་རྒྱ་མཚོའམ་རྒྱལ་ཚབ་འཛིན་པ་ཀུན་དགའ་རིན་ཆེན་རྒྱ་མཚོ་ནི། གཙང་གི་སྟེ་བ་སྣར་ཐང་བའི་སྲས་སུ་འཁྲུངས། རྗེ་བཙུན་ཀུན་དགའ་སྙིང་པོའི་ཞབས་ལ་གཏུགས་ཤིང་རབ་ཏུ་བྱུང་ཞིང་བསྙེན་པར་རྫོགས། ཁྱད་པར་དུ་ཟབ་ལམ་རྡོ་རྗེའི་རྣལ་འབྱོར་གྱི་དབང་ལུང་མན་ངག་གསན་ཏེ་བསྒོམས་པས་ཉམས་རྟོགས་མཐར་ཕྱིན། སྟོན་སྦྱངས་སད་པས་བློ་གྲོས་ནང་ནས་རྒྱས་ཏེ་གསུང་རབ་ཉིན་རེ་ལ་ཤོག་བུ་བཅོ་བརྒྱད་ཙམ་ཐུགས་ལ་ཟིན། གཞན་ཡང་མདོ་སྔགས་ཀྱི་ཆོས་བཀའ་མང་པོ་ཞུས་ནས་དེ་དག་གི་དགོངས་དོན་ཐུགས་སུ་ཆུད། རྟག་བརྟན་དམ་ཆོས་གླིང་གི་སློབ་དཔོན་ཞིང་དུ་གཤེགས་པའི་རྐྱེན་གྱིས་དེར་ཐེབས་ཏེ་རྒྱལ་ཚབ་མཛད་ནས། ལོ་བཅོ་ལྔ་ཙམ་ལ་བཤད་སྒྲུབ་ཀྱི་གྲྭ་མ་ཉམས་པར་སྐྱོང་བར་མཛད། སྐུ་ཚེའི་སྨད་ལ་གསང་སྔགས་རི་བོ་བདེ་ཆེན་དུ་བཤད་སྒྲུབ་སྤེལ་མའི་ངང་ལ་བཞུགས། ཐུགས་སྲས་ཀྱི་བུ་སློབ་ཀྱང་བློ་གྲོས་རྣམ་རྒྱལ། ཨ་མདོ་ཀུན་དགའ་དཔལ་བཟང་སོགས་མང་པོ་བྱུང་ངོ་།།

༣༠ མཁས་གྲུབ་བློ་གྲོས་རྣམ་རྒྱལ་ལ་གསོལ་བ་འདེབས།།

མཁས་གྲུབ་བློ་གྲོས་རྣམ་རྒྱལ་ནི། ཡུལ་འཛད་འཚོས་ཟ་རྣ་བ་ཞེས་པར། ཕྱི་ལོ་ ༡༨༡༩ ས་ཕོ་རྟ་ལ་ཡབ་ལྷ་དར་རྒྱས་དང་། ཡུམ་སྒྲུབ་མོ་དཔལ་འཛིན་གཉིས་ཀྱི་སྲས་སུ་ལྟེ་བས་སྒོམ་ཐག་གི་རྩུལ་འཆང་བཞིན་ངོ་མཚར་བའི་ལྟས་བཅས་འཁྲུངས། བྱིས་པ་ཤིན་ཏུ་ཆུང་ངུའི་དུས་ནས་ལྷུང་བཤགས་རང་ཤེས་དང་བྱམས་པའི་ཞལ་གཟིགས་མང་། དགུང་ལོ་བཅུ་དྲུག་པར་མཁའ་འགྲོས་བསྐུལ་བ་ལྟར་རྗེ་བཙུན་ཀུན་དགའ་སྙིང་པོའི་དྲུང་དུ་སྐྲ་ཕུད་ཕུལ། མིང་བློ་གྲོས་རྣམ་རྒྱལ་དུ་བསྟུལ། སློབ་གཉེར་མཛད་པས་རིང་པོར་མ་ལོན་པར་མཁས་པའི་གནས་ཐོབ། དེ་ནས་མཁན་རིན་ཆེན་རྒྱ་མཚོ་ལས་བསྙེན་རྫོགས་དང་དབང་བཀའ་མང་པོ་གསན་པས་མཁས་པར་གྱུར། དེ་ནས་སྒྲུབ་ལ་བརྩོན་པས་ཉམས་རྟོགས་ཀྱི་གློང་བརྡོལ། ཉམས་སྣང་དུ་རི་ཛམྦུ་ལའི་སྐུ་འདྲ་བ་ཞིག་གི་མདུན་ན་དགོན་པ་ཁྲ་ཤིག་གོ་ཞིག་འདུག་པ་ཛམ་ཐང་དུ་འདུག་པ་ཕྱིས་སུ་མངོན་གསལ་བྱུང་།

དཔལ་མགོན་གྱིས་བཀའ་ལུང་གནང་བ་ལྟར་མི་རིང་བར་སྙིང་པོ་ཁྲབ་བདག་སོགས་ཀྱི་ཆེད་དུ་ཁམས་པ་མང་པོས་ནན་གྱིས་སྐྱལ་མ་བྱས། དེའི་ཕྱིར་སྐྱིད་ཕུག་ནས་མེ་བྱ་ལོའི་ཧོར་ཟླ་ལྔ་པར་ལམ་དུ་ཞུགས། འགྲོ་ཁར་རྗེ་བཙུན་འཕྲིན་ལས་དབང་མོ་ལ་མཇལ་ཏེ་བར་ཆད་བསལ་བ་དང་རྗེས་འཛིན་གྱི་སྨོན་ལམ་བཏབ། རྗེ་བཙུན་མས་རེ་ཞིག་བཀའ་གནང་བསྟུལ་ཏེ་ལོ་གསུམ་ནས་འཁོར་ངེས་ཀྱིས་ཞེས་གསུངས།

ཧོར་ཟླ་བརྒྱད་པའི་ནང་ལ་ཛམ་ཐང་དུ་འབྱོར་བས་ཆོས་རྗེ་རྒྱལ་བ་སེང་གེ་དང་། ལྷོ་ཁ་བ་ལ་སོགས་པས་སྣེ་ལེན་རྒྱས་པར་མཛད། ཕྱི་ལོ་ ༡༨༥༩ ས་ཕྲེའི་ལོ་ནས་བཟུང་གདུལ་བྱ་རིས་མེད་ལ་དུས་ཀྱི་འཁོར་ལོའི་

དབང་ཁྲིད་སོགས་རྒྱས་པར་བསྐྱལ། རབ་བྱུང་བསྐྱེད་རྫོགས་སྒྲུབ་པ་ལྔ་བཅུ་ཙམ་དང་། རྡོ་འཛིན་སྒྲ་གསུམ་དང་ཚ་ཁོའི་རྒྱལ་པོ་སངས་རྒྱས་འབུམ་གྱིས་གདན་དྲངས་པ་ལ་སོགས་པས་དབང་བཀའ་རྗེས་གནང་སོགས་གནང་། མདོར་ན་ཡར་མགོ་ལོག་དང་མར་ཚ་ཁོའི་བར་དུ་གདུལ་བྱ་གྲངས་ལས་འདས་པར་ཆོས་ཀྱི་འཁོར་ལོ་བསྐོར།

ཁོང་གིས་ཡོན་བདག་ལ་ཕྱག་དྲུག་པའི་རྗེས་གནང་སྐབས་མགོན་པོའི་ཞལ་གསལ་བར་གཟིགས། མཆོད་ཡོན་འབྲལ་མི་ཐོད་པའི་ངང་དུ་ཕྱིར་རྫམ་ཐང་དུ་ཐེབས། དེ་ལྟར་ལོ་ངོ་བཅུ་གཉིས་ཙམ་ལ་ཁམས་ཕྱོགས་སུ་བཞུགས་ནས་བསྟན་འགྲོའི་དོན་མཛད། དེ་ནས་སེ་དགོན་འཕྲིན་སྙིང་སོགས་ཀྱིས་བཞོལ་ཀྱང་ཡར་ཐེབས་པའི་ཐུགས་ཐག་བཅད་དེ་ས་སྤྱིལ་ཏོར་ཟླ་བཞི་བའི་ཡར་ཆེས་ལ་རྫམ་ཐང་ནས་གཞི་བཏེགས། ཟླ་བ་བཅུ་གཅིག་པའི་ནང་ལྷ་སར་འབྱོར། མཐར་དགུང་གྲངས་རེ་དྲུག་པ། ཕྱི་ལོ་ ༡༨༡༣ ཆུ་ཕག་ལོར་སྐུ་གཤེགས། འདི་ཡང་ཀུན་མཁྱེན་ཆེན་པོས་རང་གི་མའི་རྣམ་སྤྲུལ་དུ་ལུང་བསྟན་ཏོ།།

༣༡ གྲུབ་ཆེན་དགེ་དབང་འཕྲིན་ལས་ལ་གསོལ་བ་འདེབས།།

མཚན་གཞན་ཆ་ལུང་བ་དགེ་དབང་འཕྲིན་ལས་ཞེས་གྲགས་པ་ཁོང་ནི། ཡུལ་ཆོས་ཟ་རུ། ཕྱི་ལོ་ ༡༨༥༩ ཤིང་ཕོ་རྟ་ལ་འཁྲུངས། བྱིས་དུས་ནས་དམ་པའི་སྤྱོད་པ་ལ་གནས་པ། དགུང་ལོ་བཅུ་དྲུག་པར་ཨ་ཁྱུ་བློ་གྲོས་རྣམ་རྒྱལ་གྱིས་རྒྱལ་ཚབ་ཆེད་རབ་བྱུང་མཛད། ཐོག་མ་ནས་ཆ་ལུང་རྡོ་རྗེ་བྲག་བཙན་ཁོང་གིས་བཀུལ་ནས་ཁོང་ལ་སྐྱེལ་བསུ་སོགས་བྱས་པར་གྲགས། ལོ་ཉི་ཤུའི་བར་འདུལ་མཛོད་དབུ་ཕར་སོགས་གཞུང་ལུགས་ལ་སྦྱངས་པས་དཀའ་བ་མེད་པར་མཁྱེན། བློ་གྲོས་རྣམ་རྒྱལ་ལས་དུས་འཁོར་བསྐྱེད་རྫོགས་སོགས་ཟབ་བཀའ་མང་པོ་གསན། སྦྱོར་དྲུག་བསྒོམས་པས་བཤད་སྟོད་དང་མཐུན་པའི་ཉམས་རྟོགས་ཤར། ལྕགས་འབྲུག་ལོར་འབྲས་སྤུངས་དགའ་ལྡན་གཉིས་སུ་ཇོ་ནང་གི་བསྟན་གཞི་བཙུགས། དེ་ནས་ཆོས་རྗེ་ཀུན་བཟང་དབང་པོ་སོགས་ལ་སྦྱོར་དྲུག་དབང་ཁྲིད་སོགས་གནང་བས། ཇོ་ནང་དུ་དེ་དག་གི་སྒྲ་རང་བྱུང་གིས་གྲགས་ཤིང་། ཡེ་ཤེས་ཐེབས་པའི་རྣམ་འགྱུར་ཀུན་མཁྱེན་ཆེན་པོའི་སྐབས་ལྟར་བྱུང་། དགུང་ལོ་བདུན་ཅུ་བ། ཕྱི་ལོ་ ༡༩༢༣ ཆུ་ཡོས་ལོའི་ཆོ་འཕྲུལ་ཟླ་བའི་ཆེས་བརྒྱད་ལ་སྐུ་འདས་སོ།། འདིའི་སློབ་མ་ཡང་དགོན་དགེ་དབང་རྣམ་རྒྱལ། རྗེ་ཀུན་བཟང་དབང་པོ། མཁན་ཆེན་ཆགས་པ་ཆོས་འཕེལ། འབྲོག་དགེ་ཆོས་སྐྱོང་དོན་གྲུབ་སོགས་མང་ངོ་།།

༣༢ དགེ་དབང་བསྟན་འཛིན་རྣམ་རྒྱལ་ལ་གསོལ་བ་འདེབས།།

དེ་ལས་གཙང་བ་ངག་དབང་བསྟན་འཛིན་རྣམ་རྒྱལ་ནི། གོང་མ་རྣམ་གཉིས་ཏེ་བློ་གྲོས་རྣམ་རྒྱལ། ངག་དབང་འཕྲིན་ལས་གཉིས་ཀྱི་དབོན་རྒྱུད་དུ། ཕྱི་ལོ་ ༡༦༩༡ ལྕགས་མོ་ལུག་གི་ལོར་བཞད་འཚོས་པ་ཏྲ་བར་མའི་ཕ་སྐྱབས་གྲོལ་དང་མ་དཔོན་མོ་བུ་ཁྲིད་ཀྱི་བུར་སྐྱེ་བ་བླངས། དགུང་ལོ་བཅུ་བར་རྡོ་རྗེ་འཆང་ཆ་ལུང་ལས་རྡོ་རྗེའི་རྣལ་འབྱོར་གྱི་དབང་མན་ངག་ཆ་ཚང་ཐོབ། བསྙེན་རྫོགས་སློབ་དཔོན་ངག་དབང་བློ་གྲོས་ཀྱིས་གནང་། དེ་ནས་ལོ་བཅུ་དྲུག་ནས་ཉི་ཤུ་མན་ལ་རྡོ་རྗེ་འཇིགས་མཛད་སོགས་ཡི་དམ་མང་པོའི་བསྙེན་སྒྲུབ་ལ་བཙད་རྒྱ་བཞུགས། སློབ་དཔོན་ངག་དབང་བློ་གྲོས་ལས་སྒྲུབ་ཐབས་བརྒྱ་རྩའི་རྗེས་གནང་སོགས་ཐོབ། པཎ་ཆེན་བློ་བཟང་ཡེ་ཤེས་ནས་སྒྲུབ་ཐབས་རྒྱ་མཚོའི་དབང་སོགས་འགའ་ཞིག་ཐོབ། ཆོས་རྗེ་ཀུན་བཟང་དབང་པོའི་དྲུང་དུ་སྦྱོར་དྲུག་གི་མན་ངག་ལུས་སྦྱོང་སྐོར་དང་། རྩ་ཐིག་རླུང་ཁྲིད་ཀྱི་སྐོར་དང་། ངེས་དོན་མདོ་དྲུམ་པ་སུམ་ཅུ་སོ་ལྔས་གཅོས་གཞུང་གདམས་ངག་ཐམས་ཅད་བུམ་པ་གང་བྱོའི་ཚུལ་དུ་ཐོབ། རྗེ་བོ་བསྟན་འཛིན་པས་ཨ་སྐྱོང་ཚུ་ཉིན་མའི་བླ་སེར་རྣམས་དང་། ཡང་སྒྲོས་སུ་འཛིན་ཀའི་ཏ་ཅེ་ཡན་ཆད་ཀྱི་སེར་སྐྱེར་གཏོགས་ཚད་གྲྭ་རྒྱུན་ལ་ཕུལ། ཛམ་ཐང་སྐུ་དགོན་ནོར་བུ་སོགས་འདུས་སྡེ་མང་པོ་ལ་དུས་འཁོར་གྱི་དབང་མོ་ཆེ་ཡོངས་རྫོགས་དང་སྒྲུབ་ཐབས་བརྒྱ་རྩ་སོགས་ཟབ་བཀའ་མང་པོ་གནང་། ཛམ་ཐང་དུ་ཐེབས། ཕྱོགས་ནས་འདུས་པའི་འདུས་སྡེ་མང་པོ་ལ་སྦྱོར་དྲུག་ཁྲིད་མོ་ཆེ་དང་། གཞན་དབང་ལུང་མན་ངག་མང་པོ་གནང་བས་བཤད་ཚོད་དང་མཐུན་པའི་ཉམས་རྟོགས་སྐྱེས་པ་ཀུན་མཁྱེན་ཆེན་པོའི་དུས་དང་མཚུངས་ཞེས་གྲགས། མགོ་ལོག་ཏུ་གདན་འདྲེན་ཞུས་ཏེ་སྦྱོར་དྲུག་ཁྲིད་ལུང་གནང་། དགུང་ལོ་ཞེ་བརྒྱད་པ། ཕྱི་ལོ་ ༡༧༣༨ ས་རྟའི་ལོར་གཟུགས་སྐུ་ཆོས་དབྱིངས་སུ་གཤེགས། འདི་གཙང་བ་གོང་མའི་སྐུ་ཕྲེང་མཐོ།

༣༣ ངག་དབང་མཁས་བཙུན་དར་རྒྱས་ལ་གསོལ་བ་འདེབས།།

མཁས་བཙུན་དར་རྒྱས་ནི། མཁས་བཙུན་བཟང་པོའི་ཡོན་ཏན་མཆོག་ཏུ་མངའ་ཞིང་ཁྱད་པར་ཉམས་རྟོགས་ཀྱི་རྩལ་ལྡན། དབང་ལུང་ཁྲིད་རྒྱུན་གྱི་མཛོད་ཆེན་འཛིན་པ་ཞིག་ཡིན་ལ། ཡན་ལག་དྲུག་གི་ཉམས་རྟོགས་ཀྱི་འཆར་སྒོ་མ་འགགས་པའི་བརྒྱུད་འཛིན་སྲོག་འཛིན་གྱི་རྟགས་མངའ་བ་ཀུན་དགའ་ཆོས་འཕེལ་གྱི་སློབ་མ། བྲ་ཡུལ་ཆོས་འཁོར་ཞེས་པ་སྟོན་གནས་རྗེས་དྲན་གྱི་རྟོགས་ལྡན་མངོན་ཤེས་ཅན་ཞིག་ཀྱང་བྱོན་པ་སོགས་དངོས་བརྒྱུད་ཅི་རིགས་པའི་སློབ་ཚོགས་མང་པོ་ཡོད་དོ།།

༣༤ ཀུན་བཟང་འཕྲིན་ལས་རྣམ་རྒྱལ་ལ་གསོལ་བ་འདེབས།།

ཀུན་བཟང་འཕྲིན་ལས་རྣམ་རྒྱལ་ནི། རྒྱལ་རོང་བག་གོ་ཤོག་ཏུ་ངོ་མཚར་བའི་ལྟས་བཟང་དང་བཅས་སྐུ་འཁྲུངས། ཆུང་དུས་ནས་དམ་པའི་ཆོས་ལ་བསླབས་པ་དང་ཉམས་ལེན་གནང་། ཁྱད་པར་ངག་དབང་

མཁས་བཙུན་དར་རྒྱས་སོགས་དམ་པ་གོང་མ་མང་པོ་ལས། རང་ལུགས་ཀྱི་དབང་ལུང་མན་ངག་སོགས་ཟབ་བཀའ་ཡོངས་རྫོགས་གསན་ཏེ་ཐུགས་དམ་མཛད་པས་ཉམས་རྟོགས་ཆེར་རྒྱས། དབུས་གཙང་དུ་ཀརྨ་པ་སོགས་མཁས་གྲུབ་དུ་མ་བསྟེན་ཏེ་སླར་ཕེབས། གཙང་བའི་གཞིམ་ཁང་གི་གདན་ས་བཟུང་ནས་སྒྲུབ་མདོ་ཕྱོགས་བཤད་སྒྲུབ་གླིང་། གསེར་ལྡོགས་མདའ་དགོན། ཛ་བ། སྣར་ཡག ཀྲྀ་ཁ་བཀྲ་ཤིས་གླིང་ཡན་ཆད་ཀྱི་སློབ་ཚོགས་སྨིན་བཞིན་བསྐྱུས་ནས་བསྟན་འགྲོའི་དོན་རྒྱ་ཆེར་མཛད་དོ།།

༣༥ ཉུས་ལྡན་ལྷུན་གྲུབ་རྒྱ་མཚོ་ལ་གསོལ་བ་འདེབས།།

ཉུས་ལྡན་ལྷུན་གྲུབ་རྒྱ་མཚོ་ནི། ཡག་མདོའི་ཕོ་བྲང་བཞེངས་ནས་གཙང་བ་ངག་དབང་འཕྲིན་ལས་ཀྱི་ཡང་སྤྲུལ་དབུས་གཙང་དུ་འཁྲུངས་པ་འཕྲིན་ལས་རྒྱ་མཚོ་ཞེས་པ་འདས་ནས། དེའི་སྤྲུལ་སྐུ་སྨྲ་ཁོག་གསེར་རིའམ་བསེ་རུ་ཞེས་པར་འཁྲུངས་པ། སྐུ་སྐྱེས་སྨིན་པ་རྒྱ་མཚོ་ཟེར་བ་དེ། དཔོན་ལྷུན་གྲུབ་ཀྱིས་ཕྱུས་ཏེ་ཡག་མདོའི་ཕོ་བྲང་ལ་བཞུགས་སུ་གསོལ། ཁོང་གིས་མི་ཆོས་ལྷ་ཆོས་ལུགས་ཟུང་གིས་འགྲོ་ཕན་སྤེལ་བར་མཛད། མགོ་ལོག་ཨ་སྐྱོང་དཔོན་དང་མཆོད་ཡོན་དུའང་གྱུར། ཁོང་ཉིད་ཀྱི་ཡང་སྤྲུལ་དེ་ཉེ་བའི་རིང་དུ་མགོ་ལོག་གཙང་ཞོལ་མའི་སྟེ་བ་རུ་བཞུགས་སྡོད་བའི་གཙང་བ་སྐུ་ངག་ཏུ་གྲགས་པ་དེའོ།།

༣༦ དཀོན་མཆོག་འཇིགས་མེད་རྣམ་རྒྱལ་ལ་གསོལ་བ་འདེབས།།

དཀོན་མཆོག་འཇིགས་མེད་རྣམ་རྒྱལ་ནི། མགོ་ལོག་ཡོ་སྟག་ཏུ་ངོ་མཚར་བའི་ལྟས་དང་བཅས་ཏེ་སྐུ་འཁྲུངས། ཤར་ཛམ་ཐང་གཙང་ཆེན་དགོན་གྱི་གདན་སར་བཀོད། ལྷ་ཆེ་བླ་མ་རྒྱལ་མཚན་དང་། དཔོན་ལྷུན་གྲུབ་རྒྱ་མཚོ་གཉིས་ལས་དུས་འཁོར་ཆོས་སྐོར་དང་། ཇོ་ནང་སྙིང་ཐུག་ཏུ་སྐུ་ཞབས་སྤྱོ་ར་བའི་དྲུང་ནས་ནི་གུའི་ཆོས་བཀའ་སོགས་བླ་མ་མང་པོ་ལས་དབང་ལུང་ཁྲིད་གསུམ་རྒྱ་ཆེར་མནོས་ཏེ། ཐོས་བསམ་སྒོམ་གསུམ་གྱི་རྟོགས་པ་མཆོག་ཏུ་རྒྱས་ནས་བསྟན་འགྲོ་ཡུན་རིང་བསྐྱངས་ཚུལ་ཡང་དེ་ཉིད་ཀྱི་རྣམ་ཐར་ལྟར་རོ།།

༣༧ ངག་དབང་ཆོས་འཕེལ་རྒྱ་མཚོ་ལ་གསོལ་བ་འདེབས།།

གཙང་བ་དགེ་སློང་ངག་དབང་ཆོས་འཕེལ་ཞབས་ནི། འཛི་ཡུལ་རབ་ཁ་ཞེས་པར་ཡབ་མགོ་ལོག་རྡོ་རྗེ་འབུམ་དང་ཡུམ་ལྷ་གས་བཟའ་སྐྱུ་མོ་རྒྱལ་གཉིས་ཀྱི་སྲས་སུ། ཕྱི་ལོ་ ༡༧༥༥ ས་སྤྲེལ་ལོར་འཁྲུངས། ཆུང་ངེད་ལ་ཚེ་དབང་སྐྱབས་འབོད། དགུང་ལོ་བདུན་ལོན་དུས་ཀློག་ལེགས་པར་བསླབས་པས་མཁས་པར་གྱུར། ཛམ་ཐང་གཙང་ཆེན་སྤྲུལ་བ་དཀོན་མཆོག་འཇིགས་མེད་རྣམ་རྒྱལ་གྱི་དྲུང་དུ་ཕེབས་ཏེ་སྐྱབས་འགྲོ་

དང་ཚངས་སྤྱོད་དགེ་བསྙེན་གྱི་སྡོམ་པ་ཞུས། མཚན་ངག་དབང་ཆོས་འཕེལ་རྒྱ་མཚོ་ཞེས་གསོལ། རིམ་བཞིན་གཙང་བ་ཉིད་བླ་མར་བསྙེན་ཏེ་བྱང་སེམས་ཀྱི་སྡོམ་པས་ཐུགས་རྒྱུད་བསྡམས། དཔོན་ལྷུན་གྲུབ་རྒྱ་མཚོའི་དྲུང་ནས་སྦྱོར་རྒྱུད། རྒྱུད་སྡེ་ལྔ་བ། དུས་འཁོར་སོགས་ཀྱི་དབང་དང་མགོན་པོའི་རྗེས་གནང་དང་། དེའི་མན་ངག་པོ་ཏི་མེ་འབར་གྱི་ལུང་བཅས་གསན། གཙང་ཆེན་སྤྲུལ་བའི་ཞལ་སྔ་ནས། དུས་འཁོར་དབང་མོ་ཆེ་ཡོངས་རྫོགས། རྒྱུད་སྡེའི་བཤད་ཁྲིད་ཟབ་ཁྱད་ཅན་དུ་མ་ཐོབ་ཅིང་། ལྷ་ཆེ་བླ་མ་ངག་དབང་རྒྱལ་མཚན་གྱི་མདུན་ནས་སྦྱོར་དྲུག་གི་ཟབ་ཁྲིད་ཞུས་ཏེ། རི་ཁྲོད་དགེ་འཕེལ་དུ་སྒོམ་འགྲོ་སྐྱབས་སེམས་ནས་བཟུང་སོར་བསམ་ཡན་ལ་ཉམས་ལེན་ལོ་གསུམ་ཙམ་མཛད་པས་སྦྱོང་བ་བཟང་རབ་ཐོན། ཕྱི་ལོ་༡༨༦༥ ཤིང་མོ་གླང་གི་ལོའི་ཟླ་བདུན་པའི་ཚེས་གཉིས་ཀྱི་ཉིན་ཕྱེད་ཡོལ་བ་ལུག་གི་དུས་ཚོད་ཙམ་ན། གཞིས་འོད་གསལ་གཉུག་མ་ཆེན་པོའི་རང་ཞལ་གྱི་དངང་གད་ཐུགས་གཉིས་མེད་རོ་མཉམ་ཆེན་པོའི་ཚུལ་དུ་དགོངས་པ་ལེགས་པར་མཐར་ཕྱིན་པའི་མཛད་ཚུལ་གནང་བའོ།།

༣༡ ངག་དབང་ཆོས་ཀྱི་འཕགས་པ་ལ་གསོལ་བ་འདེབས།།

ངག་དབང་ཆོས་ཀྱི་འཕགས་པ་ནི། འཛི་སྤྲིབ་ཕ་འབྲོ་མགོ་ཞེས་པར། ཡབ་དགྲ་བླ། ཏུས་ཨ་སྐྱབས་ལུ་གུ་དང་། ཡུམ་སློན་བཟའ་ཀླུ་སྐྱིད་གཉིས་ཀྱི་སྲས་སུ། ཕྱི་ལོ་ ༡༨༠༡ ས་འབྲུག་ལོར་བལྟམས། ཆུང་དུས་ནས་གཞན་ལས་ཁྱད་པར་འཕགས་ཤིང་། དགུང་ལོ་དྲུག་བདུན་ནས་དགེ་རྒན་ངག་དབང་ཚུལ་ཁྲིམས་ཀྱི་མདུན་ནས་ཀློག་བསླབས། རིག་པའི་གནས་དུ་མར་ཐུགས་བློ་རྒྱས། དགུང་གྲངས་བཅུ་བདུན་པར་གཙང་ཆེན་སྤྲུལ་བའི་སྐུ་དཀོན་མཆོག་འཇིགས་མེད་རྣམ་རྒྱལ་གྱི་དྲུང་ནས་རབ་ཏུ་བྱུང་བའི་སྡོམ་པ་ལེགས་མནོས་མཛད། མཚན་ངག་དབང་ཆོས་འཕགས་རྒྱ་མཚོ་ཞེས་གསོལ། དེ་ནས་བཟུང་ཤ་ཆང་ཆེ་གང་བོར་སྤངས་ཤིང་གཙང་ཆེན་མཆོག་གི་དྲུང་ནས་སྔར་ཡང་ཟབ་ཆོས་དུས་འཁོར་དབང་ཆེན། ནཻ་གུའི་ཟབ་བཀའ་ཡོངས་རྫོགས་སོགས་དང་། ཁྱད་པར་ཟབ་ལམ་སྦྱོར་དྲུག་སྔོན་འགྲོ་ནས་བཟུང་རྫོགས་རིམ་ཡན་ལག་དྲུག་པ་ཧྲིང་ངེ་འཛིན་གྱི་བར་ལེགས་པར་གསན། ཉམས་ལེན་སྐབས་རྟོགས་འབྱུལ་སོགས་ཀྱི་སློབ་དཔོན་རྟོགས་ལྡན་དྲི་མེད། སངས་རྒྱས་རྒྱ་མཚོ། རྡོ་རྗེ་འཆང་ངག་དབང་ཆོས་འཕེལ་རྒྱ་མཚོ་སོགས་བསྙེན། དེ་འདྲའི་སློ་ནས་ཉམས་ལེན་མཐའ་རྒྱས་མཛད་པས་ལམ་རང་རང་གི་རྟགས་མཚན་ཁྱད་པར་བ་བྱུང་། སྟོད་བཅུད་སྟོང་གཟུགས་ཀྱི་ལྷའི་རྣམ་རོལ་དུ་ཤར་ཞིང་ལས་རླུང་དབུ་མར་ཐིམ་རྟགས་དུ་མ་དང་། བདེ་སྟོང་གི་ཡེ་ཤེས་ལ་སེམས་ཤིན་ཏུ་གནས་པས་མཉམ་བཞག་ལས་ལྡང་དཀའ་བ་སོགས། ཉམས་དང་རྟོགས་པའི་སྒོ་རབ་ཏུ་ཡངས་པ་བྱུང་ཞིང་། ཆོས་བརྒྱུད་ལ་ཞེན་པ་གཏིང་ནས་ཆོད་པར་གྱུར། ཕྱི་ལོ་ ༡༨༧༧ མེ་མོ་གླང་ལོའི་ནག་ཟླའི་ཚེས་བཅུ་དགུ་ལ་ཁོང་ཉིད་སྐུ་ལ་སྙུང་ཟུག་གང་ཡང་མེད་པར་རྣམ་སྣང་ཆོས་

བདུན་གྱི་ངང་ནས་སྨིན་འབྲས་གྲེན་ལ་བཟློག་སྟེ། ངོན་དམ་ཆོས་དབྱིངས་ཀྱི་ངང་དུ་ཀུན་རྫོབ་གཟུགས་སྐུ་ ལེགས་བསྡུས་ཀྱི་ཚུལ་དུ་འོད་གསལ་མ་བུ་འདྲེས་པའི་ཐུགས་དམ་མཆོག་ཏུ་བཞུགས་སོ།།

༣༩ ངག་དབང་ཆོས་འཁྱོར་རྒྱ་མཚོ་ལ་གསོལ་བ་འདེབས།།

ངག་དབང་ཆོས་འཁྱོར་རྒྱ་མཚོ་ནི། ཕྱི་ལོ་ ༡༨༤༩ ལོ་འཛི་ཡུལ་ཁྲི་ལོ་མའི་གྲོང་གསེབ་ཏུ་སྐུ་འཁྲུངས་ ཤིང་། གཙང་བ་དགེ་སློང་ངག་དབང་ཆོས་འཕེལ་རྒྱ་མཚོའི་དངོས་སློབ་ཡིན་ཞིང་། ཁོང་གི་མདུན་ནས་ དཔལ་དུས་ཀྱི་འཁོར་ལོའི་དབང་ཐོབ་དུས་ཀུན་མཁྱེན་དོལ་པོ་བ་དངོས་ཞལ་མཇལ་བའི་ཉམས་སྣང་བྱུང་ ། ངག་དབང་ཆོས་འཁྱོར་རྒྱ་མཚོ་ལས་རྫོགས་རིམ་གྱི་མན་ངག་ཡོངས་སུ་རྫོགས་པ་གསན་ཅིང་། ལྷག་ པར་དུ་སྦྱོར་བ་ཡན་ལག་དྲུག་གི་ཉམས་ལེན་གནད་དུ་སྨིན་ཏེ་ཉམས་དང་རྟོགས་པའི་ཡོན་ཏན་མང་དུ་ འཁྲུངས། ལྷག་པར་དུ་རྨི་ལམ་འོད་གསལ་དུ་གྱུར་བ་བྱུང་། མཁས་བཙུན་བཟང་གསུམ་དང་ལྡ་སྒོམ་སྦྱོད་ གསུམ་གང་གི་ཐད་ནས་ཀྱང་། གཙང་བའི་གཟིམ་ཁང་གི་རྡོ་རྗེ་སློབ་དཔོན་ཞེ་ལྔ་བར་ལོས་ཤིང་འཚམ་ པར་བྱུང་། དཔལ་དུས་ཀྱི་འཁོར་ལོའི་སྒྲུབ་བརྒྱུད་ཀྱི་བསྟན་པ་རྒྱ་ཆེར་སྤེལ་ཏེ། ཕྱི་ལོ་ ༡༩༡༠ ལོར་ གཟུགས་སྐུའི་བཀོད་པ་ཆོས་ཀྱི་དབྱིངས་སུ་བསྡུས།

༤༠ ངག་དབང་ཆོས་འཛིན་རྒྱ་མཚོ་ལ་གསོལ་བ་འདེབས།།

མཚན་ཡོངས་གྲགས་སུ་ཨ་ཤུལ་ལྷ་བཟོའི་བླ་མ་ནི། མདོ་ཁམས་འཛི་ཀ་རུ་ཨ་ཤུལ་ཞེས་པའི་གྲོང་གསེབ་ ཏུ་དུས་རབས་ ༡༩ བའི་རབ་བྱུང་ ༡༥ བའི་ཆུ་མོ་ལུག ཕྱི་ལོ་ ༡༨༨༣ ལོར་ཨ་བཟང་གི་རུས་རྒྱུད་དུ་སྐུ་ འཁྲུངས་ཤིང་། ཁུ་བོ་ལྷ་བཟོ་ཀུན་ཁྱབ་ཀྱིས་གློག་བསླབས། ཤར་ཛམ་ཐང་དགོན་ཆེན་དུ་གཙང་བ་དགེ་ སློང་ངག་དབང་ཆོས་འཁྱོར་རྒྱ་མཚོ་སྒོ་གསུམ་གུས་པ་ཆེན་པོས་བསྟེན། དམ་པ་གང་གིས་བརྗེ་བས་ རྗེས་སུ་བཟུང་ནས་མཚན་ལ་ངག་དབང་ཆོས་འཛིན་རྒྱ་མཚོ་གསོལ། བླ་མ་འདིའི་དྲུང་ནས་ཟབ་ཅིང་རྒྱས་ པའི་གདམས་ངག་མང་དུ་གསན་ཅིང་ཉམས་སུ་བླངས། ལྷག་པར་དཔལ་དུས་ཀྱི་འཁོར་ལོའི་ཐུན་མོང་མ་ ཡིན་པའི་སྟོན་འགྲོ་དབེན་གསུམ་དང་། དངོས་གཞི་སྦྱོར་བ་ཡན་ལག་དྲུག་ལ་དད་བརྩོན་དྲག་དང་ཤེས་ བཞིན་བག་ཡོད་གསུམ་འདུས་ཀྱིས་ཉམས་སུ་བླངས་པས། གནས་འགྱུར་ཉམས་སྣང་ངོ་མཚར་བ་མང་དུ་ བྱུང་། དབེན་གསུམ་གྱི་སྐབས་ནས་སེམས་ཀྱི་གནས་ལུགས་རང་ངོ་འཕྲོད་ཅིང་སྟོང་གཟུགས་ཀྱི་སྣང་བ་ མཐའ་ཀླས་པ་ཤར། སོར་སྡུད་ཀྱི་སྐབས་སུ་ཐུར་ལས་སྟོང་གཟུགས་ཀྱི་སྣང་བ་འོད་གསལ་རྟགས་བཅུའི་ སྣང་བ་ཀུན་ནས་རྒྱས། བསམ་གཏན་སྐབས་སྟོང་གཟུགས་སེམས་དང་དབྱེར་མེད་དུ་གྱུར་ནས་མཉམ་ རྗེས་དབྱེར་མེད་དུ་གྱུར། སྲོག་རྩོལ་སྐབས་ལས་རླུང་དབུ་མར་བཅིངས་ནས་སྟོང་གཟུགས་རླུང་དང་རོ་

མཉམ་དུ་གྱུར། མ་དག་པའི་སྣང་བ་ཡལ་ཡུལ་དུ་གྱུར་ཞིང་རང་སྣང་གི་ཉམས་དང་སྣང་བ་རབ་འབྱམས་ཀྱིས་ཁེངས་པའི་དབང་གིས། མ་ངེས་པའི་སྤྲུལ་པ་སྣ་ཚོགས་གནང་བ་སོགས་ཤིན་ཏུ་མང་ཡང་འདིར་མི་སྤྲོ། མདོར་ན་སྐུ་ཚེའི་སྟོད་དུ་ཇམ་ཐང་གཙང་ཆེན་དགོན་པ་གཞུང་གི་ཆེད་དུ་བླ་མཆན་དུ་གྲགས་པའི་འགན་བཞེས་སྐབས། གདུལ་བྱ་སྨིན་བདག་ཁྲིམ་པ་པོ་མོ་དག་གི་ནད་གདོན་རྐྱེན་ངན་བར་ཆད་དག་ལ་གྲུབ་རྟགས་ཀྱིས་སྲུང་སྐྱོབ་བྱས་པའི་ལོ་རྒྱུས་མང་། སྐུ་ཚེའི་སྨད་དུ་བཀྲ་ཤིས་ལྷ་རྩེ་དགོན་དུ་གྲགས་པའི་དབེན་གནས་སུ་བུ་སློབ་བསྐྱངས་ཏེ་རྫོགས་རིམ་སྦྱོར་དྲུག་གིས་གདམས་པ་གནང་སྐབས་རྣམས་སུ། དག་པའི་ཉམས་སྣང་འབྱམས་སུ་ཤར་བའི་ལོ་རྒྱུས་དང་། བུ་སློབ་རྣམས་ཀྱི་དག་སྣང་དུ་ཡི་དམ་ལྷའི་སྣང་བ་མང་དུ་སྣང་ཚུལ་དང་། ཐལ་བའི་སྤྱོད་ཡུལ་ལས་འདས་པའི་གྲུབ་རྟགས་མང་དུ་གནང་བའི་ལོ་རྒྱུས་ཤིན་ཏུ་མང་བས་རྣམ་ཐར་རྒྱས་པ་དག་ཏུ་གཟིགས་རིགས།

མཐར་མི་ལོ་གསུམ་ཡས་མས་སུ་རང་བཞིན་གྱིས་མིའི་སྤྱོད་ཡུལ་ལས་འདས་པའི་མཛད་སྤྱོད་ངོ་མཚར་བ་མང་དུ་བསྟན་གནང་མཐར། ནག་པ་ཟླ་བའི་ཚེས་བཅུ་བདུན་ལ་ཐུགས་ཆོས་ཀྱི་དབྱིངས་དང་འབྲལ་མ་མྱོང་བའི་དབྱིངས་སུ་རྫོགས་པར་འཚང་རྒྱ་བར་གྱུར། སྐུ་གདུང་གི་རུས་པ་གཉིས་བྱུང་ཞིང་ལྷ་ཚོགས་སོགས་སུ་དུས་ཀྱི་འཁོར་ལོའི་ལྷ་དྲུག་བཅུ་སོ་དྲུག་གི་ཕྱག་མཚན་རྣམས་འབུར་དུ་དོད་ཡོད་པ་སོགས་བྱུང་བ་ནི་ཟུར་འཛུག་གི་སྐུ་གྲུབ་པའི་རྟགས་སུ་བཤད། ཁོང་གི་བུ་སློབ་ཐུགས་སྲས་དག་ནི། རབ་ཁ་བླ་མ་དོན་ལྡན། ཕྱགས་པ་བླ་མ་མཉམ་ཉིད། བྱ་ཡུལ་བླ་མ་བསྟན་རབ་སོགས་རེད།

༨༡ ངག་དབང་བསྟན་པ་རབ་རྒྱས་ལ་གསོལ་བ་འདེབས།།

བྱ་ཡུལ་བླ་མ་ངག་དབང་བསྟན་པ་རབ་རྒྱས་ནི། འཛོ་རྐའི་བྱ་ཡུལ་གྲོང་སྡེ་རུ། ཡབ་ཨ་ཤུལ་འབྲུག་སྒྲ་དང་། ཡུམ་ཀུ་བཟའ་པོ་ཀུ་གཉིས་ཀྱི་སྲས་སུ་དུས་རབས་ ༡༤ བའི་རབ་བྱུང་ ༡༥ པའི་ཤིང་ཐག སྤྱི་ལོ་ ༡༨༢༥ ལོར་སྐུ་འཁྲུངས། ཆུང་དུས་ནས་རིགས་ཕུན་སུམ་ཚོགས་པའི་མཚན་ལྟས་ཀྱི་སྤྱོད་བཟང་དང་ལྡན། དགུང་ལོ་བཅུ་གཉིས་སྟེང་དུ་ལས་སློབ་བཟང་པོའི་མཐུ་སྨིན་ཏེ། བཀྲ་ཤིས་ལྷ་རྩེའི་དབེན་གནས་སུ་ལྷ་བཟོའི་བླ་མ་ངག་དབང་ཆོས་འཛིན་རྒྱ་མཚོ་སྒོ་གསུམ་དང་བ་ཆེན་པོས་བསྟེན། ཐོག་མར་བླ་སློབ་མཇལ་སྐབས་ནས་བཀྲ་ཤིས་པའི་རྟགས་དང་རྟེན་འབྲེལ་ཤིན་ཏུ་འགྲིག་པོ་བྱུང་། བླ་མ་རྡོ་རྗེ་འཆང་གིས་མ་འོངས་ལེགས་པའི་ལུང་བསྟན་གྱི་བཀའ་ལུང་གསལ་པོར་གནང་། དེ་ནས་བཟུང་འདོད་པ་ཆུང་ཞིང་ཚོག་ཤེས་པའི་སྒོ་ནས། བླ་མ་གང་གིས་གཙོས་སྐྱེས་ཆེན་དམ་པ་དུ་མ་ལས་ཟབ་རྒྱས་ཆོས་ཀྱི་གདམས་ངག་མང་དུ་གསན་ཅིང་གྲུས་རྟག་བརྟན་པོས་བརྩོན་ཞིང་ཉམས་ལེན་གྱི་གནད་ལ་ཁེལ་ཐུབ་པ་བྱུང་།

གཞན་ཡང་ཡུལ་སྡེ་དང་དགོན་པ་གྲྭ་ཚང་སྲུང་སྐྱོབ་བྱེད་པའི་བླ་འགན་མང་དུ་བཞེས། སློབ་བུ་གསར་བ་དག་ལ་དམ་པའི་ཆོས་ཀྱི་ལམ་སྟོན་གྱིས་ལས་འགན་ཡང་བཞེས་པ་མི་ཉུང་། མཐར་དགུང་ལོ་ ༣༢ ནས་ཁོང་གི་རང་དགོན་བྲེ་ཡུལ་དགོན་དུ་ཕེབས་ཏེ་སླར་ཡང་འཇོང་པོ་སྐྱབས་མགོན་གྱི་མདུན་ནས་སྦྱོར་བ་ཡན་ལག་དྲུག་གི་ཉམས་ལེན་དང་། གཞན་སྐལ་ལྡན་དག་ལ་སྨྲ་ཁྲིད་སོགས་ཀྱིས་སྒྲུབ་པ་ཉམས་ལེན་དུས་ཡུན་རིང་པོར་བརྩོན་པ་ཧུར་ཐག་གནང་། དགུང་ལོ་ ༥༦ ལ་ཕེབས་སྐབས་འཇོང་པོ་སྐྱབས་མགོན་གཟུགས་སྐུའི་བཀོད་པ་བསྡུས་པས། རྡོ་རྗེ་སློབ་དཔོན་གྱི་ཐུགས་འགན་གཙང་བཞེས་ཀྱིས་སྐལ་ལྡན་སློབ་མའི་ཚོགས་མང་དུ་བསྐྱངས། དགུང་ལོ་ ༧༦ ཐོག་ཏུ་སྐུ་བསྟུན་ནས་མྱ་ངན་ལས་འདས་ཚུལ་བཞེས་པས་སློབ་བུ་དག་གིས་བརྟན་བཞུགས་ཞུས་ཀྱང་བྱང་ཤམྦྷ་ལར་རིགས་ལྡན་མ་འགག་པའི་དྲུང་དུ་ཕེབས་གཏན་ཁེལ་ཡོད་གསུངས་ནས་ཞལ་གྱིས་མ་བཞེས།

དམ་པ་འདིའི་བུ་སློབ་དག་གི་ནང་ནས་ཆེས་མཆོག་ཏུ་གྱུར་པའི་ཐུགས་སྲས་དམ་པ་དག་ནི། བླ་མ་ངག་དབང་བློ་བཟང་འཕྲིན་ལས་སམ་བསྟུས་མཚན་དུ་བླ་མ་བློས་འཕྲིན་དང་། གཞན་བླ་མ་ངག་བློས། ཡར་ཐང་རྒྱ་སྤྲུལ། བླ་མ་མཁས་ཚུལ་སོགས་མང་།

༩༢ ངག་དབང་བློ་བཟང་འཕྲིན་ལས་ལ་གསོལ་བ་འདེབས།།

བསྟུས་མཚན་དུ་བླ་མ་བློས་འཕྲིན་དུ་གྲགས་པ་མཆོག་ནི། མཁས་བཙུན་ཡོན་ཏན་རྒྱ་ཆེན་པོས་མངོན་པར་ཕྱུག་ཅིང་། ཐལ་བའི་མཛད་སྤྱོད་དང་མི་མཐུན་པ་ཅན་གྱི་དམ་པའི་སྐྱེས་བུ་མིའི་གཟུགས་སུ་བྱོན་པ་ཞིག་ཡིན། དམ་པ་འདི་ནི་རྫམ་ཐང་སྒོ་མདའ་བྲག་བར་གངས་ཅན་བོད་ཀྱི་དུས་ཆེན་བཞིའི་ཡ་གྱལ། ཨ་ལྕགས་འབྲིའི་གདུང་རྒྱུད་དུ་གཏོགས་པའི་ཡབ་དམ་པ་སྐལ་བཟང་སྐྱབས་དང་། ཡུམ་དམ་པ་ཡག་ཤུས་བཟའ་བཀྲ་ཤིས་སྐྱིད་གཉིས་ཀྱི་སྲས་སུ་རབ་བྱུང་བཅོ་ལྔ་བའི་མེ་སྦྲུལ་ལོ་དང་། ཕྱི་ལོ་ ༡༩༡༧ ལོར་ངོ་མཚར་བའི་ལྟས་བཟང་དུ་མ་དང་ལྡན་དུ་སྐུའི་ཆུ་སྐྱེས་བཞད། མེ་སྟག་ལོའི་གནམ་ལོ་གསར་ཚེས་ནས་སྐར་རྩིས་འབྱུང་ཁམས་རིག་པ་དང་། འབྱུང་རྩིས་མི་ཚེའི་འདོད་སྒྲུབ་ཀྱི་རིག་པ་སོགས་རིག་པའི་གནས་དག་ལ་སྦྱངས། དགུང་ལོ་ ༡༩ བཞེས་པ་ལྕགས་རྟ་ལོར་སྟོན་བསགས་བསོད་ནམས་རྒྱ་མཚོའི་མཐུ་སྨིན་ཏེ་དཔལ་དུས་ཀྱི་འཁོར་ལོའི་རྡོ་རྗེ་སློབ་དཔོན་ཆེན་པོ་ངག་དབང་བསྟན་པ་རབ་རྒྱས་ཉེ་བར་བསྟེན་ཅིང་། ལུས་ལོངས་སྤྱོད་དང་བཅས་པ་ཕུལ། རྒྱུད་ཀྱི་རྒྱལ་པོ་དཔལ་དུས་ཀྱི་འཁོར་ལོའི་ཐུན་མོང་དང་ཐུན་མིན་གྱི་སྔོན་འགྲོ་གྲུབ་རྗེས། རྫོགས་རིམ་སྦྱོར་བ་ཡན་ལག་དྲུག་གི་ཉམས་སུ་ལེན་པའི་སྐལ་བཟང་དང་དུ་བླངས་པས། གཟའ་འཁོར་གཅིག་གི་ནང་དུ་འོད་གསལ་རྟགས་བཅུའི་སྣང་བ་རྫོགས་པར་འཆར་

བ་སོགས། ཉམས་དང་རྟོགས་པའི་འཕེལ་རིམ་ནི་ཕལ་བའི་སྐྱེ་བོའི་སྤྱོད་ཡུལ་ལས་རིང་དུ་འདས་པ་བྱུང་། འཇིག་རྟེན་ལྟར་སྣང་དུ་གྲོང་ཚོག་ལ་ཕྱིན་པ་སོགས་མཛད་པ་ཅི་ཞིག་གནང་གིན་ཡོད་མིན་ལ་མ་ལྟོས་པར། སྐུ་ན་གཞོན་པའི་དུས་ནས་བཟུང་། རྗེ་བླ་མ་འདི་ཉིད་ཀྱི་རང་སྣང་དུ་ཡི་དམ་གྱི་ལྷ་དཔལ་གསང་བདག་འབྱུང་པོ་འདུལ་བྱེད་དང་། དཔལ་དུས་ཀྱི་འཁོར་ལོའི་ལྷ་དྲུག་བརྒྱ་སོ་དྲུག་སོགས་ཟབ་མོ་ལྷའི་སྣང་བ་ལས་འདའ་མ་མྱོང་བ་སོགས་རྟོགས་པའི་གདེང་ཚད་ཤིན་ཏུ་མཐོན་པོར་གྱུར། ཕྱིས་སུ་དགུང་ལོ་ ༣༠ ལ་སླེབས་སྐབས་སྡེ་སྣོད་འཛིན་པའི་མཁས་དབང་མཁན་ཆེན་བློ་བཟང་ཚུལ་ཁྲིམས་དགེ་བའི་བཤེས་གཉེན་དུ་བསྟེན་ཏེ། རྒྱ་ཆེན་བཤད་པའི་ལུང་གི་སྡེ་སྣོད་ལ་ལོ་གཅིག་ཙམ་ལ་སྦྱངས་པའི་རིང་དུ། བླ་སློབ་ཆོས་ཀྱི་བགྲོ་གླེང་གིས་ཉིན་མཚན་གང་དུ་འདས་མི་ཤེས་པའི་སྤྲོ་དགའི་དཔལ་ལ་རོལ།

ལོ་གཅིག་ཡས་མས་སོང་རྗེས་མཛེ་ནད་བཞེས་པའི་གླུ་ནད་ཅིག་ཡུལ་དེར་དར་ཁྱབ་ཆེ་བ་དེ་བཞིན་ཚུལ་བྱུང་། དེའི་ཆེད་དུ་ཡི་དམ་ལྷའི་དམ་མཚམས་ལ་མི་ལོ་ལྔར་བཞུགས་པས། མདོ་སྔགས་རིག་པའི་གནས་ཀུན་ཐོགས་མེད་དུ་མཁྱེན་པའི་གྲུབ་པའི་གོ་འཕང་མཐོར་པོར་ཕྱིན། མཛེ་ནད་བག་ཆགས་དང་བཅས་པ་ཙ་སྤྱངས་བྱས་ཏེ་སྨིན་མ་ཤིན་ཏུ་རིང་བོར་སྐྱེས། སྒྲུབ་གཏོར་དམ་རྫས་མྱོང་གྲོལ་དུ་གྱུར་ནས་སེམས་ཅན་ཆེས་མང་པོའི་ནད་གདོན་ཞི་བའི་བདུད་རྩིར་གྱུར། དེ་ནས་བཟུང་སྐུ་ཚེ་ཧྲིལ་པོར་མཛེ་ནད་ཅན་གྱི་ནད་པ་སྟོང་ཕྲག་མང་པོ་ནད་ལས་གྲོལ་བར་བྱས། སྐུ་ཚེའི་སྨད་དུ་བཀྲ་ཤིས་ལྷ་རྩེའི་དགོན་གྱི་བརྒྱུད་པ་ཐང་དུ་ཆགས་པ། དཔལ་བཀྲ་ཤིས་ཆོས་ཐང་དགོན་གྱི་དབུ་ཁྲིད་དགོན་བདག་གནང་ནས་ཕྱོགས་གང་ས་ནས་ཕེབས་པའི་རབ་བྱུང་བླ་སྤྲུལ་ཆོས་རྣལ་མ་དོན་གཉེར་བ་ཀུན་ལ། འགྲན་བྲལ་གྱི་བཀའ་གསུང་གིས་སྡེ་སྣོད་གསུམ་དང་རྒྱུད་སྡེ་བཞིས་མཚོན་པའི་ཆོས་ཀྱི་འཁོར་ལོ་རྒྱ་ཆེན་བསྐོར་བས། སྡེ་སྣོད་འཛིན་པའི་དགེ་བཤེས་དང་མཁན་པོ་མང་དུ་ཐོན་ཅིང་། ཆོས་ལུགས་རིས་མེད་ཀྱི་དགོན་སྡེ་ཀུན་ལ་བཤད་སྒྲུབ་ཀྱི་ཕན་བདེ་བསྐྲུན་པ་ནི་རྨད་དུ་བྱུང་བ་ཞིག་ཡིན། དེ་དག་དང་དུས་མཉམ་དུ། སྐུ་ཉིད་ཀྱི་ཡི་དམ་འབྱུང་པོ་འདུལ་བྱེད་དང་རྡོ་རྗེ་རྣམ་པར་འཇོམས་པའི་སྔགས་ནུས་ཚད་མེད་ལ་བརྟེན་ནས། ཕྱོགས་མཐའ་སོ་སོ་ནས་ཡོང་ཞིང་ནད་གདོན་བགེགས་ཀྱིས་གཟིར་བ་ཁྲི་ཕྲག་མང་པོའི་ལུས་སེམས་བདེ་ལ་བཀོད་པ་སོགས་མཛད་འཕྲིན་ནི་རྒྱ་ཆེ་ཞིང་གཏིང་ཟབ་པའོ།། དམ་པ་གང་ལ་སྐྱོང་གཞི་ཙུང་ཙམ་མེད་ཅིང་འབྱུང་ཁམས་ཤིན་ཏུ་དྭངས་བཞིན་དུ་༧སྐྱབས་རྗེ་དམ་པ་མཆོག་ཉིད་དགུང་གྲངས་༨༢ བཞེས་སྐབས་ཏེ། ཕྱི་ལོ་༡༩༩༩ ལོར། ཟླ་སོར་ནས་ད་ལོ་ང་ཤི་རན་ཡོད་པས། སློབ་ཚོགས་ཀུན་ལ་མཐའ་མཇུག་གི་ཆོས་ཀྱི་བགྲོ་གླེང་བྱ་དགོས་གསུངས་ཏེ། ཟླ་གསུམ་ཡས་མས་སུ་བཀའ་ཆོས་གནང་ནས་ཟབ་ཆོས་ཀྱི་སྒྲོ་འདོགས་མ་ལུས་པ་བསལ། ཡུལ་དེའི་མི་ཆེན་དག་བསྡུས་ཏེ་ཁོང་གི་ཡང་སྤྲུལ་ངོས་འཛིན་མི་ཚོག་པའི་བཀའ་བཏང་

། རིན་ཐང་བྲལ་བའི་རྟེན་རྫས་གསེར་སྐུ་སོགས་རྩེ་ཕོ་བྲང་པོ་ཏ་ལའི་ནང་དུ་གཏོང་དགོས་པའི་བཀའ་ཕྱོགས་མེད་དུ་གནང་། གང་ཉིད་ས་སྟག་ལོའི་ས་ག་ཟླ་བའི་ཚེས་བཅུ་གསུམ་གྱི་ཉིན་གུང་དུ་ཞབས་གཉིས་སེམས་དཔའི་དཀྱིལ་ཀྲུང་། ཕྱག་གཉིས་མཉམ་བཞག སྤྱན་གཉིས་བར་སྣང་དུ་ཧྲིག་གེར་གཟིགས་ནས། ཧྲིག་གི་རྣམ་པའི་དབུགས་ཆུང་གཉིས་ནང་དུ་རྟུབ། དེ་ནས་ཧྲིག་གི་རྣམ་པའི་དབུགས་ཆེན་པོ་གཅིག་ནང་དུ་རྟུབ་པར་བྱས་པས། གཟུགས་སྐུ་སྒྱུ་ལུས་ཀྱི་ཕུང་པོ་ཤུལ་དུ་བསྐྱུར་ཏེ་ཐུགས་ཆོས་དབྱིངས་མཉམ་ཉིད་ཆེན་པོའི་དབྱིངས་སུ་ཐིམ་པར་གྱུར་ཏོ།།

༼བླ་བརྒྱུད་འདི་ནི་ནུབ་ཕྱོགས་ཨོ་སི་ཁྲེ་ལི་ཡ་སོགས་སུ་དངོས་སུ་ཇོ་ནང་དུས་འཁོར་གྱི་བརྒྱུད་པ་སྤེལ་མཁན། ཤར་མཁན་སྤྲུལ་རིན་པོ་ཆེ་འཇམ་དཔལ་བློ་གྲོས་ཀྱི་བླ་མ་བརྒྱུད་པའི་དབང་དུ་བཏང་ཡོད་པ་རེད། སྤྱིར་བཏང་ཡིན་ན་བླ་མ་སྐུ་བཞུགས་དུས་གསོལ་འདེབས་བླ་བརྒྱུད་ནང་དུ་དངོས་སུ་ཡོད་དགོས་པའི་ངེས་པ་མེད་ཀྱང་། ཁོང་གི་དངོས་སློབ་དག་གི་རེ་བ་བཞིན་འདིར་བཀོད་པ་རེད། ཕྱག་དཔེ་འདིའི་རྩ་འགྲེལ་གཉིས་ཀ་མི་སུ་ཡིས་རང་ཉིད་སྐྱེར་སོ་སོའི་བེད་སྤྱོད་གཏོང་དུས། རང་སོ་སོ་ལ་ཆོས་འདིའི་བླ་བརྒྱུད་སོ་སོ་བ་ཡོད་ཚེ་དེ་དག་ཡར་ནང་དུ་བཙུག་ཅིང་། སོ་སོའི་བླ་བརྒྱུད་མ་ཡིན་པ་དག་མར་བཏོན་པ་དང་མ་བཏོན་པ་གང་རུང་གི་སྒོ་ནས་འདོན་ཆོག་པ་ཡིན་ནོ།། ༽

༩༣ མཁན་སྤྲུལ་འཇམ་དཔལ་བློ་གྲོས་ལ་གསོལ་བ་འདེབས།།

ཤར་མཁན་སྤྲུལ་རིན་པོ་ཆེ་འཇམ་དཔལ་བློ་གྲོས་མཆོག་འཁྲུངས་ཡུལ་ནི། མགོ་ལོག་ཁག་གསུམ་གྱི་ནང་ཚན་དུ་ཨ་སྐྱོང་ཁག་གསུམ་ཡོད་པའི་ཡ་གྲལ། ཨ་སྐྱོང་གོང་མ་ཚང་ལ་གཏོགས་པའི་གདོང་གཡང་ཟེར་བའི་འབྲོག་སྡེ་ཞིག་ཡིན། ཡབ་ཤར་ཐུབ་བསྟན་དང་། ཡུམ་ཨ་འཚབ་བཟའ་ཤེར་སྒྲོན་གཉིས་ཀྱི་སྲས་སུ་རྒྱུན་ལྡན་དུ་མིའི་འགྲོ་བ་ལ་མེད་པའི་འབྲུ་མ་དཀར་པོ་ཞིག་ན་བཟའི་ཚུལ་དུ་གྱོན་ནས། ང་སྐད་སོགས་ཅི་ཡང་མེད་པར་ཞི་བདེ་བག་ཕེབས་པ་སོགས་ངོ་མཚར་ལྟས་དང་བཅས་པའི་སྒོ་ནས་སྐུ་འཁྲུངས་ཤིང་། འཚར་ལོངས་བྱུང་བའི་བརྒྱུད་རིམ་ཁྲོད་ནས་ངོ་མཚར་དམ་པའི་ལྟས་བཟང་ཤིན་ཏུ་མང་། སྐུ་ཉིད་ཨ་སྐྱོང་གོང་མའི་དགེ་རྩ་མཁན་པོའི་ཡང་སྲིད་ཡིན་པར་སྐུ་གོང་མས་ལུང་བསྟན་ཡོད་ཐོག གྲུབ་ཆེན་ཨོ་རྒྱན་རིག་འཛིན། ཁམས་ཚང་གཏེར་ཆེན། མཁའ་འགྲོ་ཏཱ་རེ་ལྷ་མོ། གྲུབ་ཆེན་རྒྱལ་རོང་བསམ་གྲུབ་སོགས་ཀྱིས་ངོས་འཛིན་གནང་ཞིང་། སྐུ་ཚེ་དང་མཛད་འཕྲིན་ལ་བར་ཆད་བཟློག་ཕྱིར་སྤྲུལ་སྐུའི་མཚན་གནས་གསང་རྒྱ་དམ་པོ་དགོས་པར་ལུང་བསྟན་གཅིག་མཆུངས་སུ་གསུང་མཁན་མང་བས་དོན་དངོས་ཀྱི་གནས་ཚུལ་གསང་རྒྱ་བྱས་ཏེ། ལྟོ་སྐྱོ་གོས་རྡུལ་གྲྭ་རྐྱང་དཀྲུས་མའི་ཚུལ་གྱིས། ས་དགེ་བཀའ་སྙིང་ཇོ་ནང་སོགས་ཀྱི་དགོན་སྡེ་དུ་མར་གུས་རྟག་གི་བརྩོན་འགྲུས་ཀྱིས་ཐོས་བསམ་སྒོམ་པར་ནན་ཏན་གནང་། མཐར་བོད་ཀྱི་

ཆོས་བརྒྱུད་གྲུབ་མཐའ་ཀུན་ལ་ཤེས་ནས་ཐོབ་པའི་དད་པ་སྙིང་དུ་འཁྲུངས་སྟེ་ཆོས་ལུགས་རིས་མེད་ལ་མཁྱེན་རྒྱ་དང་དག་སྣང་ཆེ་བའི་སྐྱེས་བུ་དམ་པ་ཞིག་ཏུ་གྱུར། ཁྱད་པར་དུ་དཔལ་གསང་བདག་ཕྱག་ན་རྡོ་རྗེའི་རྣམ་སྤྲུལ། རྩོད་མེད་མཁས་གྲུབ་གཉིས་ལྡན། དཔལ་དུས་ཀྱི་འཁོར་ལོའི་རྣལ་འབྱོར་བ་ཡོངས་ཀྱི་རྡོ་རྗེ་སློབ་དཔོན་ཆེན་པོ། ཁམས་འཛི་སྒའི་ཡུལ་གྱི་སྐྱབས་མགོན། ༸རྗེ་བཙུན་བླ་མ་བློ་བཟང་འཕྲིན་ལས་ཚུལ་བཞིན་བསྟེན་ཏེ་བཀའ་བཞིན་བསྒྲུབས་པས། ཟབ་མོ་ནང་གི་རྟོགས་པ་འཁྲུངས་པས་༸སྐྱབས་རྗེ་བླ་མ་དམ་པ་དེའི་ཐུགས་ཀྱི་སྲས་མཆོག་ཏུ་གྱུར། ༸རྗེ་བླ་མ་འདི་ལ་གསུང་སྐྱེས་ཀྱི་བུ་སློབ་བླ་སྤྲུལ་མཁན་སློབ་མང་དུ་ཡོད་པའི་ནང་ནས། ཞར་མཁན་སྤྲུལ་ལ་༸སྐྱབས་རྗེ་བླ་མ་སྐྱ་སྐོར་གྱི་པཎ་ཞྭ་དང་། སྐུ་ཆེ་ཧྲིལ་པོར་ཉམས་བཞེས་གནང་བའི་ཕྱག་དཔེ་བྱིན་རླབས་ཅན་གཅིག་བུ་དེ་གཉིས་བསྩལ་ཏེ། རིས་མེད་ཆོས་ཀྱི་དགེ་བའི་བཤེས་གཉེན་ཆེན་པོའི་མཚན་ཐོབ་གནང་། མ་ཚད་སྐུ་ཆེ་ཧྲིལ་པོར་གསང་བ་དམ་པོ་བྱེད་དགོས་པའི་སྤྲུལ་སྐུའི་མཚན་ཐོབ་ཀྱི་གསང་རྒྱ་བསྒྲིལ་ཏེ། མ་འོངས་བསྟན་འགྲོ་ལ་སྨན་པའི་ལུང་བསྟན་གནང་། རྗེས་སོར་དཔལ་བཀྲ་ཤིས་ཆོས་ཐང་དགོན་འདུས་སྡེ་ཡོངས་ཀྱིས་ཨ་ཤུལ་ལྷ་བཟོ་བླ་མའི་མཚན་མཐོང་གིས་ཁྲི་འདོན་ཡང་བྱས། དཔལ་རྒྱལ་བ་རྗོ་ནང་བའི་བསྟན་པའི་མངའ་བདག་༸བླ་མ་ཡོན་ཏན་བཟང་པོ་མཆོག་གིས་ཞར་ཛམ་ཐང་དགོན་ཆེན་དུ། སྐུ་ཉིད་ཀྱི་འཁྲུས་འཚབ་ཀྱི་ཚུལ་དུ་དགེ་ཁྲིད་མཁན་པོ་བྱ་དགོས་པའི་བཀའ་རྒྱ་གནང་། ༸སྐྱབས་རྗེ་བླ་མ་བློ་བཟང་འཕྲིན་ལས་དགོངས་པ་ཆོས་དབྱིངས་སུ་བསྡུས་རྐྱེན་གྱིས། སྐུ་གདུང་གི་མདུན་ནས་དམ་བཅས་ཏེ་ལོ་བདུན་ལ་བྱ་བཏང་གི་ཚུལ་གྱིས་ཕྱོགས་མེད་ཡུལ་དུ་ཐེབས། ༸སྐྱབས་རྗེ་སོག་ཁལ་ཁ་རྗེ་བཙུན་དམ་པ་སོགས་ཆོས་ལུགས་རིས་མེད་ཀྱི་བྱེས་བཞུགས་གནས་ཅན་བོད་ཀྱི་སྐྱབས་མགོན་མང་པོ་ལ་མཇལ་འཛོམས་ཆོས་འབྲེལ་བརྒྱུད། མདོ་སྔགས་ཟབ་རྒྱས་ཀྱི་གལ་གནད་དག་ལ་བགྲོ་གླེང་རྟོགས་འབུལ་མཛད་པས། ཆེ་མཐོང་དང་མཚན་གནས་ཁྱད་འཕགས་དུ་མ་ཐོབ། ལྷག་པར་དུ་༸སྐྱབས་མགོན་རྒྱལ་བའི་དབང་པོ་༸གོང་ས་ལྷ་མིའི་རྣམ་འདྲེན་མཆོག་གིས་ཟག་མེད་ཐུགས་ཀྱིས་བརྩེ་གཟིགས་དང་གདེང་འཛོག་མཐོན་པོས་དམིགས་བསལ་མཇལ་ཁ་ཐེངས་གཉིས་ལ་གནང་ནས། ཟབ་བཀླིང་གདམས་པའི་ཆོས་ཀྱི་གསུང་གླེང་གིས་ཟབ་དོན་གནས་ལུགས་རྟོགས་པའི་བྱིན་རླབས་སྙིང་དུ་ཞུགས། སྟོན་པ་སངས་རྒྱས་ཀྱི་གནས་ཆེན་རྣམས་དང་འཕགས་ཡུལ་པཎ་གྲུབ་ཁག་གི་གནས་མཆོག་དག་ཏུ། ཡུན་རིང་ཉམས་བཞེས་ཕྱོད་མེད་གནང་བས་ཉམས་དང་རྟོགས་པའི་གདེང་ཚད་བརྙེས། བླ་མ་དང་མཁའ་འགྲོའི་བཀའ་ལུང་བཞིན་ནུབ་ཕྱོགས་གླིང་ཆེན་ཁག་ཏུ་བསྐྱོད་ནས་མཐའ་གཉིས་བྲལ་བའི་འཚོ་གཞིས་ཀྱི་བརྟན་པ་མ་ཤོར་བར། མཁས་བཙུན་བཟང་གསུམ་དང་། བཟོད་བརྟོན་གཉིས་ལྡན་གྱི་སྤྱོད་པའི་ངང་། ཟབ་གསལ་སྒྱུར་བའི་ཤེས་རབ་ལ་བརྟེན་ནས་དུས་ཡུན་ཤིན་ཏུ་ཐུང་ངུར། འཛམ་གླིང་སྤྱི་སྐད་ལ་མཁྱེན་པ་རྒྱས་པའི་དམ་པའི་ཆོས་ཀྱི་ལོ་ཙཱ་བ་ཆེན་པོར་

གྱུར། ནུབ་ཕྱོགས་པའི་ཤེས་རིག་སྣ་མང་གི་གལ་གནད་རགས་རིམ་མང་པོ་ཐུགས་སུ་ཆུད། ནུབ་ཕྱོགས་སུ་ནང་བསྟན་ལ་སྤྲོ་སྐྱུར་གྱི་བསམ་བློ་དང་། རྟོག་བཟོའི་བསྲེ་ལྷད་ཀྱི་རིགས་ལ་ཞིབ་འཇུག་དག་ཐེར་སོགས་མཛད་རྗེས་བཟང་པོ་བཞག ཐུགས་མཁྱེན་བརྩེ་ནུས་ལྡན་གྱི་བྱིན་རླབས་དང་། གདུལ་བྱའི་སེམས་ཁམས་ལ་མཁས་པས། ཟབ་བརླིང་གསུང་གི་ཆོས་ཀྱི་གདམས་པས་མི་མང་སྟོང་ཕྲག་མང་པོའི་བློ་སེམས་བདེ་སྐྱིད་དང་དཀར་ཆོས་དགེ་བ་ལ་བཀོད། བོད་དབྱིན་གཉིས་ཀྱི་ཐོག་ཏུ་བརྩམས་ཟིན་དང་རྩོམ་བཞིན་པའི་གསུང་འབུམ་པོད་བཅུ་གཉིས་ཙམ་དུ་ལོང་བཞིན། ད་ལྟ་སྐལ་བཟང་གདུལ་བྱའི་དཔལ་དུ་སྐུ་འཚོ་གཞེས་སུ་བཞུགས་པའོ།།

དྲིན་ཅན་རྩ་བའི་བླ་མ་ལ་གསོལ་བ་འདེབས།།

སྤྱིར་ནང་པ་སངས་རྒྱས་པའི་གཞུང་གང་ཡིན་གྱི་སྐབས་སུ་དགེ་བའི་བཤེས་གཉེན་ནམ། དགེ་བའི་ལམ་སྟོན་པ་ནི་ཤིན་ཏུ་གལ་ཆེན་ཞིག་དང་ཆེས་རྩ་ཆེན་པོ་ཞིག་ཡིན་པ་གཞིར་བཞག ཁྱད་པར་དུ་གསང་བ་སྔགས་ཀྱི་དབང་དུ་བཏང་ན་ནི། ལེགས་སྦྱར་སྐད་ལ་གུ་རུ་ཞེས་པ། བོད་སྐད་དུ་བླ་མ་ཞེས་པ་ནི་དེ་བས་ཀྱང་རྩ་ཆེ་བ་རུ་འཛིན་སྲོལ་ཡོད་ལ། རྩ་བའི་བླ་མ་ཞེས་པའི་དོན་ནི། སྤྱིར་བླ་མ་ཙམ་ཡིན་པ་དང་བརྒྱུད་པའི་བླ་མ་ཙམ་མ་ཡིན་པར། རང་ཉིད་ལ་དངོས་སུ་འཕྲད་ཅིང་ཆོས་ཀྱི་འབྲེལ་བའི་བླ་མ་ཡིན་པའི་དོན་རེད། གལ་དེ་ཆོས་འབྲེལ་ཐོབ་པའི་བླ་མ་མང་དུ་ཡོད་ན། རང་ལ་ཕན་ཐོགས་ཤོས་དེའམ། ཡང་ན་ཐུན་མོང་མ་ཡིན་པའི་ཆོས་གནང་མཁན་དེ་ལ་གོ་ན་ཡང་ཆོག་པ་རེད། གལ་ཏེ་བླ་མ་ལ་ཆེས་གཙིགས་འཛིན་དང་མཐོང་ཆེན་བྱས་ན། རང་ལ་བྱིན་རླབས་ཀྱི་ཚན་ཁ་སྨུར་བ་དང་ས་ལམ་ལ་བར་ཆད་མེད་པ་སོགས་ཀྱི་གནད་འགག་ཡོད་པར་གྲགས། དེའི་ཕྱིར་བླ་མ་ནི་གང་ཟག་སྐྱེར་ངོས་ནས་བཤད་ན་སྟོན་པ་སངས་རྒྱས་ལས་ཀྱང་དྲིན་ཆེ་བའི་ཕྱིར། དྲིན་ཅན་རྩ་བའི་བླ་མ་དེ་ལ་སྒོ་གསུམ་གུས་པ་ཆེན་པོའི་སྒོ་ནས་གསོལ་བ་འདེབས་སོ།། ཞེས་པའི་དོན་རེད།

བླ་མ་ནི་སངས་རྒྱས་ལས་ཀྱང་གང་ཟག་སྐྱེར་ངོས་ལ་བཀའ་དྲིན་ཆེ་ཞིང་དོན་གནད་ཆེ་བའི་རྒྱུ་མཚན་ནི། སངས་རྒྱས་ཀྱི་ངོས་ནས་ནུས་མཐུ་ཅི་ཙམ་ཡོད་ཀྱང་། རང་ཉིད་ལ་སངས་རྒྱས་དངོས་སུ་མཇལ་བའི་ལས་དང་སྨོན་ལམ་མ་ཡོད་པ་དང་། བླ་མ་ལ་དངོས་སུ་མཇལ་ཞིང་ཆོས་ཀྱི་བདུད་རྩི་མཉམ་དུ་ལོངས་སུ་སྤྱོད་པའི་ལས་དང་སྨོན་ལམ་ཡོད་པ། སངས་རྒྱས་ཉིད་སྐུ་འདས་ཁར། ཀུན་དགའ་བོ་སོགས་ལ་ཕྱིན་མ་འོངས་པར་དགེ་བའི་བཤེས་གཉེན་སོགས་ཀྱི་གཟུགས་སུ་བྱོན་པར་ཞལ་གྱིས་བཞེས་པ་སོགས་མང་པོ་ཞིག་ལ་བསམ་བློ་ཞིབ་ཏུ་བཏང་ན། མི་འཐད་ཅིང་རྒྱུ་མཚན་མེད་པ་ཞིག་མིན། དཔེར་ན་སངས་རྒྱས་ནི་

གྲུ་བཟོ་མཁན་དང་། ཆོས་ནི་གྲུ་གཏོང་མཁན་དང་། བླ་མ་ནི་དངོས་སུ་གྲུ་བཏང་ཏེ་ང་ཚོ་འཁོར་བའི་རྒྱ་མཚོ་ཆེན་པོ་ལས་སྲོག་སྐྱོབ་མཁན་གྱི་གྲུའི་ཁ་ལོ་བ་ལྟ་བུ་རེད། དེའི་ཕྱིར་ང་ཚོ་སངས་རྒྱས་གྲུ་བཟོ་མཁན་ལ་དགའ་སྣང་དང་དད་པ་རྗེས་མཐོང་སོགས་ཡོད་ཅིང་། གྲུ་དངོས་སུ་བཏང་ནས་རྒྱ་མཚོའི་ཉེན་ཁ་ལས་སྒྲོལ་མཁན་ལ་ཆེ་མཐོང་སོགས་ཅི་ཡང་མེད་ན་ཆེས་མི་འོས་པ་ཞིག་ཡིན་པ་ལྟ་བུ་རེད།

ཆོས་རྗེ་ལ་གསོལ་བ་འདེབས།།

ཆོས་རྗེ་ནི་ཆོས་ཀྱི་རྗེ་བོའམ་ཆོས་ཀྱི་རྒྱལ་པོའི་དོན་དང་། མདོར་ན་བརྩི་བཀུར་གཅིགས་འཛིན་ཆེ་མཐོང་བྱས་པའི་དོན་རེད། དེ་ལྟར་བྱས་ན་ཉམས་ལེན་པ་རང་གི་སེམས་རྒྱུད་ལ་བྱིན་རླབས་འཇུག་པར་བཟང་བས་རེད།

ཡབ་སྲས་ཆོས་བྱིན་གྱིས་རློབས།

ཡབ་ནི་ཕ་ཟེར་བ་ལ་ཆེ་མཐོང་དང་ཞེ་སའི་ཚིག་སྒྲར་བ་རེད། སྲས་ནི་བུའི་དོན་ལ་ཆེ་མཐོང་སམ་བརྩི་བཀུར་སྒྲར་བ་གཅིག་མཚུངས་རེད། དེ་འདྲའི་ཞེ་སའམ་རྗེས་མཐོང་གི་ཚིག་སྒྲར་བ་ནི། ཁ་ཡག་ངོ་བསྟོད་ཙམ་མ་ཡིན་པར་གོང་དུ་བཤད་པ་ལྟར་གྱི་དགོས་གནད་ཆེན་པོ་ཡོད་ཕྱིར་རེད། ཆོས་ཞེས་པ་བླ་མ་བརྒྱུད་པ་ཡོངས་རྫོགས་ལ་གསོལ་བ་བཏབ་པའི་དོན་རེད།

གང་ཞིག་དད་པའི་བླ་མའི་ཚོགས་རྣམས་ལ།།
ཚེ་འདིར་རྟག་ཏུ་གསོལ་བ་འདེབས་བྱས་ན།།
བདག་སོགས་རྒྱུད་ལ་བླ་མ་འདི་དག་གི །
ཡེ་ཤེས་སེམས་དཔའི་བྱིན་རླབས་འཇུག་པར་ཤོག །

གང་ཞིག་སྟེ་ཉམས་ལེན་པ་རང་ཉིད་དད་པ་ཡོད་སའི་བླ་མའི་ཚོགས་ཏེ་བླ་མ་དེ་རྣམས་ལ། ཚེ་འདིར་ཏེ་སྲོག་འཚོ་གཞིས་ཀྱི་དུས་ཏེ། མ་ཤི་གོང་ནས་ཡུན་རིང་པོར་དུས་རྟག་ཏུ་གསོལ་བ་འདེབས་པར་བྱས་ན་ནི། བདག་ལ་སོགས་པའི་སེམས་ཅན་ཐམས་ཅད་ཀྱི་སེམས་རྒྱུད་ལ། བརྒྱུད་པའི་བླ་མ་འདི་དག་གི་ཐུགས་རྒྱུད་དུ་བཞུགས་པའི་ཡེ་ཤེས་ཞེས་པ་རྣམ་ཤེས་ལས་འདས་པའི་གཉུག་མ་ལྷན་སྐྱེས་ཀྱི་ཡེ་ཤེས་དེ་ཉིད། སེམས་དཔའ་སྟེ་དོན་དམ་བྱང་ཆུབ་ཀྱི་སེམས། སྟོང་ཉིད་སྙིང་རྗེའི་སྙིང་པོ་ཅན་དེ་ཉིད་སེམས་རྒྱུད་ལ་སྨིན་ནུས་པར་ཤོག་ཅིག་གམ། དེ་ཉིད་སེམས་རྒྱུད་དུ་འཇུག་པར་ཤོག་ཅིག་ཅེས་པའི་དོན་ནོ།།

སྐྱེ་བ་ཀུན་ཏུ་ཡང་དག་བླ་མ་དང་།།
འབྲལ་མེད་ཆོས་ཀྱི་དཔལ་ལ་ལོངས་སྤྱོད་ཅིང་།།
ས་དང་ལམ་གྱི་ཡོན་ཏན་རབ་རྫོགས་ནས།།
རྡོ་རྗེ་འཆང་གི་གོ་འཕང་མྱུར་ཐོབ་ཤོག །

གོང་དུ་སྨོས་པ་བཞིན་བླ་མ་ལ་སངས་རྒྱས་དངོས་མཐོང་ངམ། བླ་མ་ལ་ཆེས་གཙིགས་ཆེན་དུ་འཛིན་པ་ལས་གལ་ཆེ་བ་ཞིག་མེད་ཕྱིར། སྐྱེ་བ་ནས་ཚེ་རབས་ཀུན་ཏུ་ལོག་པའི་བཤེས་གཉེན་སོགས་མ་ཡིན་པའི་ཡང་དག་པའི་བླ་མ་དག་དང་ནམ་ཡང་མི་འབྲལ་ཞིང་། དམ་པའི་ཆོས་ལ་རྒྱུན་དུ་ལོངས་སྤྱོད་པའི་སྐལ་བ་དང་ལྡན་ཞིང་། ཐར་བ་དང་ཐམས་ཅད་མཁྱེན་པའི་ལམ། ཐོས་བསམ་སྒོམ་གསུམ་ལ་གོམས་ཤིང་བརྟན་བརླིང་དུ་གྱུར་ནས་ས་དང་ལམ་ཞེས་པའི་རང་རྒྱུད་ཀྱི་ཡོན་ཏན་དག་མཐར་ཕྱིན་པའམ་རབ་ཏུ་རྫོགས་ནས། རྡོ་རྗེ་འཆང་སྟེ་གདོད་མ་དང་པོའི་སངས་རྒྱས་སམ། གཏན་དུ་འགྱུར་བ་མེད་པའི་མཐར་ཐུག་གཏན་གྱི་བདེ་བའི་གོ་འཕང་ཐོབ་པར་གྱུར་ཅིག་ཅེས་པའོ།།

སྐྱབས་ཡུལ་རྣམས་འོད་དུ་ཞུ་ནས་རང་ལ་ཐིམ་པས་བདག་རྒྱུད་བྱིན་གྱིས་བརླབ་པར་མོས།

ཞེས་པ་ཡན་ཆད་ཀྱིས་བླ་མ་བརྒྱུད་པའི་གསོལ་འདེབས་ཟིན་ནས། སྐྱབས་ཡུལ་རྣམས་ཟེར་བ་སྟེ་གོང་ནས་བསྒོམས་ཡོད་པའི་རྩ་བརྒྱུད་ཀྱི་བླ་མ་དམ་པ་དེ་དག མཐར་འོད་དུ་ཞུ་ནས་རང་ལ་ཐིམ་པའི་དབང་གིས་བདག་གི་རྒྱུད་བྱིན་གྱིས་བརླབ་པའི་མོས་པ་ཤུགས་དྲག་བྱ་དགོས་པའི་དོན་ནོ།།

གསང་སྔགས་ཐུན་མོང་སྟོན་འགྲོའི་སྐྱབས་འགྲོ།

ཐེག་པ་ཆེན་པོ་གསང་སྔགས་ལུགས་ཀྱི་སྐྱབས་ཡུལ་རྣམས་འདིར་རྩ་བའི་ཚིག་ཟིན་ཁག་ཏུ་གསལ་ལ། སྐྱབས་གནས་དེ་དག་གི་མཚན་ཉིད་དང་། དབྱེ་བ། སྐུ་གསུང་ཐུགས་ཀྱི་ཡོན་ཏན་སོགས་རྒྱས་པ་ནི་ཐུན་གྱིས་ཁྲིས་པའི་ཇོ་ནང་ལམ་རིམ་བདེ་གཤེགས་སྙིང་པོའི་འཇུག་རིམ་ཇོགས་ལྡན་གསར་པའི་ཁྲིད་ནོར་ལས་ཤེས་དགོས་ལ། ཡང་ན་སྐྱབས་འགྲོའི་རྣམ་བཞག་གཞན་ལས་ཤེས་དགོས་པ་ལས་འདིར་རྒྱས་པར་མི་སྤྲོ།

མདོར་བསྡུས་ནས་བཤད་ན། སྐབས་འདིའི་སྐྱབས་འགྲོའི་ཡུལ་ལ། བླ་མ། ཡི་དམ། སངས་རྒྱས། ཆོས། དགེ་འདུན། མཁའ་འགྲོ། ཆོས་སྐྱོང་བཅས་བདུན་པོ་དེ་ཡིན། འོན་ཀྱང་། སངས་རྒྱས་ཆོས་དགེ་འདུན་གསུམ་གྱི་ནང་དུ་བསྡུས་ན་བསྡུ་ཐུབ་པས། དེ་དག་ནི་སྐབས་འདིའི་སྐྱབས་ཡུལ་དུ་ངོས་འཛིན་བྱས་ན་ཡང་ཆོག སྐྱབས་ཡུལ་དེ་དག་ལ་སྐྱབས་སུ་འགྲོ་བར་བྱེད་པ་ལ། དང་པོ་སྐྱབས་འགྲོ་ཡང་དག་གི་རྒྱུ་དགོས་པས། དེ་ནི་ཁམས་གསུམ་འཁོར་བ་དང་། ཐེག་པ་ཐུན་མོང་བའི་ལུགས་ཀྱི་ཞི་བའི་མྱང་འདས་སམ། ཐར་བ་ཙམ་དེ་གཉིས་ལས་ངེས་པར་འབྱུང་དགོས། དེའི་དོན་ནི། ཁམས་གསུམ་འཁོར་བའི་མི་ཚད། རང་ཉིད་ཁོ་ན་ཙམ་འཁོར་བ་ལས་ཐར་བའི་ཐར་བ་ལའང་མི་ཆགས་ཤིང་། དེ་ལ་འཇིག་ཅིང་ཞེན་པ་ཞིག་དགོས་པའི་དོན་ཡིན། མ་ཟད་སྐྱབས་སུ་འགྲོ་ཡུལ་དེ་དག་གི་ཡོན་ཏན་དང་། འཕྲིན་ལས་བཅས་པ་ངོས་ཟིན་པའི་ཐོག་ནས་དེ་དག་ལ་ཁ་ཙམ་མིན་པར་སེམས་གཏིང་ནས་དད་ཅིང་ཡིད་ཆེས་དགོས། སྐྱབས་སུ་སོང་རྗེས་སུ་ངེས་པར་དུ་བསླབ་པར་བྱ་དགོས་པ་གཙོ་ཆེ་བ་ཁག་བརྗོད་ན། སྐྱབས་སྟོན་པ་སངས་རྒྱས་ལ་སྐྱབས་སུ་སོང་ཕྱིན་མི་སྟེགས་པའམ། འཇིག་རྟེན་ལས་མ་འདས་པའི་ལྷ་སོགས་ལ་གནས་སྐབས་ཀྱི་ཁེ་ཕན་ཙམ་རེའི་ཆེད་དུ་མ་གཏོགས། ཚེ་རབས་གཏན་གྱི་སྐྱབས་གནས་སུ་ནམ་ཡང་བསྟེན་མི་རུང་། སྐྱབས་དངོས་དམ་པའི་ཆོས་ལ་སྐྱབས་སུ་སོང་བའམ། དམ་པའི་ཆོས་ཉམས་སུ་བླང་རྒྱུ་ཡིན་ཕྱིན། སེམས་ཅན་སུ་ལའང་ནམ་ཡང་གནོད་པ་ཙུང་ཙམ་ཡང་བྱ་མི་རུང་། གྲོགས་སྐྱབས་གནས་དགེ་འདུན་ལ་སྐྱབས་སུ་སོང་ཕྱིན། ནང་པ་སངས་རྒྱས་པའི་ཆོས་ཀྱི་གྲོགས་པོ་རྣམས་ནི་གྲོགས་ཐམས་ཅད་ཀྱི་ནང་ནས་གལ་ཆེ་ཤོས་སུ་གཟུང་དགོས། ནང་པ་སངས་རྒྱས་པའི་ལྟ་སྤྱོད་དང་མི་མཐུན་པ་སུའང་གྲོགས་ཀྱི་མཆོག་ཏུ་བསྟེན་མི་རུང་། རྒྱུ་མཚན་ནི། དེ་དག་གི་བསམ་སྤྱོད་ཀྱིས། ནང་པ་སངས་རྒྱས་པའི་

དམ་པའི་ཆོས་ཀྱི་བསམ་སྤྱོད་ལ་ངོ་སོག་གམ། ཤུགས་སྐྱེན་ཐེབས་སླ་བས། དེ་དག་དང་མཉམ་དུ་སྤྱོད་ལམ་ཨུང་ཐབས་སུ་འབད་པ་བྱ་དགོས་ལ། སྐྱབ་པའི་ཕྱོགས་ནས། འདས་ཟིན་པའི་འཕགས་པའི་སྐྱེས་བུ་རྣམས་ཀྱི་རྣམ་ཐར་ཞིབ་དགོས་ལ། ད་ལྟའི་དགེ་བའི་བཤེས་གཉེན་དང་ཆོས་གྲོགས་ཡ་རབས་རྣམས་ཀྱི་སྤྱོད་བཟང་ལ་མིག་ལྟོས་དང་སྤྱོད་ལམ་མཐུན་ཐབས་སུ་འབད་དགོས། སྐབས་འདིའི་སྐྱབས་འགྲོའི་ཡུལ་ལ། བླ་མ། ཡི་དམ། སངས་རྒྱས། ཆོས། དགེ་འདུན། མཁའ་འགྲོ། ཆོས་སྐྱོང་རྣམས་ཡོད་པ་ལས། དགེ་འདུན་དང་མཁའ་འགྲོ། ཆོས་སྐྱོང་གི་ནང་དུ་འཇིག་རྟེན་པ་ཡོད་ཆོག་ཀྱང་། དེ་དག་ནི་གནས་སྐབས་ཀྱི་གྲོགས་ལས་གཏན་གྱི་སྐྱབས་གནས་སུ་མི་རུང་བ་ཤེས་དགོས། དེ་དག་ཚུར་བསྡུས་ན་སངས་རྒྱས། ཆོས། དགེ་འདུན་གསུམ་གྱི་ནང་དུ་རིགས་ཀྱི་སྒོ་ནས་འདུ་བའོ།།

བསྒྲུབ་དགོས་པའི་བསླབ་བྱ་ཁག གཙོ་ཆེ་ས་ནས་བརྗོད་ན་སྐྱབས་གནས་དཀོན་མཆོག་གསུམ་ལ་རྒྱུན་དུ་དད་ཅིང་དྲན་པས་ཕྱག་མཆོད་སོགས་བྱ་དགོས། དཔེར་ན་རྒྱུན་དུ་དྲན་པའི་སྒོ་ནས་ཟས་གོས་ལ་སོགས་པ། རང་ཉིད་ལ་ཡིད་དུ་འོང་བའི་དངོས་པོ་ཅི་ཡོད་རྣམས་དངོས་སུ་ནུས་ཚོད་ཀྱིས་ཕུལ་བའི་སྒོ་ནས་མཆོད་པ། མེད་པའམ་མ་ནུས་ན། ཡིད་ཡུལ་དུ་བྱུས་པའི་སྒོ་ནས་མཆོད་པ་ནི་ཤིན་ཏུ་གལ་ཆེ། ཟ་ན་བཟའ་བཏུང་གི་དུས་སུ་དྲན་ནས་སེམས་ཀྱིས་མཆོད་པ། གོས་གསར་བ་སོགས་བསྒོ་དུས་སུའང་དྲན་ནས་མཆོད་པ་ལ་སོགས་པའོ།།

དེ་ནས་སྐྱབས་སུ་འགྲོ་བའི་ཚུལ་ལ་སོགས་པ་རིམ་བཞིན་དཀྲུས་ནས་ཞེས་པར་འགྱུར་ལ། སྐྱབས་འགྲོའི་རྣམ་བཞག་རྒྱས་སྤྲོས་ཞེས་འདོད་ཡོད་མཁན་ཚོས་ནི། བདེ་གཤེགས་སྙིང་པོའི་འཇུག་རིམ་རྫོགས་ལྡན་གསར་པའི་ཁྲིད་ནོར་དང་། ཡང་ན་སྐྱབས་འགྲོའི་རྣམ་བཞག་རྣམ་དཔྱད་རྒྱས་པ་རྣམས་ལས་ཤེས་པར་འཚལ།

> ན་མཿཤྲཱི་ཀཱ་ལ་ཙཀྲཱ་ཡ། མཆོག་གསུམ་སྐྱབས་འགྲོ་དང་ནི་སེམས་བསྐྱེད་བྱ།། རྫོར་སེམས་སྒོམ་སྟེ་སྒྲིབ་སྦྱོང་ཡིག་བརྒྱ་བཟླ།། མཎྜལ་ཚོགས་ལུས་དང་ལོངས་སྤྱོད་འབུལ།། བླ་མའི་རྣལ་འབྱོར་བསྒོམས་ཤིང་གསོལ་བ་གདབ།། བསྐྱེད་པའི་རིམ་པས་ཐ་མལ་རྣམ་རྟོག་སྤང་ས།། སྒོ་གསུམ་དབེན་པར་གནས་པའི་མི་རྟོག་བསྒོམ།། ཞེས་སྨོས་སོ།།

ཞེས་ན་མཿནི་བླ་མ་དང་ལྷག་པའི་ལྷ་ལ་གུས་པས་འདུད་པ་སྟེ་ཕྱག་འཚལ་བའི་དོན་ནོ།། ཤྲཱི་ནི་དཔལ

དང་ལྡན་པ། ཀཱ་ལ་ནི་ལེགས་སྦྱར་གྱི་སྐད་དུ་དུས་དང་། ཙཀྲ་ནི་འཁོར་ལོའི་དོན་ཏེ། ཚུལ་བཞིན་བརྟེན་ན་འཁོར་འདས་ཀྱི་ལེགས་འབྱོར་དཔལ་དང་ཡོན་ཏན་ཐམས་ཅད་ཀྱི་འབྱུང་གནས་ཡིན་པའི་དོན་རེད། དུས་ནི། ཕྱི་དུས་ཀྱི་འཁོར་ལོ་སྟོང་གསུམ་འཇིག་རྟེན་གྱི་ཁམས་དང་། ཉི་ཟླ་གཟའ་སྐར་སོགས་སྣ་ཚོགས་རིགས་ཀྱི་གོ་ལ་མ་ལུས་པའི་བསྐྱོད་པ་དང་བསྐྱོད་ཚུལ་ཆེ་ཕྲ་ཀུན་གྱི་འགྲོས་དང་བཅས་པ་ལ་གོ ནང་དུས་ཀྱི་འཁོར་ལོ་གང་ཟག་གི་ལུས་ཀྱི་བཀོད་པ་སྟེ། བཀོད་པ་རྩ་བའི་དཀྱིལ་འཁོར་ཕྲ་རགས། གཡོ་བ་རླུང་ཕྲ་རགས་ཀྱི་རང་བཞིན། གནས་པའམ་བདེ་བ་ཐིག་ལེ་ཕྲ་རགས་ཀྱི་རང་བཞིན་གསུམ་གྱི་ཁོར་ཡུག་གི་བཀོད་པ། གཞོམ་བཅས་གཞོམ་མེད་ཀྱི་ངག་གི་འཁོར་ལོའི་རྒྱུན། སེམས་རྣམ་ཤེས་ཚོགས་བརྒྱད་ཀུན་གཞི་ཡེ་ཤེས་དང་བཅས་པ། གཞན་དུས་ཀྱི་འཁོར་ལོ་དོན་དམ་རང་ཆས་ཀྱི་ལྷ་དྲུག་བརྒྱ་སོ་དྲུག་གི་ལྷ་ཚོགས་ཀྱིས་མཚོན་པའི་དག་པ་སངས་རྒྱས་ཀྱི་ཞིང་གི་དཀྱིལ་འཁོར་གྱིས་བསྡུས་པ་གསུམ་དུ། བསྡུས་པ་གང་ཡིན་པ་དང་། དོན་དམ་རྣམ་པ་ཐམས་ཅད་པའི་དུས་དང་ལྷ་ཚོགས་ཀྱི་དཀྱིལ་འཁོར་དང་བཅས་པ། འཕོ་འགྱུར་བྲལ་ཞིང་མཆོག་མི་འགྱུར་བའི་བདེ་བ་ཆེན་པོའི་རང་བཞིན་དུ་གནས་པའོ།། དེ་ལྟ་བུའི་ཀུན་རྫོབ་འཁོར་བའི་དུས་ཀྱི་གནས་ལུགས་ཕྲ་གསང་གི་རང་བཞིན་ཕྲ་ཞིང་ཕྲ་བ་དཔལ་ལྡན་དུས་ཀྱི་འཁོར་ལོ་ལ་ཕྱག་འཚལ་ལོ་ཞེས་དང་། མཆོག་གསུམ་སྐྱབས་འགྲོ་དང་ནི་སེམས་བསྐྱེད་བྱ། སོགས་ཀྱིས་མཆོད་བརྗོད་མདོར་བསྡུས་སྔོན་དུ་བཏང་ནས། དུས་ཀྱི་འཁོར་ལོའི་ཐུན་མོང་བའི་སྔོན་འགྲོ་ལྔ་དང་། ཐུན་མིན་སྔོན་འགྲོ་གཉིས་ཀྱི་ས་བཅད་ཙམ་གྱི་མིང་ཙམ་བརྗོད་པ་ཡིན་པས་དེ་དག་འདིར་ཚིག་རེ་རེ་བཞིན་མི་སྤྲོ་བར་འོག་ཏུ་རང་རང་གི་སྐབས་སུ་རེ་རེ་བཞིན་རྒྱས་པར་གསལ་པོར་འཆད་པར་འགྱུར་རོ།།

འདིར་ཟབ་ལམ་རྡོ་རྗེའི་རྣལ་འབྱོར་གྱི་སྔོན་དུ་འགྲོ་བའི་དག་འདོན་མཁའ་སྤྱོད་བགྲོད་པའི་ཐེམ་སྐས་ཞེས་བྱ་བའི་ཉམས་ལེན་ལ། ཆོས་བརྒྱུད་གཞན་དང་སྔགས་བླ་མེད་གཞུང་གཞན་དང་རྩ་བ་མཐུན་པའི་ཐུན་མོང་གི་སྔོན་འགྲོ་ལྔའི་ནང་གི་ཐོག་མའི་སྔོན་འགྲོ་དང་པོ་སྐྱབས་སུ་འགྲོ་བར་བྱེད་པ་ལ། དམིགས་པ་འདི་ལྟར་བྱ་དགོས།

དབེན་པའི་གནས་སུ་སེམས་རྣལ་དུ་ཕབ་ནས།

ཞེས་པས་ལས་དང་པོ་བ་དག་ལ་ཕྱིའི་གཡེང་རྐྱེན་གཟུགས་སྒྲ་དྲི་རོ་སོགས་དབེན་པ་ཞིག་ལྡན་ན་བསྒོམ་ནུས་པ་ལ་ཉུང་ཟད་ཕན་པས་བླང་བར་བྱ་བའོ།། འོན་ཀྱང་གཟུགས་སྒྲ་སོགས་ཀྱི་གཡེང་རྐྱེན་ཉུང་ཙམ་མེད་པའི་གནས་ཤིག་རྙེད་དཀའ་བས། མཐའ་གཅིག་ཏུ་རྙེད་དགོས་པའི་ངེས་པ་མེད་ལ། གཙོ་བོ་ནང་རྐྱེན་རྣམ་རྟོག་གི་གཡེང་བ་མེད་ཐབས་ལ་འབད་དགོས་པས། རང་ཉིད་ཀྱི་ནང་གི་སེམས་དེ་ཉིད་ཕྱིའི་ཡུལ་

གྱི་གཡེང་བ་དག་གིས་མི་འཕྲོག་པའི་ཐབས་དང་ཤེས་རབ་བཅའ་ཞིང་ཉམས་སྐྱོང་དོན་ཐོག་ནས་འཚོལ་དགོས། བརྩོན་པ་ཆེན་པོས་རྣམ་རྟོག་གིས་མི་འཕྲོག་པར། སེམས་རང་ཉིད་ཀྱིས་རང་ཚུགས་ཐུབ་པར་གོམས་གཤིས་འདྲགས་པར་འཇུག་པ་ནི་སྒོམ་པའམ། གོམས་གཤིས་འདྲགས་རྒྱུ་གལ་ཆེ་ཤོས་དེ་ཡིན་པ་ཤེས་དགོས། སྐབས་འདིར་སེམས་ཀྱི་དམིགས་པ་འཕྲེར་སྟངས་ཏེ་སྐྱབས་ཡུལ་རྣམས་བསྒོམ་དགོས་པས་དེ་ཉིད་བསྒོམ་ཚུལ་ནི།

> རང་གང་དུ་གནས་པའི་ས་ཕྱོགས་འདི་ཉིད་དག་པའི་ཞིང་ཁམས་ཆེན་པོ་ཡངས་ཤིང་རྒྱ་ཆེ་བར་གྱུར་པའི་དབུས་སུ།

ཉམས་ལེན་པ་རང་ཉིད་ས་ཕྱོགས་གང་དུ་གནས་ཡོད་མེད་ལ་མ་ལྟོས་པར། རང་ལ་ལས་དབང་གིས་སྣང་བའི་ད་ལྟའི་མ་དག་སྡུག་བདེན་གྱི་ཕུང་པོའི་རང་བཞིན་གྱི་འཇིག་རྟེན་འདིའི་སྣང་བ་དེ་ཉིད་སེམས་ནས་འདོར་ཅི་ཐུབ་ཀྱིས། དེ་ཉིད་མ་དག་པར་མི་འཛིན་པར། རང་ཉིད་གནས་པའི་ས་ཕྱོགས་ཡུལ་ལུང་དེ་ཉིད་རྫོགས་པའི་སངས་རྒྱས་ཀྱི་ཐུགས་ཡེ་ཤེས་ཀྱི་སྣང་ཆ་ལས་གྲུབ་པའི་དག་པའི་ཞིང་ཁམས། རྒྱ་ཁྱོན་ཤིན་ཏུ་ཡངས་ཤིང་ཆེ་བ། མཐའ་མེད་པ་ཞིག་དངོས་སུ་སྒོམ་ནུས་ན་རབ་དང་། དེ་མ་ནུས་ན་མོས་སྒོམ་གྱིས་དེ་ལྟར་ཡིན་སྙམ་པར་མོས་པ་ཤུགས་གང་དྲག་བྱ། དེ་ལྟ་བུའི་ཡངས་པའི་དག་ཞིང་གི་དབུས་སུ།

> རིན་པོ་ཆེ་སྣ་ཚོགས་ལས་གྲུབ་པའི་གཞལ་མེད་ཁང་རྒྱན་དང་བཀོད་པ་ཕུན་སུམ་ཚོགས་པ། དེའི་དབུས་སུ་དཔག་བསམ་གྱི་སྡོང་པོ་ཡལ་ག་ལོ་འདབ་མེ་ཏོག་འབྲས་བུ་རབ་ཏུ་རྒྱས་པའི་རྩེ་མོར།

མཐའ་གཅིག་ཏུ་རིན་པོ་ཆེ་ལས་གྲུབ་མི་དགོས་ཀྱང་། གཙོ་བོ་རང་གི་དང་བ་བསྐྱེད་པའི་དངོས་པོ་ཞིག་ངེས་པར་ཡིན་དགོས། འདིའི་སྐབས་སུ་རིན་པོ་ཆེ་ཡིན་དགོས་པར་བརྗོད་པ་ནི། གཙོ་བོ་མི་རྣམས་ལ་རིན་པོ་ཆེ་སོགས་རྩ་ཆེའི་རྒྱུ་ནོར་ལ་འདོད་ཆེ་བས་དང་བ་དང་འདུན་པ་བསྐྱེད་པའི་ཆེད་དུ་ཡིན་ཞིང་། མ་ཟད་འདི་དག་དེ་སྒོན་ཉམས་ལེན་པ་སྟོང་ཕྲག་མང་པོས་འདི་ལྟར་བསྒོམས་སྐྱོང་བ་ཡིན་པས་བྱིན་རླབས་ཀྱི་ཚན་ཁ་ཡང་ཡོད་པ་ཞིག་རེད། དེའི་ཕྱིར་རིན་པོ་ཆེ་ལས་གྲུབ་པར་བསྒོམ་ན་སྐྱོན་ག་ལ་ཡོད། གཞལ་མེད་ཁང་ཟེར་བ་ནི་ལས་དབང་དང་ས་རྡོ་ཤིང་ལྕགས་སོགས་ཀྱིས་གྲུབ་པའི་ཁང་བ་དག་གི་རིན་ཚད་དང་ཆེ་ཆུང་སོགས་གཞལ་དུ་ཡོད་ཀྱང་། ད་ལྟ་འདིར་བསྒོམ་དགོས་པ་དེ་ནི་ཀུན་རྫོབ་བདེན་དངོས་ཀྱིས་གྲུབ་པའི་ཁང་བ་ཞིག་མ་ཡིན་པས། རིན་གོང་དང་ཆེ་ཆུང་སོགས་གཞལ་དུ་མེད་པ་ཞིག་ཡིན་ཕྱིར་གཞལ་མེད་

ཁང་ཟེར་གྱི་ཡོད་པ་འདྲ། དཔག་བསམ་གྱི་ཤིང་ཟེར་བ་ནི་རིག་བྱེད་ཀྱི་གཏམ་རྒྱུད་ལ་གཞི་བཅོལ་བ་ཞིག་ཡིན་ཡང་། ནང་བ་སངས་རྒྱས་པའི་དབང་དུ་བཏང་ན་གོང་སྨོས་བཞིན། ཐ་མལ་ལས་སྣང་ལས་བྱུང་བའི་ཤིང་སྡོང་ཞིག་མིན་པར་ཚད་ལས་འདས་ཤིང་དཔག་མཐའ་མེད་པའི་སྡོང་པོ་ཞིག་ཡིན་པའི་དོན་དུ་འགྲོ་བར་སེམས།

སེ་དྲིས་བརྟེགས་པའི་རིན་པོ་ཆེའི་ཁྲི་ཡངས་ཤིང་རྒྱ་ཆེ་བ་སྣ་ཚོགས་པདྨ་ཉི་ཟླ་བརྩེགས་པའི་གདན་ལ།

ཁྲི་རིན་ཆེན་སྣ་ཚོགས་ལས་གྲུབ་དགོས་པ་དང་། ཁྲི་དེ་སེ་དྲིས་བརྟེགས་དགོས་པ་སོགས་ཀུང་དོན་ལ་རང་གི་རྩ་བའི་བླ་མ་དེ་འཁོར་འདས་གཉིས་ཀྱི་བར་ཟམ་པ་ལྟ་བུའི་འདྲེན་བྱེད་ངོ་མཚར་བ་ཞིག་ཡིན་པ་གོ་ཆེད་དུ་ཡིན་པས། རིན་པོ་ཆེ་ནི་མིའི་འགྲོ་བ་དག་གི་རྩ་ཆེ་ཤོས་དང་། སེ་དྲི་ནི་དུད་འགྲོའི་རྒྱལ་པོ་རུ་གྲགས་ཤིང་མི་འཇིགས་པའི་མཚོན་དོན་ཡིན་པས། ཚད་མེད་པའི་གཙིགས་ཆེན་བྱས་པའི་དོན་ཡིན་པ་ལས་མཐའ་གཅིག་ཏུ་བླ་མའི་ཁྲི་ལ་སེ་དྲི་ཡོད་དགོས་པའི་དོན་མིན་པ་འདྲ། ཁྲི་སྟེག་གི་གདན་སྟེང་དུ་ཉི་ཟླ་དང་པདྨ་བརྒྱན་དགོས་དོན་ནི། ཉི་མས་ཟབ་གསལ་གཉིས་སུ་མེད་པའི་ཤེས་རབ་མཚོན་ཡོད་ལ། ཟླ་བས་བྱམས་སྙིང་རྗེ་བྱང་ཆུབ་ཀྱི་སེམས་མཚོན་ཡོད། པདྨ་མ་ཆགས་པ་དང་མ་དག་པ་མེད་པའམ། འཁོར་བའི་སྐྱོན་གྱིས་མ་གོས་པ་མཚོན་ཡོད། དོན་ལ་སྐྱབས་ཡུལ་བླ་མ་སོགས་སྐྱབས་གནས་རྣམས་ལ་ཡོན་ཏན་དེ་དག་ལྡན་ཡོད་པའི་མཚོན་དོན་ཡིན་པར་སྣང་།

རྩ་བའི་བླ་མ་རྡོ་རྗེ་འཆང་གི་རྣམ་པ་ཅན་ལ་བརྒྱུད་པའི་བླ་མ་རྣམས་དང་། ཡི་དམ་རྒྱལ་བའི་དཀྱིལ་འཁོར་གྱི་ལྷ་ཚོགས་ཐམས་ཅད་ཀྱིས་བསྐོར་བ།

རྩ་བའི་བླ་མའི་དོན་བཤད་མ་ཐག་པ་དང་། ལྷ་རྡོ་རྗེ་འཆང་གི་ངོ་བོར་བསྒོམ་དགོས་པ་ནི། ཉམས་ལེན་འདི་ཉིད་གསང་སྔགས་བླ་མེད་ཐེག་པའི་དགོངས་དོན་ཡིན་པས། རྡོ་རྗེ་འཆང་ནི། རྫོགས་པའི་སངས་རྒྱས་ཀྱི་སྐུ་བཞི་ཡི་མཐོ་ཤོས་ཀྱི་མཚོན་དོན་དུ་བསྒོམ་དགོས་པ་ལས། དཔེར་ན་གསང་སྔགས་ཀྱི་རྒྱུད་སྡེ་བཞི་ལས་བྱ་རྒྱུད་དང་སྤྱོད་རྒྱུད་དུ་གཏོགས་པའི་སྒྲུབ་ཐབས་རྣམས་སུ་བླ་མ་རྡོ་རྗེ་འཆང་དུ་བསྒོམ་མི་དགོས་པ་ལྟ་བུའི་མཚོན་ཡོད་པ་འདྲ། བརྒྱུད་པའི་བླ་མ་དག་ནི་རྩ་བའི་བླ་མའི་འཕྲོ་ནས་གལ་ཆེ་ཤོས་ཡིན་པས་བླ་མའི་མཐའ་སྐོར་ཁག་ཏུ་བསྒོམ། ཡི་དམ་ནི་སངས་རྒྱས་གང་རུང་ཞིག་རང་ཉིད་སྐོར་གྱིས་དམིགས་བསལ་བསྙེན་པར་བྱས་པའམ་འབྲེལ་བར་བྱས་ཡོད་པའི་ལྷ་དེ་དག་རེད། འདིའི་སྐབས་སུ་ཡི་དམ་གཙོ་

ཆེ་བ་ནི་ཐུགས་བླ་མེད་དུ་གཏོགས་པའི་ལྷ་དེ་དག་རེད། དེ་དག་ལས་ཀྱང་དཔལ་དུས་ཀྱི་འཁོར་ལོ་ནི་འདིར་གཙོ་བོའི་རྒྱལ་བ་ཡིན་པ་སྨོས་ཅི་དགོས། དེའི་ཕྱིར་སྐབས་འདིར་ཡི་དམ་ཀུན་གྱི་གཙོ་བོ་ཡིན་ནོ།།

ཞིང་དེའི་རྩ་བ་ན་མཁའ་འགྲོ་ཆོས་སྐྱོང་སྲུང་མ་ཡེ་ཤེས་ཀྱི་སྤྱན་དང་ལྡན་པ་བསྟན་སྲུང་རྒྱ་མཚོའི་ཚོགས་རྣམས་ཀྱང་བདག་ལ་སྐྱོབ་པའི་ཚུལ་གྱིས་བཞུགས་པ་དང་།

གོང་དུ་སྨོས་མ་ཐག་པ་ལྟར་གྱི་ཚད་དཔག་ཏུ་མེད་པའི་ཞིང་སྟོང་དེའི་རྩ་བར་མཁའ་འགྲོ་ཞེས་པ་ནི། ཐུགས་ལུགས་ཀྱི་སྐད་དུ་མོ་རྒྱུད་ཀྱི་བྱང་ཆུབ་སེམས་མ་དེ་དག་ལ་གོ་དགོས་ལ། དེ་དག་ནི་བྱམས་དང་སྙིང་རྗེའི་གཏེར་མཛོད། འཕྲིན་ལས་ཀྱི་རང་མདངས་ཐོགས་པ་མེད་པ། རིག་འཛིན་སྒྲུབ་པ་པོའི་ཉམས་ལེན་གྱི་མཐུན་རྐྱེན་སྒྲུབ་ཅིང་འགལ་རྐྱེན་སེལ་བའི་ནུས་མཐུ་དང་ལྡན་པའི་མོ་རྒྱུད་བྱང་ཆུབ་སེམས་མ་དང་། ཡང་ན་རྣལ་འབྱོར་བའི་ལམ་སྒྲུབ་པའི་མཐུན་རྐྱེན་ཞི་རྒྱས་དབང་དྲག་གི་སྒོ་ནས་གནང་ཞེས་མཁན་དག་ཡིན་ལ། དེ་ཡང་མཐའ་གཅིག་ཏུ་མཁའ་འགྲོ་མ་ཡིན་མི་དགོས་པར། སྒྲུབ་པ་པོ་རྣལ་འབྱོར་མ་ཡིན་ན། ཕོ་རྒྱུད་ཀྱི་མཁའ་འགྲོའམ་དཔའ་བོ་བྱང་ཆུབ་སེམ་དཔའ་འོས་ཤིང་འཚམ་པར་སྒྲུབ་པ་མོར་དེ་དག་གིས་ལམ་གྱི་མཐུན་རྐྱེན་གནང་སྲིད་པ་དང་། དེ་ལ་ཡང་དམིགས་བསལ་གྱི་ཁྱད་ཆོས་ལྡན་པའི་བོགས་འདོན་ཡོང་ངེས་པ་ཞིག་རེད། ཆོས་སྐྱོང་སྲུང་མ་དག་ནི་འཇིག་རྟེན་ལས་འདས་པ་དང་མ་འདས་པའི་ཆོས་སྐྱོང་རིགས་གཉིས་ཀྱིས་བྱང་ཆུབ་མ་ཐོབ་བར་དུ། གཙོ་བོ་དམ་ལྡན་ཆོས་པ་རྣམས་ཀྱི་ཕྱིའི་བར་ཆད་བསལ་བའི་གྲོགས་བྱེད་པའི་དམ་བཅའ་བྱས་ཡོད་ལ། འཇིག་རྟེན་འཁོར་བ་ལས་འདས་པ་འཕགས་པའི་ཆོས་སྐྱོང་དག་གིས་ཀྱང་སྣང་ཚུལ་ལ་གཅིག་མཚུངས་བྱེད་པ་ཡིན་པས། གནས་ཚུལ་དོན་དམ་པའི་ངོ་བོར་དེ་གཉིས་མི་འདྲ་ཡང་། སྣང་ཚུལ་ཀུན་རྫོབ་ཙམ་དུ་དེ་གཉིས་ཀ་དམ་པའི་ཆོས་སྐྱོང་བའི་སྲུང་མ་ཡིན་པ་ལ་འདྲ་མཉམ་ཡིན་ནོ།།

བླ་མའི་སྐུའི་མདུན་ཕྱོགས་སུ། དཔལ་རྒྱལ་བ་ཤཱཀྱ་ཐུབ་པ་སོགས་ཕྱོགས་བཅུ་དུས་གསུམ་གྱི་སངས་རྒྱས་མཆོག་གི་སྤྲུལ་པའི་སྐུ་རྣམས་དང་།

བླ་མའི་མདུན་ངོས་ཀྱི་ཕྱོགས་སུ་ད་ལྟའི་བསྟན་པ་འདིའི་སྟོན་པ། སྐལ་བཟང་སངས་རྒྱས་སྟོང་ལས་ཐུགས་བསྐྱེད་མཆོག་ཏུ་གྱུར་བ། བདག་ཅག་ལ་ཆོས་སྟོན་པ་པོ་རྒྱལ་བ་སངས་རྒྱས་དཔལ་རྒྱལ་བ་ཤཱཀྱ་ཐུབ་པ་སོགས་ཕྱོགས་བཅུ་དུས་གསུམ་གྱི་སངས་རྒྱས་མཆོག་གི་སྤྲུལ་པའི་སྐུ་རྣམས་བཞུགས་པར་བསྒོམ།

གཡས་ཕྱོགས་སུ་འཇམ་དཔལ་ལ་སོགས་པའི་བྱང་ཆུབ་སེམས་དཔའི་དགེ་འདུན་རྣམས་དང་།

དེ་བཞིན་དུ་གཡས་ཕྱོགས་སུ་བྱམས་པ་དང་། འཇམ་དཔལ་ལ་སོགས་པའི་བྱང་ཆུབ་སེམས་དཔའ་ཉེ་བའི་སྲས་ཆེན་བརྒྱད་ཀྱིས་གཙོས་བྱང་ཆུབ་སེམས་དཔའི་ཚོགས་རྣམས་བཞུགས་ཡོད་པར་བསྒོམ། ཐེག་ཆེན་འཕགས་པ་ནི། རང་གཅིག་པུའི་དོན་དུ་ཐར་བ་དོན་གཉེར་བྱེད་མཁན་དང་། རང་དོན་ཙམ་གྱི་ཐར་བའི་གོ་འཕང་ལ་མཉེས་པའི་འཕགས་པ་དེ་དག་མ་ཡིན། དེའི་ཕྱིར་ཆོས་འདི་ཉིད་ཐེག་ཆེན་པ་གཙོ་བོར་བཟུང་བའི་ཉམས་ལེན་ཡིན་པས། ཐེག་ཆེན་པའི་དགེ་འདུན་རྣམས་གཙོ་ཆེ་བས་མཆོན་དོན་དུ་གཡས་ཕྱོགས་སུ་བསྒོམ་དགོས་པ་འདྲ།

གཡོན་དུ་ཤཱ་རིའི་བུ་ལ་སོགས་པ་ཉན་རང་འཕགས་པའི་ཚོགས་རྣམས་དང་།

ཤཱ་རིའི་བུ་ནི་ཐེག་དམན་ཉན་ཐོས་ཀྱི་ཚུལ་དུ་ཡོད་ཀྱང་དོན་ལ་ཐེག་ཆེན་པ་ཡིན་པར་ཐེག་ཆེན་པས་འདོད། རྩ་བའི་ཆ་ནས་ཐེག་དམན་གྱི་དགེ་འདུན་ཟེར་དུས། སེམས་ཅན་ཐམས་ཅད་རྫོགས་པའི་སངས་རྒྱས་ཀྱི་གོ་འཕང་དོན་དུ་གཉེར་བའི་དགེ་འདུན་པ་མ་ཡིན་པར། སེམས་ཅན་ལ་བྱམས་དང་སྙིང་རྗེ་ཡོད་ཅིང་རང་ཉིད་ཐར་བ་དོན་དུ་གཉེར་མཁན་གྱི་འཕགས་པ་ལ་གོ་དགོས། གང་ལྟར་ཡང་ཉམས་ལེན་འདི་ཐེག་ཆེན་གསང་སྔགས་པ་ཡིན་ཡང་། ཐེག་དམན་པའི་དགེ་འདུན་རྣམས་ཀྱང་སྐྱབས་ཡུལ་དུ་བསྒོམ་དགོས་པ་འདི་ནི། བོད་བརྒྱུད་ནང་བསྟན་པ་དག་གིས་ཐེག་དམན་གྱི་ཆོས་དང་དགེ་འདུན་ཡང་གཙིགས་ཆེན་བྱས་ཡོད་པའི་ཁྱད་རྟགས་ངེས་ཅན་ཞིག་ཡིན་པ་ཤེས་པར་བྱའོ།།

རྒྱབ་ཏུ་ཆོས་དཀོན་མཆོག་རྣམས་རྣམ་པ་གླེགས་བམ་གྱི་ཚུལ་ཅན་རྣམས་བཞུགས་པར་མོས་ཏེ།

སྤྱིར་དམ་པའི་ཆོས་ཟེར་བ་དེ་གླེགས་བམ་མ་ཡིན་ལ། སྒྲ་ཙམ་ཡང་མ་ཡིན་པར། གང་ཟག་དག་གི་སེམས་རྒྱུད་ན་ཡོད་པའི་ནང་དོན་ཁག་དང་། དོན་བསྒོམས་ཤིང་རྟོགས་པའི་ཡོན་ཏན་སོགས་ཡིན་མོད། མོས་སྒོམ་བྱེད་པའི་སྐབས་སུ་གླེགས་བམ་པོ་ཏི་སོགས་ཀྱི་རྣམ་པ་རུ་སྒོམ་པའི་ཐུག་སྲོལ་ཡོད། དེ་ནི་སྐབས་འདི་དག་ཏུ་ལས་དང་པོ་བ་གཙོ་བོ་བྱས་པས་བསྒོམ་བྱ་ནི་མཐོང་བྱ་གཟུགས་ཀྱི་རང་བཞིན་གཙོ་བོར་སྒོམ་པའི་དུས་ཡིན་པས་རེད་སྙམ། དེའི་ཕྱིར་སྐབས་འདི་དག་ཏུ་རྒྱབ་ཕྱོགས་སུ་ཆོས་པོ་ཏི་གླེགས་བམ་གྱི་རྣམ་པ་ཁྲ་ཆིལ་ལེ་བ་ཡིད་དུ་འོང་བ་ཞིག་བསྒོམ་དགོས་པར་གསུངས།

རང་དང་ལྷན་ཅིག་ཏུ་མཁའ་མཉམ་གྱི་སེམས་ཅན་ཐམས་ཅད་ཀྱང་།

དོན་གྱི་སྐྱབས་གནས་དཀོན་མཆོག་གསུམ་ལ། སེམས་ཅན་འདི་ཐམས་ཅད་ཐར་བ་དང་ཐམས་ཅད་མཁྱེན་པའི་ལམ་དུ་འགོད་དགོས་སྙམ་ནས། བསྒོམ་ནུས་ན་སེམས་ཅན་ཐམས་ཅད་རང་ཉིད་དང་མཉམ་དུ་བསྒོམ། དེ་མ་ནུས་ན་རང་ཉིད་སེམས་ཅན་ཀུན་གྱི་འཚབ་ཡིན་སྙམ་ཏེ།

བླ་མ་དཀོན་མཆོག་སྐྱབས་གནས་རྒྱ་མཚོའི་ཚོགས་ལ་མོས་གུས་ཀྱི་གདུང་བ་ཆེན་པོས་སྐྱབས་འགྲོ་བྱེད་པར་མོས་ཤིང་།

ཞེས་གོང་སྨོས་ལྟར་གྱི་སྐྱབས་ཡུལ་དེ་ཀུན་ཡིད་དོར་བསྒོམ་ཅི་ནུས་དང་། གལ་ཏེ་བསྒོམ་མ་ནུས་ཀྱང་སྐྱབས་གནས་དེ་དག བདག་ཅག་སེམས་ཅན་ཐམས་ཅད་ཀྱི་མགོན་དུ་བཞུགས་ཡོད་སྙམ་པའི་གདུང་ཤུགས་དྲག་པོའི་ཚོར་བ་དང་ལྡན་པའི་སྒོ་ནས་མོས་པ་བྱེད།

ཁྱད་པར་སེམས་ཅན་ཐམས་ཅད་ལ་སྙིང་རྗེ་ཆེན་པོས་ཀུན་ནས་བསླངས་ཏེ། འདི་རྣམས་འཁོར་བའི་སྡུག་བསྔལ་ལས་བསྐྱབ་ཏུ་གསོལ་སྙམ་དུ་འདུན་པ་ཤུགས་དྲག་པོས་སྐྱབས་སུ་འགྲོ་བ་དངོས་ནི།

ཞེས་སྙིང་རྗེ་བསྒོམ་ཚུལ་ནི། དུས་ཐོག་མེད་ནས་སོ་སོ་རང་ཉིད་འཁོར་བར་སྐྱེ་བ་བླངས་པ་ལ་ཐོག་མ་མེད་པ་ཡིན་པས། སེམས་ཅན་ཀུན་རང་གི་ཕ་མ་དང་ཉེ་གྲོགས། མ་ཟད་གཅེས་པར་བསྐྱངས་པའི་བུ་དང་བུ་མོ་སོགས་སུ་མ་གྱུར་པའི་སེམས་ཅན་གཅིག་ཀྱང་མེད། དེ་དག་ཀུན་གྱིས་འདོད་པ་ནི་བདེ་བ་ཡིན་ཡང་དེའི་རྒྱུ་སྒྲུབ་མ་ཤེས། མི་འདོད་པ་ནི་སྡུག་བསྔལ་ཡིན་ཡང་དེའི་རྒྱུ་ནི་སྤང་མ་ཤེས་པར་ཡོད་པས། ཞེ་འདོད་དང་ལག་ལེན་ཕྱིན་ཅི་ལོག་ཏུ་སོང་ཡོད་པས། མ་དྲིན་ཅན་མ་དང་གཅེས་པའི་གཉེན་གྲོགས་དམ་པ་དེ་དག་དང་། ཕ་མ་དེ་དག་ཀུན་སྡུག་བསྔལ་རྒྱུ་དང་བཅས་པ་ལས་ཐར་ན་ཇི་མ་རུང་སྙམ་པའི་སྙིང་རྗེའི་ངོ་བོ། ཐར་བར་བྱའོ་སྙམ་པའི་འགན་འཁྲིའི་ངོ་བོ། ཐར་བའི་ཐབས་བདག་གིས་བྱེད་སྙམ་པའི་འགན་ལེན་གྱི་ངོ་བོ་སོགས་ཀྱི་ཚོར་གདུང་དང་བཅས་པས་སྐྱབས་སུ་འགྲོ་བར་བྱ། སེམས་ཅན་ཐམས་ཅད་ཐར་བ་དང་ཐམས་ཅད་མཁྱེན་པའི་གོ་འཕང་ཐོབ་ཆེད་དུ། གོང་དུ་སྨོས་ཟིན་པའི་སྐྱབས་གནས་དེ་དག་ལ་སྐྱབས་སུ་འགྲོའོ་ཞེས་ངག་ཏུ་སྐྱབས་འགྲོའི་ཚིག་བརྗོད། དེ་དང་མཉམ་དུ་འོས་འཚམ་སྐབས་བབ་དང་བསྟུན་ནས། ནུས་ན་ཐུག་དང་མཉམ་དུ་སྐྱབས་འགྲོའི་ཚིག་དོན་རྣམས་ཡིད་ལ་བརྣགས་ཏེ་ངག་ཏུ་སྐྱབས་འགྲོའི་ཚིག་རྣམས་བརྗོད་པར་བྱའོ།།

མ་ནམ་མཁའ་དང་མཉམ་པའི་སེམས་ཅན་ཐམས་ཅད། དུས་འདི་ནས་བཟུང་སྟེ། ཇི་སྲིད་བྱང་ཆུབ་སྙིང་པོ་ལ་མཆིས་ཀྱི་བར་དུ།

ཉམས་ལེན་མཁན་གྱི་གང་ཟག་ཐེག་ཆེན་པ་ཡིན་ཕྱིན་སེམས་ཅན་ཐམས་ཅད་ལ་དམིགས་དགོས་ལ། ནམ་མཁའ་དང་མཉམ་ཞེས་པའི་དོན་ནི། ནམ་མཁའ་སྔོན་པོ་མིག་གི་མཐོང་བ་དེ་ལ་མི་གོ་བར། བར་སྣང་སྟོང་པ་འདི་ལ་མཐའ་མེད་པ་བཞིན་དུ། སེམས་ཅན་ལ་ཡང་མཐའ་མེད་པར་མཚུངས་པས། དུས་ཀྱི་དབང་དུ་བྱས་ན་ཇི་སྲིད་རང་ཉིད་བྱང་ཆུབ་མ་ཐོབ་བར་དུ་སེམས་ཅན་ཐམས་ཅད་ཀྱི་ཆེད་དུ་སྐྱབས་སུ་འགྲོ་ཞེས་པའི་དོན་རེད། རྒྱུ་མཚན་ནི། རང་ཉིད་བྱང་ཆུབ་མ་ཐོབ་པ་དེ་སྲིད་དུ་རང་ཉིད་ཀྱིས་སྐྱབས་བརྟེན་དགོས་ལ། དེ་ཡང་རང་ཉིད་བྱང་ཆུབ་འཐོབ་དགོས་དོན་དེ་ཡང་སེམས་ཅན་ཐམས་ཅད་ཀྱི་དོན་ཡིན་པ་ལས་རང་ཁོ་ནའི་ཆེད་དུ་རྩ་བ་ནས་མ་ཡིན་པ་ཞིག་དགོས་པ་རེད།

ཕྱོགས་བཅུ་དུས་གསུམ་གྱི་དེ་བཞིན་གཤེགས་པ་ཐམས་ཅད་ཀྱི་སྐུ་གསུང་ཐུགས་ཡོན་ཏན་འཕྲིན་ལས་ཐམས་ཅད་ཀྱི་ངོ་བོར་གྱུར་པ།

ཐེག་ཆེན་གསང་སྔགས་ཀྱི་ལུགས་སུ་བླ་མ་ནི་སངས་རྒྱས་ཀུན་གྱི་ངོ་བོར་གྱུར་པའམ། ཀུན་གྱི་འབྱུང་གནས་ཏེ་རྩ་བ་ཡིན་པས། དེ་ལ་ཐོག་མར་སྐྱབས་སུ་འགྲོ་བའི་དོན་ཡིན་པ་ལས། མཆོག་གསུམ་གང་ལ་ཡང་མ་གཏོགས་པའི་སྐྱབས་གནས་གཞན་ཞིག་བསྒོམ་དགོས་པའི་དོན་མིན་ཡང་། འདི་དང་པོ་བླ་མའི་ཡོན་ཏན་བརྗོད་པའི་ཚེ་ན་འདི་ལྟར། ཕྱོགས་བཅུ་ནི་ཤར་ལྷོ་ནུབ་བྱང་བཞི་དང་མཚམས་བཞི། སྟེང་འོག་གཉིས་བཅས་ཕྱོགས་བཅུ་ན་བཞུགས་པའི་སངས་རྒྱས་རྣམས་དང་། དུས་གསུམ་སྟེ་འདས་མ་འོངས་ད་ལྟ་གསུམ་གྱི་སངས་རྒྱས་དག་གི་སྐུ་གསུང་ཐུགས་ཀྱི་ཡོན་ཏན་འཕྲིན་ལས་ཐམས་ཅད་ཚང་བའི་ངོ་བོ་དང་ལྡན་པ་སུ་ཡིན་པ་དེ་ནི་དཔལ་ལྡན་བླ་མ་དམ་པ་ཉིད་ཡིན་པའོ།།

ཆོས་ཀྱི་ཕུང་པོ་སྟོང་ཕྲག་བརྒྱད་ཅུ་རྩ་བཞིའི་འབྱུང་གནས།

ཉོན་མོངས་འདོད་ཆགས་ཀྱི་གཉེན་པོར་འདུལ་བའི་རིགས་ཀྱི་སྡེ་སྣོད་ཉིས་ཁྲི་ཆིག་སྟོང་། ཉོན་མོངས་ཞེ་སྡང་གི་གཉེན་པོར་མདོ་སྡེའི་རིགས་ཀྱི་སྡེ་སྣོད་ཉིས་ཁྲི་ཆིག་སྟོང་། ཉོན་མོངས་གཏི་མུག་གི་གཉེན་པོར་མངོན་པའི་རིགས་ཀྱི་སྡེ་སྣོད་ཉིས་ཁྲི་ཆིག་སྟོང་། དུག་གསུམ་ཆ་མཉམ་པ་འདུལ་བྱེད་དུ་གསང་བ་སྔགས་ཀྱི་རིགས་ཀྱི་སྡེ་སྣོད་ཉིས་ཁྲི་ཆིག་སྟོང་བཅས་ཆོས་ཀྱི་ཕུང་པོ་ཁྲི་བརྒྱད་དང་སྟོང་བཞི་རྫོགས་པའི་སངས་རྒྱས་ཀྱིས་གསུངས་པ་དེ་དག་ཀུན་གྱི་འབྱུང་ཁུངས། བླ་མ་དམ་པ་ཉིད་ཡིན་ཞེས་པའོ།།

འཕགས་པའི་དགེ་འདུན་ཐམས་ཅད་ཀྱི་མངའ་བདག ཧེ་བཙུན་རྒྱ་བ་དང་བརྒྱུད་པར་བཅས་པའི།

སོ་སོའི་སྐྱེ་བོའམ་འཇིག་རྟེན་གྱི་མི་ཕལ་བ་དག་ལས། ཐུགས་རྒྱུད་ཀྱི་ཡོན་ཏན་དག་ཁྱད་དུ་འཕགས་པའི་དགེ་འདུན་པ་ཐམས་ཅད་ཀྱི་མངའ་བདག་སྟེ་མངའ་དབང་སྒྱུར་བ་པོ། སྐྱབས་གནས་དམ་པ་དག་གི་ཧེ་བོ་དང་། བསླབ་པ་གསུམ་ལ་བཙུན་པའི་བཙུན་པ། གང་ཟག་སོ་སོའི་དམ་པའི་ཆོས་ལ་འབྲེལ་བའི་རྒྱ་བ་ཡིན་པའི་རྒྱ་བའི་བླ་མ་དང་། རྒྱ་བའི་བླ་མ་དེ་ལ་བརྒྱུད་ཏེ་རང་ལ་བརྒྱུད་ཡོད་པའི་བརྒྱུད་པའི་བླ་མ་རྣམས་ཀྱི་ཞེས་པ་དང་།

ཆོས་ཧེ་དཔལ་ལྡན་བླ་མ་དམ་པ་རྣམས་ལ་སྐྱབས་སུ་མཆིའོ།།

དེ་ལྟར་གོང་སྨོས་ཇི་བཞིན་གྱི་ཡོན་ཏན་བསམ་གྱིས་མི་ཁྱབ་པའི་བདག་ཉིད་ཡིན་པའི་ཆོས་ཀྱི་ཧེ་བོ་ཆེན་པོ་སྟེ་བླ་མ་དེ་ཉིད་ནི། ཐར་བ་དང་ཐམས་ཅད་མཁྱེན་པའི་ཡོན་ཏན་གྱི་དཔལ་དང་ལྡན་པ། བླ་མ་སྟེ་གོང་མའམ་བླ་ན་སུ་ཡང་མེད་པའི་བླ་མ་དམ་པ་དེ་ལ་བྱང་ཆུབ་མ་ཐོབ་བར་དུ། སེམས་དང་བ་དང་དད་འདུན་ཆེན་པོའི་སྒོ་ནས་སྐྱབས་སུ་མཆིའོ་སྟེ་བསྙེན་ནོ་ཞེས་པའི་དོན་ནོ།།

ཡི་དམ་དཀྱིལ་འཁོར་གྱི་ལྷ་ཚོགས་རྣམས་ལ་སྐྱབས་སུ་མཆིའོ།།

རང་གིས་ལྷག་པའི་ལྷ་གང་ཞིག་རྒྱུན་དུ་ཡིད་ལ་དམ་དུ་བཅངས་ཤིང་། བསྙེན་པར་བྱ་བ་ནི་ཡི་དམ་གྱི་དོན་ཡིན་ལ། སྤྱིར་བཏང་བོད་བརྒྱུད་ནང་བའི་རྒྱུད་སྡེ་བཞིའི་ལྷ་ཚོགས་རྣམས་ནི་སྤྱིར་བཏང་ནས་བསྙེན་པར་བྱ་བའི་ཡི་དམ་གྱི་རིགས་གང་ཡིན་རྣམས་ཡིན་ལ། དགོས་བཀར་གྱི་དབང་དུ་བྱས་ན་ནི་དེའི་ངེས་པ་མེད། དཀྱིལ་འཁོར་ནི་སངས་རྒྱས་ཀྱི་ཞིང་ཁམས། ཟག་མེད་ཀྱི་ལྷའི་ཡུལ་གླིང་ངམ། དག་ཞིང་གི་ལྷ་ཚོགས་ལ་སོགས་པའི་དོན་ཡིན་ལ། ཡོངས་གྲགས་སུ་རྡུལ་ཚོན་དང་བྲིས་དཔར་ལ་སོགས་ཀྱི་དཀྱིལ་འཁོར་སུ་གྲགས་པ་རྣམས་ནི་མཚོན་དོན་ཙམ་ཡིན་པ་ལས། དཀྱིལ་འཁོར་དངོས་ནི་མ་ཡིན་ནོ། མདོར་བསྡུས་ན། ཡི་དམ་ལྷའི་རང་བཞིན་གྱི་ཚོགས་ལ་སྐྱབས་སུ་མཆིའོ་ཞེས་པའི་དོན་ཡིན་ནོ།།

རྫོགས་པའི་སངས་རྒྱས་བཅོམ་ལྡན་འདས་རྣམས་ལ་སྐྱབས་སུ་མཆིའོ།།

གོང་དུ་བཤད་པའི་ཡི་དམ་ཀྱི་ལྷ་ཚོགས་དེ་དག རྫོགས་པའི་སངས་རྒྱས་ཀྱི་རང་བཞིན་ཡིན་པ་གཞི་ལ་བཞག་ཏེ། དེ་ཉིད་གང་ཟག་སོ་སོ་སྐྱེར་གྱི་ཡི་དམ་ཡིན་པས་ཆ་ནས་བཞག་པའམ། ཡང་ན་སྤྱིའི་ཡི་དམ་གྱི

ཆ་ནས་བཞག་མོད། འདིར་རྫོགས་པའི་སངས་རྒྱས་བཅོམ་ལྡན་འདས་རྣམས་ཟེར་དུས་གང་ཟག་སྔེར་གྱི་ལྷག་ལྷ་ཡིན་མིན་ལ་མ་ལྟོས་པར། ཡི་དམ་རྒྱུད་སྡེ་བཞིའི་ལྷ་ཚོགས་དག་མ་ཡིན་པའི་སངས་རྒྱས་སྤྱི་ལ་ཁྱབ་པ་རྣམས་ཏེ། བདག་ཅག་གི་སྟོན་པ་སྟེ་མི་མཇེད་འཇིག་རྟེན་གྱི་རྣམ་འདྲེན་བཞི་བ་གཙོར་བྱས། སྐལ་བཟང་གི་སངས་རྒྱས་སྟོང་རྩ་གཉིས་ལ་སོགས་པ་རྣམས་ལ་སྐྱབས་སུ་མཆིའོ་ཞེས་པའི་དོན་ཡིན་ནོ།།

དམ་པའི་ཆོས་རྣམས་ལ་སྐྱབས་སུ་མཆིའོ།།

དམ་པ་ཏེ་ལེགས་པའི་ཡོན་ཏན་ལྡན་པའི་ལུང་གི་ཆོས། བརྗོད་བྱ་བསླབ་པ་གསུམ་དང་རྗོད་བྱེད་སྡེ་སྣོད་གསུམ་ཡིན་ལ། རྟོགས་པའི་ཆོས་ནི། འཕགས་པ་གསུམ་གྱི་ཐུགས་རྒྱུད་དུ་བཞུགས་པའི་ས་བཅུ་ལམ་ལྔ་སྟེ། མདོར་ན་འགོག་ལམ་གཉིས་ཀྱིས་བསྡུས་པའི་ཡོན་ཏན་དེ་དག་ཡིན། དེ་ལྟ་བུའི་ལུང་རྟོགས་གཉིས་ཀྱིས་བསྡུས་པའི་དམ་པའི་ཆོས་དེ་དག་ལ། དད་འདུན་དང་བ་ཆེན་པོས་སྐྱབས་སུ་བསྟེན་པ་སྟེ། རང་གི་ནུས་ཚོད་ལྡོགས་ཚོད་ཀྱིས་ཉམས་སུ་བླངས་ཏེ་རང་རྒྱུད་ལ་ཉམས་མྱོང་གསར་བ་ཞིག་སླེབ་ཐུབ་པར་ཡང་ནས་ཡང་དུ་འབད་པར་བྱ། ནམ་ཡང་འདོར་བར་མི་བྱའོ།། ཞེས་པའི་དོན་དུ་གོ་བ་ཡིན་ནོ།།

འཕགས་པའི་དགེ་འདུན་རྣམས་ལ་སྐྱབས་སུ་མཆིའོ།།

འཕགས་པ་སྟེ་སྐྱེ་བོ་ཕལ་བའི་རང་བཞིན་ལས་ཁྱད་པར་དུ་འཕགས་པ་སྟེ། ཉན་རང་བྱང་ཆུབ་སེམས་དཔའི་ཐེག་པ་གང་རུང་གི་ས་དང་ལམ་གྱིས་བསྡུས་པའི་གང་ཟག་རྣམས་ཡིན་ལ། དེ་འདྲའི་འཕགས་པའི་སྐྱེས་བུ་རྣམས་ལམ་སྐྱབ་པོ་རང་གིས་གྲོགས་ཀྱི་མཆོག་ཏུ་བསྟེན་པའི་སྒོ་ནས་སྐྱབས་སུ་མཆིའོ།། འཕགས་པའི་ལམ་ལ་ཁ་ཕྱོགས་ཤིང་འཕགས་ལམ་དུ་ད་དུང་མ་ཞུགས་པ་དག་ལའང་། དད་འདུན་བརྩེ་གདུང་ཤུགས་དྲག་པོ་དང་ལྡན་པའི་སྒོ་ནས་དེ་དག་ལ་བློ་ཐག་ཉེ་བོའི་གྲོགས་སུ་བསྟེན་པར་བྱའོ།།

མཁའ་འགྲོ་ཆོས་སྐྱོང་སྲུང་མ་ཡེ་ཤེས་ཀྱི་སྤྱན་དང་ལྡན་པ་རྣམས་ལ་སྐྱབས་སུ་མཆིའོ།།

མཁའ་འགྲོ་ནི་མཐའ་གཅིག་ཏུ་མཁའ་ལ་རྫུ་འཕྲུལ་གྱིས་འགྲོ་མཁན་ཞིག་ཡིན་མི་དགོས་པར། བྱང་ཆུབ་སེམས་མའམ་འཕགས་མ་ཞེས་པའི་དོན་ལྟ་བུ་ལ་གོ་ན་མཛེས། ལྷག་པར་དུ་གནས་ཉེར་བཞི་སོགས་མོ་རྒྱུད་ཀྱི་ལྷ་མོ་དང་ཞིང་སྐྱེས་མ་སོགས་ཉམས་ལེན་ནང་གི་བར་ཆད་སེལ་བའི་ཡེ་ཤེས་ཀྱི་སྤྱན་ལྡན་རྣམས་ལ་གོ་དགོས་སོ།།

ཆོས་སྐྱོང་ནི། འཕགས་ལམ་དུ་ཞུགས་ཤིང་སངས་རྒྱས་བསྟན་པ་སྲུང་བའི་དམ་སྒོམ་ལྡན་པའི་འཕགས་པ་ཡེ་ཤེས་ཀྱི་སྤྱན་དང་ལྡན་པ་དང་། དེ་བཞིན་དུ་བསྟན་པ་སྲུང་བར་དམ་སྒོམ་ལྡན་པ་གཞིར་བཞག་པའི་གང་ཟག འཕགས་ལམ་ལ་འགྲོ་བར་དམ་བཅའ་བརྟན་ཅིང་། འཇིག་རྟེན་ཐུན་མོང་དང་ཐུན་མོང་མ་ཡིན་པ་གང་རུང་གི་རྫུ་འཕྲུལ་ལྡན་པའམ། གལ་ཏེ་རྫུ་འཕྲུལ་དང་མ་ལྡན་ནའང་། དཀར་ཕྱོགས་དགེ་བ་ལ་གཅིག་ཏུ་སྦྱོར་བའི་བློ་ནུས་ལྡན་པའི་མི་དང་མི་མ་ཡིན་པ། གཙོ་བོ་རྒྱལ་འབྱོར་བའི་ལམ་གྱི་ཕྱིའི་བར་ཆད་བསལ་ནུས་པ་ཡིན་ལ། དེ་དག་ལས་འཕགས་པ་རྣམས་མཐར་ཐུག་གཏན་གྱི་སྐྱབས། གནས་དང་འཇིག་རྟེན་པ་རྣམས་གནས་སྐབས་ཀྱི་ལམ་བསྒྲུབ་པའི་གྲོགས་སུ་གཟུང་བར་བགྱིའོ།། ཞེས་པའི་དོན་ནོ།།

ལན་གསུམ་སོགས་ཅི་ནུས་སུ་བྱའོ།།

ཞེས་ཉམས་ལེན་མཁན་དེའི་ཉམས་ལེན་དེ་དག་ངག་འདོན་བྱེད་པའི་དུས་སུ་གོང་གི་སྐྱབས་འགྲོའི་ཚིག་དེ་དག་ཐེངས་གསུམ་ལས་མི་ཉུང་བར་བཟླག་དགོས་པའི་དོན་ཡིན་ནོ།།

གལ་ཏེ་སྐྱབས་འགྲོ་ངག་འདོན་བསྐྱར་འདོན་གྱིས་གྲངས་འབུམ་ཐེར་སོགས་གསོག་འདོན་བྱེད་དགོས་པའི་དུས་སུ་ནི། སྐྱབས་འགྲོའི་ཚིག ཆོས་རྗེ་དཔལ་ལྡན་བླ་མ་དམ་པ་ཞེས་པ་ནས། མཁའ་འགྲོ་ཆོས་སྐྱོང་སྲུང་མ་ཡེ་ཤེས་ཀྱི་སྤྱན་དང་ལྡན་པ་རྣམས་ལ་སྐྱབས་སུ་མཆིའོ།། ཞེས་པའི་བར་ཡང་ཡང་བསྐྱར་འདོན་བྱས་ན་ཆོག་པ་ལས། དེ་དག་གི་གོང་ནས་འདོན་མི་དགོས་པ་ནི་ཐུག་སྒྲོལ་ཡིན་པ་ཤེས་པར་བྱ། ཐུན་གྱི་རྗེས་སུ་སྐྱབས་འགྲོ་མཚམས་འཛོག་པའམ། དེ་མིན་སྐྱབས་འགྲོ་བསྡུས་པ་བྱེད་པའི་དུས་གང་ཡིན་ཡང་། གང་ལྟར་ཚར་དུས་མཇུག་ཏུ་སྐྱབས་འགྲོའི་ཚིགས་ཞིང་བསྒོམས་ནས་གསལ་ཡོད་པ་རྣམས་མཐའ་ནས་རིམ་བཞིན་རང་ལ་ཐིམ་པའི་སྒོ་ནས་བསྡུ་དགོས། དེ་ནི་རང་རྒྱུད་དུ་བྱིན་རླབས་ཀྱི་ཚན་ཁ་འཇུག་ཆེད་ཡིན། དེ་ནི་འདི་ལྟར་འོག་གི་ཚིག་འདི་དག་ངག་ཏུ་འདོན་ཞིང་ཡིད་ནས་དགའ་སྤྲོ་དང་བཅས་པས་རང་ཉིད་ལ་བསྡུ་བར་བྱའོ།།

> བླ་མ་དང་དཀོན་མཆོག་རིན་པོ་ཆེ་རྣམ་པ་གསུམ་ལ་བདག་ཕྱག་འཚལ་ཞིང་སྐྱབས་སུ་མཆིའོ།། ཁྱེད་རྣམས་ཀྱིས་བདག་གི་རྒྱུད་བྱིན་གྱིས་བརླབ་ཏུ་གསོལ། ལན་གསུམ།

ཞེས་པ་ནི་གོང་དུ་བརྗོད་ཟིན་པ་དག་བསྡུས་པའི་སྒོ་ནས་བསྐྱར་ཟློས་བྱས་ཏེ་ཉམས་སུ་བླངས་པའི་དོན་ལས་གཞན་ཅི་ཡང་མེད། བླ་མ་དང་སངས་རྒྱས་ཆོས་དགེ་འདུན་བཞི་ལ་གོང་དུ་སྨོས་པ་བཞིན་སྐྱབས་

སྐྱབས་བསྟེན་པར་བྱའོ་ཞེས་དང་། དེ་ལྟར་ཚུལ་བཞིན་དུ་སྐྱབས་སུ་སོང་ན། ཁོང་ཚོའི་ཐུགས་རྒྱུད་ཀྱི་ཡོན་ཏན་དག་གིས་རས་ཡུག་ཚོན་གྱིས་བསྒྱུར་བ་བཞིན་རང་གི་རྒྱུད་ལ་ཡང་འགྱུར་བ་ཆེན་པོ་ཞིག་ཐེབས་པར་ཤོག་ཅིག དེ་ལྟར་ཡོང་བར་སྨོན་ལམ་ཕུགས་དྲག་པོས་འདེབས་སོ།། ཞེས་གསོལ་བཏབ་ཞུ་བ་སྙིང་ནས་འདོན་ནོ།། དེའི་ཕྱིར་མཐུན་པའི་རྒྱུ་རྐྱེན་གྱིས་རང་རྒྱུད་ལ་ལེགས་པའི་ཕུགས་རྐྱེན་ཐེབས་པར་བྱ། ཞེས་པའི་དོན་དེ་ལན་གསུམ་དུ་ངག་འདོན་བྱ་དགོས་སོ།།

གསོལ་བ་གདབ། སྐྱབས་ཡུལ་རྣམས་འོད་དུ་ཞུ་ནས་རང་ལ་ཐིམ།

དགེ་བ་འདི་ཡིས་སྐྱེ་བོ་ཀུན།།
བསོད་ནམས་ཡེ་ཤེས་ཚོགས་རྫོགས་ཤིང་།།
བསོད་ནམས་ཡེ་ཤེས་ལས་བྱུང་བའི།།
དམ་པ་གཉིས་པོ་ཐོབ་པར་ཤོག

དེ་ལྟར་ཚུལ་བཞིན་དུ་སྐྱབས་འགྲོ་བྱས་པ་ལ་སོགས་པས། འཇིག་རྟེན་དང་འཇིག་རྟེན་ལས་འདས་པའི་དགེ་བའི་བསོད་ནམས་ཀྱི་ཚོགས་དང་། དམིགས་པ་མཚན་མའི་རྟོགས་པ་བྲལ་བའི་ཡེ་ཤེས་ཀྱི་ཚོགས་དངོས་དང་། དེ་དག་དང་ཆ་འདྲ་བའི་ཚོགས་རྣམས་ཀྱི་མཐུ་ལ་བརྟེན་ཏེ། ནམ་ཞིག་ཚོགས་གཉིས་ཡོངས་སུ་རྫོགས་ཏེ། དེ་གཉིས་ལས་བྱུང་བའི་ཆོས་ཀྱི་སྐུ་དང་གཟུགས་ཀྱི་སྐུ་དམ་པ་གཉིས་པོ་ཐོབ་ནས། འགྲོ་བ་སེམས་ཅན་ཐམས་ཅད་ཀྱི་དོན་ཆེན་འགྲུབ་པར་ཤོག་ཅིག་ཅེས་པའོ།། དེ་ལྟར་ཡོང་བར་སྨོན་ལམ་ཕུགས་དྲག་པོས་འདེབས་སོ།། གསོལ་བཏབ་ཞུ་བ་སྙིང་ནས་འདོན་ནོ།། ཞེས་པའོ།།

དཔལ་ལྡན་རྒྱལ་བ་ཇོ་ནང་བའི་ལུགས་ལ། དཔལ་དུས་ཀྱི་འཁོར་ལོའི་རྫོགས་རིམ་སྦྱོར་བ་ཡན་ལག་དྲུག་ཉམས་སུ་ལེན་དུས། ཐོག་མར་འདིའི་ལུགས་ཀྱི་ཐུན་མོང་གི་སྔོན་འགྲོ་ལྔའི་ཐོག་མ་སྐྱབས་འགྲོ་བྱ་སྐབས་སུ། རང་གཞན་སེམས་ཅན་ཐམས་ཅད་ལ་དམིགས་མི་དགོས་པ་མིན་ཡང་། སྐྱབས་འགྲོ་རང་གི་སྐབས་བྱང་ཆུབ་མཆོག་ཏུ་སེམས་བསྐྱེད་པའི་ཚིག་གསལ་པོ་མེད་ཀྱང་སེམས་ཅན་ཐམས་ཅད་ཀྱི་དོན་ཡིན་པ་ཤེས་བྱེད་ཀྱི་ཚིག་ཡོད་པ་བཞིན་དུ་ཤེས་དགོས། སྙིང་ནས་སྐྱབས་སུ་འགྲོ་བའི་མཚོན་དོན་དག་གིས་བརྗོད་པ་ཙམ་མིན་པར། ལུས་ཐོག་ནས་ཕྱག་འབུམ་འཚལ་བ་དང་། སྒྲིབ་པ་སྦྱོང་བའི་མཐུན་རྐྱེན་དུ་འང་འགྲོ་བས་ཕྱག་དང་སྦྲགས་དགོས། ཕྱག་འབུམ་གྱི་ཕྱག་རེ་རེ་དང་སྐྱབས་འགྲོའི་ཚིག་རེ་སྦྲགས་དགོས་པའི་སྒོ་ནས་ཉམས་སུ་ལེན་པ་ལས། སྐྱབས་འགྲོའི་ཚིག་ཆ་ཚང་འབུམ་འགྲོ་དགོས་པའི་ངེས་པ་མེད།

སྒྲོན་མེད་རབ་གསལ་སྣང་བ།

གང་ལྟར་ཕྱག་འབུམ་གཅིག་མ་རྫོགས་བར་དུ། དེའི་རིམ་པ་རྗེས་མའི་ཉམས་ལེན་རྣམས་མི་འཇུག་པ་ནི་དམ་པ་གོང་མ་རྣམས་ཀྱིས་ཕྱག་སྲོལ་ཡིན། དེ་རྗེས་དེ་མ་ཐག་ཏུ་རང་གི་སེམས་ནང་དུ་བསྒོམས་ཡོད་པའི་ཚོགས་ཞིང་སྐྱབས་ཡུལ་རང་ཉིད་ལ་ཐིམ་པའི་དམིགས་པ་བྱེད་དགོས་པ་ནི་གོང་ནས་བཤད་ཟིན་པ་ལྟར་ཡིན། དེ་ནས་བསྔོ་བ་དང་སྨོན་ལམ་གྱི་མཐའ་བརྒྱན་པར་བྱའོ།།

ཐེག་པ་ཆེན་པོ་གསང་སྔགས་ཀྱི་ལུགས་སུ་མཆོག་གསུམ་ལ་སྐྱབས་སུ་འགྲོ་ཚུལ་ལ། སྐྱབས་འགྲོ་ཡང་དག་གི་རྒྱུ། སྐྱབས་སུ་འགྲོ་ཡུལ་ངོས་འཛིན་དང་དེ་དག་གི་ཡོན་ཏན་ཤེས་པ། སྐྱབས་སུ་འགྲོ་བའི་ཕན་ཡོན། སྐྱབས་སུ་འགྲོ་ཚུལ་སོགས་གསར་དུ་ཤེས་དགོས་ཀྱང་། འདིར་གཙོ་བོ་ཚིག་འགྲེལ་གཙོ་བོ་བྱེད་པའི་སྐབས་ཡིན་པས་དེ་དག་ཆ་ཚང་ཞིག་རྒྱས་སྤྲོས་བྱས་མེད། དེ་དག་ནི་ཕྲན་གྱི་རྫོ་ནང་ལམ་རིམ་བདེ་གཤེགས་སྙིང་པོའི་འཇུག་རིམ་རྫོགས་ལྡན་གསར་པའི་ཁྲིད་ནོར་རམ། ཡང་ན་གཞུང་གཞན་རྣམས་ལས་ཤེས་དགོས་པས་དྲན་པར་འཚལ།

གསང་སྔགས་ཐུན་མོང་སྔོན་འགྲོའི་ཐེག་ཆེན་སེམས་བསྐྱེད།

ཐེག་ཆེན་ལམ་གྱི་རྩ་བའི་གཞུང་ཤིང་བྱང་ཆུབ་མཆོག་ཏུ་སེམས་བསྐྱེད་པ་ཉམས་སུ་ལེན་དུས། སྐྱབས་འགྲོ་མེད་པར་སེམས་བསྐྱེད་བྱེད་པའི་གནས་དང་ལུགས་གཉིས་ཀ་མེད་པས། བོད་བརྒྱུད་ནང་པའི་བརྒྱུད་འཛིན་སུས་ཀྱང་མི་བྱེད་པ་འདྲ། རྒྱལ་བ་ཇོ་ནང་པའི་དུས་འཁོར་རྫོགས་རིམ་གྱི་སྔོན་འགྲོ་འདིའི་ཆ་ཤས་གང་ཞིག་ཉམས་སུ་ལེན་སྐབས་སུ་ཡང་། ཕྱག་སྲོལ་དུ། བློ་ལྡོག་རྣམ་བཞི་ནས་བཟུང་སྟར་བཞིན་རིམ་པས་སྐྱབས་འགྲོ་དང་བཅས་པ་བྱེད་པའི་སྲོལ་རྒྱུན་ཡོད།

གནས་སྐབས་རེད། སེམས་བསྐྱེད་ནི་རང་ཉིད་དངོས་གཞིའི་ཉམས་ལེན་ཡིན་པའི་སྐབས་ཡིན་ན། དེའི་སྐབས་སུ་སྐྱབས་འགྲོ་སོགས་བསྡུས་པ་ཞིག་སྔོན་དུ་བཏང་ནས། དེ་ནས་སེམས་བསྐྱེད་དངོས་གཞིའི་ཚུལ་དུ་ཐུན་རེ་ལ་ཅི་ནུས་སུ་བསགས་ཏེ། མཐར་འབུམ་གཅིག་གསོག་པའམ། ཡང་ན་གྲངས་ཀ་ལ་ཆེར་མི་ལྟ་བར་དོན་གྲངས་བྱས་ནས་ཉིན་རེར་ཐུན་བཞི་རེ་བྱས་ནས་བདུན་ཕྲག་ཁ་ཤས་ལ་ཉམས་ལེན་མཛད་སྲོལ་ཡོད་དོ།།

སེམས་བསྐྱེད་ནི་བརྗོད་བྱ་ཤིན་ཏུ་རྒྱ་ཆེན་པོ་ཞིག་ཡིན། འདི་ཉིད་ཏ་ཙང་རྒྱས་པར་བསླབ་ན། དགོན་སྡེ་འགའ་ཞིག་གིས་ཕྱག་སྲོལ་དུ་མི་ལོ་བཅུ་གཉིས་རེར་སློབ་སྦྱོང་བྱེད་སྲོལ་ཡོད་འདུག འོན་ཀྱང་། འདིའི་སྐབས་ཀྱི་ནང་དོན་སྙིང་བསྡུས་ནི། སེམས་ཅན་ཐམས་ཅད་ཀྱི་དོན་དུ་རྫོགས་པའི་སངས་རྒྱས་ཀྱི་གོ་འཕང་འཐོབ་པར་བྱ། དེའི་ཆེད་དུ་ཟབ་ལམ་རྡོ་རྗེའི་རྣལ་འབྱོར་བསྒོམ་པར་བགྱིའོ་ཟེར་བ་དེས་གནད་དུ་མ་འདུས་པ་ཞིག་མེད། དེ་དང་འདྲ་བ་ལ་སྙིང་ཐག་པ་ནས་དམིགས་པའི་སེམས་རྒྱ་བསྐྱེད་པ་ནི་སྨོན་པ་སེམས་བསྐྱེད་ཟེར། དེ་འདྲའི་སྨོན་སེམས་ཡོད་པ་གཞི་ལ་བཞག་ནས་དེའི་ཆེད་དུ་བྱ་བ་ལ་འཇུག་པས་ཟིན་པའི་སེམས་བསྐྱེད་ལ་འཇུག་པ་སེམས་བསྐྱེད་ཟེར།

ད་ནི་དེའི་འདྲའི་སེམས་བསྐྱེད་དེ་ཉིད་རང་གི་རྒྱུད་ལ་ཇི་ལྟར་བསྐྱེད་དགོས་བསམ་ན་ནི་འདི་ལྟར། སྔར་སྐྱེ་བ་ཚེ་རབས་དུ་མར་བསགས་པའི་དགེ་བའི་ཚོགས་ཅི་ཡོད་རྣམས་དང་། ད་ལྟའི་གནས་སྐབས་སུ་དམ་པའི་ཆོས་གང་ཉམས་སུ་ལེན་བཞིན་པས་མཚོན། མ་འོངས་གསོག་འགྱུར་གྱི་དགེ་བའི་བྱ་བ་གང་བྱ་

ཐམས་ཅད། མཐའ་ཡས་པའི་སེམས་ཅན་མ་ལུས་པའི་ཆེད་ཁོ་ན་དང་། དེ་ཡང་གཙོ་བོའི་དམིགས་ཡུལ་སེམས་ཅན་ཐམས་ཅད་རྣམ་གྲོལ་གཏན་གྱི་བདེ་བ་རྫོགས་པའི་སངས་རྒྱས་ཀྱི་གོ་འཕང་ཁོ་ན་ལ་དམིགས་ནས། སེམས་ཅན་དེ་དག་ཐམས་ཅད་གནས་སྐབས་བདེ་དགའི་དོན་ཐམས་ཅད་འགྲུབ་ཅིང་ལོངས་སུ་སྤྱོད་ནུས་པ་དང་། རིམ་གྱིས་རྡེ་ལེགས་དང་རྡེ་བཟང་དུ་ཕྱིན་ཏེ། མཐར་སྐྱོན་ཀུན་ཟད་ཡོན་ཏན་ཀུན་ལྡན། བླ་ན་མེད་པ་རྫོགས་པའི་སངས་རྒྱས་ཀྱི་གོ་འཕང་ལ་བདག་གིས་འགོད་པར་བྱ། དེ་ཡང་སེམས་ཐག་གཅང་བཅད་དང་། བློ་ཐག་གཏན་ཆོད་ཀྱི་སྒོ་ནས་བསམ་དགོས་པའོ།།

དེའི་ཆེད་དུ་འདིར་ངས་དཔལ་དུས་ཀྱི་འཁོར་ལོའི་ཟབ་ལམ་རྡོ་རྗེའི་རྣལ་འབྱོར་སྦྱོར་བ་ཡན་ལག་དྲུག་བསྒོམ་པར་བགྱིའོ།། ཞེས་ཐེག་ཆེན་པའི་ལམ་དུ་འཇུག་འདོད་ཅིང་ཐེག་ཆེན་པ་དངོས་གནས་ཤིག་བྱེད་འདོད་ཕྱིན། སྙིང་རྗེ་ཆེན་པོས་སེམས་ཅན་མཐའ་ཡས་པ་ལ་དམིགས་དགོས་ཤིང་། ཤེས་རབ་ཀྱིས་དམིགས་ཡུལ་རྫོགས་པའི་བྱང་ཆུབ་ཀྱི་གོ་འཕང་ཁོ་ན་ལ་དམིགས་དགོས་པར་བསྟན་པ་རེད།

འདི་དག་གི་མཚན་ཉིད། མཚན་གཞི། དབྱེ་བ། བྱེད་ལས། གོ་རིམ་དང་ས་མཚམས་སོགས་རྒྱས་པར་དབྱེ་ན་ཆེས་མང་མོད་དེ། མདོར་དོན་སྙིང་པོ་སྲོག་རྩ་ནི། ཉེ་རིང་བྲལ་བའི་སེམས་ཅན་མཐའ་ཡས་པ་ལ་བྱམས་དང་སྙིང་རྗེ་བཅོས་མ་མ་ཡིན་པ་ཞིག་སྐྱེ་བའི་ཆེད་དུ། བཅོས་མ་ཚུན་ཆད་ནས་འགོ་བཙུགས་ཏེ་སེམས་རྒྱ་བསྐྱེད་དེ་བློ་སྦྱོང་དགོས་པ་དང་གཅིག ཤེས་རབ་ཀྱིས་རྫོགས་བྱང་ལ་དམིགས་ཞེས་པ། སེམས་ཅན་རྣམས་ལ་གནས་སྐབས་ཀྱི་བདེ་བ་སྟོབས་འབྱོར་ལོངས་སྤྱོད་ཀྱི་བདེ་འབྱོར་ལ་དམིགས་པ་ཙམ་མ་ཡིན་པར། རྣམ་པར་གྲོལ་བ་གཏན་གྱི་བདེ་བ་རྫོགས་པའི་སངས་རྒྱས་ཀྱི་གོ་འཕང་ལ་བདག་གིས་འགོད་པར་བྱ་སྙམ་པའི་སྙིང་སྟོབས་ཆེན་པོ་ཞིག་འཆང་དགོས་པས་གཉིས་པ་འདི་ཁོ་ན་རེད་དོ།།

དེ་ཡང་དང་པོ་བཅོས་མ་དང་། བཙན་གྱིས་བྱེད་དགོས་ན་ཡང་བྱེད། རིམ་གྱིས་གོམས་པ་དང་བོ་དེ་ཙམ་ནས་འགོ་བཙུགས་ཏེ་རིམ་བཞིན་བྱ་དགོས་སོ།། གང་ཟག་འགའ་རེས་ནི་བཙན་གྱིས་འགོ་འཛུགས་མི་དགོས་པར། སེམས་ནང་དུ་རང་ཆས་སུ་ཡོད་ནི་རེད། གང་ཟག་འགའ་རེ་ནི་གནས་སྐབས་སུ་དེ་ཙམ་བློ་ལ་རྩ་བ་ནས་མི་ཤོང་མཁན་ཡང་ཡོད་ནི་རེད། གང་ལྟར་ཡང་། དེ་འདྲའི་སེམས་བསྐྱེད་དེ་བློ་ལ་ཅི་ཙམ་གོམས་ན་དེ་ཙམ་གྱིས་ཕན་བདེ་བླ་ན་མེད་པའི་རྨང་གཞི་འཛུགས་ཐུབ་པ་ནི་ངེས་པ་ཅན་ཡིན་ནི་རེད། དེའི་ཕྱིར་མཐའ་གཅིག་ཏུ་འབད་དགོས་པའོ།། དེ་འདྲའི་སེམས་བསྐྱེད་དེ་ཉིད་དང་པོ་བཅོས་མ་རྒྱུད་ལ་སྐྱེས། བར་དུ་འདྲེས་མ། ཐ་མར་བཅོས་མ་མ་ཡིན་པ་ཞིག་རྒྱུད་ལ་སྐྱེས་ན་ཐེག་པ་ཆེན་པོའི་ཚོགས་ལམ་ལ་ཞུགས་པ་རེད། དེ་འདྲའི་བཅོས་མིན་དེ་ལ་ཡང་ཡང་གོམས་ན་རིམ་པས་ཚོགས་ལམ་འབྲིང་དང་ཆེན་

པོ་སོགས་བརྒྱད་དེ། མཐར་ཐུན་མིན་ཁྱད་འཕགས་ཀྱི་དབང་པོ་ལྔ་ལ་སོགས་པ་འགྲུབ་དུས་སྦྱོར་ལམ་ལ་ཞུགས་པ་རེད། སྦྱོར་ལམ་གྱི་ངོ་བོར་གྱུར་བའི་སེམས་བསྐྱེད་དེ་ཡང་ཚོགས་ལམ་ལས་ཁྱད་དུ་འཕགས་པ་སློས་ཅི་དགོས། དེ་ནི་མཐོང་ལམ་གྱི་ངོ་བོར་སྦྱོར་བྱེད་ཀྱི་ལམ་ཡིན་པའི་རྒྱུ་མཚན་གྱིས་སྦྱོར་ལམ་ཟེར། མཐོང་ལམ་ནི་ཆོས་ཀུན་གྱི་གནས་ལུགས་མཐར་ཐུག་མངོན་སུམ་དུ་རྟོགས་པའི་ཡེ་ཤེས་དེ་ཉིད་རེད་ལ། དེའི་ངོ་བོར་གྱུར་བའི་སེམས་བསྐྱེད་དེ་ཡང་དམིགས་མེད་ཡེ་ཤེས་ཀྱི་སེམས་བསྐྱེད་ཞིག་ཏུ་འགྱུར། མཐོང་ལམ་གྱི་ཡེ་ཤེས་དེ་ཉིད་ལ་གོམས་པས་ས་དང་པོ་ནས་རིམ་བཞིན་ས་བདུན་པ་བར་ཏེ། མ་དག་ས་བདུན་ཟེར་བས་དེ་བར་དུ་རྩོལ་བཅས་ཀྱི་སེམས་བསྐྱེད་ཡིན་མོད། ས་བརྒྱད་པ་ནས་དག་པ་ས་གསུམ་ཡིན་པས་རྩོལ་བ་མི་དགོས་པར་རྩོལ་མེད་ཀྱི་ངོ་བོར་གྱུར་བའི་སེམས་བསྐྱེད་དུ་འགྱུར། མི་སློབ་ལམ་མམ། སངས་རྒྱས་ཀྱི་སའི་སེམས་བསྐྱེད་ཀྱི་བར་དུ་ཡོད་དོ།། དེ་འདྲའི་གནས་སྐབས་གསུམ་གྱི་སེམས་བསྐྱེད་དེ་ཡང་དཔེ་དང་། གྲོགས་དང་། མཚུངས་ཆོས་སོགས་ཀྱི་སྒོ་ནས་དབྱེ་ན་སོ་བདུན་དུ་དབྱེ་ཚུལ་སོགས་ཡོད། དེ་དག་ནི། ཐྲན་གྱི་ཇོ་ནང་ལམ་རིམ་འགྲེལ་ཆེན་བདེ་གཤེགས་སྙིང་པོའི་འཇུག་རིམ་ལ་སོགས་པ་ལས་ཤེས་པར་བྱ་བ་ལས་འདིར་རྒྱས་པར་མི་སྤྲོའོ།། འོ་ན་སྐབས་འདིར་སེམས་བསྐྱེད་དངོས་ལ་ཇི་ལྟར་འཇུག་པའི་སྒོ་ནས་ལག་ལེན་དུ་བྱ་དགོས་སྙམ་ན་འདི་ལྟར་བྱའོ།། དེ་ནི་བག་ཡངས་པའི་ཚོར་བ་དང་བཅས་བདེ་བའི་གདན་ལ་འདུག་སྟེ་ངག་ཏུ་འདི་ལྟར་བཟླ།

སེམས་ཅན་ཐམས་ཅད་ཀྱི་དོན་དུ་རྫོགས་པའི་སངས་རྒྱས་ཀྱི་གོ་འཕང་ཐོབ་པར་བྱ།
དེའི་ཆེད་དུ་ཟབ་ལམ་རྡོ་རྗེའི་རྣལ་འབྱོར་བསྒོམ་པར་བགྱིའོ།།

སྐབས་འདིའི་ཉམས་ལེན་དང་འབྲེལ་དགོས་ན། ཉམས་ལེན་ག་དུས་བྱེད་ན་སེམས་བསྐྱེད་ངག་འདོན་འདི་ཉིད་ལན་གསུམ་ལས་མི་ཉུང་བ་ཞིག་བཟླག་དགོས་པ་རེད། སེམས་ཅན་ཐམས་ཅད་ཀྱི་དོན་དུ་ཟེར་བ་དེས། བྱམས་པ་དང་སྙིང་རྗེའི་དམིགས་ཡུལ་མཐའ་ཡས་པའི་སེམས་ཅན་ཐམས་ཅད་ལ་དམིགས་དགོས་པར་བསྟན་པ་རེད། རྫོགས་པའི་སངས་རྒྱས་ཀྱི་གོ་འཕང་ཐོབ་པར་བྱ། ཟེར་བ་དེས་ཆོས་རབ་རྣམ་འབྱེད་ཀྱི་ཤེས་རབ་དང་། གནས་ལུགས་མཐར་ཐུག་རྟོགས་པའི་ཤེས་རབ་གཉིས་ཀྱིས། ཐར་བ་དམ་པ་མཐར་ཐུག་པའི་ཡེ་ཤེས་སམ། རྣམ་གྲོལ་གཏན་གྱི་བདེ་བ་རྫོགས་པའི་སངས་རྒྱས་ཀྱི་གོ་འཕང་ལ་དམིགས་ཡོད་པར་བསྟན། ཟབ་ལམ་རྡོ་རྗེའི་རྣལ་འབྱོར་བསྒོམ་པར་བགྱིའོ་ཞེས་པའི་སྨོན་པ་བྱང་ཆུབ་ཀྱི་སེམས་ཙམ་མ་ཡིན་པར། འཇུག་པ་བྱང་ཆུབ་ཀྱི་སེམས་དེ་ལ་འཇུག་པའི་བསླབ་བྱ་ལ་བསླབ་དགོས་པར་བསྟན་པ་རེད། གོང་དུ་སློས་པ་ནང་བཞིན་དུ། སེམས་བསྐྱེད་ངག་འདོན་དེ་ཉུང་མཐའ་ལན་གསུམ་ལས་མི་ཉུང་

བ་དག་ཏུ་སྐྱོར་བའི་ཐུག་སྲོལ་ཡོད་པས་དེ་ལྟར་འདོན་དགོས། དམིགས་བསལ་སེམས་བསྐྱེད་དངོས་གཞིའི་ཉམས་ལེན་བྱེད་དུས་གྲངས་ཀ་བརྒྱ་སྟོང་ཁྲི་འབུམ་སོགས་ལ་ལྟོས་པ་མེད་པར་སེམས་རྒྱུད་དུ་སེམས་བསྐྱེད་སྐྱེ་ཙི་ཐུབ་བྱ་དགོས་པ་རེད། སྦྱོད་པ་ཉམས་ལེན་གང་ཟག་གི་རྒྱུད་ལ་སྐྱེ་རིམ་གྱི་དབང་དུ་བཏང་ན། རྒྱུ་འབྲས་མན་ངག་བདུན་དང་། ཚད་མེད་བཞིར་གྲགས་པའི་ཉམས་ལེན་དག་གིས་རང་རྒྱུད་ལ་ཐོག་མར་སྐྱེ་དགོས་པས། དེ་དག་གིས་ཐོག་མར་བློ་སྦྱངས་ཏེ། དེ་ནས་བྱང་ཆུབ་ཀྱི་སེམས་ལ་གཞོལ་དགོས་སོད། རྒྱུ་མཚན་ནི། དང་པོ་སེམས་ཅན་ཀུན་ལ་ཉེ་རིང་ཆགས་སྡང་མེད་པའི་བཏང་སྙོམས་ཀྱི་བློ་མེད་ན། སེམས་ཅན་ཐམས་ཅད་ཡིད་འོང་དུ་ཤར་བ་སྟེ་བྱམས་པ་ཚད་མེད་སྐྱེ་བའི་གཞི་མེད། བྱམས་པ་ཚད་མེད་མེད་ན་སེམས་ཅན་ཐམས་ཅད་ཀྱི་སྡུག་བསྔལ་བྲལ་འདོད་ཀྱི་སྙིང་རྗེ་སྐྱེ་བའི་གཞི་མེད། དེ་མེད་ན་སེམས་ཅན་ཐམས་ཅད་ཀྱི་བདེ་བ་རྒྱུ་འབྲས་དང་བཅས་པ་རང་གི་སྤྱོད་བ་ལྟ་བུའི་དགའ་བ་སྐྱེ་བའི་གཞི་མེད། དེ་དག་མེད་པར་མཐའ་གཉིས་དང་བྲལ་ཞིང་ཟུར་གཉིས་ལྡན་གྱི་བྱང་ཆུབ་ཀྱི་སེམས་བསྐྱེད་སྐྱེ་བའི་གནས་མེད་པ་ཤེས་པར་བྱའོ།། ཡིན་ཡང་འདིར་སེམས་བསྐྱེད་སྔོན་དུ་དག་འདོན་བྱས་ཏེ་ཚད་མེད་བཞི་རྗེས་ལ་བྱ་བ་ནི་དམ་པ་གོང་མ་རྣམས་ཀྱི་ཐུག་སྲོལ་ཡིན། ཅིའི་ཕྱིར་ཡིན་སྙམ་ན། དག་འདོན་གྱི་རིམ་པ་ནི་སེམས་བསྐྱེད་རྒྱུད་ལ་སྐྱེ་རིམ་མ་ཡིན་པར། བསྐྱེད་རུང་གི་རིམ་པ་ཡིན་པས། དང་པོ་སེམས་བསྐྱེད་ཀྱི་དམིགས་ཡུལ་གཏན་ལ་ཕབ་ནས། དེ་ནས་སྦྱོད་པ་ཉམས་ལེན་གྱི་རིམ་པ་ཚད་མེད་བཞིའི་བློ་སྦྱོང་ལ་འཇུག་པའི་དབང་དུ་བཏང་བ་འདྲ།

ཚད་མེད་བཞིའི་སྒོ་ནས་བློ་སྦྱོང་བ་ནི།

སེམས་ཅན་ཐམས་ཅད་བདེ་བ་དང་བདེ་བའི་རྒྱུ་དང་ལྡན་པར་གྱུར་ཅིག
སྡུག་བསྔལ་དང་སྡུག་བསྔལ་གྱི་རྒྱུ་དང་བྲལ་བར་གྱུར་ཅིག
སྡུག་བསྔལ་མེད་པའི་བདེ་བ་དམ་པ་དང་མི་འབྲལ་བར་གྱུར་ཅིག
ཉེ་རིང་ཆགས་སྡང་གཉིས་དང་བྲལ་བའི་བཏང་སྙོམས་ཚད་མེད་པ་ལ་གནས་པར་
གྱུར་ཅིག

ཅེས་ལན་གསུམ་སོགས་ཅི་ནུས་བྱའོ།། མཐར་དགེ་བ་བསྔོ།

ཚད་མེད་བཞིར་གྲགས་པ་ནི། དམིགས་ཡུལ་སེམས་ཅན་མཐའ་ཡས་པའམ་ཚད་མེད་པ་ལ་དམིགས་པའི་བྱམས་སྙིང་རྗེ་དགའ་བ་བཏང་སྙོམས་བཞི་ཡིན་པས་རེད། དེ་བཞིན་དུ་དམིགས་བྱེད་ཀྱི་བློ་དང་

དམིགས་ཚུལ་སོགས་ཀྱང་རིམ་གྱིས་ཚད་མེད་དུ་འགྱུར་བར་བསྒོམ་དགོས་པ་དང་། རིམ་གྱིས་དངོས་སུ་རྫོགས་པའི་བྱང་ཆུབ་ཀྱི་ཚད་མེད་པའི་ཡེ་ཤེས་ཀྱི་རྒྱུ་རུ་འགྱུར་དགོས་པ་ལ་སོགས་པས་ཚད་མེད་བཞིའི་མཚན་གྱིས་བསྟན་པ་འདྲ། ཞེས་པའང་གོང་དུ་སྨོས་པ་ནང་བཞིན་དུ་སེམས་བསྐྱེད་དག་འདོན་དེ་ལན་གསུམ་ལས་མི་ཉུང་བ་བསྒྱུར་དགོས་པའི་དོན་རེད། དམིགས་བསལ་སེམས་བསྐྱེད་དངོས་གཞིའི་ཉམས་ལེན་བྱེད་དུས། གྲངས་ཀ་བརྒྱ་སྟོང་ཁྲི་འབུམ་སོགས་ལ་ལྟོས་པ་མེད་པར་དོན་གྱི་སེམས་བསྐྱེད་རང་རྒྱུད་ལ་སྐྱེ་ཐབས་སུ་འབད་ན། འདིའི་ནང་དུ་མ་འདུས་པ་མེད་ལ། འདིའི་ནང་དུ་ཐེག་པ་ཆེན་པོའི་ཆོས་ཀྱི་གནད་རྩ་དེ་ཟིན་ཡོད་ལ། འདིས་ཟབ་ལམ་རྡོ་རྗེའི་རྣལ་འབྱོར་ལ་བསྟེན་ཡོད་པའི་གསང་སྔགས་བླ་མེད་པའི་ལམ་གྱི་རྣམ་པ་ཅན་གྱི་ཐེག་ཆེན་པ་རུ་འགྱུར་ཡོད་པ་རེད་ལ། སེམས་བསྐྱེད་ཀྱིས་མ་ཟིན་ན་ནི་གསང་སྔགས་བླ་མེད་ཀྱི་ཉམས་ལེན་པར་ཞོག ཐེག་ཆེན་པའི་ལམ་ཙམ་དུ་འགྱུར་བའི་གནས་མེད་པ་ཞེས་པར་འཚལ་ལོ།།

གསང་སྔགས་ཐུན་མོང་སྔོན་འགྲོའི་ སྡིག་སྦྱོང་རྡོར་སེམས་སྒོམ་བཟླས།

གསུམ་པ་རྡོར་སེམས་སྒོམ་བཟླས་ནི།

སྡིག་སྒྲིབ་མ་དག་ན་ཆོས་ཀྱི་ཉམས་ལེན་གོང་འཕེལ་ལམ། ཉམས་དང་རྟོགས་པའི་ཉམས་མྱོང་ལ་སོགས་པ་སྐྱེ་བའི་ཐབས་མེད་ལ། དེ་མེད་ན་ཐར་བ་དང་ཐམས་ཅད་མཁྱེན་པའི་གོ་འཕང་ཞིག་ལ་སྦྱོར་བའི་ཐབས་ཞིག་ག་ལ་ཡོད། དེའི་ཕྱིར་སྡིག་སྒྲིབ་ནི་ངེས་པར་དུ་སྦྱང་དགོས། དེ་སྦྱོང་བའི་ཐབས་ནི་གཉེན་པོ་བསྟེན་པ་དེ་རེད། སྤྱིར་སྡིག་སྒྲིབ་དང་དེའི་གཉེན་པོ་དགེ་བ་གཉིས་ནི་ཚ་བ་དང་གྲང་བ་གཉིས་ལྟར་དུ། གཅིག་གིས་གཅིག་གི་མགོ་གནོན་ཐུབ་པའི་རང་བཞིན་དུ་གནས་ཡོད་པས། བསོད་ནམས་དང་དགེ་བ་ཅི་ཞིག་བསགས་ཀྱང་སྡིག་སྒྲིབ་དག་པའི་གཉེན་པོར་མི་འགྱུར་བ་གཅིག་ཀྱང་མེད། ཡིན་ནའང་ཀུན་སློང་དམ་དམིགས་ཡུལ་འཛིན་ལུགས་ཀྱིས་ཁྱད་པར་ཆེན་པོ་ཡོད་དགོས་པ་ཆོས་ཉིད་ཡིན། དཔེར་ན། དམིགས་བསལ་སྡིག་བཤགས་ཀྱི་ཚིག་སོགས་སྡིག་པ་དག་པའི་ཆེད་དུ་དམིགས་ན། སྡིག་སྒྲིབ་དག་སྟོབས་ཆེ་བའི་རྒྱུ་མཚན་གྱིས། མདོ་ཕྱོགས་ནས་བདེ་གཤེགས་སོ་ལྔ་ལྟ་བུའི་ལྷ་ཁྱད་པར་བ་ཡོད་པ་དང་། སྔགས་ཕྱོགས་ནས་རྡོ་རྗེ་སེམས་དཔའི་སྒོམ་བཟླས་ལྟ་བུ་ཉམས་སུ་ལེན་རྒྱུ་ཡོད་ནི་རེད།

སྡིག་ལྟུང་ལ་འགྱོད་པ་ཙུང་ཟད་ཀྱང་མ་ཡོད་ན། གཟུངས་སྔགས་བཟླས་པ་ལ་སོགས་པ་ཅི་བྱས་ཀྱང་སྡིག་སྒྲིབ་དག་རྒྱུ་ནི་ཤིན་ཏུ་དཀའ་བ་སྲིད་མཐའ་ཙམ་ཡིན། དེ་བཞི་རེ་རེ་བཞིན་འདི་ལྟར་ཡིན། དང་པོ་འགྱོད་པའི་སྟོབས་ནི། རང་གི་སེམས་སུ་ཤེས་པའི་ཉེས་པ་བཅས་པའི་ཁ་ན་མ་ཐོ་བ་ཁས་བླང་བའི་སྡོམ་དམ་ཚིག་སོགས་དང་འགལ་བ། རང་བཞིན་གྱི་ཁ་ན་མ་ཐོ་བ། སྲོག་གཅོད་རྐུ་རྫུན་ལ་སོགས་པ་བྱས་ཚད་ལ་ངོ་ཚ་དང་འགྱོད་པ་དང་། རང་གིས་ངོས་སུ་མི་ཤེས་པའི་ཚེ་རབས་ཐོག་མ་མེད་པ་ནས་བསགས་པའི་སྡིག་སྒྲིབ་རྒྱ་ཆེ་ལ། གཉིང་ཟབ་པ་ཞིག་ཡོད་ཚོད་པ་ལ་ཡིད་ཆེས་བྱས་ནས་དེ་དག་ལ་ཡང་འགྱོད་པ་བསྐྱེད་ཅི་ཐུབ་དགོས། གཉིས་པ་རྟེན་གྱི་སྟོབས་ནི། སྡིག་པ་བཤགས་པའི་རྟེན་ཞིག་ལ་བརྟེན་ནས་བཤགས་དགོས་པ་ལས། སྡིག་པ་དག་པར་ཤོག་ཅིག་སྨྲམ་པ་ཙམ་གྱིས་ནི་སྡིག་སྒྲིབ་དག་མི་ནུས་པས། སྐབས་འདི་ལྟ་བུ་ལ་ནི། བཅོམ་ལྡན་འདས་རྡོ་རྗེ་སེམས་དཔའ་ཡབ་ཡུམ་ལ་བརྟེན་དགོས་པས། རྡོ་རྗེ་

སེམས་དཔའི་བསྒོམ་བཟླས་ལ་བརྟེན་ནས་གཟུངས་སྔགས་བཟླས་སྒོམ་བྱེད་པ་ལ་སོགས་པའི་སྒོ་ནས་སྡིག་པ་བཤགས་དགོས། གསུམ་པ་ཀུན་ཏུ་སྤྱོད་པའི་སྟོབས་ནི། རང་གི་ཀུན་སློང་དང་ཀུན་སྤྱོད་ཀྱི་སྒོ་ནས། དངོས་སུ་སྡིག་པ་བཤགས་པའི་ཐབས་ལ་ཀུན་ནས་སམ་ཡོངས་སུ་སྤྱོད་དགོས། དེའི་དོན་ནི་ཤུགས་ཆེན་དང་རྒྱུན་མཐུད་ནས་སྤྱོད་པར་འཇུག་དགོས་པའི་དོན་ནོ།། དཔེར་ན། འདིའི་སྐབས་སུ་རྡོར་སེམས་སྒོམ་བཟླས་བྱེད་པ་དང་གཟུངས་སྔགས་བཟླ་བ་ལྟ་བུ་སོགས་ལ་ཀུན་ནས་ཡང་དག་པར་འཇུག་པ་ལྟ་བུ་རེད། བཞི་བ་སླར་ལྡོག་པའི་སྟོབས་ནི། རང་ཉིད་ཀྱིས་སྡིག་པ་བཤགས་པའི་ཐབས་བརྟེན་པ་ཀུན་གྱིས་སྡིག་པ་དག་ཡོད་པར་ཡིད་ཆེས་ཡོད་པའི་ཐོག་ནས། ཕྱིན་ཆད་དེ་ལྟ་བུའི་སྡིག་ལྟུང་གི་ལས་རྣམས་མི་གསོག་པར་དམ་བཅའ་བརྟན་པོ་ཡོད་པ་གཉིས་ཚང་ན་སྡིག་སྒྲིབ་དག་པར་ནུས་ཤུགས་ཆེ་བ་རེད།

མདོར་བསྡུས་ནས་བཤད་ན། སྡིག་སྒྲིབ་ཅི་ཙམ་དག་སྟོབས་ཆེ་དང་མི་ཆེ་ནི། སྡིག་ལྟུང་ལ་འགྱོད་པ་ཤུགས་ཆེ་ཆུང་དང་། མ་འོངས་པར་མི་བྱེད་པའི་དམ་བཅའ་ཤུགས་ཆེ་ཆུང་ལ་རག་ལས་ཚབས་ཤིན་ཏུ་ཆེ་བ་ལས། གཟུངས་སྔགས་བཟླས་པའི་གྲངས་ཀྱི་མང་ཉུང་དང་། མཆོད་མེ་དང་རྫོ་དར་སོགས་ཀྱི་ཁ་གྲངས་མང་ཉུང་གཅིག་པོས་ཁྱད་པར་ཙུང་ཟད་རེ་ཕྱེ་ཐུབ་ན་མ་གཏོགས། གཉེན་པོ་སྟོབས་བཞིའི་ནང་གི་གཙོ་བོ་འགྱོད་པ་དང་སླར་ལྡོག་པ་གཉིས་ལྟ་བུའི་ནུས་པ་ཞིག་མེད་ཐག་ཆོད་ཡིན་པ་རེད། མདོར་ན་རང་གིས་བྱས་བསགས་ཀྱི་སྡིག་ལྟུང་ལ་འགྱོད་པ་དང་། གཉེན་པོ་ལ་ཡིད་ཆེས། སླར་ཡང་མི་བྱེད་པར་དམ་བཅའ་སོགས་ཡོད་ན་ནི། སྟོབས་གཞན་དག་ཤུགས་ཀྱིས་འོང་བ་ཆོས་ཉིད་ཡིན་ལ། དེ་དག་འཛོམ་ན་བསྐལ་པ་ཁྲི་འབུམ་མང་པོའི་སྡིག་པའང་། དུས་ཡུན་སྐར་ཆ་ཁ་ཤས་ནང་བཤགས་ཐུབ་སྲིད་པ་ཞིག་ཡིན་པར་ཤེས་དགོས་པ་ནི་གནད་དམ་པ་ཞིག་ཡིན། བྱས་བསགས་གཉིས་ཞེས་པའི་དོན་མདོར་བསྡུས་ནས་བཤད་ན། སྡིག་པ་ཞིག་བསྒྲུབ་འདོད་ཙམ་ཡོད་ཀྱང་། གཞན་དབང་སྟོབས་བཙན་གྱིས་དངོས་སུ་ལས་ལ་མ་འཇུག་པ་ནི་བྱས་ལ་མ་བསགས་པའི་སྡིག་པ་ཟེར། བྱེད་འདོད་ཀྱི་ཀུན་སློང་མེད་ཀྱང་གཞན་དབང་སྟོབས་བཙན་གྱིས་ལས་དེ་བསགས་ན། བསགས་ལ་མ་བྱས་པའི་སྡིག་པ་ཟེར་རོ།། ཀུན་སློང་ཡང་ཡོད། སྡིག་པའི་བྱ་བ་ཡང་བྱས་ཡོད་ན། བྱས་བསགས་གཉིས་ག་ཚང་ཡོད་པའི་སྡིག་པ་ཡིན་པས་གོང་མ་གཉིས་ལས་ལྕི་བ་རེད།

སྐབས་འདིར་རྡོར་སེམས་སྒོམ་བཟླས་ཀྱི་སྒོ་ནས་སྡིག་སྒྲིབ་སྦྱོང་བར་བྱེད་པ་ལ། གཉེན་པོ་སྟོབས་བཞི་བརྟེན་དགོས་པ་གང་ཞིག་ལ། འདི་ནི་གོང་གི་སྐྱབས་སེམས་གཉིས་ཀྱི་སྔོན་འགྲོ་ལས་གཏིང་ཟབ་ཅིང་དོན་བརླིང་བ་ཡིན། རྒྱུ་མཚན་ནི། ཉམས་ལེན་འདི་དངོས་སུ་སྔོན་འགྲོའི་གྲས་སུ་བཞག་ཀྱང་། དོན་ལ་གསང་སྔགས་བླ་མེད་ཀྱི་བསྐྱེད་རིམ་གྱི་ངོ་བོར་གྱུར་བའི་བསྒོམ་བྱ་རྣམས་ཚིག་ཤིན་ཏུ་བསྡུས་པའི་སྒོ་

ནས་བཞག་ཡོད་པས། འདི་ལ་བསམ་ཞིབ་གཟབ་ནན་དང་། བསྒོམ་པའི་གནད་གསང་རྣམས་ལ་ངེས་པ་འཇོངས་པའི་སྒོ་ནས། འབད་པ་ལྷུར་ལེན་དང་རྩུར་བརྩོན་ཆེར་བསྐྱེད་ཀྱིས་ཉམས་ལེན་དགོས་ངེས་ཀྱི་གནས་ཆེས་གལ་ཆེན་ཞིག་ཡིན་པ་ཤེས་ཤིང་། དེ་བཞིན་དུ་ཉམས་སུ་བླང་བར་འཚལ་ལོ།། དེ་ནི་བདག་མེད་དམ་སྟོང་ཉིད་ཀྱི་ལྟ་བས་ཟིན་པར་འབད་པ་ནི་ཆེས་གལ་ཆེ་ཞིང་དེ་ཆགས་ཡོད། དེའི་ཕྱིར་ཤེས་ན་ཐོག་མར་ཆོས་ཐམས་ཀྱི་གནས་ལུགས་སྟོང་བ་ཉིད་ལ་སེམས་མཉམ་པར་འཇོག དེ་ནི་ད་ལྟའི་རང་ཅག་ལ་སྣང་བའི་བདེན་གྲུབ་ཚུགས་ཐུབ་པའི་ཆོས་ཐམས་ཅད་ཀྱི་ངོ་བོའམ། རང་བཞིན་ནམ། གནས་ལུགས་དངོས་ཀྱི་ངོར་དེ་ལྟར་དུ་གྲུབ་མེད་པའི་རང་བཞིན་སྟོང་བ་དེ་ཉིད་ངེས་པའི་ངེས་ཤེས་ཀྱི་ངང་དུ་རྣམ་རྟོག་དང་བྲལ་བར་གནས་དགོས་པ་དེ་རེད། གལ་ཏེ་དེ་འདྲའི་ལྟ་བ་སྐྱོང་མ་ཤེས་ན་མ་མཐའ། ཆོས་ཐམས་ཅད་ཀྱི་གནས་ལུགས་སྟོང་བ་ཉིད་ཡིན་ནོ་སྙམ་པའི་དང་ནས་མོས་པ་ཤུགས་དྲག་ཙམ་བྱས་ན་ཡང་སྡིག་པ་བཤགས་པའི་མཐུན་རྐྱེན་དུ་འགྲོ་ངེས་དང་ཕན་ནུས་ཆེའོ།།

ཨོཾ་སྭ་བྷཱ་ཝ་ཤུདྡྷ་སརྦ་དྷརྨཿསྭ་བྷཱ་ཝ་ཤུདྡྷོ྅ཧཾ།

ཞེས་སྟོང་སྦྱངས་ཀྱི་སྔགས། ཨོཾ་སྭ་བྷཱ་ཝ་ཤུདྡྷ་སརྦ་དྷརྨཿསྭ་བྷཱ་ཝ་ཤུདྡྷོ྅ཧཾ། ཞེས་པ་དེས་གོང་སྨོས་བཞིན་དུ་ཆོས་ཐམས་ཅད་ངོ་བོ་ཉིད་ཀྱིས་སྟོང་བའི་ངང་དུ་སྦྱངས་པའི་གྲོགས་བྱེད། ནང་པ་སངས་རྒྱས་པའི་དམ་པའི་ཆོས་ཀྱི་སྙིང་པོ་ཟབ་བཅས་ཀུན་རྫོབ་ཀྱི་ཆོས་ཀུན་ངོ་བོས་སྟོང་བའི་སྟོང་ཉིད་ཀྱི་དོན་ཡིན་ལ། རང་ཅག་སེམས་ཅན་ཐམས་ཅད་ཀྱིས་མི་འདོད་པའི་རིགས་དང་སྡུག་བསྔལ་གྱི་རིགས་ཡོད་ཚད་ལ། རྒྱུ་རྐྱེན་ཆེས་མང་པོ་ཞིག་བགྲང་རྒྱུ་ཡོད་ཀྱང་། རྩ་བ་མཐར་གཏུགས་ན་ནི་ཀུན་རྫོབ་ཀྱི་ཆོས་ཐམས་ཅད་རྩ་བ་འཛིན་ས་མེད་པའི་ངོ་བོ་ཉིད་ཀྱི་བདེན་མེད་དང་། དཔྱད་ན་རང་གི་ངོ་བོའི་གྲུབ་མ་མྱོང་བའི་སྒོ་ནས་སྟོང་བས་ཕྱིར། ངོ་བོ་གདོད་ནས་གྲུབ་མ་མྱོང་བའི་སྟོང་ཉིད་ཡིན་བཞིན་དུ། མ་བརྟག་མ་དཔྱད་པའི་ངོ་བོར་སེམས་ཅན་རྣམས་ཀྱི་རྣམ་ཤེས་ཚོགས་དྲུག་གི་ངོར། བདེན་གྲུབ་དང་ཚུགས་ཐུབ་ཏུ་སྣང་བ་རེད། དེའི་ཕྱིར་དམ་ཆོས་ངེས་གསང་ཟབ་མོ་གང་ཞིག་ཉམས་སུ་ལེན་པའི་སྔ་རོལ་དུ། སྟོང་སྦྱངས་ཟེར་བ་སྟོང་ཉིད་ཀྱི་སྔགས་བརྗོད་ཅིང་། ཤེས་ན་སྟོང་ཉིད་ལ་མཉམ་པར་བཞག མ་ཤེས་ཀྱང་ཆོས་ཐམས་ཅད་རང་གི་ངོ་བོས་སྟོང་བའི་སྟོང་ཉིད་ཀྱི་རང་བཞིན་ཞིག་ཡིན་སྙམ་པའི་མོས་སྒོམ་བྱ་དགོས། དེ་ཙམ་ལས་མ་ཐུབ་ཀྱང་དེ་ལ་འབད་པ་ནི་ཤིན་ཏུ་གལ་ཆེ། དེའི་ཕྱིར་འདིར། ཨོཾ་སྭ་བྷཱ་ཝ་ཤུདྡྷ་སརྦ་དྷརྨཿསྭ་བྷཱ་ཝ་ཤུདྡྷོ྅ཧཾ། ཞེས་པ་ནི་སྟོང་སྦྱངས་ཀྱི་སྔགས་དེ་ཉིད་ལན་ཅིག་བཟླས་ཏེ་འཁོར་འདས་ཀྱིས་བསྡུས་པའི་ཆོས་ཐམས་ཅད་མི་དམིགས་པར་སྟོང་བར་གྱུར་སོང་བར་མོས། དེའི་དོན་ནི། སྟོང་ཉིད་དེ་བཞིན་ཉིད་ངེས་པའི་ངེས་ཤེས་དེའི་ངང་དུ་འཇོག་ཅི་ཐུབ་ཏུ་གཞག ཐ་ན་ཡང་། རྩེ་གཅིག་པའི་ངེས་ཤེས་དེ་ཉིད་ཀྱི་ངང་དུ་སྐར་ཆ་ལྔ་ནས་བཅུ་

ཡས་མས་སུ་མཉམ་པར་བཞག་ནས་འདུག་དགོས།

> སྟོང་པའི་ངང་ལས་རང་གི་སྤྱི་བོར་པཾ་ལས་པདྨ་དང་། ཨཱཿལས་ཟླ་བའི་དཀྱིལ་
> འཁོར་གྱི་སྟེང་དུ། ཧཱུྃ་ལས་རྡོ་རྗེ་དཀར་པོ་རྩེ་ལྔ་པ། ལྟེ་བ་ལ་ཧཱུྃ་གིས་མཚན་པ།

ཞེས་དེའི་རྗེས་སུ་འཁོར་འདས་ཀྱིས་བསྡུས་པའི་ཆོས་ཐམས་ཅད། སྟོང་པར་སོང་བའི་སྟོང་སྣང་དེའི་ངང་ནས་སླར་སྒྱུར་དུ་རང་ཉིད་ཐ་མལ་རང་ག་བར་གསལ། དེ་ནས་རང་གི་སྤྱི་གཙུག་ཁྲུ་གང་ཙམ་གྱི་ཡང་ཐོག་ཏུ་ཡི་གེ་པཾ་ཡིག་འདི་སྒོམ། པཾ་ཡིག་འདིས་འཁོར་བ་ལ་ངེས་འབྱུང་མཚོན་ཡོད། པཾ་ཡིག་དེ་ཉིད་གནས་འགྱུར་ཏེ་མེ་ཏོག་པད་མ་ཞིག་ཏུ་གྱུར། དེས་ནི་ངེས་འབྱུང་དེ་ཉིད་སྲིད་ཞི་གཉིས་ཀྱི་མཐའ་ལ་མི་གནས་པའི་ངེས་འབྱུང་གི་ངོ་བོ་ཡིན་པའི་མཚོན་དོན་ཡིན། དེའི་སྟེང་དུ་ཡི་གེ་ཨཱཿའདི་འདྲ་ཞིག་སྒོམ། ཨཱཿཡིག་དེས་བྱང་ཆུབ་ཀྱི་སེམས་མཚོན་ཡོད། ཨཱཿདེ་ཉིད་གནས་འགྱུར་ནས་ཟླ་བའི་དཀྱིལ་འཁོར་ཏེ་ཟླ་བ་ཟླུམ་པོའི་གདན་ཞིག་ཏུ་གྱུར། དེའི་སྟེང་ཏུ་ཡི་གེ་ཧཱུྃ་ཡིག་འདི་འདྲ་ཞིག་བསྒོམ། ཧཱུྃ་ཡིག་གིས་ཆོས་སྐུའི་ངོ་བོ་གཉུག་མ་ལྷན་ཅིག་སྐྱེས་པའི་ཡེ་ཤེས་མཚོན་ཡོད། ཧཱུྃ་ཡིག་དེ་ཡང་གནས་འགྱུར་ནས་རྡོ་རྗེ་མདོག་དཀར་པོ་རྩེ་ལྔ་བ་གཅིག་ཏུ་གྱུར། དེ་ནི་སྒྲུབ་པ་དག་ཟིན་གྱི་ཆོས་སྐུ་དེ་བཞིན་ཉིད་དམ། ཡང་ན་ངོ་བོ་ཉིད་སྐུ་རུ་གྲགས་པ་དེ་ཉིད་མཚོན་ཡོད། དེ་ནས་རྡོ་རྗེ་རྩེ་ལྔ་བ་དེ་ཉིད་ཀྱི་ལྟེ་བའི་དཀྱིལ་དུ་སླར་ཡང་ཡི་གེ་ཧཱུྃ་ཡིག་གི་མཚན་པ་དེ་ནི་རྣམ་པ་ཐམས་ཅད་མཁྱེན་པའི་རྣམ་མཁྱེན་ནམ་ཡེ་ཤེས་ཆོས་སྐུ་མཚོན་པ་ཡིན་ནོ།།

> དེ་ལས་འོད་འཕྲོས། འཕགས་པ་མཆོད། སེམས་ཅན་ཐམས་ཅད་ཀྱི་སྡིག་སྒྲིབ་
> སྦྱངས། ཚུར་འདུས་ཧཱུྃ་ལ་ཐིམ། དེ་འོད་དུ་ཞུ་བ་ཡོངས་སུ་གྱུར་པ་ལས།

དེ་ནས་རྡོ་རྗེ་རྩེ་ལྔ་དེ་ལས་འོད་ཆེན་པོ་ཕྱོགས་ཀུན་ཏུ་འཕྲོ་བར་སྒོམ། འོད་ཟེར་དེ་དག་ལས་འོད་ཀྱི་རང་བཞིན་དུ་གྱུར་པའི་མཆོད་པའི་རྫས་དང་ཡོ་བྱད་བསམ་གྱིས་མི་ཁྱབ་པ། སྒྲུབ་པ་པོ་རང་གི་བློས་དམིགས་ཚོད་དང་བློ་འདོད་བཞིན་དུ་གྱུར་ཏེ། ཐེག་པ་གསུམ་གྱིས་བསྡུས་པའི་འཕགས་པ་སློབ་དང་མི་སློབ་པ་ཀུན་ལ་མཆོད་པ་རྒྱ་ཆེན་པོ་བྱེད་པར་སྒོམ། དེ་ནས་ཡང་འོད་ཟེར་དེ་དག་མར་འཕྲོས་ནས་སེམས་ཅན་ཐམས་ཅད་ལ་ཕོག་པས། སེམས་ཅན་ཐམས་ཅད་ཀྱི་འཁོར་བ་ཐོག་མེད་ནས་བསགས་པའི་སྡིག་པ་དང་སྒྲིབ་པ་རྣམས་དང་། དེ་དག་གི་ས་བོན་བག་ཆགས་དང་བཅས་པ་བྱང་ཞིང་དག་པར་བསམ། དེ་ནས་ཡང་འོད་ཟེར་དེ་དག་ཚུར་འདུས། རྡོ་རྗེ་རྩེ་ལྔ་བ་དེའི་ལྟེ་བའི་དབུས་ཀྱི་ཧཱུྃ་དེ་ཉིད་ལ་ཐིམ་པར་བསྒོམ། དེ་དག་ནི་སངས་རྒྱས་ཀྱི་གཟུགས་སྐུའི་འགྲོ་དོན་བྱེད་པའི་མཚོན་དོན་དང་། ད་ལྟ་སྒྲུབ་པ་པོས་དེ་ལྟར་བྱེད་

པ་ནི་གསང་ཆེན་སྔགས་ཀྱི་ཁྱད་ཆོས་ལྡན་པའི་སྒོ་ནས། སྒྲུབ་པ་པོའི་གཟུགས་སྐུའི་རྒྱུ་བསོད་ནམས་ཀྱི་ཚོགས་ཆེན་གསོག་པའི་ཆེད་དུ་ཡིན་ནོ།།

བཅོམ་ལྡན་འདས་རྡོ་རྗེ་སེམས་དཔའ་སྐུ་མདོག་དཀར་པོ་ཞལ་གཅིག་ཕྱག་གཉིས་པ།

ཞེས་རང་ཉིད་ཀྱི་སྤྱི་གཙུག་ཁྲ་གང་གི་ནམ་མཁར། སྔར་བསྒོམས་ཡོད་པ་ཇི་ལྟ་བ་བཞིན་གྱི་པདྨའི་གདན་ཞིག་སྣང་ཙམ་ལ་གསལ། དེའི་སྟེང་དུ་ཟླ་བའི་གདན་ཡང་གསལ། དེའི་སྟེང་དུ་ངོ་བོ་རང་ཉིད་ཀྱི་རྩ་བའི་བླ་མ་ཡིན་པ་ལ། རྣམ་པ་བཅོམ་ལྡན་འདས་རྡོར་སེམས་ཡབ་ཡུམ་གཉིས་མཉམ་པར་སྦྱོར་བ་ཞིག་བསྒོམ། གོང་དུ་ས་བོན་ལ་སོགས་པའི་སྒོ་ནས་འཆང་རྒྱུ་ཚུལ་དང་འགྲོ་དོན་མཛད་ཚུལ་སོགས་བསྒོམ་པ་ནི། སངས་རྒྱས་བྱེད་ཀྱི་ལམ་ཚོགས་གསོག་པའི་ཆེད་དུ་བསྒོམ་པ་ཡིན་མོད། འདིར་འབྲས་བུ་སངས་རྒྱས་ཀྱི་སྐུ་དངོས་ཤིག་བསྒོམ་པ་ནི། འབྲས་བུ་སངས་རྒྱས་ཀྱི་སྐུ་དངོས་དེ་ཉིད་བསྒོམ་པ་ཡིན་ལ། དེ་ཡང་ལོངས་སྐུ་རྡོ་རྗེ་སེམས་དཔའི་ངོ་བོ་རུ་བསྒོམ་པ་ཡིན་པར་ཤེས་འཚལ། བཅོམ་ལྡན་འདས་ཞེས་པའི་གོ་དོན་ནི། སྒྲིབ་གཉིས་ཀྱི་ཟག་པ་དང་བཅས་པའི་ཕུང་པོ་ཕྲ་རགས་ཀུན་གྱིས་བསྡུས་པའི་ཕུང་པོའི་བདུད་བཅོམ་པ། ལས་ཀྱི་འབྲས་བུ་འཁོར་འཁྲུར་དང་བཅས་ཀྱིས་མཚོན་པའི་འཆི་བདག་གི་བདུད་བཅོམ་པ། ཉོན་མོངས་པ་ཕྲ་རགས་ཀུན་གྱིས་བསྡུས་པའི་ཉོན་མོངས་པའི་བདུད་བཅོམ་པ། ཟག་བཅས་ཀྱི་བྱེད་ལས་ནུས་པ་དང་བཅས་པའམ། ཟག་བཅས་ཟག་མེད་གཉིས་ཀྱི་དཀར་པོ་དགེ་བ་ལ་བར་དུ་གཅོད་པའི་ལྷའི་བུའི་བདུད་དེ། བདུད་བཞི་ཕྲ་རགས་དང་བཅས་པ་བཅོམ་ཞིང་། སངས་རྒྱས་ཀྱི་ཐུན་མོང་མ་ཡིན་པའི་ཆེ་བའི་ཡོན་ཏན་ནམ་ལེགས་པའི་ཡོན་ཏན་དྲུག་དང་ལྡན་པ་སྟེ། དབང་ཕྱུག་དང་གཟུགས། དཔལ། གྲགས་པ། བརྗོད་འགྲུས། ཤེས་རབ་སོགས་ཕུན་སུམ་ཚོགས་པ་དེ་དག་དང་ལྡན་པ། མཐའ་གཉིས་ཏེ་སྲིད་པ་འཁོར་བའི་མཐའ་དང་། ཞི་བ་སྟེ་རང་ཉིད་འཁོར་བ་ལས་ཐར་བའི་ཐར་བ་དོན་དུ་གཉེར་བའི་ཞི་བའི་མཐའ་གཉིས་ལས་འདས་པའམ་གྲོལ་བ། རྣམ་པ་ཐམས་ཅད་པའི་ཐུགས་ཡེ་ཤེས་ཀུན་རྫོབ་ཉོན་མོངས་པས་ཚུགས་པ་མེད་པའི་རྡོ་རྗེའམ། ཡང་ན་སེམས་ཅན་ཐམས་ཅད་ཀྱི་སྡིག་སྒྲིབ་བག་ཆགས་དང་བཅས་པ་སྦྱོང་བར་བྱེད་པ་ལ། ཐུགས་ཞུམ་པ་མེད་པའི་རྡོ་རྗེ་ལྟ་བུའི་སེམས་དཔའ་ཆེན་པོ་མཆོག་སྟེ། དེ་འདྲའི་ཁྱད་ཆོས་སྣ་མང་དང་ལྡན་པའི་ལྷ་རྡོ་རྗེ་སེམས་དཔའ་དེ་ནི་སྐུ་མདོག་དཀར་པོ་གངས་ལ་ཉི་གཞོན་འཆར་བ་ལྟ་བུ། ཞལ་གཅིག་དང་ཕྱག་གཉིས་པ་ཅན་ཞིག་བསྒོམས་ཤིང་།

གཡས་རྡོ་རྗེ་དང་གཡོན་དྲིལ་བུ་འཛིན་པས་ཡུམ་ལ་འཁྱུད་པ། ཡུམ་རྡོ་རྗེ་སྙེམ་མ་དཀར་མོ་གྲི་གུག་དང་ཐོད་པ་འཛིན་པ་དང་མཉམ་པར་སྦྱོར་བ། གཉིས་ཀའང་རུས་པ་དང་རིན་པོ་ཆེའི་རྒྱན་གྱིས་བརྒྱན་པ།

ཕྱག་གཡས་པས་གསེར་གྱི་རྡོ་རྗེ་འཛིན་ཅིང༌། ཕྱག་གཡོན་པས་དངུལ་དཀར་གྱི་དྲིལ་བུ་འཛིན་པ། དེ་ཡང་ཕྱག་གཉིས་ཀ་ཐུགས་ཀར་བསྣོལ་ཏེ་ཡུམ་ལ་འཁྱུད་པའི་སྒོ་ནས་རྡོར་དྲིལ་འཛིན་ཅིང་བཞུགས་པ། རྡོ་རྗེ་སེམས་དཔའི་ཡུམ་རྡོ་རྗེ་སྙེམ་མ་དཀར་མོ་དེ་ཉིད་ཡབ་ལ་འཁྱུད་པ། ཡུམ་གྱི་ཕྱག་གཡས་པས་གྲི་གུག་འཛིན་ཅིང་དེ་ཡང་ཕྱག་གཡས་ཡབ་ཀྱི་མགུལ་ནས་འཁྱུད་པའི་ཚུལ་གྱིས་གྲི་ཁྱུག་འཛིན་པ་དང༌། ཕྱག་གཡོན་པས་ཐོད་པ་བདུད་རྩི་དང་བཅས་པ་འཛིན་ཅིང་ཕྱག་གཡོན་མ་ཡབ་ཀྱི་མགུལ་ནས་འཁྱུད་པ། ཡབ་ཡུམ་གཉིས་ཀ་ཞབ་ཚུལ་མཉམ་པར་སྦྱོར་བ། ཡབ་ཡུམ་གཉིས་ཀ་རུས་པ་དང་རིན་པོ་ཆེའི་རྒྱན་སྣ་ཚོགས་ཀྱིས་བརྒྱན་པ་ཞིག་ཏུ་སྒོམ།

> རྡོ་རྗེ་དང་པདྨའི་སྙོལ་མོ་ཀྱང་གིས་བཞུགས་པའི་དཔྲལ་བར་ཨོཾ། མགྲིན་པར་ཨཱཿ ཐུགས་ཀར་ཧཱུྃ། ལྟེ་བར་ཧོཿ ཐུགས་ཀའི་ཧཱུྃ་ལས་འོད་འཕྲོས།

རྡོ་རྗེ་སེམས་དཔའ་ཞབས་གཉིས་རྡོ་རྗེ་སྙོལ་ཀྱང་དང་ཡུམ་རྡོ་རྗེ་སྙེམ་མ་དཀར་མོ་ནི། པདྨའི་སྙོལ་ཀྱང་གིས་ཡབ་ལ་འཁྱུད་དེ་གཉིས་སུ་མེད་པར་ཡོད་པའི་དཔྲལ་བར་ཨོཾ་ཡིག་འདི་འདྲ་ཞིག་བསྒོམ། མགྲིན་པར་ཨཱཿཡིག་འདི་འདྲ་ཞིག་བསྒོམ། ཐུགས་ཀར་ཧཱུྃ་ཡིག་འདི་འདྲ་ཞིག་སྒོམ། ལྟེ་བར་ཧོཿའདི་འདྲ་ཞིག་བསྒོམ། ཐུགས་ཀའི་ཧཱུྃ་ཡིག་འདི་འདྲ་ཞིག་བསྒོམས་ནས། ཡིག་འབྲུ་དེ་དག་ལས་ཕར་འོད་ཟེར་ཤར་ལྷོ་ནུབ་བྱང་བཞི་དང༌། དེ་དག་གི་མཚམས་བརྒྱད་དང༌། སྟེང་དང་འོག་སྟེ་ཕྱོགས་བཅུ་ཀུན་ཏུ་འཕྲོས།

> ཕྱོགས་བཅུའི་སངས་རྒྱས་དང་བྱང་ཆུབ་སེམས་དཔའ་ཐམས་ཅད་ཀྱི་བྱིན་རླབས་ཡེ་ཤེས་ཀྱི་བདུད་རྩིའི་རྣམ་པར་སྤྱན་དྲངས།

ཤར་ལྷོ་ནུབ་བྱང༌། མཚམས་བཞི་དང་སྟེང་འོག་གཉིས་ཏེ་ཕྱོགས་བཅུའི་སངས་རྒྱས་དང་བྱང་ཆུབ་སེམས་དཔའ་ཐམས་ཅད་ལ་ཐིམ། དེ་ནས་ཁོང་ཚོའི་བྱིན་རླབས་དང་ནུས་མཐུ་རྣམས་ངོ་བོ་རང་བྱུང་གི་ཡེ་ཤེས་ཡིན་པ་ལ། རང་བཞིན་བདུད་རྩི་དྲི་མ་མེད་པའམ། ཆེས་དྭངས་མ་འོད་ཕུང་ལྟ་བུའི་རྣམ་པའི་བདུད་རྩིའི་རང་བཞིན་ཅན་ཞིག་ཏུ་གྱུར་ནས་ཚུར་སྤྱན་དྲངས་ཏེ་རྡོ་རྗེ་སེམས་དཔའ་ཡབ་ཡུམ་ལ་ཐིམ་པར་གྱུར།

> ཛཿཧཱུྃ་བཾ་ཧོཿ གཉིས་སུ་མེད་པར་བསྟིམས།

དེ་ཡང་ཐིམ་ལུགས་ནི། ཐོག་མར་ཡི་གེ་ཛཿབརྗོད་པས་བྱིན་རླབས་བདུད་རྩིའི་རྣམ་པར་སྤྱན་དྲངས་ཤིང༌། དེ་ནས་ཡི་གེ་ཧཱུྃ་བརྗོད་པས་རྡོར་སེམས་ཡབ་ཡུམ་ལ་ཐིམ་ཞིང༌། དེ་ནས་བཾ་བརྗོད་པས་རྒྱུད་དུ་བརྟན་པར་

བྱས། དེ་ནས་ཧཱུཾཿ བརྗོད་པས་རྡོར་སེམས་ཡབ་ཡུམ་དང་དབྱེར་མེད་རོ་གཅིག་ཏུ་གྱུར་པར་བསྒོམ།

བཅོམ་ལྡན་འདས་བདག་དང་སེམས་ཅན་ཐམས་ཅད་ཀྱིས་འཁོར་བ་ཐོག་མ་མེད་པ་ནས་བསགས་པའི་སྡིག་སྒྲིབ་ཉེས་ལྟུང་དྲི་མའི་ཚོགས་ཐམས་ཅད་བྱང་ཞིང་དག་པར་མཛད་དུ་གསོལ། ཞེས་གསོལ་བ་བཏབ་ལ།

དེ་ནས་བཅོམ་ལྡན་འདས་རྡོ་རྗེ་སེམས་དཔའ་ཡབ་ཡུམ་ལ་སྙིང་ཁོང་རུས་པའི་གཏིང་ནས་གསོལ་བ་བཏབ། གསོལ་འདེབས་ནི། མ་གྱུར་ནམ་མཁའི་མཐའ་དང་མཉམ་པའི་སེམས་ཅན་ཐམས་ཅད་ཚེ་རབས་ཐོག་མ་མེད་པ་ནས་ད་ལྟའི་བར་དུ་ལས་དང་། ཉོན་མོངས་པའི་གཞན་དབང་དུ་གྱུར་ཏེ། ཁམས་གསུམ་གྱིས་བསྡུས་པའི་འགྲོ་བ་རིགས་དྲུག་ཏུ་འཁོར་བའི་ཚེ་ན། ཉོན་མོངས་ཆགས་སྡང་རྨོངས་གསུམ་གྱི་དབང་དུ་སོང་ནས། སྒོ་གསུམ་གྱིས་བསགས་པའི་སྡིག་པ་ནི་གྲངས་ལས་འདས་པ་ཞིག་ཡོད་པ་དང་། གཞན་ཡང་མཚམས་རེར་དཀར་པོ་དགེ་བ་ལ་འཇུག་འདོད་ཀྱི་བློས་རྒྱུད་ལ་སྡོམ་པ་བླངས་པ་ལ་སོགས་པ་བྱས་ཀྱང་། མི་ཤེས་པ་དང་། མ་གུས་པ། བག་མེད་པ་དང་ཉོན་མོངས་པ་མང་བ་ལ་སོགས་པའི་དབང་གིས། སྡོམ་པའི་སྲུང་མཚམས་ལས་འདའ་བར་གྱུར་པ་ལ་སོགས་པའི་ཉེས་ལྟུང་གི་སྡིག་སྒྲིབ་ཡོད་དོ་ཅོག་གི་དྲི་མ་བག་ཆགས་དང་བཅས་པ་བྱང་ཞིང་དག་པའི་གྲོགས་དམ་པ་གནང་བར་སྙིང་ཐག་པ་ནས་ཞུ་བ་ལགས་ན། དེ་དེ་བཞིན་དུ་བཅོམ་ལྡན་འདས་རྡོ་རྗེ་སེམས་དཔའི་ཐུགས་རྗེ་དང་བཀའ་དྲིན་མི་ཆུང་བར་འཚལ། ཞེས་སེམས་གདུང་ཤུགས་དྲག་པོའི་སྒོ་ནས་གསོལ་བ་གདབ་དགོས་པའོ།། དེ་ནས་སྡིག་པ་མི་དགེ་བས་མཚོན་པའི་སྒྲིབ་པ་ཀུན་སྦྱོང་བྱེད་ཀྱི་ཡི་གེ་བརྒྱ་བའི་སྔགས་འདི་ཉིད་བགྲང་དགོས། སྔགས་འདི་ནི་ལེགས་པར་སྦྱར་བ་སཾ་སྐྲྀ་ཏའི་སྐད་ཡིན་པས་སྐད་ཡིག་གཞན་ལས་བྱིན་རླབས་སྟོང་འགྱུར་གྱིས་ཆེ་བ་ཡིན་པས་འདིར་བཀོད་པ་རེད། གདུལ་བྱ་འགའ་ལ་སྔགས་དོན་ཤེས་འདོད་ཆེར་མེད་ལ། མ་ཤེས་ན་ཕན་རླབས་ཆེ་བའི་གང་ཟག་ཡང་ཡོད། དེ་དག་ལ་རང་སྐད་དུ་བསྒྱུར་ན་ཕན་རླབས་ཆུང་བས། དེ་རིགས་ཀྱིས་སྔགས་དོན་ལ་མ་བལྟས་ན་ཡང་ཆོག ཡང་འགའ་ཞིག་གིས་སྔགས་དོན་ཤེས་འདོད་ཡོད་ཅིང་ཤེས་ན་བྱིན་རླབས་ཀྱི་ནུས་ཤུགས་ཆེ་བ་ཡང་ཡོད་སྲིད་པས། གང་ཟག་སོ་སོའི་མོས་འདུན་དང་རྒྱུད་ཚོད་ལྟར་བྱ་དགོས། གལ་ཏེ་ཤེས་པར་འདོད་ན་སྔགས་དོན་ཤིན་ཏུ་བསྡུས་ནས་བརྗོད་ན་འདི་ལྟར་ཡིན།

ཨོཾ་ཤྲཱི་བཛྲ་ཧེ་རུ་ཀ་ས་མ་ཡ་མ་ནུ་པཱ་ལཱ་ཡ། ཨོཾ་རྡོ་རྗེ་ཁྲག་འཐུང་དམ་ཚིག་རྗེས་སུ་སྐྱོངས། བཛྲ་ཧེ་རུ་ཀ་ཏྭེ་ནོ་པ་ཏིཥྛ། རྡོ་རྗེ་ཁྲག་འཐུང་ཉིད་ཀྱིས་ཉེ་བར་གནས་པར་མཛོད། དྲྀ་ཌྷོ་མེ་བྷ་ཝ། བདག་ལ་བརྟན་པར་མཛད་དུ་གསོལ། སུ་ཏོ་ཥྱོ་མེ་བྷ་ཝ། བདག་ལ་ཤིན་ཏུ་དགྱེས་པར་མཛོད། ཨ་ནུ་རཀྟོ་མེ་བྷ་ཝ། བདག་ལ་རྗེས་སུ་ཆགས་པར་མཛོད། སུ་པོ་ཥྱོ་མེ་བྷ་ཝ། བདག་ལ་ཤིན་ཏུ་རྒྱས་པར་མཛོད། སརྦ་སིདྡྷིམྨེ་པྲ་ཡཙྪ།

བདག་ལ་དངོས་གྲུབ་ཐམས་ཅད་སྩོལ། སརྦ་ཀརྨ་སུ་ཙ་མེ། ཙིཏྟཾ་ཤྲི་ཡཾ་ཀུ་རུ་ཧཱུྃ། ལས་ཀུན་ལ་ཡང་བདག་སེམས་ལ། དགེ་ལེགས་སུ་མཛོད་ཧཱུྃ། ཧ་ཧ་ཧ་ཧཿ ཧོ། རྣ་ག་ཝཱན། བཛྲ་ཧེ་རུ་ཀ་མཱ་མེ་མུཉྩ། ཧ་ཧ་ཧ་ཧ་ཧོཿབཅོམ་ལྡན་འདས་རྡོ་རྗེ་ཁྲག་འཐུང་། བདག་མ་འདོར། ཧེ་རུ་ཀོ་བྷ་ཝ། ཁྲག་འཐུང་ཉིད་དུ་མཛོད། མཧཱ་ས་མ་ཡ་སཏྭ་ཨཱཿཧཱུྃ་ཕཊ། དམ་ཚིག་སེམས་དཔའ་ཆེན་པོ་ཨཱཿཧཱུྃ་ཕཊ།

ནང་དོན་ལ་ཐད་གར་བསམ་ན་འདི་ལྟར། ཨོཾ་རྡོ་རྗེ་ཁྲག་འཐུང་དམ་ཚིག་རྗེས་སུ་སྐྱོངས། རྡོ་རྗེ་ཁྲག་འཐུང་ཉིད་ཀྱིས་ཉེ་བར་གནས་པར་མཛོད། བདག་ལ་བརྟན་པར་མཛད་དུ་གསོལ། བདག་ལ་ཤིན་ཏུ་དགྱེས་པར་མཛོད། བདག་ལ་རྗེས་སུ་ཆགས་པར་མཛོད། བདག་ལ་ཤིན་ཏུ་རྒྱས་པར་མཛོད། བདག་ལ་དངོས་གྲུབ་ཐམས་ཅད་སྩོལ། ལས་ཀུན་ལ་ཡང་བདག་སེམས་ལ། དགེ་ལེགས་སུ་མཛོད་ཧཱུྃ། ཧ་ཧ་ཧ་ཧ་ཧོཿབཅོམ་ལྡན་འདས་རྡོ་རྗེ་ཁྲག་འཐུང་། བདག་མ་འདོར། ཁྲག་འཐུང་ཉིད་དུ་མཛོད། དམ་ཚིག་སེམས་དཔའ་ཆེན་པོ་ཨཱཿཧཱུྃ་ཕཊ། དེ་ནས་སྡིག་སྒྲིབ་སྦྱོང་བྱེད་ཀྱི་ཡི་གེ་བརྒྱ་པའི་སྔགས་འདི་ཉིད་བགྲང་བའི་དུས་སུ། སྐད་འདི་ཉིད་ལེགས་པར་སྦྱར་བ་སཾ་སྐྲི་ཏའི་སྐད་ཡིན་པས་སྐད་ཡིག་གཞན་ལས་བྱིན་རླབས་སྟོང་འགྱུར་གྱི་ཆེ་བ་ཡིན་པས། རང་གཞན་གྱི་སྡིག་སྒྲིབ་བག་ཆགས་དང་བཅས་པ་དག་བྱེད་ཡིན་སྙམ་དུ་དགའ་སྤྲོབས་དང་བཅས་པས་བཟླ་བར་བྱ།

དེ་ལས་བཟླས་དམིགས་རྒྱས་པ་དང་། ཡང་ན་མོས་སྒོམ་ཤུགས་ཆེན་བྱེད་པའི་སྒོ་ནས་སྔགས་བཟླ་ཐུབ་ན་བཟླས་དམིགས་དག་འདི་ལྟར་བྱ་དགོས། བཅོམ་ལྡན་འདས་རྡོ་རྗེ་སེམས་དཔའ་ཡབ་ཡུམ་གཉིས་ཀའི་སྐུ་ལུས་སྦྱོར་བའི་སྦྱོར་མཚམས་ནས། ངོ་བོ་སྟོང་ཉིད་སྙིང་རྗེ་ཟུང་དུ་འཇུག་པའི་ངོ་བོ་ཡིན་པ་ལ། རྣམ་པ་ཡབ་ཡུམ་སྙོམ་པར་ཞུགས་པའི་བདེ་བ་ཆེན་པོ་ལས་བྱུང་བའི་བདུད་རྩི་བྱང་སེམས་དཀར་དམར་དག་བྱུང་བ་ཟགས་ཏེ། རང་ཉིད་ཀྱི་སྤྱི་གཙུག་ཚངས་པའི་བུ་ག་ནས་ཞུགས། རང་གི་ཚེ་རབས་ཐོག་མེད་ནས་བསགས་པའི་སྡིག་སྒྲིབ་ཉེས་ལྟུང་བག་ཆགས་དང་བཅས་པ་དག་པར་བསྒོམ། དེ་ཡང་རང་བཞིན་གྱི་ཁ་ན་མ་ཐོ་བའི་སྡིག་སྒྲིབ་དག་སྲོལ་སྲོལ་ཉ་གཅིང་སྡོམ་སྡིག་སོགས་ཀྱི་ངོ་བོར་བྱུང་། བཅས་པའི་ཁ་ན་མ་ཐོ་བའི་ཉེས་ལྟུང་དམ་ཚིག་ཉམས་ཆགས་སོགས་ནི་དུད་ཁུ་དང་སོལ་ཁུའི་རྣམ་པར་བྱུང་བར་མོས་ལ། དེ་དག་ཐམས་ཅད་ས་འོག་ཏུ་སོང་ནས། རང་གི་ཚེ་རབས་ཐོག་མེད་ནས་བུ་ལོན་ལན་ཆགས་སུ་དང་གང་ལ་ཡོད་ཚད་དེ་དག་གི་ཁ་ནང་ནས་ཁོག་ནང་དུ་སོང་སྟེ་དེ་དག་གི་ཡིད་ཚིམས་ཏེ་བུ་ལོན་ལན་ཆགས་ཐམས་ཅད་དག་པར་བསྒོམ་མོ། ཞེས་ཅི་ནུས་བཟླས་མཐར།

ཞེས་དམིགས་རྣམ་འདི་དག་ཡི་གེ་བརྒྱ་པའི་སྔགས་ཟློ་བཞིན་པའི་སྐབས་སུ་བྱ་དགོས་པ་ཡིན་པས། ཞེས་ཅི་ནུས་བཟླས་མཐར་གསུངས་པ་རེད། རབ་ན་སྔགས་བཟླ་བ་དང་དམིགས་རྣམ་སྒོམ་པ་གཉིས་ཀ་ཐུབ་ན་བཟང་ཡང་། སྡིག་ལྟུང་ལ་འགྱོད་པའི་ཚོར་བ་གདུང་ཤུགས་དྲག་པོ་དང་། དམིགས་རྣམ་གསལ་

བའི་དྲན་པ་གཉིས་ཡོད་ན་གཟུངས་སྔགས་བཟླ་བ་ལས་དུང་འགྱུར་གྱིས་སྡིག་པ་བཤགས་པ་ལ་ནུས་པ་ཐོན་ཐུབ། དེ་གཉིས་ཀྱི་ཡ་གྲལ་འགྱོད་པའི་ཚོར་གདུང་དྲག་པོ་གཅིག་པུ་ཙམ་ཡོད་ན་ཡང་གཟུངས་སྔགས་བཟླས་པ་ལས་ནུས་ཤུགས་ཆེ་བ་སྨོས་ཅི་དགོས།

སྡིག་སྒྲིབ་ལ་འགྱོད་པའི་སྟོབས། རྟེན་གྱི་སྟོབས། ཀུན་དུ་སྤྱོད་པའི་སྟོབས། སླར་ལྡོག་པའི་སྟོབས་བཞི་དེ་དག་ལས་ཀྱང་སྡིག་སྒྲིབ་ཅི་ཙམ་དག་སྟོབས་ཆེ་དང་མི་ཆེ་ནི། སྟོབས་བཞིའི་ཡ་གྲལ། སྡིག་ལྟུང་ལ་འགྱོད་པ་ཤུགས་ཆེ་ཆུང་དང་། སླར་ལྡོག་པ་སྟེ་མ་འོངས་པར་མི་བྱ་བའི་དམ་བཅའ་བརྟན་པ་དེ་གཉིས་ནི་གཙོ་བོ་ཡིན། དེ་བཞིན་དུ་སྡིག་པ་དག་ཡོད་པའི་ཡིད་ཆེས་བརྟན་བརླིང་གི་ཤུགས་ཆེ་ཆུང་ལ་ཡང་ཤིན་ཏུ་རག་ལས། དེ་གཉིས་དང་ལྡན་ན། རྟེན་གྱི་སྟོབས་དང་ཀུན་ཏུ་སྤྱོད་པའི་སྟོབས་གཉིས་ནི་རང་ཤུགས་ཀྱིས་མི་འོང་ཐབས་མེད་རེད། སྡིག་ལྟུང་ལ་འགྱོད་པ་ཙུང་ཟད་ཀྱང་མ་ཡོད་ན་གཟུངས་སྔགས་བཟླས་པ་གཅིག་པོས་ནི་སྡིག་ལྟུང་སོགས་དག་པ་ནི་སྲིད་མཐའ་ཙམ་ལས་མེད་པ་ཤེས་གལ་ཆེ།

མདོར་བསྡུས་ནས་བཤད་ན། སྡིག་སྒྲིབ་ཅི་ཙམ་དག་སྟོབས་ཆེ་དང་མི་ཆེ་ནི། སྡིག་ལྟུང་ལ་འགྱོད་པ་ཤུགས་ཆེ་ཆུང་དང་། མ་འོངས་པར་མི་བྱ་བའི་དམ་བཅའི་ཤུགས་ཆེ་ཆུང་ལ་ཧ་ཅང་རག་ལས་པ་མ་གཏོགས། གཟུངས་སྔགས་བཟླས་པའི་གྲངས་ཀྱི་མང་ཉུང་དང་། མཆོད་མེ་དང་རྡོ་དར་གྱི་ཁ་གྲངས་ཀྱི་མང་ཉུང་གཅིག་པོས་ཁྱད་པར་ཙུང་ཟད་རེ་ཕྱེ་ཐུབ་པ་ཙམ་ལས། གཉེན་པོ་སྟོབས་བཞིའི་ནང་གི་གཙོ་བོ་འགྱོད་པ་དང་སླར་ལྡོག་པ་གཉིས་ལྟ་བུའི་ནུས་པ་ཞིག་མེད་ཐག་ཆོད་ཡིན་པ་རེད། དེའི་ཕྱིར་རང་གིས་བྱས་བསགས་ཀྱི་སྡིག་ལྟུང་ལ་འགྱོད་པ་དང་། གཉེན་པོ་ལ་ཡིད་ཆེས། སླར་ཡང་མི་བྱ་བར་དམ་བཅའ་སོགས་ཡོད་ན། བསྐལ་པ་འབུམ་མང་པོའི་སྡིག་པ་ཡང་དུས་ཡུན་སྐར་ཆ་ཁ་ཤས་ནང་བཤགས་ཐུབ་སྲིད་པ་ཞིག་ཡིན་པ་གོང་ནས་བཤད་ཟིན། དེ་ལྟར་དགེ་བའི་ཕན་ཡོན་དང་སྡིག་པའི་ཉེས་དམིགས་གཉིས་ལ་ཡིད་ཆེས་ཟབ་མོ་དང་། གཉེན་པོ་བརྟེན་པར་གདུང་ཤུགས་དྲག་པོའི་སྒོ་ནས་གསོལ་བ་འདི་ལྟར་འདེབས།

མགོན་པོ་བདག་ནི་མི་ཤེས་རྨོངས་པ་སྟེ།།
དམ་ཚིག་ལས་ནི་འགལ་ཞིང་ཉམས།།
བླ་མ་མགོན་པོས་སྐྱབས་མཛོད་ཅིག །
གཙོ་བོ་རྡོ་རྗེ་འཛིན་པ་སྟེ།།
ཐུགས་རྗེ་ཆེན་པོའི་བདག་ཉིད་ཅན།།
འགྲོ་བའི་གཙོ་ལ་བདག་སྐྱབས་མཆི།།

ཀྱི་མགོན་པོ་ཞེས་དད་འདུན་དང་གདུང་ཤུགས་དྲག་པོའི་སྒོ་ནས་བོས་ཏེ། གང་ཟག་ཐ་མལ་བ་བདག་ནི། མི་ཤེས་པ་གཏི་མུག་རྨོངས་པའི་གཞན་དབང་དུ་སོང་ཞིང་། གཅེས་འཛིན་དང་ཆགས་སྡང་སོགས་ཀྱིས་མཐར་བའི་དབང་གིས། གསང་ཆེན་སྔགས་ཀྱི་སྡོམ་པ་དང་དམ་ཚིག་དག་ལས་འགལ་ཞིང་ཉམས་པ་ཤིན་ཏུ་མང་བའི་ལས་ངན་བདག་འཇིག་རྟེན་ན་བླ་ན་མེད་པའི་བླ་མ་སྐྱབས་མགོན་དམ་པ། བཅོམ་ལྡན་འདས་རྡོ་རྗེ་སེམས་དཔའ་མཆོག་གིས་ཐུགས་བརྩེ་བ་ཆེན་པོས། བདག་འཁོར་བ་དང་ངན་སོང་གི་ཉེས་པ་ལས་སྐྱོབས་པར་མཛོད་ཅིག བཅོམ་ལྡན་འདས་རྡོ་རྗེ་སེམས་དཔའ་ཁྱེད་ནི་རིགས་དང་དཀྱིལ་འཁོར་རྒྱ་མཚོའི་ཁྱབ་བདག་བླ་མ་རྡོ་རྗེ་འཛིན་པ་དང་གཉིས་སུ་མ་མཆིས་པ། ཐུགས་མཁྱེན་པ་དང་བརྩེ་བ་ཆེན་པོའི་བདག་ཉིད་ཅན། འགྲོ་བ་སེམས་ཅན་ཐམས་ཅད་ཐར་བ་དང་ཐམས་ཅད་མཁྱེན་པའི་ལམ་དུ་འདྲེན་པའི་གཙོ་བོ་ཁྱེད་ལ། བདག་གིས་སྒོ་གསུམ་གུས་པ་ཆེན་པོའི་སྒོ་ནས་སྐྱབས་སུ་མཆིའོ།། ཞེས་གསོལ་བ་རྩེ་གཅིག་ཏུ་བཏབ་པའོ།།

> སྐུ་གསུངས་ཐུགས་རྩ་བ་དང་ཡན་ལག་གི་དམ་ཚིག་ཉམས་པ་ཐམས་ཅད་མཐོལ་ལོ་བཤགས་སོ།། འཁོར་བ་ཐོག་མ་མེད་པ་ནས་བསགས་པའི་སྡིག་སྒྲིབ་ཉེས་ལྟུང་དྲི་མའི་ཚོགས་ཐམས་ཅད་བྱང་ཞིང་དག་པར་བྱིན་གྱིས་བརླབ་ཏུ་གསོལ།

དེ་ལྟར་གདུང་ཤུགས་དྲག་པོས་གསོལ་བ་བཏབ་ནས། ཡི་དམ་རྡོ་རྗེ་སེམས་དཔའ་སོགས་རྫོགས་པའི་སངས་རྒྱས་རྣམས་ཀྱིས་གསུངས་པའི་གསང་ཆེན་སྔགས་ཀྱི་རྩ་བ་དང་ཡན་ལག་གི་དམ་ཚིག་རྣམས་དང་། སྐུ་ཡི་དམ་ཚིག གསུང་གི་དམ་ཚིག ཐུགས་ཀྱི་དམ་ཚིག་སོགས་རེ་རེ་བཞིན་མ་ཤེས་པ། མ་གུས་པ། བག་མ་མཆིས་པ། ཉོན་མོངས་པའི་དབང་དུ་ཤོར་བ་ལ་སོགས་པའི་དབང་གིས་བསླབ་སྡོམ་གང་དག་ལ་བདག་འགལ་བ། འདས་པ། ཉམས་པ། རལ་བ་ལ་སོགས་པ་གང་བྱུང་བ་ཐམས་ཅད་མི་འཆབ་ཅིང་མི་སྦེད་དོ།། མཐོལ་ལོ།། འཆགས་སོ།། དཔལ་རྡོ་རྗེ་སེམས་དཔའ་སྡིག་པ་བཤགས་པའི་རྟེན་དུ་བཞུགས་པའི་བསྐལ་བ་བཟང་པོ་ལ་བརྟེན་པའི་མཐུ་སྟོབས་ནུས་པ་ཡིས་འཁོར་བ་ཐོག་མ་མེད་པ་ནས་བསགས་ཤིང་། ད་ལྟ་ད་དུང་ཡང་ཡང་གསོག་བཞིན་པ་ལ་སོགས་པའི་སྡིག་ལྟུང་སྒྲིབ་པ། ཉེས་ལྟུང་དྲི་མའི་ཚོགས་ཐམས་ཅད་བྱང་ཞིང་དག་པར་བྱིན་གྱིས་བརླབ་ཏུ་གསོལ། ཞེས་གསོལ་བ་ཤུགས་དྲག་ཏུ་འདེབས་པའོ།།

> རྡོ་རྗེ་སེམས་དཔའ་ཡབ་ཡུམ་ཟླ་བ་ཞུ་བ་ལྟར་གྱུར་བ་ལས་རང་གི་སྤྱི་གཙུག་ནས་ཐིམ། རྡོ་རྗེ་སེམས་དཔའ་ཡབ་ཡུམ་གྱི་སྐུ་གསུང་ཐུགས་དང་རང་གི་ལུས་ངག་ཡིད་གསུམ་ཡེ་ཤེས་རྡོ་རྗེའི་རྣམ་པ་དབྱེར་མེད་དུ་གྱུར།

དེ་ལྟར་སྙིང་ཐག་པ་ནས་གསོལ་བ་ཞུགས་དྲག་བཏབ་པས། དཔལ་རྡོ་རྗེ་སེམས་དཔའ་ཡབ་ཡུམ་གཉིས་སྡིག་སྒྲིབ་སྦྱོང་མཁན་ནམ་སྦྱོང་པ་པོ་རང་ལ་ཐུགས་ཞེན་ཏུ་དགྱེས། རྒྱུ་མཚན་ནི། དཔལ་རྡོ་རྗེ་སེམས་དཔའ་ཡབ་ཡུམ་གྱིས་སེམས་ཅན་ཐམས་ཅད་ལ་མ་ཡིས་བུ་གཅིག་པུ་ལ་བརྩེ་བ་བཞིན་དུ་བརྩེ་བས། དེ་ལྟ་བུས་རང་གི་སྡུག་བསྔལ་གྱི་རྒྱུ་བ་སྡིག་སྒྲིབ་ཡིན་པར་ཤེས་ཤིང་། དེ་བཤགས་ཚུལ་ཡང་ཤེས། དེ་བཤགས་པའི་ཚོད་སེམས་ལྡན་པ་མཁྱེན་པས་སོ།། དེའི་དབང་གིས་རྡོར་སེམས་ཡབ་ཡུམ་མཐར་ཟླ་བ་ལྟར་དཀར་བའི་ཟག་མེད་ཡེ་ཤེས་ཀྱི་ཕུང་པོ་དག་འོད་དཀར་པོའི་རྣམ་པ་ལྟར་དུ་ཞུ་ནས། རང་ཐ་མལ་བའི་སྤྱི་གཙུག་ནས་ལུས་ཀུན་ཏུ་ཐིམ་པས། ལུས་སེམས་གཉིས་ཀ་དགའ་བ་དང་བདེ་བའི་ཁེངས་པར་གྱུར། དེས་རྡོ་རྗེ་སེམས་དཔའ་ཡབ་ཡུམ་གྱི་སྐུ་གསུང་ཐུགས་དང་། རང་གི་ལུས་ངག་ཡིད་གསུམ་དབྱེར་མེད་པ་ཡེ་ཤེས་རྡོ་རྗེ་སེམས་དཔའི་རྣམ་པར་གྱུར་པར་སྒོམ། འདི་འདྲའི་སྐོར་རྒྱས་པ་སྒོམ་ཐུབ་ན་བཟང་ཞིང་། མི་ཐུབ་ན་ཐ་ན་མོས་པ་ཙམ་བྱ་བ་ཡང་ཤིན་ཏུ་གལ་ཆེ། དེ་ནས་ཡིད་དང་བ་ཆེན་པོའི་སྒོ་ནས་ངག་ཏུ་འདི་ལྟར་བརྗོད།

> དགེ་བ་འདི་ཡིས་མྱུར་དུ་བདག །
> རྡོ་རྗེ་སེམས་དཔའ་འགྲུབ་གྱུར་ནས།།
> འགྲོ་བ་གཅིག་ཀྱང་མ་ལུས་པ།།
> དེ་ཡི་ས་ལ་འགོད་པར་ཤོག །

དེ་ལྟར་ཚེ་རབས་ཐོག་མེད་ནས་བསགས་པའི་སྡིག་སྒྲིབ་བཤགས་ཆེད་དུ། དཔལ་རྡོ་རྗེ་སེམས་དཔའི་སྒོམ་བཟླས་བྱས་ནས་སྡིག་སྒྲིབ་སྦྱངས་པ་ལ་སོགས་པའི་དགེ་བ་འདི་དག་ལ་བརྟེན་ནས། མྱུར་བ་ཉིད་དུ་བདག་གིས་སེམས་ཅན་ཐམས་ཅད་ཀྱི་ཆེད་དུ་དཔལ་རྡོ་རྗེ་སེམས་དཔའི་གོ་འཕང་མངོན་དུ་གྲུབ་པར་གྱུར་ཏེ། འགྲོ་བ་སེམས་ཅན་ཐམས་ཅད་ཀྱི་སྡིག་སྒྲིབ་མ་ལུས་པ་སྦྱོང་བའི་ལམ་སྟོན་པར་གྱུར་ནས། འགྲོ་བ་མ་ལུས་པ་མཐར་དཔལ་རྡོ་རྗེ་སེམས་དཔའི་གོ་འཕང་དངོས་ཀྱི་ས་ལ་འགོད་ནུས་པར་གྱུར་ཅིག

> དགེ་བ་འདི་ཡིས་སྐྱེ་བོ་ཀུན།།
> བསོད་ནམས་ཡེ་ཤེས་ཚོགས་རྫོགས་ཤིང་།།
> བསོད་ནམས་ཡེ་ཤེས་ལས་བྱུང་བའི།།
> དམ་པ་གཉིས་པོ་ཐོབ་པར་ཤོག །

དེ་ལྟར་སྡིག་སྦྱོང་བཟླས་བརྗོད་བྱས་པའི་དགེ་བ་འདི་ཡིས། མར་གྱུར་འགྲོ་བའི་སྐྱེ་བོ་ཀུན་གྱི་བསོད་ནམས་དང་ཡེ་ཤེས་ཀྱི་ཚོགས་གཉིས་པོ་རྫོགས་པའི་རྒྱུ་རུ་འགྱུར་བར་སྨོན་ཞིང་བསྔོས་ན། བསོད་ནམས་དང་ཡེ་ཤེས་མཐར་ཕྱིན་པ་ལས་བྱུང་བའི་རྫོགས་པའི་སངས་རྒྱས་ཀྱི་ཆོས་སྐུ་དང་། གཟུགས་སྐུ་དམ་པ་གཉིས་པོ་འཐོབ་པར་འགྱུར་བའི་རྒྱུར་གྱུར་ཅིག ཅེས་པ་ལ་སོགས་པའི་དོན་ནོ།།

གསང་སྔགས་ཐུན་མོང་སྔོན་འགྲོའི་ ཚོགས་གསོག་པ་མཎྜལ་མཆོད་པ།

བཞི་པ་མཎྜལ་རྣམས་བྱ་བ་ནི།

གང་གི་དྲིན་གྱིས་བདེ་ཆེན་ཉིད།།
སྐད་ཅིག་ཉིད་ལ་འཆར་བ་གང་།།
བླ་མ་རིན་ཆེན་ལྟ་བུའི་སྐུ།།
རྡོ་རྗེ་ཅན་ཞབས་པད་ལ་འདུད།།

ཐོག་མར་མཎྜལ་ཞེས་པའི་གོ་དོན་ནི། དཀྱིལ་འཁོར་གྱི་གོ་དོན་ཡིན་ལ། དཀྱིལ་འཁོར་ཞེས་པའི་གོ་དོན་ཡང་། ཚུར་ས་ནས་བསམ་ན་དབྱིབས་ཟླུམ་པོ། ནང་དུ་རིགས་སྣ་ཚོགས་ཀྱིས་བཅུད་དང་ལྡན་པ་ཞིག་ལ་གོ་དགོས། ཆེ་ས་ནས་བསམ་བློ་བཏང་ན་མཐའ་གཅིག་ཏུ་དབྱིབས་ལ་མ་ལྟོས་པའི་འཇིག་རྟེན་གྱི་ཁམས་དང་། འཇིག་རྟེན་ལས་འདས་པའི་ཁམས་ཀྱི་དག་པ་ལྷའི་དཀྱིལ་འཁོར་རྣམས་ལ་གོ་དགོས། ནམ་རྒྱུན་དུ་རང་ཅག་གི་མིག་ལམ་དུ་མཐོང་རྒྱུ་ཡོད་པའི་དཀྱིལ་འཁོར་རིས་བྲིས་དང་རྡུལ་ཚོན་གྱིས་བྱས་པ་ལ་སོགས་པ་ནི། འཇིག་རྟེན་ལས་འདས་པའི་དག་པ་ལྷའི་དཀྱིལ་འཁོར་རྣམས་མཚོན་བྱེད་ཙམ་ཡིན་པ་ལས་དཀྱིལ་འཁོར་དངོས་མིན་པ་ཤེས་སླ། དེ་དག་ནི་གསང་སྔགས་ཀྱི་ཆོས་ཉམས་སུ་ལེན་པོ་དག་གི་བསྒོམ་བྱ་ལྷ་ཡི་དཀྱིལ་འཁོར་རྣམས་ཡིན་ནོ།།

སྐབས་འདིའི་མཎྜལ་ཞེས་པ་ནི། གཙོ་བོ་འཇིག་རྟེན་ལས་འདས་པ་ལྷ་ཡི་དཀྱིལ་འཁོར་མཚོན་བྱེད་མ་ཡིན་པས་བསྒོམ་བྱ་ལྷའི་དཀྱིལ་འཁོར་ཡང་མིན། འདི་ནི་གཙོ་བོ་འཇིག་རྟེན་གྱི་ཁམས་མ་དག་པའི་དཀྱིལ་འཁོར་རམ། རང་ཅག་གི་འཇིག་རྟེན་ཁམས་འདི་མཚོན་བྱེད་ཡིན་པ་རེད། མ་དག་འཇིག་རྟེན་གྱི་ཁམས་འདི་ཉིད་རང་ཅག་ལ་ལས་ཀྱི་འབྲེལ་བ་ཡོད་པས་རང་ཅག་གིས་མཆོད་འོས་ཤིང་འཚམ་པའི་ངོ་བོ་ཅན་ཡིན་པའི་རྒྱུ་མཚན་གྱིས། རང་ཅག་གིས་མཆོད་པར་བྱ་བའི་མཎྜལ་ནི་དེ་ཉིད་མཚོན་བྱེད་ཡིན་ནོ།། གོང་སྨོས་ཀྱི་རྒྱུ་མཚན་དེ་དག་གིས། སྐབས་འདིའི་མཎྜལ་གྱི་མཚོན་དོན་ནི། རང་ཅག་གི་སྤྱི་མཐུན་ལས་ཀྱིས

གྲུབ་པའི་འཇིག་རྟེན་གྱི་ཁམས་འདི་ཉིད་ཡིན་ལ། དེ་ནི་དབུས་སུ་རིའི་རྒྱལ་པོ་རི་རབ་དང་། མཐའ་སྐོར་དུ་གླིང་བཞི་དང་། དགྲ་གཅན་ཉི་ཟླ་དུས་མེ་དགུ་དང་། དེ་དག་གི་སྟེང་དུ་ལྷ་དང་མི་ཡི་དཔལ་དང་འབྱོར་བ་ལ་སོགས་པ་མ་ཚང་བ་མེད་ཅིང་བློ་ཡི་དཔོག་ཚོད་ཐམས་ཅད་ལ་དམིགས་ཏེ། མཆོད་བྱེད་ཀྱི་མཎྜལ་གཞི་དང་ལྷུགས་རི་རྫོག་དང་། ནང་དུ་རབ་ན་རིན་པོའི་རིགས་སྣ་ཚོགས་དང་། ཐ་ན་ཡང་འབྲི་རིགས་ལ་སོགས་པའི་བཀང་བ་དེ་ཉིད་མཆོད་པ་འདི་ནི། སྐབས་སུ་དམ་པ་གོང་མ་རྣམས་ཀྱི་ཕྱག་སྲོལ་གྱི་མཎྜལ་ཚོམ་བུ་དགུ་མ་ཡིན་ལ།

སྐབས་གཞན་དུ་ཚོམ་བུ་བདུན་མ། ལྔ་མ། གཅིག་མ། མཎྜལ་ཚོམ་བུ་སོ་མདུན་མ་ལ་སོགས་པ་ཁ་སྐོང་གི་ཚུལ་དུ་བཀོད་ན་ཆོག་ལ། དེ་དག་གི་བཀོད་ལུགས་དང་བཤམས་ལུགས་སོགས་ཡོད་པ་འདིར་རྒྱས་པར་མི་སྤྲོ་ལ། ཐུན་གྱི་ཇོ་ནང་བའི་ལམ་རིམ་སོགས་གཞན་དུ་ཤེས་པར་བྱའོ།།

ཐོག་མར་མཎྜལ་གྱི་མཆོད་པ་དངོས་གཞི་ལ་མ་འཇུག་པའི་སྔོན་དུ། མཎྜལ་དབུལ་བའི་ཡུལ་གཙོ་བོ་ནི་སྐབས་གསུམ་དཀྱིལ་འཁོར་ཀུན་འདུས་རང་གི་རྩ་བའི་བླ་མ་ཉིད་ཡིན་པས། དེ་ལ་ཐོག་མར་མཆོད་པར་བརྗོད་དེ་མཆོད་པ་དབུལ་བ་ནི་གལ་ཆེ་བས་མཆོད་བརྗོད་ཀྱི་ཚིག་ཟིན་ལྟར་བྱས་ན་འདི་ལྟར། བླ་མ་རིན་པོ་ཆེ་གང་ཞིག་གི་གསང་བ་གསུམ་གྱི་བཀའ་དྲིན་དང་བྱིན་རླབས་ཀྱིས། ཐུགས་ཟག་པ་མེད་པའི་ཡེ་ཤེས་བདེ་བ་ཆེན་པོའི་རང་བཞིན་ཅན་གང་ཞིག་གིས། ཉིད་ཀྱི་རྟོགས་པ། ཐ་མལ་བ་ཐུན་གྱི་རྒྱུད་ལ་སྐད་ཅིག་མ་གཅིག་ཉིད་ལ་གནང་ཞིང་འཆར་བར་བྱེད་པ་པོ་གང་ཞིག་སྟེ། རྩ་བའི་བླ་མ་དམ་པ་ཡིད་བཞིན་རིན་པོ་ཆེ་དབང་གི་རྒྱལ་པོ་ལྷ་བུའི་སྐུ་གསུང་ཐུགས་ལ། སྒོ་གསུམ་དང་བ་ཆེན་པོའི་སྒོ་ནས་ཕྱག་འཚལ་ཞིང་། ལྷག་པར་དུ་ཐུགས་ཟག་པ་མེད་པ་རྡོ་རྗེའི་ཐུགས་ཅན་ཁྱེད་ཀྱི་ཞབས་ཀྱི་པདྨོ་ལ་རབ་ཏུ་གུས་ཤིང་དང་བས་འདུད་དོ།།

གང་གི་བཀའ་དྲིན་འོད་ཀྱིས་གསལ་བྱས་བདག་ཉིད་ཀྱི།།
དེ་ཉིད་རིན་ཆེན་འོད་ཀྱི་ཚོགས་ཀྱིས་མུན་བཅོམ་ནས།།
མིག་སྐྱོན་མེད་རྣམས་རོལ་བར་བཅས་པའི་སྟེང་དུ་ནི།།
ལྟར་གྱུར་བླ་མ་ཉི་མ་དེ་ལ་ཕྱག་འཚལ་ལོ།།

གོང་དེ་མ་ཐག་ཏུ་བཤད་པའི་བླ་མ་དམ་པ་གང་ཞིག བཀའ་དྲིན་དང་། བྱིན་རླབས་ཀྱི་འོད་སྣང་གིས་བདག་ཐ་མལ་བའི་བསལ་བྱ་ཉོན་མོངས་པ་དང་དེའི་འབྲས་བུ་སྡུག་བསྔལ་བཅོམ་པར་བྱེད་པའི་བདག་

ཉིད་ཁྱེད་ཀྱི་དེ་ཉིད། རིན་པོ་ཆེའི་འོད་ཀྱི་སྣང་བའི་ཚོགས་ཀྱིས་ཐུན་ཐ་མལ་བའི་མ་རིག་པའི་མུན་པ་བཅོམ་ནས། ཤེས་རབ་ཀྱི་སྤྱན་དང་ལྡན་ཞིང་མ་རིག་པའི་མིག་དེ་ཉིད་འགག་མེད་སྐྱོན་མེད་པའི་རྣམ་པའི་དཔལ་རྣམས་ལ་རོལ་བར་བྱས་པའམ། བཅས་པར་བཞུགས་པ་དང་། བདེ་བ་ཆེན་པོའི་ཏིང་དེ་འཛིན་བཅས་པའི་སྙིང་དབུའམ་དང་དུ་གནས་པར་བྱས་ནས་ནི། བླ་མ་དམ་པ་ཉིད་ཇི་ལྟ་བར་འགྱུར་བར་བྱེད་པ་པོ། ཀུན་ལ་བྱམས་བརྩེའི་བདག་ཉིད་བླ་མ་ཉི་མ་ལྟ་བུ་དེ་ལ་སྒོ་གསུམ་གུས་པ་ཆེན་པོའི་སྒོ་ནས་ཕྱག་འཚལ་ལོ།།

ཞེས་པས་ཕྱག་བྱ།

ཁྱོད་ནི་མ་དང་ཁྱོད་ནི་ཕ་སྟེ་ཁྱོད་ནི་འགྲོ་བའི་བླ་མ་ཁྱོད་ནི་གཉེན་དང་གྲོགས་བཟང་
ཡང་།། ཁྱོད་ནི་མགོན་པོ་ཁྱོད་ནི་བྱེད་པོ་ཕན་དང་སྡིག་འཇོམ་ཁྱོད་ནི་གོ་འཕང་ཕུན་
སུམ་ཚོགས་པ་ཡང་།། ཁྱོད་ནི་འབབ་ཞིག་གནས་དང་ཁྱོད་ནི་ཡོན་ཏན་མཆོག་གི་
གནས་ཏེ་སྐྱོན་རྣམས་བཅོམ་པ་ཁྱོད་ཉིད་དོ།། ཁྱོད་ནི་དམན་པ་རྣམས་ཀྱི་མགོན་དང་
ཡིད་བཞིན་ནོར་བུ་རྒྱལ་བའི་དབང་པོ་ཁྱོད་ལ་བདག་སྐྱབས་མཆི།།

དེ་ལྟ་བུའི་བླ་མ་རིན་པོ་ཆེ་ཁྱོད་ནི་འགྲོ་བ་ཀུན་ལ་བྱམས་བརྩེ་བླ་ན་མེད་པའི་མ་ཡུམ་མཆོག་དང་། ཁྱོད་ནི་འགྲོ་བ་མ་ལུས་པ་སྐྱོབ་པའི་སྐྱོབ་པ་མཆོག་སྟེ་ཟླ་དང་བྲལ་བའི་ཕ་དམ་པ་སྟེ་དཔུང་གཉེན་མཆོག ཁྱོད་ནི་འགྲོ་བ་མ་ལུས་པ་ཀུན་ལ་ཕྱོགས་རིས་བྲལ་བའི་འགྲོ་བའི་བླ་མ། ཁྱོད་ནི་སེམས་ཅན་ཀུན་ལ་ནམ་ཡང་འབྲལ་བ་མེད་པའི་གཉེན་གྱི་མཆོག་དང་ནམ་ཡང་བསླུ་བ་མེད་པའི་གྲོགས་ཀྱི་མཆོག་གམ་གྲོགས་བཟང་པོ་དེ་ཡང་ཁྱོད་ཡིན་པས། ཁྱོད་ནི་སྐྱབས་པ་ཆེན་པོ་སྟེ་མགོན་པོ་མཆོག་དང་། ཁྱོད་ནི་ལེགས་ཚོགས་ཡོན་ཏན་མ་ལུས་པའི་བྱེད་པོ། ཕན་དང་བདེ་བ་མ་ལུས་པའི་འབྱུང་གནས། ཉོན་མོངས་དང་སྡིག་པ་རྣམས་འཇོམ་པར་བྱེད་པའི་ཆོམ་རྐུན་མཆོག་དང་། ཁྱོད་ནི་ནམ་ཞིག་གཏན་གྱི་དོན་དུ་གཉེར་བྱའི་གོ་འཕང་ཕུན་སུམ་ཚོགས་པ་དང་གཉིས་སུ་མ་མཆིས་པས། ཁྱོད་ནི་འབབ་ཞིག་གམ་ཁོ་ན་འཇུག་པའི་གནས་དམ་པ་དང་། ཁྱོད་ནི་ཡོན་ཏན་མཐར་ཐུག་པ་མཆོག་གི་གནས་དང་སྐྱོན་རྣམས་ཏེ། སྐྱོན་མ་ལུས་པ་བཅོམ་པ་ནི་ཁྱོད་ཉིད་ཁོ་ན་དང་། ཁྱོད་ནི་འཁོར་བ་ལ་དབང་མེད་དུ་འཁོར་དགོས་པའི་དམན་པ་རང་ཅག་ལྟ་བུ་དང་། ཉོན་མོངས་པའི་གཞན་དབང་དུ་གྱུར་པ་རྣམས་ཀྱི་མགོན་མཆོག་གཅིག་པོ་དང་། ཡིད་བཞིན་ནོར་བུ་ཡིན་པས་རྒྱལ་བ་རྫོགས་པའི་སངས་རྒྱས་པ་དག་གི་དབང་པོ་ལྟ་བུ་ཁྱོད་ལ། བདག་དུས་འདི་ནས་བཟུང་ཇི་སྲིད་བྱང་ཆུབ་མ་ཐོབ་ཀྱི་བར་དུ་སྐྱབས་སུ་མཆི་ཞིང་བརྟེན་ནོ།།

སྟོན་མེད་རབ་གསལ་སྣང་བ།

ཞེས་པའམ་བསྡུ་ན།

དཔལ་ལྡན་བླ་མ་དམ་པ་དུས་གསུམ་གྱི་སངས་རྒྱས་རིན་པོ་ཆེ་ལ་སྐྱབས་སུ་མཆིའོ།། ཞེས་པས་སྐྱབས་འགྲོ་བྱ།

གཏན་གྱི་ལེགས་ཚོགས་དང་བདེ་བ་མཆོག་གི་དཔལ་དང་ལྡན་པའི་བླ་མ་དམ་པ། དུས་གསུམ་གྱི་སངས་རྒྱས་ཐམས་ཅད་ཀྱི་ངོ་བོ་བླ་མ་རིན་པོ་ཆེ་ལ་སྐྱབས་སུ་མཆིའོ།། དེ་འདྲའི་བླ་མ་དམ་པ་དེ་ལ་ཕྱག་འཚལ་ཞིང་སྐྱབས་སུ་མཆིའོ་ཞེས་པའི་དོན་ཡིན། ཞེས་སོགས་ཀྱིས་མཚོན་པར་བརྗོད་དེ། མཎྜལ་དངོས་ཕུལ་བ་ལ་འཇུག་པའོ།།

མཎྜལ་འབུལ་བ་ནི་ཉམས་ལེན་མཁན་གྱིས་བསོད་ནམས་ཀྱི་ཚོགས་གསོག་ཆེད་དུ་འབུལ་དགོས་པ་ཡིན་པས། རང་ཉིད་ལ་དབང་བའི་རྒྱུ་ནོར་ལོངས་སྤྱོད་ཀྱིས་འབུལ་དགོས་ལ། དེ་བཞིན་དུ་རང་ཉིད་ལ་སྐབས་དང་དུས་སུ་འཚམ་པའི་འབུལ་བའི་དངོས་པོ་མ་ཡོད་ན། ཡིད་དུ་འོང་བའི་ལོངས་སྤྱོད་དབུལ་རྒྱུ་ཡོད་ན་ཅི་མ་རུང་སྙམ་པའི་འདུན་པ་ཤུགས་དྲག་དང་ལྡན་དུ་ཡིད་ཀྱིས་སྤྲུལ་བ་ཡང་འབུལ་ན་བསོད་ནམས་ཀྱི་ཚོགས་གསོག་ཐུབ། དེའི་མི་ཚད་རང་ཉིད་གཅིག་པོ་ལ་མི་དབང་ཡང་། རང་ཉིད་དང་སེམས་ཅན་གཞན་རྣམས་དང་ཐུན་མོང་གི་བསོད་ནམས་ལས་བྱུང་བའི་ད་ལྟའི་རང་ཅག་གི་འཇིག་རྟེན་ཁམས་དང་། འཇིག་རྟེན་ཁམས་གཞན་རྣམས་འབུལ་ན་ཡང་ཕན་ཡོན་ཆེ་བས་དབུལ་བར་བགྱི་དགོས་པའོ།།

ད་ནི་མཎྜལ་དངོས་སུ་འབུལ་དགོས་དོན་ནི། ཉམས་ལེན་མཁན་གྱིས་བསོད་ནམས་ཀྱི་ཚོགས་གསོག་ཆེད་དུ་འབུལ་དགོས་པ་ཡིན་པས། རང་ཉིད་ལ་དབང་བའི་རྒྱུ་ནོར་ལོངས་སྤྱོད་འབུལ་དགོས་ལ། དེ་བཞིན་དུ་རང་ཉིད་ལ་སྐབས་དང་དུས་སུ་འོས་འཚམ་གྱི་འབུལ་བའི་དངོས་པོ་མ་ཡོད་ན། ཡིད་དུ་འོང་བའི་ལོངས་སྤྱོད་དབུལ་རྒྱུ་ཡོད་ན་ཅི་མ་རུང་སྙམ་པའི་འདུན་པ་ཤུགས་དྲག་དང་ལྡན་དུ་ཡིད་ཀྱིས་སྤྲུལ་བ་ཡང་འབུལ་ན་བསོད་ནམས་ཀྱི་ཚོགས་གསོག་ཐུབ། དེའི་མི་ཚད་རང་ཉིད་གཅིག་པོ་ལ་མི་དབང་ཡང་། རང་ཉིད་དང་སེམས་ཅན་གཞན་རྣམས་དང་ཐུན་མོང་གི་བསོད་ནམས་ལས་བྱུང་བའི་ད་ལྟའི་རང་ཅག་གི་འཇིག་རྟེན་ཁམས་དང་། འཇིག་རྟེན་ཁམས་གཞན་རྣམས་འབུལ་ན་ཡང་ཕན་ཡོན་ཆེ་བས་དབུལ་བར་བགྱི་དགོས་པའོ།།

རག་ཏུ།

ཨོཾ་བཛྲ་བྷཱུ་མི་ཨཱཿཧཱུྃ གཞི་ཡོངས་སུ་དག་པ་དབང་ཆེན་གསེར་གྱི་ས་གཞི།

དེའི་ཕྱིར་ཐོག་མར་འཇིག་རྟེན་ཁམས་འབུལ་བ་ལ་འཇིག་རྟེན་ཁམས་ཇི་འདྲ་ཡིན་ཕྱོགས་ཙམ་ཤེས་པའི་སྒོ་ནས་སྒོམ་པའམ་མོས་པ་བྱ་དགོས་པས་འདི་ལྟར་བྱ། ཨོཾ་སྐྱེ་མཆོག་དང་དཔལ་གྱི་ངོ་བོ་ལྡན་པའི་དབུ་དྲངས་ཏེ། བཛྲ་ཞེས་པ་མི་འཇིག་ཅིང་སྲ་བརྟན་གྱི་རང་བཞིན་དུ་གྱུར་པའི་བྷཱུ་མི་ཞེས་པ། གཞི་ཡོངས་སུ་དག་པ་དབང་ཆེན་གསེར་གྱི་ས་གཞི་སྲ་ཞིང་བརྟན་པ་དང་། ཨཱཿདོན་དམ་རང་བྱུང་གི་ངོ་བོ་ལ་ཀུན་རྫོབ་སྐྱེ་བ་མེད་ནའང་། ཀུན་རྫོབ་རྟེན་འབྱུང་གི་དངོས་པོ་མང་དུ་སྐྱེ་བའི་འབྱུང་གཞི་སྲ་བརྟན་གྱི་རང་བཞིན་ཅན་རྣམས་བསྟན། ཧཱུཾ་ནི་ངོ་བོ་ཕུན་སུམ་ཚོགས་པའི་རང་བཞིན་བསོད་ནམས་རྒྱ་མཚོའི་ངོ་བོར་གྱུར་པའི་དབུལ་བྱའི་མཎྜལ་དེ་དག་ཀྱང་། དོན་ལ་རང་བཞིན་སྟོང་པ་ཆེན་པོའི་ངོ་བོ་ཡིན་པའི་དོན་བསྟན་པའོ།།

ཨོཾ་བཛྲ་རེ་ཁེ་ཨཱཿཧཱུཾ། ཕྱི་ལྕགས་རིའི་ཁོར་ཡུག་གིས་བསྐོར་བའི་དབུས་སུ།

བཤད་མ་ཐག་པ་བཞིན་ཨོཾ་དང་བཛྲ་གོང་ལྟར་གཅིག་ཏུ་མཚུངས་ཤིང་། རེ་ཁེ་ནི་ལྕགས་རི་ཡི་དོན་ཡིན་ལ། ཨཱཿཧཱུཾ་ཡང་གོང་ལྟར་དུ། དོན་དམ་སྐྱེ་མེད་ལས་སྐྱེས་པའི་རྟེན་འབྱུང་སྲ་ཞིང་བརྟན་པ་ཕུན་སུམ་ཚོགས་པའི་འཇིག་རྟེན་ཁམས་ཀྱི་ཕྱི་ལྕགས་རིའི་ཁོར་ཡུག་གིས་བསྐོར་བའི་དབུས་སུ།

རིའི་རྒྱལ་པོ་རི་རབ།

ཞེས་པ་འཛམ་གླིང་འདིའི་དབུས་སུ། འབྱོར་ཕྱུག་དཔལ་དང་ལྡན་པའི་རིའི་རྒྱལ་པོ་རི་རབ་དཔག་ཚད་འབུམ་ཕྲག་གཅིག་ཏུ་ཡོད་པ། དབུས་མཐའ་ལྷུང་གྲུ ཤར་བཻཌཱུརྱ་སྔོན་པོ། ལྷོ་པདྨ་རཱ་ག་དམར་པོ། ནུབ་ཀརྐེ་ཏ་སེར་པོ། བྱང་ཆུ་ཤེལ་དཀར་པོ་ལ་སོགས་པ་ཐམས་ཅད་རིན་པོ་ཆེའི་རིགས་སྣ་ཚོགས་ལས་གྲུབ་པ། ཁ་ཁྱེར་གཡེར་ཞིང་སྟེང་དུ་རྡོ་རྗེའི་ར་ལྭ་ཡོད་པ། དེ་ཡང་ཕྱི་དུས་ཀྱི་འཁོར་ལོ་འཇིག་རྟེན་གྱི་བཀོད་པ། ནང་དུས་ཀྱི་འཁོར་ལོ་གང་ཟག་གི་རྡོ་རྗེའི་ལུས་ལ་སྦྱར་ན། རི་རབ་ཀྱི་སྐྲ་མཚམས་ནས་སྤྱི་གཙུག་བར་གཟུགས་མེད་ཁམས་དང་། མགྲིན་པ་དང་གདོང་ནི་གཟུགས་ཁམས། དེ་མན་ལྟག་མ་དག་ནི་འདོད་ཁམས་ཏེ་ཁམས་གསུམ་གྱི་ས་ཡི་བསྡུས་པར་གསུངས་པའོ།། རི་རབ་ཀྱི་རྩ་བ་ནས་གླིང་དྲུག་སྟེ་ནང་ནས་ཕྱི་རིམ་བཞིན་དུ་ཛམྦུ་བའི་གླིང་། དཀར་པོའི་གླིང་། རབ་མཆོག་གླིང་། ཀུ་ཤའི་གླིང་། མིའམ་ཅིའི་གླིང་། ཁྲུང་ཁྲུང་གླིང་བཅས་དྲུག་ཡོད་ཅིང་། དེ་ནས་རིམ་བཞིན་དུ་མཚོ་དྲུག་སྟེ་སྦྲང་རྩིའི་མཚོ། མར་ཁུའི་མཚོ། ཞོའི་མཚོ། འོ་མའི་མཚོ། ཆུའི་མཚོ། ཆང་གི་མཚོ་སྟེ་མཚོ་དྲུག་ཡོད། དེ་དག་རེ་རེའི་མཐའ་ལ་འཁྱིལ་བྱེད་ཀྱི་རི་དྲུག་སྟེ། འོད་སྡོན་རི། མནྡ་རའི་རི། མཚན་མོའི་རི། ནོར་བུའི་འོད་ཀྱི་རི། བྲེའོ་ཡི་རི། བསིལ་རི་སྟེ་རི་དྲུག་གིས་མཚོ་དྲུག་ལ་བསྐོར་ཡོད།

ཤར་ལུས་འཕགས་པོ། ལྷོ་འཛམ་བུ་གླིང་། ནུབ་བ་ལང་སྤྱོད། བྱང་སྒྲ་མི་སྙན། སྒྲ་གཅན། ཉི་མ། ཟླ་བ། དུས་མེ།

དེ་དག་གི་ཕྱི་ལ་འཛམ་གླིང་ལས་ཀྱི་ས་པ་སྟེ་རང་ཅག་གི་སྤྱོད་ཡུལ་དུ་གྱུར་པ། ཤར་ལུས་འཕགས་གླིང་། ལྷོ་འཛམ་བུ་གླིང་། ནུབ་བ་ལང་སྤྱོད། བྱང་སྒྲ་མི་སྙན་སོགས་གླིང་ཆེན་བཞི་དང་། གླིང་ཕྲན་གྲངས་ལས་འདས་པ་དང་། དེ་བཞིན་དུ་འཛམ་གླིང་འདིར་གཏོགས་པའི་སྐར་མ། གཟའ་སྒྲ་གཅན་དུ་གྲགས་པ་ནི། ད་ལྟའི་འཇིག་རྟེན་དུ་སྣང་བའི་རྒྱ་སྐར་རགས་པའི་ངོ་བོ་མ་ཡིན་པའི་ཕྲ་ཕུང་གི་བདག་ཉིད་ཅན་སྟོང་བའི་ལུས་ཅན་ཞེས་གྲགས་པ་ཞིག་ཡིན། སྐྱི་ཁྲིམ་ནག་པ་ཞེས་འཇིག་རྟེན་དུ་གྲིབ་མ་བཞིན་ནག་པོའི་རང་བཞིན་དུ་གྲགས་པ་ཞིག་ཡིན་ཡང་། ནང་རྡོ་རྗེའི་ལུས་དང་སྦྱར་དུས་ནི་རྩ་དབུ་མ་དགྲ་གཅན་ཞེས་གྲགས་པས་ཕྲ་ཕུང་གི་བདག་ཉིད་ཡིན་པ་ཤེས་ནུས་པ་འདྲའོ།། ཉི་མ་སྟེ་རགས་པའི་རྒྱ་སྐར་ཚེས་ཆེན་པོ་འཇིག་རྟེན་ཀུན་ལ་མཐོང་ཆོས་སུ་ཚ་བའི་རང་བཞིན་དུ་ཡོད་པ་དེ་དང་། ཟླ་བ་སྟེ་འཇིག་རྟེན་མཐོང་ཆོས་མདོག་དཀར་ཞིང་། བསིལ་བའི་རང་བཞིན་དུ་གྲགས་པ་དེ་དང་། དུས་མེ་སྟེ་སྒྲ་གཅན་གྱི་མཇུག་མ་དང་ཡང་ན་ཕྱོགས་ཁ་གཏད་དུ་གྲགས་པ། མ་འོངས་འཇིག་རྟེན་འདི་འཇིག་དུས་ཀྱི་དུས་མཐའི་མེ་འབྱུང་བའི་གཞི་རྩ་འདི་ཉིད་དུ་ཡང་གྲགས་པ་སྟེ། མདོར་ན་ཕྲ་བའི་རང་བཞིན་གྱི་གཟུགས་ལས་བཀྲལ་བའི་གཟའ་སྐར་ཞིག་ཏུ་ངོས་འཛིན་རུང་བ་ཞིག་ཡིན་པ་འདྲ། དེ་ལྟར་འཇིག་རྟེན་དུ་མངོན་གྱུར་དུ་སྣང་མི་སྣང་དང་ཕྲ་རགས་ཀྱིས་བསྡུས་པ་ཐམས་ཅད་དང་།

དབུས་སུ་ལྷ་དང་མིའི་དཔལ་འབྱོར་ཕུན་སུམ་ཚོགས་པ་གང་ཡང་མ་ཚང་བ་མེད་པ།

དེ་ལྟ་བུའི་ཁམས་གསུམ་རིགས་དྲུག་གིས་བསྡུས་པའི་འཛམ་གླིང་ཆེན་པོ་དེའི་དབུས་སུ། ལྷ་དང་མིའི་དཔལ་འབྱོར་ཡིད་དུ་འོང་ཞིང་ཕུན་སུམ་ཚོགས་པ་གང་ཡང་མ་ཚང་བ་མེད་པ་ཞིག་ངོས་སུ་བསྒོམ་ཐུབ་ན་རབ་དང་། དེ་མ་ཐུབ་ཀྱང་དེ་ལྟར་ཡིད་འོང་ཕུན་སུམ་ཚོགས་པ་བསམ་གྱིས་མི་ཁྱབ་པ་ཞིག་ཡོད་པར་མོས་ལ། དེ་ལྟ་བུའི་མོས་པའི་ཚོར་འདུ་ཤུགས་དྲག་པོའི་སྒོ་ནས། དམ་པ་གོང་མ་རྣམས་ཀྱི་གསུང་བྱིན་རླབས་ཅན་གྱི་ངག་འདོན་འདི་ཉིད་བསྒྲགས་ཏེ་བསྒོམ་དགོས་པའོ།།

བརྒྱུད་པར་བཅས་པའི་ཆོས་རྗེ་དཔལ་ལྡན་བླ་མ་དམ་པ་རྣམས་དང་།

དེ་བཞིན་གོང་ནས་བཤད་པ་བཞིན་རང་ལ་བཀའ་དྲིན་ཤིན་ཏུ་ཆེ་བའི་རྩ་བའི་བླ་མ་དམ་པ་མཆོག་དང་། རྩ་བའི་བླ་མ་ལ་མ་ཐུག་གི་བར་དུ་བརྒྱུད་པར་བཅས་པའི་ཆོས་ཀྱི་རྗེ་བོ་དཔལ་ལྡན་བླ་མ་དམ་པ་རྣམས་དང་།

ཡི་དམ་དཀྱིལ་འཁོར་གྱི་ལྷ་ཚོགས།

ཡི་དམ་རྒྱུད་སྡེ་བཞི་སྟེ། བྱ་རྒྱུད། སྤྱོད་རྒྱུད། རྣལ་འབྱོར་གྱི་རྒྱུད། རྣལ་འབྱོར་བླ་ན་མེད་པའི་རྒྱུད་དེ་དག་ཏུ་གདོགས་པའི་དཀྱིལ་འཁོར་གྱི་ལྷ་ཚོགས་ཐམས་ཅད་དང་།

སངས་རྒྱས་དང་བྱང་ཆུབ་སེམས་དཔའ་འཕགས་པ་ཉན་རང་གི་ཚོགས་དང་
བཅས་པ་རྣམས་དང་།

ཡི་དམ་གྱི་ངོ་བོར་གྱུར་བའི་སངས་རྒྱས་དེ་དག་ལས་གཞན་པའི་སངས་རྒྱས་དང་བྱང་ཆུབ་སེམས་དཔའ་ཐམས་ཅད་ཀྱི་ཚོགས་དང་བཅས་པའི་ཁོངས་སུ། འཕགས་པ་ཉན་ཐོས་སློབ་པ་དང་མི་སློབ་པ། རང་སངས་རྒྱས་སློབ་པ་དང་མི་སློབ་པ་ཀུན་གྱི་ཚོགས་དང་བཅས་པ་རྣམས་དང་།

མཁའ་འགྲོ་ཆོས་སྐྱོང་སྲུང་མ་ཡེ་ཤེས་ཀྱི་སྤྱན་དང་ལྡན་པ་རྣམས་ལ་དབུལ་བར་བགྱིའོ།

གནས་ཡུལ་ཉེར་བཞིའི་མཁའ་འགྲོ་མ་རྣམས་ཞིང་སྐྱེས། འཛམ་གླིང་གང་སར་ཁམས་དྲུག་ལྡན་གྱི་སྔགས་སྐྱེས་ཀྱི་མཁའ་འགྲོ་མའི་ཚོགས་བསམ་གྱིས་མི་ཁྱབ་པ་རྣམས་དང་། དམ་པའི་ཆོས་སྐྱོང་ཞིང་ཆོས་ལྡན་གྱི་སྐྱེ་བོ་དག་ལ་སྲུང་ཞིང་སྐྱོབ་པར་བྱེད་པའི་སྲུང་མ་ཡེ་ཤེས་ཀྱི་སྤྱན་དང་ལྡན་པ་རྣམས་ལ། མཎྜལ་འདིས་མཆོད་པའི་འཇིག་རྟེན་ཁམས་སུ་ཡོད་འོང་གི་ཆོས་རྣམས་གང་དག་ཅི་མཆིས་པ་ཐམས་ཅད་དང་འདུན་སྤྲོ་དགའ་ཆེན་པོའི་ངང་ནས་དབུལ་བར་བགྱིའོ།།

ཐུགས་རྗེས་འགྲོ་བའི་དོན་དུ་བཞེས་སུ་གསོལ།། བཞེས་ནས་བྱིན་གྱིས་བརླབ་ཏུ་གསོལ།།

ཞེས་པས་རང་ཉིད་ཀྱིས་དེ་ལྟར་དབུལ་བར་བྱས་པ་ཇི་བཞིན་དུ། ཡུལ་དམ་པ་བླ་མ་དང་། དཀོན་མཆོག་གསུམ་གྱི་ཐུགས་རྗེ་བརྩེ་བ་ཆེན་པོས་འགྲོ་བ་བདག་དང་། བདག་ལྟ་བུ་རྣམས་ཀྱི་བསོད་ནམས་ཀྱི་ཚོགས་རྫོགས་ཤིང་གནས་སྐབས་ནད་མེད་བདེ་སྐྱིད་དང་། མཐར་ཐུག་རྫོགས་པའི་སངས་རྒྱས་ཀྱི་གོ་འཕང་འཐོབ་པའི་དོན་རྒྱ་ཆེན་པོ་འགྲུབ་པའི་ཆེད་དུ་བཞེས་སུ་གསོལ། བཞེས་ནས་ཀྱང་བདག་གི་བློ་ཆོས་ལས་ནམ་ཡང་མི་འདའ་བར་བྱིན་གྱིས་བརླབ་ཏུ་གསོལ།

བདག་གཞན་ལུས་ངག་ཡིད་གསུམ་དུས་གསུམ་དགེ་ཚོགས་བཅས།།
རིན་ཆེན་མཎྜལ་བཟང་པོ་ཀུན་བཟང་མཆོད་པའི་ཚོགས་བཅས་པ།།
བློ་ཡིས་དམིགས་ནས་བླ་མ་དཀོན་མཆོག་རྣམས་ལ་འབུལ།།
ཐུགས་རྗེས་དབང་གིས་བཞེས་ནས་བྱིན་གྱིས་བརླབ་ཏུ་གསོལ།།

ཞེས་པ་འདིས་གོང་དུ་གསུངས་པའི་མཎྜལ་ཕུལ་བ་དེ་དག་འདིར་བསྡུས་པའི་སྒོ་ནས་གསུངས་པ་ཡིན་པས། གོང་གི་ཐམས་ཅད་བྱེད་པའི་ཁོམ་ལོང་མེད་དུས་བསྡུས་པ་འདི་བྱས་ན་ཆོག དེའི་དོན་ནི། ཐུན་གྱིས་བདག་དང་གཞན་སེམས་ཅན་མ་ལུས་པའི་ཚབ་བྱས་ཏེ། རང་གཞན་སྤྱི་ལ་དབང་བའི་ཕྱི་ཡུལ་གྱི་འཇིག་རྟེན་ནས་རང་ཅག་སྒེར་སོ་སོ་ལ་དབང་བའི་ལོངས་སྤྱོད། མ་ཟད་རང་ཅག་གི་ཐོག་མེད་ནས་ལུས་ངག་ཡིད་གསུམ་དང་དུས་གསུམ་དུ་བསགས་པའི་དགེ་ཚོགས་དང་བཅས་པ། རིན་པོ་ཆེ་སྣ་ཚོགས་ལས་གྲུབ་པའི་མཎྜལ་གྱི་མཆོད་བྱེད་བཟང་པོ་དང་བཅས་པ། ཀུན་ཏུ་བཟང་པོའི་མཆོད་པའི་ཚོགས་རྒྱ་ཆེན་པོར་འགྱུར་བར་དམིགས་པ་དང་བཅས་པ་འདི། རང་གི་བློ་ཡིས་དམིགས་ནས་བླ་མ་དཀོན་མཆོག་རྣམས་ལ་དབུལ་བར་བགྱི་ན། ཐུགས་བརྩེ་བ་ཆེན་པོ་དང་བཅས་པའི་རྗེས་སུ་གཟུང་བའི་སྒོ་ནས་བཞེས་སྟེ། བདག་ཅག་ལ་བྱིན་གྱིས་བརླབས་ཤིང་ནུས་པའི་མཐུ་སྩལ་དུ་གསོལ་ཞེས་པའོ།།

ས་གཞི་སྤོས་ཆུས་བྱུགས་ཤིང་མེ་ཏོག་བཀྲམ།།
རི་རབ་གླིང་བཞི་ཉི་ཟླས་བརྒྱན་པ་འདི།།
སངས་རྒྱས་ཞིང་དུ་དམིགས་ཏེ་ཕུལ་བ་ཡིས།།
འགྲོ་ཀུན་རྣམ་དག་ཞིང་ལ་སྤྱོད་པར་ཤོག །

གུ་རུ་ཨི་དཾ་རཏྣ་མཎྜལ་ཀཾ་ནིརྱཱ་ཏ་ཡ་མི།

ཡང་མཎྜལ་བསྡུས་པ་གཞན་འདི་ནི། གོང་དུ་རྒྱས་པར་སྨོས་པའི་མཎྜལ་ཚོམ་བུ་དགུ་བ་སོགས་ཚིག་བསྡུས་པའི་སྒོ་ནས་གསུངས་པ་ཡིན་ནོ།། ས་གཞི་ཆེན་པོ་འདི་ཉིད་ལྷན་སྐྱེས་ཀྱིས་སྤོས་སོགས་དྲི་བཟང་གི་ཆུས་བྱུགས་ཤིང་། རི་ལུང་ནགས་ཚལ་མེ་ཏོག་སོགས་ཡིད་འོང་གི་དངོས་པོ་སོགས་བཀྲམ་པའམ་བཀང་ཞིང་། དེའི་ཐོག་ཏུ་གོང་སྨོས་བཞིན་གྱི་རིའི་རྒྱལ་པོ་རི་རབ་དང་མཐའ་སྐོར་དུ་གླིང་བཞི་གླིང་ཕྲན་རྣམས་དང་། དེའི་སྟེང་གི་ནམ་མཁའ་སོགས་སུ་ཉི་མ་དང་ཟླ་བས་བརྒྱན་པ་འདི་དག་ཐམས་ཅད། ཡི་དམ་དུས་ཀྱི་འཁོར་ལོ་ལ་སོགས་པའི་སངས་རྒྱས་རྣམས་ཀྱི་ཞིང་དུ་དམིགས་ཏེ་ཕུལ་བའི་བསོད་ནམས་ཀྱིས། འགྲོ་བ་སེམས་ཅན་ཀུན་མ་ལུས་པར་སྡུག་བདེན་གྱིས་རྣམ་པར་དག་པའི་ཞིང་ཁམས་དག་ལ་སྐྱེ་ཐུབ་ཅིང་སྤྱོད་ནུས་པར་ཤོག་ཅིག ཅེས་ཁོམ་ལོང་ཡོད་དུས་མཎྜལ་རྒྱས་བསྡུས་ཀུན་སུ་མཐུད་དུ་འབུལ་བ་དང་། ཁོམ་ལོང་མེད་པའམ་ཡང་ན་ཁྲི་འབུམ་མང་པོ་གསོག་དུས་མཎྜལ་ཐུང་བ་འདི་དག་གང་རུང་རེ་སྐྱོར་དགོས་པའོ།། གུ་རུ་ཨི་དཾ་རཏྣ་མཎྜལ་ཀཾ་ནིརྱཱ་ཏ་ཡ་མི། ཞེས་པའི་སྔགས་དོན་ཙུང་བསྡུས་ན། བླ་མ་དཀོན་མཆོག་རྣམས་ལ་མཎྜལ་འདི་དབུལ་བར་བགྱིའོ་ཞེས་པའི་དོན་ནོ།། འདི་ཡན་ཆད་ཀྱིས་ཚོགས་གསོག་མཎྜལ་གྱི་ཉམས་ལེན་སོང་ཟིན་པའོ།།

གསང་སྔགས་ཐུན་མོང་སྔོན་འགྲོའི་བླ་མའི་རྣལ་འབྱོར།

ད་ནི་ཟབ་ལམ་རྡོ་རྗེ་རྣལ་འབྱོར་གྱི་རྟོགས་པ་སྐྱེ་བར་བྱེད་ནུས་པ་རང་རྒྱུད་ལ་འཇུག་བྱེད་ཀྱི་བླ་མའི་རྣལ་འབྱོར་ཞེས་བྱ་བ་ཉམས་སུ་ལེན་པ་ལ། དཔལ་ལྡན་རྒྱལ་བ་རྡོ་ནང་བ་ལ་ཡུན་རིང་དུ་དར་བའི་རང་ལུགས་གཞི་ལ་བཞག་ན། བླ་སྤྲུལ་དགེ་བཙུན་དག་སྦྱོར་བ་ཡན་ལག་དྲུག་གི་སྔོན་འགྲོ་དངོས་གཞི་དང་བཅས་པ་ཉམས་སུ་ལེན་པ་ལ། མ་མཐའ་ཡང་མི་ལོ་གསུམ་ལ་སྦྱོར་དྲུག་ཞེས་གྲགས་པའི་མཚམས་ལ་འདུག་སྲོལ་ཡོད། སྔོན་འགྲོའི་ངག་འདོན་འདི་ཉིད་དག་ཐོག་ཏུ་མཐར་ཆགས་སུ་ཀློག་འདོན་སྒོམ་པ་སོགས་ཀྱིས་ཉམས་སུ་ལེན་གནང་སྲོལ་ཡོད་མོད། དེའི་དུས་སུ་ཉི་མ་རེ་རེ་བཞིན་དུ་ཐུན་བཞི་རེ་དགོས་པ་ལ། དེ་ནི་བླ་མའི་རྣལ་འབྱོར་འདི་ཉིད་དང་། དེ་མིན་འོག་ཏུ་ལོགས་སུ་ཡོད་པའི་བླ་མའི་རྣལ་འབྱོར་གཉིས་ཡོད་པ་དང་གསུམ་ག་ཐུན་རེ་རེ་བཞིན་སྦྱ་མཐུད་དུ་རེ་མོས་བྱས་ནས་ཀློག་འདོན་དགོས་པ་ལས། གསུམ་ག་ཐུན་རེ་རེ་ལ་ཀློག་འདོན་མི་དགོས། མི་སྐྱ་ཕོ་མོ་ལ་སོགས་པ་དུས་ཚོད་མང་དུ་མེད་པ་དག་གིས་ཀྱང་ཉིན་རེར་ཐུན་གཅིག་གམ། མ་མཐའ་ལ་གཟའ་འཁོར་རེར་ཐུན་རེ་ལས་བྱེད་མི་ཁེམ་མཁན་ཞིག་ཡིན་ཡང་། བླ་མའི་རྣལ་འབྱོར་གསུམ་པོ་རེ་མོས་བྱས་ཏེ་སྔོན་འགྲོའི་ངག་འདོན་གྱི་གཞུང་ཁོག་ཏུ་སྦྲད་ན་ཆོག་པར་སེམས།

བླ་རྣམ་འདི་ཉིད་སྒོམ་འདོན་བྱེད་དུས་བསྒོམ་བྱའི་བླ་མ་ནི། ངོ་བོ་རང་ཉིད་ལ་གསང་ཆེན་སྔགས་ཀྱི་དབང་ལུང་མན་ངག་གི་ཁྲིད་རྣམས་གནང་མཁན་གྱི་རྩ་བའི་བླ་མ་ཉིད་གཙོ་བོར་བཞག་དེ། ངོ་བོ་བླ་མ་དེ་ཉིད་ཡིན་པ་ལ། རྣམ་པ་ཆོས་སྐུ་རྡོ་རྗེ་འཆང་གི་རྣམ་པ་ཅན་དང་། ཡང་ན་རང་ཉིད་རྩ་བའི་བླ་མ་ལ་ཆེས་ཁྱད་དུ་འཕགས་པའི་ཐུན་མོང་མ་ཡིན་པའི་དད་པ་དང་དག་སྣང་ཡོད་མཁན་ཞིག་ཡིན་ན། བླ་མ་སྐུ་དངོས་ཀྱི་རྣམ་པར་བསྒོམ་ན་མི་ཆོག་པ་མེད། དེའི་སྐོར་རྒྱས་པ་འོག་ནས་འབྱུང་ངོ༎

ལྔ་པ་བླ་མའི་རྣལ་འབྱོར་སྒོམ་པ།

བླ་མའི་རྣལ་འབྱོར་སྒོམ་པ་ནི། སྔོན་འགྲོ་དག་གི་ཁྲིད་ནས་དངོས་གཞི་ལྟ་བུར་ཆགས་ཡོད། རྒྱུ་མཚན་ནི། བླ་མའི་རྣལ་འབྱོར་གྱི་སྐབས་སུ་བླ་མ་ནི་དཀྱིལ་འཁོར་གྱི་གཙོ་བོ་དང་། སངས་རྒྱས་ཀུན་གྱི་ཁྱབ་བདག་དང་། མ་ཟད་འཁོར་འདས་ཀུན་གྱི་སྤྱི་དཔལ་སོགས་ཡིན་པར་ཤེས་དགོས་ལ་བསྒོམ་ཡང་དགོས་

པའི་ཕྱིར། དག་སྣང་གཞི་ལ་བཞག་པའི་ཉམས་ལེན་ཡིན་པས། གསང་བ་སྔགས་ཀྱི་དངོས་གཞི་དག་དང་མཐུན་པར་གྱུར་པས་སོ།། ཉམས་ལེན་འདིའི་དངོས་བསྟན་གཙོ་བོ་ནི་རྩ་བ་དང་བརྒྱུད་པའི་བླ་མ་རྣམས་དང་། ལྷག་པར་དུ་རྩ་བའི་བླ་མ་གཅིག་པུ་ལ་བསྟེན་ན། ཚེ་གཅིག་ལ་འཚང་རྒྱ་བའི་གོ་འཕང་བརྙེས་ཐུབ་ཅིང་། གཞན་ཅི་ཡང་མི་དགོས་པའི་དོན་རེད། མི་འགའ་ཞིག་ལ་བླ་མ་སངས་རྒྱས་ལས་ཀྱང་ལྷག་པར་བསམ་བློ་འཁོར་ཐུབ་དཀའ་བ་ཞིག་ཡིན། རྒྱུ་མཚན་ནི། བླ་མ་ལ་རྫུ་འཕྲུལ་དང་མངོན་ཤེས་ཡོད་པར་སྣང་དཀའ་བ་དང་། ནད་ལ་སོགས་མི་འདོད་པ། སྐྱེ་འཆི་དང་བཀྲེས་ཀྲུད་ཡོད་པར་སྣང་བ། མ་ཟད་ཚོར་བ་བདེ་སྡུག་སོགས་ཀྱང་ཡོད། ཧོབ་ཏེ་ལྟ་དུས་བླ་མ་ནི་སོ་སོའི་སྐྱེ་བོ་རང་བཞིན་པ་ཞིག་ལས་ཁྱད་ཆོས་ཤིག་མཐོང་དཀའ་བས་རེད། ཡིན་ནའང་། དེའི་གནད་འགག་ནི། གཅིག་ནས་དག་སྣང་འཆར་དཀའ་ཞིང་། འཆར་མི་ཐུབ་པ་ཞིག་ཡིན་ཡང་། སློབ་མ་གང་ཞིག་ལ་དག་སྣང་འཆར་ཐུབ་སོང་ན། དེས་གསང་སྔགས་ཀྱི་ལམ་དེ་ཉིད་ཁྱད་འཕགས་སུ་གྱུར་པས་རེད་ལ། དེ་འདྲ་མ་ཐུབ་ན་ཁྱད་དུ་འཕགས་པར་མི་འགྱུར་བ་རེད། གཉིས་ནས་བླ་མ་ཟེར་དུས་རང་ལ་ཆོས་གསུང་མཁན་གྱི་མི་རང་བཞིན་པ་འདི་ཁོ་ན་ཡིན་པར་བློ་ཡིས་ཆུང་ལྟ་དང་ཆུང་བཟུང་མི་བྱེད་པར། སྣང་ཚུལ་སོ་སྐྱེ་རང་བཞིན་པ་ཏུ་སྣང་མིན་ལ་མ་ལྟོས་པར། སེམས་ཀྱིས་འཛིན་ཚུལ་གྱིས་བླ་མ་ཁོ་ན་ལས་རང་ལ་ཟབ་རྒྱས་མན་ངག་གི་བརྒྱུད་པ་རྣམས་བྱུང་བ་རྒྱུ་མཚན་དུ་བྱས་ཏེ། སངས་རྒྱས་ཀུན་གྱིས་རང་ལ་དངོས་སུ་གནང་མ་བྱུང་བ་དེ་དག་བླ་མས་གནང་བ་ཡིན་པས། དམིགས་བསལ་དུ་བླ་མ་ནི་རང་ལ་འབྲེལ་བ་དང་བཀའ་དྲིན་གཉིས་ཕྱོགས་ནས་ཁྱད་དུ་འཕགས་ཡོད་པ་ཤེས་དགོས། མ་ཚད་བླ་མ་ལ་ཐུག་དུས་སྣང་ཚུལ་གཙོ་བོར་མི་འཛིན་པར་དག་སྣང་གཙོ་བོར་གཟུང་དགོས། དེ་འདྲའི་འཛིན་ཚུལ་ཡང་དག་པ་ལ་གོམས་ཐུབ་ན་གསང་སྔགས་ཀྱི་ཁྱད་ཆོས་ལེན་ཐུབ་པ་ལས། རྣམ་རྟོག་སྣ་ཚོགས་ཀྱིས་བླ་མ་འདི་བ་ལ་དག་སྣང་བསྒོམ་ཐུབ་དང་། ག་བ་ལ་མི་ཐུབ་སོགས་བསམ་ན། གསང་སྔགས་ཀྱི་ཟབ་དོན་རྟོགས་པའི་གནས་མེད། དེ་ཡང་སུ་ཡིན་ལ་མིག་མེད་ཀྱུ་མཆོང་གིས་བླ་མའི་འདུ་ཤེས་བཞག་དགོས་པའི་དོན་མ་རེད་དེ། ཐོག་མར་རང་གིས་ཕ་རོལ་བའི་བླ་མ་དེ་ཉིད་ཀྱི་གདམས་ངག་ལ་མཐོང་ཆེན་བྱེད་པའི་སྒོ་ནས་རང་ཉིད་ཆོས་ཀྱི་སྣོད་ལྡན་བྱེད། དེ་རྗེས་ཕ་རོལ་བའི་བླ་མ་ལས་བློ་སྐྱེད་ཆུང་དུ་ལས་མ་ཐོན་ཡང་། གཙིགས་ཆེན་དུ་བཟུང་། དེའི་མི་ཚད་ཁོང་ཉིད་རང་གི་དགེ་བའི་བཤེས་གཉེན་ནམ། བླ་མའི་འདུ་ཤེས་བཞག གང་ལྟར་ཁོང་ལ་མཐོང་ཐུབ་པའི་ཡོན་ཏན་ཆུང་དུ་འདི་ཙམ་གྱིས་མི་ཚད་པར་ཡོན་ཏན་གྱི་མཛོད་དུ་ཡིད་ཆེས་བསྐྱུན་ཅི་ཐུབ་བྱ། དེ་གཅིག་པོ་མ་ཡིན་པར་ཁོང་དང་རང་ཉིད་གཉིས་བར་གྱི་འབྲེལ་བ་དེ་ཉིད། དམ་པའི་ཆོས་ཀྱི་འབྲེལ་བ་ཆགས་ཡོད་པས། དེ་ཉིད་ལམ་འགྲོ་ཡག་པོར་སོང་ན། རྣམ་གྲོལ་གཏན་གྱི་བདེ་བ་འཐོབ་བྱེད་ཡིན་པས། རང་ཉིད་ལ་སྣང་ཚུལ་ཙམ་དུ་མི་འཛིན་པར་བཀའ་དྲིན་ཆེས་ཆེན་པོ་ཏུ་འཛིན་ཅི་ཐུབ་བྱེད་ནུས་ན། ལེགས་ཚོགས་ཐམས་ཅད་འགྲུབ་པའི་

གཞི་རྩ་བརྟན་ཐུབ་པའི་རྒྱུ་མཚན་གྱིས་བླ་མའི་རྣལ་འབྱོར་འདི་གལ་ཆེ་བ་རེད། དེ་འདྲ་བསམ་མ་ཐུབ་ན། རང་བཞིན་གྱི་མི་དང་མིའི་བར་གྱི་འབྲེལ་བ་ལས་གཞན་འདུ་ཤེས་ཅི་ཡང་མེད་པས། དེ་ལ་འབྲས་བུ་ཆེན་པོ་ཞིག་འབྱུང་རྒྱུ་ཡོད་པར་ངོས་འཛིན་བྱས་ན་ནོར་བ་མིན་ནམ་སྙམ། མ་ཟད་ད་དུང་དེ་ལས་ཀྱང་ལམ་ལོག་པར་གཏོང་བའི་རྒྱུ་རྐྱེན་དུའང་འགྱུར་མི་སྲིད་པ་མིན་ནོ།།

> སྐྱབས་སེམས་སོགས་སྔར་བཞིན། གནས་ཁང་དག་པའི་ཞིང་དུ་གསལ་བའི་དབུས་སུ། སེང་ཁྲི་པདྨ་ཉི་ཟླའི་གདན་ལ་རྩ་བའི་བླ་མ་ཁྱབ་བདག་རྡོ་རྗེ་འཆང་སྐུ་མདོག་སྔོན་པོ་ཞལ་གཅིག་ཕྱག་གཉིས་པ། རྡོ་རྗེ་དང་དྲིལ་བུ་ཐུགས་ཀར་བསྣོལ་ནས་བཟུང་བ། ཞབས་རྡོ་རྗེ་སྐྱིལ་མོ་ཀྲུང་གིས་བཞུགས་པ། དར་དང་རིན་པོ་ཆེའི་རྒྱན་ཐམས་ཅད་ཀྱིས་བརྒྱན་པ། མཚན་དཔེ་ཡོངས་སུ་རྫོགས་ཤིང་། རང་ལ་དགྱེས་པའི་ཞལ་འཛུམ་བག་དང་ལྡན་པ། འོད་དང་འོད་ཟེར་གྱི་ཚོགས་མཐའ་ཡས་པ་འཕྲོ་བའི་སྐུ་ཅན། མཐའ་སྐོར་དུ་བརྒྱུད་པའི་བླ་མ་རྣམས་དང་། ཡི་དམ་དཀྱིལ་འཁོར་གྱི་ལྷ་ཚོགས། སངས་རྒྱས་བྱང་སེམས། འཕགས་པ་ཉན་རང་། མཁའ་འགྲོ་ཆོས་སྐྱོང་སྲུང་མ་ཐམས་ཅད་བཞུགས་པར་མོས། དངོས་བཤམས་ཡིད་སྤྲུལ་གྱི་མཆོད་པ་བསམ་གྱིས་མི་ཁྱབ་པ་བློས་ཕུལ་ཏེ་དད་པ་ཤུགས་དྲག་པོས་གསོལ་བ་འདེབས་པ་ནི།

ཞེས་པ་འདིའི་སྐབས་བཞིན་དུ། བླ་མའི་རྣལ་འབྱོར་ཁོ་ན་ཉམས་ལེན་དངོས་གཞི་བྱེད་པའི་སྐབས་ཡིན་ཡང་། སྐྱབས་སེམས་གཉིས་དང་། རྡོར་སེམས་སྒོམ་བཟླས། མཎྜལ་ཀུན་བསྡུས་པ་ཞིག་སྔོན་དུ་འགྲོ་དགོས་པ་ནི་སྔར་ཡང་ཡང་བཤད་པ་དེ་བཞིན་ཡིན་ནོ།། དེ་ནས་དང་པོ་རྩ་བརྒྱུད་ཀྱི་བླ་མ་དག་བསྒོམ་ཡུལ་གྱི་གནས་ཁང་ལ་སོགས་པ་ནི། རང་ཅག་སོ་སྐྱེ་རྣམས་ཀྱི་གནས་སྐབས་ཀུན་རྫོབ་ཀྱི་སྣང་བ་འདི་དག་ལྟ་བུ་མ་ཡིན་པར། མ་མཐའ་ཡང་། དག་པའི་ཞིང་ཁམས་ཡིད་དུ་འོང་བ་ཞིག་ཡིན་སྙམ་པའི་འདུན་པ་ཤུགས་དྲག་པོའི་སྒོ་ནས། དག་པའི་གཞལ་མེད་ཁང་གསལ་ཅི་ཐུབ་ཞིག་གསལ་བཏབ། གཞལ་མེད་ཁང་དེའི་དབུས་སུ། སེངྒེ་བརྒྱད་ཀྱིས་བཏེགས་པའི་ཁྲི་ཡི་ཐོག་ཏུ་པདྨ་འདབ་མ་སྟོང་ལྡན་གྱི་གདན། དེའི་སྟེང་དུ་ཉི་མའི་གདན། དེའི་སྟེང་དུ་ཟླ་བའི་གདན་ལ་སོགས་པ་བསྒོམ། གདན་དེ་དག་གི་སྟེང་དུ་ངོ་བོ་རྩ་བའི་བླ་མ་ཡིན་པ་ལ། རྣམ་པ་ཁྱབ་བདག་རྡོ་རྗེ་འཆང་གི་རྣམ་པ་སྐུ་མདོག་སྔོན་པོ་ཞལ་གཅིག་ཕྱག་གཉིས་པ། རྡོ་རྗེ་དང་དྲིལ་བུ་ཐུགས་ཀར་བསྣོལ་ནས་བཟུང་བ། ཞབས་རྡོ་རྗེ་སྐྱིལ་མོ་ཀྲུང་གིས་བཞུགས་པ། དར་གྱི་ཚས་གོས་ལྟ་སྟེ། དར་གྱི་སྟོད་གཡོགས། སྨད་གཡོགས། དར་གྱི་ཐུ་དུང་། སྐ་རགས། དར་དཔྱངས་སོགས་དང་། ལོངས་སྐུའི་རྒྱན་ཆ་བརྒྱད་དེ་རིན་པོ་ཆེ་དང་མེ་ཏོག་གི་ཆོམ་བུའི་དབུ་རྒྱན། སྙན་རྒྱན། མགུལ་རྒྱན། དོ་ཤལ། དཔུང་རྒྱན། སེ་མོ་དོ། ཕྱག་གདུབ། ཞབས་གདུབ་སོགས་རྒྱན་ཐམས་ཅད་ཀྱིས་བརྒྱན་པ། མཚན་བཟང་པོ་སོ་གཉིས་དང་། དཔེ་བྱད་བཟང་པོ་བརྒྱད་ཅུ་ཡོངས་སུ་རྫོགས་ཤིང་།

སྒྲོན་མེད་རབ་གསལ་སྣང་བ།

རང་ལ་ཐུགས་བརྩེ་བ་ཆེན་པོས། དགྱེས་པའི་ཞལ་འཛུམ་བག་དང་ལྡན་པ། ཟབ་མེད་ཀྱི་འོད་དང་འོད་ཟེར་གྱི་ཚོགས་མཐའ་ཡས་པ་འཕྲོ་བའི་སྐུ་ཅན་ཞིག་ཏུ་བསྒོམས་ཤིང་མོས། དེ་ནས་བླ་མ་དེའི་མཐའ་སྐོར་དུ་བརྒྱུད་པའི་བླ་མ་རྣམས་ཁྲ་སྤུང་ངེ་། འོད་འཕིགས་སེ་བཞུགས་པར་མོས། དེ་དག་གི་མཐའ་སྐོར་དག་ཏུ་ཡི་དམ་དཀྱིལ་འཁོར་གྱི་ལྷ་ཚོགས་རྣམས་དང་། སངས་རྒྱས་དང་བྱང་ཆུབ་སེམས་དཔའ་རྣམས་དང་། ཐེག་དམན་དུ་འབོད་པ། ཐེག་པ་ཐུན་མོང་གི་འཕགས་པ་ཉན་ཐོས་དང་། རང་རྒྱལ་གྱི་ཚོགས་དང་བཅས་པའི་འཕགས་ཚོགས་རྣམས་དང་། མཁའ་འགྲོ་ཆོས་སྐྱོང་སྲུང་མ་ཐམས་ཅད་མཐའ་སྐོར་ཀུན་ཏུ་བཞུགས་པར་མོས་གུས་ཤུགས་དྲག་པོ་བསྐྱེད། བླ་མ་ལ་རྒྱུན་དུ་དངོས་བཤམས་ཀྱི་མཆོད་པ་གོ་སྐབས་དམ་འཛིན་གྱི་སྒོ་ནས་གང་དག་ལ་མཁོ་ཆེ་བའི་ཡོ་བྱད་དག་འབུལ། མ་ཟད་ཡིད་ཀྱིས་སྤྲུལ་བའི་མཆོད་པ་བསམ་གྱིས་མི་ཁྱབ་པ་གོང་དུ་མཚུལ་ཀྱི་སྐབས་རྣམས་སུ་ཅི་ལྟར་གསུངས་པ་ལྟ་བུ་རྣམས་ཡིད་ལ་ཤར་བར་བྱས། དེ་ལས་ཀྱང་ལྷག་པའི་མཆོད་པ་དག རང་གི་བློས་དཔོག་ཚོད་ཀྱིས་ཡིད་ངོར་ཤར་བར་བྱས་ཏེ་ཕུལ་ནས། གཞན་སུ་དང་གང་གིས་མཆོད་པ་རང་ལས་ལྷག་པ་འབུལ་བ། ཡང་ན་འདྲ་མཉམ་དུ་ཕུལ་བ་ལ་སོགས་པ་ལ་རྗེས་སུ་ཡི་རང་དང་། མོས་གུས་དད་འདུན་ཡི་རང་དང་བཅས། དད་འདུན་གདུང་ཤུགས་དྲག་པོས་རྩ་བརྒྱུད་ཀྱི་བླ་མར་གསོལ་བ་འདེབས་པ་ནི་འདི་ལྟར།

བླ་མ་རེ་རེ་བཞིན་གྱི་བླ་མའི་རྣལ་འབྱོར་དངོས་ནི།
དྲིན་ཅན་རྩ་བའི་བླ་མ་རིན་པོ་ཆེ།།
སྲིད་དང་ཞི་བའི་ཕུན་ཚོགས་མ་ལུས་པ།།
མགོན་པོ་ཁྱོད་ཀྱི་ཐུགས་རྗེའི་སྟོབས་ལས་བྱུང་།།
དགོས་འདོད་ཀུན་འབྱུང་ཁྱེད་ལ་གསོལ་བ་འདེབས།།

བཀའ་དྲིན་གཞལ་མཐའ་བྲལ་བའི་དྲིན་ཅན། ཐད་ཀར་དུ་རང་ཉིད་ལ་ཆོས་དང་དམ་ཚིག་གིས་འབྲེལ་བའི་རྩ་བའི་བླ་མ། བླ་མ་ནི་རིན་ཐང་གཞལ་མཐའ་བྲལ་བས་རིན་པོ་ཆེ་ཡིད་བཞིན་གྱི་ནོར་བུ་དབང་གི་རྒྱལ་པོ་ལས་ཀྱང་གཞལ་དུ་མེད་པ། སྲིད་པ་འཁོར་བ་དང་ཞི་བ་མྱང་འདས་གཉིས་ཀྱི་ཕུན་ཚོགས་མ་ལུས་པའི་འབྱུང་གནས། སྡུག་བསྔལ་མཐའ་དག་ལས་སྐྱོབ་པའི་སྐྱབས་དམ་པའམ། ལེགས་པའི་ལམ་དུ་འཁྲིད་མཁན་གྱི་མགོན་པོ། ཁྱོད་ཀྱི་ཐུགས་རྗེའི་མཁྱེན་བརྩེ་བླ་ན་མེད་པའི་སྟོབས་ལས་མ་བྱུང་བའི་ལེགས་ཚོགས་ཅི་ཡང་མེད་པ། འགྲོ་བ་ཀུན་གྱི་དགོས་འདོད་ཀུན་ཏུ་འབྱུང་བས་ཡིད་བཞིན་གྱི་ནོར་བུ་ཁྱེད་ལ་སྙིང་ཁོང་རུས་པའི་གཏིང་ནས་གསོལ་བ་འདེབས་སོ།།

ཀུན་ཁྱབ་བདེ་ཆེན་དང་པོའི་རྫོགས་སངས་རྒྱས།།
འོག་མིན་གནས་སུ་ཆོས་སྐུ་རྡོ་རྗེ་འཆང་།།
ལོངས་སྐུ་དུས་འཁོར་སྤྲུལ་སྐུ་ཤཱཀྱའི་ཏོག །
བཞི་ལྡན་སྐུ་བཞིའི་ཚོགས་ལ་གསོལ་བ་འདེབས།།

འཁོར་འདས་ཀུན་ལ་ཆོས་ཉིད་ཀྱི་ཚུལ་དུ་ཁྱབ་ཅིང་། བདེ་བ་ཆེན་པོའི་ཡེ་ཤེས་དང་པོའི་སངས་རྒྱས་དུས་ཀྱི་འཁོར་ལོ་རྫོགས་པའི་སངས་རྒྱས་ཀུན་འདུས་ཏེ། འོག་མིན་སྟུག་པོ་བཀོད་པའི་གནས་མཆོག་ཏུ་ཆོས་སྐུ་རྡོ་རྗེ་འཆང་གི་མཚན་གྱིས་བསྟན་པ། འཁོར་ངེས་པ་ལྷ་ལྡན་གྱི་ཞིང་མཆོག་དག་ཏུ་ལོངས་སྐུ་དུས་ཀྱི་འཁོར་ལོ་མཆོག་དང་། མི་མཇེད་འཇིག་རྟེན་གྱི་ཞིང་ཁམས་སུ་མཆོག་གི་སྤྲུལ་སྐུ་ཤཱཀྱ་ཐུབ་པར་ཤར་བ། ཤཱཀྱའི་རིགས་རྣམས་ཀྱི་ཕུལ་དང་ཏོག་ལྟར་དུ་གྱུར་པ། སོཨུ་ཧླ་ཏི་གཽཨུ་ཏ་མ་མཆོག་སྟེ། སྐུ་བཞིའི་བདག་ཉིད་ཀྱི་ཚོགས་འདུས་པ་བླ་མ་དམ་པ་ཉིད་ལ་དད་འདུན་དང་བ་ཆེན་པོས་གསོལ་བ་འདེབས་སོ།།

རྒྱལ་བའི་རྣམ་སྤྲུལ་ཆོས་རྒྱལ་སུམ་ཅུ་ལྔ།།
མཁས་གྲུབ་དམ་པ་དུས་ཞབས་ཆེ་ཆུང་གཉིས།།
པཎ་ཆེན་ནཱ་ལེནྡྲ་དང་བླ་མགོན་ཞབས།།
ཆོས་རྒྱལ་ལོ་པཎ་རྣམས་ལ་གསོལ་བ་འདེབས།།

རྒྱལ་བ་རྫོགས་པའི་སངས་རྒྱས་རྣམས་ཀྱི་རྣམ་པར་སྤྲུལ་པའི་ཟློས་གར། བྱང་ཤམྦྷ་ལའི་ཆོས་རྒྱལ་ཟླ་བ་བཟང་པོ་དང་། དེའི་རྗེས་ཀྱི་ཆོས་རྒྱལ་བདུན་དང་རིགས་ལྡན་ཉེར་ལྔ། རྒྱལ་སྲས་གཉིས་བཅས་ཆོས་རྒྱལ་སུམ་ཅུ་རྩ་ལྔ་ལ། དད་འདུན་གདུང་ཤུགས་དྲག་པོས་གསོལ་བ་འདེབས་སོ་ཞེས་པ་ལ་སོགས་པའི་དོན་ཏེ། ཞིང་མཆོག་ཤམྦྷ་ལའི་རྫོགས་ལྡན་ཡོངས་སྐུའི་ཟབ་ཆོས་དཔལ་དུས་ཀྱི་འཁོར་ལོའི་རྒྱུད་ཞུ་བ་པོ་ཆོས་རྒྱལ་ཟླ་བ་བཟང་པོ་དང་། ༡ རྒྱལ་པོ་ཟླ་བ། ༢ ལྷ་དབང་། ༣ གཟི་བརྗིད་ཅན། ༤ ཟླ་བའི་བྱིན། ལྷའི་དབང་ཕྱུག ༦ སྣ་ཚོགས་གཟུགས། ༧ ལྷའི་དབང་ལྡན་རྣམས་དང་། བྱང་ཤམྦྷ་ལའི་རིགས་ཐམས་ཅད་གསང་ཆེན་སྔགས་སུ་གཅིག་ཏུ་བསྡུ་བ་པོ། ༡ རིགས་ལྡན་འཇམ་དཔལ་གྲགས་པ། དེ་ནས་རིམ་པ་བཞིན་དེའི་བརྒྱུད་འཛིན་པ། ༢ པདྨ་དཀར་པོ། ༣ བཟང་པོ། ༤ རྣམ་རྒྱལ། ༥ བཤེས་གཉེན་བཟང་པོ། ༦ རིན་ཆེན་ཕྱུག ༧ ཁྱབ་འཇུག་སྦས་པ། ༨ ཉི་མ་གྲགས། ༩ ཤིན་ཏུ་བཟང་། ༡༠ རྒྱ་མཚོ་རྣམ་རྒྱལ། ༡༡ རྒྱལ་དཀའ། ༡༢ ཉི་མ། ༡༣ སྣ་ཚོགས་གཟུགས། ༡༤ ཟླ་བའི་འོད། ༡༥ མཐའ་ཡས། ༡༦ ས་སྐྱོང་། ༡༧ དཔལ་སྐྱོང་། ༡༨ སེངྒེ། ༡༩ རྣམ་པར་གནོན། ༢༠ སྟོབས་པོ་ཆེ། ༢༡ མ་འགགས་པ། ༢༢

མི་ཡི་སེངྒེ། ༢༣ དབང་ཕྱུག་ཆེན་པོ། ༢༤ མཐའ་ཡས་རྣམ་རྒྱལ། ༢༥ རིགས་ལྡན་དྲག་པོ་འཁོར་ལོ་ཅན་གྱི་བར་ཉེར་ལྔ་དང་། དེའི་སྟེང་དུ་ཆོས་རྒྱལ་བདུན་བརྩིས་པས་སོ་གཉིས། དེའི་སྟེང་དུ་དཔལ་དུས་ཀྱི་འཁོར་ལོའི་རྒྱུད་ཞུ་བ་པོ་ཆོས་རྒྱལ་ཟླ་བ་བཟང་པོ་དང་། རིགས་ལྡན་ཉེར་ལྔ་བ་དྲག་པོ་འཁོར་ལོ་ཅན་གྱི་སྲས་ ༡ ཚངས་པ་དང་། ༢ ལྷ་དབང་གཉིས་བཅས་ཆོས་རྒྱལ་སུམ་ཅུ་རྩ་ལྔ་དང་། ཡང་ན་རྒྱུད་ཞུ་བ་པོ་ཟླ་བཟང་མ་བརྩིས་པར། རིགས་ལྡན་ཉེར་ལྔ་བའི་སྲས་ལྷ་དབང་རྒྱུད་ཀྱི་སྲས་འོད་སྲུང་བསྣན་ནས་སོ་ལྔ་བགྲང་མཁན་ཡང་ཡོད། གང་ལྟར་ཆོས་རྒྱལ་རིགས་ལྡན་དེ་དག་ལ་བཅོས་མིན་དད་འདུན་ཞུས་པ་ཆེན་པོས་གསོལ་བ་འདེབས་སོ།།

དེ་ནས་རེས་གསང་ཤམྦྷ་ལའི་ཟབ་ཆོས་འཛིན་རྟེན་མི་ཡུལ་དུ་འདྲེན་པ་པོ། གྲུབ་པའི་དབང་ཕྱུག་དུས་ཞབས་པ་ཆེན་པོ། རྒྱ་གར་ལྷོ་ཕྱོགས་ཨ་ཏ་ཞེས་པར་འཁྲུངས། མཚན་དུ་མཉྫུ་བཛྲ། བོད་སྐད་དུ་འཇམ་པའི་རྡོ་རྗེར་གྲགས། རིགས་ལྡན་གྱི་སྤྲུལ་པ་དང་མཇལ། དབང་བསྐུར་ཞིང་ཟབ་མོའི་རྣལ་འབྱོར་ཟླ་བ་དྲུག་ལ་བསྒོམས་པས་རྫུ་འཕྲུལ་གྱིས་ཤམྦྷ་ལར་བྱོན། རིགས་ལྡན་དངོས་དང་མཇལ། དུས་འཁོར་སོགས་རྒྱུད་སྡེ་མང་པོ་དང་། སེམས་འགྲེལ་སྐོར་གསུམ་སོགས་ཟབ་བཀའ་རྣམས་མི་ཡུལ་དུ་དྲངས་ཏེ་སྤེལ། མཐར་འཇའ་ལུས་སུ་གཤེགས། རྗོགས་ལྡན་ཤམྦྷ་ལའི་ཟབ་ཆོས་དུས་ཀྱི་འཁོར་ལོ་འཛམ་གླིང་འདིར་ནང་འདྲེན་ཁོ་ན་ཡིན་པས། མཚན་གྲུབ་ཆེན་དུས་ཞབས་པ་ཆེན་མོ་རུ་གྲགས་པའི་ཞབས་ཀྱི་པདྨོ་ལ་སྒོ་གསུམ་དང་བ་ཆེན་པོས་གསོལ་བ་འདེབས་སོ།།

དམ་པ་དེའི་ཐུགས་སྲས་མཆོག་ཤྲཱི་བྷ་དྲའམ་དུས་ཞབས་ཆུང་བ། པ་རོལ་སྨྲ་བ་ཟིལ་གྱིས་གནོན། མངོན་ཤེས་རྫུ་འཕྲུལ་ཐོགས་པ་མེད་ཅིང་། མུ་སྟེགས་པའི་ལྟ་བ་ཚར་བཅད་ཅིང་། ཁྱད་པར་དུ་དཔལ་དུས་ཀྱི་འཁོར་ལོའི་ཟབ་ཆོས་སྙན་ནས་སྙན་དུ་བརྒྱུད་པའི་སྐལ་བཟང་འདྲེན་མཁན་ཐུགས་ཀྱི་ས་བཅུ་གཉིས་ཐོབ་ཅིང་། ཟབ་ཆོས་ཀྱི་ཡང་དག་པའི་བརྒྱུད་འཛིན་གཉིས་པ་དཔལ་ནཱ་རོ་བ་ལ་སོགས་པའི་སློབ་བརྒྱུད་ཅན། གྲུབ་ཆེན་དུས་ཀྱི་འཁོར་ལོའི་སྐུ་ཞབས་པ་གཉིས་པ་རུ་གྲགས་པ་དེ་ལ་སྒོ་གསུམ་གུས་པས་གསོལ་བ་འདེབས་སོ།།

གྲུབ་ཆེན་ཤྲཱི་བྷ་དྲའི་ཐུགས་སྲས་བོ་དྷི་བྷ་དྲའམ་བོད་སྐད་དུ་བྱང་ཆུབ་བཟང་པོ། ཕྱི་ནང་གཉིས་ཀྱི་ཆོས་ལ་ཤིན་ཏུ་མཁས་ཤིང་། ནང་བའི་ཆོས་ཡོད་དོ་ཅོག་ལ་མཁས་པས་དཔལ་ན་ལེནྡྲའི་གནས་གཞིའི་བདག་པོར་གྱུར། ལས་བཞི་གང་སྒྲུབ་ཀྱང་རླུང་གི་རྣལ་འབྱོར་ཁོ་ནས་འགྲུབ་པར་ངེས་སོ།། ལྷག་པར་དུ་དཔལ་དུས་ཀྱི་འཁོར་ལོའི་ཟབ་ཆོས་ཐུགས་དམ་དུ་བཞུང་བའི་བརྒྱུད་འཛིན་མཆོག རྫོགས་པའི་སངས་རྒྱས་

ཀྱི་ཐུགས་སྲས་སུ་གྱུར་པ། མཚན་རྒྱལ་སྲས་ནཱ་ལེནྡྲ་པའམ་ཛྙོ་ཧྲི་ཛྷ་དྲ་ལ་དད་འདུན་གུས་པ་ཆེན་པོས་གསོལ་བ་འདེབས་སོ།།

རྒྱ་གར་ཁ་ཆེའི་རིགས་དང་ཆོས་ལུགས་སུ་སྐུ་འཁྲུངས་པས་ཕྱི་རོལ་བའི་གཞུང་ལུགས་མཐར་ཕྱིན་པ། མདོ་སྡེ་སྐྱིད་འདུས་ལས་ངེས་དོན་བསྟན་པའི་བརྒྱུད་འཛིན་ཡང་དག་ཏུ་ལུང་གིས་ཟིན་པ། མ་ཕྱུམ་ནང་བ་སངས་རྒྱས་པ་ལ་མོས་པ་ཆེ་བས་མ་ཕྱུམ་གྱིས་བསྐུལ་ཏེ་ནང་བའི་གཞུང་ལ་སྦྱངས་པས་མཐར་ཕྱིན་ནས་པཎྜི་ཏ་མཆོག་ཏུ་གྱུར་པ། ལྷག་པར་དུ་དཔལ་དུས་ཀྱི་འཁོར་ལོའི་ཟབ་ཆོས་ཀྱིས་རིགས་སད་པ། དབུགས་ཐེངས་རེ་ལ་ཤློ་ཀ་བཅུ་དྲུག་ཙམ་ཟིན་པ། དུས་འཁོར་རྫོགས་རིམ་གྱི་སྦྱོག་འཛིན་མཐར་ཕྱིན་ནས་སྐུ་ལ་བཤད་གཅིའི་རྒྱ་བ་ཆད་པ། རྗེ་རིགས་ལྡན་གྱི་སྤྲུལ་པས་བོད་དུ་གདུལ་བྱ་ཡོད་པར་ལུང་བསྟན་པ། རྫོགས་ལྡན་དུས་ཀྱི་འཁོར་ལོའི་ཟབ་ཆོས་བོད་གངས་ཅན་དུ་འདྲེན་པའི་མགོན་པོ་མཆོག་ལ་བཀའ་དྲིན་སྙིང་དུ་བཅངས་ཏེ་གསོལ་བ་ལན་སྙིང་དུ་འདེབས་སོ།།

སྒྲ་སྒྱུར་འབྲོ་སྟོན་ལོ་ཙཱ་བའམ་མཚན་གཞན་འབྲོ་ལོ་ཙཱ་བ་ཤེས་རབ་གྲགས་པ། དཔལ་དང་འབྱོར་བའི་ལོངས་སྤྱོད་ཐམས་ཅད་དམ་ཆོས་ཟབ་མོ་ཁོ་ནའི་ཡོན་དུ་ཕུལ་ཞིང་། པཎ་ཆེན་ཟླ་མགོན་གྱི་མདུན་ནས་དཔལ་དུས་ཀྱི་འཁོར་ལོའི་ཆོས་ཟབ་རྒྱས་ཡོངས་སུ་རྫོགས་པ། གངས་རིའི་ཁྲོད་དུ་སྒྲུབ་བརྒྱུད་དུས་ཀྱི་འཁོར་ལོའི་བཀའ་ཐོག་མར་བབས་པ། དཔལ་མཆོག་དུས་ཀྱི་འཁོར་ལོའི་རྫོགས་ལྡན་ཟབ་ཆོས་སྐད་གཉིས་སྨྲ་བའི་སྒྲ་སྒྱུར་ཤིང་རྟ་ཆེན་པོ། འབྲོ་ལོ་ཙཱ་བ་ཤེས་རབ་གྲགས་པ་ལ་དད་འདུན་གདུང་ཤུགས་དྲག་པོས་གསོལ་བ་འདེབས་སོ།།

འགྲོ་བའི་སྐྱབས་གནས་སྒོམ་པ་དཀོན་མཆོག་བཟང་།།
ཟབ་ལམ་མཐར་ཕྱིན་སྒྲོ་སྟོན་གནམ་ལ་བརྟེགས།།
གྲུབ་ཆེན་ཡུ་མོ་ཆོས་ཀྱི་རྡོ་ཆེན་ཞབས།།
དངོས་གྲུབ་མཆོག་བརྙེས་གསུམ་ལ་གསོལ་བ་འདེབས།།

བོད་ནུབ་བརྒྱུད་འཕན་ཡུལ་དུ་སྐུ་འཁྲུངས། མཚན་གཞན་བླ་མ་ལྷ་རྗེ་སྒོམ་པ་དཀོན་མཆོག་སྙིང་དུའང་གྲགས་པ། ཁོང་གིས་ལུས་ངག་ཡིད་གསུམ་ལོངས་སྤྱོད་དང་བཅས་པ་བླ་མ་ཁ་ཆེ་པཎ་ཆེན་ཟླ་བ་མགོན་པོར་ཕངས་མེད་དུ་ཕུལ་ནས་པའི་ཟླ་གྲལ་གྱི་གཏོང་ཕོད་ལྡན་པས། པཎ་ཆེན་ཟླ་མགོན་ལས་དབང་རྒྱུད་བཤད་མན་ངག་མཐའ་དག་གསན། བླ་མའི་ཐུགས་ཟིན་ཏེ་གདམས་ངག་མ་ལུས་ཐོབ་ཅིང་། སྒྲུབ་པ་ཉམས་ལེན་བླ་ན་མེད་པའི་འབྲས་བུར་སྔགས་ཀྱི་ཡི་དམ་ཡོངས་རྫོགས་ཀྱིས་ཞལ་གཟིགས་ཤིང་ལུང་

བསྟན་ཐོབ། དམ་པའི་ཆོས་སྒྲུབ་མཁན་རྣལ་མ་མཆོག་ཏུ་གྱུར། བླ་མ་ལྷ་རྗེ་སྒོམ་པ་དགོན་མཆོག་སྐྱུང་ལ་སྒོ་གསུམ་གུས་པ་ཆེན་པོས་གསོལ་བ་འདེབས་སོ།།

སྒྲོ་སྟོན་གནམ་ལ་བརྩེགས་ནི། མཚན་གཞན་བླ་མ་སྒྲོ་སྟོན་གནམ་བརྩེགས་ཞེས་པ་དང་། ཡུལ་ཁྲིད་འཕགས་ནོར་བཟང་དུ་ཕ་མ་རིགས་བཟང་གི་སྲས་སུ་འཁྲུངས། འཁོར་བའི་ཆོས་ལ་ངེས་པར་འབྱུང་ཞིང་དམ་པའི་ཆོས་ལ་དད་བརྩོན་དྲན་པ་བརྟན་པོས་དམ་པའི་བཤེས་གཉེན་མང་དུ་བསྟེན་ཅིང་གདམས་ངག་གི་རྒྱུད་ཡོངས་སུ་གང་། པཎ་ཆེན་ཟླ་མགོན་ལས་དབང་དང་རྒྱུད་བཤད་ཡོངས་སུ་རྫོགས་པའི་ཟབ་ཆོས་དུས་ཀྱི་འཁོར་ལོ་ལ་ཉམས་ལེན་རྣལ་མ་བྱས། ལྷག་པར་ཏུ་བླ་མ་ལྷ་རྗེ་སྒོམ་པ་དགོན་མཆོག་སྐྱུང་ཡུན་རིང་བསྟེན་ནས། གདམས་ངག་མང་དུ་ཐོབ་ནས་ཉམས་ལེན་ལ་གཅིག་ཏུ་གཞོལ་བ་ཉིད་ལ་སྒོ་གསུམ་གུས་པ་ཆེན་པོས་གསོལ་བ་འདེབས་སོ།།

བླ་མ་གྲུབ་ཆེན་ཡུ་མོ་མི་བསྐྱོད་རྡོ་རྗེ་ནི་རབ་བྱུང་དང་པོའི་དུས་སུ། གངས་དཀར་ཏི་སེའི་ཟུར་བར་ཡབ་ཁྲིམས་པ་ཞེས་བྱ་དང་། ཡུམ་མཚན་ལྡན་མ་ཞིག་གི་སྲས་སུ་སྐུ་འཁྲུངས། ཁ་ཆེ་པཎ་ཆེན་ལས་ཆོས་འབྲེལ་ཙམ་ལས་མ་ཐོབ་ཀྱང་། བླ་མ་སྒྲོ་སྟོན་གནམ་བརྩེགས་མི་ལོ་ལྔར་བསྟེན། དཔལ་དུས་ཀྱི་འཁོར་ལོའི་དབང་རྒྱུད་མན་ངག་མཐའ་དག་ཉམས་སུ་བླངས། ཕྱིས་འུ་ཡུག་གི་རྒྱལ་གནས་སུ་བཞུགས། རྫུ་འཕྲུལ་མང་དུ་བསྟན་པ་ནི་ཡོངས་གྲགས་ཡིན། གཞན་སྟོང་དབུ་མའི་ལྟ་བ་དཔལ་དུས་ཀྱི་འཁོར་ལོ་སྐོགས་ཀྱི་གཞན་སྟོང་གྲུབ་མཐའི་སྲོལ་འབྱེད་པར་གྲགས། དེ་ལྟ་བུའི་གྲུབ་པའི་ཁྱུ་མཆོག་ཆེན་པོ་བླ་མ་གྲུབ་ཆེན་ཡུ་མོ་བ་རུ་གྲགས་པ་དང་། མཆོག་གི་དངོས་གྲུབ་ཐོབ་པར་གྲགས་པའི་བླ་མ་གསུམ་ལ་སྒོ་གསུམ་གུས་པ་ཆེན་པོས་གསོལ་བ་འདེབས་སོ།།

> སྤྲུལ་སྐུ་རྣམ་ཤཱ་ཀ་ར་སྲས་ཀྱི་མཆོག
> ཐོས་དོན་མཐར་ཕྱིན་མཁས་པ་ནམ་མཁའ་འོད།།
> མདོན་ཤེས་དང་ལྡན་མ་ཅིག་སེ་མོ་ཆེ།།
> ངོ་མཚར་སྐྱབས་མགོན་རྣམས་ལ་གསོལ་བ་འདེབས།།

སྤྲུལ་སྐུ་རྣམ་ཤཱ་ཀ་ར་སྟེ་ཆོས་ཀྱི་དབང་ཕྱུག་ནི། གྲུབ་ཆེན་ཡུ་མོ་བ་དགུང་ལོ་༥༠བཞེས་དུས། སྲས་སུ་ལས་སྨོན་བཟང་པོའི་མཐུ་ལས་འཁྲུངས་པར་གྲགས། ཤེས་རབ་ཤིན་ཏུ་རྣོ་བས་གྲུབ་ཆེན་ལ་མངའ་བའི་གདམས་ངག་ཐམས་ཅད་དགུང་ལོ་ཉི་ཤུ་ཚུན་ལ་ཐུགས་སུ་ཆུད། དཔྱལ་ཀུན་དགའ་རྡོ་རྗེ། བརྒྱ་གླིང་བ། ས་སྐྱ་པཎ་ཆེན་སོགས་ཀྱིས་རྩོད་ཀྱང་མ་ཐུབ། གསང་རྒྱ་དམ་པོའི་སྒོ་ནས་སྒྲུབ་པ་ཉམས་ལེན་གནད་སྨིན་

བྱས་པས་ཡབ་ཀྱི་ཐུགས་དམ་ཟིན། སྲས་ཀྱི་མཆོག་ཏུ་གྱུར་པ་ཧླཱ་མེ་ཤྭ་ར་བ་ཆེན་པོ་ལ་སྒོ་གསུམ་གུས་པ་ཆེན་པོས་གསོལ་བ་འདེབས་སོ།།

སྲས་མཆོག་ཆོས་ཀྱི་འབྱུང་གནས་ཀྱི་ཐུགས་སྲས་མཆོག་སྟེ། བུ་ཆེན་ནམ་མཁའ་འོད་ཟེར་མདོ་སྔགས་ལ་མཁས་ཤིང་གྲུབ་པའི་ཚད་དུ་བརྙེས་པ་ཞིག་བྱུང་། གྲུབ་འབྲས་སུ་འོད་ཟེར་ཕྲེང་བ་དང་བྱམས་ཆོས་སྡེ་ལྔ་ལ་ཤིན་ཏུ་མཁས་ཤིང་མཆོག་ཏུ་གྱུར་པ་དེ་ལ་དད་པ་ཆེན་པོའི་སྒོ་ནས་ཕྱག་གིས་མཆོད་དོ།།

སྲས་མོ་རྗེ་འབུམ་ནི་ཨོཌྜ་བོ་ཌྷིའི་ལྕམ་ལི་ཀཱི་ཀ་རའི་སྤྲུལ་སྐུ་ཡིན་པར་གྲགས་པ། གཟུགས་བྱད་ཤིན་ཏུ་མཛེས་ཤིང་དཀའ་སྤྱད་ཆེན་པོ་བྱུང་བས། མཐུ་དང་སྔགས་བསླབས་པས་ཀུན་གྱིས་སླགས་མི་ཚུགས་ཤིང་བཀའ་གནན་པར་གྱུར། དེ་རྗེས་དཔལ་དུས་ཀྱི་འཁོར་ལོ་ལ་སྐལ་བཟང་ཡོད་པས། སྒོམ་ཁང་དུ་ཞུགས་མ་ཐག་ལས་རླུང་དབུ་མར་རྒྱུ་འགོ་ཚུགས། རིམ་གྱིས་སྦྱོར་བ་ཡན་ལག་དྲུག་བསྒོམས་པས་ཞག་གཅིག་ལ་རྟགས་བཅུ་རྫོགས། དུས་འཁོར་རྒྱུད་འགྲེལ་ཡོངས་རྫོགས་ཐུགས་ལ་བཞུགས། ཞག་བདུན་ལ་རླུང་དབུ་མར་ཐིམ། གྲུབ་ཐོབ་ཆེན་མོར་གྱུར་པས་དཔལ་དུས་ཀྱི་འཁོར་ལོའི་བསྟན་པ་ལ་ཕན་པ་རྒྱ་ཆེན་བྱུང་། གྲུབ་པའི་དབང་ཕྱུག་མ་ཆེན་མོ་མ་ཅིག་སྤྲུལ་པའི་རྗེ་མོ་ཁྱེད་ལ་སྒོ་གསུམ་དང་བ་ཆེན་པོའི་སྒོ་ནས་གསོལ་བ་འདེབས་སོ།།

དེ་ཉིད་ཀྱི་མིང་པོ་སེ་མོ་ཆེ་བ་ནམ་མཁའ་རྒྱལ་མཚན་ཡང་། ཡན་ལག་དྲུག་བསྒོམས་པས་ཉམས་རྟོགས་དང་མཁྱེན་རབ་ནང་ནས་བརྡོལ། ནམ་མཁའ་འོད་ཟེར་ལས་རྒྱུད་འགྲེལ་དང་། རྗེ་འབུམ་ལས་དབང་མདོར་བསྟན་བཀའ་འགྲེལ་པདྨ་ཅན་གསན། རང་གི་སྐྱེ་བ་༧༨ དྲན་པ་སོགས་གྲུབ་པའི་རྟགས་མཚན་མང་ཞིང་ལུང་གིས་ཟིན་པ། མཚན་སྙན་གྱི་གྲགས་པ་ཤིན་ཏུ་ཆེ། གཙང་འོ་ཡུང་སེ་མོ་ཆེའི་དགོན་པ་བཏབ། ཕུ་ལུང་ཕུག་ཏུ་སྐུ་བསྟུང་བ་མེད་པར་འོད་གསལ་དང་དུ་སྐུ་གཤེགས་པ་ཁྱེད་ལ་སྒོ་གསུམ་དང་བ་ཆེན་པོས་གསོལ་བ་འདེབས་སོ།།

འགྲོ་བའི་མུན་སེལ་འཇམ་གསར་ཞེས་རབ་འོད།།
ཞེས་བྱ་ཀུན་མཁྱེན་ཆོས་སྐུ་འོད་ཟེར་འཕྲོ།།
འགྱུར་མེད་བདེ་ཆེན་མཐར་ཕྱིན་ཀུན་སྤངས་རྗེ།།
འདྲེན་མཆོག་མཐར་ཐུག་གསུམ་ལ་གསོལ་བ་འདེབས།།

འགྲོ་བའི་མྱུན་སེལ་འཇམ་གསར་བ་ཤེས་རབ་འོད་ཟེར་མཆོག ཁོང་ནི་ཡུལ་ཉང་རོས་དབུས་སུ་སྐུ་འཁྲུངས། ལྷག་པའི་ལྷ་འཇམ་དཔལ་དབྱངས་ཀྱིས་ལུང་བསྟན་པ་ལྟར། སེ་མོ་ཆེ་བ་ལས་དུས་འཁོར་གྱི་དབང་གསན་བསྒོམས་པས་ཉམས་རྟོགས་མཐར་ཕྱིན། རྒྱུད་འདུར་གྱི་འཆད་ཉན་མཛད། བཤད་སྒྲུབ་སྤེལ་མའི་ངང་ལ་བཞུགས། སྤྲིངས་ཡིག་བེཏྟུཏྲའི་ཕྲེང་བ་སོགས་མཛད། འདི་མན་ལ་དུས་འཁོར་ཅུང་ཟད་བཀའ་སྒྲོ་ཡངས་སུ་སོང་། མཁས་གྲུབ་གཉིས་ལྡན་གྱི་ཆོས་ཀྱི་རྗེ་བོ་དམ་པ་འཇམ་དབྱངས་གསར་མ་ལ་སྙིང་ནས་གསོལ་བ་འདེབས་སོ།།

ཀུན་མཁྱེན་ཆོས་སྐུ་འོད་ཟེར་གྱིས་ཆོས་རྗེ་འཇམ་གསར་བ་ལས། དུས་འཁོར་གྱི་དབང་རྒྱུད་མན་ངག་རྫོགས་པར་གསན་པས་ཉམས་རྟོགས་བརྒྱ་འགྱུར་དུ་འཕེལ། དབང་གི་ཡེ་ཤེས་སྐབས་བླ་མ་རྡོར་ཤུགས་སུ་གཟིགས། ཡེ་ཤེས་ཕེབས་པ་ཉིན་ཕྱེད་ཙམ་མ་བཏང་། འདུས་པའི་རྒྱུད་ཡོངས་རྫོགས་རྒྱ་སྐད་དུ་སངས་ཀྱིས་བཏོན། མནལ་ཐམས་ཅད་འོད་གསལ་དུ་སོང་བའི་ངང་ནས་སྒོམ་བཟླས་སོགས་བྱེད་ཅིང་། སྐུའི་བཀོད་པ་ཡང་ཅིག་ཅར་མང་དུ་སྟོན་པ་དེ་ལ་སྒོ་གསུམ་གུས་པ་ཆེན་པོས་གསོལ་བ་འདེབས་སོ།།

མཚན་གཞན་ཀུན་སྤངས་པ་ཐུགས་རྗེ་བརྩོན་འགྲུས་སུ་གྲགས་པ་ནི། རིགས་ལྡན་སྤྲུལ་པ་དངོས་ཡིན་པ། མཁས་བཙུན་བཟང་པོའི་མཐར་ཐུག རྟགས་མངོན་གྱུར་གྱི་གྲུབ་ཐོབ་ཆེན་པོ་བ། འཇིག་རྟེན་གྱི་རྟེན་བདེ་གྲགས་བསྟོད་སོགས་སྤངས་པས་ཀུན་སྤངས་ཐུགས་རྗེ་བརྩོན་འགྲུས་ཞེས་དང་། གཞན་ཀུན་སྤངས་ཆེན་པོ་ཀུན་ཏུ་བཟང་པོ་ཞེས་བྱ་བར་གྲགས། ཀུན་མཁྱེན་ཆོས་སྐུ་བ་ལ་མདའ་བའི་གཞུང་གདམས་ངག་ཐམས་ཅད་དང་། འབྲོ་ལུགས་ཀྱི་དབང་རྒྱུད་བཤད་དང་སྦྱོར་དྲུག་ཉམས་ཁྲིད་དུ་མ་གསན་པས་ཉམས་རྟོགས་ཀྱི་ཀློང་བརྡོལ། རྡོ་མོ་ནགས་སྨན་རྒྱལ་མོ་དང་ཕྱི་བྲག་ནགས་གསུམ་གྱི་ཚེ་སྒོ་ཀུན་གྱིས་གདན་འདྲེན་བྱས་པ་བཞིན་ཇོ་ནང་དུ་གདན་ས་མཛད། སྤྱིར་སྦྱོར་བ་ཡན་ལག་དྲུག་པའི་གདམས་པ་མི་འདྲ་བ་བཅུ་བདུན་ཙམ་གསན་ཅིང་ཉམས་སུ་བླངས། ཕྱོགས་ཀྱི་གཞན་སྟོང་དབུ་མ་ཆེན་པོ་བདེ་སྟོང་ཟུང་འཇུག་གི་ངོ་བོ་ཏུ་ཐབས་མཆོག་རྣལ་འབྱོར་ཡན་ལག་དྲུག་ལ་ཉམས་ལེན་གྱི་མཐིལ་དུ་མཛད། བུ་སློབ་ཆེས་མང་བོར་སྤེལ་བས་དཔལ་ལྡན་རྒྱལ་བ་ཇོ་ནང་བ་ཞེས་པའི་མཚན་གྱི་སྙན་པ་གང་སར་ཁྱབ། མཐར་དགའ་ལྡན་ཡིད་དགའ་ཆོས་འཛིན་དུ་གཤེགས་པར་གྲགས་པ་ཁྱེད་ལ་སྒོ་གསུམ་གུས་པ་ཆེན་པོས་གསོལ་བ་འདེབས་སོ།།

རྒྱལ་བའི་ཡེ་ཤེས་གཅིག་བསྡུས་བྱང་སེམས་ཆེ།།
མཁས་བཙུན་བཟང་པོ་ཡོན་ཏན་རྒྱ་མཚོར་འཁྱིལ།།
ཀུན་མཁྱེན་དུས་གསུམ་སངས་རྒྱས་དོལ་པོ་བ།།
མཚུངས་མེད་བླ་མ་གསུམ་ལ་གསོལ་བ་འདེབས།།

བྱང་སེམས་རྒྱལ་བ་ཡེ་ཤེས་ནི། མེ་སྤྲུལ་ལོར་ཡུལ་མདོ་ཁམས་སུ་འཁྲུངས། ཆོས་རྗེ་ཀུན་སྤངས་ཆེན་པོ་དང་མཇལ་ནས་ཤིན་ཏུ་དད་པ་ཐོབ། རྣལ་འབྱོར་ཡན་ལག་དྲུག་གསན་པས་ཉམས་རྟོགས་མཐར་ཕྱིན། གཞུང་གདམས་ངག་ཐམས་ཅད་བུམ་པ་གང་བྱོར་གནང་། ཀུན་སྤངས་ཆེན་པོའི་བཀའ་གནང་ལ་བརྟེན་ཇོ་ནང་གི་གདན་སར་ཐེབས། ཆོས་རྗེ་ཀུན་སྤངས་པའི་གདན་སར་ལོ་བརྒྱད་བཞུགས། མཁས་བཙུན་ཡོན་ཏན་རྒྱ་མཚོ་ལ་གདན་ས་གཏད་ནས་དགུང་ལོ་རེ་བཞི། ལྕགས་ཕོ་སྤྲེལ་ལོའི་དབྱིད་འབྲིང་པོའི་ཚེའི་བཅུའི་ཉི་དྲོས་ལ། ཕྱུག་མོ་ཆོས་སྡིང་གི་རི་ཁྲོད་དུ་སྐུ་ཆོས་ཀྱི་དབྱིངས་སུ་གཤེགས་པ་ཉིད་ལ་སྒོ་གསུམ་དང་བ་ཆེན་པོས་གསོལ་བ་འདེབས་སོ།།

དེ་ནས་མཁས་བཙུན་ཡོན་ཏན་རྒྱ་མཚོ་ནི། བྱང་སེམས་ཆེན་པོ་ཉིད་ཀྱི་མཆེད་གྲོགས་སློབ་མ་རྒྱལ་ཚབ་གསུམ་ཀ་ཡིན། མདོག་གི་མཁར་རྙིང་དུ་སྔགས་རྙིང་མ་བའི་རྒྱུད་དུ་ལྕགས་སྤྲེལ་ལ་འཁྲུངས། གསང་སྔགས་ཕྱོགས་ཀྱི་བླ་མ་མང་དུ་བསྟེན། ཇོ་ནང་དུ་ཐེབས། ཀུན་སྤངས་ཆེན་པོ་ལས་ཟབ་ལམ་གྱི་ཁྲིད་གསན། མཚན་མོའི་རྣལ་འབྱོར་ཞག་ཉེར་གཅིག་ལ་རྟགས་བཅུ་རྫོགས་པར་མཐར་ཕྱིན། ཉིན་མོའི་རྣལ་འབྱོར་གྱི་སྐབས་འཕར་གཡོའི་ཉམས་ཆེར་བྱུང་སྟེ་མདའ་རྒྱང་ཙམ་དང་རྡོ་རྒྱང་ཙམ་དུ་འཕར་བའི་འཕར་གཡོས་ཇོ་ནང་གི་རི་ཀླུང་མེད་པར་བྱོན་པ་ཞག་བདུན་གྱི་བར་དུ་བྱུང་། དེ་སྐབས་རྗེས་སུ་མཉམ་ཉིད་ཆེན་པོ་གཅིག་གི་ངང་དུ་གྱུར། མངོན་མཁྱེན་ཐོགས་མེད་མངའ། ཆོས་འདི་མ་གསན་དང་འདི་མི་མཁྱེན་མེད་པ། སྐུ་བཙུན་པ་རབ་ཀྱི་མཐར་ཐུག་པས་ཚུལ་ཁྲིམས་ཀྱི་དྲི་བསུང་རྒྱ་ཆེར་འཕྲོ་བ་ཞིག་སྟེ། དང་པོ་ཀུན་སྤངས་ཆོས་རྗེ་བླ་མ་བསྟེན་ཚུལ་རྒྱུད་ནས་བཤད་པ་ལྟར་བསྟེན། དེ་རྗེས་བྱང་སེམས་ཆེན་པོ་གདན་སར་ཐེབས་པ་ལའང་ཀུན་སྤངས་ཆེན་པོ་དང་ཁྱད་མེད་དུ་བསྟེན། བྱང་སེམས་ཆེན་པོ་སྐུ་འདས་ནས་ཇོ་ནང་གི་གདན་སར་སྒྲུབ་བརྒྱུད་ཀྱི་བསྟན་པ་རྒྱ་ཆེར་བསྐྱངས། རྗེས་སུ་ཀུན་མཁྱེན་ཆེན་པོ་གདན་སར་བསྐོས། དགུང་ལོ་རེ་བརྒྱད་མེ་མོ་ཡོས་ཀྱི་ལོར་སྟོན་ཟླ་འབྲིང་པོའི་ཚེས་ལྔ་ལ་དག་ཞིང་དུ་གཤེགས་པ་པོ་ཁྱེད་ལ་སྒོ་གསུམ་གུས་པས་གསོལ་བ་འདེབས་སོ།།

དོལ་པོ་བ་ཤེས་རབ་རྒྱལ་མཚན་ནི། གཞན་སྟོང་དབུ་མ་ཆེན་པོ་སེངྒེའི་ང་རོའི་སྒྲ་གངས་རིའི་ཁྲོད་དུ་བསྒྲགས་པར་མཛད་པ་པོ། དཔལ་རྒྱལ་བ་ཇོ་ནང་བའི་གདན་རབས་བཞི་བ་པ། དཔལ་དུས་ཀྱི་འཁོར་ལོའི་བྱིན་རླབས་དོན་བརྒྱུད་བཅོ་ལྔ་པ། ཀུན་མཁྱེན་རྟེན་པ་བཞི་ལྡན་དུ་གྲགས་པ་ནི། ཕྱི་ལོ་ ༡༢༩༢ སྔགས་རྙིང་མ་བའི་ཁྱིམ་རྒྱུད་དུ་སྐུ་འཁྲུངས། མདོ་རྒྱུད་མང་པོ་ནས་རྒྱལ་བ་རྫོགས་པའི་སངས་རྒྱས་ཀྱི་ལུང་གིས་ཟིན་ཅིང་། གཞན་སྟོང་དབུ་མ་ཆེན་པོའི་ལྟ་བ་ནི་རྒྱལ་བའི་གསུང་རབ་མ་ལུས་པའི་དགོངས་པ་མཐར་ཐུག་ཏུ་རྒྱ་ཆེར་བསྒྲུབས་ཤིང་། དེ་ཉིད་ཐེག་པ་ཐམས་ཅད་ཀྱི་ཡང་རྩེ་དང་དཔལ་ལྡན་དུས་ཀྱི་འཁོར་ལོའི་དགོངས་པ་ཟླ་མེད་པར་བསྒྲགས་པ་རྩོད་གྲལ་དུ་གྱུར་པའི་བྱེད་པོ་གང་ཉིད་ཀྱི་ཞབས་ཀྱི་པདྨོ་ལ་སྒོ་

སྤྲོན་མེད་རབ་གསལ་སྣང་བ།

གསུམ་གྲུས་པ་ཆེན་པོའི་ཕྱག་འཚལ་ཞིང་སྐྱབས་སུ་མཆིའོ།།

ཕྱོགས་ལས་རྣམ་རྒྱལ་མི་མཐུན་ཕྱོགས་ལས་རྒྱལ།།
ཀུན་ལ་དགའ་སྟེར་དཔལ་གྱི་ཉ་དགོན་མཚན།།
མཁྱེན་བརྩེའི་དབང་ཕྱུག་ཀུན་དགའ་བློ་གྲོས་ཞབས།།
བསྟན་པའི་སྲོག་ཤིང་གསུམ་ལ་གསོལ་བ་འདེབས།།

ཀུན་མཁྱེན་ཆེན་པོའི་གདན་ས་འཛིན་པའི་མངའ་བདག་བྱང་ཆུབ་སེམས་དཔའ་ས་ཡི་སྙིང་པོའི་སྤྲུལ་བར་གྲགས་པ་ཕྱོགས་ལས་རྣམ་རྒྱལ། ཕྱི་ལོ་ ༡༣༠༨ མེ་ཕོ་རྟ་ཡི་ལོར་མངའ་རིས་ཡ་ཚ་རྒྱལ་པོའི་བླ་མཆོད་བླ་ཆེན་ཞིག་གི་སྲས་སུ་འཁྲུངས། ཡབ་ཁུ་བོ་སོགས་ལས་སྔགས་ཆོས་མང་པོ་སྦྱངས། དགུས་གཙང་དུ་ཕྱིན་ནས་ཞར་ཚད་དགུ་གསུམ་སྦྱངས་པས་གཞུང་ལུགས་ཐམས་ཅད་ལ་མཁྱེན་པ་རྒྱས། དགུང་ལོ་ཉེར་གཅིག་ལ་དབུས་གཙང་ཀུན་ཏུ་གྲྭ་སྐོར་མཛད། ཇོ་ནང་དུ་ཕེབས། ཆོས་རྗེས་སྐྱ་འབུམ་ལ་བསྐོར་བ་བྱེད་པ་དང་མཇལ་ནས་བླ་བྲང་དུ་ཞག་བདུན་ལ་འབེལ་གཏམ་ཤིན་ཏུ་འཕེལ་བར་མཛད་པས། གཞན་སྟོང་གི་གྲུབ་མཐའ་སངས་རྒྱས་ཐམས་ཅད་ཀྱི་དགོངས་པ་ཆོས་ཐམས་ཅད་ཀྱི་ཆོས་ཉིད་དུ་ངེས་པ་སྐྱེད། ཀུན་མཁྱེན་ཆེན་པོ་ལ་མི་ཕྱེད་པའི་དད་པ་འཁྲུངས། དུས་ཀྱི་འཁོར་ལོའི་དབང་ཞུས། ཟབ་ལམ་གྱི་ཁྲིད་བསྐྱངས་པས་ཉམས་རྟོགས་ཕུན་སུམ་ཚོགས་པ་འཁྲུངས། དུས་འཁོར་གྱི་རྒྱུད་སོགས་ཐུགས་ལ་བཟུང་བས་ཐུགས་ཀྱི་སྲས་སུ་གྱུར་པ་ཁྱེད་ལ་སྙི་གསུམ་གུས་པ་ཆེན་པོའི་སྒོ་ནས་ཕྱག་འཚལ་ལོ།།

འཇམ་དཔལ་སྤྲུལ་པར་གྲགས་པ་མཚུངས་མེད་ཉ་དབོན་ཀུན་དགའ་དཔལ། ཕྱི་ལོ་ ༡༢༨༥ ཤིང་མོ་བྱའི་ལོར་ཐ་སྐར་ཟླ་བའི་ཚེས་བརྒྱད་ལ་ཡུལ་ཉང་པོར་འཁྲུངས། ཁམས་པའི་དགེ་བཤེས་ཉ་དར་མ་རིན་ཆེན་གྱི་དབོན་པོ་ཡིན། ཆུང་དུ་ནས་མཁྱེན་རབ་ཤིན་ཏུ་ཆེ། ཀུན་མཁྱེན་ཆེན་པོ་དང་ཡང་ཡང་མཇལ། ཕྱིས་མདོ་སྔགས་ཀྱི་གཞུང་ཐམས་ཅད་ལ་མཁྱེན་པ་རྒྱས་ཤིང་རིག་པའི་དབང་ཕྱུག་ཆེན་པོར་གྱུར། ཕྱོགས་ལས་རྣམ་རྒྱལ་ཡུན་རིང་བསྟེན། ཉམས་རྟོགས་ཀྱང་མཐར་ཕྱིན། དུས་འཁོར་སོགས་མདོ་སྔགས་ཀྱི་ཆོས་མང་པོ་ལ་མཁས་པའི་མཁྱེན་པ་རྒྱས། ལྷག་པར་ཚད་མ་ཉ་ལ་ཁྲུངས་གཏུགས་ཟེར་བའི་ཚད་དུ་གྱུར། རྗེ་ཙོང་ཁ་པ་ཆེན་པོ་སོགས་བརྒྱུད་འཛིན་གཞན་གྱི་བདག་ཉིད་ཆེན་པོ་ཡང་མང་པོ་སློབ་མར་གྱུར་པ་སོགས་ངོ་མཚར་བའི་མཛད་རྣམ་མང་བ་དེ་ལ་སྙི་གསུམ་གུས་པས་གསོལ་བ་འདེབས་སོ།།

དེ་ཡང་ཉ་དབོན་པའི་ཐུགས་སྲས་གྲུབ་ཆེན་ཀུན་དགའ་བློ་གྲོས་ནི། ཤར་ཁ་བའི་སྐུ་རུས་སུ་འཁྲུངས།

ཕར་ཚད་མངོན་འདུལ་དབུ་མ་སོགས་མདོ་ཕྱོགས་རྣམས་དང་། དུས་འཁོར་གྱི་བཤད་སྒྲུབ་ཉ་དབོན་པ་ལས་གསན། བླ་མ་གཞན་མང་པོ་ལ་དབང་གདམས་ངག་རྒྱ་ཆེར་ཞུས། རྒྱལ་རིགས་སུ་འཁྲུངས་ཀྱང་སྲིད་ལ་མ་ཆགས་པར་བས་མཐའ་རྣམས་སུ་སྒྲུབ་པ་ཁོ་ན་ལ་གཞོལ། ཇོ་ནང་བའི་ཆོས་བརྒྱུད་འཛིན་སྤེལ་བཅས་སྐུ་ཚེའི་སྨད་ལ་འཁྲུལ་ཞིག་ཆེན་པོར་བཞུགས་ཤིང་། བུ་སློབ་རིན་ཆེན་དོན་གྲུབ་ཀྱི་སྐྱེ་བར་གྲགས་པ་དེ་ལ་གསོལ་བ་འདེབས་སོ།།

དཀོན་མཆོག་གསུམ་འདུས་འཕྲིན་ལས་བཟང་པོའི་ཞབས།།
ནམ་མཁའི་མཐའ་ཁྱབ་ངེས་དོན་དམ་ཆོས་སྐྱོང་།།
མདོ་སྔགས་པཎ་ཆེན་ནམ་མཁའ་དཔལ་བཟང་པོ།།
ངོ་མཚར་བླ་མ་གསུམ་ལ་གསོལ་བ་འདེབས།།

འཇམ་དབྱངས་དཀོན་མཆོག་བཟང་པོའམ། མཚན་གཞན་དཀོན་མཆོག་འཕྲིན་ལས་བཟང་པོ་ཡང་གྲགས། འཁྲུངས་ཡུལ་ལ་སྟོད་བྱང་བའི་ཕྱོགས་ཤིག་ཡིན། ས་སྐྱ་སོགས་གྲྭ་ས་ཕལ་ཆེ་བར་བྱོན་ནས་མཁན་འཇམ་དབྱངས་རིན་རྒྱལ་བ་དང་། གྲུབ་ཆེན་ཀུན་དགའ་བློ་གྲོས་ལས་དུས་འཁོར་སོགས་ཟབ་དོན་མཐའ་དག་གསན་ཏེ་ཐུགས་སུ་ཆུད། སི་ཏུ་ཀུན་བཟང་རབ་བརྟན་འཕགས་ཀྱིས་བླ་མར་བཀུར། ཉང་སྟོད་ཀྱི་ཆོས་སྡེ་གསར་བའི་ཆོས་དཔོན་མཛད། ཇོ་ནང་བའི་གྲྭ་ཚང་གསར་དུ་བཙུགས། ཕྱིས་རྩེ་ཤར་ནུབ་ཀྱིས་གུས་པས་བཏུད། ཆོས་སྡེ་གཉིས་ཆ་དང་ཇོ་ནང་གི་གདན་ས་མཛད། མཁས་གྲུབ་རྗེ་དཔོན་སློབ་ཀྱིས་བྱད་ཁ་བྱས་པ་ཡང་བྱང་སེམས་དང་རྡོར་བཟླས་སྤེལ་བས་ཕྱིར་ལོག་ཏུ་སོང་། བླ་མ་ས་སྐྱ་བའི་སྤྲུལ་པར་གྲགས་པ་དེར་སྒོ་གསུམ་གུས་པ་ཆེན་པོས་ཕྱག་འཚལ་ལོ།།

མཚན་གཞན་ནམ་མཁའ་ཆོས་སྐྱོང་དུ་གྲགས་པ་ནི། ཀུན་མཁྱེན་བསོད་ནམས་ཆེན་མོ་ལས་མཚན་ཉིད་ཀྱི་གཞུང་རྣམས་མཁས་པར་སྦྱངས། སླར་འཇམ་དབྱངས་དཀོན་བཟང་གི་ཆོས་གྲྭར་བྱོན། ཆོས་དང་གང་ཟག་ལ་དད་དེ་མཚན་ཉིད་ཀྱི་གཞུང་རྣམས་ཐོས་བསམ་གྱིས་མཁས་པར་སྦྱངས། གཞན་སྟོང་ལ་ངེས་པ་ཆུགས། སྦྱོར་དྲུག་ཞུས་ཏེ་ཉམས་རྟོགས་ཀྱང་ཤིན་ཏུ་བཟང་། དུས་འཁོར་གྱི་རྒྱུད་ལ་མཁས་པར་བྱས། ངམ་རིང་སོགས་འཆད་ཉན་འགའ་རེའི་སར་ཕེབས། རྩེ་ཤར་ནུབ་དང་ཁྱད་པར་སེང་གེ་རྩེ་བས་ཡོན་བདག་བྱས། རྩེ་ཆེན་དང་ཇོ་ནང་གི་གདན་ས་ཡུན་རིང་མཛད། བཤད་སྒྲུབ་གཉིས་ཀ་བཟུང་། སྐུ་འབུམ་ཆེན་མོའི་ཆོས་འཁོར་གསེར་ཟངས་ཀྱིས་གཡོགས་པར་མཛད་པ་སོགས་མཛད་པ་བཟང་པོ་མང་དུ་བསྐྱངས་པ་དེ་ལ་གསོལ་བ་འདེབས་སོ།།

ནམ་མཁའ་དཔལ་བཟང་དང་པོ་རྩ་བའི་གྲུབ་མཐའ་ས་སྐྱ་ཡིན། མོས་པ་རབ་འབྱམས་ཐུགས་རྗེ་དཔལ་བཟང་གི་གྲྭ་སར་སློབ་གཉེར་མཛད། བརྒྱ་སྟེར་འཆད་ཉན་ཡང་ལོ་ཤས་ཚུགས་པ་བྱུང་། ལྷུན་སྡིངས་སུ་བདག་ཆེན་པའི་སློབ་མ་ཤངས་སྟོན་བྱ་བ་ལས་དུས་འཁོར་བྱང་ལུགས་ཞུས་ཏེ་དེ་ལས་མཁས་པར་སྤྱངས། རྒྱལ་བ་ནམ་མཁའི་མཚན་ཅན་ལས་སྦྱོར་དྲུག་མན་ངག་ཇོ་ནང་ལུགས་འདི་སྔ་དུས་ཤིག་ནས་གསན་པས་ཉམས་རྟོགས་བཟང་པོ་འཁྲུངས། འབྲས་སྤུངས་དགོན་པ་བཏབ་ནས་འགྲོ་དོན་ཅུང་ཟད་མཛད་དོ།།

སྤྲ་སྤྲུར་མཚན་ཅན་རཏྣ་བྷ་དྲ་དང་།།
འགྲོ་ཀུན་དགའ་བའི་བླ་མ་གྲོལ་མཆོག་རྗེ།།
སྐྱེ་མེད་དོན་གཟིགས་ལུང་རིགས་རྒྱ་མཚོའི་ཞབས།།
གཞན་ཕན་མཐོན་གྲུར་གསུམ་ལ་གསོལ་བ་འདེབས།།

ལོ་ཆེན་རཏྣ་བྷ་དྲ་ནི། འཁྲུངས་ཡུལ་འབྲོག་པའི་ས་ཁུལ་ནས་ཡིན། གྲྭ་ས་བཞད་ཀྱི་གྲྭ་ཚང་ཆེན་པོ་ནས་ཡིན། ཨོ་རྒྱན་རྗོགས་པ་སོགས་བླ་མ་མང་པོ་བསྟེན། གསང་སྔགས་གསར་རྙིང་སོགས་ཀུན་ལ་མཁས། ཁྱད་པར་པཎ་ཆེན་ནམ་མཁའ་དཔལ་བཟང་ལས་དུས་འཁོར་གྱི་ཆོས་སྐོར་གསན་པས་ཉམས་རྟོགས་རྒྱས། སྤྱན་རས་གཟིགས་སོགས་ཡི་དམ་མང་པོའི་ཞལ་གཟིགས། མདོག་གི་སྨན་སྡིངས་དང་། བཞད་རི་བོ་གྲུ་འཛིན་སོགས་དགོན་གནས་མང་དུ་བཏབ། ཐུགས་རྗེ་ཆེན་པོའི་དམར་ཁྲིད་དང་། སྦྱོར་དྲུག་ཁྲིད་ཡིག་སོགས་ཀྱང་མཛད་པ་གང་དེ་ལ་གསོལ་བ་འདེབས་སོ།།

རྗེ་ཀུན་དགའ་གྲོལ་མཆོག་ནི་མངའ་རིས་སྨད་ཀྱི་གློ་བོ་སྨན་ཐང་ཞེས་པར། གཉག་སྟོན་ཤཱཀྱ་སུ་ནེའི་རིགས་རྒྱུད་དུ་ཡབ་དཔོན་དྲུང་ཚེ་དབང་བཟང་པོ་ལོ་ང་བརྒྱད་དང་། ཡུམ་བཙུན་མོ་སྤྲ་ཁྱི་གཉིས་ཀྱི་ཁྱི་མ་ལོ་ཉེར་གཉིས་བཞེས་པ་གཉིས་ཀྱི་སྲས་སུ་མེ་ཡོས་ལོར་འཁྲུངས། ཇོ་ནང་། ཤངས་པ། ས་སྐྱ་སོགས་ཀྱི་དབང་བཀའ་མང་པོ་དང་། རྙིང་ཕྱོགས་ཀྱི་ཆོས་སྐོར་དང་བཅས་ཟབ་ཆོས་ཀྱི་མཛོད་ཆེན་པོར་བཞུགས་ལ། རྒྱལ་བ་དགེ་འདུན་རྒྱ་མཚོ་དང་ལན་གཉིས་མཇལ་བས་དང་པོའི་སྐབས་འབེལ་གཏམ་དང་ཕན་ཚུན་ཐུགས་མཉེས་མཛད། རྗེས་སུ་མཇལ་དུས་ཆོས་འབྲེལ་བཀའ་གདམས་ནོར་ཕྲེང་གི་རྩ་བའི་ལུང་ཞུས། བར་སྐབས་རེར་ཇོ་ནང་གི་གདན་ས་མཛད། སྐུ་ཚེའི་སྨད་དུ་ཆོས་ལུང་བྱང་རྩེ་བཏབ་ནས་སྒྲུབ་སྡེ་ལ་གཙོ་བོར་མཛད།། དེ་ནས་སྔོན་གྱི་སྐྱེས་རབས་དང་རྗེས་ནས་ཡང་སྲིད་ངོས་འཛིན་སོགས་ཀྱི་ལུང་བསྟན་གསལ་བར་མཛད་དེ་བསྟན་འགྲོའི་དོན་རེ་ཞིག་རྫོགས་ཚུལ་གྱིས་དགུང་ལོ་དྲུག་ཅུ་བ། མེ་སྟག་ལོའི་ཟླ་བ་

དང་པོའི་ཚེས་བརྒྱད་ལ་གཟུགས་སྐུ་ཆོས་དབྱིངས་སུ་ཐིམ་པ་དེ་ཉིད་ལ་གསོལ་བ་འདེབས་སོ།།

ལོ་ཙཱ་བ་ལོ་ཆེན་རཏྣ་བྷ་དྲ་ཡི་དངོས་སློབ་མཁན་ཆེན་ལྷུང་རིགས་རྒྱ་མཚོ་ནི། ཉང་སྟོད་དུ་སྐྱེ་བ་གཙང་ཁང་བའི་སྐུ་རུས་སུ་འཁྲུངས། གསེར་མདོག་ཅན་དུ་མདོ་སྔགས་ལ་གསན་སྦྱོང་རྒྱ་ཆེར་མཛད། ཁྱད་པར་རྗེ་ཀུན་དགའ་གྲོལ་མཆོག་ལས་དུས་འཁོར་གྱི་དབང་རྒྱུད་མན་ངག་མཐའ་དག་གསན། མ་འོངས་ལུང་བསྟན་ཡང་སྲིད་ངེས་འཛིན་སོགས་ཀྱི་ཞལ་བཀོད་དང་། རྒྱལ་རྩེའི་མཁན་པོར་མངའ་གསོལ། གཞན་སྟོང་ཁང་ཚོགས་པ་སོགས་ཀྱི་མཁན་པོར་ཡུན་རིང་བཞུགས། རྗེ་དམ་པའི་ཡང་སྤྲུལ་ཁྲི་འདོན་མཛད་ནས། བཀའ་ཆོས་ཐམས་ཅད་ཐུལ་གྲུབ་སྐྱེ་ཐུགས་དགོངས་རྫོགས་ནས་འདས་ཚུལ་བསྟན་པ་དེ་ལ་གསོལ་བ་འདེབས་སོ།།

འགྲོ་ཀུན་ཐར་བར་འདྲེན་མཛད་སྒྲོལ་བའི་མགོན།།
ཀུན་དགའ་རིན་ཆེན་ཡོན་ཏན་རྒྱ་མཚོའི་གཏེར།།
རིགས་ཀུན་བདག་པོའི་མཁས་གྲུབ་རྣམ་པར་རྒྱལ།།
བཀའ་དྲིན་མཚུངས་མེད་གསུམ་ལ་གསོལ་བ་འདེབས།།

མཚན་གཞན་རྗེ་བཙུན་ཀུན་དགའ་སྙིང་པོ་སྟེ། ཡོངས་གྲགས་སུ་ཏཱ་ར་ནཱ་ཐ་ནི། སྔོན་རྟ་ལོ་ཙཱ་བ་ཆེན་པོའི་བརྒྱུད་པ་རིམ་པར་བྱོན་པའི་བསྐྱེ་གནས་སུ། དེའི་གདུང་རྒྱུད་སྔགས་འཆང་ཚུལ་ཁྲིམས་རྒྱ་མཚོ་ལ་སྲས་བཞི་འཁྲུང་བའི་ཆེ་ཤོས་རྣམ་རྒྱལ་ཕུན་ཚོགས་དང་། ཡུམ་རྡོ་རྗེ་བུ་དགའ་ལྷ་མོ་གཉིས་ཀྱི་སྲས་སུ་ཤིང་མོ་ཕག་གི་ལོར་སྐུ་འཁྲུངས། ཕྱག་ཞབས་ལ་འཁོར་ལོ་དང་སྐུ་ལ་གུར་གུམ་གྱི་དྲི་ངད་ལྡན་པ། སྤྱན་གྱིས་ཕྱོགས་ཐམས་ཅད་ལ་གཟིགས་བཞིན་ཞལ་ནས་སུམ་བྷ་ནིའི་སྔགས་ལན་གསུམ་བརྗོད་པར་གྲགས། དེ་སྐབས་མེས་པོས་པདྨ་སྲི་གཅོད་རྡོ་རྗེ་ཞེས་པའི་མཚན་གསོལ། སྐུ་ཤེས་ཙམ་ནས་ང་བླ་མ་ཀུན་དགའ་གྲོལ་མཆོག་ཡིན་ཞེས་ཡང་ཡང་གསུངས། མཚན་ཀུན་དགའ་སྙིང་པོ་བཀྲ་ཤིས་རྒྱལ་མཚན་དུ་གསོལ་ཞིང་། དག་སྣང་དུ་སྤྲུལ་པའི་བཀྲ་ཤིས་གཉེན་རྒྱ་གར་བ་ཛྙ་ལ་ནཱ་ཐས། ཏཱ་ར་ནཱ་ཐ་ཞེས་པའི་མིང་བསྩལ། མཁས་མཆོག་བྱམས་པ་ལྷུན་གྲུབ་གནས་ཀྱི་བླ་མར་བསྟེན་ནས་མདོ་རྒྱུད་ལ་གསན་སྦྱངས་མཛད་དེ་མཁས་པའི་གནས་ཐོབ། གངས་ཅན་རྒྱུད་སྡེ་རྒྱ་མཚོའི་འབྱུང་གནས་སུ་གྱུར་པ་དེ་ལ་གསོལ་བ་འདེབས་སོ།།

སྔོན་སྦྱངས་རིན་ཆེན་རྒྱ་མཚོའམ་རྒྱལ་ཚབ་འཛིན་པ་ཀུན་དགའ་རིན་ཆེན་རྒྱ་མཚོ་ནི། གཙང་གི་སྐྱེ་བ

སྣར་ཐང་བའི་སྲས་སུ་འཁྲུངས། རྗེ་བཙུན་ཀུན་དགའ་སྙིང་པོའི་ཞབས་ལ་གཏུགས་ཤིང་རབ་བྱུང་དང་བསྙེན་རྫོགས་ཀྱང་མཛད། ཁྱད་པར་ཟབ་ལམ་རྡོ་རྗེའི་རྣལ་འབྱོར་གྱི་དབང་ལུང་མན་ངག་གསན་ཏེ་བསྒོམས་པས་ཉམས་རྟོགས་མཐར་ཕྱིན། སྔོན་སྦྱངས་སད་པས་བློ་གྲོས་ནང་ནས་རྒྱས་ཏེ་གསུང་རབ་ཉིན་རེ་ལ་ཤོག་བུ་བཅོ་བརྒྱད་ཙམ་ཐུགས་ལ་ཟིན། གཞན་ཡང་མདོ་སྔགས་ཀྱི་ཆོས་བཀའ་མང་པོ་ཞུས་ནས་དེ་དག་གི་དགོངས་དོན་ཐུགས་སུ་ཆུད། རྟག་བརྟན་དམ་ཆོས་གླིང་གི་སློབ་དཔོན་ཞིང་ལ་གཤེགས་པའི་རྐྱེན་གྱིས། དེར་ཕེབས་ཏེ་རྒྱལ་འཚབ་མཛད་ནས་ལོ་བཅོ་ལྔ་ཙམ་ལ་བཤད་སྒྲུབ་ཀྱི་གྲྭ་མ་ཉམས་པར་སྐྱོང་བར་མཛད། སྐུ་ཚེའི་སྨད་ལ་གསང་སྔགས་རི་བོ་བདེ་ཆེན་དུ་བཤད་སྒྲུབ་སྤེལ་མའི་ངང་ལ་བཞུགས་པ་དེ་ལ་གསོལ་བ་འདེབས་སོ།།

མཁས་གྲུབ་བློ་གྲོས་རྣམ་རྒྱལ་ནི། ཡབ་ལྷ་དར་རྒྱས་དང་ཡུམ་ཕྱུག་མོ་དཔལ་འཛིན་གཉིས་ཀྱི་སྲས་སུ་ལྟེ་བས་སྒོམ་ཐག་གི་ཚུལ་འཆང་བཞིན་ངོ་མཚར་བའི་ལྟས་བཅས་འཁྲུངས། ཆུང་དུ་ནས་ལྷུང་བཤགས་རང་ཤེས་དང་བྱམས་པའི་ཞལ་གཟིགས་མང་། དགུང་ལོ་བཅུ་དྲུག་པར་མཁའ་འགྲོས་བསྐུལ་བ་ལྟར་རྗེ་བཙུན་ཀུན་དགའ་སྙིང་པོའི་དྲུང་དུ་སྐྲ་ཕུད་ཕུལ། དེ་ནས་སྒྲུབ་ལ་བརྩོན་པས་ཉམས་རྟོགས་ཀྱི་གློང་བརྡོལ། རི་ཛམྦྷ་ལའི་སྐུ་འདྲ་བ་ཞིག་གི་མདུན་ན་དགོན་པ་ཁྲ་ཤིག་གེ་ཞིག་ལུང་དུ་བསྟན་པ་ཕྱིས་ཛམ་ཐང་ཡིན་པར་ཤེས། ཏཱ་ར་ནཱ་ཐའི་ལྷུམ་སྨིན་རྗེ་བཙུན་འཕྲིན་ལས་དབང་མོས་བཀའ་གནང་བ། ཕྱི་ལོ་ ༡༦༥༨ ས་ཁྱིའི་ལོ་ནས་བཟུང་གདུལ་བྱ་རིས་མེད་རྣམས་ལ་དུས་ཀྱི་འཁོར་ལོའི་དབང་ཁྲིད་སོགས་རྒྱས་པར་བསྩལ། ཕྱག་དྲུག་པའི་རྗེས་གནང་སྐབས་མགོན་པོའི་ཞལ་གསལ་བར་གཟིགས། མདོ་སྨད་ཀྱི་མཆོད་ཡོན་འབྲལ་མི་ཐོད་བཞིན་ཛམ་ཐང་དུ་ཕེབས། ཀུན་མཁྱེན་ཆེན་པོས་རང་གི་མའི་རྣམ་སྤྲུལ་དུ་ལུང་བསྟན་པ་དེ་ལ་གསོལ་བ་འདེབས་སོ།།

ངག་གི་དབང་ཕྱུག་ཐུགས་རྗེའི་འཕྲིན་ལས་བདག །
བསྟན་འཛིན་མཆོག་གྱུར་རྣམ་པར་རྒྱལ་བའི་སྡེ།།
སྒྲུབ་བརྒྱུད་རྒྱན་སྤེལ་མཁས་བཙུན་དར་རྒྱས་ཞབས།།
གདམས་པའི་མཛོད་འཛིན་གསུམ་ལ་གསོལ་བ་འདེབས།།

ངག་དབང་ཐུགས་རྗེ་འཕྲིན་ལས་སམ། མཚན་གཞན་ཆ་ལུང་བ་ངག་དབང་འཕྲིན་ལས་ཞེས་གྲགས་པ་ནི། ཡུལ་ཆོས་ཟར་དུ་ཤིང་པོ་རྟ་ལ་འཁྲུངས། ཆུང་དུ་ནས་དམ་པའི་སྤྱོད་པ་ལ་གནས་པ། ཐོག་མ་ནས་ཆ་ལུང་རྡོ་རྗེ་བྲག་བཙན་ཁོང་གིས་བཏུལ་ནས་སྐྱེལ་བསྲུ་སོགས་བྱས་ལ། བློ་གྲོས་རྣམ་རྒྱལ་ལས་དུས་འཁོར་བསྐྱེད་རྫོགས་སོགས་ཟབ་བཀའ་མང་པོ་གསན། སྦྱོར་དྲུག་བསྒོམས་པས་བཤད་ཆོད་དང་མཐུན་

པའི་ཉམས་རྟོགས་ཤར། ལྕགས་འབྲུག་ལོར་འབྲས་སྤུངས་དགའ་ལྡན་གཉིས་སུ་རྗོ་ནང་གི་བསྟན་གཞི་བཙུགས། དེ་ནས་ཆོས་རྗེ་ཀུན་བཟང་དབང་པོ་སོགས་ལ་སྦྱོར་དྲུག་དབང་ཁྲིད་སོགས་གནང་བས་རྗོ་ནང་གི་རང་སྐད་གྲགས་ཤིང་། ཡེ་ཤེས་ཕེབས་པའི་རྣམ་འགྱུར་ཀུན་མཁྱེན་ཆེན་པོའི་སྐབས་ལྟར་བྱུང་། ཆུ་ཡོས་ལོའི་ཆོ་འཕྲུལ་ཟླ་བའི་ཚེས་བརྒྱད་ལ་སྐུ་འདས་པ་དེ་ལ་གསོལ་བ་འདེབས་སོ།།

གཙང་བ་ངག་དབང་བསྟན་འཛིན་རྣམ་རྒྱལ། གོང་མ་བློ་གྲོས་རྣམ་རྒྱལ། ངག་དབང་འཕྲིན་ལས་གཉིས་ཀྱི་དབོན་རྒྱུད་ཡིན། ལྕགས་མོ་ལུག་གི་ལོར་འཁྲུངས། དགུང་ལོ་བཅུ་དྲུག་ནས་ཉི་ཤུ་མན་ལ་རྡོ་རྗེ་འཇིགས་མཛད་སོགས་ཡི་དམ་མང་པོའི་བསྙེན་སྒྲུབ་ལ་བཅད་རྒྱར་བཞུགས། སློབ་དཔོན་ངག་དབང་བློ་གྲོས་ལས་སྒྲུབ་ཐབས་བརྒྱ་རྩའི་རྗེས་གནང་སོགས་ཐོབ། པཎ་ཆེན་བློ་བཟང་ཡེ་ཤེས་ནས་སྒྲུབ་ཐབས་རྒྱ་མཚོའི་དབང་སོགས་འགའ་ཞིག་ཐོབ། ཆོས་རྗེ་ཀུན་བཟང་དབང་པོའི་དྲུང་དུ་སྦྱོར་དྲུག་གི་མན་ངག་ལུས་སྦྱོང་སྙོར་དང་། རྩ་ཐིག་རླུང་ཁྲིད་ཀྱི་སྙོར་དང་། ངེས་དོན་མདོ་དྲུམ་པ་སུམ་ཅུ་སོ་ལྔས་གཙོར་བྱས་གཞུང་གདམས་ངག་ཐམས་ཅད་བུམ་པ་གང་བྱོའི་ཚུལ་དུ་ཐོབ། རྗེ་བོ་བསྟན་འཛིན་པས་ཨ་སྐྱིད་ཆུ་ཉིན་མའི་བླ་སེར་རྣམས་དང་། ཡང་སློས་སུ་འཛི་རཱའི་ཏ་ཅེ་ཡན་ཆད་ཀྱི་སེར་སྐྱེར་གཏོགས་ཚད་གྲྭ་རྒྱུན་ལ་ཕུལ། དབང་ལུང་མན་ངག་མང་པོ་གནང་བས། བཤད་ཚོད་དང་མཐུན་པའི་ཉམས་རྟོགས་སྐྱེས་པ་ཀུན་མཁྱེན་ཆེན་པོའི་དུས་དང་མཚུངས་ཞེས་གྲགས། མགོ་ལོག་ཏུ་གདན་འདྲེན་ཞུས་ཏེ་སྦྱོར་དྲུག་ཁྲིད་ལུང་གནང་། དགུང་ལོ་ཞེ་བརྒྱད་པ། ཕྱི་ལོ་ ༡༨༣༥ ས་རྟའི་ལོར་སྐུ་ཆོས་དབྱིངས་སུ་གཤེགས་པ་པ་གཙང་བ་གོང་མའི་སྐུ་ཐོག་མ་ཡིན་པ་དེ་ལ་གསོལ་བ་འདེབས་སོ།།

མཁས་བཙུན་དར་རྒྱས་སམ་ཀུན་དགའ་ཆོས་འཕེལ་ནི། མཁས་བཙུན་བཟང་པོའི་ཡོན་ཏན་མཆོག་ཏུ་མངའ་ཞིང་ཁྱད་པར་ཉམས་རྟོགས་ཀྱི་རྩལ་ལྡན། དབང་ལུང་ཁྲིད་ཀྱི་ཆོས་བརྒྱུད་འཛིན་པ་ཞིག་ཡིན་ལ། ཡན་ལག་དྲུག་གི་ཉམས་རྟོགས་ཀྱི་འཆར་སྒོ་མ་འགགས་པའི་བརྒྱུད་འཛིན། སྲོག་འཛིན་རྟགས་མངའ་ཀུན་དགའ་ཆོས་འཕེལ་གྱི་སློབ་མ་བྲ་ཡུལ་ཆོས་འཁོར་ཞེས་པ། རྗེས་དྲན་རྟགས་ལྡན་མངོན་ཤེས་ཅན་ཞིག་ཀྱང་བྱོན་པ་སོགས་དངོས་བརྒྱུད་ཅི་རིགས་པའི་སློབ་ཚོགས་མང་པོ་གྲོལ་བའི་ལམ་དུ་བཀོད་པ་དེ་ལ་གསོལ་བ་འདེབས་སོ།།

ཀུན་བཟང་སྤྱོད་པའི་འཕྲིན་ལས་རྣམ་པར་རྒྱལ།།
གྲུབ་པའི་རྣམ་རོལ་ཆོས་ཀྱི་དཔལ་འབྱོར་རྗེ།།
མན་ངག་མཆོག་སྙེར་རྒྱལ་བའི་མཚན་འཆང་བ།།
མཛད་པ་ལྷུན་གྲུབ་གསུམ་ལ་གསོལ་བ་འདེབས།།

སྟོན་མེད་རབ་གསལ་སྣང་བ།

ཀུན་བཟང་འཕྲིན་ལས་རྣམ་རྒྱལ་ནི། རྒྱལ་རོང་བག་ཀོ་ཤོག་ཏུ་སྐུ་ངོ་མཚར་བའི་ལྟས་བཅས་འཁྲུངས། ཆུང་ངུ་ནས་ཆོས་ལ་བསླབས། ཁྱད་པར་དག་དབང་མཁས་བཙུན་དང་རྒྱས་སོགས་དམ་པ་གོང་མ་མང་པོ་ལས་རང་ལུགས་ཀྱི་དབང་ལུང་མན་ངག་སོགས་ཟབ་བཀའ་ཡོངས་རྫོགས་གསན། ཐུགས་དམ་མཛད་པས་ཉམས་རྟོགས་ཆེར་རྒྱས། དབུས་གཙང་དུ་ཀརྨ་པ་སོགས་མཁས་གྲུབ་དུ་མ་བསྟེན། སླར་ཕེབས། གཙང་བའི་གཞིམ་ཁང་གི་གདན་ས་བཟུང་ནས་སྒྲ་མདོ་སྔགས་བཤད་སྒྲུབ་གླིང་། གསེར་ལྡུགས་མདའ་དགོན། ཇ་བ། སླར་ཡག རྒྱ་ཁ་བཀྲ་ཤིས་གླིང་ཡན་ཆད་ཀྱི་སློབ་ཚོགས་སྨིན་བཞིན་བསྐྱུས་ནས་བསྟན་འགྲོའི་དོན་རྒྱ་ཆེན་མཛད་པ་དེ་ལ་གསོལ་བ་འདེབས་སོ།།

ཆོས་འབྱོར་རྒྱ་མཚོ་ནི། མཁས་བཙུན་དང་རྒྱས་ལས་སྦྱོར་བ་ཡན་ལག་དྲུག་གི་ཉམས་རྟོགས་ཀྱི་འཆར་སྒོ་མ་འགགས་པའི་བརྒྱུད་འཛིན་པར་གྱུར་བ། སྲོག་འཛིན་རྟགས་མངའ་བ་ཀུན་དགའ་ཆོས་འཕེལ་གྱི་སློབ་མ་བྲོ་ཡུལ་ཆོས་འབྱོར་ཞེས་པ་རྗེས་དྲན་རྟགས་ལྡན་མངོན་ཤེས་ཅན་ཞིག་ཀྱང་བྱོན་པ་དེ་ཡིན་ནོ།།

ནུས་ལྡན་ལྷུན་གྲུབ་རྒྱ་མཚོ་ནི། འཛི་ཁོག་ཡག་མདོའི་པོ་བྲང་བཞེངས་ནས། གཙང་བ་དག་དབང་འཕྲིན་ལས་ཀྱི་ཡང་སྤྲུལ་དབུས་གཙང་དུ་འཁྲུངས་པ། འཕྲིན་ལས་རྒྱ་མཚོ་ཞེས་པ་འདས་པ་དེའི་ཡང་སྲིད་སྤྲ་ཁོག་གསེར་རིའམ་བསྙེའི་རྟ་ཞེས་པར་འཁྲུངས་པ་སྐུ་སྐྱེས་སྨིན་པ་རྒྱ་མཚོ་ཟེར་བ་དེ། དཔོན་ལྷུན་གྲུབ་པས་བླུས་ཏེ་ཡག་མདོའི་པོ་བྲང་དེར་བཞུགས་སུ་གསོལ་ནས་ལུགས་བཟུང་གིས་འགྲོ་ཕན་སྤེལ་བར་མཛད། ཨ་སྐྱོང་དཔོན་དང་མཆོད་ཡོན་དུ་གྱུར་ཏེ་ཉིད་ཀྱི་ཡང་སྤྲུལ་ཉེ་ཚར་གཙང་བ་སྐུ་དག་ཏུ་གྲགས་པ་དེ་ལ་གསོལ་བ་འདེབས་སོ།།

དཀོན་མཆོག་གསུམ་དངོས་འཇིགས་མེད་རྣམ་རྒྱལ་ཞབས།།
སྐྱབས་གནས་ཀུན་འདུས་རཏྣ་ཕཎྜེའི་མཚན།།
ཟུང་འཇུག་སྐུ་བརྙེས་ཆོས་འཛིན་རྒྱ་མཚོའི་ཞབས།།
མཐོང་ཐོས་འདྲེན་མཛད་གསུམ་ལ་གསོལ་བ་འདེབས།།

དཀོན་མཆོག་འཇིགས་མེད་རྣམ་རྒྱལ། མགོ་ལོག་ཡོ་སྟག་ཏུ་ངོ་མཚར་བ་དང་བཅས་ཏེ་འཁྲུངས། གཙང་བའི་གདན་སར་བཀོད། ལྷ་ཆེ་བླ་མ་རྒྱལ་མཚན་དང་། དཔོན་ལྷུན་གྲུབ་རྒྱ་མཚོ་གཉིས་ལས་དུས་འཁོར་ཆོས་སྐོར་དང་། རྫོ་ནང་སྙིང་ཐུག་ཏུ། སྐུ་ཞབས་སྟོ་ར་བའི་དྲུང་ནས་ནཻ་གུའི་ཆོས་བཀའ་སོགས་བླ་མ་མང་པོ་ལས་དབང་ལུང་ཁྲིད་གསུམ་རྒྱ་ཆེར་མནོས་ཏེ་ཐོས་བསམ་སྒོམ་གསུམ་གྱིས་རྟོགས་པ་མཆོག་ཏུ་རྒྱས་ནས། བསྟན་འགྲོ་ཡུན་རིང་བསྐྱངས་ཏེ་བཞུགས་པ་དེ་ལ་གསོལ་བ་འདེབས་སོ།།

གཙང་བ་དགེ་སློང་ངག་དབང་ཆོས་འཕེལ་ཞབས་པ་ནི། འཛི་ཡུལ་རབ་ཁ་ཞེས་པར་ཡབ་མགོ་ལོག་རྡོ་རྗེ་འབུམ་དང་ཡུམ་ལྷུགས་བཟའ་ཀླུ་མོ་རྒྱལ་གཉིས་ཀྱི་སྲས་སུ་འཁྲུངས། རྫམ་ཐང་གཙང་ཆེན་སྤྱུལ་བའི་དཀོན་མཆོག་འཇིགས་མེད་རྣམ་རྒྱལ་གྱི་དྲུང་དུ་ཕེབས་ནས། སྐྱབས་འགྲོ་དང་ཚངས་སྤྱོད་དགེ་བསྙེན་གྱི་སྡོམ་པ་ཞུས་ཏེ་མཚན་ངག་དབང་ཆོས་འཕེལ་རྒྱ་མཚོ་ཞེས་གསོལ། དེ་ནས་བཟུང་གཙང་བ་ཉིད་བླ་མར་བསྟེན་ནས་བྱང་སེམས་ཀྱི་སྡོམ་པས་ཐུགས་རྒྱུད་སྨིན་བཞིན་རིམ་པས་དབོན་ལྷུན་གྲུབ་རྒྱ་མཚོའི་དྲུང་ནས། སྨྱོང་རྒྱུད། རྒྱུད་སྡེ་ལྔ་བ། དུས་འཁོར་སོགས་ཀྱི་དབང་དང་མགོན་པོའི་རྗེས་གནང་། དེའི་མན་ངག་པོ་ཏི་མེ་འབར་གྱི་ལུང་བཅས་གསན། རྒྱུད་སྡེའི་བཤད་ཁྲིད་ཟབ་ཁྱད་ཅན་དུ་མ་ཐོབ་ཅིང་། ལྷ་ཆེ་བླ་མ་ངག་དབང་རྒྱལ་མཚན་གྱི་མདུན་ནས་སྦྱོར་དྲུག་གི་ཟབ་ཁྲིད་ཞུས་ཏེ། རི་ཁྲོད་དགེ་འཕེལ་དུ་སྨོན་འགྲོ་སྐྱབས་སེམས་ནས་བཟུང་སོར་བསམ་ཡན་ལ་ཉམས་ལེན་ལོ་གསུམ་ཙམ་མཛད་པས་སྦྱོང་བ་བཟང་རབ་ཐོན། ཕྱི་ལོ་ ༡༩༨༥ ལོར་འོད་གསལ་གཉུག་མ་ཆེན་པོའི་རང་ཞལ་གྱི་ངང་དང་། གང་ཐུགས་གཉིས་མེད་རོ་མཉམ་ཆེན་པོའི་ཚུལ་དུ་དགོངས་པ་ལེགས་མཐར་ཕྱིན་པའི་མཛད་ཚུལ་གནང་ངོ་།།

ཡོང་གྲགས་སུ་ཨ་ཤུལ་ལྷ་བཟོའི་བླ་མ་ནི། མདོ་ཁམས་འཛི་ཀ་རུ་ཨ་ཤུལ་ཞེས་པའི་གྲོང་གསེབ་ཏུ་སྐྱུ་འཁྲུངས་ཤིང་། ཤར་རྫམ་ཐང་གཞིམ་ཁང་དུ་གཙང་བ་དགེ་སློང་ངག་དབང་ཆོས་འབྱོར་རྒྱ་མཚོ་སློ་གསུམ་ཀུས་པ་ཆེན་པོས་བསྟེན། དམ་པ་གང་གིས་བརྗེ་བས་རྗེས་སུ་བཟུང་ནས་མཚན་ལ་ངག་དབང་ཆོས་འཛིན་རྒྱ་མཚོ་གསོལ། བླ་མ་འདིའི་དྲུང་ནས་ཟབ་ཅིང་རྒྱས་པའི་གདམས་ངག་མང་དུ་གསན་ཅིང་ཉམས་སུ་བླངས། དབེན་གསུམ་གྱི་སྐབས་ནས་སེམས་ཀྱི་གནས་ལུགས་རང་ངོ་འཕྲོད་ཅིང་སྟོང་གཟུགས་ཀྱི་སྣང་བ་མཐའ་གླུས་པ་ཤར། སོར་སྡུད་ཀྱི་སྐབས་སུ་སྔར་ལས་སྟོང་གཟུགས་ཀྱི་སྣང་བ་འོད་གསལ་རྟགས་བཅུའི་སྣང་བ་ཀུན་ནས་རྒྱས། བསམ་གཏན་སྐབས་སྟོང་གཟུགས་སེམས་དང་དབྱེར་མེད་དུ་གྱུར་ནས་མཉམ་རྗེས་དབྱེར་མེད་དུ་གྱུར། སྲོག་རྩོལ་སྐབས་ལས་རླུང་དབུ་མར་བཅིངས་ནས་སྟོང་གཟུགས་རླུང་དང་རོ་མཉམ་དུ་གྱུར། མདོར་ན་སྐུ་ཚེའི་སྟོད་དུ་རྫམ་ཐང་གཙང་ཆེན་དགོན་པ་གཞུང་གི་ཆེད་དུ་བླ་མཆན་དུ་གྲགས་པའི་འགན་བཞེས་སྐབས་སུ། གདུལ་བྱ་སྨིན་བདག་ཁྲིམ་པ་ཕོ་མོ་ངག་གི་ནད་གདོན་རྐྱེན་ངན་བར་ཆད་དག་ལ་གྲུབ་རྟགས་ཀྱིས་སྲུང་སྐྱོབ་བྱས་པའི་ལོ་རྒྱུས་མང་། སྐུ་ཚེའི་སྨད་དུ་བཀྲ་ཤིས་ལྷ་རུ་དགོན་དུ་གྲགས་པའི་དབེན་གནས་སུ་བུ་སློབ་བསྐྱངས་ཏེ་རྫོགས་རིམ་སྦྱོར་དྲུག་གིས་གདམས་པ་གནང་སྐབས་དག་ཏུ། དག་པའི་རང་སྣང་གི་ཉམས་སྣང་འབྲུམས་སུ་གླུས་པའི་ལོ་རྒྱུས་དང་། བུ་སློབ་རྣམས་ཀྱིས་དག་སྣང་དུ་ཡང་ཡི་དམ་ལྷའི་རྣམ་པ་མང་དུ་སྣང་ཚུལ་དང་། ཐལ་བའི་སྤྱོད་ཡུལ་ལས་འདས་པའི་གྲུབ་རྟགས་གནང་བའི་ལོ་རྒྱུས་ཤིན་ཏུ་མོད་པས། རྣམ་ཐར་རྒྱས་པ་དག་ཏུ་གཟིགས་རིགས། མཐར་

མི་ལོ་གསུམ་ཡས་མས་སུ་རང་བཞིན་གྱི་མིའི་སྤྱོད་ཡུལ་ལས་འདས་པའི་མཛད་སྤྱོད་ངོ་མཚར་བ་དུ་མ་བསྟན་གནང་། ཁོང་གི་བུ་སློབ་ཐུགས་སྲས་དག་ནི། རབ་ཁ་བླ་མ་དོན་ལྡན། སྤགས་པ་བླ་མ་མཉམ་ཉིད། བྱ་ཡུལ་བླ་མ་བསྟན་རབ་སོགས་རེད། མཐར་གཤེགས་དུས་སྐུ་གདུང་གི་རུས་པ་གཉིས་བྱུང་ཞིང་། ལྷུ་ཚིགས་སོགས་སུ་དུས་ཀྱི་འཁོར་ལོའི་ལྷ་དྲུག་བཅུ་སོ་དྲུག་གི་སྤགས་རྣམས་འབུར་དུ་དོད་ཡོད་པ་སོགས་བྱུང་བ་ནི། ཟུང་འཇུག་གི་སྐུ་གྲུབ་པའི་རྟགས་བྱུང་བ་དེ་ལ་གསོལ་བ་འདེབས་སོ།།

རྫོགས་ལྡན་བསྟན་པ་རབ་ཏུ་རྒྱས་མཛད་མགོན།།
ཟླ་གྲལ་བློ་གྲོས་བཟང་པོའི་འཕྲིན་ལས་རྒྱས།།
འཇམ་དཔལ་དབྱངས་དངོས་བློ་གྲོས་ཕྱོགས་མཐར་ཁྱབ།།
བསྟན་པའི་གསལ་བྱེད་གསུམ་ལ་གསོལ་བ་འདེབས།།

བྱ་ཡུལ་བླ་མ་ངག་དབང་བསྟན་པ་རབ་རྒྱས་ནི། འཛི་ཀའི་བྱ་ཡུལ་གྲོང་སྡེ་རུ་སྐྱ་འཁྲུངས། དགུང་ལོ་བཅུ་གཉིས་སྟེང་དུ་ལས་སྨོན་བཟང་པོའི་མཐུ་སྨིན་ཏེ། བཀྲ་ཤིས་ལྷ་རུའི་དབེན་གནས་སུ་ལྷ་བཙོའི་བླ་མ་ངག་དབང་ཆོས་འཛིན་རྒྱ་མཚོ་སྒོ་གསུམ་དང་བ་ཆེན་པོས་བསྟེན། ཐོག་མར་བླ་སློབ་མཇལ་སྐབས་ནས་བཀྲ་ཤིས་པའི་རྟགས་དང་རྟེན་འབྲེལ་ཤིན་ཏུ་འགྲིག་པོ་བྱུང་། བླ་མ་རྡོ་རྗེ་འཆང་གིས་མ་འོངས་ལེགས་པའི་ལུང་བསྟན་གྱི་བཀའ་ལུང་གསལ་པོར་གནང་། དེ་ནས་བཟུང་འདོད་པ་ཆུང་ཞིང་ཆོག་ཤེས་པའི་སྒོ་ནས། བླ་མ་དམ་པ་དེས་གཙོས་སྐྱེས་ཆེན་དམ་པ་དུ་མ་ལས་ཟབ་རྒྱས་ཆོས་ཀྱི་གདམས་ངག་མང་དུ་གསན་ཅིང་གུས་རྟག་བརྟན་པོས་བརྩོན་ཞིང་ཉམས་ལེན་གྱི་གནད་ལ་ཁེལ་ཐུབ་པ་བྱུང་། དགུང་ལོ་ ༥༨ ལ་ཐེབས་དུས་འཛིང་པོ་སྐབས་མགོན་གཟུགས་སྐུའི་བཀོད་པ་བསྐྲུན་པས། རྡོ་རྗེ་སློབ་དཔོན་གྱི་ཐུགས་འགན་གཙང་བཞེས་ཀྱིས་སྐལ་བཟང་སློབ་མའི་ཚོགས་མང་དུ་བསྐྲུངས། དམ་པ་འདིའི་བུ་སློབ་དག་གི་ནང་ནས་ཆེས་མཆོག་ཏུ་གྱུར་པའི་ཐུགས་སྲས་དམ་པ་དག་ནི། བླ་མ་ངག་དབང་བློ་བཟང་འཕྲིན་ལས་སམ་བསྟུས་མཚན་དུ་བླ་མ་བློས་འཕྲིན་དང་། བླ་མ་ངག་བློས། ཡར་ཐང་རྒྱ་སྤྲུལ། བླ་མ་མཁས་ཚུལ་སོགས་མང་། དགུང་ལོ་ ༧༨ ཐོག་ཏུ་སྐུ་མྱ་ངན་ལས་འདས་ཚུལ་བཞེས་པས། སློབ་བུ་དག་གིས་བརྟན་བཞུགས་ཞུས་ཀྱང་བྱང་ཤམྦྷ་ལར་རིགས་ལྡན་མ་འགག་པའི་དྲུང་དུ་ཐེབས་གཏན་ཁེལ་ཡོད་གསུངས་ནས་ཞལ་གྱིས་མ་བཞེས་པ་དེ་ལ་གསོལ་བ་འདེབས་སོ།།

བླ་མ་བློ་བཟང་འཕྲིན་ལས་སམ་བསྟུས་མཚན་དུ་བླ་མ་བློས་འཕྲིན་དུ་གྲགས་པ་མཆོག་ནི། མཁས་བཙུན་

ཡོན་ཏན་རྒྱ་ཆེས་མངོན་པར་ཐུག་ཅིང་། ཐལ་བའི་མཛད་སྤྱོད་དང་མི་མཐུན་པ་ཅན་གྱི་དམ་པའི་སྐྱེས་བུ་མིའི་གཟུགས་སུ་བྱོན་པ་ཞིག་ཡིན། དགུང་ལོ་ ༡༥ བཞེས་དུས་ཏེ། ལྕགས་རྟ་ལོར་སྦྱོན་བསགས་བསོད་ནམས་རྒྱ་མཚོའི་མཐུ་སྨིན་དེ་དཔལ་དུས་ཀྱི་འཁོར་ལོའི་རྡོ་རྗེ་སློབ་དཔོན་ཆེན་པོ་ངག་དབང་བསྟན་པ་རབ་རྒྱས་ཉེ་བར་བསྟེན། རྫོགས་རིམ་སྦྱོར་བ་ཡན་ལག་དྲུག་ཉམས་ལེན་གནང་དུས་། གཟའ་འཁོར་གཅིག་གི་ནང་དུ་འོད་གསལ་རྟགས་བཅུའི་སྣང་བ་རྫོགས་པར་འཆར་བ་སོགས་སོ་སོའི་སྐྱེ་བོའི་སྤྱོད་ཡུལ་ལས་རིང་དུ་འདས་པ་བྱུང་། ཡི་དམ་གྱི་ལྷ་དཔལ་གསང་བདག་འབྱུང་པོ་འདུལ་བྱེད་དང་། དཔལ་དུས་ཀྱི་འཁོར་ལོའི་ལྷ་དྲུག་བརྒྱ་སོ་དྲུག་སོགས་ཟབ་མོ་ལྷའི་སྣང་བ་ལས་འདའ་མ་མྱོང་བ་སོགས། རྟོགས་པའི་གདེང་ཚད་ཀྱིས། ཚུལ་བསྟན་དུ་གླུ་ནད་བཞེས་པ་བག་ཆགས་དང་བཅས་པ་རྩ་བ་གཏན་སྤངས་གནང་སྟེ་སྐུ་ཚེ་ཕྱིལ་བོར་གླུ་ནད་ཅན་བརྒྱ་ཕྲག་མང་པོ་ནད་ལས་ཐར་བར་མཛད་པ་སོགས་གྲུབ་ཐོབ་ཀྱི་མཛད་རྣམ་ཤིན་ཏུ་མང་། མ་ཟད་སྐུ་ཚེ་ཕྱིལ་བོར་སྐལ་བཟང་གི་གདུལ་བྱ་སྟོང་ཕྲག་བརྒྱལ་བར་ཟབ་རྒྱས་ཆོས་ཀྱི་གདམས་ངག་མང་དུ་བསྩལ་ཞིང་། ཕྱོགས་ཀུན་གྱི་མཁས་ཆེན་ཀུན་མདུན་སར་འདུས་ཤིང་གུས་པས་བཀུར་བསྟི་བྱས། མཐར་དམ་པ་གང་ལ་བསྟུང་གཞི་ཙུང་ཙམ་ཡང་མེད་བཞིན་དུ། དགུང་གྲངས་ ༨༢ བཞེས་སྐབས། ཕྱི་ལོ་ ༡༩༩༩ ལོའི་སྤྱུ་སོར་ནས། ད་ལོ་སྐུ་འདས་པར་ལུང་བསྟན་དེ་སློབ་ཚོགས་ཀུན་ལ་མཐའ་མཇུག་གི་ཆོས་ཀྱི་བགྲོ་གླེང་བྱ་དགོས་གསུངས་ཏེ། ཟླ་གསུམ་ཡས་མས་སུ་བཀའ་ཆོས་གནང་ནས་དམ་ཆོས་ཟབ་མོ་ལ་ཡོད་པའི་སྒྲོ་འདོགས་མ་ལུས་བསལ། ཡུལ་དེའི་མི་སྣ་གལ་ཆེན་ཁག་བསྡུས་ཏེ་ཁོང་གི་ཡང་སྤྲུལ་ངོས་འཛིན་མི་ཚོག་པའི་བཀའ་བཏང་། ས་སྟག་ལོའི་ས་ག་ཟླ་བའི་ཚེས་བཅུ་གསུམ་གྱི་ཉིན་ཕྱག་གཉིས་མཉམ་བཞག སྤྱན་གཉིས་བར་ནང་དུ་ཧྲིག་གེར་གཟིགས་ནས་རིག་གི་རྣམ་པའི་དབུགས་ཆེན་པོ་གཅིག་ནང་དུ་རྡུབ་པར་བྱས་པས། ཐུགས་ཆོས་དབྱིངས་མཉམ་ཉིད་ཆེན་པོའི་དབྱིངས་སུ་བསྡུས།

ཤར་མཁན་སྤྲུལ་རིན་པོ་ཆེ་འཇམ་དཔལ་བློ་གྲོས་མཆོག་ནི། མགོ་ལོག་གདོང་གཡང་ཟེར་བའི་འབྲོག་སྡེ་ཚུང་དུ་རུ་སྐྱ་འཁྲུངས། ཨ་སྐྱོང་གོང་མའི་དགེ་རྩ་མཁན་པོའི་ཡང་སྲིད་ཡིན་པར་སྐུ་གོང་མས་ལུང་བསྟན་ཡོད་ཐོག གྲུབ་ཆེན་ཨོ་རྒྱན་རིག་འཛིན། མཁའ་འགྲོ་ཏཱ་རེ་ལྷ་མོ་སོགས་ཀྱིས་ངོས་འཛིན་གནང་། སྐུ་ཆེ་དང་མཛད་འཕྲིན་གྱི་བར་ཆད་ཟློག་ཕྱིར་སྤྲུལ་སྐུའི་མཚན་གནས་གསང་རྒྱ་དམ་པོ་དགོས་པར་ལུང་བསྟན་པས། ལྷོ་སྐྱ་གོས་རྩལ་གྲྭ་རྐྱང་དཀྲུས་མའི་ཚུལ་གྱིས་གངས་ཅན་བོད་ཀྱི་ཆོས་བརྒྱུད་གྲུབ་མཐའ་ཀུན་ལ་ཞུགས་ཤིང་། ཉམས་སུ་ལེན་པར་མཁས་པའི་སྐྱེས་བུ་དམ་པ་ཞིག་ཏུ་གྱུར། སྐྱབས་རྗེ་བླ་མ་བློ་

བཟང་འཕྲིན་ལས་བསྟེན་ཏེ་མདོ་སྔགས་ཆོས་ཀྱི་གནད་མང་དུ་གསན། དཔལ་དུས་ཀྱི་འཁོར་ལོའི་རྫོགས་རིམ་སྦྱོར་བ་ཡན་ལག་དྲུག་སོགས་ཉམས་ལེན་གཙོ་བོ་བྱས། ཤར་ཛམ་ཐང་དགོན་ཆེན་དུ་༧རྗེ་བཙུན་ངག་དབང་ཡོན་ཏན་བཟང་གིས་ཁོང་གི་སྐུ་འཚབ་ཏུ་བསྐོས་ཀྱང་ཡུན་རིང་མ་བཞུགས། ༧སྐྱབས་རྗེ་བླ་མ་བློ་བཟང་འཕྲིན་ལས་དགོངས་པ་ཆོས་དབྱིངས་སུ་བསྡུས་རྐྱེན་གྱིས་སྐུ་གདུང་ལས་དམ་བཅས་ཏེ་གནས་ངེས་མེད་དུ་ཐེབས། གངས་ཅན་བོད་ཀྱི་༧སྐྱབས་མགོན་རྒྱལ་བའི་དབང་པོ་མཆོག་ལ་དམིགས་བསལ་མཇལ་ཁ་དང་རྟོགས་འབུལ་བྱས་པས། དབུག་དབྱུང་བྱིན་རླབས་ཁྱད་དུ་འཕགས་པ་བྱུང་། སྟོན་པ་སངས་རྒྱས་ཀྱི་གནས་ཆེན་རྣམས་དང་འཕགས་ཡུལ་པཎ་གྲུབ་ཁག་གི་གནས་མཆོག་དག་ཏུ་ཡུན་རིང་ཉམས་བཞེས་མཛད་པས་ཉམས་དང་རྟོགས་པའི་གདེང་ཚད་བརྙེས། བླ་མ་དང་མཁའ་འགྲོའི་བཀའ་ལུང་བཞིན་ཟབ་གསལ་སྒྱུར་བའི་ཤེས་རབ་ལ་བརྟེན་ནས། ཐུབ་ཕྱོགས་པའི་ནང་བསྟན་གྱི་སྒྲོ་བསྒྱུར་བསྲེ་ལྷད་རིགས་གཙང་བསལ་གནང་། མཁྱེན་བརྩེ་གཉིས་ལྡན་དང་གདུལ་བྱའི་སེམས་ཁམས་ལ་མཁས་པས་གསུང་ཆོས་ཀྱིས་མི་མང་སྟོང་ཕྲག་མང་པོའི་ལུས་སེམས་བདེ་སྐྱིད་དང་དཀར་ཆོས་དགེ་བ་ལ་བཀོད། ཐུན་མིན་ཁྱད་ཆོས་ལྡན་པའི་གསུངས་འབུམ་མང་བ་ལ་སོགས་པའི་མཛད་འཕྲིན་རིགས་སྣ་མང་དང་བཅས་སྐུ་འཚོ་ཞིང་གཞེས་པའོ།།

བསླུ་མེད་གཏན་གྱི་སྐྱབས་མཆོག་ཁྱེད་རྣམས་ལ།།
ལུས་ངག་ཡིད་གསུམ་གུས་པས་ཕྱག་འཚལ་ལོ།།
དངོས་བཤམས་ཡིད་སྤྲུལ་མཆོད་སྤྲིན་དཔག་མེད་འབུལ།།
ཐོག་མེད་བསགས་པའི་སྡིག་ལྟུང་སོ་སོར་བཤགས།།

འཁོར་འདས་དགེ་བ་ཀུན་ལ་རྗེས་ཡི་རང་།།
ཆོས་འཁོར་རྒྱུན་ཆད་མེད་པར་བསྐོར་དུ་གསོལ།།
མྱ་ངན་མི་འདའ་བཞུགས་པར་གསོལ་བ་འདེབས།།
བདག་གཞན་བླ་མེད་བྱང་ཆུབ་མྱུར་ཐོབ་ཤོག །

ཅེས་པ་འདི་ཨགཱུཧྲ་ཀཱཧྣའི་མིང་གིས་སྦྱར་པའོ། །

དུས་གཏན་དུའམ་ནམ་ཡང་བསླུ་བ་མེད་པའི་གཏན་གྱི་སྐྱབས་མཆོག་བླ་མ་དམ་པ་ཁྱེད་རྣམས་ལ། བདག་གིས་ལུས་ངག་ཡིད་གསུམ་གུས་པ་ཆེན་པོའི་སྒོ་ནས་ཕྱག་འཚལ་ལོ།། དངོས་བཤམས་ཏེ་

དངོས་སུ་འབྱོར་བའམ་རང་ལ་ཡོད་པའི་དངོས་པོ་དག་གིས་ཅི་ནུས་སུ་མཆོད་ཅིང་། དངོས་སུ་རང་ཉིད་ལ་མེད་པ་རང་གི་ཡིད་ཀྱིས་སྤྲུལ་ནུས་པའི་མཆོད་པའི་ཚོགས་སྤྲིན་བཞིན་མང་བ་དཔག་ཏུ་མེད་པ་ཞིག་བློ་ཡིས་དམིགས་ཏེ། རྩ་བརྒྱུད་ཀྱི་བླ་མ་དམ་པ་ཀུན་ལ་དབུལ་བར་བགྱིའོ།། ཚེ་རབས་འཁོར་བ་ཐོག་མ་མེད་པ་ནས་བསགས་པའི་སྡིག་པ་དང་སྡོམ་པའི་ཕྱོགས་ཉམས་པ་ལ་སོགས་པའི་བཅས་པ་དང་རང་བཞིན་གྱི་ལྟུང་བ་གང་དག་ཅི་ཡོད་ཐམས་ཅད་སོ་སོར་བཤགས་སོ།། རང་གཞན་གཉིས་ཀྱི་ཟག་བཅས་ཀྱི་དགེ་བའམ་འཁོར་བའི་དགེ་བ་དང་། ཟག་མེད་ཀྱི་དགེ་བའམ་མྱང་འདས་ཀྱི་དགེ་བ་གཉིས་ཀྱིས་མཚོན་པའི་དགེ་བ་ཀུན་ལ་རྗེས་སུ་ཡི་རང་བྱ་ཞིང་། གང་དག་འཕགས་པའི་སྐྱེ་བོ་ཀུན་གྱིས་ཆོས་འཁོར་རྒྱུན་ཆད་མེད་པར་འགྲོ་བ་སེམས་ཅན་རྣམས་ཀྱི་ཆེད་དུ་བསྐོར་དུ་གསོལ། ཞེས་གསོལ་བ་རྩེ་གཅིག་ཏུ་འདེབས་སོ།། འཕགས་པའི་སྐྱེ་བོ་སོགས་གང་འཁོར་བ་ལ་སྐྱོ་སྟེ་མྱ་ངན་ལས་འདའ་བར་འདོད་པ་གང་དག་སུ་ཞུགས་ཀུན། མྱ་ངན་ལས་མི་འདའ་བར་ད་དུང་འཁོར་བ་མ་སྟོང་བར་དུ་འགྲོ་བ་སེམ་ཅན་ཀུན་གྱི་སྡུག་བསྔལ་སྐྱོབ་ཕྱིར་དུ་བཞུགས་པར་གསོལ་བ་འདེབས་སོ།། ཞེས་དང་། བདག་གིས་འདིར་སེམས་ཅན་གྱི་དོན་བསམ་པ་སོགས། དགེ་བའི་དངོས་པོ་འདིས་མཚོན་པའི་དུས་གསུམ་དུ་དགེ་རྩ་ཅི་བསགས་ཐམས་ཅད། བདག་གཞན་སེམས་ཅན་ཐམས་ཅད་བླ་ན་མེད་པ་བྱང་ཆུབ་ཀྱི་གོ་འཕང་མྱུར་དུ་འཐོབ་པར་ཤོག་ཅིག ཅེས་དགེ་བ་ཡན་ལག་བདུན་ཕུལ་བའོ།། དེ་ལྟར་ཡན་ལག་བདུན་པའི་སྒོ་ནས་ཚོགས་བསགས་པའི་མཐའ་བརྒྱན་པར་བྱས་ཏེ། དྲིན་ཅན་རྩ་བརྒྱུད་ཀྱི་བླ་མ་ཀུན་གྱི་ཡོན་ཏན་དང་བཀའ་དྲིན་ཤེས་ཤིང་དྲན་པའི་སྒོ་ནས། བསམ་པར་བྱ་བ་ཁག་ལ་འཇུག་པར་བྱའོ།།

འདི་མན་ཆད་ཀྱི་བླ་རྣམ་འདིའི་རྩ་བའི་ཚིག་རྣམས་ཤིན་ཏུ་ཁ་གསལ་བའི་སྒོ་ནས་པར་ཆེ་བ་གོང་དུ་སྨོན་འགྲོའི་ཁོག་གཞུང་རྣམས་སུ་ཚིག་འགྲེལ་བྱས་ཟིན་པས། ཡང་བསྐྱར་འདི་ནས་རྩ་ཚིག་དང་འགྲེལ་བ་རྣམས་ལོགས་སུ་བྱས་ཏེ་ཚིག་འགྲེལ་བྱས་ན་བསྐྱར་བཟློས་དང་སྣག་ཤོག་གྲོན་པའི་རྒྱུ་ཙམ་ལས་དོན་ཆེས་ཆེར་མེད་ཤས་ཆེ་བས། འདིར་ཡང་བསྐྱར་རྩ་ཚིག་རྣམས་ལོགས་སུ་བཀར་ཏེ། རེ་རེ་བཞིན་ཚིག་འགྲེལ་མི་དགོས་པར་རྩ་ཚིག་ཁག་གྱི་བར་མཚམས་འགའ་རེ་ལ་ཚིག་ལྷག་ཅུང་ཙམ་རེའི་གསལ་ཁ་ཙམ་ཟུར་བཀོད་དེ་བཞག་ན་ལེགས་པ་འདྲ་བས་དེ་ལྟར་བགྱི་བར་བྱའོ།།

ཕྱོགས་བཅུ་དུས་གསུམ་གྱི་སངས་རྒྱས་ཀུན་འདུས་ཀྱི་ངོ་བོ་ཆོས་རྗེ་དཔལ་ལྡན་བླ་མ་རིན་པོ་ཆེ་ལ་གསོལ་བ་འདེབས་སོ།། ངོ་བོ་ཉིད་སྐུ། ཡེ་ཤེས་ཆོས་སྐུ། ལོངས་སྐུ། སྤྲུལ་སྐུ་སྟེ། སྐུ་བཞིའི་བདག་ཉིད་ཀྱི་ཆོས་རྗེ་དཔལ་ལྡན་བླ་མ་རིན་པོ་ཆེ་ལ་གསོལ་བ་འདེབས་སོ།། སྲིད་པ་འཁོར་བ་དང་ཞི་བ་མྱང་འདས་གཉིས་ལས་སྐྱོབ་པའི་སྐྱབས་མཆོག འཇིག་རྟེན་པའི་སྐྱབས་ལ་སོགས་པ་དང་འདྲ་མཚུངས་བྲལ་བའི་

ཆོས་ཀྱི་རྗེ་བོ། ཐར་བ་དང་ཐམས་ཅད་མཁྱེན་པའི་ལོངས་སྤྱོད་ཀྱི་དཔལ་དང་ལྡན་པའི་བླ་མ་རིན་པོ་ཆེ་ལྷ་བུའམ། རིན་པོ་ཆེ་ལས་ཀྱང་ལྷག་པ་དེ་ལ་གསོལ་བ་འདེབས་སོ།། སྲིད་ཞི་གཉིས་ལས་འདྲེན་པའི་འདྲེན་མཆོག་གཞན་སུ་དང་ཡོན་ཏན་དང་ནུས་པ་མཚུངས་པ་མེད་པའི་ཆོས་རྗེ་དཔལ་ལྡན་བླ་མ་རིན་པོ་ཆེ་ལ་གསོལ་བ་འདེབས་སོ།། ཐར་བ་མཆོག་གི་ལམ་སྟོན་པ་པོ་ཆོས་རྗེ་དཔལ་ལྡན་བླ་མ་རིན་པོ་ཆེ་ལ་གསོལ་བ་འདེབས་སོ།། མཆོག་གི་དངོས་གྲུབ་སངས་རྒྱས་ཀྱི་གོ་འཕང་གི་དངོས་གྲུབ་དང་། རལ་གྲི་ལ་སོགས་པའི་ཐུན་མོང་གི་དངོས་གྲུབ་བདུན་ལ་སོགས་པ་འབྱུང་བའི་གནས་ཆོས་རྗེ་དཔལ་ལྡན་བླ་མ་རིན་པོ་ཆེ་ལ་གསོལ་བ་འདེབས་སོ།། མ་རིག་ཉོན་མོངས་དང་ཤེས་བྱའི་སྒྲིབ་པ་གཉིས་ཀྱི་མུན་པ་སེལ་བྱེད་ཀྱི་ཆོས་རྗེ་དཔལ་ལྡན་བླ་མ་རིན་པོ་ཆེ་ལ་གསོལ་བ་འདེབས་སོ།། ཞེས་སོགས་ཀྱིས་གསོལ་བ་སྙིང་གི་གཏིང་ནས་བཏབ་ཏེ། གསོལ་བ་བཏབ་པའི་རེ་འདོད་གང་ཞིག་ཞུ་བར་འདོད་པ་ནི། བདག་ལ་ཟབ་ཅིང་གསང་བའི་ལམ་ལ་འཇུག་ཐུབ་པའི་དབང་ཐང་དམ་ནུས་པ་བསྐུར་བའམ་གནང་བར་བྱིན་གྱིས་བརླབ་ཏུ་གསོལ། བདག་གིས་ད་ནས་བཟུང་སྟོ་སེམས་རྩེ་གཅིག་གིས་སྒྲུབ་པ་ཟབ་མོ་ཟབ་ལམ་རྡོ་རྗེའི་རྣལ་འབྱོར་ཉམས་སུ་ལེན་ནུས་པར་བྱིན་གྱིས་བརླབ་ཏུ་གསོལ། སྐལ་བ་བཟང་པོའི་སྒྲུབ་པ་ཉམས་ལེན་འདི་ཉིད་ལ་བར་ཆད་ཅི་ཡང་མི་འབྱུང་བར་བྱིན་གྱིས་བརླབ་ཏུ་གསོལ། སྒྲུབ་པའི་སྙིང་པོའམ་གནད་གསང་ཉམས་ལེན་བྱ་ལ་མི་འཆུག་ཅིང་མི་ནོར་བའི་སྒོ་ནས་ལོངས་སུ་སྤྱོད་ནུས་པར་བྱིན་གྱིས་བརླབ་ཏུ་གསོལ། ཟབ་ཅིང་གཏིང་མེད་པའི་སྒྲུབ་པ་ཉམས་ལེན་རབ་ཀྱིས་མཐར་ཕྱིན་པར་བྱིན་གྱིས་བརླབ་ཏུ་གསོལ། འགྲོ་བ་ཀུན་ལ་བུ་སྡུག་པོ་བཞིན་གྱི་བྱམས་པ་དང་། རྒྱུ་མཚན་ལ་མ་ལྟོས་པའི་སྙིང་རྗེ་ཆེན་པོ་དང་། དོན་གཉིས་སམ་ཟུང་གཉིས་དང་ལྡན་པའི་བྱང་ཆུབ་ཀྱི་སེམས་རང་རྒྱུད་ལ་འཁྲུང་བར་བྱིན་གྱིས་བརླབ་ཏུ་གསོལ། སེམས་བཏང་སྙོད་ལ་དབང་ཐོབ་པའི་ཞི་གནས་དང་། བདག་མེད་པའི་དོན་གཙོ་བོར་གྱུར་བའི་དངོས་པོ་རྣམས་ཀྱི་གནས་ལུགས་ཡང་དག་པའམ། ལྷག་གེར་མཐོང་ནུས་པའི་ལྷག་མཐོང་སྟེ་ཞི་ལྷག་ཟུང་དུ་འབྲེལ་བའི་ཏིང་ངེ་འཛིན་ལ་དབང་འཐོབ་པར་བྱིན་གྱིས་བརླབ་ཏུ་གསོལ། སྲིད་པ་འཁོར་བ་ལས་འདས་ཤིང་། ཞི་བ་དམ་པའི་རང་མདངས་སྟོང་གཟུགས་རབ་འབྱམས་ལ་སོགས་པའི་ཉམས་མྱོང་དང་། བདག་གཉིས་ཀྱི་དབེན་པའི་དོན་རྟོགས་པའི་རྟོགས་པ་ཁྱད་པར་ཅན་རྒྱུད་ལ་སྐྱེ་བར་བྱིན་གྱིས་བརླབ་ཏུ་གསོལ། ཟབ་ཅིང་རྒྱ་ཆེ་བའི་ལམ། མི་འཇིགས་ཅིང་མི་ཤིགས་པ་རྡོ་རྗེའི་རང་བཞིན་ཅན་གྱི་རྣལ་འབྱོར་གྱི་རིམ་པ་རྣམས་མཐར་ཕྱིན་པར་བྱིན་གྱིས་བརླབ་ཏུ་གསོལ། གནས་ལུགས་དོན་དམ་པ་ནམ་ཡང་འགྱུར་བ་བྲལ་བའི་ཕྱག་རྒྱའམ་དམ་རྒྱ་ལས་ཀྱང་དམ་པའི་རང་བཞིན་ཅན་གྱི་ཕྱག་རྒྱ་ཆེན་མོ་སྟེ། ཕྱག་རྒྱ་ཆེན་པོའི་མཆོག་གི་དངོས་གྲུབ་རྫོགས་པའི་སངས་རྒྱས་ཀྱི་གོ་འཕང་དེ་ཉིད་ཚེ་འདི་ཉིད་ལ་དབང་འཐོབ་པར་བྱིན་གྱིས་བརླབ་ཏུ་གསོལ། ཞེས་པ་ལ་སོགས་ཀྱིས་ཉམས་ལེན་པ་རང་གིས་ལམ་འདི་ལ་བརྟེན་ནས་གང་ཞིག་འདོད་པ་ཀུན་ལ་འདོད་གསོལ་བྱ་བའོ།།

དེ་ནས་འདོད་པའི་དངོས་སྒྲུབ་དེ་དག་ཐོབ་པའི་ཆེད་དུ་དབང་བཞི་ལེན་དགོས་པས་དབང་བཞི་ལེན། དེ་
ལ་དབང་བཞི་ལེན་ཚུལ་མང་དུ་ཡོད་པ་དག་འདིར་རྒྱས་པར་མི་སྤྲོ་མོད། འདིར་ནི་བྱེད་སླ་སྐབས་བདེ་
ཞིག་གིས་བླ་མ་རང་སེམས་ཀྱི་ངོར་བསྒོམས་ནས་བྱ་བའམ། ཡང་ན་རང་གི་རིག་པ་བླ་མར་ངོ་ཤེས་པའི་
སྒོ་ནས་བྱེད་པ་ནི་འདི་ལྟར་རོ།། ངོ་བོ་དྲིན་ཅན་རྩ་བའི་བླ་མ་ཉིད་ཡིན་པ་ལ། རྣམ་པ་རྡོ་རྗེ་འཆང་ཆེན་སྐུ་
མདོག་སྔོན་པོ་ཅན་གྱི་རྣམ་པ་ཅན་དུ་བློ་ངོར་གསལ་བར་བྱས་ཏེ། བླ་མ་དེ་ཉིད་ཀྱི་དཔྲལ་བའི་ཨོཾ་ལས་
འོད་ཟེར་འཕྲོས་པས་བདག་ཉིད་སྟེ། རང་ཉིད་ཀྱི་དཔྲལ་བ་རུ་ཐིམ་པས། རང་ཉིད་ཀྱི་ལུས་ཀྱི་སྡིག་སྒྲིབ་
མ་ལུས་པ་རྣམ་པར་དག དེ་ཉིད་ནི་གསང་སྔགས་བླ་ན་མེད་པའི་བུམ་པའི་དབང་ཉིད་ཡིན་པར་མོས།
བུམ་པའི་དབང་ཞེས་པ་ནི། ཤེས་བྱའི་ཆོས་ཀྱི་གཞི་རྩ་བོ་མོའི་རང་བཞིན་གྱི་ནུས་མཐུ་ལ་ཕན་ཚུན་རེག་
པ་ཙམ་ལས་བྱུང་བའི་བྱིན་རླབས་ནུས་མཐུ་སྟེ། བུམ་པའི་མིང་གིས་བསྟན་ཅིང་། བུམ་པ་དང་བུམ་ཆུའི་
གཟུགས་ཀྱིས་མཚོན་བྱེད་ཀྱི་དབང་བསྐུར་བ་ཅན་ཏེ། དེ་ཉིད་ཀྱི་དབང་ངམ་མཐུ་ཐོབ་པར་ཤོག་ཅིག དེས་
སངས་རྒྱས་ཀྱི་སྐུའི་བྱིན་རླབས་རྣམས་རང་རྒྱུད་ལ་ཞུགས་པར་ཤོག་ཅིག་ཅེས་པའོ།། བླ་མའི་མགྲིན་པ་
ན་གསལ་བའི་ཨཱཿལས་འོད་ཟེར་འཕྲོས་པས། བདག་ཉིད་ཀྱི་མགྲིན་པར་ཐིམ་པས། བདག་ཉིད་ཀྱི་ངག་གི་
སྡིག་སྒྲིབ་ཐམས་ཅད་དག་པར་བསམ། དེས་གསང་བའི་དབང་ཞེས་པ་དེ་ཐོབ། གསང་བའི་དབང་ནི་ཕོ་
མོའི་རང་བཞིན་གྱི་རེག་ནུས་ཙམ་གྱིས་མི་ཚད་པར། གསང་བའི་རྫས་རིགས་རོ་ལ་མྱོང་བས་ནུས་མཐུ་
ལས་བྱུང་བའི་བྱིན་རླབས་ནུས་མཐུའོ།། དེ་ཉིད་རང་རྒྱུད་ལ་ཐོབ་པས་རྒྱལ་བ་ཐམས་ཅད་ཀྱི་གསུང་གི་
བྱིན་རླབས་རྣམས་རང་རྒྱུད་ལ་ཞུགས་པར་ཤོག་ཅིག་ཅེས་པའོ།། བླ་མའི་ཐུགས་ཀའི་ཧཱུྃ་ལས་འོད་ཟེར་
འཕྲོས་པས་བདག་ཉིད་ཀྱི་སྙིང་གར་ཞུགས་ཤིང་ཐིམ་པས། བདག་རང་ཉིད་ཀྱི་སྡིག་སྒྲིབ་རྣམས་དག་སྟེ།
ཤེས་རབ་ཕྱག་རྒྱ་ཆེན་མོའི་དབང་ཞེས་པ་ཐོབ་ཅིང་། དེ་ནི་ཕོ་མོའི་གསང་རྫས་ལ་རེག་པ་ཙམ་གྱིས་མི་
ཚད་པར། རྩ་རླུང་སེམས་གསུམ་སྨིན་པ་གང་ཞིག་གིས་ཕན་ཚུན་གསང་བའི་དབང་པོ་སྦྱིབ་སྦྱོར་སོགས་
མཉམ་སྦྱོར་ཆེན་པོའི་ཕྱག་རྒྱ་ལས་བྱུང་བའི་བདེ་སྟོང་གི་ཡེ་ཤེས་སྐྱེ་ནུས་ཤིང་། དེ་ལ་བསྟེན་ཏེ་སངས་
རྒྱས་ཀྱི་ཐུགས་ཀྱི་བྱིན་རླབས་རྣམས་རང་རྒྱུད་ལ་ཞུགས་པར་ཤོག་ཅིག་ཅེས་པའོ།། བླ་མ་དམ་པ་མཆོག་
གི་ལྟེ་བའི་ཧོཿཡིག་ལས་འོད་ཟེར་འཕྲོས་ཏེ་བདག་ཉིད་ཀྱི་ལྟེ་བར་ཐིམ་པས། ཐ་མལ་རྣམ་རྟོག་གི་ཆགས་
པའི་ཚོར་བ་དང་། རྟོག་པའི་རྣམ་པར་རྟོག་པའི་འདུ་ཤེས་དང་། དེ་དག་གིས་བཞག་པའི་ཕྲ་བའི་བག་
ཆགས་དག་དང་བྲལ་ཏེ། རྟོད་མེད་རང་བྱུང་གི་ཡེ་ཤེས་སྟོང་གཟུགས་ཕྱག་རྒྱ་ཆེན་མོའི་དབང་བཞི་བའི་
དོན་ཐོབ་པར་ཤོག དེས་རྒྱལ་བ་རྡོ་རྗེ་འཆང་གི་སྐུ་བཞིའི་ས་བོན་ཐེབས་པར་ཤོག དེས་ཡེ་ཤེས་རྡོ་རྗེའི་
བྱིན་རླབས་དེ་ཉིད་ཀྱི་དབང་ཐོབ་སྟེ་ཡེ་ཤེས་ཡང་དག་པའི་གློང་དུ་ཞུགས་པར་གྱུར་ཅིག དེ་དག་གི་དབང་
དང་མཐུ་ཡིས་རྩ་བའི་བླ་མ་དེ་ཉིད་འོད་དུ་ཞུ་སྟེ། བླ་མའི་སྐུ་གསུང་ཐུགས་དང་བཅས་པ་རང་ལ་ཐིམ། དེ་
ནས་བླ་མའི་གསང་གསུམ་མི་ཤིགས་པའི་འཁོར་ལོ་དང་། རང་གི་སེམས་ཉིད་གཉུག་མའི་གཞི་དབྱིངས་

སྨོན་མེད་རབ་གསལ་སྣང་བ།

གཉིས་དབྱེར་མེད་ཆོས་སྐུའི་རང་རྩལ་དང་དུ་བདག་ཉིད་གཅིག་ཏུ་གྱུར་ཅིང་། གཉིས་འཛིན་འགྱུ་བ་ཡེ་ནས་མེད་པའི་རྩ་བྲལ་ལྷུན་གྲུབ་ཆེན་པོའི་ངང་དུ་དུས་གཏན་དུ་བཞག་པར་བྱ་བའོ།། ཞེས་པ་ལ་མོས་གུས་ཀྱི་ངང་དུ་འཛོག་ཅི་ཐུབ་སུ་བཞག་དགོས་པའོ།།

རྩ་བ་དང་བརྒྱུད་པའི་བླ་མ་ཁྱེད་ཀྱི་སྐུ་གསུང་ཐུགས་ཀྱི་གསང་བ་ཟབ་མོ་རྣམས་ཇི་འདྲ་དང་། ཁྱེད་ཀྱི་འཁོར་དང་སྐུ་ཚེའི་ཚད་དང་ཞིང་ཁམས་ཀྱི་ཡོན་ཏན་ལ་སོགས་པ་དང་། ཐ་ན་ཁྱེད་ཀྱི་མ་འོངས་པའི་སངས་རྒྱས་ཀྱི་ངོ་བོའི་མཚན་མཆོག་བཟང་པོ་དེ་དག་ཇི་འདྲ་བ་དེ་བཞིན་དུ། བདག་དང་སེམས་ཅན་ཐམས་ཅད་ཀྱང་དེ་འདྲ་ཁོ་ན་ཇི་ལྟ་བར་འགྱུར་བར་ཤོག་ཅིག ཁྱེད་ཀྱི་སྐུ་གསུང་ཐུགས་ལ་བསྟོད་ཅིང་གསོལ་བ་བཏབ་པའི་མཐུ་ལས། བདག་སོགས་སེམས་ཅན་ཀུན་གང་དུ་གནས་པའི་ས་ཕྱོགས་དེ་ལ། ནད་དང་དབུལ་ཕོངས་འཐབ་རྩོད་ལ་སོགས་པ་མི་འདོད་པའི་རིགས་རྣམས་ཞི་བ་དང་། ཟབ་ཅིང་རྒྱ་ཆེ་བའི་དམ་པའི་ཆོས་དང་སྲིད་འབྱོར་དཔལ་ཡོན་ལ་སོགས་པ་བཀྲ་ཤིས་ཤིང་གོང་ནས་གོང་དུ་འཕེལ་བར་མཛད་དུ་གསོལ། ཞེས་སོགས་འདོད་གསོལ་བྱས་པའོ།།

འདི་ཡན་གྱིས་གསང་སྔགས་ཀྱི་ཉམས་བཞེས་གཞན་དང་ཆ་འདྲ་བའི་ཐུན་མོང་བའི་སྔོན་འགྲོའི་ཆོས་ལྔ་ཡོངས་སུ་རྫོགས་པའི་གཞི་རྩ་རྣམས་གྲུབ་པ་ཡིན་ནོ།། བླ་མའི་རྣལ་འབྱོར་གཞན་གཉིས་བླ་རྣམ་འདིའི་འཚབ་ཏུ་རེ་མོས་སུ་གློག་འདོན་བསྒོམ་པའི་སྒོ་ནས་ཉམས་སུ་ལེན་དགོས་པ་དྲན་པར་བྱའོ།།

དུས་འཁོར་རྫོགས་རིམ་ཐུན་མིན་གྱི་སྔོན་འགྲོ་བསྐྱེད་རིམ།

འདིར་དཔལ་དུས་ཀྱི་འཁོར་ལོའི་རྫོགས་རིམ་སྦྱོར་བ་ཡན་ལག་དྲུག་གི་ཐུན་མོང་མ་ཡིན་པའི་སྔོན་འགྲོ་གཉིས་ཡོད་པའི་དང་པོ་ནི། དུས་འཁོར་ལྷན་སྐྱེས་ཀྱི་བསྐྱེད་རིམ་འདི་ཉིད་རེད། སྤྱིར་བསམ་ན་བསྐྱེད་རྫོགས་གཉིས་ཀ་གསང་སྔགས་ཀྱི་དངོས་གཞིའི་ཉམས་ལེན་ཡིན་ཞིང་། དེ་གཉིས་ཀར་བསྟེན་ནས་སྒྲིབ་པ་ཆེ་ཕྲའི་རིགས་དག་རྒྱུ་ཡོད་ཅིང་། དག་པའི་ལྷ་སྐུ་འགྲུབ་རྒྱུ་ཡོད་པས་བསྐྱེད་རིམ་ཉིད་ཀྱང་ཆེས་རྒྱ་ཆེ་གཏིང་ཟབ་ཀྱི་གནས་ཞིག་ཡིན་པ་དང་། མ་ཟད་སྐབས་མང་པོར་བསྐྱེད་རིམ་ཡང་དག་ཅིག་མ་འགྲུབ་བར་དུ་རྫོགས་རིམ་བསྒོམ་རྒྱུ་མེད་པའི་རྣམ་བཞག་བྱས་ཡོད་མོད། འོན་ཀྱང་འདིའི་སྐབས་སུ་བསྐྱེད་རིམ་དེ་ཉིད་རྫོགས་རིམ་སྦྱོར་དྲུག་གི་སྔོན་འགྲོར་བཞག་པ་མ་ཟད། ཤིན་ཏུ་བསྡུས་པ་ཙམ་ལས་མེད་པ་དེ་ནི་ཐུན་མོང་མ་ཡིན་པའི་ཁྱད་ཆོས་ཤིག་ཡིན།།

སྤྱིར་བསྐྱེད་རིམ་ནི། དོན་གྱི་གནད་ཙ་གནས་སྐབས་བཞིའི་སྦྱོང་བ་ཟད་བྱེད་དེ། སད་པའི་གནས་སྐབས། རྨི་ལམ་གྱི་གནས་སྐབས། གཉིད་མཐུག་གི་གནས་སྐབས། སྙོམ་འཇུག་གི་གནས་སྐབས་བཞིས་བསྡུས་པའི་མ་དག་ཀུན་རྫོབ་གཟུང་འཛིན་གྱིས་བསྡུས་པ་ཐམས་ཅད་དག་པ་ལྷའི་རང་བཞིན་དུ་སྦྱོང་བྱེད་དམ་མངོན་དུ་འགྱུར་བྱེད་ཅིག་རེད། འདིའི་གནས་སྐབས་སུ་རྒྱལ་བ་ཇོ་ནང་པའི་གྲུབ་བརྙེས་རིག་འཛིན་གོང་མ་རྣམས་ཀྱི་ཕྱག་སྲོལ་ལྟར་ན། དཔལ་དུས་ཀྱི་འཁོར་ལོ་ལྷན་སྐྱེས་ཞེས་ཞལ་གཅིག་ཕྱག་གཉིས་པའི་སྐུར་བསྡུས་པའི་བསྐྱེད་རིམ་ས་བཅད་མ་སྟོང་ཙམ་ཞིག་གིས། རྫོགས་རིམ་སྦྱོར་བ་ཡན་ལག་དྲུག་གི་སྔོན་འགྲོ་བྱས་ཏེ་ཐད་ཀར་རྫོགས་རིམ་ལ་འཇུག་སྲོལ་ཡོད་པ་མ་ཟད། ཕྱག་སྲོལ་འདི་ལ་བསྟེན་ནས་གྲུབ་པའི་གོ་འཕང་བརྙེས་པ་ཆེས་མང་དུ་བྱུང་བ་ནི་གནད་འགག་ཆེན་པོ་ཞིག་ལ་ཐུག་ཡོད་སྙམ། སྤྱིར་ཇོ་ནང་པའི་བསྐྱེད་རིམ་ནི། གཞན་སྟོང་དབུ་མ་ཆེན་པོའི་ལྟ་བ་གཞི་ལ་བཞག་པའི་དཔལ་དུས་ཀྱི་འཁོར་ལོའི་ལྷ་དྲུག་བརྒྱ་སོ་དྲུག་པོ་གང་ཟག་སོ་སོའི་རང་རྒྱུད་དུ་གདོད་མ་ནས་བཞུགས་པ་དེ་ཉིད། མ་རིག་པས་སྒྲིབ་ཡོད་པ་འདག་བྱེད་ཀྱི་རྣལ་འབྱོར་རྒྱ་ཆེ་ཞིང་གཏིང་ཟབ་པའི་མངོན་རྟོགས་ཤིག་ཡིན་ཞིང་། དོན་ལ་འདི་དངོས་གཞི་ཟབ་མོ་ཡིན་པས། འདིར་རྫོགས་རིམ་སྦྱོར་དྲུག་གི་སྔོན་འགྲོ་བསྡུས་པ་ཙམ་གྱི་ས་བཅད་དུ་བཞག་ཡོད་པས། འདི་གོང་གི་ཐུན་མོང་སྔོན་འགྲོ་རྣམ་བཞིན་དུ་གོ་སླ་ཤེས་ཐུབ་ཅིག་མིན་པར་ཚུང་ཟད་གོ་བ་ལོན་དཀའ་ཡང་། འདིའི་སྐབས་སུ་དད་པ་དང་དག་སྣང་གཙོ་ཆེ་བའི་སྒོ་ནས་ཡུན་དུ་གོམས་པར་

བྱས་ན། གོ་བ་ཡོན་པ་དང་མ་ཡོན་པ་གཉིས་ཀྱི་སྒོ་ནས་ཉམས་ལེན་ལ་གནད་དུ་འགྲོ་ཐུབ་པ་སེམས་ལ་ནན་འཛིན་བྱེད།།

འདི་དག་གི་སྐོར་རྒྱས་སྤྲོས་ནི་སློབ་དཔོན་དང་སློབ་མ་མཉམ་དུ་འཛོམས་པའི་སྐབས་བ་བཟང་པོ་ཞིག་གི་གནས་སྟངས་འོག་ནས་མཐར་ཆགས་སུ་འཁྲིད་དགོས་པ་ཞིག་ཡིན། འདིར་གནས་སྐབས་སུ་འཆད་ཁྲིད་མེད་མཁན་རྣམས་ལ་ཤིན་ཏུ་བསྡུས་པ་ཞིག་གོ་སླ་བཟུང་བདེ་ཡིས་ཙུང་ཟད་ཙམ་བཤད་ཁུལ་གྱིས་བྲིས་པའོ།། དེ་ཡང་བསྐྱེད་རིམ་འདི་བསྒོམ་དུས། ཐོག་མར་གནས་ལུགས་དོན་དམ་སྟོང་བ་ཉིད་ལ་རྣམ་རྟོག་དང་རྣམ་པར་མི་རྟོག་པའི་རིགས་གང་རུང་གིས་གནས་ལུགས་ལ་མཉམ་པར་འཇོག་པའི་སྒོ་ནས་འགོ་འཛུགས་དགོས་པས། དང་པོ་ཐབ་མོ་སྟོང་ཉིད་ཀྱི་དོན་ཤཱུ་ནྱ་ཏཱས་སྔགས་ཀྱིས་སྟོང་པར་སྦྱང་བ་ནི།

ཨོཾ་ཤཱུ་ནྱ་ཏཱ་ཛྙཱ་ན་བཛྲ་སྭ་བྷཱ་ཝ་ཨཱཏྨ་ཀོ྅ཧཾ།

ཞེས་པ་སྟོང་སྦྱངས་སུ་གྲགས་པ། ཤཱུ་ནྱ་ཏཱའི་སྔགས་བརྗོད་བཞིན་གཟུང་འཛིན་གཉིས་དང་བྲལ་བའི་སྟོང་ཉིད་ཡེ་ཤེས་རྡོ་རྗེ་བདེ་གཤེགས་སྙིང་པོའི་རང་བཞིན་གྱི་བདག་ཉིད་དེ་ང་ཡིན་ནོ་སྙམ་དུ་ང་རྒྱལ་འཛིན། ཡང་ན། དོན་ལ་གཉུག་མ་ལྷན་ཅིག་སྐྱེས་པའི་ཡེ་ཤེས་དོན་དམ་བདེ་གཤེགས་སྙིང་པོ། གནས་ལུགས་དོན་དམ་བདེན་པའི་ངོ་བོར་ཀུན་རྫོབ་གཟུང་འཛིན་གྱིས་བསྡུས་པའི་ཆོས་ཐམས་ཅད་རང་བཞིན་གདོད་མ་ཉིད་ནས་སྟོང་བ་ཡིན་པ་ལ་ཡིན་པར་ཤེས་པའི་ངང་དུ་གནས། ཐ་ན་ཡང་དཔྱད་པའི་ཀུན་རྫོབ་གཟུང་འཛིན་གྱི་ཆོས་ཐམས་ཅད་སྟོང་བར་གྱུར་སོང་སྙམ་སྟེ་སྟོང་བའི་ངང་དུ་སེམས་གློད་དེ་བཞག

སྟོང་པའི་ངང་ལས་རང་སྐད་ཅིག་གིས་དུས་འཁོར་ལྷན་སྐྱེས་སུ་གྱུར་པ་ནི། འབྱུང་བཞི་རི་རབ་པད་ཟླ་ཉི་མ་སྒྲ་གཅན་རྣམས་བརྩེགས་པའི་གདན་ལ།

ཞེས་པ་འདིས་མ་དག་པའི་ཕྱུང་ཁམས་སྐྱེ་མཆེད་ཐམས་ཅད་སྟོང་བར་གྱུར་པ་དེའི་ངང་ལས། སྐད་ཅིག་གིས་རང་ཉིད་དུས་འཁོར་ལྷན་སྐྱེས་སུ་གྱུར་པར་བསམ། དེ་ཡང་འོག་གཞིའི་གདན་རྣམས་མ་དག་ཟག་བཅས་ཀྱི་ལས་ཀྱིས་གྲུབ་པ་མ་ཡིན་པར། རང་ཉིད་དུས་ཀྱི་འཁོར་ལོའི་ཐུགས་ཡེ་ཤེས་ཀྱི་སྣང་ཆ་ཟག་མེད་ལས་གྲུབ་པའི་རླུང་གི་དཀྱིལ་འཁོར་ཡངས་ཤིང་རྒྱ་ཆེ་བ་འོག་གཞི་དང་པོ་དང་། དེའི་སྟེང་དུ་མེ་ཚུ་ས་ཡི་དཀྱིལ་འཁོར་རྣམས་སྟེང་ནས་རིམ་བརྩེགས་ཀྱིས་འོག་མ་འོག་མ་ལས་སྟེང་མ་སྟེང་མ་མཐའ་རྒྱ་ཆུང་བ། ས་ཡི་དཀྱིལ་འཁོར་གྱི་དབུས་སུ་རིའི་རྒྱལ་པོ་རི་རབ་དཔག་ཚད་འབུམ་ཕྲག་གཅིག་ཏུ་མཐོ་བ་ཡོད་པ། རི་རབ་ཀྱི་དབུས་རིན་པོ་ཆེ་མཆོད་ལྡང་གཱ་ལས་གྲུབ་པ། དེ་བཞིན་དུ་ཤར་བེཌཱུརྻ་སྔོན་པོ། ལྷོ་པདྨ་རཱ་ག་དམར་པོ། ནུབ་ཀརྐེ་ཏ་སེར་པོ། བྱང་ཆུ་ཤེལ་དཀར་པོ་སོགས་རིན་པོ་ཆེའི་རིགས་སྣ་ཚོགས་

ལས་གྲུབ་པ། ཁ་ཁྱེར་གཡེར་ཞིང་སྟེང་དུ་རྡོ་རྗེའི་རྭ་ལྔ་ཡོད་པ། དེའི་སྟེང་དུ་རི་རབ་ཀྱི་ཁ་ཁྱེར་ལས་མཐའ་རྒྱ་ཙམ་ཟད་ཆུང་བའི་སྣ་ཚོགས་པདྨ། དེའི་སྟེང་དུ་པདྨའི་ལྟེ་བར་ཟླ་བ་དང་། ཉི་མ། སྒྲ་གཅན། དུས་མེའི་གདན་རྣམས་རིམ་བརྩེགས་ཀྱི་སྟེང་དུ་ཡོད་པའོ།།

བདག་ཉིད་དཔལ་དུས་ཀྱི་འཁོར་ལོ་སྐུ་མདོག་སྔོན་པོ་ཞལ་གཅིག་ཕྱག་གཉིས་སྤྱན་
གསུམ་པ། རྡོ་རྗེ་དང་དྲིལ་བུ་འཛིན་པས་ཡུམ་ལ་འཁྱུད་པ།

དོན་དམ་སྟོང་ཉིད་བདེ་བར་གཤེགས་པའི་སྙིང་པོ་དེ་ཉིད། དཔལ་དུས་ཀྱི་འཁོར་ལོ་ཡེ་ནས་ཡིན་པ་ལ་ཡིན་པར་ཤེས་པའི་འདུ་ཤེས་ཀྱི་སྒོ་ནས། སྐད་ཅིག་མ་གཅིག་གིས་རང་ཉིད་དཔལ་དུས་ཀྱི་འཁོར་ལོ་རུ་གྱུར། དེ་ཡང་རྩ་དབུ་མ་རྣམ་པར་དག་པའི་བརྡ་རུ་སྐུ་མདོག་སྔོན་པོ་ཅན་དུ་བསམ། ཆོས་ཐམས་ཅད་ཀྱི་དེ་བཞིན་ཉིད་ངོ་བོར་རོ་གཅིག་པའི་བརྡ་རུ་ཞལ་གཅིག་ཅན་དུ་བསམ། དེ་བཞིན་དུ་རིམ་པར། ཐབས་མི་འགྱུར་བའི་བདེ་བ་ཆེན་པོ་དང་། ཤེས་རབ་སྟོང་པ་ཉིད་སྟོང་གཟུགས་ཀྱི་སྐུ་གཉིས་དབྱེར་མེད་ཟུང་འཇུག་གི་བདག་ཉིད་ཡིན་པའི་བརྡ་རུ་ཕྱག་གཉིས་པ། དུས་གསུམ་གྱི་ཤེས་བྱ་ཐམས་ཅད་ཆགས་ཐོགས་མེད་པར་མཁྱེན་པའི་བརྡ་རུ་སྤྱན་གསུམ་པ། ཐབས་ཤེས་གཉིས་ཀྱི་དོན་སྟོན་པའི་བརྡ་རུ་ཕྱག་གཡས་རྡོ་རྗེ་དང་། གཡོན་དྲིལ་བུ་ཐུགས་ཀར་བསྣོལ་ནས་འཛིན་པས་ཡུམ་ལ་འཁྱུད་པར་བསམ།

ཞབས་གཡོན་པ་དཀར་པོ་བསྐུམ་པས་དབང་ཕྱུག་དཀར་པོ་དང་། གཡས་པ་དམར་
པོ་བརྐྱང་བས་འདོད་ལྷ་དམར་པོའི་སྙིང་ཁར་མནན་པ།

ཕྱི་རོལ་གྲངས་ཅན་པའི་ཐ་སྙད་ལས་བྱུང་བའི་རྡུལ་མུན་སྙིང་སྟོབས་གསུམ་སྤྱངས་པའི་བརྡ་རུ། མགྲིན་པ་དབུས་ནག་པོ་ཅན་དང་། དེ་བཞིན་དུ། གཡས་དམར་གཡོན་དཀར་བའི་མགྲིན་པ་གསུམ་པ། སྲིད་ཞིའི་མཐའ་གཉིས་གནོན་པའི་བརྡ་རུ་ཞབས་གཉིས་པ། སྐུ་བཞེངས་ཏེ་བཞུགས་པ་ལས་རྩ་རྐྱང་མ་རྣམ་པར་དག་པའི་བརྡ་རུ་ཞབས་གཡོན་པ་དཀར་པོ་ནང་དུ་བསྐུམས་པ། འདོད་ཆགས་ཞེ་སྡང་གཏི་མུག་ང་རྒྱལ་བཞི་སྤངས་པའི་བརྡ་རུ། དབང་ཕྱུག་དྲག་པོ་དཀར་པོ་གདོང་གཅིག་པ། གན་རྒྱལ་མགོ་གཡོན་དུ་བསྟན་པ་དྲན་མེད་དུ་བརྒྱལ་བའི་སྙིང་ཁར་མནན་པ། རོ་མ་རྣམ་པར་དག་པའི་ཞབས་གཡས་པ་དམར་པོ་བརྐྱངས་པ། བདུད་བཞི་སྤངས་པའི་བརྡ་རུ་འདོད་ལྷའམ་བདུད་དམར་པོ་ཞི་བའི་ཉམས་ཅན། གན་རྒྱལ་མགོ་གཡས་སུ་བསྟན་པ་དྲན་མེད་དུ་བརྒྱལ་བའི་སྙིང་ཁར་མནན་པ།

རོལ་པའི་ཐོར་ཚུགས་དང་། ཡིད་བཞིན་གྱི་ནོར་བུ་དང་།
ཟླ་བ་ཕྱེད་པས་དབུ་ལ་བརྒྱན་པ།

དབུ་སྐྲ་རལ་བའི་ཐོར་ཚུགས་སམ་ཅོད་པན་སྤྱི་བོའི་གཙུག་ཏུ་བཅིངས་པའི་སྣེ་མོ་སྐུ་རྒྱབ་ཏུ་དཔྱངས་པ། ཐོར་ཚུགས་ཀྱི་རྩེ་མོར་ཡིད་བཞིན་གྱི་ནོར་བུ་མཐའ་སྐོར་དུ་པ་ཏྲའི་རིས་ཀྱིས་སྤྲས་ཤིང་ཏོག་གིས་བརྒྱན་པ། རལ་བའི་ཅོད་པན་གྱི་མདུན་ངོས་སུ་འཕྲིན་ལས་རྣམ་པ་བཞིའི་སྒོ་ནས་སེམས་ཅན་རྣམས་འདུལ་བར་བྱ་བའི་བརྡར། སྣ་ཚོགས་རྡོ་རྗེ་གྱེན་དུ་བསླངས་པ། ཐོར་ཚུགས་ཀྱི་རྩེ་མོར་གཡོན་ངོས་སུ་མི་འགྱུར་བའི་བདེ་བའི་ཆ་ཤས་ཡོངས་སུ་རྫོགས་པའི་བརྡ་རུ་ཟླ་བ་ཕྱེད་པས་བརྒྱན་པ་དང་།

> རྡོ་རྗེའི་རྒྱན་དང་། སྟག་གི་པགས་པའི་ཤམ་ཐབས་ཅན། ཕྱག་སོར་རྣམས་ཁ་དོག་ལྔ་པ། སོར་ཚིགས་རྣམས་ཁ་དོག་གསུམ་པ།

རྒྱུ་བདེ་སྟོང་ཡེ་ཤེས་ཀྱི་ངོ་བོར་གྱུར་པའི་རྡོ་རྗེ་ཕ་ལམ་ལས་གྲུབ་ཅིང་རྣམ་པ་ཡང་རྡོ་རྗེ་རྩེ་ལྔ་བའི་གཟུགས་ཀྱིས་མཚོན་པའི་རྡོ་རྗེའི་ན་རྒྱན་དང་། རྡོ་རྗེའི་མགུལ་རྒྱན་དང་། རྡོ་རྗེའི་གདུ་བུ་དང་། རྡོ་རྗེའི་སྐ་རགས་དང་། རྡོ་རྗེའི་རྐང་གདུབ་དང་། རྡོ་རྗེའི་ཕྲེང་བ་དང་། མགུལ་བའི་རྒྱབ་ནས་ཁུག་ཀློན་བྱས་ཏེ་མདུན་ངོས་སུ་དཔྱངས་པའི་རྡོ་རྗེའི་དར་དཔྱངས་དང་རྡོ་རྗེའི་རྒྱན་རྣམས་ཀྱིས་བརྒྱན་པ། ང་རྒྱལ་རྣམ་པར་དག་པའི་བརྡར་སྟག་གི་པགས་པའི་ཤམ་ཐབས་ཅན། ཟླ་བའི་ཡོན་ཏན་ལྔ་སྟེ་ཙ་རྐྱང་མའི་སྒྲིབ་པ་ལྔ་དག་ཅིང་། དེ་དག་ཆོས་ཉིད་ཡེ་ཤེས་ལྔ་དང་ལྡན་པའི་བརྡར་མཐེ་བོང་སེར་པོ། མཛུབ་མོ་དཀར་པོ། གུང་མོ་དམར་པོ། སྲིན་ལག་ནག་པོ། མཐེའུ་ཆུང་ལྗང་གུ་སྟེ་ཕྱག་སོར་རྣམས་ཁ་དོག་ལྔ་བ་དང་། ཉི་མའི་ཡོན་ཏན་གསུམ་སྟེ། ཙ་རོ་མའི་སྒྲིབ་པ་གསུམ་དག་ཅིང་། དེ་དག་གི་ཆོས་ཀྱི་སྐུ་གསུང་ཐུགས་ཀྱི་རྡོ་རྗེ་གསུམ་དང་ལྡན་པའི་བརྡ་རུ་ཕྱག་གི་སོར་མོ་རྣམས་ཀྱི་ཚིགས་ཀྱི་ཕྲེང་བ་དང་པོ་རྣམས་ནག་པོ། གཉིས་པ་རྣམས་དམར་པོ། གསུམ་པ་རྣམས་དཀར་པོ་སྟེ། སོར་ཚིགས་རྣམས་ཁ་དོག་གསུམ་པ།

> རྡོ་རྗེ་སེམས་དཔས་དབུ་ལ་བརྒྱན་ཅིང་། མེ་རི་ཁ་དོག་སྣ་ལྔ་བའི་དབུས་ན་བཞུགས་པ། ཁྲོ་ཆགས་འཛེས་པའི་ཉམས་ཅན་ནོ།།

རང་ཉིད་དུས་ཀྱི་འཁོར་ལོའི་དབུའི་ཐོར་ཅོག་གི་སྟེང་དུ། དཔལ་དུས་ཀྱི་འཁོར་ལོ་ཉིད་རྡོ་རྗེ་སེམས་དཔའི་རིགས་སུ་གནས་པ་ཡིན་པའི་མཚོན་བྱེད་དུ་རྡོ་རྗེ་སེམས་དཔའ་སྐུ་མདོག་སྔོན་པོ་ཅན་གྱིས་དབུ་བརྒྱན་པ། དེ་ནི་རང་རྒྱུད་ལ་ཡེ་ནས་བཞུགས་པའི་དུས་ཀྱི་འཁོར་ལོ་དེ་ཉིད་ད་ལྟ་མངོན་དུ་གྱུར་པ་འདི། ཡེ་ནས་རྡོ་རྗེ་སེམས་དཔའི་རིགས་སུ་གྲུབ་པ་ཡིན་པར་གོ་བྱེད་དམ་མཚོན་བྱེད་ཡིན་པར་བཤད། རང་ཉིད་དུས་ཀྱི་འཁོར་ལོའི་སྐུ་ལས་འོད་ཟེར་སྣ་ལྔ་འཕྲོས་པ་འདོམ་གང་ཚུན་ཆད་དུ་མཆེད་པའི་དབུས་ན་བཞུགས་པ།

དེའི་ཕན་ཆད་རིམ་བཞིན་དུ་འོད་ཟེར་སྣ་ལྔའི་རྩེ་མོར་མེ་རི་ཁ་དོག་སྣ་ལྔ་མཐའ་མེད་དུ་འཁྱུག་པའོ།། མཆེ་བ་ཕྱེད་གཙིགས་པ་དང་། ཅུང་ཟད་དམར་ལ་ཟླུམ་པའི་སྤྱན་གསུམ་དང་ལྡན་པ་སོགས་ཁྲོ་བའི་ཉམས་དང་ཆགས་པའི་ཉམས་གཉིས་ཀ་འདྲེས་པའི་ཉམས་ཅན། ཐབས་དམིགས་པ་མེད་པའི་སྙིང་རྗེའམ་མི་འགྱུར་བའི་བདེ་བ་ཆེན་པོ་ལས་གྲུབ་པའི་བདག་ཉིད་དོ།།

དེ་ལ་འཁྱུད་པའི་སྣ་ཚོགས་ཡུམ་སྐུ་མདོག་སེར་མོ། ཞལ་གཅིག་ཕྱག་གཉིས་སྤྱན་གསུམ་མ། གཡས་གྲི་གུག་དང་། གཡོན་ཐོད་པ་འཛིན་པས་ཡབ་ལ་འཁྱུད་ཅིང་། ཞབས་གཡས་བསྐུམ་གཡོན་བརྐྱང་བས་ཡབ་དང་སྦྱོར་བ། གཅེར་བུ་རུས་པའི་ཕྱག་རྒྱ་ལྔས་བརྒྱན་ཅིང་། དབུ་སྐྲ་ཕྱེད་དཀྲོལ་བའོ།།

ངོ་བོ་དཔལ་དུས་ཀྱི་འཁོར་ལོ་ཉིད་དང་དབྱེར་མ་མཆིས་ཤིང་རྣམ་པ་དེ་ལ་འཁྱུད་པའི་སྣ་ཚོགས་ཡུམ། སྐུ་མདོག་སེར་མོ་གསེར་གྱི་མདངས་དང་ལྡན་པ། ཞལ་གཅིག་ཕྱག་གཉིས། སྤྱན་གསུམ་མ། གཡས་གྲི་གུག་འཛིན་པས་ཡབ་ཀྱི་མགུལ་བ་གཡོན་ནས་འཁྱུད་པ། གཡོན་ཐོད་པ་བདུད་རྩིས་གང་བ་ཡབ་ཀྱི་ཞལ་ལ་སྟོབ་པའི་ཚུལ་གྱིས་ཡབ་ཀྱི་མགུལ་བ་གཡས་ནས་འཁྱུད་ཅིང་། ཞབས་གཡས་བསྐུམ་པས་ཡབ་ཀྱི་སྐུ་སྐེད་ནས་འཁྱིལ་ཞིང་། གཡོན་བརྐྱང་བས་ཡབ་ཀྱི་ཞབས་གཡས་པ་དང་མཉམ་པར་སྦྱོར་བའི་སྒོ་ནས་ཡབ་དང་གསང་བའི་གནས་སྦྱོར་ཏེ་འཁྱུད་པ། སྐུ་གཅེར་བུ་ལ། སྤྱི་བོར་རུས་པའི་འཁོར་ལོ། རྣ་བར་རུས་པའི་རྣ་རྒྱན། མགུལ་བར་རུས་པའི་མགུལ་རྒྱན། དཔུང་བ་དང་མཁྲིག་མ། སོར་མོ། རྐང་གདོང་རྣམས་སུ་རུས་པའི་གདུ་བུ། སྐེད་པར་རུས་པའི་སྐ་རགས་ཏེ་རུས་པའི་ཕྱག་རྒྱ་ལྔས་བརྒྱན་ཅིང་། དབུ་སྐྲ་ཕྱེད་སྤྱི་བོར་ཐོར་ཚུགས་སུ་བཅིངས་ཤིང་། ཕྱེད་མར་སྐུ་རྒྱབ་སུ་གྲོལ་བ་སྟེ་ཤེས་རབ་རྣམ་ཀུན་མཆོག་ལྡན་གྱི་སྟོང་བ་ཉིད་ཀྱི་ངོ་བོའོ།།

དཔྲལ་བར་ཨོཾ། མགྲིན་པར་ཨཱཿ ཐུགས་ཀར་ཧཱུྃ། ལྟེ་བར་ཧོཿ གསང་གནས་སུ་སྭཱ། གཙུག་ཏོར་དུ་ཧཱཿརྣམས་འཁོད་པར་གྱུར།

ཡབ་ཡུམ་གཉིས་ཀའི་དཔྲལ་བར་ཆུ་ཁམས་རྣམ་པར་དག་པ། སྣང་བ་མཐའ་ཡས་ཀྱི་རིགས་ཐམས་ཅད་ཀྱི་བདག་ཉིད་དང་། སྐུ་རྡོ་རྗེའི་བདག་ཉིད་ཡིན་པའི་བརྡ་རུ་ཨོཾ་དཀར་པོས་མཚན་པ། མགྲིན་པར་མེ་ཁམས་རྣམ་པར་དག་པ་རིན་ཆེན་འབྱུང་ལྡན་གྱི་རིགས་ཐམས་ཅད་འདུས་པའི་བདག་ཉིད་དང་། གསུང་རྡོ་རྗེའི་བདག་ཉིད་ཡིན་པའི་བརྡ་རུ་ཨཱཿདམར་པོས་མཚན་པ། ཐུགས་ཀར་རླུང་ཁམས་རྣམ་པར་དག

པ། དོན་ཡོད་གྲུབ་པའི་རིགས་ཐམས་ཅད་འདུས་པའི་བདག་ཉིད་དང་། ཐུགས་རྡོ་རྗེའི་བདག་ཉིད་ཡིན་པའི་བཛྲ་ཧཱུྃ་ནག་པོས་མཚན་པ། ལྟེ་བར་ས་ཁམས་རྣམ་པར་དག་པ། རྣམ་པར་སྣང་མཛད་ཀྱི་རིགས་ཐམས་ཅད་འདུས་པའི་བདག་ཉིད་དང་། ཡེ་ཤེས་རྡོ་རྗེའི་བདག་ཉིད་ཡིན་པའི་བཛྲ་ཧོཿསེར་པོས་མཚན་པ། གསང་གནས་སུ་ཡེ་ཤེས་ཀྱི་ཁམས་རྣམ་པར་དག་པ། རྡོ་རྗེ་སེམས་དཔའི་རིགས་ཐམས་ཅད་འདུས་པའི་བདག་ཉིད་ཡིན་པའི་བཛྲ་སྭ་སྔོན་པོས་མཚན་པ། གཙུག་ཏོར་དུ་ནམ་མཁའི་ཁམས་རྣམ་པར་དག་པ། མི་བསྐྱོད་པའི་རིགས་ཐམས་ཅད་འདུས་པའི་བདག་ཉིད་ཡིན་པའི་བཛྲ་ཧཱ་ལྗང་གུས་མཚན་པ་ཅན་དུ་གྱུར་པར་བསམ་སྟེ། དཔལ་དུས་ཀྱི་འཁོར་ལོ་ཡབ་ཡུམ་གཉིས། རིགས་དྲུག་འདུས་པའི་བདག་ཉིད་ཡིན་པར་གོ་བྱེད་ཡིན་པས་ན་དེ་ལྟར་སྒོམ་དགོས་པའི་ཕྱིར་རོ།།

རང་གི་སྙིང་ཁ་ནས་འོད་ཟེར་འཕྲོས། སྣོད་ཐམས་ཅད་གཞལ་ཡས་ཁང་དང་།
བཅུད་ཐམས་ཅད་དུས་ཀྱི་འཁོར་ལོའི་ལྷ་ཚོགས་སུ་གྱུར།

དེ་ནས་རང་དུས་ཀྱི་འཁོར་ལོའི་སྙིང་ག་སོགས་གནས་དྲུག་གི་ཡི་གེ་དྲུག་ལས། རིགས་དྲུག་པོ་རང་རང་གི་རང་བཞིན་ལས་གྲུབ་པའི་འོད་ཟེར་རང་རང་གི་མདོག་ཅན་དཔག་ཏུ་མེད་པ་འཕྲོས་པས། ཕྱི་སྣོད་ཀྱི་འཇིག་རྟེན་ཐམས་ཅད་ལ་ཕོག་པས། དུས་ཀྱི་འཁོར་ལོའི་སྐུ་གསུང་ཐུགས་ཀྱི་གཞལ་མེད་ཁང་དང་བཅས་པར་གྱུར། ནང་བཅུད་ཀྱི་སེམས་ཅན་ཐམས་ཅད་ལ་ཕོག་པས། དུས་ཀྱི་འཁོར་ལོའི་ཐུགས་གསུང་སྐུའི་ལྷ་ཚོགས་ཅན་དུ་གྱུར་པར་བསམ་མོ།། དེ་ནས་ལྷ་སྐུ་གསལ་བཞིན་དུ་སྟོང་ཞིང་། སྟོང་བཞིན་དུ་གསལ་བར་སྣང་བའི་བདག་ཉིད་དུ་ཤར་བའི་ངང་ནས་ལྷ་ལ་སེམས་འཛིན་པས་གསལ་སྣང་དང་ང་རྒྱལ་བསྐྱེད་དེ་སྔགས་འདི་བཟླ་བར་བྱའོ།། ཨོཾ་ཧ་ཀྵ་མ་ལ་ཝ་ར་ཡཾ་སྭཱ་ཧཱ། ཞེས་བཟླ་བཞིན་དུ་སྣང་སྲིད་ཐམས་ཅད་དཔལ་དུས་ཀྱི་འཁོར་ལོའི་རང་བཞིན་འབའ་ཞིག་ཏུ་བསྒོམ་མོ།།

དེ་ནས་བཟླས་པ་བྱ་བའི་དམིགས་རིམ་རྒྱས་པ་ཁག་བྱེ་ན་འདི་ལྟར་རོ།། རང་ཉིད་དཔལ་དུས་ཀྱི་འཁོར་ལོར་གསལ་བའི་སྙིང་ཁར་ཟླ་བ་ཉི་མ་སྒྲ་གཅན་གསུམ་མམ་དུས་མེ་དང་བཅས་པའི་གདན་བཞི་བརྩེགས་ཀྱི་སྟེང་དུ། རྣམ་བཅུ་དབང་ལྡན་བསྒོམ་པ་ནི་འདི་ལྟར་རོ།། ནཱ་ད་ནག་པོ། ཐིག་ལེ་དམར་པོ། རྣམ་བཅད་དཀར་པོ། ཧ་དཀར་པོ། ཀྵ་ལྗང་གུ། མ་ཤར་ནག ལྷོ་དམར། བྱང་དཀར། ནུབ་སེར། དབུས་ལྗང་གུ་སྟེ་སྣ་ཚོགས་མདོག་ཅན། ལ་སེར་པོ། ཝ་དཀར་པོ། ར་དམར་པོ། ཡ་ནག་པོའི་མདོག་ཅན་གསལ་བཏབ། དེ་ལ་དམིགས་ནས་བདེ་སྟོང་གི་ཚོར་གདུང་དང་། མོས་པ་དྲག་པོས་མོས་སྒོམ་བྱས་ནས་སྔགས་འདི་ཉིད་བཟླ། ཨོཾ་ཧ་ཀྵ་མ་ལ་ཝ་ར་ཡཾ་སྭཱ་ཧཱ། ཞེས་པའི་སྔགས་གཟུགས་འདི་ལ་དམིགས་ནས་ངག་ཏུ་ཡང་གཟུང་སྔགས་དེ་ཉིད་བཟླའོ།།

བཟླས་དམིགས་གཞན་གྱི་སྒོ་ནས་བཟླ་ཚུལ་ཁག་ནི་འདི་ལྟར་རོ།།

༡ རང་ཉིད་དཔལ་དུས་ཀྱི་འཁོར་ལོར་གསལ་བའི་སྙིང་གར་རྣམ་བཅུ་དབང་ལྡན་ཡི་གེ་རེ་རེ་བཞིན་གྱི་ཁ་མདོག་རྣམས་གསལ་བོར་བསྒོམ་པར་དཀའ་ན། ཁ་དོག་ཐམས་ཅད་འདུས་པའི་ངོ་བོའམ་བདག་ཉིད་ཅན་ཁ་མདོག་ལྗང་གུའི་རྣམ་པ་ཅན་བསྒོམ་མོ།། སྙིང་གའི་རྣམ་བཅུ་དབང་ལྡན་ལས་འོད་ཟེར་དཔག་ཏུ་མེད་པ་ལོངས་སྐུའི་ཞིང་ཁམས་གཙོ་བོར་གྱུར་པའི་ཞིང་ཁམས་རྣམས་སུ་འཕྲོས་པས། དཔལ་དུས་ཀྱི་འཁོར་ལོའི་ལྷ་ཚོགས་ལ་སོགས་པ་ཡི་དམ་རྒྱུད་སྡེ་བཞིའི་ལྷ་ཐམས་ཅད་སྤྱན་དྲངས་ཏེ་རང་ལ་ཐིམ་པས། རང་ཉིད་ཡི་དམ་ཀུན་འདུས་སུ་གྱུར་པར་བསམ་ནས་སྔགས་བཟླ་བར་བྱ་བའོ།། ཡང་འོད་ཟེར་འཕྲོས་པས་རང་ལ་ཟབ་ལམ་སྟོན་པའི་རང་གི་རྩ་བའི་བླ་མ་དེ་ཉིད་སྤྱན་དྲངས་ཏེ། དེས་བདག་ལ་དབང་བཞི་རྫོགས་པར་བསྐུར་ནས། རིགས་བདག་རྡོ་རྗེ་སེམས་དཔའ་དང་དབྱེར་མེད་དུ་བཞུགས་པར་བསམ་བཞིན་དུ་ཡང་སྔགས་བཟླ་བར་བྱའོ།།

༢ ཡང་ན་དམིགས་པ་གཞན་བྱ་འདོད་ན། སྙིང་གའི་རྣམ་བཅུ་ལས་འོད་ཟེར་འཇིག་རྟེན་གྱི་ཁམས་ཐམས་ཅད་ཁྱབ་པར་འཕྲོས། ཕྱི་སྣོད་ལ་ཕོག་པས་ཕྱི་སྣོད་དག་པའི་གཞལ་ཡས་ཁང་རྣམས་སུ་གྱུར། ཡང་འོད་ཟེར་དག་ནང་བཅུད་ལ་ཕོག་པས་ནང་བཅུད་སེམས་ཅན་ཐམས་ཅད་དུས་ཀྱི་འཁོར་ལོའི་སྐུར་གྱུར། འོད་ཟེར་རྣམས་སླར་འདུས། རང་ལ་ཐིམ་པར་བསམ་ཏེ་སྔགས་བཟླ་བར་བྱ་བའོ།།

༣ གཞན་དོན་སྣོད་བཅུད་ཞིང་སྦྱོང་གི་བཟླས་དམིགས་ཏེ། མདོ་ལམ་དུ་ཞིང་སྦྱོང་བ་འདི་གཉིས་ཚོགས་བསགས་པའི་དོན་ཡིན་ཞིང་། བཟླས་དམིགས་དེ་གཉིས་ནི་གསང་སྔགས་ཉམས་ལེན་པ་ཐམས་ཅད་ཀྱི་ཐུན་མོང་ཁྱད་མེད་དུ་ཉམས་སུ་ལེན་ཚོག་པ་ཞིག་གོ །

༤ ཡང་གནས་ལུགས་སྟོང་ཉིད་དྲན་པ་དང་། འཁོར་འདས་ཀྱི་ཆོས་ཐམས་ཅད་རང་དུས་ཀྱི་འཁོར་ལོའི་བདག་ཉིད་ཡིན་པར་ཞེ་ཕུགས་ལ་དྲན་བཞིན་པའི་ངང་ནས། གོང་གི་གཟུངས་སྔགས་ཧ་ཀྵཱའི་ཡིག་འབྲུ་རྣམས་གཅིག་གི་འོག་ཏུ་གཅིག་གི་མགོ་ཆུད་པའི་ཕྲེང་བ་རྒྱུན་མ་ཆད་པར་རང་གི་ཁ་ནས་སྒློ་བུར་དུ་བྱུང་སྟེ། རང་གི་ལུས་ཀྱི་ནང་གང་སའི་ནང་དུ་སོང་། དེ་ནས་རང་ཉིད་ཡབ་དུས་ཀྱི་འཁོར་ལོའི་རྡོ་རྗེའི་ལམ་ནས་བདེ་ཁྲིལ་ལི་ལི་བྱུང་ཏེ། རང་ཉིད་ཀྱི་ངོ་བོའི་ཡུམ་གྱི་པདྨར་ཞུགས། རང་ཉིད་ཡུམ་གྱི་རྩ་དབུ་མའི་ནང་བརྒྱུད་དེ་ཡུམ་གྱི་ཞལ་ནས་རང་ཉིད་ཡབ་ཀྱི་ཞལ་དུ་ཞུགས། སྙིང་གའི་རྣམ་བཅུ་དབང་ལྡན་ལ་ཐིམ་པར་བསམ་ལ་བཟླ་བ་ཡང་གནད་ཤིན་ཏུ་ཆེ་བར་གསུང་སོ།།

༥ ཡང་སྔར་བཞིན་སྔགས་ཕྲེང་རང་ཡབ་ཀྱི་ཞལ་ནས་སྒློ་བུར་དུ་བྱུང་སྟེ། རང་ཉིད་ཡུམ་གྱི་ཞལ་དུ་ཞུགས། སྐུའི་ནང་བརྒྱུད་དེ་བྷ་ག་ནས་བདེ་ཁྲི་ལི་ལི་རང་ཉིད་ཡབ་ཀྱི་གསང་བའི་རྡོ་རྗེར་ཞུགས། དབུ་

 སྟོན་མེད་རབ་གསལ་སྣང་བ།

མའི་ནང་ནས་བརྒྱུད་དེ་སྙིང་གའི་རྣམ་བཅུ་དབང་ལྡན་ལ་ཐིམ་པར་བསམ་བཞིན་བཟླ་སྟེ། བཟླས་དམིགས་འདི་གཉིས་ནི་རྒྱ་གར་པཎ་ཆེན་དུ་མས་གསུངས་ཤིང་སྔགས་བླ་མེད་ཀྱི་ཐུན་མོང་མ་ཡིན་པའི་བཟླས་པ་སྟེ། རྫོགས་རིམ་གྱི་བདེ་སྟོང་གི་ཡེ་ཤེས་འདྲེན་པ་སོགས་དགོས་པ་དུ་མ་ཡོད་པས། བླ་མེད་ཀྱི་ལྷའི་བཟླས་དམིགས་ཐམས་ཅད་ཀྱི་གཙོ་བོ་དང་བཟླས་དམིགས་ཀྱི་དངོས་གཞི་ཡིན་པས་འདིའི་སྒོ་ནས་བཟླས་པ་གཙོ་བོར་བྱ་བ་ནི་གལ་ཆེ་བ་ཡིན་ནོ།།

ཐུན་འཇོག་ཁར་སྔོན་བཅུད་རྟེན་དང་བརྟེན་པའི་དཀྱིལ་འཁོར་དུ་གསལ་བ་དེ་ཐམས་ཅད་འོད་དུ་ཞུ་ནས་རང་ལ་ཐིམ། རང་ཉིད་ཡུམ་གྱི་རྣམ་པ་དེ་ཉིད་ཡབ་ལ་ཐིམ། ཡབ་ཀྱང་ནས་རིམ་བཞིན་སྙིང་གའི་རྣམ་བཅུ་དབང་ལྡན་ལ་ཐིམ། དེ་ནས་རིམ་པས་སྟེང་གི་ནཱ་དཱ་ལ་ཐིམ། ནཱ་དཱ་སྟོང་བར་ཡལ་བའི་ངང་ནས་སྤྲོས་བྲལ་ལ་ཅུང་ཟད་མཉམ་པར་བཞག་ཏེ་ཅུང་ཟད་མི་རྟོག་པའི་ངང་དུ་བཞག་གོ། སླར་ཡང་སྐད་ཅིག་ལ་རང་ཉིད་དུས་ཀྱི་འཁོར་ལོ་ཡབ་ཡུམ་གྱི་སྐུ་གསལ་འདེབས་པར་བྱ་དགོས་པའོ།།

ཐུན་མཚམས་སུ་རང་ཉིད་དུས་ཀྱི་འཁོར་ལོ་ཡིན་པའི་ང་རྒྱལ་དང་མ་བྲལ་བར་བྱ་ཐུབ་ན་རབ་དང་། མ་མཐར་ཡང་མཚམས་མཚམས་སུ་དྲན་ཅི་ནུས་བྱ། གང་སྣང་ཐམས་ཅད་དུས་ཀྱི་འཁོར་ལོའི་སྐུ་རྡོ་རྗེའི་ངོ་བོ། སྒྲ་གང་གྲགས་ཐམས་ཅད་དུས་ཀྱི་འཁོར་ལོའི་གསུང་གཞོམ་མེད་རྡོ་རྗེའི་རང་སྒྲ། བདག་གི་སེམས་ལ་རྣམ་རྟོག་གང་སྐྱེ་ཐམས་ཅད་དུས་ཀྱི་འཁོར་ལོའི་ཐུགས་བདེ་སྟོང་གི་ཡེ་ཤེས་སུ་མོས་པའི་ངང་ནས་རྗེས་ཐོབ་ཀྱི་དུས་འདའ་བར་བྱ་དགོས་ཀྱི། ཚ་ལོ་དང་ཚ་ལོ་རྒྱ་བ་སོགས་ཁ་ན་མ་ཐོ་བ་དང་། གཞན་རྣམ་གཡེང་དང་ལོང་གཏམ་སོགས་ཀྱི་ངང་དུ་ལུས་མི་རུང་ངོ་།།

སྔགས་ཀྱི་བཟླས་པ་ཅི་ནུས་སུ་བྱས་པའི་མཐར།

དེ་ཐམས་ཅད་འོད་དུ་ཞུ་ནས་རང་ལ་ཐིམ།

ལྷ་སྐུ་གསལ་སྟོང་དེ་ལ་ཅི་ནུས་སུ་མཉམ་པར་བཞག

དགེ་བ་འདི་ཡིས་མྱུར་དུ་བདག །
དུས་ཀྱི་འཁོར་ལོ་འགྲུབ་གྱུར་ནས།།
འགྲོ་བ་གཅིག་ཀྱང་མ་ལུས་པ།།
དེ་ཡི་ས་ལ་འགོད་པར་ཤོག །

དགེ་བ་འདི་ཡིས་སྐྱེ་བོ་སོགས་དང་གོང་བཞིན་དགེ་བ་བསྔོ།

དཔལ་དུས་ཀྱི་འཁོར་ལོའི་བསྐྱེད་རིམ་སྒོམ་པ་ལ་སོགས་པའི་དགེ་བ་འདི་ཡིས་མཚོན་པའི་དུས་གསུམ་དུ་རང་གཞན་ཀུན་གྱི་དགེ་རྩ་ཇི་སྙེད་ཅིག་བསགས་ཡོད་པ་ཐམས་ཅད་ཀྱི་མཐུ་ལ་བརྟེན་ནས། མྱུར་བ་མྱུར་དུ་བདག་གིས་སེམས་ཅན་ཐམས་ཅད་ཀྱི་དོན་དུ། དཔལ་ལྡན་དུས་ཀྱི་འཁོར་ལོའི་གོ་འཕང་བརྙེས་པར་གྱུར་ཏེ། མཐའ་ཡས་པའི་འགྲོ་བ་གཅིག་ཀྱང་མ་ལུས་པ། དཔལ་ལྡན་དུས་ཀྱི་འཁོར་ལོའི་ས་ལ་འགོད་པར་ཤོག་ཅིག་ཅེས་པའོ།།

དགེ་བ་འདི་ཡིས་སྐྱེ་བོ་ཀུན།།
བསོད་ནམས་ཡེ་ཤེས་ཚོགས་རྫོགས་ཤིང་།།
བསོད་ནམས་ཡེ་ཤེས་ལས་བྱུང་བའི།།
དམ་པ་སྐུ་གཉིས་ཐོབ་པར་ཤོག

ཟབ་ལམ་རྡོ་རྗེ་རྣལ་འབྱོར་གྱི་སྔོན་འགྲོའི་རིམ་པ་ནས་རིམ་བཞིན་བསྒོམས་པས་དགེ་བ་འདི་ཡིས། འགྲོ་བའི་སྐྱེ་བོ་རང་གཞན་སེམས་ཅན་ཀུན་གྱི། བསོད་ནམས་དང་ཡེ་ཤེས་ཀྱི་ཚོགས་རྒྱ་ཆེན་པོ་རྫོགས་ཏེ། དེའི་བསོད་ནམས་དང་ཡེ་ཤེས་ལས་བྱུང་བའི་དགེ་ཚོགས་རྒྱ་ཆེན་པོས། ཀུན་རྫོགས་གཞན་སྣང་གི་ཆོས་ཀྱི་སྐུ་དང་གཟུགས་ཀྱི་སྐུ་སྟེ་དམ་པ་སྐུ་གཉིས་པོ་འཐོབ་པའི་རྒྱུར་གྱུར་ཅིག ཞེས་བསྔོ་སྨོན་བྱས་པའོ།།

དུས་འཁོར་རྫོགས་རིམ་ཐུན་མིན་གྱི་སྔོན་འགྲོ་དབེན་གསུམ།

སྔོན་འགྲོ་ཆོས་བདུན་གྱི་ཡ་གྱལ་བདུན་པ། དཔལ་དུས་ཀྱི་འཁོར་ལོའི་རྫོགས་རིམ་སྦྱོར་བ་ཡན་ལག་དྲུག་གི་ཐུན་མོང་མ་ཡིན་པའི་སྔོན་འགྲོ་གཉིས་པའམ། སྔོན་འགྲོ་མཐོ་ཤོས་འདི་ནི་ཤིན་ཏུ་ཟབ་པའི་མན་ངག་དབེན་པ་གསུམ་ཞེས་གྲགས་ལ། གོང་དུ་ཡོད་པའི་སྔོན་འགྲོ་ཆོས་དྲུག་པོ་ཉམས་ལེན་ཟིན་རྗེས་སུ་ཁག་བདུན་པ་འདི་ཉིད་བསྒོམས་ཏེ་ཉམས་སུ་ལེན་པར་བྱ་དགོས་པ་ཞིག་གོ། འདི་ལ་དགོས་བཙུགས་ཀྱི་ངག་འདོན་རྩ་བ་ནས་མེད་ལ། འདི་ཉིད་ཐུན་མིན་བླ་མ་དགེ་བའི་བཤེས་གཉེན་ལས་དངོས་ཁྲིད་འབོག དེ་ནས་བླ་མས་བྱིན་རླབས་ཀྱི་ཚིག་དང་འགྲོགས་ཏེ་རྒྱས་པར་བྱ་དགོས་པ་སྲོལ་རྒྱུན་ལྟར་ཡིན་པས་ཁྲིད་དམ། འགྲེལ་བཤད་སོགས་བྱ་སྲོལ་མེད་པའི་ཐུན་མོང་མ་ཡིན་པའི་ཞི་གནས་སྒྲུབ་ཐབས་ཤིག་གོ། གཞན་ཡང་དབང་དང་ཚིག་སོགས་སྔོན་དུ་འགྲོ་མི་དགོས་པར་མདོ་ལམ་གྱི་ཞི་གནས་སྒྲུབ་ལུགས་དང་ཆ་འདྲ་བར་བཀའ་རྒྱ་སྒྲོ་ཡངས་པོ་བྱས་ནས་འགྲོ་མི་ཚོག་པ་ཚེར་མེད་པ་འདྲ་བས། འདིར་དེའི་དབང་དུ་བཏང་ཏེ་བཤད་པར་བྱའོ།།

ལུགས་འདི་དག་གང་ལ་ཡང་དང་པོ་བསྒོམ་པའི་གནས་ནི། བསྒོམ་ཁང་ཅ་ཅོ་སོགས་མེད་པའི་གནས་སུ་མུན་ནག་གི་ཁང་བ་སྐྱེའུ་ཁུང་སྒོ་སོགས་མེད་པའམ་ཡོད་ན་དེ་དག་བསུམས་ཏེ་བསྒོམ་དགོས། དེ་ཡང་ཐུན་མོང་མ་ཡིན་པའི་ལུས་གནད་འཛོག་ཚུལ་ཡོད་ཀྱང་དེ་དག་ནི་བླ་སློབ་ཞལ་འཛོམ་པའི་དུས་སུ་ཁྲིད་བཏབ་ན་ལེགས་པར་སྙམ། སྤྱིར་བཏང་ལུས་ཀྱི་ལུས་གནད་རྣམ་སྣང་གི་ཆོས་བདུན་དུ་གྲགས་པ་འདིར་བསྒྲང་ན། གང་ཟག་སུ་ཞིག་གིས་དངོས་སུ་དབེན་གསུམ་ཉམས་སུ་ལེན་དུས་བླ་མ་རྡོ་རྗེ་སློབ་དཔོན་གྱིས་དངོས་སུ་ཁྲིད་པའི་དུས་སུ་ཤེས་སླ་བས། དེ་དག་འདིར་ངེས་པར་དུ་སྤྲོ་མི་དགོས་ལ། དེས་ན་འདིར་སྤྱིར་བཏང་གི་རྣམ་སྣང་ཆོས་བདུན་ཙམ་ཞིག་སྤྲོ་ན་དེ་དག་ནི་རིམ་པ་བཞིན། ༡ རྐང་བ་གཉིས་རྡོ་རྗེ་དཀྱིལ་ཀྲུང་། ༢ ལག་གཉིས་རྡོ་རྗེ་ཁུ་ཚུར་གྱིས་ཐེ་བོང་གཉིས་ཀྱིས་སྲིན་མཛུབ་གཉིས་ཀྱི་རྩ་བར་མནན་ཏེ་བཙུར། ༣ སྒལ་ཚིགས་དྲང་པོར་བསྲིང་། ༤ མིག་གིས་རང་གི་མིག་ལས་ཐུང་ཙམ་མཐོ་སའི་སོར་བཅུ་དྲུག་གི་ནམ་མཁའ་ནག་ཁུང་ལ་ཅེར་གྱིས་གཏད། ༥ སོ་མཆུ་རང་སོར་བཞག ༦ ལྕེ་རྩེ་ཡ་རྐན་ལ་སྦྱར། ༧ མགྲིན་པ་ནང་དུ་གུག་པ་རྣམས་ཡིན་ནོ།།

དེ་ནས་སེམས་དེ་ཡིད་ཀྱི་རྣམ་པར་ཤེས་པ་དབང་ལྟའི་ཡུལ་དུ་གཡེང་བའི་རྒོད་པ་དང་། ལྷོད་དྲགས་ནས་

བྱེད་རྫུགས་སུ་མི་འཇུག་པར་བསྒོམ། ཏ་ཙང་སྒྲིམ་མི་ཆེ། ལྷོད་མི་ཆེ་བར་མཐའ་གཉིས་སུ་མ་ལྷུང་བའི་ངོ་བོར་གནས་པར་བྱེད། གལ་ཏེ་བྱིང་རྒོད་ཅི་ཞིག་བྱུང་ཡང་དང་པོ་དྲན་པས་ངོ་བོ་དེ་ཉིད་དྲན། ཤེས་བཞིན་གྱིས་དེ་ཉིད་ཤེས་པའམ་ཏ་གོ་ བག་ཡོད་ཀྱིས་དེ་ཉིད་ལ་འཇུག་ལྡོག་བྱ་ཤེས་དགོས། དེ་ཡང་ལས་དང་པོ་བ་ཞིག་ཡིན་ན། གལ་ཏེ་བྱིང་རྒོད་གང་རུང་དང་བྲལ་ཚུལ་མ་ཤེས་པའམ་བྲལ་ཐབས་མ་ཐོན་ན། འབྱུང་མཁན་གྱི་རྣམ་རྟོག་ཁོ་རང་ལ་ཐད་ཀར་ཅེར་གྱིས་ལྟ་བ་དང་། རྒོད་པ་བྱུང་ན་ཡང་དེ་ལྟར་རྒོད་པ་རང་ལ་ཅེར་གྱིས་ལྟ་བར་བྱ་དགོས། དེ་ནི་བྱིང་རྒོད་རང་ཉིད་ལ་བློ་སེམས་གཏད་དགོས་པའི་དོན་ཡིན།

དེ་ཡང་སེམས་འཇུག་ལུགས་དང་དེ་དག་གི་ངོ་བོ་ཇི་ལྟར་ཡིན་སོགས་འདིར་ལུང་དྲངས་ཏེ་ཙུང་ཟད་སྨྲས་ན་འདི་ལྟར། ༡ དང་པོ་སྒོམ་ལ་བརྩོན་པའི་ཐོག་མར་རང་སེམས་དེ་ཉིད་རི་གཟར་གྱི་ཆུ་འབབ་པ་ལྟར་སེམས་སྐད་ཅིག་ཀྱང་མི་སྡོད་པ་ལ་མི་གནས་པར་རྣམ་རྟོག་བརྒྱུད་མར་འཕྲོ་ཞིང་། སྔར་ལས་ཀྱང་རྣམ་རྟོག་ཇེ་མང་དུ་སོང་བར་སྣང་བ་འོང་སྟེ། སྔར་དེ་ལས་ཀྱང་མང་བའི་རྣམ་རྟོག་རྒྱ་འབྱམས་སུ་འགྲོ་བ་ཡིན་ཀྱང་། སེམས་ཁ་ཕྱིར་ལྟས་སུ་སོང་བས་རྣམ་རྟོག་ངོས་མ་ཟིན་པ་ཡིན། ཏིང་ངེ་འཛིན་ལ་སེམས་ཙུང་ཟད་གནས་པར་འོང་བའི་རྐྱེན་གྱིས་མི་གནས་ཤིང་འཕྲོ་བའི་རྣམ་རྟོག་ངོས་ཟིན་པ་ཡིན་པས། གཡོ་བའི་ཉམས་རི་གཟར་གྱི་འབབ་ཆུ་ལྟ་བུ་དེ་བྱུང་བ་ཡིན། འདིའི་སྐབས་སེམས་མི་རྟོག་པ་ལ་དྲན་ཤེས་ཀྱིས་ཆེད་དུ་བཞག་པའི་རྐྱེན་གྱིས་ཙུང་ཟད་རེ་གནས་པ་ཡིན། འདི་སེམས་རང་གི་ངོ་བོ་རང་ཤུགས་ཀྱིས་མི་སྡོད་པར་གཡོ་བའི་རང་བཞིན་ཅན་ལས། གཡོ་བའི་ཏིང་ངེ་འཛིན་ཐོབ་པ་ཡིན་པས་དགའ་བ་སྒོམ་དགོས་པ་ཞིག་ཡིན་པ་ལས། བློ་ཕམ་དགོས་པའི་དོན་ནི་མ་ཡིན།

༢ དེའི་ཚེ་སེམས་མི་སྡོད་པ་ལ་ཅི་ཡང་མི་སེམས་པར་ཏིང་ངེ་འཛིན་ལ་ཡིད་ཆེས་བསྐྱེད། དྲན་ཤེས་ཡང་ཡང་བསྟེན། སྒོམ་མི་བསམ་པའི་ལེ་ལོ་བྱུང་ན་དང་བའི་དད་པ་སྐྱེད་བྱེད་ཀྱི་རྣམ་ཐར་ཀློག་པ་སོགས་འདུན་པ་བསྐྱེད་པའི་ལས་སོགས་ལ་འཇུག བྱིང་རྒོད་བྱུང་ན་གཉེན་པོ་དྲན་ཤེས་གཉིས་བརྟེན་ཏེ་བྱིང་རྒོད་འབྱུང་མཁན་རང་གི་ངོ་ལ་ལྟ་བའི་སྒོ་ནས་ཡང་ཡང་བསྒོམ། བར་སྐབས་རེ་ལ་རྔོང་ཁོག་རྟོག་པོའི་ཆུ་སྒྲ་ལ་རྒྱུན་དུ་ཉན་ན་མཐར་སྒྲ་ཡོད་པ་མི་ཤེས་པར་འགྱུར་བ་ལྟར། སེམས་རང་བཞིན་གྱིས་ཁད་ཆགས་པའམ་རང་ཤུགས་ཀྱིས་བབ་ཆགས་ནས་ཕྱིའི་གཟུགས་སྒྲ་སོགས་ཀྱིས་མི་གནོད་པར་ཤིག་གེར་གནས་པ་ཡོང་། དེ་ནས་ཡང་བསྒྱུར་སྔར་བཞིན་རྣམ་རྟོག་དུ་མ་འཕྲོ་ཞིང་སེམས་གཡོ་བའི་རང་བཞིན་དུ་འགྱུར་བ་ཞིག་འོང་སྟེ། འདི་སེམས་རང་ཤུགས་ཀྱིས་གནས་པའི་ཏིང་ངེ་འཛིན་ཞིག་ཐོབ་པ་ཡིན་པས་ཐོབ་པའི་ཏིང་ངེ་འཛིན་ཞེས་བྱ།

༣ དེ་ནས་ཡང་གོང་བཞིན་ཡང་ཡང་བསྒོམས་པས་སྤྲུལ་བ་མཆོང་མ་ཐག་མི་ལྷུང་བར་ཅེར་གྱིས་སྡོད་པ་ལྟར། སྡོད་པ་ནི་སེམས་འཕྲོ་བའམ་རྣམ་རྟོག་ཤུགས་ཆུང་དུ་རེ་སྐྱེས་ནས་ཏིང་ངེ་འཛིན་ལ་བར་གཅོད་ཀྱང་། དེ་མ་ཐག་རང་ཞིར་འགྲོ་བའམ། དེ་མ་ཐག་རྣམ་རྟོག་གི་འཕྲོ་བཅད་ནས་མི་རྟོག་པ་ལ་སེམས་ཁད་ཆགས་

ཏེ་གནས་པའི་སྟེང་དུ་འཇོག་ནུས་པ་འོང་སྟེ། གོང་གི་ཐོབ་པའི་ཏིང་ངེ་འཛིན་ལ་གོམས་འདྲིས་སོང་བའི་ཏིང་ངེ་འཛིན་ཡིན་པས་གོམས་པའི་ཏིང་ངེ་འཛིན་ཡིན། དེ་ནས་ཡང་ཡང་བསྒོམས་པས་མཚོ་ཆུང་བསེར་བུས་བསྐྱོད་ཀྱང་གཞན་དུ་མི་བསྐྱིལ་བ་ལྟར་རྣམ་རྟོག་སྐྱེད་དཀའ་ཞིང་། རེས་འགའ་རྣམ་རྟོག་ཙུང་ཟད་རེ་སྐྱེས་ཀྱང་རྟོག་མེད་ཀྱི་ཏིང་ངེ་འཛིན་ལ་གནས་པ་ལས་གཞན་དུ་མི་བསྐྱོད་ཅིང་རྣམ་རྟོག་གིས་ཏིང་ངེ་འཛིན་གྱི་བར་མི་གཅོད་པ་འོང་སྟེ། གོམས་པ་སོང་བའི་གོམས་པ་དེ་འདིར་བརྟན་པའི་ཏིང་ངེ་འཛིན་ཡིན།

༤ དེ་ནས་ཀྱང་ཡང་ཡང་བསྒོམས་པས་རྒྱ་མཚོ་རྦབས་དང་བྲལ་བ་ལྟར་སེམས་ལ་རྣམ་རྟོག་ཡེ་མི་སྐྱེ་ལ། བཞག་ན་རང་ཤུགས་ཀྱིས་ཁད་ཆགས་ཏེ་སྡོད། བཏང་ན་དམིགས་པ་ཀུན་ལ་འགྲོ་བ་ཞིག་འོང་སྟེ། གོང་གི་བརྟན་པའི་ཏིང་ངེ་འཛིན་ཙམ་མཐར་ཕྱིན་པའི་ཏིང་ངེ་འཛིན་ཡིན།

༥ བཞག་སྡོད་ལ་དབང་ཐོབ་པའི་ཏིང་ངེ་འཛིན་ནི་ཞི་གནས་དང་། ངོ་བོ་གསལ་སྟོང་དུ་ལྷག་གེར་མཐོང་བ་ལ་ལྷག་མཐོང་དུ་ངོ་སྤྲོད་པ་དམ་པ་གོང་མའི་ཕྱག་སྲོལ་དུ་མཛད། སེམས་རྟོག་མེད་ལ་ཆེད་དུ་བཞག་མི་དགོས་པར་རང་ཤུགས་ཀྱིས་སྡོད་པའི་དུས་འདིར། དེ་གའི་ངང་ནས་ཆོས་གཞན་རྣམས་མ་ཟད་སེམས་ཀྱི་ངོ་བོ་རེས་གསལ་བའི་ཆ་དང་། རེས་སྟོང་བའི་ཆ་དང་། རེས་བདེ་བའི་ཆ་དང་། རེས་གསལ་སྟོང་ཆ་མཉམ་པ་དང་། རེས་གསུམ་ག་ཆ་མཉམ་པ་གང་ཤར་ཡང་དེ་ལ་འང་སེམས་གཏད་པ་དང་ཆེད་འཛིན་གང་ཡང་མི་བྱ་བར། སེམས་བསམ་མེད་རང་བབ་ཁོ་ནར་བཞག་པ་ལ་ཡང་ཡང་གོམས་པས་སེམས་ཀྱི་ངོ་བོ་གསལ་སྟོང་སོགས་ཤར་འདུག་ཀྱང་། གང་ལ་ཡང་ཆེད་འཛིན་མི་བྱེད་པར་གསལ་རིག་གི་ཆ་དེ་ཡིད་ཞབས་སུ་སྐྱོང་འདུག་པའི་ངང་དུ་སེམས་རང་ཤུགས་ཀྱིས་ཁད་ཆགས་ནས་གནས་པ་ཞིག་འོང་སྟེ། ཆོས་ཉིད་ཡེ་ཤེས་ཀྱི་རིག་པ་དང་རྟོག་མེད་དང་། ཆེད་འཛིན་མེད་པ་ཙམ་ལ་རིགས་འདྲ་བའི་ཀུན་གཞིའི་རྣམ་ཤེས་ཡིན་ལ། དེ་ནས་ཀྱང་གསལ་རིག་སྐྱོང་བ་ཡིད་ཞབས་སུ་ཤར་འདུག་པ་དེ་ཡང་ལྟོས་མེད་དང་འཛིན་མེད་དུ་བཏང་སྟེ། སེམས་གང་ཡང་གཏད་པ་མེད་པ་ཁོ་ནའི་ངང་དུ་ཡང་ཡང་གོམས་པར་བྱས་པས་གསལ་རིག་གི་སྐྱོང་སྣང་ཡང་ནུབ། འཛིན་པ་ཐམས་ཅད་ཞིག མཉམ་བཞག་གི་ངོ་ལ་གོ་རྒྱུ་རིག་རྒྱུ་ཤེས་རྒྱུ་གང་ཡང་མེད་པར་ཡུལ་ཡུལ་ཅན་གཅིག་ཐ་དད་ལ་སོགས་པའི་སྣང་བ་ཐམས་ཅད་ཆམ་གྱིས་དག་པས། ཡེ་ཤེས་སྤྲོས་པ་དང་བྲལ་བའི་རྣམ་པར་མི་རྟོག་པའི་ཡེ་ཤེས་ཤིག་སྐྱེ་བར་འགྱུར་ཏེ། དེ་ནི་མཚན་མེད་ཀྱི་སྟོང་ཉིད་དང་། ཆོས་ཉིད་བདེ་གཤེགས་སྙིང་པོའོ།། འདི་མ་རྟོགས་པའི་དུས་སུ་སོར་སྡུད་བསྒོམས་ནས་དུ་རྟགས་སོགས་ཤར་བ་ནི་དེ་འདྲའི་བདེ་གཤེགས་སྙིང་པོའི་ཡེ་ཤེས་ཀྱི་སྣང་ཆ་ཡིན་ཀྱང་། དེ་སྣང་མཁན་གྱི་མི་རྟོག་པའི་ཡེ་ཤེས་དེ་སྟོང་ཉིད་བདེ་གཤེགས་སྙིང་པོ་དངོས་མ་ཡིན་ལ། འོན་ཀྱང་སྟོང་ཉིད་བསྒོམ་པ་ནི་ཡིན་ནོ།།

འདིར་ཞིབ་ཆ་དང་དཔྱད་རྒྱུ་མང་ཡང་རེ་ཞིག་དེ་ཙམ་གྱིས་བཞག དངོས་སུ་སློབ་དཔོན་དང་མཉམ་དུ་ཉམས་ལེན་དམར་ཁྲིད་བྱེད་དུས་རྒྱས་སྤྲོས་ཆོག་པ་ལས། དེ་མིན་འདི་ཙམ་ལས་རྒྱས་པར་སྤྲོ་མི་དགོས་

སྐམ་མོ།། དབེན་གསུམ་འདི་ཉིད་ཞག་བརྒྱ་དང་ཡང་ན་ཞག་ཞེ་ལྔ་ལས་མི་ཉུང་བར་བསྒོམ་པའི་ལུགས་སྲོལ་ཡོད་པ་རེད། དུས་ཚོད་དེ་དག་གི་རིང་ལ་ཉིན་རེ་ལ་ཐུན་བཞི་བྱ་དགོས་པ་རྒྱུན་ལྡན་ལྟར་ཡིན་ལ། ཐུན་བར་རྣམས་སུ་ཡང་དྲན་ཤེས་བག་ཡོད་ཆེས་གཟབ་ནན་གྱིས་བརྟེན་དགོས། དེ་ཡང་དབེན་པ་གསུམ་བརྟེན་དགོས་ལ། མ་ཟད་ལྷོད་མེད་བཞི་ལ་གནས་ཤིང་ལྷོད་ཆོས་དེ་དག་དང་བྲལ་བ་དགོས། རྒྱུ་མཚན་དེ་དག་གི་ཕྱིར། དཔེར་ན། འགྲོ་དུས་གོམ་པའི་འདེགས་འཛོག་རེ་རེ་བཞིན་ལ་དྲན་ཤེས་བརྟེན་དགོས་པས་གོམ་པ་ཐུང་དུར་སྤོས་ཏེ་ཆེས་དལ་མོའི་ངང་དུ་བསྐྱོད་དགོས་པ། མིག་གིས་འདོམ་གང་ལས་ལྷག་མི་རྒྱང་ཕྱིར་ཞྭ་མོ་ཐོད་རིང་གྱོན་ནས་འགྲོ་སྲོལ་ཡོད་པ། ངག་གིས་ཙ་ཅོ་སོགས་མི་སྨྲ་ཅིང་ཁུ་སིམ་མེར་བཞུགས་པ། མདོར་ན་སྤྱོད་ལམ་ཀུན་ཏུ་དབེན་པ་གསུམ་ཞེས་པ་བརྟེན་དགོས་པ་སྟེ། མི་གཡོ་བ་གསུམ་གྱི་སྒོ་ནས་དབེན་པ་གསུམ་བརྟེན་དགོས་པ་ལ། ལྷོད་མེད་བཞི་ལ་གནས་པར་བྱ་དགོས། དང་པོ་དབེན་པ་གསུམ་ནི། ལུས་བྱ་སྤྱོད་ཀྱིས་དབེན་ཅིང་མི་གཡོ་བ་ལྷ་ཁང་ནང་གི་སྐུ་བཞེངས་ལྟ་བུ་དགོས་པ་ལ། ངག་གཏམ་བརྗོད་ཀྱིས་དབེན་ཅིང་མི་གཡོ་བ་པི་ཝཾ་གི་རྒྱུད་ཐག་བཅད་པ་ལྟ་བུ་དང་། སེམས་རྣམ་རྟོག་གིས་དབེན་ཅིང་མི་གཡོ་བ་ཆུ་ཡི་རགས་ཐག་བཅད་པ་ལྟ་བུ་དགོས་སོ།།

ལྷོད་མེད་བཞི་ནི། ལུས་ཀྱི་ལོངས་སྤྱོད་ལ་མི་ལྷོད་པ་ཟེར་བ་སྟེ། ལུས་ཀྱི་ལོངས་སྤྱོད་རྒྱས་སྤྲོས་ལ་མི་ལྷོད་པར་འདོད་ཆུང་ཆོག་ཤེས་ཀྱི་ངང་བསྐྱང་བ། ངག་གི་ལོངས་སྤྱོད་ལ་མི་ལྷོད་པ་སྟེ། ངག་ཀྱལ་ཀ་དང་གླུ་རྩེད་སོགས་བག་མེད་ངག་འཁྱལ་ལ་མི་ལྷོད་པར་ངག་བཙུན་ཞིང་དོན་ལྡན་ཁོ་ན་ལས་མི་གླེང་བ། སེམས་རྣམ་རྟོག་སྣ་ཚོགས་ལ་མི་ལྷོད་པ་སྟེ། སེམས་རྣམ་གཡེང་དང་རྟོག་དཔྱོད་སོགས་ལ་རྒྱུན་གོམས་མི་བྱེད་པར། རྣམ་པར་མི་རྟོགས་པའི་ངང་བསྐྱང་ཅི་ཐུབ་བྱ་བ། འཚོ་བའི་ལོངས་སྤྱོད་ལ་མི་ལྷོད་པ་སྟེ། རང་བཞིན་གྱི་མི་བཞིན་དུ་ཟ་གནས་ཀྱི་ཐིག་ལེའི་མགུལ་སྐྱོད་དང་དེའི་འཇགས་བདེ་ཡི་འཚོ་བའི་ལོངས་སྤྱོད་ལ་དོན་དུ་མི་གཉེར་བར། འཚོ་མེད་ཞི་ཞིང་དབེན་པའི་ངང་བསྐྱང་ཅི་ཐུབ་བྱ་དགོས་པའི་དོན་ནོ།། འདི་ཉིད་བསྒོམ་པའི་ལོ་རྒྱུད་དང་ཆས་གོས་སོགས་ནི་བླ་སློབ་ཞལ་འཛོམས་པའི་དུས་སུ་ཤེས་སླ་བས་འདིར་བཤད་པས་དགོས་པ་ཆེར་མ་མཐོང་བས་འདིར་རེ་ཞིག་མི་སྤྲོའོ།།

> ཞེས་ཟབ་ལམ་རྡོ་རྗེའི་རྣལ་འབྱོར་གྱི་ངག་འདོན་མཁའ་སྤྱོད་བགྲོད་པའི་ཐེམ་སྐས་འདིའང་། ཀུན་མཁྱེན་ཆོས་ཀྱི་རྒྱལ་པོ་ཇོ་ནང་བ་ཡབ་སྲས་ཀྱི་ཕྱག་ལེན་ཇི་ལྟ་བ་སྟེ། གྲུབ་ཐོབ་གོང་མ་རྣམས་ཀྱི་ཡི་གེ་སོ་སོའི་གནད་ཚང་བར་བྱས་ཤིང་གཞུང་འདི་སྲོལ་བའི་མགོན་པོས་མཛད་པ་དར་རྒྱས་འཕེལ།

དེ་ཡན་ཆད་ཀྱིས་ཐུན་མོང་གི་སྔོན་འགྲོ་ལྔ་དང་ཐུན་མིན་གྱི་སྔོན་འགྲོ་གཉིས་ཏེ་བདུན་པོ་སོང་ཟིན་ཏོ།།

དངོས་གཞི་སྦྱོར་བ་ཡན་ལག་དྲུག་མདོར་བསྡུས།

དངོས་གཞི་སྦྱོར་བ་ཡན་ལག་དྲུག་ནི། བླ་སློབ་ཞལ་འཛོམས་པའི་སྒོ་ནས་ཁྲིད་སྒོམ་སྤྲུགས་མ་བྱས་ཏེ་ཉམས་སུ་ལེན་དགོས་པས་འདིར་ས་བཅད་མ་སྟོང་ཙམ་ཞིག་ཚིག་འགྲེལ་ཙམ་བྱེད་པ་ལས་རྒྱས་པར་མི་སྤྲོའོ།། རྒྱ་མཚན་ནི། གཞུང་ལུགས་ཀྱི་སྤྱི་ཁོག་འདི་ཉིད། ལས་དང་པོ་བ་རྣམས་ཀྱི་ཆེད་དུ་སྟོན་འགྲོའི་ངག་འདོན་གྱི་ཚིག་འགྲེལ་ཙམ་ཡིན་པ་དང་། རྒྱ་མཚན་གཙོ་བོ་ནི། སྟོན་འགྲོའི་སྐབས་སུ་དངོས་གཞིའི་ཁྲིད་ཡིག་ལ་རྒྱས་སྤྲོས་བྱས་ན་མི་སུ་ཡིན་གྱིས་བསླབ་མི་ཆོག་པའི་བཀག་རྒྱ་ཏུ་ཡང་འགྱུར་འགྲོ་བས་སོ།།

ཨོཾ་ཨཱཿཧཱུྃ་ཧོཿཧཾ་ཀྵཿ

དང་པོ་ཨོཾ་ཨཱཿཧཱུྃ་ཧོཿཧཾ་ཀྵཿཞེར་བ་དེས། ཁམས་དྲུག་ལྡན་གྱི་གང་ཟག་གིས་སྦྱོང་བྱེད་སྦྱོར་བ་ཡན་ལག་དྲུག་གི་སྒོ་ནས། སྦྱང་བྱ་མ་དག་པའི་ཕུང་པོ་དྲུག་དག་པའི་ཤུལ་ཏུ། མངོན་དུ་འགྱུར་བྱ་ཡེ་ནས་བཞུགས་པའི་རྒྱལ་བ་རིགས་དྲུག་པོ་མངོན་དུ་བྱ་དགོས་པས། དེ་དག་མངོན་དུ་འགྱུར་བྱེད་ཀྱི་ས་བོན་ནམ་མཚོན་དོན་གྱི་ཐུགས་དྲུག་སྨོས་པའོ།།

ལྷ་བདེ་གཤེགས་སྙིང་པོའི་བཀའ་དྲིན་གྱིས།།
ཡིད་རྣམ་རྟོག་འགྱུ་བ་སོ་སོར་བཅད།།
ཉམས་འོད་གསལ་རྟགས་བཅུ་རྫོགས་གྱུར་ནས།།
ལམ་སོར་སྡུད་འབྱོང་བར་བྱིན་གྱིས་རློབས།།
པ་དྲིན་ཅན་བླ་མ་ལ་གསོལ་བ་འདེབས།།
འདྲེན་མཆོག་ཡབ་སྲས་རྣམས་ཀྱིས་བྱིན་གྱིས་རློབས།།

སེམས་ཅན་ཐམས་ཅད་ཀྱི་རྒྱུད་ལ་ཡེ་གདོད་མ་ནས་ཆོས་ཉིད་དུ་གནས་པའི་ལྷ་བདེ་གཤེགས་སྙིང་པོ་སྟེ། གཞི་རྒྱུད་བདེ་བར་གཤེགས་པའི་སྙིང་པོ་ཡི་བཀའ་དྲིན་ནམ། ཆོས་ཉིད་ཀྱི་བྱེད་ལས་ཀྱིས། སྦྱོར་བ་ཡན་ལག་དྲུག་གི་དང་པོ་སོར་སྡུད་ཅེས་པ། ཉམས་ལེན་པ་གང་ཟག་སོ་སོའི་རང་རིག་པའི་ཡེ་ཤེས་དེ་ཉིད།

རྣམ་པར་མི་རྟོག་པའི་ཡེ་ཤེས་མངོན་དུ་འགྱུར་ཆེད་དུ། ཕྱི་ཡུལ་དྲུག་གི་ཡུལ་དུ་རྒྱུ་བའི་ཡིད་རྣམ་རྟོག་གི་འགྱུ་བ་དག་སོ་སོ་ནས་བཅད་པའམ་སྤྱུད་ཏེ། ནང་མི་རྟོག་པའི་ཡེ་ཤེས་འཆར་བའི་ཉམས་འོད་གསལ་རྟགས་བཅུ་པོ་ཡོངས་སུ་རྫོགས་པར་གྱུར་ནས་བརྟན་པར་གྱུར་པ་ནི། ལམ་སོར་སྤྱུད་ཡང་དག་དུ་འབྱོང་བ་ཡིན་པས་དེ་ཉིད་རྒྱུད་ལ་སྐྱེ་བར་བྱིན་གྱིས་རློབས་ཤིག་ཅེས་སོ།། དེ་འདྲའི་སྐལ་བ་བཟང་པོ་འབྱུང་བར་འགྱུར་ཞིང་། འགལ་རྐྱེན་བར་ཆད་མེད་པར་ཕ་དྲིན་ཅན་རྩ་བརྒྱུད་ཀྱི་བླ་མ་རྣམས་ལ་གསོལ་བ་སྙིང་ཐག་པ་ནས་འདེབས་ན། རྣམ་རྟོག་ཡོ་ལང་གི་འཁོར་བ་ལས་འདྲེན་པའི་འདྲེན་པ་མཆོག བླ་མ་ཡབ་སྲས་དང་བཅས་པ་རྣམས་ཀྱིས་བྱིན་གྱིས་རློབས་ཤིག གསོལ་བ་བཞིན་དུ་འགྲུབ་པར་གྱུར་ཅིག

ལྷ་བདེ་གཤེགས་སྙིང་པོའི་བཀའ་དྲིན་གྱིས།།
ཡིད་རླུང་སེམས་དག་རྣམས་མི་གཡོ་ཞིང་།།
ཉམས་ཤེས་རབ་རྟོགས་དཔྱོད་དགའ་བདེ་འཕེལ།།
ལམ་བསམ་གཏན་འབྱོང་བར་བྱིན་གྱིས་རློབས།།
ཕ་དྲིན་ཅན་བླ་མ་ལ་གསོལ་བ་འདེབས།།
འདྲེན་མཆོག་ཡབ་སྲས་རྣམས་ཀྱིས་བྱིན་གྱིས་རློབས།།

སེམས་ཅན་ཐམས་ཅད་ཀྱི་རྒྱུད་ལ་ཡེ་གདོད་མ་ནས་ཆོས་ཉིད་དུ་གནས་པའི་ལྷ་བདེ་གཤེགས་སྙིང་པོ་སྟེ། གཞི་རྒྱུད་བདེ་གཤེགས་སྙིང་པོ་ཡི་བཀའ་དྲིན་ནམ། ཆོས་ཉིད་ཀྱི་ནུས་པ་ཡིས། ཆོས་སྦྱོར་བ་ཡན་ལག་དྲུག་གི་གཉིས་པ་བསམ་གཏན་སྟེ། རང་ཡིད་དང་རླུང་སེམས་སམ། ཕྲ་བའི་ཡིད་ཤེས་དང་བཅས་པ་གཡོ་བ་མེད་པའི་སྒོ་ནས། རྣམ་པར་མི་རྟོག་པའི་ཡེ་ཤེས་ལ་གནས་ཐུབ་པའི་གནས་ཆ་གོམས་པ་སྟོབས་ཆེན་དུ་གྱུར་ཏེ། རིམ་བཞིན་མི་རྟོག་པའི་ཉམས་འཕར་དགོས་པ་ཅན་ནོ།། ༡ དེ་ཡང་དང་པོ་ཤེས་རབ་ཅེས་པ་འོད་གསལ་རྟགས་བཅུ་ལ་རྩེ་གཅིག་ཏུ་སེམས་པ་ཡིན། སྟོང་གཟུགས་ལ་དངོས་པོའི་མིང་གིས་བཏགས་ཤིང་། དེའི་མཚན་ཉིད་ཤེས་པ་ཡིན་པས་ཤེས་རབ་ཀྱིས་མིང་གིས་བསྟན།

༢ དེ་ནས་རིམ་བཞིན་འཕར་ཏེ་རྟོགས་པས། དེའི་སྟེང་དུ་སྟོང་གཟུགས་སེམས་སུ་ཤེས་པ་ཙམ་ཡིན། འོན་ཀྱང་རྟོགས་པས་སྟོང་གཟུགས་སེམས་ལས་གཞན་དུ་གཏན་ནས་མེད་མཐའ་ཆོད་པར་ཤེས་མེད།

༣ དཔྱོད་པས་ནི་སྟོང་གཟུགས་དེ་སེམས་ཉིད་གཅིག་པུ་ལས་གཞན་དུ་ཡུལ་ཡུལ་ཅན་ནམ་གཟུང་འཛིན་གཉིས་རྟོག་བྱ་རྟོག་བྱེད་སོ་སོའི་དབྱེ་བ་མེད་པ་ཁོ་ནར་རྟོགས་ཤིང་། དུ་བའི་སྣང་བ་ལ་དུ་བ་མེད་པ་དང་།

དཀར་པོ་འབར་བ་ལ་དཀར་པོ་མེད་པ་སོགས་གཟུང་བ་དང་བྲལ་བའི་རྟོགས་ཚུལ་ཡིན། དེ་ཕྱིར་དབྱེད་པའི་ཡན་ལག་ནི་མཉམ་གཞག་ཏུ་སྟོང་གཟུགས་ལ་ཐ་དད་པའི་གཉིས་སྣང་འགག་པའི་རང་བཞིན་ཅན་ཡིན་ནོ།།

༤ དགའ་བའི་ཡན་ལག་ནི། སྟོང་གཟུགས་ལ་དམིགས་པས་སེམས་ལ་དགའ་བདེ་འཆར་བ་ཡིན་ལ། དེ་ཡང་ནང་དུ་བདེ་བ་ཙུང་ཟད་ཤར་བའི་ཚེ་འདི་བདེའོ་སྙམ་དུ་རྗེས་སུ་ཙུང་ཟད་འཛིན་པ་དང་ཆགས་པ་དང་བཅས་པ་འཆར། བོད་པ་སྔ་མ་པལ་ཆེར་ནི་གཟུགས་ལ་ཆགས་པའི་དོན་རྣལ་འབྱོར་བའི་བློ་ངོར། སྟོང་གཟུགས་དང་སེམས་གཉིས་འབྲལ་མ་ཤེས་པ་དང་བྲལ་མི་བྲ་བའི་དོན་དུ་གནས་པའོ།།

༥ དགའ་བ་འདི་སྟོང་གཟུགས་ཀྱིས་དྲངས་པའི་དགའ་བདེ་ཡིན་ལ། དེ་ལའང་ཞེན་པ་དང་བཅས་པ་ཡིན་པས་ཆགས་པའི་སྒྲས་སྨོས་པ་ཡིན་ལ། དེས་ན་ཡན་ལག་འདིའི་ངོ་བོ་ནི་སྟོང་གཟུགས་ལས་བྱུང་བའི་བདེ་བ་ཙམ་ཡིན་པས་གཡོ་མེད་བདེ་བའི་ཧིང་ངེ་འཛིན་གྱི་ངོ་བོར་གྱུར་ཅིང་། འོན་ཀྱང་དེ་ལ་མངོན་པར་ཆགས་པ་ཡང་མེད། སྟོང་གཟུགས་དང་བདེ་བ་དང་སེམས་ཉིད་གསུམ་མཉམ་གཞག་ཏུ་ཐ་དད་དུ་འཛིན་པ་ནུབ་ཅིང་། ཐ་དད་པ་རོ་སྙང་བ་སྲབ་པའི་བདེ་བ་ཤིན་ཏུ་སྦྱངས་པའི་མཚན་ཉིད་ཅན་སྟེ། རིམ་པ་ལྔའི་བསྡུས་པའི་བསམ་གཏན་ནོ།།

དེ་ལྟར་བསྒོམ་པས་རིམ་བཞིན་དུ། རྟགས་བཅུ་སྟོང་གཟུགས་མ་ལུས་པ་ཡིད་མི་རྟོག་པ་དང་དབྱེར་མེད་དུ་གྱུར་པའི་ལམ། རྣམ་པར་དག་པ་བསམ་གཏན་རང་རྒྱུད་ལ་འཁྲུངས་བར་བྱིན་གྱིས་རློབས་ཤིག དེ་འདྲའི་སྐལ་བ་བཟང་པོ་འབྱུང་བར་འགྱུར་ཞིང་། འགལ་རྐྱེན་བར་ཆད་མེད་པར་པ་དྲིན་ཅན་རྩ་བརྒྱུད་ཀྱི་བླ་མ་རྣམས་ལ་གསོལ་བ་འདེབས་ན། འདྲེན་མཆོག་བླ་མ་ཡབ་སྲས་རྣམས་ཀྱིས་བྱིན་གྱིས་རློབས་ལ་དངོས་དོན་བདེ་གཤེགས་སྙིང་པོ་ལ་རེག་པར་གྱུར་ཅིག

ལྷ་བདེ་གཤེགས་སྙིང་པོའི་བཀའ་དྲིན་གྱིས།།
རྩ་རོ་རྐྱང་རླུང་བཅུ་དབུ་མར་ཚུད།།
ཉམས་གཏུམ་མོ་འབར་བའི་ཧཾ་ཡིག་ཞུ།།
ལམ་སྲོག་རྩོལ་འཁོར་བར་བྱིན་གྱིས་རློབས།།
པ་དྲིན་ཅན་བླ་མ་ལ་གསོལ་བ་འདེབས།།
འདྲེན་མཆོག་ཡབ་སྲས་རྣམས་ཀྱིས་བྱིན་གྱིས་རློབས།།

སེམས་ཅན་ཐམས་ཅད་ཀྱི་རྒྱུད་ལ་ཡེ་གདོད་མ་ནས་ཆོས་ཉིད་དུ་གནས་པའི་ལྷ་བདེ་གཤེགས་སྙིང་པོ་སྟེ། གཞི་རྒྱུད་བདེ་གཤེགས་སྙིང་པོ་ཡི་བཀའ་དྲིན་ནམ། ཆོས་ཉིད་ཀྱིས་དབང་དམ་སྟོབས་ཤུགས་ཀྱིས། སྦྱོར་བ་ཡན་ལག་དྲུག་གི་གསུམ་པ་སྲོག་རྩོལ། རྣལ་འབྱོར་བའི་སྟོང་གཟུགས་དང་རྣམ་པར་མི་རྟོག་པའི་ཡེ་ཤེས་དབྱེར་མེད་དུ་བསྲེས་ཟིན་ནས་གོམས་པ་ཉིད། རླུང་དང་བསྲེས་ཏེ་རྩ་རོ་མ་དང་རྐྱང་མ་གཉིས་ཀྱིས་མཚོན་པའི་རྩ་དག་ཏུ་རྒྱུ་བའི་རྩ་བའི་རླུང་། སྲོག་འཛིན་དང་། གྱེན་རྒྱུ། ཁྱབ་བྱེད། མེ་མཉམ། ཐུར་སེལ་བཅས་ལྔ་དང་། ཡན་ལག་གི་རླུང་། རྒྱུ་བ་དང་། རྣམ་པར་རྒྱུ་བ། ཡང་དག་པར་རྒྱུ་བ། རབ་ཏུ་རྒྱུ་བ། ངེས་པར་རྒྱུ་བ་བཅས་ལྔ་སྟེ། དེ་བཅུ་པོ་ལ་གནད་དུ་བསྣུན་དེ་རླུང་དེ་དག་དབུ་མར་ཚུད་ཅིང་འཆིང་ཐུབ་བྱེད་ཀྱི་ལམ། སྲོག་རྩོལ། དེ་འདྲའི་སྦྱོར་བ་ཡི་དབང་གིས་མས་བརྟན་གཏུམ་མོ་འབར་བས། སྤྱི་བོའི་ཧཾ་ཡིག་ཞུ་སྟེ་དེའི་དབང་གིས་ཡེ་ཤེས་ཀྱི་བདེ་བ་ལ་གནས་ཐུབ་འོང་བར་གསོལ་བའོ།། འདི་དག་ནི་ཉམས་ལེན་མཁན་གང་ཟག་སྤྱིར་བཏང་བའམ་སྤྱིའི་ཆ་ནས་བཤད་པ་ཡིན། དེའི་ཕྱིར་འདི་དག་ནི་གཙོ་བོ་ལམ་རང་ལུས་ཐབས་ལྡན་ལ་བརྟེན་ཏེ་ཞུ་བདེའི་ཡེ་ཤེས་འདྲེན་པར་རྩལ་སྦྱོང་བྱ་ཚུལ་གཙོ་བོ་བྱས་ནས་བཤད་པ་ཡིན་ནོ།། ཡིན་ནའང་གདུལ་བྱ་བྱེ་བྲག་པ་ལ་རགས་པའི་ལས་རྒྱ་སོགས་གཞན་ལུས་ཐབས་ལྡན་ཡང་གང་ཟག་དང་ཡུལ་དུས་འོས་འཚམ་དུ་འོང་མི་ཆོག་པའང་མེད་དོ།། དེ་ལྟ་བའི་སྲོག་རྩོལ་དེ་ཉིད་རྒྱུད་ལ་སྐྱེ་བར་བྱིན་གྱིས་རློབས་ཤིག སྐལ་བ་བཟང་པོ་འདི་དང་མི་འབྲལ་བར་གོང་ནས་གོང་དུ་འབྲུང་བར་འགྱུར་ཞིང་། འདི་ལ་འགལ་རྐྱེན་བར་ཆད་མེད་པར། པ་དྲིན་ཅན་རྩ་བརྒྱུད་ཀྱི་བླ་མ་རྣམས་ལ་གསོལ་བ་སྙིང་ནས་འདེབས་ན། ཟླ་གྲལ་འདྲེན་མཆོག་བླ་མ་ཡབ་སྲས་རྣམས་ཀྱིས་བྱིན་གྱིས་བརླབ་པར་མཛད་དུ་གསོལ།

འཛིན་པ་ལ་ལྷ་བདེ་གཤེགས་སྙིང་པོའི་བཀའ་དྲིན་གྱིས།།
ཁམས་འཛག་མེད་ཐིག་ལེ་དཔྲལ་བར་བརྟན།།
ཉམས་ཞི་བདེ་འགྱུར་མེད་རྒྱུད་ལ་སྐྱེས།།
ལམ་འཛིན་པ་འགྲོང་བར་བྱིན་གྱིས་རློབས།།
པ་དྲིན་ཅན་བླ་མ་ལ་གསོལ་བ་འདེབས།།
འདྲེན་མཆོག་ཡབ་སྲས་རྣམས་ཀྱིས་བྱིན་གྱིས་རློབས།།

སེམས་ཅན་ཐམས་ཅད་ཀྱི་རྒྱུད་ལ་ཡེ་གདོད་མ་ནས་ཆོས་ཉིད་དུ་བཞུགས་པའི་ལྷ་བདེ་གཤེགས་སྙིང་པོ་སྟེ། གཞི་རྒྱུད་བདེ་གཤེགས་སྙིང་པོ་ཡི་བཀའ་དྲིན་ནམ། རང་བཞིན་ཆོས་ཉིད་ཀྱི་བྱིན་རླབས་ཀྱིས། སྦྱོར་བ་ཡན་ལག་དྲུག་གི་བཞི་བ་འཛིན་པ། སྟོང་གཟུགས་རླུང་དང་བསྲེས་ཟིན་ཐིག་ལེར་བསྲེས་པའི་སྦྱོར་

བརྟར་ལ་ཡང་ཡང་གོམས་པས། འདི་ཡན་ཆད་དུ་ཁམས་གཏན་ནས་འཛགས་མེད་དུ་གྱུར་ཐུབ་མེད་ཀྱང་། རྣལ་འབྱོར་འདི་ལ་གོམས་པ་རྫོགས་པས། ཁམས་མི་ཞིགས་པའི་ཐིག་ལེ་ནམ་ཡང་འཛགས་པ་མེད་པར་བརྟན་པར་གྱུར་ཏེ། རང་རིག་ཡེ་ཤེས་ཀྱི་མས་བརྟན་གཏུམ་མོ་འབར་བས་ཞི་བདེ་ཙམ་མ་ཡིན་པར། ཞི་བདེ་འགྱུར་བ་མེད་པའི་ལམ་འཛིན་པ་ཉིད། མྱུར་བ་མྱུར་དུ་རྒྱུད་ལ་སྐྱེ་བར་བྱིན་གྱིས་རློབས་ཤིག དེ་འདྲའི་སྐལ་བ་བཟང་བོ་ཞིག་རང་རྒྱུད་ལ་འབྱུང་བར་འགྱུར་བ་ལ། འགལ་རྐྱེན་དང་བར་ཆད་ཀྱིས་དབེན་པར་བྱིན་གྱིས་རློབས་ཤིག ཕ་དམ་པ་དྲིན་ཅན་རྩ་བརྒྱུད་ཀྱི་བླ་མ་རྣམས་ལ་གསོལ་བ་འདེབས་ན། འདྲེན་པའི་མཆོག་བླ་མ་ཡབ་སྲས་རྣམས་དང་བཅས་པས་བྱིན་གྱིས་རློབས་ཤིག དེའི་དབང་གིས་རང་རྒྱུད་ཀྱི་རྟོགས་པ་གོང་ནས་གོང་དུ་འཕེལ་བར་གྱུར་ཅིག

ལྷ་བདེ་གཤེགས་སྙིང་པོའི་བཀའ་དྲིན་གྱིས།།
ལུས་རྩ་འདབ་བདེ་ཆེན་ཐིག་ལེས་གང་།།
ཉམས་ཕྱག་རྒྱ་གསུམ་ལ་མངའ་བརྙེས་པའི།།
ལམ་རྗེས་དྲན་འཁྱོང་བར་བྱིན་གྱིས་རློབས།།
ཕ་དྲིན་ཅན་བླ་མ་ལ་གསོལ་བ་འདེབས།།
འདྲེན་མཆོག་ཡབ་སྲས་རྣམས་ཀྱིས་བྱིན་གྱིས་རློབས།།

སེམས་ཅན་ཐམས་ཅད་ཀྱི་རྒྱུད་ལ་ཡེ་གདོད་མ་ནས་ཆོས་ཉིད་དུ་གནས་པའི་ལྷ་བདེ་གཤེགས་སྙིང་པོ་སྟེ། གཞི་རྒྱུད་བདེ་གཤེགས་སྙིང་པོ་ཡི་བཀའ་དྲིན་ནས། ཆོས་ཉིད་རྣམ་པར་དག་པའི་སྟོབས་ཀྱིས། སྦྱོར་བའི་ཡན་ལག་ལྔ་བ་རྗེས་དྲན། ནང་སྟོང་གཟུགས་རླུང་དང་ཐིག་ལེ་དང་བཅས་པར་དབང་འབྱོར་བས། ཁམས་ལ་འཛགས་པ་མེད་པའི་ནུས་སྟོབས་རྩལ་དུ་རྫོགས་ཏེ། ཞུ་བདེ་འཛགས་མེད་ཙམ་པོ་བ་ཙམ་མ་ཡིན་པར། ལུས་ཀྱི་རྩ་འདབ་ཀུན་ཏུ་བདེ་བ་ཆེན་པོའི་ཐིག་ལེ་འབབ་ཞིག་གིས་ཁེངས་པས། རང་སྣང་ཡེ་ཤེས་ཀྱི་ཉམས་ཀྱི་ཕྱག་རྒྱ་གསུམ་སྟེ། ལས་རྒྱ། ཡེ་རྒྱ། སྟོང་གཟུགས་ཕྱག་རྒྱ་ཆེན་མོ་གསུམ་ལ་མཉམ་པར་སྦྱོར་བ་དང་། དེས་དྲངས་པའི་བདེ་བའི་ཡེ་ཤེས་ལ་རོལ་བའི་ལམ། སྔར་སྦྱངས་ཟིན་པའི་ཞི་བདེའི་ཡེ་ཤེས་ཡང་ཡང་འདྲེན་པའི་རྒྱུ་མཚན་གྱིས་རྗེས་དྲན་དུ་གྲགས་པའི་ལམ་རང་རྒྱུད་ལ་འཁྱོང་བར་བྱིན་གྱིས་རློབས་ཤིག དེ་འདྲའི་སྐལ་བ་བཟང་བོ་འབྱུང་བ་ལ་ཕྱི་ནང་གི་བདུད་ཀྱི་འགལ་རྐྱེན་བར་ཆད་ལས་ཐར་བར་བྱིན་གྱིས་རློབས་ཤིག སྔར་སྦྱངས་ཟིན་གྱི་ཡེ་ཤེས་ཡང་ཡང་རྒྱུད་ལ་བསྐྱེད་པའི་ཕ་དྲིན་ཅན་རྩ་བརྒྱུད་ཀྱི་བླ་མ་རྣམས་ལ་གསོལ་བ་སྙིང་ནས་འདེབས་ན། ཞི་བསིལ་དམ་པ་རྒྱལ་བའི་གོ་འཕང་ལ་འདྲེན་པའི་

སྔོན་མེད་རབ་གསལ་སྣང་བ།

འདྲེན་མཆོག་བླ་མ་ཡབ་སྲས་རྣམས་ཀྱིས་བྱིན་གྱིས་རློབས་ཤིག བདེ་གཤེགས་སྙིང་པོ་མངོན་དུ་བྱེད་ནུས་པར་གྱུར་ཅིག

ལྷ་བདེ་གཤེགས་སྙིང་པོའི་བཀའ་དྲིན་གྱིས།།
རྩ་འཁོར་ལོ་དྲུག་པོ་བདེ་བའི་གདང་།།
སེམས་སྤྲོས་པ་མེད་ལ་དབང་འགྱུར་ཞིང་།།
ལམ་ཏིང་འཛིན་འབྱོང་བར་བྱིན་གྱིས་རློབས།།
ཕ་དྲིན་ཅན་བླ་མ་ལ་གསོལ་བ་འདེབས།།
འདྲེན་མཆོག་ཡབ་སྲས་རྣམས་ཀྱིས་བྱིན་གྱིས་རློབས།།

རང་གཞན་སེམས་ཅན་ཐམས་ཅད་ཀྱི་རྒྱུད་ལ་ཡེ་གདོད་མ་ནས་ཆོས་ཉིད་དུ་གནས་པའི་ལྷ་བདེ་གཤེགས་སྙིང་པོ་སྟེ། གཞི་རྒྱུད་རང་བཞིན་བདེ་གཤེགས་སྙིང་པོ་ཡི་བཀའ་དྲིན་ནམ། རང་བྱུང་ལྷན་སྐྱེས་ཀྱི་ཆོས་ཉིད་ཀྱི་ནུས་སྟོབས་ཀྱིས། རྣལ་འབྱོར་པས་རྟེན་དྲན་གྱི་སྐབས་ནས་སྟོང་གཟུགས་ཀྱི་ཕྱག་རྒྱ་ལ་བརྟེན་ཏེ། ཁམས་འཛགས་པ་མེད་པའི་མི་འགྱུར་བའི་བདེ་བ་ཆེན་པོ་འགྲུབ་ཟིན་པ་ལ་ཡང་ཡང་གོམས་པས་གོམས་པ་མཐར་ཕྱིན་ཏེ། རྩ་འཁོར་ཁ་ཤས་ཙམ་མ་ཡིན་པར། གཙུག་ཏོར་ནས་གསང་གནས་བར་གྱི་རྩ་འཁོར་ལོ་དྲུག་པོ་བདེ་བ་ཆེན་པོའི་ཡེ་ཤེས་འབབ་ཞིག་གིས་གང་། གཙུག་སེམས་བདེ་བ་ཆེན་པོའི་ཡེ་ཤེས་དེ་ཉིད་ཀྱིས་ཡོ་ལང་འབབ་ཞིག་ལས་ཀུན་རྫོབ་རྣམ་རྟོག་གི་སྤྲོས་པ་བྲལ་བས། ཀུན་ཁྱབ་རྟག་པའི་བདེ་ཆེན་ལ་དབང་འབྱོར་བས། གཉུག་མ་ལྷན་ཅིག་སྐྱེས་པའི་ཡེ་ཤེས་དེ་ཁོ་ན་ལ་ལོངས་སུ་སྤྱོད་པས། ཚེས་ཟབ་གསང་སྔ་བའི་ལམ་ཏིང་ངེ་འཛིན་རྒྱུད་ལ་སྐྱེ་བར་བྱིན་གྱིས་རློབས་ཤིག བསྐལ་བ་གྲངས་མེད་མང་པོར་མ་སྐྱེད་པའི་སྐལ་བ་བཟང་པོ་འདི་འབྱུང་བ་དོན་ལྡན་མཐར་ཕྱིན་པར་ཤོག་ཅིག དེ་ལ་ཕྱི་ནང་གསང་གསུམ་གྱི་འགལ་རྐྱེན་བར་ཆད་དང་བྲལ་བར་ཕ་བླ་མ་དམ་པ་མཆོག དྲིན་ཅན་རྩ་བ་དང་བརྒྱུད་པའི་བླ་མ་རྣམས་དང་། རང་རྒྱུད་ལ་ཡེ་བཞུགས་པའི་ངེས་པ་དོན་གྱི་དཔལ་ལྡན་གྱི་བླ་མ་ལ་ཡང་གསོལ་བ་འདེབས་ན། འདྲེན་མཆོག་གཏན་གྱི་སྐྱབས་གནས་བླ་མ་ཡབ་སྲས་རྣམས་ཀྱིས་དེ་བཞིན་འབྱོང་བར་བྱིན་གྱིས་རློབས་ཤིག

ལྷ་བདེ་གཤེགས་སྙིང་པོའི་བཀའ་དྲིན་གྱིས།།
ལུས་བྱེད་བཅིངས་གནད་དང་མ་བྲལ་ཞིང་།།
ཆོས་མ་ནོར་མན་ངག་ཟབ་མོ་ཡིས།།

ལམ་སྦྱོར་དྲུག་འགྲུབ་བར་བྱིན་གྱིས་རློབས།།
ཕ་དྲིན་ཅན་བླ་མ་ལ་གསོལ་བ་འདེབས།།
འདྲེན་མཆོག་ཡབ་སྲས་རྣམས་ཀྱིས་བྱིན་གྱིས་རློབས།།

འགྲོ་བ་སེམས་ཅན་ཐམས་ཅད་ཀྱི་རྒྱུད་ལ་ཡེ་གདོད་མ་ནས་ཆོས་ཉིད་ཀྱི་ཚུལ་དུ་གནས་པའི་ལྷ་བདེ་གཤེགས་སྙིང་པོ་སྟེ། གཞི་རྒྱུད་བདེ་གཤེགས་སྙིང་པོ་ཡོད་པའི་བཀའ་དྲིན་ནམ་ཆོས་ཉིད་ཀྱིས། སྦྱོར་བའི་ཡན་ལག་དྲུག་པོ་སོ་སོའི་སྐབས་ཀྱི་ལུས་བྱེད་བཅིངས་ཀྱི་གནད་རྣམས་དང་མི་འབྲལ་བར། ཆོས་དམ་པ་མ་ནོར་བའི་མན་ངག་ཟབ་མོའི་རང་རྒྱུད་གྲོལ་བར་བྱེད་པ་ལམ་སྦྱོར་བ་ཡན་ལག་དྲུག་པོ་རྒྱུད་ལ་བསྐྱེད་ནུས་པར་གྱུར་ཅིག དེ་ལྟར་དུ་འགྱུར་ཞིང་དེ་འདྲའི་སྐལ་བ་བཟང་པོ་འབྱུང་བ་དང་ལྡན་ཞིང་། གསང་བ་གསུམ་གྱི་འགལ་རྐྱེན་བར་ཆད་ཀུན་དང་བྲལ་བར་ཕ་དྲིན་ཅན་རྩ་བརྒྱུད་ཀྱི་བླ་མ་རྣམས་ལ་གསོལ་བ་འདེབས་ན། འདྲེན་མཆོག་བླ་མ་ཡབ་སྲས་རྣམས་ཀྱིས་དེ་བཞིན་དུ་འགྲུབ་བར་བྱིན་གྱིས་རློབས་ཤིག

སྦྱོར་དྲུག་ངོས་འཛིན་གསོལ་འདེབས་བདེ་སྟོང་གསལ་བྱེད་ཅེས་པ་འདི་ཡང་རྟོན་པ་བཞི་ལྡན་གྱིས་སྦྱར་བའོ། །བར་གྱི་ཕ་དྲིན་ཅན་ཞེས་པའི་ཚིག་རྐང་གཉིས་པོ་ཨཀློ་ཀརྨའི་མིང་གིས་མཛད་པའོ།།

དེ་ཉིད་ཁ་གསལ་བའི་འགྲེལ་བ་ཡོགས་སུ་བྱེད་མི་དགོས་སྙམ་སྟེ་རང་སོར་བཞག་གོ །

དགེ་བ་འདི་ཡིས་འགྲོ་བ་མ་ལུས་པ།།
དོན་མེད་འཁོར་བའི་བྱ་བ་རབ་སྤངས་ནས།།
དོན་ཆེན་རྡོ་རྗེའི་རྣལ་འབྱོར་ལེགས་བསྒོམས་ཏེ།།
དུས་ཀྱི་འཁོར་ལོའི་གོ་འཕང་མྱུར་ཐོབ་ཤོག །

དེ་ལྟར་དཔལ་དུས་ཀྱི་འཁོར་ལོའི་རྫོགས་རིམ་སྦྱོར་བ་ཡན་ལག་དྲུག་གི་ལམ་ཉམས་སུ་བླངས་པས་མཚོན་པའི་དགེ་བ་འདི་དག་གིས། འགྲོ་བ་སེམས་ཅན་གཅིག་ཀྱང་མ་ལུས་པ་ཀུན་གྱིས་དོན་མེད་འཁོར་བའི་བྱ་བ་རྣམས་རབ་ཏུ་སྟེ་གཏན་དུ་སྤངས་ནས། དོན་ཆེན་གཏན་གྱི་བདེ་བ་རྡོ་རྗེའི་རྣལ་འབྱོར་ཡན་ལག་དྲུག་ལེགས་པར་བསྒོམས་ཏེ། དང་པོའི་སངས་རྒྱས་དུས་ཀྱི་འཁོར་ལོའི་གོ་འཕང་མྱུར་དུ་འཐོབ་པར་ཤོག་ཅིག

སྒྲོན་མེད་རབ་གསལ་སྣང་བ།

དགེ་བ་འདི་ཡིས་མྱུར་དུ་བདག །
སྦྱོར་བ་ཡན་ལག་དྲུག་པོ་འགྲུབ་གྱུར་ནས།།
འགྲོ་བ་སེམས་ཅན་གཅིག་ཀྱང་མ་ལུས་པ།།
ཐམས་ཅད་དེ་ཡི་ས་ལ་འགོད་པར་ཤོག །

རྣམ་པར་དཀར་བའི་དགེ་བ་འདི་ཡི་བསོད་ནམས་ཀྱིས། མྱུར་དུ་བདག་དང་འགྲོ་བ་ཀུན་གྱིས་ཟབ་ལམ་རྡོ་རྗེའི་རྣལ་འབྱོར་སྦྱོར་བ་ཡན་ལག་དྲུག་པོ་འགྲུབ་པར་གྱུར་ནས། མཐའ་ཡས་པའི་འགྲོ་བ་སེམས་ཅན་གཅིག་ཀྱང་མ་ལུས་པ་ཐམས་ཅད་དཔལ་དུས་ཀྱི་འཁོར་ལོའི་ས་ལ་འགོད་པར་ཤོག་ཅིག་ཅེས་པའོ།།

སྦྱོར་དྲུག་བརྒྱུད་པའི་
བླ་ནམ་བྱིན་རླབས་ཆར་འབེབས།

༄༅། །ན་མཿཤྲཱི་ཀཱ་ལ་ཙཀྲ་ཡ། ཞེས་ན་མ་ནི་ཕྱག་འཚལ་བ་སྟེ་གུས་ཤིང་འདུད་པའི་དོན་དང་། ཤྲཱི་དཔལ། ཀཱ་ལ་ནི་དུས་དང་། ཙཀྲ་ནི་འཁོར་ལོའི་དོན། དོན་དངོས་ནི། བླ་མ་དང་དབྱེར་མ་མཆིས་པའི་དཔལ་དུས་ཀྱི་འཁོར་ལོར་ཕྱག་འཚལ་ལོ་ཞེས་པའི་དོན་ནོ། །བླ་མའི་རྣལ་འབྱོར་བསྒོམ་དུས་ཉམས་ལེན་མཁན་རང་ཉིད་ཀྱི་རྩ་བའི་བླ་མ་དེ་ཉིད་ཁྱབ་བདག་རྡོ་རྗེ་འཆང་གི་ངོ་བོར་བསྒོམ་དགོས་པ་སྤྱི་མཚུངས་ལྟར་དང་། བླ་ནམ་འདིའི་ཚིག་ཟིན་དུ་ཡོད་མོད། འོན་ཏེ་དམ་པ་གོང་མ་རྣམས་ཀྱི་ཕྱག་བཞེས་དང་མན་ངག་ལྟར་ན། རང་གི་རྩ་བའི་བླ་མ་ཀུན་མཁྱེན་དོལ་པོ་བའི་རྣམ་པར་བསྒོམ་དགོས་པར་ཡང་གསུངས་འདུག་པས། དེ་ནི་ཉམས་ལེན་མཁན་སོ་སོས་རང་གི་མོས་འདུན་ལ་བསྟུན་ཏེ་གདམ་ག་བྱས་ཏེ་བསྒོམ་ན་ལེགས་པར་སྣང་བས། དེ་ལུགས་ཀྱིས་རྩ་བརྒྱུད་ཀྱི་བླ་མ་རྣམས་མདུན་ཀྱི་ནམ་མཁར་བསྒོམ་དགོས་པ་གཞི་ལ་བཞག་ཏེ་བསྒོམ་པར་བྱའོ། །

བླ་མ་ཡི་དམ་དཀོན་མཆོག་གསུམ་ལ། །
བདག་ཡིད་དང་བས་སྐྱབས་སུ་མཆིའོ། །

དང་པོ། གོང་དུ་ཡང་ཡང་འགྲེལ་ཟིན་པ་བཞིན་དུ་གོང་ན་མེད་ཅིང་བླ་ན་མེད་པའི་བླ་མ་དང་། བསྐྱེད་སྒྲུབ་ལ་སོགས་པའི་སྒོ་ནས་རང་སེམས་སམ། རང་གི་ཡིད་ལ་དམ་པོར་འཛིན་པའི་ལྷ་བྱེ་བྲག་པའི་ཡི་དམ་དང་། དེ་བཞིན་དུ་འཇིག་རྟེན་ན་ཤིན་ཏུ་དཀོན་ཞིང་མཆོག་ཏུ་གྱུར་པའི་རྫོགས་པའི་སངས་རྒྱས། དེས་གསུངས་པའི་དམ་པའི་ཆོས། དེ་འཛིན་སྐྱོང་སྤེལ་མཁན་གྱི་འཕགས་པའི་དགེ་འདུན་དཀོན་མཆོག་གསུམ་ལ། བདག་གི་ཡིད་དང་བ་ཆེན་པོའི་སྒོ་ནས་རྗེ་སྲིད་བྱང་ཆུབ་སྙིང་པོ་མ་མཆིས་པའི་བར་དུ་སྐྱབས་སུ་བརྟེན་ནོ་དང་སྐྱབས་སུ་མཆིའོ། །ཞེས་སྐྱབས་འགྲོ་བསྡུས་པ་ཞིག་བྱས་ཤིང་།

སེམས་ཅན་རྣམས་ལ་བྱམས་དང་སྙིང་རྗེ། །
དགའ་དང་བཏང་སྙོམས་སྐྱེ་བར་གྱུར་ཅིག །

དེ་ནས་ནམ་མཁའ་དང་མཉམ་པའི་སེམས་ཅན་རྣམས་ཏེ་སེམས་ཅན་གཅིག་ཀྱང་མ་ལུས་པ་ཀུན་ལ་བདེ་བ་དང་ལྡན་འདོད་ཀྱི་བྱམས་པ་བསྒོམ། སྡུག་བསྔལ་དང་བྲལ་འདོད་ཀྱི་སྙིང་རྗེ་བསྐྱེད། སེམས་ཅན་སུ་དང་གང་ཡིན་ཀུན་གྱི་གཟུགས་བཟང་ལང་ཚོ་དཔལ་འབྱོར་སྐལ་གྲགས་སོགས་ཀུན་ལ་རྗེས་སུ་ཡི་རང་གི་སྒོ་ནས་དགའ་བ་སྒོམ། དེ་བཞིན་དུ་སེམས་ཅན་ཐམས་ཅད་ཚེ་རབས་འཁོར་བ་ཐོག་མེད་ནས། རང་གི་སྙིང་དུ་སྡུག་པའི་གཉེན་དང་གྲོགས་བྱས་པ་ལ་འདྲ་མཉམ་ཡིན་པས། དེ་ཀུན་ལ་ཉེ་རིང་ཆགས་སྡང་ལ་སོགས་པ་ཅུང་ཟད་ཙམ་ཡང་མེད་པའི་བཏང་སྙོམས་བསྒོམས་ཤིང་རང་རྒྱུད་དུ་སྐྱེ་བར་གྱུར་ཅིག ཅེས་བྱང་ཆུབ་ཀྱི་སེམས་རྒྱུད་ལ་སྐྱེད་བྱེད་ཀྱི་ཚད་མེད་བཞི་ཞེས་པ་སྔོན་དུ་བཏང་ནས། དེ་རྗེས་བྱང་ཆུབ་ཀྱི་སེམས་དངོས་སུ་བསྐྱེད་པ་ནི།

སེམས་ཅན་དོན་དུ་ཟབ་ལམ་བླ་མའི།།
རྣལ་འབྱོར་ཉིད་ལ་བརྩོན་པར་བགྱིའོ།།

ནམ་མཁའི་མཐའ་དང་མཉམ་པའི་སེམས་ཅན་ཐམས་ཅད་ཀྱི་མཐར་ཐུག གཏན་གྱི་བདེ་བའི་གོ་འཕང་འཛིན་པའི་དོན་ཆེན། རྫོགས་པའི་སངས་རྒྱས་ཀྱི་གོ་འཕང་ཐོབ་པའི་ཆེད་དུ། གོ་སྐབས་བླ་ན་མེད་པའི་སྐལ་བ་བཟང་པོ་འདི་ཉིད་དང་དུ་བླངས་ཏེ། ཟབ་ལམ་རྡོ་རྗེ་རྣལ་འབྱོར་གྱི་བླ་མའི་རྣལ་འབྱོར་འདི་ཉིད་ལ་འཇུག་པར་བྱའོ།། འདི་ལ་དད་འདུན་དང་བ་ཆེན་པོས་བརྩོན་པར་བགྱིའོ།། ཞེས་སྙིང་རྗེས་སེམས་ཅན་ལ་དམིགས་ཤིང་། ཤེས་རབ་ཀྱིས་རྫོགས་བྱང་ལ་དམིགས་པའི་བྱང་ཆུབ་མཆོག་ཏུ་སེམས་བསྐྱེད་པར་བྱའོ།། ཞེས་སེམས་བསྐྱེད་བསྡུས་པ་ཞིག་ཀྱང་བྱས་པ་སོགས་ཀྱིས་བླ་རྣམ་འདི་ཉིད་གཅིག་པོ་ཉམས་སུ་བླངས་ཀྱང་ནང་བ་སངས་རྒྱས་པའི་ཉམས་ལེན་ཁ་ཚང་བར་བྱས་པར་སོང་ཡོད་པ་འདྲའོ།།

མ་དག་སྣོད་བཅུད་འཇིག་རྟེན་ཐམས་ཅད།།
ཅིར་ཡང་མི་དམིགས་སྟོང་པར་གྱུར་ཅིག །

འདིར་རང་ཅག་ལ་ལས་ཀྱི་དབང་གིས་སྣང་བའི་འཇིག་རྟེན། ཀུན་རྫོབ་མ་དག་པ་ཕྱིའི་སྣོད་དང་ནང་བཅུད་སེམས་ཅན་རྣམས་ཀྱིས་བསྡུས་པའི་འཇིག་རྟེན་ཐམས་ཅད། དོན་ལ་བདེན་དངོས་སུ་ཅུང་ཟད་ཙམ་ཡང་མ་གྲུབ་པའི་ངེས་ཤེས་ཟབ་མོ་བསྐྱེད། ཐ་ན་མོས་སྒོམ་ཙམ་གྱིས་ཀྱང་སྣང་གྲགས་ཀྱི་ཆོས་ཐམས་ཅད་ཅི་ཡང་མི་དམིགས་པ་སྟོང་བར་གྱུར་སོང་སྙམ་དུ་གནས་སྐབས་སྐར་ཆ་ཁ་ཤས་ལ་ཡང་བསྒོམ་པར་གྱིས་ཤིག

རང་གི་སྤྱི་བོར་རིན་ཆེན་ཁྲི་སྟེང་།། པད་ཟླ་ལ་སོགས་གདན་ལྔའི་སྟེང་དུ།། རྩ་བའི་བླ་མ་རྡོ་རྗེ་འཆང་ཆེན།། སྐུ་མདོག་སྔོན་པོ་ཞལ་གཅིག་ཕྱག་གཉིས།། ཞབས་གཉིས་རྡོ་རྗེ་སྐྱིལ་ཀྲུང་གིས་བཞུགས།། སྣ་ཚོགས་དར་གྱི་ན་བཟའ་བརྒྱན་བས་མཛེས།། རིན་ཆེན་རུས་རྒྱན་འཕྲེང་བག་དང་ལྡན།། རྡོ་རྗེ་དྲིལ་བུ་ཐུགས་ཀར་བསྣོལ་ཞིང་།།

དེ་ནས་སྐད་ཅིག་ལ། རང་གི་སྤྱི་བོའི་སྟེང་གི་ནམ་མཁའ་ལ་རིན་པོ་ཆེའི་ཁྲི་ཡངས་ཤིང་རྒྱ་ཆེ་བ་ཞིག་གི་སྟེང་དུ་པདྨ་དང་དེའི་སྟེང་དུ་ཟླ་བ། དེའི་སྟེང་དུ་ཉི་མ་དང་། དེའི་སྟེང་དུ་སྒྲ་གཅན། ཡང་དེའི་སྟེང་དུ་དུས་མེ་ལ་སོགས་པའི་གདན་ལྔའི་སྟེང་དུ། ངོ་བོ་རང་གི་རྩ་བའི་བླ་མ་ཡིན་པ་ལ། རྣམ་པ་རྡོ་རྗེ་འཆང་ཆེན་པོའམ། གལ་ཏེ་རྡོ་རྗེ་འཆང་ཆེན་སྒོམ་པའི་དབང་དུ་བཏང་ན། སྐུ་མདོག་སྔོན་པོ་ནམ་མཁའི་མདོག་ལྟ་བུ་ལ་ཞལ་གཅིག་ཕྱག་གཉིས། ཞབས་གཉིས་རྡོ་རྗེ་སྐྱིལ་ཀྲུང་གིས་བཞུགས་པ། དར་རྣམ་པ་སྣ་ཚོགས་ཀྱི་ན་བཟའ་བརྒྱན་པའི་མཛེས་པར་སྤྲས་པ། རིན་པོ་ཆེ་དང་རུས་པའི་རྒྱན་ལ་སོགས་པའི་རྒྱན་གྱིས་སྤྲས་ཤིང་། སྐུ་འཕྲེང་བག་དང་ལྡན་ཞིང་། རྡོ་རྗེ་དང་དྲིལ་བུ་གཉིས་ཐུགས་ཀར་བསྣོལ་ཞིང་འཛིན་པ་ཅན་དུ་བསྒོམ། ཡང་ན་ཀུན་མཁྱེན་ཆོས་ཀྱི་རྒྱལ་པོ་རྟོན་པ་བཞི་ལྡན། རྒྱལ་བ་རྡོ་ནང་བ་ཆེན་པོ། དོལ་པོ་བ་ཤེས་རབ་རྒྱལ་མཚན་བསྒོམ། ཀུན་མཁྱེན་དོལ་པོ་བ་ནི་ཆོས་གོས་རྣམ་གསུམ་གསོལ་བའི་དགེ་སློང་གི་ཆ་བྱད་ཅན། ཞབས་གཉིས་རྡོ་རྗེ་དཀྱིལ་ཀྲུང་གིས་བཞུགས་པ། ཕྱག་གཉིས་སེམས་ཉིད་ངལ་གསོའི་ཕྱག་རྒྱས་པུས་མོ་བྲུང་བཀབ་པ། སྐུ་མདོག་དཀར་ལ་སྐྱ་ཤ་རྒྱས་པ། སྤྱན་གཉིས་ནམ་མཁར་ཧར་གྱིས་གཟིགས་ཤིང་། ཐུགས་བདེ་སྟོང་གཉིས་སུ་མེད་པའི་ཡེ་ཤེས་ལ་གནས་པའི་རྣམ་པ་ཅན་དུ་སྒོམ།

སྐུ་ཡི་གནས་བཞིར་ཡི་གེ་བཞིས་མཚན།།
ཐུགས་ཀའི་ཧཱུྃ་ལས་འོད་ཟེར་འཕྲོས་པས།།
རྩ་བརྒྱུད་བླ་མ་སྐྱབས་གནས་ཐམས་ཅད།།
ཛཿཧཱུྃ་བཾ་ཧོཿགཉིས་མེད་ཐིམ་གྱུར།།

རྡོ་རྗེ་འཆང་དང་ཡང་ན་ཀུན་མཁྱེན་དོལ་པོ་བ་གང་བསྒོམ་ཡང་། ཁོང་གི་དཔྲལ་བ་མགྲིན་པ་སྙིང་ག་ལྟེ་བ་སྟེ་སྐུ་ཡི་གནས་བཞི་ལ་ཡི་གེ་བཞི་སྟེ་ལྟེ་བ་ལ་ཛ། སྙིང་ག་ལ་ཧཱུྃ། མགྲིན་པ་ལ་བཾ། དཔྲལ་བ་ལ་ཧོཿབཞི་ཡིས་མཚན་ཡོད་པར་བསྒོམ་ལ། དེའི་ནང་གི་ཐུགས་ཀའི་ཧཱུྃ་ལས་འོད་ཟེར་ཕྱོགས་བཅུ་ཀུན་ཏུ་འཕྲོས་པས། རྩ་བ་དང་བརྒྱུད་པར་བཅས་པའི་བླ་མ་རྣམས་དང་། སྐྱབས་གནས་དམ་པ་ཐམས་ཅད་སྤྱན་དྲངས་ཏེ། བླ་མ་རང་གི་གནས་བཞིའི་ཡི་གེ་ཛཿཧཱུྃ་བཾ་ཧོཿབཞི་གསལ་བ་བཞིན་དུ། རག་ནས་ཀྱང་དེ་ལྟར་བཟློད་པས། རིམ་པ་བཞིན་དུ་བླ་མ་དང་རྒྱལ་བ་སྲས་བཅས་རང་ལ་ཐིམ་ཏེ་དབྱེར་མེད་རོ་གཅིག་ཏུ་གྱུར་པར་བསྒོམ་མོ།།

མི་འགྱུར་ཡིད་འོང་མཚན་དཔེས་ལེགས་སྤྲས།། འགགས་མེད་ཚངས་དབྱངས་
ཕྱོགས་བཅུར་སྒྲོག་མཛད།། འཁྲུལ་མེད་ཕྱག་རྒྱ་ཆེ་ལ་གནས་པ།། བླ་མའི་སྐུ་གསུང་
ཐུགས་ལ་ཕྱག་འཚལ།།

གལ་ཏེ་ཇི་ལྟ་བ་བཞིན་དུ་སྒོམ་ཐུབ་ཀྱང་མ་ཐུབ་རུང་། བླ་མ་དེ་ཉིད་སྐུ་མི་འགྱུར་ཞིང་གཡོ་བ་མེད་པ་ཡིད་དུ་འོང་བའི་མཚན་དང་དཔེ་བྱད་ཀྱིས་ལེགས་པར་སྤྲས་པ། གསུང་འགག་པ་མེད་པ་ཚངས་པའི་དབྱངས་ཡན་ལག་དྲུག་ཅུ་དང་ལྡན་པ་ཕྱོགས་བཅུ་ཀུན་ཏུ་སྒྲོག་པར་མཛད། ཐུགས་འཁྲུལ་བ་བྲལ་བའི་གནས་ལུགས་ཀྱི་ཕྱག་རྒྱ་ཆེ་ལ་གནས་པ། དེ་དག་ཇི་ལྟ་བ་བཞིན་དུ་བསྒོམ་མ་ཤེས་པའམ་མ་ནུས་ཡང་། མོས་གུས་ཆེན་པོའི་སྒོ་ནས་མོས་སྒོམ་ཙམ་ཡང་བྱེད་པ་གལ་ཆེ། དེ་ལྟ་བུའི་བསམ་ཡུལ་ལས་འདས་པའི་བླ་མ་དེའི་སྐུ་གསུང་ཐུགས་ལ་དང་བ་ཆེན་པོས་ཕྱག་འཚལ་ཞིང་དད་པས་འདུད་དོ།། ཞེས་མོས་པ་ཤུགས་དྲག་པོ་བསྒོམ་པར་བྱའོ།།

སོར་སྡུད་ལ་སོགས་སྦྱོར་བྱེད་དྲུག་གིས།། ཕུང་པོ་ལ་སོགས་སྦྱང་བྱ་དྲུག་དྲུག
ལེགས་པར་སྦྱངས་པས་བདེ་གཤེགས་སོ་དྲུག གཅིག་ཏུ་བསྡུས་པའི་སྐུ་ལ་
ཕྱག་འཚལ།།

སྦྱོར་བ་ཡན་ལག་དྲུག་གི་ཐོག་མ་རྣམ་ཤེས་ཚོགས་དྲུག་ཕྱི་རོལ་ཡུལ་ལས་རྣམ་པར་སོ་སོར་སྡུད་དེ། ནང་རྣམ་པར་མི་རྟོག་པའི་ཡེ་ཤེས་ཀྱི་ངོ་བོར་འཛིན་པར་བྱེད་པ་ལ་སོགས་པས། སྦྱང་བྱ་མ་དག་པའི་ཕུང་པོ་དྲུག་པོ་འདི་རྣམས། སྦྱོང་བྱེད་སྦྱོར་བ་ཡན་ལག་དྲུག་གིས་བྱང་བར་བྱེད་དོའམ། སྦྱང་བར་བྱའོ།། ཞེས་པའི་དོན་ཏེ། དེ་ཡང་ཞིབ་ཙིང་ཕྲ་བའི་སྒོ་ནས་འདི་དག་ལ་འཇུག་ན། ཕུང་པོ་ལ་སོགས་སྦྱང་བྱ་དྲུག་པོ་རེ་རེ་ལ་དྲུག་རེ་དྲུག་རེར་བྱས་ཏེ། སྦྱོང་བྱེད་ཀྱང་དྲུག་རེ་དྲུག་རེས་ལེགས་པར་སྦྱངས་པས་ཐོབ་པ་སྟེ་བདེ་བར་གཤེགས་པ་སུམ་ཅུ་སོ་དྲུག་དག་གི་བདག་ཉིད་དམ། དེ་དག་གཅིག་ཏུ་བསྡུས་པའམ་འདུས་པའི་སྐུ་བླ་མ་དམ་པ་དེར་སྒོ་གསུམ་དང་བ་ཆེན་པོའི་སྒོ་ནས་ཕྱག་འཚལ་ལོ།།

ལུས་ངག་ཡིད་གསུམ་དུས་གསུམ་དགེ་ཚོགས།། མཆོད་པའི་སྤྲིན་ཕུང་དཔག་
ཏུ་མེད་པ།། ཀུན་ཏུ་བཟང་པོའི་རྣམ་འཕྲུལ་ཇི་བཞིན།། བདག་ཡིད་དང་བས་
མཆོད་པར་འབུལ་ལོ།།

གསང་ཆེན་སྔགས་ཀྱི་རྟོགས་པ་ཁྱད་པར་ཅན་རྒྱུད་ལ་སྐྱེ་བར་བྱེད་པ་ལ། རང་ལ་དབང་བའི་ལུས་ངག་

ཡིད་གསུམ་དང་། རང་གིས་བསགས་པའི་དུས་གསུམ་གྱི་དགེ་ཚོགས་དང་བཅས་པ། མཆོད་པའི་སྤྲིན་ཕུང་དཔག་ཏུ་མེད་པ་སྟེ་ཚད་མེད་པ་ཞིག་ཏུ་ཡིད་ཀྱིས་དམིགས་ཏེ། དེ་ཡང་མཆོད་བྱ་དེ་དག་རྒྱ་ཆེན་པོ་གྲངས་ལས་འདས་པ་ཀུན་ཏུ་བཟང་པོའི་མཆོད་པའི་རྣམ་པར་འཕྲུལ་སྟེ། གྲངས་དང་ཚད་ལས་འདས་པ་ཅན་དུ་དམིགས་ནས། བདག་ཡིད་དང་བ་ཆེན་པོ་དང་དད་པ་ཆེན་པོའི་སྒོ་ནས་མཆོད་ཅིང་འབུལ་བར་བགྱིའོ།། ཞེས་པའི་དོན་སྟེ། ཀུན་ཏུ་བཟང་པོའི་མཆོད་པ་ཇི་ལྟ་བར་དམིགས་མ་ཤེས་ན་ཡང་མོས་བསྒོམ་ཙམ་ངེས་པར་དུ་བྱ་དགོས་པའོ།།

ལུས་ངག་ཡིད་ཀྱི་སྒོ་ནས་བསགས་པའི།། སྡིག་པའི་ཚོགས་ཀུན་མཐོལ་ལོ་བཤགས་སོ།། དགེ་ལ་ཡི་རང་ཆོས་འཁོར་བསྐོར་མཛོད།། རྟག་ཏུ་བཞུགས་པར་གསོལ་བ་འདེབས་སོ།།

རང་གི་ཚེ་རབས་འཁོར་བ་ཐོག་མེད་ནས་བསགས་པའི་ལས་དང་ཉོན་མོངས་པའི་སྒྲིབ་པ་དག་གིས། རང་ཉིད་ཀྱི་རྒྱུད་ལ་ཉམས་དང་རྟོགས་པ་སོགས་མི་སྐྱེ་བར་གནོད་པའི་ཕྱིར་ན། ཚེ་རབས་ཐོག་མེད་ནས་རང་གི་ལུས་ངག་ཡིད་ཀྱི་སྒོ་ནས་བསགས་པའི་སྡིག་པ་དང་སྒྲིབ་པའི་ཚོགས་ཀུན་མ་ལུས་པ་མཐོལ་ཞིང་བཤགས་སོ།། འཕགས་པ་དང་སོ་སོའི་སྐྱེ་བོ་ཀུན་གྱིས་བསགས་པའི་དགེ་བ་ཀུན་ལ་རྗེས་སུ་ཡི་རང་ཞིང་། འཇིག་རྟེན་ན་སངས་རྒྱས་ཟིན་ཅིང་ད་དུང་ཆོས་འཁོར་མ་བསྐོར་བར་ཡོད་པ་གང་དག་ཅི་མཆིས་པ་ཀུན་ལ་ཆོས་ཀྱི་འཁོར་ལོ་བསྐོར་བར་བསྐུལ་བར་མཛོད་ཅིག ཅེས་བསྐུལ་བར་བྱའོ།། དེ་བཞིན་དུ་འཇིག་རྟེན་ཁམས་མྱ་མཐའ་མེད་པ་དག་ཏུ་བཞུགས་པའི་འཕགས་པའི་སྐྱེ་བོ་གང་དག་སུ་བཞུགས་ཀུན་ལས། དགོངས་པ་མྱ་ངན་ལས་འདའ་བར་ཐུགས་དགོངས་གཏོང་བཞིན་པ་དེ་དག་ཀུན་ལ་མྱ་ངན་ལས་མི་འདའ་བར་རྟག་ཏུ་སེམས་ཅན་གྱི་ཆེད་དུ་བཞུགས་པར་བསྐུལ་ཞིང་གསོལ་བ་འདེབས་སོ།།

ཚོགས་གསུམ་མཐར་ཕྱིན་བཅུ་གཉིས་ལམ་བགྲོད།། རྡོ་རྗེ་འཛིན་པ་ཀུན་གྱི་གཙོ་བོ།། སྐུ་བཞིའི་མངའ་བདག་དཔལ་ལྡན་བླ་མར།། གསོལ་བ་འདེབས་སོ་བྱིན་གྱིས་རློབས་ཤིག །

ཚོགས་གསུམ་སྟེ། བསོད་ནམས་ཀྱི་ཚོགས། ཡེ་ཤེས་ཀྱི་ཚོགས། འཐོ་མེད་ཚུལ་ཁྲིམས་ཀྱི་ཚོགས་གསུམ་མཐར་ཕྱིན་པར་བྱིན་གྱིས་རློབས་ཤིག ཞེས་པའོ།། འཐོ་བ་མེད་པའི་དོན་ནི། བདེ་སྟོང་རྒྱུ་སྐྱེན་མཚོན་དོན་དང་བཅས་པ་འཐོ་བ་མེད་པར་དུས་ཀུན་འགོང་བའི་དོན་ནོ།། དེ་འདྲའི་འཐོ་མེད་ཀྱི་ཚོགས་ནི་དཔལ་དུས་ཀྱི་འཁོར་ལོའི་གཞུང་ལས་གསུངས་པའི་ཐུན་མིན་གྱི་ཚོགས་ཏེ། འཐོ་མེད་བདེ་བ་ཆེན་པོའི་

ཡེ་ཤེས་ཀྱི་ནང་དུ་ཟག་མེད་ལྷན་ཅིག་སྐྱེས་པའི་ཡེ་ཤེས་ཀྱི་ཚོགས་གཉིས་དང་ཚོགས་གསུམ་ཀུན་འདུས་ཚུལ་སོགས་མང་ཡང་འདིར་བསྡུས་པའི་སྐབས་ཡིན་པས་རྒྱས་པར་མི་སྤྲོའོ།། ཡང་ན་ཆོས་སྐུའི་ཚོགས། ལོངས་སྐུའི་ཚོགས། སྤྲུལ་སྐུའི་ཚོགས་ཟེར་བའི་ལུགས་ཀྱང་འདུག་སྙམ། གང་ལྟར་ཚོགས་གསུམ་ཡོངས་སུ་རྫོགས་པ་མཐར་ཕྱིན་ཅིང་། སྦྱོར་བ་ཡན་ལག་དྲུག་པ་ཉིད་དེ་འཛིན་གྱི་ས་བཅུ་གཉིས་ཀྱི་སེམས་བསྡུས་པའི་ལམ་བཅུ་གཉིས་བགྲོད་དེ། གསང་ཆེན་སྔགས་ཀྱི་རྡོ་རྗེ་འཛིན་པ་ཀུན་གྱི་གཙོ་བོ་བླ་ན་མེད་པ། སྐུ་བཞི་ཡེ་ཤེས་ལྔའི་བདག་ཉིད་དམ་མདའ་བདག་དཔལ་ལྡན་བླ་མ་དམ་པ་མཆོག་ལ། སྒོ་གསུམ་དང་བ་ཆེན་པོའི་སྒོ་ནས་གསོལ་བ་འདེབས་སོ།། མྱུར་བ་མྱུར་དུ་བྱིན་གྱིས་རློབས་ཤིག

> གཉིས་མེད་ཡེ་ཤེས་རྩེ་གཅིག་བསྒོམས་པས།། གཉིས་སྣང་ཚོགས་བརྒྱད་གནས་འགྱུར་ཐོབ་པ།། ཡེ་ཤེས་ལྔ་ལྡན་དཔལ་ལྡན་བླ་མར།། གསོལ་བ་འདེབས་སོ་བྱིན་གྱིས་རློབས་ཤིག

སྣང་སྟོང་གཉིས་སུ་མེད་པ་དང་ཡུལ་ཡུལ་ཅན་གཉིས་སུ་མེད་པའི་ཡེ་ཤེས་རྩེ་གཅིག་པ་བསྒོམས་པས། གཉིས་སྣང་ཅན་གྱི་བློ་ཚོགས་བརྒྱད་པོ་འདི་རྣམས་གནས་འགྱུར་ཐོབ་པའི་བླ་མ་དམ་པ། ཆོས་དབྱིངས་ཡེ་ཤེས། མེ་ལོང་ཡེ་ཤེས། སོར་རྟོགས་ཡེ་ཤེས། མཉམ་ཉིད་ཡེ་ཤེས། བྱ་གྲུབ་ཡེ་ཤེས་ཏེ་ཡེ་ཤེས་ལྔ་མངོན་དུ་གྱུར་བའི་དཔལ་ལྡན་བླ་མ་དེ་ལ། སྒོ་གསུམ་གུས་པས་གསོལ་བ་འདེབས་སོ།། དེའི་དགེ་འབྲས་བདག་ལ་མྱུར་དུ་སྨིན་ནས་བདག་ལ་ད་ལྟ་ཉིད་དུ་བླ་མ་ཉིད་ཇི་ལྟ་བ་བཞིན་དུ་བྱིན་གྱིས་རློབས་ཤིག

> བསྐྱེད་རྫོགས་མཐར་ཕྱིན་བཅུ་གཉིས་དབང་གིས།། སྐལ་ལྡན་གདུལ་བྱ་སྨིན་གྲོལ་མཛད་པའི།། བླ་མ་ཀུན་འདུས་དཔལ་ལྡན་བླ་མར།། གསོལ་བ་འདེབས་སོ་བྱིན་གྱིས་རློབས་ཤིག །

བསྐྱེད་རིམ་ལྷའི་སྣང་བའི་སྒོ་ནས་གནས་སྐབས་བཞིའི་དག་སོགས་དང་། རྫོགས་རིམ་རྩ་ཐིག་རླུང་གསུམ་ལ་དངོས་སུ་བསྟུན་པས་མཆོག་མི་འགྱུར་བའི་ཡེ་ཤེས་མཐར་ཕྱིན་པ་ཉིད་དེ་འཛིན་གྱི་ས་བཅུ་གཉིས་ལ་དབང་བས། སྐལ་བ་དང་ལྡན་པའི་གདུལ་བྱའི་རྒྱུད་སྨིན་ཅིང་གྲོལ་བར་མཛད་པའི་བླ་མ་དམ་པ། འཁོར་འདས་ཀྱི་ལེགས་པའི་དངོས་པོ་གང་དག་ཅི་ཡོད་ཐམས་ཅད་འདུས་པའི་བླ་མ་ཀུན་འདུས་པའི་དཔལ་དང་ལྡན་པའི་བླ་མ་དེ་ལ། སྙིང་ཐག་པ་ནས་གསོལ་བ་འདེབས་སོ།། དེ་ལྟར་གདུང་ཤུགས་དྲག་པོའི་སྒོ་ནས་གསོལ་བ་འདེབས་ན་ཐུན་ཀྱང་མྱུར་དུ་ཚེད་ཇི་ལྟ་བ་བཞིན་དུ་མྱུར་བར་བྱིན་གྱིས་རློབས་ཤིག

> ཁྱེད་ཕུང་རིགས་དྲུག་སྐྱེ་མཆེད་སྲས་བརྒྱད།། ཕྱག་ཞབས་ལ་སོགས་ཁྲོ་བོའི་ཚོགས་ཀུན།། ཡི་དམ་ཀུན་འདུས་དཔལ་ལྡན་བླ་མར།། གསོལ་བ་འདེབས་སོ་བྱིན་གྱིས་རློབས་ཤིག

དཔལ་ལྡན་བླ་མ་དམ་པ་ཁྱེད་ཀྱི་ཕུང་པོ་དྲུག་པོ་ནི་རྒྱལ་བ་རིགས་དྲུག་ཡེ་ནས་ཡིན་པ་དང་། དེ་བཞིན་དུ་ཁྱེད་ཀྱི་སྐྱེ་ཞིང་མཆེད་པའི་ཤེས་པ་བརྒྱད་ནི་བྱང་ཆུབ་སེམས་དཔའ་སྲས་བརྒྱད་དང་། ཕྱག་དང་ཞབས་ལ་སོགས་པ་ནི་སྒོ་སྐྱོང་གི་ཁྲོ་བོ་དང་ཁྲོ་མོའི་རང་བཞིན་གྱི་ཚོགས་ཀུན་ཏེ། ཁྱེད་ནི་ཡི་དམ་ཀུན་འདུས་པའི་དཔལ་ལྡན་བླ་མ་ཁྱེད་ཡིན་པས། བདག་གིས་དད་འདུན་གུས་པ་ཆེན་པོས་ཁྱེད་ལ་རྩེ་གཅིག་ཏུ་གསོལ་བ་འདེབས་སོ།། གསོལ་བ་བཏབ་པ་དེས་བདག་ཐམས་ཅད་ཀྱི་ཉམས་ཡི་དམ་གྱི་དངོས་གྲུབ་དང་བྱིན་གྱིས་རློབས་ཤིག

> དོན་གཉིས་མཐར་ཕྱིན་ཆོས་སྐུའི་ངོ་བོ།། སྣ་ཚོགས་སྤྲུལ་བས་འགྲོ་བའི་དོན་མཛད།། སངས་རྒྱས་ཀུན་འདུས་དཔལ་ལྡན་བླ་མར།། གསོལ་བ་འདེབས་སོ་བྱིན་གྱིས་རློབས་ཤིག །

དཔལ་ལྡན་བླ་མ་ཁྱེད་ནི། རང་དོན་ཆོས་སྐུ་དང་གཞན་དོན་གཟུགས་སྐུ་གཉིས་མཐར་ཕྱིན་པ། སྐྱེ་མེད་ཆོས་ཀྱི་སྐུ་མངོན་དུ་བྱས་པའི་ངོ་བོ་ཅན་ཡིན་པའི་ཕྱིར་ན། སྣ་ཚོགས་གཟུགས་ཀྱི་སྐུའི་སྤྲུལ་པ་བསམ་གྱིས་མི་ཁྱབ་པའི་སྒོ་ནས་སྣ་ཚོགས་འགྲོ་བ་གང་དག་གི་གནས་སྐབས་དང་མཐར་ཐུག་གི་དོན་གཏན་དུ་མཛད་པ་ཅན། སངས་རྒྱས་ཀུན་འདུས་ཀྱི་ངོ་བོ་དཔལ་ལྡན་བླ་མ་དམ་པ་དེ་ལ་གསོལ་བ་འདེབས་སོ།། དེའི་ཕྱིར་ན་བདག་ལ་ཉིད་ཀྱི་བྱིན་རླབས་ཉུས་མཐུ་མ་ལུས་པ་སྩོལ་ཅིག

> དོན་དམ་བརྗོད་བྲལ་རྣམ་བྱང་བདེན་པའི།། གསུང་རབ་གླེགས་བམ་རྣམ་པར་སྟོན་མཛད།། དམ་ཆོས་ཀུན་འདུས་དཔལ་ལྡན་བླ་མར།། གསོལ་བ་འདེབས་སོ་བྱིན་གྱིས་རློབས་ཤིག

ཆོས་ཀུན་གྱི་གནས་ལུགས་མཐར་ཐུག་དོན་དམ་སྒྲ་ཚིག་གིས་བརྗོད་པ་བྲལ་བའི་རྣམ་བྱང་བདེན་པའི་ངོ་བོ་ཡེ་ནས་ཡིན་ཡང་། དེ་ཉིད་ཀུན་རྫོབ་ཏུ་རྣམ་པ་གསུང་རབ་གླེགས་བམ་དང་། རྗོད་བྱེད་ཀྱི་སྒྲ་ལ་སོགས་པའི་རྣམ་པ་སྟོན་པར་མཛད་པའི་དམ་ཆོས་ཀུན་འདུས་པ། དཔལ་ལྡན་བླ་མ་དམ་པ་ཁྱེད་ལ་གསོལ་བ་སྙིང་ནས་འདེབས་ན་བདག་གི་རྒྱུད་ཟབ་རྒྱས་དམ་པའི་ཆོས་བཞིན་དུ་བྱིན་གྱིས་རློབས་ཤིག

རིག་གྲོལ་གཉིས་ལྡན་ས་བཅུའི་མངའ་བདག འགྲོ་བའི་མགོན་སྐྱབས་བཤེས་གཉེན་དམ་པ།། དགེ་འདུན་ཀུན་འདུས་དཔལ་ལྡན་བླ་མར།། གསོལ་བ་འདེབས་སོ་བྱིན་གྱིས་རློབས་ཤིག །

རིག་པ་ཆོས་ཀུན་གྱི་གནས་ལུགས་རིག་པ་དང་། གྲོལ་བ་སྒྲིབ་གཉིས་དང་བྲལ་བའི་བྲལ་བ་གཉིས་ལྡན་པའི་ས་བཅུའི་མངའ་བདག་གམ། དེ་འདྲའི་གོ་འཕང་ལ་གནས་པ། འགྲོ་བ་མ་ལུས་པའི་མགོན་དང་སྐྱབས་གནས་དམ་པ། དགེ་བའི་བཤེས་གཉེན་དམ་པ་མཆོག་སྟེ། དགེ་འདུན་ཀུན་འདུས་པའི་ངོ་བོ་དཔལ་ལྡན་བླ་མ་མཆོག་ལ། སྒོ་གསུམ་གུས་པས་སྙིང་ནས་གསོལ་བ་འདེབས་སོ།། ད་ལྟ་ཉིད་ནས་བདག་ཡང་དག་པའི་དགེ་འདུན་གྱི་ངོ་བོ་རུ་བྱིན་གྱིས་རློབས་ཤིག

དམིགས་མེད་སྙིང་རྗེ་བདེ་ཆེན་ངོ་བོ།། ཐབས་ཀྱི་སྒོ་ནས་དགྲ་བགེགས་འཇོམས་མཛད།། ཆོས་སྐྱོང་ཀུན་འདུས་དཔལ་ལྡན་བླ་མར།། གསོལ་བ་འདེབས་སོ་བྱིན་གྱིས་རློབས་ཤིག

དམིགས་པ་མེད་པའི་སྙིང་རྗེའམ་དོན་དམ་པའི་སྙིང་རྗེ་སྟེ། གཉུག་མ་ལྷན་ཅིག་སྐྱེས་པའི་ཡེ་ཤེས་བདེ་བ་ཆེན་པོའི་ངོ་བོ་ཉིད་བླ་མ་ཁྱེད་ཡིན་ཡང་། གདུལ་བྱ་སེམས་ཅན་གྱི་ལས་དབང་མི་འདྲ་བ་དག་ལ་ཐབས་ཀྱི་སྒོ་ནས་དྲག་པོའི་རྣམ་པར་འཕོས་པ་ལ་སོགས་པས། ཉོན་མོངས་རྒྱུ་རྐྱེན་དང་བཅས་པའི་དགྲ་བགེགས་འཇོམས་པར་མཛད་པའི་ཁྲོ་བོ་འཛིགས་སུ་རུང་བ་ཁྱེད་ཉིད། བསྟན་པའི་དཔལ་དང་འགྲོ་བའི་བདེ་ལ་གནོད་པའི་དགྲ་བགེགས་འདུལ་བའི་ཆོས་སྐྱོང་ཀུན་འདུས་པའི་ངོ་བོ་དཔལ་ལྡན་བླ་མ་དམ་པ་དེ་ལ་གསོལ་བ་འདེབས་སོ།། ནུས་མཐུ་དེ་དག་རང་རྒྱུད་ལ་འཁྲུངས་པར་བྱིན་གྱིས་རློབས་ཤིག

ཞི་རྒྱས་དབང་དྲག་ལས་ལ་མངའ་བརྙེས།། མཆོག་དང་ཐུན་མོང་དངོས་གྲུབ་སྩེར་མཛད།། དངོས་གྲུབ་འབྱུང་གནས་དཔལ་ལྡན་བླ་མར།། གསོལ་བ་འདེབས་སོ་བྱིན་གྱིས་རློབས་ཤིག

སེམས་ཅན་ལ་ཕན་པ་ཁོ་ནའི་ཆེད་དུ་ནད་གདོན་རྐྱེན་ངན་སོགས་ཞི་བའི་ལས་འགྲུབ་ཅིང་། དེ་བཞིན་དུ་ཚེ་བསོད་དཔལ་འབྱོར་རྒྱས་པར་བྱེད་པའི་རྒྱས་པའི་ལས་དང་། འཁོར་འདས་ལེགས་པའི་དབང་ཐང་སྣན་གྲགས་སོགས་ལ་དབང་བའི་དབང་གི་ལས་དང་། དགྲ་བགེགས་གདུག་པ་ཅན་སོགས་དྲག་པོ་ཁོ་ནས་འཇོམས་དགོས་པ་དག་འཇོམས་པར་བྱེད་པའི་དྲག་པོའི་ལས་ཏེ། ལས་བཞི་ལ་མངའ་བརྙེས་པའི་

ལས་བཞི་ལྷུན་གྱིས་གྲུབ་པ་པོ། དེ་འདྲའི་འཇིག་རྟེན་གྱི་དངོས་གྲུབ་ཙམ་གྱིས་ཀྱང་མི་ཚད་པ། མཆོག་དང་ཐུན་མོང་གི་དངོས་གྲུབ་མ་ལུས་པ་སྩེར་བར་མཛད་པ་པོ། དངོས་གྲུབ་ཀུན་གྱི་འབྱུང་གནས་དཔལ་ལྡན་བླ་མ་དམ་པ་དེ་ལ་སྙིང་ཐག་པ་ནས་གསོལ་བ་འདེབས་ན། བདག་གི་རྒྱུད་མཆོག་ཐུན་གྱི་དངོས་གྲུབ་བྱིན་རླབས་སྩོལ་ཅིག

མདོ་རྒྱུད་མན་ངག་བསྟན་བཅོས་ཀུན་ལ།། འཆད་རྩོད་རྩོམ་གྱིས་ལོག་རྟོག་སེལ་མཛད།།
མ་རིག་མུན་སེལ་དཔལ་ལྡན་བླ་མར།། གསོལ་བ་འདེབས་སོ་བྱིན་གྱིས་རློབས་ཤིག

ཐེག་པ་ཐུན་མོང་བ་མདོ་དང་ཐུན་མོང་མིན་པ་གསང་བ་སྔགས་སམ་རྒྱུད་དང་། བླ་མ་དམ་པའི་ཐུན་མོང་མ་ཡིན་པའི་མན་ངག་ལ་སོགས་པའི་བསྟན་བཅོས་ཀུན་ལ་འཆད་པ་དང་རྩོད་པ། རྩོམ་པ་ལ་སོགས་ཀྱི་སྒོ་ནས་གདུལ་བར་བྱ་བའི་སེམས་ཅན་རྣམས་ཀྱི་རྒྱུད་ཀྱི་ལོག་རྟོག་སེལ་བར་མཛད་པ་པོ། མ་རིག་པའི་མུན་པ་སེལ་བར་མཛད་ནུས་པའི་ནུས་པ་མཆོག་ཏུ་མངའ་བ། དཔལ་ལྡན་བླ་མ་མཆོག་དེ་ལ་སྒོ་གསུམ་གུས་པ་ཆེན་པོས་གསོལ་བ་འདེབས་ན། དེས་བདག་གི་ཐ་མལ་བའི་འདུ་ཤེས་དང་། ཡིད་དཔྱོད་ལ་སོགས་པའི་ཉེས་ཚོགས་དག་སྟེ། རང་རྒྱུད་ཡང་དག་ཤེས་རབ་ཀྱི་དྲི་དང་མི་འབྲལ་བར་བྱིན་གྱིས་རློབས་ཤིག

དེང་ནས་བདག་ནི་བླ་མ་ཁྱེད་དང་།། ལུས་དང་གྲིབ་མ་ལྟ་བུར་འགྲོགས་ཏེ།། ཟབ་
དོན་མན་ངག་བདུད་རྩི་འཐུང་བར།། དཔལ་ལྡན་བླ་མས་བྱིན་གྱིས་རློབས་ཤིག

དེང་ནས་ཏེ་དུས་ད་ལྟ་ནས་བཟུང་། བདག་ནི་བླ་མ་དམ་པ་ཁྱེད་དང་། ཚེ་རབས་ཀུན་ཏུ་ལུས་དང་གྲིབ་མ་ཇི་ལྟ་བར་འགྲོགས་ཏེ། ཟབ་མོའི་དོན་གྱི་མན་ངག་བདུད་རྩི་ཡང་ནས་ཡང་དུ་འཐུང་བར་གསོལ་བ་འདེབས་ན། ཇི་ལྟར་སྨོན་པ་དེ་བཞིན་དུ་དཔལ་ལྡན་བླ་མས་བདག་རྒྱུད་བྱིན་གྱིས་རློབས་ཤིག བདག་ལ་དེ་ལྟ་བུའི་སྐལ་བ་བཟང་པོ་དང་ནམ་ཡང་མི་འབྲལ་བར་ཤོག་ཅིག དེ་ལ་བདུད་ཀྱིས་བར་ཆད་མི་འབྱུང་བར་གྱུར་ཅིག

མ་དག་ལོག་པའི་འཚོ་བ་སྤངས་ནས།། བདུད་རྩི་ལྟེ་སྦྱོར་ཉམས་སུ་བླངས་ཏེ།། ཟས་
གོས་སོགས་ལ་ལྟོས་པ་མེད་པར།། དཔལ་ལྡན་བླ་མས་བྱིན་གྱིས་རློབས་ཤིག

མི་ཆོས་བླ་མའི་རྫུན་དང་། ཁ་གསག་དང་གཞོག་སློང་འདོད་རྫམ་ལ་སོགས་པ་མ་དག་ལོག་པའི་འཚོ་

བའི་རིགས་ཀུན་གཏད་ནས་སྤྲངས་ཏེ། སྤྱགས་དང་ཏིང་འཛིན་གྱི་ནུས་པའི་བདུད་རྩི་ལྡེ་སྦྱོར་ལ་སོགས་པ་ཉམས་སུ་བླངས་ཏེ། རགས་པ་ཁམས་ཀྱི་ཟས་དང་གོས་ལ་སོགས་པར་ལྟོས་མི་དགོས་ཤིང་། འཇིག་རྟེན་གྱི་འདོད་པ་ལ་ལྟོས་པ་མེད་པར་གནས་ཏེ་ཟབ་མོའི་དོན་ལ་ལོངས་སྤྱོད་ནུས་པར་དཔལ་ལྡན་བླ་མ་མཆོག་གིས་བྱིན་གྱིས་བརླབ་པར་མཛད་དུ་གསོལ།

དབེན་པའི་གནས་སུ་ཟབ་མོའི་དོན་ལ།། རྩེ་གཅིག་བསམ་གཏན་སྒྲུབ་པ་བྱས་ནས།།
ཚེ་འདི་ཉིད་ལ་ཕྱག་ཆེན་འཐོབ་པར།། དཔལ་ལྡན་བླ་མས་བྱིན་གྱིས་རློབས་ཤིག

ལུས་ངག་ཡིད་གསུམ་གྱི་འདུ་འཛི་དབེན་པའི་གནས་སུ། གནས་ལུགས་ཟབ་མོ་ཟབ་ལམ་རྡོ་རྗེ་རྣལ་འབྱོར་གྱི་དོན་ལ་རྩེ་གཅིག་ཏུ། བསམ་གཏན་སྒྲུབ་པ་རང་དབང་བ་བྱས་ནས། ད་ལྟའི་ཚེ་འདི་ཉིད་ལ་ཕྱག་རྒྱ་ཆེན་པོ་མཆོག་གི་གོ་འཕང་ཐོབ་ནུས་པར་དཔལ་ལྡན་བླ་མ་དམ་པ་མཆོག་གིས་བྱིན་གྱིས་རློབས་ཤིག

བླ་མའི་གནས་ཀྱི་ཡི་གེ་བཞི་པོ།། སངས་རྒྱས་ཀུན་གྱི་སྐུ་བཞིར་མོས་ཤིང་།། དེ་ལ་
དམིགས་ཏེ་དབང་བཞི་ལེན་པར།། དཔལ་ལྡན་བླ་མས་བྱིན་གྱིས་རློབས་ཤིག

རྩ་བའི་བླ་མ་དམ་པའི་སྐུ་ཡི་གནས་བཞི་ལ། ཡི་གེ་ཨོཾ་ཨཱཿཧཱུྃ་ཧོཿབཞི་པོ་དེ་དག་དུས་གསུམ་གྱི་སངས་རྒྱས་ཀུན་གྱི་སྐུ་བཞི་ཡེ་ནས་ཡིན་པ་ལ་ཡིན་པར་མོས་ཤིང་བསྒོམ་པར་བྱའོ།། ཡི་གེ་དེ་དག་ལ་དམིགས་ཏེ་བུམ་དབང་ལ་སོགས་པའི་དབང་བཞི་ལེན་ཐུབ་པར་དཔལ་ལྡན་བླ་མ་དམ་པས་བྱིན་གྱིས་བརླབས་ཏེ་རང་རྒྱུད་སྨིན་ནུས་པར་གྱུར་ཅིག

དཔྲལ་བའི་ཨོཾ་ལས་ཨོཾ་ཡིག་དཀར་པོ།། རང་གི་ལུས་ཀྱི་དཔྲལ་བར་ཞུགས་ཤིང་།།
དེ་ལ་བརྟེན་ནས་བུམ་དབང་འཐོབ་པར།། དཔལ་ལྡན་བླ་མས་བྱིན་གྱིས་རློབས་
ཤིག ལུས་དང་སད་པའི་སྒྲིབ་པ་དག་ནས།། དགའ་བའི་དགའ་བཞི་ཉམས་སུ་སྨྱོང་
བས།། སྐུ་ཡི་རྡོ་རྗེ་སྤྲུལ་སྐུ་ཐོབ་པར།། དཔལ་ལྡན་བླ་མས་བྱིན་གྱིས་རློབས་ཤིག

དེ་ནས་རིམ་པ་བཞིན་དུ་བླ་མ་དམ་པ་མཆོག་གི་དཔྲལ་བའི་ཨོཾ་ལས་ཨོཾ་ཡིག་དཀར་པོ་ཞིག་འཕྲོས་ཏེ། ཐ་མལ་བ་རང་ཉིད་ཀྱི་ལུས་ཀྱི་དཔྲལ་བ་ནས་ནང་དུ་ཞུགས་ཤིང་ཐིམ་པར་གྱུར་བར་བསམ། བྱིན་རླབས་ཀྱི་འོད་ཀྱི་རྣམ་པ་དེ་ཉིད་ལ་བརྟེན་ནས། ལུས་ཀྱི་སྒྲིབ་པ་སྦྱོང་བྱེད་སྐུ་བུམ་པའི་དབང་ཐོབ་པར་མོས། དཔལ་ལྡན་བླ་མ་དམ་པ་མཆོག་གི་སྐུ་ཡི་བྱིན་རླབས་ནུས་མཐུ་ཐམས་ཅད་ཀྱིས་བྱིན་གྱིས་རློབས་ཤིག་ཅེས་

སླས་པས། ལུས་ཀྱི་སྒྲིབ་པ་དང་སད་པའི་གནས་སྐབས་ཀྱི་སྒྲིབ་པ་རྣམས་དག་པར་གྱུར་ནས། བདེ་སྟོང་དགའ་བའི་དགའ་བ་བཞི་ཉམས་སུ་མྱོང་བར་གྱུར། སྐུ་ཡི་རྡོ་རྗེ་རྫོགས་པའི་སངས་རྒྱས་སྤྲུལ་པའི་སྐུ་ཐོབ་པར་བྱིན་གྱིས་རློབས་ཤིག དཔལ་ལྡན་བླ་མ་དམ་པ་མཆོག་གིས། སྐུའི་ཡོན་ཏན་ཚད་མེད་བསམ་གྱིས་མི་ཁྱབ་པས་ད་ལྟ་ཉིད་ནས་བྱིན་གྱིས་རློབས་ཤིག

མགྲིན་པའི་ཨཱཿལས་ཨཱཿཡིག་དམར་པོ།། རང་གི་ལུས་ཀྱི་མགྲིན་པར་ཞུགས་ཤིང་།། དེ་ལ་བརྟེན་ནས་གསང་དབང་འཐོབ་པར།། དཔལ་ལྡན་བླ་མས་བྱིན་གྱིས་རློབས་ཤིག ངག་དང་རྨི་ལམ་སྒྲིབ་པ་དག་ནས།། མཆོག་གི་དགའ་བཞི་ཉམས་སུ་མྱོང་བས།། གསུང་གི་རྡོ་རྗེ་ལོངས་སྐུ་འཐོབ་པར།། དཔལ་ལྡན་བླ་མས་བྱིན་གྱིས་རློབས་ཤིག

དེ་བཞིན་དུ་རིམ་པ་ལྟར་བླ་མ་དམ་པ་མཆོག་གི་མགྲིན་པའི་ཨཿལས་ཨཿཡིག་དམར་པོ་ཞིག་འཕྲོས་ཏེ། ཐ་མལ་བ་རང་ཉིད་ཀྱི་ལུས་ཀྱི་མགྲིན་པ་ནས་ནང་དུ་ཞུགས་ཤིང་ཐིམ་པར་གྱུར། བྱིན་རླབས་ཀྱི་འོད་ཀྱི་རྣམ་པ་ཅན་དེ་ཉིད་ལ་བརྟེན་ནས་རང་ཉིད་ཀྱི་ངག་གི་སྒྲིབ་པ་སྦྱོང་བྱེད་གསུང་གསང་བའི་དབང་ཐོབ་པར་མོས། མགྲིན་པར་དཔལ་ལྡན་བླ་མ་དམ་པ་མཆོག་གི་གསུང་གི་བྱིན་རླབས་ནུས་མཐུ་ཐམས་ཅད་ཀྱིས་བྱིན་གྱིས་རློབས་ཤིག དེས་ངག་གི་སྒྲིབ་པ་དང་རྨི་ལམ་གྱི་གནས་སྐབས་ཀྱི་སྒྲིབ་པ་རྣམས་དག་པར་གྱུར་ནས། བདེ་སྟོང་དགའ་བའི་མཆོག་དགའ་བཞི་ལ་སོགས་པ་ཉམས་སུ་མྱོང་བར་གྱུར། གསུང་གི་རྡོ་རྗེ་རྫོགས་པའི་སངས་རྒྱས་ལོངས་སྐུ་འཐོབ་པར་བྱིན་གྱིས་རློབས་ཤིག དཔལ་ལྡན་བླ་མ་དམ་པ་མཆོག་གི་ཚད་ལས་འདས་པའི་ཐུགས་རྗེ་ཆེན་པོས་བདག་ལ་ད་ལྟ་ཉིད་ནས་བྱིན་གྱིས་རློབས་ཤིག

ཐུགས་ཀའི་ཧཱུྃ་ལས་ཧཱུྃ་ཡིག་ནག་པོ།། རང་གི་ལུས་ཀྱི་སྙིང་གར་ཞུགས་ཤིང་།། དེ་ལ་བརྟེན་ནས་ཤེར་དབང་འཐོབ་པར།། དཔལ་ལྡན་བླ་མས་བྱིན་གྱིས་རློབས་ཤིག ཡིད་དང་གཉིད་འཐུག་སྒྲིབ་པ་དག་ནས།། ཁྱད་པར་དགའ་བཞི་ཉམས་སུ་མྱོང་བས།། ཐུགས་ཀྱི་རྡོ་རྗེ་ཆོས་སྐུ་ཐོབ་པར།། དཔལ་ལྡན་བླ་མས་བྱིན་གྱིས་རློབས་ཤིག

ཡང་དེ་ནས་རིམ་པ་བཞིན་དུ་བླ་མ་དམ་པ་མཆོག་གི་ཐུགས་ཀའི་ཧཱུྃ་ལས་ཧཱུྃ་ཡིག་ནག་པོ་ཞིག་འཕྲོས་ནས། རང་ཐ་མལ་བ་ཉིད་ཀྱི་སྙིང་ག་ནས་ནང་དུ་ཞུགས་ཤིང་ཐིམ་པར་གྱུར། བྱིན་རླབས་ཀྱི་འོད་ཀྱི་རྣམ་པ་ཅན་དེ་ཉིད་ལ་བརྟེན་ནས། ཡིད་དང་གཉིད་འཐུག་གི་སྒྲིབ་པ་སྦྱོང་བྱེད་ཐུགས་ཤེས་རབ་ཀྱི་དབང་ཐོབ་པར

སོལ། སྙིང་གར་དཔལ་ལྡན་བླ་མ་དམ་པ་མཆོག་གི་ཐུགས་ཀྱི་བྱིན་རླབས་ནུས་མཐུ་ཐམས་ཅད་ཀྱིས་བྱིན་གྱིས་རློབས་ཤིག དེས་ཡིད་ཀྱི་སྒྲིབ་པ་དང་། གཉིད་འཐུག་གནས་སྐབས་ཀྱི་སྒྲིབ་པ་རྣམས་དག་པར་གྱུར་ནས། བདེ་སྟོང་ཁྱད་པར་ཅན་གྱི་དགའ་བ་བཞི་ཉམས་སུ་མྱོང་བར་གྱུར། ཐུགས་ཀྱི་རྡོ་རྗེ་རྫོགས་པའི་སངས་རྒྱས་ཆོས་སྐུ་འཐོབ་པར་བྱིན་གྱིས་རློབས་ཤིག དཔལ་ལྡན་བླ་མ་དམ་པ་མཆོག་གིས་བསམ་གྱིས་མི་ཁྱབ་པའི་བྱིན་རླབས་བདག་ལ་ད་ལྟ་ཉིད་དུ་སྩོལ་ཅིག

ལྟེ་བའི་ཧོཿལས་ཧོཿཡིག་སེར་པོ།། རང་གི་ལུས་ཀྱི་ལྟེ་བར་ཞུགས་ཤིང་།། དེ་ལ་
བརྟེན་ནས་བཞི་དབང་འཐོབ་པར།། དཔལ་ལྡན་བླ་མས་བྱིན་གྱིས་རློབས་ཤིག
ཆགས་པའི་བག་ཆགས་དྲི་མ་དག་ནས།། ལྷན་སྐྱེས་དགའ་བཞི་ཉམས་སུ་མྱོངས་
པས།། ཡེ་ཤེས་རྡོ་རྗེ་བདེ་སྟོང་འཐོབ་པར།། དཔལ་ལྡན་བླ་མས་བྱིན་གྱིས་རློབས་ཤིག

མཐར་ཐུག་གི་དབང་ཐོབ་ཆེད་དུ་ལྟེ་བའི་ཧོཿལས་ཧོཿཡིག་སེར་པོ་འོད་ཀྱི་རང་བཞིན་ཅན་འཕྲོས་ཏེ། རང་གི་ལུས་ཀྱི་ལྟེ་བའི་ནང་དུ་ཞུགས་ཤིང་། དེ་ལ་བརྟེན་ནས་བཞི་དབང་སྟེ། དབང་བཞི་བ་གསང་བའི་ཚིག་གི་དབང་ཐོབ་པར་སོམས། དཔལ་ལྡན་བླ་མ་དམ་པ་དེ་ཉིད་ཀྱིས་ད་ལྟ་ཉིད་ནས་བདག་གི་རྒྱུད་བྱིན་གྱིས་རློབས་ཤིག ཞེས་གསོལ་བ་བཏབ་པས། ཆགས་པའི་བག་ཆགས་དྲི་མ་དང་བཅས་པ་དག་ནས། བདེ་སྟོང་ལྷན་ཅིག་སྐྱེས་པའི་དགའ་བ་བཞི་ཆ་མཉམ་དུ་ཉམས་སུ་མྱོང་བའི་སྐལ་བ་དང་ལྡན་པར་གྱུར། མཐར་ཐུག་པ་གདོད་མའི་ཡེ་ཤེས་རྡོ་རྗེ་བདེ་སྟོང་འཐོབ་པར་བྱིན་གྱིས་རློབས་ཤིག དེ་ལྟར་ཇི་ལྟར་གསོལ་བ་བཏབ་པ་བཞིན་དུ་དཔལ་ལྡན་བླ་མ་དམ་པ་མཆོག་གིས་བྱིན་གྱིས་བརླབ་པར་མཛད་དུ་གསོལ།

སྤྱི་བོའི་བླ་མ་འོད་དུ་ཞུ་ནས།། རང་གི་ལུས་ལ་གཉིས་མེད་ཐིམ་ཞིང་།། སྙིང་གའི་པདྨ་
འདབ་བརྒྱད་དབུས་སུ།། བརྟན་པར་བཞུགས་ནས་བྱིན་གྱིས་རློབས་ཤིག དེ་ལྟར་
བསྒོམས་པས་བདག་སོགས་སེམས་ཅན།། རང་རྒྱུད་ཁམས་ཀྱི་དྲི་མ་དག་ནས།།
བདེ་གཤེགས་སྙིང་པོ་མྱུར་དུ་ཐོབ་པར།། དཔལ་ལྡན་བླ་མས་བྱིན་གྱིས་རློབས་ཤིག

དེ་ལྟར་དབང་བཞི་བླངས་པས། སྤྱི་བོའི་གཙུག་གི་རྩ་བའི་བླ་མ་འོད་ཀྱི་རང་བཞིན་དུ་ཞུ་ནས་རང་གི་ལུས་ངག་ཡིད་གསུམ་ལ་ཐིམ་སྟེ། རང་དང་གཉིས་སུ་མེད་པར་དབྱེར་མེད་རོ་གཅིག་ཏུ་གྱུར་པར་སོམས། དེ་ནས་སླར་ཡང་རང་ཉིད་ཀྱི་སྙིང་གའི་དབུས་སུ་པདྨ་འདབ་མ་བརྒྱད་པ་ཅན་ཞིག་བསྒོམ། དེའི་དབུས་སུ་འགྱུར་མེད་བརྟན་པར་བཞུགས་སུ་གསོལ། བཞུགས་ནས་བདག་ལ་བྱིན་གྱིས་བརླབས་ཤིང་བརྟན་པར་བཞུགས་ཤིག དེ་ལྟར་བསྒོམས་པའི་བྱིན་རླབས་ཀྱིས་བདག་སོགས་སེམས་ཅན་ཐམས་ཅད་ཀྱི། རང་

རྒྱུད་ཁམས་ཀྱི་དྲི་མ་གློ་བུར་བ་མ་ལུས་ཤིང་ལུས་མེད་པར་དག་ནས། རང་ཅག་གི་རྒྱུད་ཀྱི་ཡེ་བཞུགས་གདོད་མའི་རང་ཞལ་རང་ཆས་སུ་བཞུགས་པ། བདེ་གཤེགས་སྙིང་པོ་མྱུར་དུ་མངོན་དུ་བྱེད་ནུས་པའམ། འཐོབ་ནུས་པར་དཔལ་ལྡན་བླ་མ་དམ་པ་རྫོགས་པའི་སངས་རྒྱས་དངོས་དེས་བྱིན་གྱིས་རློབས་ཤིག དེ་ལྟར་གོང་སྨོས་བཞིན་དཔལ་ལྡན་བླ་མའི་ཐུགས་དང་རང་སེམས་དབྱེར་མི་ཕྱེད་པའི་ངོ་བོ་བསྲེས་ཏེ། ཐ་ནའང་དུས་ཡུན་སྐར་ཆ་ཁ་ཤས་ལ་བསྒོམ་པར་བྱའོ།།

ཅེས་སྦྱོར་བ་ཡན་ལག་དྲུག་གི་བླ་མའི་རྣལ་འབྱོར་བྱིན་རླབས་ཆར་འབེབས་མ་ཞེས་བྱ་བ་འདི་ནི་རྟོན་པ་བཞི་ལྡན་གྱིས་སྦྱར་བའོ།།

ཞེས་པའི་དོན་མི་གོ་བ་མེད་ཀྱང་། རྟོན་པ་བཞི་ལྡན་ཞེས་པ་ལ་འགྲེལ་བཤད་ཙམ་བྱས་ན། དེ་ནི་དོལ་པོ་བ་ཤེས་རབ་རྒྱལ་མཚན་གྱི་མཚན་གྱི་རྣམ་གྲངས་ཡིན། རྟོན་པ་བཞིའི་དོན་ནི། ཚིག་ལ་མི་རྟོན་དོན་ལ་རྟོན། གང་ཟག་ལ་མི་རྟོན་ཆོས་ལ་རྟོན། ཀུན་རྫོབ་ལ་མི་རྟོན་དོན་དམ་ལ་རྟོན། རྣམ་ཤེས་ལ་མི་རྟོན་ཡེ་ཤེས་ལ་རྟོན། ཞེས་པ་སོགས་བཞི་པོ་རེད། དང་པོ་ཚིག་ལ་མི་རྟོན་དོན་ལ་རྟོན་ཞེས་པ་ནི། བདེན་གཉིས་ཀྱི་བསྡུས་པའི་ཆོས་གང་ཞིག་བཤད་ཡང་། དཔེ་ལ་གཞི་ལམ་འབྲས་གསུམ་གང་ཞིག་གཏན་ལ་ཕབ་ཆེ། སྐབས་སུ་བབས་པ་དང་། གང་ལ་ཐོབ་པ་དང་། ཅིག་ལ་ཕན་པ་སོགས་ཀྱི་ཆེད་དུ། དོན་གང་ཞིག་དཔེ་དེ་ཉིད་ཀྱིས་རྟོན་དགོས་ཤིང་། དེའི་ཕྱིར་ཐད་ཀར་གོམས་འདྲིས་ཀྱི་དབང་གིས་སྣང་བའི་ཚིག་ཙམ་དང་། དོན་གང་ཞིག་ལ་ཞེན་པ་ཙམ་གྱིས་གནད་དོན་དམ། གནས་ལུགས་དངོས་སམ། དོན་ངོ་མ་རྣམས་ནམ་ཡང་མི་རྟོགས་ན་ཡང་། ཀུན་མཁྱེན་དོལ་པོ་བ་ནི་དེ་འདྲ་རྩ་བ་ནས་མ་ཡིན་པའི་རྒྱུ་མཚན་གྱིས་སོ།། གང་ཟག་ལ་མི་རྟོན་ཆོས་ལ་རྟོན་ཟེར་བ་ནི། གང་ཟག་གང་ཞིག་གིས་ཆོས་ཅི་ཞིག་ལ་འགྲེལ་བ་བཤད་དུས། ཆོས་དེ་ཉིད་ལ་དགོས་པའི་ཟབ་དོན་ཡོད་མེད་དང་། ཡང་དག་ཡོད་མེད་ལ་ལྟ་དགོས་པ་ལས། བཤད་མཁན་གྱི་གང་ཟག་དེ་ཉིད་བཟང་ངན་བར་གསུམ་གང་ཞིག་ཡིན་པའི་རྒྱུ་མཚན་གྱིས། དེས་བཤད་པའི་གཏམ་གྱི་རིན་ཐང་ལས་སླ་བོས་སྒོ་ནས་གཞལ་བ་ནི་ཤིན་ཏུ་ནོར་འཁྲུལ་ཆེ། སྤྱིར་བཏང་མི་རྣམས་ནི་དེ་འདྲའི་བླུན་ཞེན་ཤིན་ཏུ་ཆེ་མོད། དོལ་པོ་བ་ནི་དེ་འདྲ་ལས་གྲོལ་ཏེ། དོན་དངོས་ཀྱི་གནས་ལུགས་ངོ་མ་དེ་ཉིད་ལ་ལྟ་ཐུབ་ཅིང་། ཚིག་གི་ཡག་སྡུག་དང་རྣ་བར་སྙན་མིན་སོགས་ཀྱིས་གང་ཟག་ལ་མི་གཞལ་བར། དོན་ངོ་མ་གང་ཞིག་དམར་ལྗེན་དུ་ཤེས་ཤིང་རྟོགས་མཁན་ཞིག་ཡིན་པའི་དོན་རེད། ཀུན་རྫོབ་ལ་མི་རྟོན་དོན་དམ་ལ་རྟོན། ཞེས་པ་ནི། ཕལ་བའི་སྐྱེ་བོ་རྣམས་ཀུན་རྫོབ་སྣང་གྲགས་ཀྱི་བསྡུས་པའི་ཆོས་རྣམས་ལ་ཆགས་ཤིང་ཞེན་ཏེ། དེ་ལས་གཞན་དུ་ལྟ་མི་ཤེས་ལ། དེ་ཉིད་ཁོ་ན་བདེན་པར་བཟུང་ཏེ་འཁོར་བར་ཡང་ཡང་འཁོར་བའི་རྒྱུ་བསགས་ཀྱི་ཡོད་མོད། ཀུན་མཁྱེན་དོལ་པོ་བ་ནི་དེ་ལས་གྲོལ་ཏེ་དོན་དམ་གནས་ལུགས་མཐར་ཐུག་ཤེས་ཤིང་རྟོགས་ཏེ། དེ་ཉིད་ཉམས་སུ་སྦྱོང་ནས་དེ་ལ་ལོངས་སུ་སྤྱོད་པའི་

དང་དུ་གནས་པའི་གང་ཟག་ཅིག་ཅེས་པས་དོན་རེད། རྣམ་ཤེས་ལ་མི་རྟེན་ཡེ་ཤེས་ལ་རྟེན། ཞེས་པ་ནི། ཐ་མལ་བའི་བློ་མ་རིག་གྲིས་སླད་པ་ཅན། ཀུན་རྫོབ་ཀྱི་རྣམ་པར་ཤེས་པ་ཚོགས་བརྒྱད་པོ་ཁོ་ན་ལ་བསྟེན་ནས་གཞི་ལམ་འབྲས་གསུམ་སོགས་གཏན་ལ་མི་ཕབ་པར། གནས་ལུགས་ཡང་དག་པ་མཐར་ཐུག་པའི་ལྟ་བ་གཏན་ལ་ཕབ་མཁན་ཡིན་པས། གང་ཟག་ཐ་མལ་བ་བཞིན་དུ་རྣམ་ཤེས་ཀྱི་ཡོ་ལང་དང་། རྣམ་ཤེས་ཀྱི་སྤྱོད་ཡུལ་ཤ་སྟག་ལ་མི་ལྟོས་ཤིང་མི་རེག་པར། སྒྲ་དང་རྟོག་པའི་ཡུལ་ལས་འདས་པའི་དོན་དམ་རྣམ་པ་ཐམས་ཅད་པ་རྟོགས་ཤིང་ཉམས་སུ་སྤྱོང་བ་དང་། དེ་ལ་ལོངས་སུ་སྤྱོད་མཁན་གྱི་སྐྱེས་བུ་དམ་པ་ཞིག་ཡིན་པས། དོལ་པོ་བ་ཤེས་རབ་རྒྱལ་མཚན་ལ་རྟེན་པ་བཞི་ལྡན་དུ་གྲགས་ཤིང་གྲུབ་པའོ།།

> དཔལ་ལྡན་བླ་མའི་རྣམ་པར་ཐར་པ་ལ།། སྐད་ཅིག་ཙམ་ཡང་ལོག་ལྟ་མི་སྐྱེ་ཞིང་།།
> ཅི་མཛད་ལེགས་པར་མཐོང་བའི་མོས་གུས་ཀྱིས།། བླ་མའི་བྱིན་རླབས་སེམས་ལ་
> འཇུག་པར་ཤོག

ལེགས་པའི་ཡོན་ཏན་ཐམས་ཅད་ཀྱི་དཔལ་དང་ལྡན་པའི་བླ་མ་ཡི་རྣམ་པར་ཐར་བ་སྟེ། བླ་མའི་མཚན་ཉིད་དང་ངོ་བོ། ཡང་ན་བྱ་བ་དང་སྤྱོད་པ་ལ་སོགས་པ་གང་འདྲ་དང་ཇི་ལྟར་སྣང་ཡང་། རང་ཉིད་ཀྱི་ལས་སྣང་དང་སེམས་ཅན་གྱི་བསོད་ནམས་ཀྱི་འདང་ཚོད་ཙམ་ཡིན་པ་མ་གཏོགས། བླ་མ་རང་ངོས་སུ་རང་བཞིན་གྱིས་གྲུབ་པའི་སྐྱོན་སོགས་ཅི་ཡང་མེད་པར་རྟོགས་པའི་བློ་ནས་སེམས་ལ་སྐད་ཅིག་ཙམ་ཡང་ལོག་ལྟ་དང་སྐུར་འདེབས་སོགས་མི་སྐྱེ་ཞིང་། བླ་མས་ཅི་མཛད་ཀུན་ཆོས་སུ་ཤེས་ནུས་པའི་དག་སྣང་གིས་ལེགས་པར་མཐོང་བའི་མོས་གུས་དང་ལྡན་པའི་བློ་ནས། དྲིན་ཅན་རྩ་བ་དང་བརྒྱུད་པར་བཅས་པའི་བླ་མ་དམ་པ་རྣམས་ཀྱི་བྱིན་རླབས་རང་གི་སེམས་རྒྱུད་ལ་འཇུག་ནུས་པར་ཤོག་ཅིག ཅེས་པའི་དོན་ནོ།།

> སྐྱེ་བ་ཀུན་ཏུ་ཡང་དག་བླ་མ་དང་།། འབྲལ་མེད་ཆོས་ཀྱི་དཔལ་ལ་ལོངས་སྤྱོད་ཅིང་།།
> ས་དང་ལམ་གྱི་ཡོན་ཏན་རབ་རྫོགས་ནས།། རྡོ་རྗེ་འཆང་གི་གོ་འཕང་མྱུར་ཐོབ་ཤོག

དུས་འདི་ནས་བཟུང་སྟེ་སྐྱེ་བ་ནས་ཚེ་རབས་ཀུན་ཏུ། ཡང་དག་པའི་རྩ་བརྒྱུད་ཀྱི་བླ་མ་དམ་པ་རྣམས་དང་ནམ་ཡང་འབྲལ་བ་མེད་པའི་སྒོ་ནས། དམ་པའི་ཆོས་ཟབ་མོའི་དཔལ་ལ་ལོངས་སུ་སྤྱོད་ནུས་ཤིང་། དེ་ལ་ཕྱི་ནང་གསང་བ་གསུམ་གྱི་རྐྱེན་ངན་བར་ཆད་སོགས་གང་ཡང་མེད་པར། ས་ཡི་མཐར་ཐུག་གམ་ཡོན་ཏན་གྱི་མཐར་ཐུག་རྫོགས་པའི་སངས་རྒྱས་ཀྱི་གོ་འཕང་ལ་འགྲོ་བའི་ས་དང་ལམ་གྱི་ཡོན་ཏན་ཐམས་ཅད་རིམ་པ་བཞིན་དུ་འཕེལ་ཏེ། ཡང་དག་པར་རབ་ཏུ་རྫོགས་ནས། མཐར་སྐུ་བཞི་ཡེ་ཤེས་ལྔའི་བདག་ཉིད་ཅན་རྒྱལ་བ་རྫོགས་པའི་སངས་རྒྱས་རྡོ་རྗེ་འཆང་གི་གོ་འཕང་མྱུར་བ་མྱུར་དུ་ཐོབ་པར་ཤོག་ཅིག ཅེས་པ་ལ་སོགས་པའོ།།

བླ་རྣམ་དངོས་གྲུབ་འགུགས་པའི་ལྕགས་ཀྱུ།

༄༅།། ཨོཾ་སྭ་སྟི བླ་མའི་རྣལ་འབྱོར་དངོས་གྲུབ་འགུགས་པའི་ལྕགས་ཀྱུ་
ཞེས་བྱ་བ། བླ་མ་དམ་པའི་ཞབས་ལ་ཕྱག་འཚལ་ལོ།།

ཨོཾ་སྭ་སྟི། ཞེས་བཀྲ་ཤིས་པའི་ཚིག་གིས་དབུ་བྲངས་ཏེ། འདི་ནི་རྩ་བ་དང་བརྒྱུད་པའི་བླ་མ་རྣམས་ལ་ཡོད་པའི་བྱིན་རླབས་དང་དངོས་གྲུབ་མཐའ་དག་འགུགས་ཏེ། རང་རྒྱུད་ལ་སྦྱོར་ནུས་པའི་བླ་མའི་རྣལ་འབྱོར་དངོས་གྲུབ་འགུགས་པའི་ལྕགས་ཀྱུ་ཞེས་བྱ་བའོ།། སྐབས་སུ་རང་གིས་རང་ལ་དྲན་སྐུལ་བཏང་བའོ།། ལྷག་པར་དུ་རྩ་བའི་བླ་མ་དམ་པའི་ཞབས་ཀྱི་པདྨོ་ལ་སྒོ་གསུམ་གུས་པ་ཆེན་པོས་ཕྱག་འཚལ་ལོ།། ཞེས་བཀའ་གཉན་ཞིང་གལ་ཆེ་བའི་མཚོན་དོན་དུ། སྒོ་གསུམ་གུས་པས་མཆོད་ཕྱག་ཕྱོན་དུ་བཏང་སྟེ། ཡིད་མ་གཡེང་བར་འདི་ལྟར་བརྗོད་ཅིང་དོན་བསམ་པར་བྱ་སྟེ།

ཆོས་རྣམས་ཐམས་ཅད་རང་གི་སེམས་སྣང་ཙམ།། རང་གི་སེམས་ཀྱང་གསལ་
སྟོང་བརྗོད་དུ་མེད།། སྣང་བ་མ་འགགས་སྣ་ཚོགས་ཅི་ཤར་ཡང་།། རང་རིག་
སྐད་ཅིག་འདི་ལ་གཡོ་བ་མེད།། ཨོཾ་ཤཱུ་ནྱ་ཏཱ་ཛྙཱ་ན་བཛྲ་སྭ་བྷཱ་ཝ་ཨཱཏྨ་ཀོ྅ཧཾ།

ཞེས་ངག་ཏུ་སྒྲོར་དུས། སྣང་སྲིད་འཁོར་འདས་ཀྱིས་བསྡུས་པའི་ཆོས་ཐམས་ཅད་རང་གི་ལས་ཀྱི་རྣམ་སྨིན་གྱིས་སྣང་བ་ཙམ་སྟེ། བཟང་ངན་བར་མ་ཐམས་ཅད་སེམས་ལས་སྣང་བ་ཙམ་མ་གཏོགས་མེད་ལ། རང་གི་སེམས་འདི་ཉིད་ཀྱང་ཕར་གང་དུ་ཡོད་བཙལ་ཆེ་གསལ་སྟོང་བརྗོད་དུ་མེད་པ་ཙམ་ལས་སྐྱེད་རྒྱུ་མེད་ལ། ཕར་མ་བརྟག་མ་དཔྱད་པར་བལྟས་ན་འཁོར་འདས་ཀྱི་སྣང་བ་མ་འགགས་པར་སྣ་ཚོགས་ཅི་ཤར་ཐམས་ཅད་ཀྱང་། རང་གི་རིག་པ་སྐད་ཅིག་མ་འདི་ཉིད་ལས་ནམ་ཡང་གཡོ་བ་མེད་ཅིང་ཀུན་རྫོབ་ཀྱི་སྣང་བ་རྣམས་གནས་ལུགས་སྟོང་བ་ཙམ་དུ་ཟད་དོ།། ཞེས་བསམ་པའི་འདུ་ཤེས་དང་ཆོར་བ་ཤུགས་དྲག་པོའི་སྒོ་ནས། ཨོཾ་ཤཱུ་ནྱ་ཏཱ་ཛྙཱ་ན་བཛྲ་སྭ་བྷཱ་ཝ་ཨཱཏྨ་ཀོ྅ཧཾ། ཞེས་པའི་སྔགས་འདི་ངག་ནས་བརྗོད་ཅིང་དོན་དམ་སྟོང་བ་ཉིད་དམིགས་པ་མེད་པའི་ངང་དུ་ཅི་ནུས་པར་མཉམ་པར་བཞག

རང་སེམས་དག་པའི་སྣང་བ་འོག་མིན་ཞིང་།། ཞིང་འདིའི་དབུས་སུ་གཞལ་མེད་
ཁང་པ་མཛེས།། དེ་དབུས་སེང་ཁྲི་པདྨ་ཉི་ཟླའི་སྟེང་།། དྲིན་ཅན་རྩ་བའི་བླ་མ་
དམ་པ་བཞུགས།།

ད་ལྟའི་མ་དག་པའི་སྣང་བ་འདི་ལ་སྣང་བ་ལྟར་དུ་མི་ལྟ་བར། རང་སེམས་དག་པར་སྦྱང་བ་སྟེ་རང་ཉིད་ལ་གང་སྣང་བ་ཐམས་ཅད་འོག་མིན་སྟུག་པོ་བཀོད་པའི་ཞིང་ལ་སོགས་པའི་ཞིང་ཁམས་སུ་མོས་པ་ཤུགས་དྲག་བསྐྱེད། དེ་འདྲའི་དག་པའི་ཞིང་ཁམས་འདིའི་དབུས་སུ་གཞལ་མེད་ཀྱི་ཁང་བ་ལྟ་ན་སྡུག་ཅིང་མཛེས་པ་ཞིག་བསྒོམ། གཞལ་མེད་ཀྱི་ཁང་བ་དེའི་དབུས་སུ་སེང྄ྒེ་ཆེན་པོ་བརྒྱད་ཀྱིས་བཏེགས་པའི་ཁྲི་པདྨ་ཉི་ཟླ་སྒྲ་གཅན་དུས་མེ་དང་བཅས་པའི་སྟེང་དུ། བཀའ་དྲིན་མཚུངས་པ་མེད་པའི་དྲིན་ཅན་རྩ་བའི་བླ་མ་དམ་པ་མཆོག ངོ་བོ་རང་ཉིད་ཀྱི་རྩ་བའི་བླ་མ་ཡིན་པ་ལ། རྣམ་པ་རྡོ་རྗེ་འཆང་དམ། ཡང་ན་རྗེ་བཙུན་ཏཱ་ར་ནཱ་ཐའི་རྣམ་པ་ཅན་གཞི་བརྗོད་དཔག་ཏུ་མེད་པའི་ངོ་བོར་བཞུགས་པར་བསམ་པའི་གསལ་འདེབས་ཅི་ནུས་བྱའོ།།

གཞི་བརྗོད་དཔག་མེད་གསེར་གྱི་ལྷུན་པོ་འདྲ།། འོད་ཟེར་ཉི་མ་འབུམ་གྱི་
མདངས་དང་ལྡན།། བདག་ལ་དགྱེས་པས་ཞལ་རས་འཛུམ་དཀར་གཡོ།།

ཐུགས་ཟག་པ་མེད་པའི་ཡེ་ཤེས་ལས་འཁྲུངས་པའི་གཞི་བརྗོད་དཔག་ཏུ་མེད་པའི་ངོ་བོ་ཅན་གྱི་བླ་མ་དེ་ཉིད། ལྟ་ན་སྡུག་པའི་བརྗིད་ཉམས་ནི་གསེར་གྱི་ལྷུན་པོ་དང་འདྲ་བ། ཟག་པ་མེད་པའི་སྐུ་ལས་འོད་ཟེར་ཉི་མ་འབུམ་གྱི་མདངས་དང་ལྡན་པ་ཕྱོགས་ཀུན་ཏུ་འཕྲོ་བར་བསྒོམ་ལ། བདག་རང་ཉིད་ལ་ཐུགས་མཉེས་པ་ཚད་མེད་པའི་རྣམ་པས་ཞལ་རས་འཛུམ་དཀར་གྱི་དགྱེས་འཛུམ་པདྨའི་འདབ་མ་ལྟར་གཡོ་བར་བསྒོམ།

སྟེང་གི་ཕྱོགས་ལ་བརྒྱུད་པའི་བླ་མ་རྣམས།། རྫུ་འཕྲུལ་བཀོད་པ་སྣ་ཚོགས་
བཅས་པ་དང་།། སྐུ་ཡི་མཐའ་སྐོར་ཕྱོགས་རྣམས་ཐམས་ཅད་དུ།། ཧེ་རུ་ཀ་དང་
རྡོ་རྗེ་ཕག་མོ་སོགས།། ཡི་དམ་ལྷ་ཚོགས་ཐམས་ཅད་སྤྲིན་ལྟར་འཐིབས།།

དེ་འདྲའི་རྩ་བའི་བླ་མ་དམ་པ་མཆོག་བཞུགས་པའི་སྟེང་གི་ནམ་མཁའི་ཕྱོགས་ཀུན་ཏུ་བརྒྱུད་པའི་བླ་མ་རྣམས་ཀྱིས་ཁེངས་པར་མོས། བརྒྱུད་པའི་བླ་མ་དེ་དག་རེ་རེས་ཀྱང་རྫུ་འཕྲུལ་གྱི་བཀོད་པ་སྣ་ཚོགས་པ་དང་བཅས་པའི་སྒོ་ནས་བཞུགས་པ་དང་། དེ་དག་རེ་རེ་བཞིན་སྐུ་ཡི་མཐའ་སྐོར་གྱི་

ཕྱོགས་རྣམས་ཐམས་ཅད་ཀུན་ཏུ་ཁྲོ་བོ་ཧེ་རུ་ཀ་སྟེ་རྡོ་རྗེ་ཁྲོ་བོ་དང་ཁྲོ་མོའི་ལྷ་ཚོགས་རྣམས་དང་། རྡོ་རྗེ་ཕག་མོ་ལ་སོགས་པ་ཞི་མ་ཁྲོའི་རྣམ་ཅན་གྱི་ཡི་དམ་རྒྱུད་སྡེ་བཞིའི་ལྷ་ཚོགས་ཐམས་ཅད་སྤྲིན་ལྟར་འཐིབས་ཤིང་ཁྲ་སྟུང་རེར་འོད་འཐིབས་སེར་བཞུགས་པར་བསྒོམ་དགོས་ལ། མ་མཐར་མོས་གུས་དྲག་པོ་ནི་ངེས་པར་དུ་བྱ་དགོས་པའོ།།

> སངས་རྒྱས་བྱང་སེམས་ཕྱོགས་བཅུའི་མཁའ་དབྱིངས་ཁྱབ།། སྤྲུལ་པའི་དགྲ་
> བཅོམ་ས་གཞི་ཁྱབ་པ་དང་།། མཁའ་འགྲོ་ཆོས་སྐྱོང་སྲུང་མའི་ཚོགས་རྣམས་
> ཀྱང་།། རང་རང་འཁོར་དང་རྫུ་འཕྲུལ་དཔག་མེད་བཅས།། བཀའ་ལ་ཉན་ཅིང་
> གསུང་བཞིན་སྒྲུབ་པས་བཞུགས།།

དེ་ལྟ་བུའི་རྩ་བ་དང་བརྒྱུད་པའི་བླ་མ་རྣམས་ཀྱི་མ་ཚད། ཐམས་ཅད་མཁྱེན་པ་རྫོགས་པའི་སངས་རྒྱས་ཀྱི་གོ་འཕང་དུ་གཤེགས་ཟིན་པའི་སངས་རྒྱས་རྣམས་དང་། ས་དང་པོ་ནས་ས་བཅུའི་བར་དུ་གནས་པའི་བྱང་ཆུབ་སེམས་དཔའ་བསམ་གྱིས་མི་ཁྱབ་པས་ཤར་ལྷོ་ནུབ་བྱང་དང་། མཚམས་བཞི་སྟེང་འོག་གཉིས་ཏེ་ཕྱོགས་བཅུའི་མཁའ་དབྱིངས་ཀུན་ཏུ་ཁྱབ་ཡོད་པར་མོས། དེའི་མ་ཚད་ཐེག་པ་དམན་པའི་ཚུལ་འཛིན་ཅིང་སྤྲུལ་པའི་ཉན་རང་དགྲ་བཅོམ་པ་རྣམས་ཀྱིས་རང་ཉིད་གནས་པའི་ས་གཞི་ཐམས་ཅད་དུ་ཁྱབ་པར་མོས། དེ་བཞིན་དུ་གནས་ཉེར་བཞི་དང་ཡུལ་སོ་དྲུག་སོགས་སུ་གནས་པ། མཁའ་འགྲོ་དང་། མཁའ་འགྲོ་མའི་ཚུལ་བཟུང་བ། ལྷན་སྐྱེས། ཞིང་སྐྱེས། སྔགས་སྐྱེས་ཀྱི་མཁའ་འགྲོ་མའི་ཚོགས་རྣམས་དང་། དམ་པའི་ཆོས་སྐྱོང་བ་དང་སྲུང་ཞིང་སྒྲུབ་པ་པོའི་གང་ཟག་གི་ལས་བྱེད་པའི་དམ་ལྡན་སྲུང་མའི་ཚོགས་རྣམས་ཀྱང་། རང་རང་གི་འཁོར་དང་ལྡན་ཞིང་། རྫུ་འཕྲུལ་དཔག་ཏུ་མེད་པའི་ནུས་མཐུ་ལྡན་པ་དང་བཅས་པའི་སྒོ་ནས། གཙོ་བོ་རྒྱལ་བ་རྩ་བའི་བླ་མ་དང་བརྒྱུད་པའི་བླ་མ་དེ་དག་གི་བཀའ་ལ་ཉན་ཅིང་། སྐད་ཅིག་ལ་གསུང་བཞིན་སྒྲུབ་ནུས་པའི་མཐུ་རྩལ་དང་བཅས་པའི་སྒོ་ནས་བཞུགས་པར་གྱུར་ཡོད་པར་མོས།

> གང་ལ་གང་འདུལ་སྤྲུལ་བ་སོ་ཉའི་ཚོགས།། གློག་ལྟར་འཁྱུགས་ཤིང་བུ་ཡུག་
> འཚུབས་པ་བཞིན།། ས་དང་བར་སྣང་རི་ཀླུང་མེད་པར་ཁྱབ།། ཐམས་ཅད་སྐུ་
> ནི་བཀྲག་མདངས་འོད་དང་ལྡན།། གསུང་ནི་ཐེག་ཆེན་དམ་པའི་ཆོས་སྒྲ་སྒྲོག
> ཐུགས་ནི་འོད་གསལ་བདེ་བ་ཆེན་པོའི་ངང་།། མཛད་པ་འཕྲིན་ལས་མ་ངེས་ཅིར་
> ཡང་སྟོན།།

རྩ་བརྒྱུད་ཀྱི་བླ་མ་དང་། ཡི་དམ་འཁའ་འགྲོ་ཆོས་སྐྱོང་དང་བཅས་པ་དེ་དག་རེ་རེ་བཞིན་གྱིས། མ་གྱུར་འགྲོ་བ་སེམས་ཅན་རྣམས་ལ་གང་ལ་གང་འདུལ་གྱི་སྤྲུལ་པ་བསམ་གྱིས་མི་ཁྱབ་པ་དང་ལྡན་པ་དང་། དེ་དག་རེ་རེ་བཞིན་གྱི་སྤྲུལ་པའི་ཟློས་གར་རམ་མངགས་པའི་པོ་ཉ་ལྟ་བུའི་ཚོགས་བསམ་གྱིས་མི་ཁྱབ་པ་མང་པོ། སློག་འཁྲུགས་པ་ལྟར་གྱི་རྫུ་འཕྲུལ་སྟོན་ཞིང་ཁ་བ་བུ་ཡུག་འཚུབས་པ་བཞིན་དུ་བྱོན་ཏེ། ཐབས་སྣ་ཚོགས་ཀྱིས་འགྲོ་བ་མཐའ་མེད་པའི་དོན་རྒྱ་ཆེན་པོ་བྱེད་པ་དང་། དེ་འདྲའི་སྤྲུལ་བའམ་པོ་ཉ་བ་རྣམས་ས་གཞི་དང་བར་སྣང་། རི་ལུང་དང་ཆུ་ཀླུང་གི་དབྱེ་བ་མེད་པར་ཁེངས་ཤིང་ཁྱབ་པར་མོས་ལ། དེ་དག་ཐམས་ཅད་ཀྱི་སྐུ་ནི་བཀྲག་མདངས་འོད་དང་ལྡན་ཞིང་། གསུང་ལ་ནི་ཐེག་པ་ཆེན་པོའི་དམ་པའི་ཆོས་ཀྱི་སྒྲ་དབྱངས་སྒྲོག་པ་དང་། ཐུགས་ནི་འོད་གསལ་བདེ་བ་ཆེན་པོའི་ངང་ལས་གཡོ་བ་སྐད་ཅིག་ཀྱང་མེད་པ། མཛད་པ་དང་འཕྲིན་ལས་ནི་མ་ངེས་ཤིང་། ངེས་པ་ཅི་ཡང་མེད་པའི་སྒོ་ནས་འགྲོ་བ་སེམས་ཅན་གྱི་ཕན་པ་དང་བདེ་དོན་ཁོ་ན་སྒྲུབ་པར་སྟོན་པའོ།།

> ཀུན་ཀྱང་རྗེ་བཙུན་བླ་མའི་སྤྲུལ་པ་སྟེ།། གཞན་ཡང་འཁོར་འདས་སྣང་བ་མ་ལུས་པ།། མཚན་ལྡན་བླ་མའི་ཡེ་ཤེས་ཆོ་འཕྲུལ་ཙམ།།

དེ་ལྟ་བུའི་བསམ་གྱིས་མི་ཁྱབ་པའི་སྣང་བ་འབྱུང་བ་དེ་དག་ཀུན་ཀྱང་མདོར་རྟིལ་གྱིས་དྲིལ་ན། རྗེ་བཙུན་བླ་མ་དམ་པ་ཁོ་ནའི་སྤྲུལ་པ་ཡིན་པ་སྟེ་ཡིན་པར་ཤེས་པའི་མོས་སྒོམ་ཤུགས་དྲག་པོ་བྱ། དེས་ཀྱང་མི་ཚད་པར་གཞན་ཡང་འཁོར་འདས་ཀྱི་སྣང་བ་མ་ལུས་པ་ཡོད་དོ་ཚོག་ཀུན་ཀྱང་། མཚན་ལྡན་རྗེ་བཙུན་བླ་མ་ཁོ་ནའི་ཐུགས་ཡེ་ཤེས་ཚད་མེད་པ་དེའི་ཆོ་འཕྲུལ་ཙམ་ལས་གཞན་ཅི་ཡང་མིན་པ་ཤེས་པར་བྱ་བ་ནི་གལ་ཆེའོ།།

> བདག་གི་ལུས་དང་ལོངས་སྤྱོད་ཅི་མཆིས་དང་།། དུས་གསུམ་བསགས་པའི་དགེ་བ་ཅི་ཡོད་དང་།། ཕྱོགས་བཅུའི་ཞིང་ན་བདག་པོས་མ་བཟུང་བའི།། མཆོད་པའི་བྱེ་བྲག་ཧི་སྙེད་མཆིས་པ་དང་།། དགྲ་གཉེན་བར་མས་བསྡུས་པའི་སེམས་ཅན་རྣམས།། འགྲོ་དྲུག་ནམ་མཁའི་མཐས་གཏུགས་ཧི་སྙེད་དང་།། སྲིད་པ་གསུམ་གྱི་ལོངས་སྤྱོད་གང་མཆིས་དང་།།

བདག་ལ་ད་ལྟར་ཡོད་པའི་ལུས་དང་ལོངས་སྤྱོད་ཅི་མཆིས་དང་། ཚེ་རབས་ཐོག་མེད་ནས་བསགས་པའི་དགེ་བ་དང་། གཞན་ཡང་དུས་གསུམ་དུ་བསགས་ཤིང་གསོག་པར་འགྱུར་བའི་དགེ་བ་ཅི་

ཡོད་དང་། དེའི་སྟེང་དུ་རང་ཉིད་ཁོ་ན་ལ་དབང་བ་མ་ཡིན་པའི་ཕྱོགས་བཅུའི་ཞིང་ན། བདག་པོས་མ་བཟུང་བའི་མཆོད་པའི་བྱེ་བྲག་གང་དག་ཇི་སྙེད་མཆིས་པ་ཐམས་ཅད་དང་། བདག་གི་དགྲ་དང་གཉེན་དང་། དེ་གཉིས་ཀ་མ་ཡིན་པའི་བར་མ་ཡིས་བསྡུས་པའི་སེམས་ཅན་རྣམས་དང་། གཞན་ཡང་ཁམས་གསུམ་འགྲོ་དྲུག་ནམ་མཁའི་མཐས་གཏུགས་པ་ཇི་སྙེད་མཆིས་པ་དེ་དག་དང་། མ་ཟད་སྲིད་པ་གསུམ་གྱི་དངོས་རྫས་ཡོངས་སྤྱོད་གང་དག་ཅི་རྙེད་ཅིག་མཆིས་པ་ཐམས་ཅད་དང་།

བདག་གི་ཡིད་ཀྱིས་སྤྲུལ་དང་སྨོན་ལམ་མཐུས།། སངས་རྒྱས་བྱང་སེམས་དཔའ་བོ་མཁའ་འགྲོར་བཅས།། དུས་གསུམ་ཕྱོགས་བཅུར་འབྱུང་བ་ཐམས་ཅད་ཀྱི།། ཡེ་ཤེས་རང་སྣང་ལས་གྲུབ་མཆོད་པའི་ཚོགས།། གྲངས་མེད་ཚད་མེད་བསམ་གྱིས་མི་ཁྱབ་པ།། མཆོག་ཏུ་བརྗོད་བག་ཆགས་པའི་ཚུལ་དང་བཅས།། བླ་མའི་ཐུགས་དང་རང་སེམས་དབྱེར་མེད་པ།། སྐྱེ་མེད་ཆོས་སྐུའི་ཚོ་འཕྲུལ་ཙམ་དུ་སྒོམ།།

ད་ལྟ་བདག་ལ་ཧིང་ངེ་འཛིན་ཡོད་མེད་ལ་མ་ལྟོས་པར། བདག་གི་ཡིད་ཀྱིས་སྤྲུལ་བ་གང་དག་ཅི་ཡོད་རྣམས་དང་། དེ་བཞིན་དུ་ཡིད་ཀྱིས་སྨོན་ལམ་འདེབས་པའི་སྒོ་ནས་བྱས་པ་དག་གིས་མཐུས། རྫོགས་པའི་སངས་རྒྱས་བྱང་སེམས་དཔའ་བོ་མཁའ་འགྲོ་དང་བཅས་པ། དེ་ཡང་ད་ལྟ་བ་ཙམ་མ་ཡིན་པར་དུས་གསུམ་དུ་འབྱུང་བ་དག་དང་། ཕྱོགས་བཅུ་ནས་འབྱུང་བ་ཐམས་ཅད་ཀྱི་ཐུགས་ཡེ་ཤེས་ཀྱི་ངོ་བོའི་རང་སྣང་ལས་གྲུབ་པའི་མཆོད་པའི་ཚོགས་གྲངས་མེད་པ། ཚད་མེད་པ། བསམ་གྱིས་མི་ཁྱབ་པ། དེ་དག་ནི་ཡང་དག་པར་དང་། མཆོག་རབ་ཀྱི་རབ་དང་། མཆོག་ཏུ་བརྗོད་ཉམས་ལྡན་པའི་གཟི་བརྗིད་ཀྱི་བབ་ཆགས་པའི་ཉམས་དང་ལྡན་ཞིང་ཚུལ་དང་བཅས་པ་བསམ་གྱིས་མི་ཁྱབ་པ་ཀུན། དོན་ལ་བླ་མའི་ཐུགས་དང་རང་སེམས་དབྱེར་མེད་པ་དེ་ཉིད་ཡིན་པས། དོན་ལ་ནམ་ཡང་སྐྱེ་བ་མེད་ཅིང་འགག་པ་ཡང་མེད་པའི་ཆོས་སྐུ་དོན་དམ་པའི་ཚོ་འཕྲུལ་ཁོ་ན་ཙམ་དུ་ཟད་པར་བསྒོམ་ལ་མོས་གུས་ཤུགས་དྲག་པོ་བྱའོ།།

སངས་རྒྱས་ཀུན་འདུས་བླ་མ་རིན་པོ་ཆེ།། དམ་ཆོས་ཀུན་འདུས་ཆོས་རྗེ་རིན་པོ་ཆེ།། དགེ་འདུན་ཀུན་འདུས་འདྲེན་མཆོག་རིན་པོ་ཆེ།། བླ་མ་ཀུན་འདུས་གཅིག་ཆོག་རྒྱལ་བོ་ཁྱོད།། ཡི་དམ་ཐམས་ཅད་ཁྱོད་ཀྱི་སྐུ་ལ་ཚང་།། མཁའ་འགྲོ་ཆོས་སྐྱོང་ཐམས་ཅད་པོ་ཉར་སྤྲུལ།། རྡོ་རྗེ་འཆང་ཆེན་ཁྱོད་ལ་གསོལ་བ་འདེབས།

དུས་གསུམ་གྱི་ཕྱོགས་ཀུན་གྱི་སངས་རྒྱས་ཀུན་འདུས་པའི་བླ་མ་རིན་པོ་ཆེ། ལུང་དང་རྟོགས་པའི་བསྡུས་པའི་དམ་པའི་ཆོས་ཀུན་འདུས་པའི་ཆོས་རྗེ་དཔལ་ལྡན་བླ་མ་རིན་པོ་ཆེ། ཐེག་པ་གསུམ་གྱི་ལམ་ལྡ་དང་ཐེག་ཆེན་ས་བཅུའི་བསྡུས་པའི་དགེ་འདུན་གྱི་སྡེ་ཀུན་འདུས་པ། འཁོར་བ་དང་ངན་སོང་གི་འགྲོ་བ་མ་ལུས་པ་ཐར་བར་འདྲེན་པའི་འདྲེན་མཆོག་རིན་པོ་ཆེ། རིགས་དང་དཀྱིལ་འཁོར་རྒྱ་མཚོའི་ཁྱབ་བདག སྲིད་པ་གསུམ་གྱི་རྣམ་པ་མ་ལུས་པ་ཅན་གྱི་བླ་མ། སངས་རྒྱས་ཀུན་འདུས་དང་མཆོག་གསུམ་གཅིག་ཆོག་གི་ཆོས་ཀྱི་རྒྱལ་པོ་ཁྱོད། གང་ཟག་སྐྱེར་སོ་སོ་ལ་ལས་དང་སྨོན་ལམ་གྱིས་གྲུབ་ཅིང་། ཡིད་ལ་དམ་དུ་བཅངས་ན་མཆོག་དང་ཐུན་མོང་གི་དངོས་གྲུབ་མཐའ་དག་སྐྱེར་བ་པོ་ཐམས་ཅད་ཁྱོད་ཀྱི་སྐུ་ལ་ཚང་བ། དཔའ་བོ་དང་དཔའ་མོ་མཁའ་འགྲོ་དང་མཁའ་འགྲོ་མ་དང་། དམ་པའི་ཆོས་སྐྱོང་བའི་སྲུང་མ་ཐམས་ཅད་དང་དེ་དག་གི་པོ་ཉ་ཡང་སྤྲུལ་དང་བཅས་པ། མ་ཟད་རང་གི་རྩ་བའི་བླ་མ་དེ་ཉིད་འཁོར་འདས་ཀུན་གྱི་ཁྱབ་བདག་དང་། མི་འགྱུར་གཡུང་དྲུང་གི་གོ་འཕང་བརྙེས་པ། རྡོ་རྗེའི་ས་བརྙེས་པ་རྡོ་རྗེ་འཆང་ཆེན་ཁྱེད་ལ་གསོལ་བ་འདེབས། ཞེས་དང་།

སོས་པའི་བུ་ལ་ད་ལྟ་བྱིན་གྱིས་རློབས།། སྤྱུག་པོ་བཀོད་པའི་ཞིང་དུ་རྡོ་རྗེ་
འཆང་།། དྲག་པོ་འདུལ་ཚེ་ཧེ་རུ་ཀ་དཔལ་སྐུ།། ཆགས་བྲལ་རྣམས་ལ་ཤཱཀྱ་ཐུབ་
པར་བསྟན།། དཀའ་ཐུབ་ཅན་ལ་དྲང་སྲོང་ཚུལ་འཛིན་ཅིང་།། ཐེག་གསུམ་ལམ་
དུ་ཞུགས་པའི་སེམས་ཅན་ལ།། བྱང་སེམས་རང་རྒྱལ་ཉན་ཐོས་ཚུལ་དུ་སྟོན།།

དེ་ལྟ་བུའི་འཁོར་འདས་གཉིས་ཀྱི་ཁྱབ་བདག་དེ་ལ་སོས་ཤིང་གྲུས་པའི་སྒོ་ནས་གསོལ་བ་བཏབ་ན། དད་འདུན་སོས་པའི་བུ་ང་ལ་ད་ལྟ་ཉིད་ནས་བྱིན་གྱིས་རློབས་ཤིག་ཅེས་དང་། འོག་མིན་སྤྱུག་པོ་བཀོད་པའི་ཞིང་དུ་ཡང་བླ་མ་དེ་ཉིད་ལོངས་སྐུ་རྡོ་རྗེ་འཆང་གི་ངོ་བོ་རུ་བཞུགས་པ། བསྟན་པ་དང་འགྲོ་བ་ལ་གནོད་ཅིང་། ཞི་བས་མི་འདུལ་བ་དག་ལ་དྲག་པོས་འདུལ་དགོས་ཚེ་ཁྲོ་བོ་ཧེ་རུ་ཀ་དཔལ་ལ་སོགས་པའི་སྐུ་ཅན་དང་། འཁོར་བ་ལ་ངེས་འབྱུང་སོགས་ཀྱིས་འདུལ་དགོས་པ་རྣམས་ལ་ཆགས་བྲལ་གྱི་རྣམ་པ་སྟེ། མཆོག་གི་སྤྲུལ་སྐུ་ཤཱཀྱ་ཐུབ་པ་ལྟ་བུའི་གཟུགས་སྐུ་བསྟན་པ། འདོད་ཡོན་གྱི་དངོས་པོ་ཀུན་ལ་ཁ་གཏད་དུ་ལངས་པའི་དཀའ་ཐུབ་ཅན་གྱི་ཆོས་ལུགས་ལ། དྲང་སྲོང་དཀའ་ཐུབ་ཅན་གྱི་ཚུལ་ཡང་འཛིན་ཅིང་། གདུལ་བྱ་འདུལ་བར་བྱེད་པ་ལ་སོགས་པ། མདོར་ན་ཕྱི་ནང་གི་ཐེག་པ་ཐུན་མོང་བ་དང་། ཐུན་མིན་ནང་བ་སངས་རྒྱས་པའི་ཐེག་གསུམ་གང་གི་ལམ་དུ་ཞུགས་ཤིང་གཞུག་པར་གྱུར་པའི་སེམས་ཅན་ཐམས་ཅད་ལ། གང་ལ་གང་འདུལ་གྱིས་བྱང་ཆུབ་

སེམས་དཔའ་དང་རང་རྒྱལ་དགྲ་བཅོམ་པ། ཉན་ཐོས་དགྲ་བཅོམ་པ་ལ་སོགས་པའི་ཚུལ་དུ་སྟོན་པའོ།།

ཚངས་དང་ཁྱབ་འཇུག་འདོད་ལྷ་དབང་པོ་དང་།། དབང་ཕྱུག་ལ་སོགས་ལྷ་ཡི་
གཟུགས་སུའང་སྟོན།། ཁ་ཅིག་ཏུ་ནི་རྒྱལ་སྲིད་སྤྱོད་ལ་དགྱེས།། གཞན་དུ་རིག་
པའི་བརྟུལ་ཞུགས་སྤྲོད་པ་སྤྱོད།། ལ་ལར་དུར་སྒྲིག་འཛིན་པའི་གཟུགས་ཀྱང་
འཆང་།། གང་ལ་གང་འདུལ་སྐུ་ལ་གསོལ་བ་འདེབས།།

ཚོས་འདི་ལས་ཕྱི་རོལ་དུ་གྱུར་པའི་མུ་སྟེགས་ཚངས་པ་བ་དག་ལ་ཚངས་པའི་ཚུལ་དུ་མངོན་ཞིང་། ཁྱབ་འཇུག་པ་དག་ལ་ཡང་དེ་ལྟར་དང་། འདོད་ཁམས་པའི་ལྷ་ལ་སོགས་པ་ལྷའི་དབང་པོ་བརྒྱ་བྱིན་ལྟ་བུ་སོགས་གང་ལ་གང་འདུལ་གྱི་གཟུགས་སུ་ཡང་སྟོན་པ། དེ་བཞིན་དུ་སྤྲུལ་པའི་རྣོས་གར་ཁག་ཅིག་ཏུ་ནི་རྒྱལ་སྲིད་ཀྱི་སྤྱོད་པ་ལ་སོགས་པར་དགྱེས་པའི་སྒོ་ནས་འགྲོ་བའི་དོན་མཛད་ཅིང་། ཡང་གདུལ་བྱའི་འགྲོ་བ་འགའ་ཞིག་གཞན་ལ་རིག་པ་འཛིན་པ་དང་། མ་ངེས་པའི་བརྟུལ་ཞུགས་ཏེ་སྤྱོད་པ་སྣ་ཚོགས་པར་སྤྱོད་ཅིང་། ཡང་ལ་ལ་ནི་དུར་སྒྲིག་འཛིན་པའི་དགེ་སློང་གི་གཟུགས་ཀྱང་འཆང་བ་ལ་སོགས་པའི་གང་ལ་གང་འདུལ་གྱི་སྐུ་ཅན་གྱི་བླ་མ་དམ་པ་དེ་ལ་སྙིང་ནས་དད་ཅིང་གུས་པས་གསོལ་བ་འདེབས་སོ།།

སེམས་ཅན་ཀུན་གྱི་བསམ་པ་ཇི་བཞིན་དུ།། ཁྱོད་ཀྱི་བསྟན་པ་འདི་ཡང་བསམ་
མི་ཁྱབ།། ཇི་ལྟར་མཁའ་ལ་སྤྲིན་དང་འཇའ་ཚོན་སོགས།། རྣམ་པ་སྣ་ཚོགས་
གཟུགས་བརྙན་སྣང་ན་ཡང་།། ནམ་མཁའ་ལས་བྱུང་ནམ་མཁའི་ངོ་བོ་དང་།།
ནམ་མཁའི་ངང་དུ་ཐིམ་པར་འགྱུར་བ་བཞིན།། སྤྲོས་བྲལ་ཅི་ཡང་མ་ཡིན་ཚོས་
ཀྱི་སྐུ།། འབད་རྩོལ་མེད་ཀྱང་ལྷུན་གྲུབ་འཕྲིན་ལས་ཅན།།

མདོར་ན་གོང་དུ་བཤད་པ་ཇི་ལྟ་བ་བཞིན་དུ། མར་གྱུར་སེམས་ཅན་ཀུན་གྱི་བསམ་པ་ཇི་ལྟར་ཕན་དང་བདེ་བའི་དངོས་པོ་སྟེར་ནུས་པ་དེ་བཞིན་དུ། བླ་མ་སངས་རྒྱས་མཆོག་ཁྱོད་ཀྱི་བསྟན་པ་འདི་ཡང་བསམ་གྱིས་མི་ཁྱབ་པའི་ངོར་འབྱུང་ཞིང་། ཡིན་ན་ཡང་ཀུན་རྫོབ་ཐ་སྙད་ཙམ་དུ་མ་གཏོགས་གནས་ལུགས་དོན་དམ་བདེན་པའི་ངོ་བོར་ནི་ཇི་ལྟར་མཁའ་ལ་སྤྲིན་དང་འཇའ་ཚོན་སོགས་བྱུང་བ། རྣམ་པ་སྣ་ཚོགས་ཀྱི་གཟུགས་བརྙན་ཞིག་ཏུ་མང་པོ་སྣང་ན་ཡང་། པར་ལྟ་དུས་ནམ་མཁའ་ལས་བྱུང་བའི་འཇའ་ཚོན་དང་སྤྲིན་པ་ལ་སོགས་པ། ནམ་མཁའི་ངོ་བོར་པར་ནམ་མཁའི་ངང་དུ་འཐིམ་པར་

འགྱུར་བར་སྣང་བ་ཙམ་ཡིན་པ་བཞིན་དུ། ཆོས་ཀྱི་སྐུ་དེ་ཉིད་ནི་སྤྲོས་བྲལ་ཅི་ཡང་མ་ཡིན་པ་ནམ་མཁའ་ལྟ་བུའི་སྐུ་སྟེ། ནམ་མཁའ་བཞིན་དུ་འབད་རྩོལ་སོགས་ཅི་ཡང་མེད་ཀྱང་། རྒྱལ་སྣང་སོགས་ལྷུན་གྱིས་གྲུབ་པའི་འཕྲིན་ལས་ཅན་དུ་ཤེས་པར་བྱའོ།།

གང་ལ་གང་འདུལ་མཛད་པ་སྤྱིར་བསྟན་ཀྱང་།། རང་རིག་རང་གསལ་སྤྲོས་བྲལ་
དབྱིངས་ཀྱི་ངང་།། སྐྱེ་འགག་མེད་ཅིང་འགྲོ་འོང་གནས་དང་བྲལ།། དོན་དམ་
སྐུ་ཅན་ཁྱེད་ལ་གསོལ་བ་འདེབས།། རྟག་ཏུ་གུས་པའི་ཡིད་ཀྱིས་ཕྱག་འཚལ་
ཞིང་།། སྐྱབས་གནས་ཀུན་འདུས་ཁྱེད་ལ་སྐྱབས་སུ་མཆི།།

དེ་ལྟར་ཡང་ནས་ཡང་དུ་སྨྲས་པ་ཇི་བཞིན་དུ། མ་གྱུར་འགྲོ་བ་སུ་ཞིག་གམ་གང་ཞིག་ལ་འཕྲིན་ལས་གང་གིས་འདུལ་བའི་མཛད་པ་སྤྱིར་སྣ་ཚོགས་ཤིག་བསྟན་ཀྱང་། དོན་དུ་རང་རིག་ནང་དབྱིངས་རང་གསལ་སྤྲོས་པ་བྲལ་བའི་དབྱིངས་ཀྱི་ངང་རོ་གཅིག་པ། དེ་ལ་སྐྱེ་འགག་དང་འཕོ་འགྱུར་འགྲོ་འོང་གནས་སྡོད་དང་བྲལ་བ། དོན་དམ་རྣམ་པ་ཐམས་ཅད་ཀྱི་སྐུ་ཅན་ཁྱེད་ལ་དུས་རྟག་པར་རྒྱུན་གྱི་འཁོར་ལོའི་ངོ་བོར་ཕྱག་འཚལ་ལོ། བདག་གིས་དུས་རྟག་ཏུ་དོན་དམ་བླ་མའི་ངོ་བོའི་གནས་ལུགས་ལ་སྒོ་གསུམ་གུས་པའི་ཡིད་ཀྱིས་སྐྱབས་གནས་ཀུན་འདུས་སུ་ཤེས་པའི་སྒོ་ནས། སྲིད་ཞིའི་འཇིགས་པ་མ་ལུས་པ་ལས་སྐྱོབ་པར་སྐྱབས་སུ་མཆིའོ།།

མཆོད་པ་ཐམས་ཅད་དབྱེར་མེད་ངང་དུ་འབུལ།། རང་བཞིན་མེད་ཀྱང་སྡིག་
ཀུན་མཐོལ་ལོ་བཤགས།། འཁོར་འདས་དགེ་བ་ཀུན་ལ་རྗེས་ཡི་རང་།། གྲགས་
སྟོང་བརྗོད་བྲལ་གསུང་ལ་ཆད་པ་མེད།། ཆོས་ཀྱི་སྐུ་ལ་སྐྱེ་འཆི་མི་མངའ་ཡང་།།
ཆོས་འཁོར་རྒྱུན་མི་འཆད་པར་བསྐོར་བ་དང་།། འགྲོ་བའི་དོན་ལ་རྟག་ཏུ་
བཞུགས་སུ་གསོལ།། ཐུགས་ཡིད་དབྱེར་མེད་དོན་དུ་བསྔོ་བར་བགྱི།།

དོན་དམ་སྐྱེ་འགག་འགྲོ་འོང་བྲི་གང་བྲལ་ཡང་། ཀུན་རྫོབ་རྒྱུ་འབྲས་ཀྱི་ཚོགས་ནམ་ཡང་མི་བསླུ་བས། དངོས་བཤམས་ཡིད་སྤྲུལ་གྱི་མཆོད་པ་ཐམས་ཅད། མཆོད་བྱ་མཆོད་བྱེད་དབྱེར་བ་མེད་པའི་རིག་པའི་ངང་དུ་འབུལ་བར་བགྱིའོ།།

སྒྲིབ་གཉིས་རང་བཞིན་གྱིས་གྲུབ་པ་མེད་ཀྱང་། ཀུན་རྫོབ་བདེན་པའི་ངོ་བོ་རུ་སྡིག་པའི་ཚོགས་ཀུན་སྙིང་ནས་མཐོལ་ལོ་བཤགས་སོ།། ཟག་བཅས་ཟག་མེད་གཉིས་ཀྱི་དགེ་བ་སྟེ་འཁོར་བ་དང་མྱང་

འདས་ཀྱིས་བསྡུས་པའི་དགེ་བ་ཀུན་ལ་རྗེས་སུ་ཡི་རང་ཞིང་། དོན་དམ་གནས་ལུགས་སུ་སྒྲ་གྲགས་ཀུན་གྱི་སྟོང་བ། བརྗོད་བྲལ་གྱི་གསུང་རྒྱུན་ཆད་པ་མེད་པ་ཡིན་པའི་ཆོས་ཀྱི་སྐུ་ལ་སྐྱེ་འཆི་མི་མངའ་ཡང་། རྒྱུ་འབྲས་རྟེན་འབྱུང་གི་ངོ་བོ་ཤེས་པའི་སྒོ་ནས། འགྲོ་བ་ཀུན་ལ་ཆོས་འཁོར་རྒྱུན་མི་ཆད་པར་ཡང་ནས་ཡང་དུ་བསྐོར་བར་བསྐུལ་ལོ།། དོན་ལ་མྱ་ངན་ལས་འདའ་བའམ། འཆི་བ་མེད་ཀྱང་ཀུན་རྫོབ་སྣང་བ་བསླུ་མེད་ཀྱི་ངོ་བོར་འགྲོ་བ་སེམས་ཅན་ཀུན་གྱི་བདེ་དོན་དུ། བསྐལ་བ་རྒྱ་མཚོའི་བར་དུ་འཆི་བ་མེད་པའི་གོ་འཕང་དུ་རྟག་ཏུ་བཞུགས་པར་གསོལ་བ་འདེབས་སོ།། རང་གཞན་སྐྱེ་འཕགས་ཀུན་གྱིས་དུས་གསུམ་དུ་བསགས་པའི་དགེ་བའི་དངོས་པོ་ཀུན་མ་ལུས་པ། བླ་མ་དོན་དམ་སངས་རྒྱས་དངོས་དང་ཐུགས་ཡིད་དབྱེར་མེད་རོ་གཅིག་ཏུ་འདྲེས་པའི་དོན་དུ་བསྔོ་བར་བགྱིའོ།།

བླ་མེད་བྱང་ཆུབ་མཆོག་ཏུ་སེམས་བསྐྱེད་བགྱི།། རྗེ་བཙུན་སྒྲོལ་བའི་མགོན་པོ་ཁྱེད་ཉིད་ཀྱི།། སྐུ་གསུང་ཐུགས་ཀྱི་བྱིན་གྱིས་རློབས་པ་དང་།། དབང་བཞི་རྫོགས་པར་ད་ལྟར་བསྐུར་དུ་གསོལ།། ལུས་ལ་ལྷན་སྐྱེས་བདེ་ཆེན་བསྐྱེད་པ་དང་།། ངག་ལ་རིགས་སྔགས་ནུས་པ་བརྟན་པ་དང་།། སེམས་ལ་འོད་གསལ་ཡེ་ཤེས་འཆར་བ་རུ།། མཚན་ལྡན་བླ་མས་ད་ལྟར་བྱིན་གྱིས་རློབས།།

དེ་ལྟར་ཡན་ལག་བདུན་གྱི་སྒོ་ནས་ཚོགས་བསགས་ཏེ། ཚོགས་བསགས་སྒྲིབ་སྦྱོང་གི་དགེ་རྩ་དེ་དག་ཀུན། ཐེག་ཆེན་ལམ་གྱི་གཞུང་ཤིང་དུ་གྱུར་པ་བླ་ན་མེད་པ་བྱང་ཆུབ་མཆོག་ཏུ་སེམས་བསྐྱེད་པར་བགྱི་ན། ཁྱབ་བདག་རྗེ་བཙུན་སྒྲོལ་བའི་མགོན་པོ་ཏྭ་ར་ནཱ་ཐ་ཁྱེད་ཉིད་མཆོག་གིས། སྐུ་དང་གསུང་དང་ཐུགས་ཀྱིས་དགེ་བ་དེ་དག་ཐམས་ཅད་ལམ་མཆོག་ཏུ་གྱུར་བར་བྱིན་གྱིས་རློབས་པར་མཛད་དུ་གསོལ། དོན་དམ་གནས་ལུགས་རྟོགས་པར་བྱིན་རླབས་ཀྱི་དབང་བཞི་པོ་རྫོགས་པར་ད་ལྟ་ཉིད་ནས་གསོལ་བ་འདེབས་ན་ད་ལྟ་ཉིད་ནས་བསྐུར་དུ་གསོལ། དབང་གི་ནུས་པས་ཐུན་གྱི་ལུས་ལ་ལྷན་སྐྱེས་ཀྱི་བདེ་བ་ཆེན་པོའི་ཡེ་ཤེས་བསྐྱེད་དུ་གསོལ། བདག་གི་ད་ལྟའི་ཐ་མལ་བའི་ངག་ལ་ཡང་རིགས་སྔགས་ཀྱི་ནུས་པའི་རང་བཞིན་ཞུགས་ཤིང་བརྟན་པར་གྱུར་ཅིག གསོལ་བ་འདེབས་པ་པོ་བདག་ལ། གནས་སྐབས་ལུས་ཀྱི་བདེ་བ་ཙམ་མ་ཡིན་པར་རང་སེམས་ཀྱི་གནས་ལུགས་འོད་གསལ་བདེ་བའི་ཡེ་ཤེས་ཉིད་ད་ལྟ་ནས་འཆར་བ་རུ། མཚན་ཉིད་ཅི་ལྟ་བ་བཞིན་ལྡན་པའི་དཔལ་ལྡན་བླ་མ་དམ་པ་མཆོག་དེས་དུས་ད་ལྟ་ཉིད་ནས་བྱིན་གྱིས་རློབས་ཤིག

བླ་མའི་དཔྲལ་མགྲིན་ཐུགས་ཀ་ལྟེ་བ་ལས།། འོད་ཟེར་བྱུང་ནས་བདག་གི་གནས་བཞིར་ཐིམ།། སྐུ་གསུང་ཐུགས་དང་ཡེ་ཤེས་རྡོ་རྗེ་ཡི།། བྱིན་གྱིས་བརླབས་ཤིང་དབང་བཞི་ཐོབ་པར་གྱུར།། སླར་ཡང་བུམ་པའི་ཆུ་ཡིས་བུམ་དབང་བསྐུར།། བྱང་ཆུབ་སེམས་ཀྱིས་གསང་བའི་དབང་བསྐུར་ཞིང་།། མཉམ་སྦྱོར་བདེ་བའི་ཤེས་རབ་ཡེ་ཤེས་དང་།། འཛིན་མེད་ཕྱག་ཆེན་བཞི་པའི་དབང་ཡང་བསྐུར།།

རྩ་བའི་བླ་མ་དམ་པ་མཆོག་གི་དཔྲལ་བ་མགྲིན་པ་ཐུགས་ཀ་ལྟེ་བ་སོགས་ལས། རིམ་བཞིན་འོད་ཟེར་དཀར་དམར་མཐིང་ག་དང་ནག་པོ་བཞི་འཕྲོས་ཏེ་བྱུང་ནས། རིམ་བཞིན་རང་ཉིད་ཀྱི་དཔྲལ་བ། མགྲིན་པ། སྙིང་ག ལྟེ་བ་བཅས་པའི་གནས་བཞི་ལ་ཐིམ་པར་མོས། དེའི་དབང་གིས་རིམ་པ་བཞིན་དུ་སྐུ་དང་གསུང་། ཐུགས་དང་ཡེ་ཤེས་རྡོ་རྗེའི་ངོ་བོ་བཞི་ཡི་རང་བཞིན་དུ་བྱིན་གྱིས་བརླབས་ཤིང་། དབང་བཞི་པོ་མདོར་བསྡུས་ནས་ཐོབ་པར་མོས་གུས་བསྐྱེད། སླར་ཡང་དབང་བཞི་པོ་རེ་རེ་བཞིན་དུ་ཐོབ་པར་བསམ་པ་ནི། བླ་མའི་དཔྲལ་བའི་འོད་ཟེར་རང་གི་དཔྲལ་བར་ཐིམ་པས། བླ་མ་ཡབ་ཡུམ་གྱི་ཆ་ཤས་རང་ལ་རེག་པ་བུམ་པའི་ཆུ་ཡིས་བུམ་དབང་བསྐུར་ཞིང་ཐོབ་པར་གྱུར། བླ་མའི་མགྲིན་པའི་འོད་ཟེར་རང་གི་མགྲིན་པར་ཐིམ་པས། བླ་མ་ཡབ་ཡུམ་གྱི་བྱང་སེམས་ཞུ་བ་རང་གིས་མྱང་བས་རང་ཉིད་ལ་གསང་བའི་དབང་བསྐུར་ཞིང་ཐོབ། བླ་མའི་ཐུགས་ཀའི་འོད་ཟེར་རང་གི་སྙིང་གར་ཐིམ་པས། དངོས་སུ་བླ་མས་རྒྱལ་བའི་ཡབ་ཡུམ་དང་མཉམ་པར་སྦྱོར་བས་བདེ་བ་ཆེན་པོའི་ཤེས་རབ་ཡེ་ཤེས་ཀྱི་དབང་ཐོབ། བླ་མའི་ལྟེ་བའི་འོད་ཟེར་རང་གི་ལྟེ་བར་ཐིམ་པས། རང་རིག་རང་གསལ་འཛིན་པ་མེད་པའི་ལྷན་སྐྱེས་ཀྱི་ཕྱག་རྒྱ་ཆེན་པོའི་དབང་བཞི་བ་ཡང་བསྐུར་ཞིང་། དབང་བཞིའི་ཡེ་ཤེས་ཐོབ་པར་མོས་པ་ཤུགས་དྲག་པོ་བྱའོ།། ཚོར་གདུང་ཤུགས་ཧྲིང་ཟབ་མོ་བསྐྱེད་པར་གལ་ཆེའོ།།

རེ་ས་གཞན་ན་མེད་དོ་ཆོས་ཀྱི་རྗེ།། སྐྱབས་གནས་གཞན་ན་མེད་དོ་རིན་པོ་ཆེ།། ཆུ་ལ་ཆུ་བཞག་བཞིན་དུ་དབྱེར་མེད་ཅིང་།། འབྲལ་མེད་གནས་ལུགས་རྟོགས་པར་བྱིན་གྱིས་རློབས།། བླ་མ་བྱང་ཆུབ་སེམས་ཀྱི་བདུད་རྩིར་ཞུ།། རྩ་འཁོར་བཞི་པོ་གང་བས་དབང་བཞི་ཐོབ།། བླ་མ་རང་སེམས་དབྱེར་མེད་ཆོས་སྐུའི་ངང་།། རྩ་བྲལ་ལྷུན་གྲུབ་ཆེན་པོའི་ངང་དུ་བཞག །

ཞེས་རྒྱ་ཆེན་གཏིང་ཟབ་ཀྱིས་གསོལ་བ་ཚོར་ཤུགས་དྲག་པོས་བཏབ་མཐར། ཡང་བསྐྱར་བླ་མ་ལ་

གདུང་ཤུགས་དྲག་པོའི་སྒོ་ནས་བདག་ཅག་སེམས་ཅན་ཐམས་ཅད་འཁོར་བ་དང་ངན་སོང་ལས་སྐྱོབ་པའི་སྐྱབས་ནི། ཁྱེད་ཉག་གཅིག་ལས་རེ་ས་དང་བརྟེན་ས་གཞན་ན་སུ་ཡང་མེད་དོ།། དེའི་ཕྱིར་ཆོས་ཀྱི་རྗེ་བོ་མཆོག་ཉིད་ལས་སྐྱབས་གནས་གཞན་ནི་སུ་ཡང་མེད་དོ།། ཀྱེ། བླ་མ་རིན་པོ་ཆེ། ཞེས་དག་སྣང་དད་འདུན་ཤུགས་དྲག་པོས་གསོལ་བ་བཏབ་པས། བླ་མའི་ཐུགས་དང་རང་ཉིད་ཀྱི་སེམས་གཉིས་ཆུ་ཡི་ནང་དུ་ཆུ་བླུག་པའམ། ཆུ་ཡི་ནང་དུ་ཆུ་བཞག་པ་བཞིན་དུ་དབྱེར་མེད་རོ་གཅིག་ཏུ་གྱུར་པར་མོས། དེ་ལྟ་བུའི་དབྱེར་མེད་རོ་གཅིག་ཏུ་འབྲལ་བ་མེད་པར་གནས་ལུགས་དོན་དམ་པ་ཉག་གཅིག་པུའི་ངང་དུ་བཞག ནམ་པར་མི་རྟོག་པའི་ངོ་བོར་ཅི་ཙམ་གནས་ཐུབ་པ་དེ་ཙམ་དུ་གནས་པར་བྱའོ།། དེ་ནས་བླ་མའི་སྐུ་གསུང་ཐུགས་དང་བཅས་པ། བྱང་སེམས་བདེ་བའི་ཐིག་ལེའམ། ཀུན་དྷ་བྱང་ཆུབ་ཀྱི་སེམས་ཀྱི་བདུད་རྩིའི་ངོ་བོ་ཧཱུྃ་ཞུ་ནས། རང་གི་རྩ་འཁོར་བཞི་པོ་སྟེ། དཔྲལ་མགྲིན་སྙིང་ག་ལྟེ་བ་བཞི་པོའི་རྩ་འཁོར་རྣམས་ལ་བཞུར་ཏེ་གང་། དེ་ལྟ་བུའི་སྒོ་ནས་ཡང་བསྐྱུར། བུམ་དབང་། གསང་དབང་། ཤེར་དབང་སྤྲོས་བྲལ་མཆོག་གི་དབང་བཞི་པོ་ཐོབ་པའི་མོས་གུས་ཤུགས་དྲག་པོ་བྱའོ།། དེ་འདྲའི་ངང་དུ་རྩ་བའི་བླ་མ་དང་རང་སེམས་དབྱེར་མེད་པ་ཆོས་སྐུ་གདོད་མའི་གོ་འཕང་གི་ངང་དུ། རྩ་བྲལ་དེ་ཡུལ་ཡུལ་ཅན་གྱི་རྣམ་པའམ་རྩ་བའི་གཏད་སོ་དང་བྲལ་བ་རང་བྱུང་གདོད་མ་ལྷུན་གྲུབ་ཆེན་པོའི་ངང་དུ་བཞག་ནས། ཡུན་ཅི་ཙམ་གནས་ཐུབ་པ་དེ་ཙམ་ཏུ་གནས་པར་བྱའོ།།

> ཞེས་པ་འདི་ནི་མཆོག་ཏུ་གྱུར་པའི་བླ་མའི་རྣལ་འབྱོར་ཏེ་ཚེ་གཅིག་ལུས་གཅིག་ལ་སངས་རྒྱས་སྟེར་བར་ཐེ་ཚོམ་མེད་དོ།། རྒྱལ་ཁམས་པ་ཏྭ་ར་ནཱ་ཐས་རང་ལོ་ཉེར་དགུ་བ་ལ་དཔལ་བཟང་ལྡན་དུ་བྲིས་པའོ།།

ཞེས་བླ་རྣམ་ལྕག་མ་འདི་ཉིད་མཛད་པ་པོས་གཏམ་གྱི་མཐའ་བརྒྱན་པའོ།། འདི་ལ་འགྲེལ་བ་བྱ་མི་དགོས་ལ་བྱ་ཡང་མི་ནུས། འདི་ལ་དད་པ་དང་དག་སྣང་བྱ་བ་ལས་གལ་ཆེ་བ་ཅི་ཡང་བྱ་རྒྱུ་མེད་པར་སྣང་།

> སྐྱེ་ཞིང་སྐྱེ་བ་དག་ནི་ཐམས་ཅད་དུ།། རིགས་བཟང་བློ་གསལ་ང་རྒྱལ་མེད་པ་དང་།། སྙིང་རྗེ་ཆེ་ཞིང་བླ་མ་ལ་གུས་ཤིང་།། དཔལ་ལྡན་བླ་མའི་དམ་ཚིག་ལ་གནས་ཤོག

ཇི་སྲིད་སྐུ་བཞིའི་བདག་ཉིད་རྡོ་རྗེ་འཆང་གི་གོ་འཕང་ལ་མ་རེག་བར་དུ། འཁོར་བ་ལ་སྐྱེ་བ་བླང་དགོས་པ་གང་ཞིག་བྱུང་རུང་། སྐྱེ་བ་དེ་དག་ལེན་དགོས་པ་དེ་སྲིད་དུ། དེ་དག་གི་དུས་ཐམས་ཅད་དུ། རིགས་ངན་པའི་དབང་གིས་དགེ་བ་སྒྲུབ་ཏུ་མི་བཏུབ་པ་ལ་སོགས་པའི་རིགས་སུ་ནམ་ཡང་མི་

སྐྱེ་ཞིང་། རིགས་བཟང་པོ་དམ་ཆོས་དགེ་ལ་དགའ་ཞིང་ཀུན་གྱིས་བཀུར་འོས་ཤིང་བཀུར་བ། བློ་གྲོས་གསལ་ཞིང་ཆོས་ཀྱི་གནས་ལུགས་རྟོགས་ནུས་པ། ཉོན་མོངས་པ་ང་རྒྱལ་དང་ཕྲག་དོག་སོགས་མེད་པའམ་ཧ་ཅང་སྲབ་པ་དང་། གཞན་གྱི་སྡུག་བསྔལ་འབྲལ་འདོད་ཀྱི་སྙིང་རྗེ་ཤུགས་དྲག་པ། སེམས་ཅན་ཀུན་ལ་སྙིང་ཉེ་ཞིང་། ལྷག་པར་དུ་རང་གི་དགེ་བའི་བཤེས་གཉེན་དང་བླ་མ་ལ་གུས་པ་ཆེ་ཞིང་། བརྩོན་པས་དུས་ཀུན་ཏུ་བསྐུར་བ། དམ་པའི་ཆོས་ཀྱི་དཔལ་ཡོན་ཁྱད་དུ་འཕགས་པའི་དཔལ་དང་ལྡན་པ། རང་གི་བླ་མ་ལ་བརྟེན་པའི་རྩ་བ་དང་ཡན་ལག་གི་དམ་ཚིག་རྣམས་མིག་འབྲས་བཞིན་དུ་སྲུང་ནུས་པ་སྟེ། དེ་འདྲའི་སྐལ་བཟང་ལ་གནས་པར་ཤོག་ཅིག་ཅེས། སྔར་ལམ་གསང་སྔགས་རྡོ་རྗེ་ཐེག་པའི་ལམ་གྱི་གནད་ལ་བརྟེན་ཏེ། ཐམས་ཅད་མཁྱེན་པ་སངས་རྒྱས་ཀྱི་གོ་འཕང་ལ་རེག་པ་ནི་དམ་ཚིག་སྲུང་བ་ལ་རག་ལས་ཡོད་པར་ནན་ཏན་དུ་བརྗོད་པའོ།།

> དཔལ་ལྡན་བླ་མའི་རྣམ་པར་ཐར་པ་ལ།། སྐད་ཅིག་ཙམ་ཡང་ལོག་ལྟ་མི་སྐྱེ་ཞིང་།།
> ཅི་མཛད་ལེགས་པར་མཐོང་བའི་མོས་གུས་ཀྱིས།། བླ་མའི་བྱིན་རླབས་སེམས་
> ལ་འཇུག་པར་ཤོག

སྔར་ལམ་རྡོ་རྗེ་ཐེག་པའི་ཟབ་ཆོས་ཀྱི་དཔལ་དང་ལྡན་པ། དམ་པའི་ཡོན་ཏན་གྱི་གོང་ན་མེད་པའམ་བླ་ན་མེད་པའི་བླ་མ་ཡི་སྐྱེ་རབས་ལོ་རྒྱུས་སམ། རྣམ་པར་ཐར་བ་སྟེ་འདས་མ་འོངས་ད་ལྟ་གསུམ་གྱི་བྱུང་རིམ་དང་བརྒྱུད་རིམ་ཐམས་ཅད་ལ། ཐུང་མཐའི་དུས་སྐད་ཅིག་མ་ཙམ་གྱི་བར་དུ་ཡང་། མ་རྟོགས་པ་དང་ལོག་པར་རྟོགས་པའི་བློ་ཡི་དྲི་མ་ཙམ་ཡང་རང་རྒྱུད་ལ་ནམ་ཡང་མི་སྐྱེ་ཞིང་། བླ་མ་མཆོག་གིས་སྐུ་གསུང་ཐུགས་ཀྱིས་བྱ་སྤྱོད་ཅི་མཛད་ཐམས་ཅད། བསྟན་འགྲོ་གཉིས་ལ་གནས་སྐབས་དང་མཐར་ཐུག་གི་ཕན་པ་དང་བདེ་བའི་ལེགས་དོན་ཁོ་ན་ཡིན་པར། མཐོང་ནུས་པའི་མོས་གུས་ཀྱིས། བླ་མེད་བསྐལ་བཟང་གི་བྱིན་རླབས་དངོས་གྲུབ་འདི་ཉིད། དུས་གསུམ་སངས་རྒྱས་ཀུན་འདུས་ཀྱི་བླ་མའི་བྱིན་རླབས་ནུས་མཐུ་ཁོ་ན་ཡིན་པས། དོན་དམ་ཆོས་སྐུའི་ངོ་བོ་བླ་མའི་ཐུགས་རྒྱུད་ཀྱི་མངོན་རྟོགས་ཡོན་ཏན་ཐམས་ཅད་པོ། རང་གི་སེམས་ཀྱི་གཏིང་དུ་ཞུགས་ནུས་པར་ཤོག་ཅིག ནུས་པ་ཞིག་རང་གིས་བྱའོ་སྙམ་དུ་གདུང་ཤུགས་དྲག་པོའི་སྒོ་ནས་དུས་ཀུན་ཏུ་དྲན་ཤེས་བག་ཡོད་གསུམ་ལྡན་གྱིས་ཉམས་སུ་ལེན་དགོས་པའི་དོན་ནོ།།

མཇུག་བྱང་སྨོན་ཚིག

འདིར་སྨྲས་པ། རྒྱུད་ཀྱི་རྒྱལ་པོ་དུས་ཀྱི་འཁོར་ལོ་ཞེས།།
གངས་རིའི་ཁྲོད་དུ་མཁས་བླུན་ཀུན་ལ་གྲགས།།
གངས་ཅན་མགོན་པོ་ལ་སོགས་དམ་པ་ཚོས།།
དུས་ཀྱི་འཁོར་ལོའི་དབང་ཆེན་ཡང་ཡང་བསྐུལ།།

དབང་ཐོབ་མོས་ལྡན་སྨིན་པའི་གདུལ་བྱ་དག
རིམ་པར་འཇུག་པའི་ལག་ལེན་རྣལ་མ་ཞིག
ད་ལྟ་གངས་རིའི་ཁྲོད་ན་འདི་ཙམ་ལས།།
སྲིད་མཐར་གྱུར་པས་འདི་ཡང་དོན་ཡོད་སྙམ།།

ཟང་ཟིང་གཡེང་བ་འཁྲིགས་པའི་ཡུལ་དུས་ནས།།
བརྩོན་པའི་གོ་ཆ་ལེ་ལོས་འཕྲོག་པ་ཡིས།།
རྟོགས་དཔྱོད་དབུལ་བས་ལེགས་བཤད་བླ་མེད་ཅིག
མིན་ཡང་ལེགས་པའི་ལམ་འཁྲིད་མཁན་དུ་ངེས།།

དེའི་ཕྱིར་ཁོ་བོའི་བསམ་བཟང་དལ་བའི་སྐྱེས།།
བློ་གསར་དོན་གཉེར་ཅན་ལ་ཕན་བདེའི་སྨན།།
གྱུར་ལ་རྟེན་འབྱུང་བདེན་པས་མཐུ་དཔུང་བསྐྱེད།།
མཁའ་འགྲོ་སྲུང་མས་གདོང་གྲོགས་ཀུན་ནས་མཛོད།།

ད་ནས་བཟུང་སྟེ་ངེས་གསང་ཟབ་མོའི་ལམ།།
འཕོ་མེད་རྩ་རླུང་ཕྲ་བའི་སྦྱོར་དྲུག་གིས།།
སྟོང་གཟུགས་ཕྱག་ཆེན་དགའ་མའི་བདེ་བ་ཆེ།།
བཅུ་དྲུག་དགའ་བཞིའི་དཔལ་ལ་རོལ་ནུས་ཤོག

སྨོན་མེད་རབ་གསལ་སྣང་བ།

གལ་ཏེ་རང་གཞན་འགྲོ་བ་སུ་ཡིས་ཀྱང་།།
ཟབ་གསང་ཆོས་ཀྱི་གནད་སྙིགས་མ་ཁྲོལ་ཡང་།།
མ་འོངས་རིགས་ལྡན་དྲག་པོའི་དཀྱིལ་འཁོར་དུ།།
ངེས་གསང་རྫོགས་ལྡན་ཆོས་ལ་སྤྱོད་ནུས་ཤོག

ཨོཾ་ཨཱཿཧཱུྃ་ཧོ༔ གངས་རིའི་ཕྲེང་བས་ཀུན་ནས་བསྐོར་བའི་དབུས།། ཆུ་སྐྱེས་འདབ་བརྒྱད་ལྟེ་བར་ཀེ་ལ་ཤའི།། རི་བོའི་སྙིང་ན་ལྷ་ཡི་བཀོད་པའི་གྲོང་།། ཤམྦྷ་ལ་ཡི་གཙོ་བོ་ཀ་ལྤ་བར།། ཉེ་བའི་ཡུལ་དང་བཅྭ་དཀར་པོའི་མཚོ།། ཙན་དན་ནགས་དབུས་དཀྱིལ་འཁོར་འཁོར་ལོ་དང་།། ཕྱི་རོལ་པད་འདབ་སོ་སོར་གནས་པའི་གྲོང་།། བྱེ་བ་དགུ་བཅུ་ཙ་དྲུག་ལ་སོགས་པ།། ཕྱགས་ཀྱི་ཞིང་མཆོག་ཁྱད་འཕགས་རིགས་བཞུགས་པའི།། ཆོས་རྒྱལ་རིགས་ལྡན་ཡེ་ཤེས་ལྷ་ཚོགས་དང་།། སྤྲུལ་བའི་རྒྱལ་པོ་དགུ་བཅུ་ཙ་དྲུག་སོགས།། མཆོད་འོས་ཀུན་ལ་ཕྱག་འཚལ་སྐྱབས་སུ་མཆིའོ།། འདིར་འབད་དགེ་བ་རྣམ་པར་དཀར་བའི་མཐུས།། བདག་ལུས་བོར་ཚེ་དཔལ་ལྡན་ཤམྦྷ་ལར།། རིགས་ལྡན་རྒྱལ་པོའི་འཁོར་དུ་ལེགས་སྐྱེས་ནས།། དུས་འཁོར་བསྟན་ལ་བྱ་བ་བྱེད་པར་ཤོག

ཨོཾ་ཨཱཿཧཱུྃ་ཧོ༔ཧྲཱི་ཀྵཿ

About the Author

Khentrul Rinpoche is a Non-Sectarian Master of Tibetan Buddhism. He has devoted his life to a wide variety of spiritual practices, studying with more than 25 masters from all of the major Tibetan traditions. While he has genuine respect and appreciation for all spiritual systems, he has the greatest confidence and experience with his personal path of the Kalachakra Tantra as taught in the Jonang-Shambhala Tradition.

Rinpoche brings a sharp and inquisitive mind to everything he does. His teachings are accessible and direct, often emphasising a very pragmatic sensibility. Over the years Rinpoche has authored a variety of books to guide his students and has specifically made great efforts to translate and provide commentary on texts which present the gradual stages of the Kalachakra Path.

Rinpoche has no doubt that our world has the potential to develop genuine peace and harmony while still preserving its environment and humanity. He believes this *Golden Age of Shambhala* is possible through the study and practice of the Kalachakra System. To this end, Rinpoche has begun travelling the world to share his knowledge of this unique lineage, free from sectarian bias.

RINPOCHE'S VISION

The Tibetan Buddhist Rimé Institute was founded with the express purpose of supporting Khentrul Rinpoche in realising his vision for greater peace and harmony in this world. As our community continues to grow and develop, more and more people are becoming involved with this extraordinary effort.

To give you a sense of the scope of Rinpoche's vision, we can speak of eight goals that reflect Rinpoche's short and long term priorities:

Immediate Goals

Ultimately speaking, lasting genuine happiness is only possible through profound personal transformation. Now more than ever we need methods to develop our wisdom and actualise our greatest potential. It is for this reason Rinpoche places such a heavy priority on the preservation of the Jonang Kalachakra Lineage. There are four ways in which Rinpoche hopes to do this:

1. **Create opportunities to connect with an authentic and complete Kalachakra lineage in close collaboration with dedicated meditators in remote Tibet.** Our goal is to create all of the supports for practicing Kalachakra in accordance with the authentic lineage masters who have upheld this tradition for thousands of years. We do this by commissioning statues and paintings, writing books and giving teachings around the world. We place particular emphasis on ensuring the authenticity of our material, drawing on the profound experience of highly realised meditators who dedicate their lives to these practices.

2. **Establish international retreat centres for the study and practice of Kalachakra.** In order to integrate the teachings into our mind it is crucial to have the opportunity to engage in periods of intensive practice. We are working to create the necessary infrastructure that will support and nurture the members of our community to engage in both short and long-term retreat. This includes the purchase of land and the construction necessary to conduct group and solitary retreats. Our long-term aim is to develop a network of centres around the world, forming a global community that is able to support a wide variety of practitioners.

3. **Translate and publish the unique and rare texts of Kalachakra masters.** The Kalachakra System has been the subject of countless texts over the course of Tibet's long history. So far only a small

fraction of these texts has been translated and made accessible in the West. While the theoretical texts are important, we aim to focus particularly on the pith instructions that can guide dedicated practitioners to a deeper experience of these profound teachings.

4. **Develop the tools and programs for a structured learning experience.** With pockets of students distributed throughout the world, we believe it is important to make the most of modern technology to facilitate the process of learning. Our aim is to develop a robust online educational platform that allows our international community to access quality study programs which are intuitive, structured and engaging.

Long-Term Goals

While we each work towards achieving ultimate peace and harmony in our own mind, we must not lose sight of the fact we exist within the greater context of a world filled with incredible diversity. Individuals give rise to a variety of beliefs and practices that in turn shape how we relate and interact with each other. In this interdependent reality, it is vital to find viable strategies for promoting greater tolerance and respect. As such, Rinpoche proposes four specific areas of activity:

1. **Promote the development of a Rimé Philosophy through dialogue with other traditions.** With the desire to be constructive members of a pluralistic society, we need to learn ways of reconciling our differences. To this end we aim to help people develop the positive qualities that promote an attitude of mutual respect, openness to new ideas and an inquisitive desire to overcome our ignorance.

2. **Develop highly realised role models by offering financial support to dedicated practitioners.** In order to ensure the authenticity of our spiritual traditions, it is imperative that there

are people who actualise the highest realisations. Therefore we aim to create a financial scholarship program which facilitates genuine practitioners who wish to dedicate their lives to spiritual development, regardless of their system of practice. By helping people actualise the teachings they become positive role models for those around them, inspiring and guiding generations to come.

3. **Actualise the great potential of female practitioners by developing specialised training programs.** The Tibetan culture has a long history of cultivating highly realised masters through the intensive training of those who are recognised to have great potential. Unfortunately the search for potential has focused mostly on male candidates. Rinpoche believes it is increasingly important to have strong, highly realised female role models who can help bring greater balance into our world. For this reason we are working to develop a unique training program for providing women with the opportunity to actualise their spiritual potential. It is our aim to design a specialised curriculum as well as the financial infrastructure to fully support all aspects of their education.

4. **Promote greater flexibility of mind and a broader understanding of reality through modern educational programs.** In a world that is rapidly evolving, we need to rethink the type of skills we are teaching our children. The rigid structures of the past are often ill equipped to prepare students for the challenges they will face during their lives. We aim to develop a variety of educational programs that can help children become more flexible and capable of adapting within their context. An important part of these programs is to develop greater awareness of the role our mind plays in our day-to-day experiences. We also aim to reform the monastic education system to increase its relevance in our modern world.

HOW CAN YOU HELP?

None of this will be possible without your support and participation. This vision requires a vast amount of merit and generosity from multiple benefactors over the course of many years. If you would like to help, please do not hesitate to contact us.

Tibetan Buddhist Rimé Institute
1584 Burwood Highway
Belgrave VIC 3160
AUSTRALIA

temple@rimebuddhism.com
www.rimebuddhism.com

Other Books Published by the Tibetan Buddhist Rimé Institute

www.rimebuddhism.com/product-category/books/

Unveiling Your Sacred Truth through the Kalachakra Path *

Book One: The External Reality — Book Two: The Internal Reality
Book Three: The Enlightened Reality

Demystifying Shambhala

The perfection of peace and harmony
as revealed by the Jonang Tradition of Kalachakra

Divine Ladder

Preliminary practices for the Gradual Path to Kalachakra Completion

Hidden Treasure of the Profound Path

A word-by-word commentary on the Kalachakra Preliminary Practices

Ocean of Diversity

An unbiased summary of views and practices,
gradually emerging from the teachings of the world's wisdom traditions

Rimé Prayer Book

A collection of essential prayers and practices from the
diverse traditions of Tibetan Buddhism

A Happier Life

How to develop genuine happiness and wellbeing
during every stage of your life

An Authentic Guide to Meditation

A Secret Incarnation

Reflections of a Tibetan Lama

* *Some books are currently in development and*
may not yet be available for purchase.

Ingram Content Group UK Ltd.
Milton Keynes UK
UKHW020910140323
418545UK00012B/1497

9 780994 610690